THE MODERN LANGUAGE ASSOCIATION
OF AMERICA

MONOGRAPH SERIES

XIX

THE REDISCOVERY
OF SIR JOHN MANDEVILLE

SIR JOHN MANDEVILLE TAKING LEAVE OF THE KING OF ENGLAND

# The Rediscovery of Sir John Mandeville

BY

JOSEPHINE WATERS BENNETT

NEW YORK

*The Modern Language Association of America*

1954

Copyright 1954 by The Modern Language Association
of America
London, Oxford University Press

## IN THE NAME OF GOD ALMIGHTY:

there was a man of the land of Genoa, a hawker of printed books, who carried on his trade in this land of Andalusia, whom they called Christopher Columbus, a man of great intelligence, though with little book learning, very skilled in the art of cosmography and the mapping of the world. From that which he had read in Ptolemy and in other books, and by his own natural ingenuity, he formed an opinion as to how and in what way this world, in which we were born and in which we live, is fixed in the arc of heaven, so that in no part does it reach to the skies, nor is there anything firm to which it is joined, but there is only land and water, formed in a circle, amid the space of the heavens. And he conceived of a way in which a land, rich in gold, might be attained, and he had the opinion that, as this world and the firmament of land and water can be traversed round about by land and water, as John Mandeville relates, it followed that one who had such ships as were suitable and who was ready to persevere through sea and land, of a surety would be able to go and to pass by the westward . . . which would be to compass all the earth and the roundness of the world.

*Andrés Bernáldez*

Approved for publication in the Monograph Series.

WILLIAM CHARVAT
HENRY A. GRUBBS
JOHN M. HILL
HARRY LEVIN
ROBERT A. PRATT
LIONEL STEVENSON
ROSEMOND TUVE
CURTIS C. D. VAIL
*Committee of Award*

# PREFACE

THE PROBLEM of who wrote *Mandeville's Travels* first presented itself to me ten years ago when a Guggenheim Fellowship gave me a year's leisure for research and the War restricted me to the resources of American libraries. Since that time I have worked at it piecemeal as school holidays permitted. As the manuscript has grown and changed over the years, in successive revisions and reorganizations, inconsistencies of form have crept in which have left traces, even in the finished work. The bibliographies of manuscripts and editions have grown until they threatened to overweigh the text, and therefore I have omitted the further list of references cited in the footnotes. Where the same work has been referred to more than once, and the reader comes upon an abbreviated reference, the complete reference can be found through the index, except where it occurs on the immediately preceding page.

In the process of working out a convincing argument, and of finding a publisher, I have had help and advice from several readers to whom I am indebted for criticism, and suggestions. I am especially indebted to Professor Rosemond Tuve of Connecticut College, who read both the first draft and the final copy, and whose continuing interest has been a sometimes needed spur. Professor B. J. Whiting of Harvard University, Professor Edward B. Ham of the University of Michigan, and Mrs. Beatrice Daw Brown have each sent me detailed and most valuable criticism. Professor Charlotte D'Evelyn of Mount Holyoke College read the manuscript and gave me useful advice. Professor Robert Pratt of the University of North Carolina has been most helpful in the final stages of the work. I am glad to have this opportunity to thank all of the readers, who have accepted as one of the duties of scholarship the task of contributing from their store of learning toward the improvement of this book. Many others have kept my interest in Mandeville (the writing of a monograph is a kind of monomania) in mind, and have helped with bits of information which came to their attention. Professor Eugene M. Waith of

Yale University, Mrs. Laura Hibbard Loomis, Miss Bertha H. Putnam, Professor Roger Sherman Loomis of Columbia University, Professor Franklin B. Williams of Georgetown University, and Professor James M. Osborn of Yale University have all helped in this way. The Very Reverend Vincent J. Flynn has loaned me some of his materials about Rhodes. Professor Carl Selmer of Hunter College has interpreted some difficult German verses. Mr. W. A. Jackson, Director of the Houghton Library of Harvard University, has supplied information about some of the rare editions.

To Mr. Malcolm Letts I am indebted for several courtesies. It would have been a great convenience if I could have had his edition of three rare texts, just published by the Hakluyt Society, while I was writing my book, but at least I am pleased to note that his observations about the 1371 manuscript support my contentions about it.

Like my author, I have read more than I have traveled, and in describing the manuscripts and rare early editions I have had to depend much upon others for what I should have been most happy to observe for myself. To Mr. R. A. B. Mynors, Master of Pembroke College, Cambridge, my obligation is so great that it would be no exaggeration to say that everything of value in the descriptions of the French manuscripts in England I owe to him; only the mistakes and omissions are mine. He has collated test passages and described for me all but one (which I overlooked until too late) of the French manuscripts in English public libraries, and he has used precious vacation time to examine for me those at Brussels and Bern also. Without his help the classification of the French manuscripts would have had to wait indefinitely. I must thank also M. Marcel Thomas, Bibliothicaire du Cabinet des Manuscripts, of the Bibliothèque Nationale, for supplying me with similar information about the French manuscripts not only in Paris, but in some of the provincial libraries also. My husband, Dr. Roger E. Bennett, gave up precious leisure while in Vienna to examine the manuscripts there for me. Professor Guy de Poerck of the Rijksuniversitiet of Ghent most kindly sent me descriptions of the four Brussels manuscripts. I am indebted to M. J. Porcher, Conservateur du Cabinet des Manuscripts, of the Bibliothèque Nationale, for permission to reproduce the pictures, as well as for answering inquiries. Professor Caterine Santoro, Director of the Biblioteca Trivulziana in Milan, provided me with a full description of a manuscript in her care. Mme. J. Gobeaux-Thonet, Librarian in Chief of the University of Liège, has put me in her debt by answering inquiries.

The Harvard College Library has repeatedly made its resources available to me, and Miss Alice Reynolds of the Interlibrary Loan Department has been most helpful both in arranging loans and in securing photostats and microfilm for my use. The Columbia University Library has been equally cooperative. And I am further indebted for special services to the staffs of the Folger Shakespeare Library, the Library of Congress, the New York Public Library, the Pierpont Morgan Library, and the Newberry Library. Private collectors in America have been most generous in allowing me to examine their treasures. I take this opportunity to thank especially Mr. Lessing J. Rosenwald, Mr. Boies Penrose, and Mr. H. P. Kraus for allowing me to examine incunabula and manuscripts in their possession.

I wish to thank Dr. Curt F. Bühler of the Pierpont Morgan Library, not only for helping in the examination and description of treasures in that library, and supplying information about copies elsewhere, but especially for a most helpful review of the manuscript of my bibliography of editions. If he failed to make a complete bibliographer out a tyro in one lesson, at least he brought some order out of chaos. What imperfections remain must be attributed to the waywardness and inattention of the pupil and not to any imperfection in the instruction.

To Professor Paul O. Kristeller of Columbia University I am especially indebted for information about the present state of European libraries, and for doing what he could in the proofs to bring the nomenclature of those libraries up-to-date in Appendix I, and for much valuable suggestion and advice.

I am very pleased to be able to thank Professor Ray Nash of Dartmouth College for designing the title page, and for making other suggestions for improving the appearance of the preliminary pages. For a grueling week of typing the manuscript, I shall always be indebted to Mrs. Sophia Sternfeld. For careful reading of the proof I owe a debt of gratitude to my colleagues, Mrs. Lavinia B. Eves and Dr. Roland Blenner-Hassett, as well as to Professor and Mrs. Loomis, and to Professor B. Q. Morgan of Stanford University.

Finally, I am deeply indebted to the staff of the Modern Language Association for much help in the various stages and processes of publication. Professor W. R. Parker has given council and comfort over the years. Professor John Fisher of New York University has given time and thought beyond the call of duty, and, with Donald D. Walsh, has devoted many hot summer hours to editing the manuscript. But of the making of books there is no end. It is good that it should be so, for these are the munitions of peace, the bonds of fellowship, and the roots of understanding. Their making is a way of life whose aim is truth. If they never quite achieve it fully, they nevertheless create a world of the mind in which the natural climate is the temperate air of peace and understanding. And so, to the making of books, and the reading of books, may there never be an end.

# TABLE OF CONTENTS

Introduction ........................................ 1

### PART I: The *Travels* as Literature

1. The Materials ................................. 15
2. The Transformation of the Materials .............. 26
3. The Romance of Travel ........................ 39
4. The Experience of a Traveler .................... 54
5. Motives and the Man .......................... 69

### PART II: The Identity of the Author

6. Two Liège Traditions .......................... 89
7. The Chantilly Manuscript ...................... 111
8. The Apocryphal Works ........................ 123
9. Three Families of French Manuscripts .......... 135
10. The Case Against Jean d'Outremeuse.............. 147
11. Doctor Jean de Bourgogne ..................... 158
12. The Place of Writing of the *Travels* ............... 170
13. The English Mandevilles ........................ 181
14. Some Further Clues .......................... 205

### PART III: The Reputation and Influence of the *Travels*

15. The First Two Centuries ....................... 219
16. A Bright Imaginary World ..................... 244

### Appendices

I. Checklist of Manuscripts ...................... 263
II. Bibliography of Editions ...................... 335
    List of References Cited in Appendices .......... 387
III. The Castle of the Sparrowhawk ................. 407
IV. Harley 4383, Cotton and Egerton Translations .... 411
    Locations of Manuscripts ...................... 415
    Index ......................................... 421

# ILLUSTRATIONS

All of the illustrations are reproduced, through the courtesy of the Bibliothèque Nationale, from the *Livre des Merveilles* [ancien fonds français 2810] described on pages 228-229 and 270.

Sir John [here called Guillaume] Mandeville taking leave
    of the King of England [fol. 141] .......... *frontispiece*

Tartars eating strange food, such as foxes [fol. 173] ...  14

The Castle of the Sparrowhawk. Its fairy mistress re-
    ceives the King of Armenia [fol. 178] ...........  15

The lake at Ceylon formed by the repentant tears of
    Adam and Eve [fol. 193] ......................  88

The race of men and women without heads [fol. 194$^v$]  89

Prester John honors the Cross [fol. 205] .............  218

The vegetable lamb and some barnacle geese [fol. 210$^v$]  219

The quotation from Andrés Bernáldez, on page v, is from his *History of Two Catholic Sovereigns, Don Ferdinand and Dona Isabella,* translated by Cecil Jane (Oxford University Press, 1932), page 309.

# INTRODUCTION

MANDEVILLE'S TRAVELS is a book important in the history of almost every literature of Europe. Historians of travel have rejected it as spurious, yet its influence on the discoverers of the New World was direct and incontestable. It belongs primarily to the history of imaginative literature, where it has an important place; but it has a place also in the history of geographical discovery because it did much to disseminate, in popular and inviting form, the general fund of knowledge and belief which prepared the minds of men for the great voyages. Then, when new travels had put it out-of-date, it achieved a fresh vogue as a book of wonders which stimulated the imaginations of readers for many generations. It was read by Ariosto and Tasso, Cervantes, Rabelais, and Montaigne, as well as by every great English writer from the *Pearl* poet to William Morris. It belongs to the history of imaginary and imaginative travel, from the *Chemin de Long Estude* of Christine de Pisan to *Alice's Adventures in Wonderland*. Indeed, in the course of six centuries it has found readers of all ages and of many interests. It has a secure place in the history of English prose, and in the history of popular literature—not the cheap and transitory, but that imaginative and enduring popular literature which eventually finds a secure place on the bookshelves of the young.

The *Travels* was written in French in the third quarter of the fourteenth century, and by the end of that century it had been translated into every major language of Europe. Over 250 manuscripts survive even today, and many have been lost. It has an important place in the history of early printing, since at least thirty-five editions were produced in the incunabular period. Indeed, the record of popular editions shows that the *Travels* retained a large audience well into the twentieth century. Even in our time it has been called one of the most readable books ever written.

Within the last hundred years, however, it has suffered a curious fate. Both the book and its author have fallen victims of a series of mistakes and misunderstandings. The *Travels* has been condemned as a dishonest book, an account of travels which never took place, and the author has been denied the name and even the nationality which he claimed for himself. The truth is that an attempt, made in his own day, to steal credit for the book, has in the twentieth century achieved complete, if temporary, success.

The magnitude of such a crime depends, however, after so long a time, on the value of the work involved. "A good book is the precious life-blood of a master spirit, embalmed and treasured up on purpose to a life beyond life," but a dishonest book is no such treasure and owes its author no such immortality. The *Travels* must, first of all, be shown to be "a good book," and then the identity of the author can most profitably be investigated—although, since personality plays so important a part in literary quality, and the two are so inextricably bound together, if the reader prefers, he may turn immediately to Part II and the discussion of authorship. A brief sketch of Mandeville's influence on the discoverers of America, and on the explorers of that even greater world, the land of make-believe, will be found in Part III.

It was surmised at least as early as the fifteenth century, and probably from the beginning, that the *Travels* was not a factual and pedestrian (or equestrian) account of its author's own experiences. However, until well into the nineteenth century Mandeville enjoyed the reputation of having been the greatest English traveler of the Middle Ages. Because he told such wonderful tales, he was also frequently described, at least from the sixteenth century onward, as the greatest liar. In the eighteenth century he enjoyed a renewed respectability, fostered by Dr. Johnson, as "the father of English prose."[1] But

---

[1] Samuel Johnson, in the "History of the Language" prefixed to his *Dictionary* (1755), quotes Mandeville first after the Anglo-Saxons and

this title was taken from him in the nineteenth century when it was demonstrated that French was the language of the original text, and that the author of the earliest English translation made some absurd mistakes because he was translating from a faulty manuscript. He could not, therefore, have been the author of the original.

Finally, in the 1880's, the source-hunters and the biographers, between them, reduced the book and its author to almost complete nonentity. A theory was put forward that the author was not an Englishman named Sir John Mandeville, but a Liège[*] physician named Jean de Bourgogne, or Jean à la Barbe, who used the name "Mandeville" as a pseudonym.[2] Many bibliographers, as well as the historians of medicine, travel, and letters, have adopted this theory, to the confusion of indices and library catalogues. In 1923 the editor of the Early English Text Society edition of the *Travels* went a step further and argued that the real author was not the Liège doctor, Jean de Bourgogne, but his friend and biographer, Jean d'Outremeuse, author of some verse romances and of a prose world chronicle.[3]

---

before Gower, whom he calls "the father of our poetry." George Burnett, *Specimens of English Prose-Writers* (1807), prepared as a companion to Ellis's famous *Specimens of Early English Poets* (1790), I, 3, calls Mandeville "the first prose writer in the English language." Robert Chambers, *Cyclopaedia of English Literature* (1844), I, 32, says he "is usually held as the first English prose writer." Henry Morley, *English Writers* (1864), I, 750, calls him "our first prose writer in formed English." William Minto, *Manual of English Prose Literature* (1872), p. 211, uses the phrase "the Father of English prose."

[*] The grave accent on this word was officially adopted recently, but the older acute accentuation has been preserved in quotations and titles.

[2] First argued by E. B. Nicholson in the article (with Sir Henry Yule) on "Mandeville, Jehan de," *The Encyclopaedia Britannica*, 9th ed. (1883). See further his article, "John of Burgundy, alias 'Sir John Mandeville,'" *The Academy*, xxv (April 12, 1884), 261-262. The theory was adopted by G. F. Warner, "Mandeville, Sir John," in the *Dictionary of National Biography* (1893), and developed fully in his Introduction to *The Buke of Sir John Maundeuill*, ed. for the Roxburghe Club (1889), hereafter cited as "Introduction."

[3] Paul Hamelius, ed., *Mandeville's Travels, Translated from the French*

As Jusserand observed, "Mandeville first lost his character as a truthful writer, then out of three versions of his book [French, English, and Latin] . . . two were withdrawn from him. . . . Existence now has been taken from him and he is left with nothing at all."[4] The *Cambridge History of English Literature* asserts that "Sir John never lived, . . . his travels never took place, and . . . his personal experiences . . . were compiled out of every possible authority."[5] This dismal picture has not been effectively changed by Mr. Malcolm Letts's recent study, *Sir John Mandeville: the Man and his Book*,[6] although he gives it as his opinion, unsupported by fresh evidence, or even by argument, that the author was an Englishman named Sir John Mandeville, who practised medicine at Liège under the name of Jean à la Barbe.

It is time, however, that someone undertook the whole complex problem of text and authorship; because the *Travels* is an important fact of literary history as well as a most entertaining book. In Part I, I hope to show that the *Travels* is not, as it has so often been called, merely a plagiarized travel book. The author has done much more than collect materials from the reports of genuine travelers. He has selected and pruned and arranged. More important still, he has imagined. He knew how to select picturesque details, and how to invent them. He knew how to secure that "willing suspension of disbelief" which is the foundation of all great fiction—in fact, of all imaginative literature. He is a master of the technique, known also to Defoe and Swift, of representing himself as the doubting Thomas whose sceptical approach to the marvelous effectively reassures the reader.

The author of the *Travels* had something more than great

---

of Jean d'Outremeuse, for the Early English Text Society, O.S., 153 (1919 for 1916) text, and 154 (1923 for 1916) Introduction and Notes.

[4] J. J. Jusserand, *A Literary History of the English People* (New York, 1895), I, 403.

[5] (New York, 1933), II, 90.

[6] (London, 1949).

plausibility. He succeeded in creating a character. Sir John Mandeville is a personality who gives inner coherence and life to the book. If he is a fictitious creation, the author deserves to be ranked with the foremost creators of characters in literature. It is much easier to believe that the personality stamped upon the book is the author's own; that he projected himself into his work (no mean literary feat), and that he actually was the modest, reasonable, and tolerant man, the man of culture and wide reading, which he represents himself to be. The Sir John Mandeville who appears in the *Travels* is full of reverence for the God who made all things, secure in a firm faith, yet free from intolerance and narrow orthodoxy. He is gentle and charitable toward the strange beliefs of the heathen, and even toward the "heretics," i.e., the Greeks, Nestorians, and other non-Roman Christian sects of whom he writes. He treats all that he reports with the respect due to God's handiwork, and the humility of a modest observer who does not pretend to understand the ways of God. He is fond of quoting Scripture (in the Latin of the Vulgate), and he has amazed even his detractors by the extent and variety of his reading. He has a sense of humor not unlike Chaucer's. He makes use of the same sly juxtaposition of details, so as to suggest a comment on human foibles without actually making one and so passing from humor to satire. He has the "gentilesse" which is the core of Chaucer's urbanity, the wholesomeness which is the flower of a well-balanced personality, and the kindliness which puts understanding before judgment. He has the sympathetic imagination to credit the remote people dwelling on the other side of the earth with the feelings, desires, and human failings which he had observed at home.

A comparison of the author's text with his sources will most clearly demonstrate these literary qualities in the *Travels*, and since these sources have been quoted, in the original languages, in the Early English Text Society and Roxburghe Club editions of the *Travels*, I shall quote in English, as far as possible, for the convenience of the reader. However, since there are four translations of Mandeville into English to choose from, it is necessary to include a summary account of these translations here, although a discussion of the texts upon which they are based must be reserved for Part II.

It was long believed that Mandeville wrote in three languages, and that the popular Latin and the earliest English,[7] as well as the French version, were by him. The first English translator represented him as saying, "And ye shall understand, that I have put this book out of Latin into French, and translated it again out of French into English, that every man of my nation may understand it."[8] The original French text says at this point, "Sachez que ieusse cest [liuerette] mis en latyn pur pluis briefment deuiser; mes, pur ceo que plusours entendent mieltz romantz que latin, ieo lay mys en romance . . ."[9] Perhaps the Englisher, in translating *ieusse* (should have) as "have" was merely mistaken in the mode of the French verb, but when he makes the author claim to have translated the book into English, he is perpetrating a deliberate falsehood. The translator was not the author. He was not able to correct mistakes in the copy before him, which was not the author's holograph but an imperfect copy. Largely as a result of his great fidelity to this imperfect text, he is led into a few absurd blunders.[10] Hamelius, the most recent editor, exaggerates the amount of error in the English of the Cotton manuscript. In general it is a very faithful and literal translation of the Norman-French version, which I shall show was the original

[7] This is the translation in Cotton MS. Titus C XVI, edited by Hamelius for E.E.T.S.

[8] *The Travels of Sir John Mandeville: the Version of the Cotton Manuscript in Modern Spelling*, ed. A. W. Pollard (London, 1905), p. 6. My quotations will all be from this edition, unless otherwise indicated.

[9] Warner printed the best Norman-French text he could find in the Roxburghe Club edition of *The Buke* (note 2, above), see p. 3, l. 26.

[10] Described by Warner, in his Introduction, p. xiii. For example, *nonains cordelieres* becomes "nonnes of an hundred ordres" (C ordres), and *signes du ciel* becomes "swannes of heauene" (cignes).

version of the *Travels*. I shall quote, therefore, from this version, taking care to avoid the few interpolations, and to call attention to the few inaccuracies, such as the ones just quoted.

The English translator had before him a French text which was certainly not the author's holograph, but was an early copy which a study of the proper names (see p. 143) shows to have been as good as, or better than, any now surviving. The translation is important, therefore, not only for its literary merits, but as evidence of what the author actually wrote. It exists in a single manuscript (British Museum, Cotton Titus C XVI) which has been edited several times, and since the archaic spelling is of philological rather than literary interest I shall quote from the transcription into modern spelling made by A. W. Pollard, except where reference to the French is absolutely necessary.

There are three other English versions, a short popular one printed by Pynson in 1496 and frequently reprinted from that date until 1725, when the full text of the Cotton manuscript was edited for the first time. This is commonly called the "Pynson version" and it has a history and a place of its own in the story of English literature. It was made from the first, or Cotton manuscript version, with the help of an imperfect French text.[11] A new and complete translation, made in the fifteenth

---

[11] Nicholson, op. cit., and Warner, Introduction, pp. x-xiv, argue that the short version is the earlier, because the translator had the French before him and corrected most of the mistakes of the Cotton text. However, at one point a leaf of the French manuscript ended with the words, *tant a dire come roys. Il y so.* The next leaf began, *et est celle vallee mult froid,* and the translation reads, "That ys to say among hem *Roys Ils* and this vale ys ful cold." He did not discover that there was a gap in his manuscript, extending from p. 18, l. 21, to p. 32, l. 16, of the French published by Warner. The Cotton text gives this passage correctly, but this translator was correcting the Cotton text from a defective French manuscript. He does not, however, fill in a gap which occurs in the Cotton manuscript (but not in the Egerton or in Warner's French text). The short version agrees with the Cotton closely. Hamelius argues (against Nicholson and Warner) that it is unreasonable to suppose that the *later* version introduced errors of translation not in the earlier one. The

century, was not printed until 1889 when it was edited for the Roxburghe Club by G. F. Warner.[12] Its scholarly author knew both the earlier translation and a French text, and he seems also to have had one of the unprinted Latin translations before him. His work is therefore interesting and important, but less significant than the Cotton text. A fourth version in English, discovered by Vogels, was made from a Latin text which was known at St. Albans before 1400. It is being edited for the Hakluyt Society by Mr. Malcolm Letts.

Mandeville's reputation has suffered in many ways from too great success. His text was tampered with by over-zealous enthusiasts.[13] His materials were borrowed and appropriated in various ways. His book was cut and garbled in popular editions, such as the Pynson text of the English version which by no means does justice to its original. And his great plausibility was disastrous in the end.

For centuries he was looked upon as a genuine traveler, though a great liar; and when the source-hunters discovered that his book was not a report of first-hand observations, but the product of much reading, they condemned the author as a "mere plagiarist" and his book as worthless. It is natural enough that the historians of travel, discovering that they had been duped, should retaliate by extravagant condemnation of the book. But historians of literature are in a different position entirely. The successful fabrication of a travel book, the creation of imaginary travels, is a literary achievement. And Mandeville's success cannot be questioned. He uses his ma-

---

process of abbreviation, in successive revisions, is the usual one in the progressive degeneration of a text, as described, for example, by the latest editor of Marco Polo. And that process would indicate that the Cotton version is the older.

[12] Preserved in a single copy, Egerton MS. 1982 in the British Museum. For discussion of the relations among the English versions, see J. Vogels, *Handschriftliche Untersuchungen über die englische Version Mandeville's,* in *Jahresbericht über das Realgymnasium zu Crefeld* (Crefeld, 1891).

[13] See below, chaps. 5-10.

terials like a creative artist, arousing the reader's imagination by every device of sense impression and pictorial association known to the literary craftsman.

Mandeville belongs, not to the history of exploration (though he has a larger place there than is commonly recognized today), but to the history of European literature. He left a mark on the literatures of France, Italy, Spain, Portugal, Germany, Denmark, the Low Countries, and Bohemia; but he has a special place in English literature because he claimed that nationality and was accepted by the English, who took a proprietary pride in him. They believed that he was a great traveler, and his example had a stimulating effect on what was already a notable English characteristic.[14] They were great wanderers, but it was this book which made the English traveler articulate and so exerted an influence which the mere traveler, whose experiences died with him, could never have.

The first translation into English has an important place in the history of English prose although the translator will probably remain nameless. He was not the original author, but the praise which has been bestowed upon his work by the ablest critics, from Dr. Johnson to George Saintsbury, is no less deserved because we can no longer call him "Sir John Mandeville," nor "the Father of English Prose." With the help of the author of the *Travels*, he produced one of the most delightful and deservedly popular books ever written. It has subtle humor and charm for the mature reader. It has marvels and wonders to arouse the imagination of the young. It is full

[14] Wyclif, Gower, and Higden all comment on the Englishman's love of travel, and Chaucer gives his knight that characteristic, but all of these comments were written *after* the *Travels* had begun to circulate. The opposite was equally true to fact, and might as easily have been embodied in tradition. An Italian visitor to England about 1500 reports that criminals, forced to abjure the realm, were lamented by women and children saying, "'they had better have died than go out of the world,' as if England were the whole world!" *A Relation . . . of the Island of England* . . . trans. C. A. Sneyd, Royal Historical Society Publications, XXXVII (1847), 35.

of memorable stories and graphic descriptions as well as of absurdities and quaint beliefs. Henry Morley called it "the most entertaining book written in Early English prose."[15] Richard Garnett went much further, saying that it is "one of the most remarkable books in our literature."[16] Saintsbury describes it as "the first book of *belles lettres* in English prose,"[17] and he goes on to say, "here for the first time distinctly, the subject and the idiosyncrasy of the author produce between them a *style*." For "author" we must read "translator," yet all of the subject and most of the idiosyncrasy of the English derive from the French original, and there is glory enough in the result for two to share.

The truth is that the English is a translation of the Norman-French version of the *Travels*, which has an English word-order and a cadence that sounds rough and crude to a French ear but converts easily into idiomatic English. Credit is due to the author, therefore, for much of the style of the translation.

Moreover, the literary merits of the work are not confined to the happy union of subject matter and language. The form, the selection and arrangement of the materials, and the skillful management of the narrative, both in small units and in the composition as a whole, represent an accomplishment which belongs to the original, and which compares favorably with the best work of a much later time. The author shows great artistic tact in the handling of his matter. He knew when to stop, how to round out a book without padding it, and how to arrange his material with due consideration for proportion and variety. This he was free to do because he was writing a work of fiction and not a factual account of his own experiences.

The *Travels* is a finished artistic composition, not a mere travel-book. It has both style and form, as well as delightful

[15] *English Writers*, 3d ed., IV (1889), 284.
[16] With Edmund Gosse, *English Literature* (New York, 1903), I, 194-195.
[17] *A Short History of English Literature* (1898), pp. 150-151.

subject matter and an author whose charm of personality survives even in translation. He has, as we shall see, not only humor and skill, but interpretation, a "reading of life," which brings him into Milton's charmed circle of master-spirits. His is a work much too important to the literary historian, and much too valuable in itself, to be left where it lies at present, in the limbo of exploded myths and literary hoaxes.

The present study will undertake, therefore, to clear away the debris of misinformation and misunderstanding which has been accumulating around both the book and its author for six centuries. I propose to deal with the book first, because upon its quality depends the importance of the authorship, and because a discussion of the book provides an approach to the much more complex problem of authorship. Since the *Travels* has been condemned as "mere plagiarism" and even as "mere translation," it seems best to begin with a brief account of its sources. This will be followed by an account of the author's handling of his materials, his techniques and methods, the possible extent of his travel experience, and his reasons for writing as they devolve from the work itself.

With the true character of the *Travels* in mind, the reader will be ready to examine the evidences of the author's identity, beginning with the well-known Liège records which identify Sir John Mandeville with the famous doctor, Jean de Bourgogne. Here the history of the French texts, never before brought to bear upon the problem, throws a flood of new light upon the whole subject of authorship and enables us to see the Liège romancer, Jean d'Outremeuse, almost in the very act of tampering with the text and creating the myth that Mandeville wrote his *Travels* at Liège and was buried there.

When the ghost of Jean de Bourgogne is finally laid in its own grave, and the Norman-French text of the *Travels* has been established as the original version, it will be time to turn to England and look among the multitude of Mandevilles there for some trace of our author.

In a final section I have tried to indicate Mandeville's influence, not only on his contemporaries, but on the discoverers and explorers of the New World, and on such English writers as Sir Thomas More and his contemporaries, and on Spenser and Shakespeare and Milton, as well as on Swift and Defoe and Coleridge. Such a list of readers is proof enough of the author's importance, but the breadth of his appeal can best be seen in the record of manuscripts and editions which will be found in the appendices.

If in this process of clearing away the mistakes, misunderstandings, and stark falsehoods which have come to obscure the *Travels*, I can leave with the reader a fresher and more vivid appreciation of the book itself, and a desire to read it again, then this book will have been worth much long and difficult labor.

# PART I
# THE *TRAVELS* AS LITERATURE

THE TARTARS EAT FOXES

THE CASTLE OF THE SPARROWHAWK

… 1 …

# THE MATERIALS

*Mandeville's Travels* purports to have been completed in 1356, and to be a report of travels upon which the author set out from England in 1322.[1] Translated into terms of English history this would mean that he set out a few months after the defeat of the Barons at Boroughbridge by the supporters of Edward II, and that he finished the book in the year of the great victory of Edward III over the French king at Poitiers. In the larger perspective of European history this was a period of constant agitation for a new crusade which kept interest in the Near East at a fever heat. It was the end of a period of exploration of the Far East which had excited the imaginations and aroused the cupidity of all Europe. The fall of Acre in 1291 was a challenge to Christendom rivaled only by the book of Marco Polo (1290) about the wonders and riches of the Orient. When the author of the *Travels* was growing up, two of the strongest impulses, religion and greed, drew men's interests toward the East. There was also curiosity.

The *Travels* falls into two unequal parts of which the first and shorter is concerned with the Holy Land and the Near East. The second, and somewhat longer, part purports to describe a journey "throughout Turkey, Armenia the little and the great; through Tartary, Persia, Syria, Arabia, Egypt the high and the low; through Lybia, Chaldea, and a great part of Ethiopia; through Amazonia, Ind the less and the more, a great part; and throughout many other Isles, that be about Ind" (p. 5), including Marco Polo's fabulous Cathay.

It is now well established that whether or not Mandeville performed any part of these travels, he made his book out of accounts of the Near and Far East which were circulating in

---

[1] For a discussion of these dates, see below, pp. 149 ff.

his day. Many reports of the Near East, and especially of the Holy Places in Palestine, were available, and the *Travels* is indebted to many of them, but Mandeville used as a kind of framework a journey through Palestine and Egypt written about 1336 by a renegade German friar called William of Boldensele.[2] For his travels in Eastern Palestine, from Bethlehem through Galilee to Damascus he makes extensive use of an Itinerary written about 1330 and attributed, probably erroneously, to a Franciscan Friar, Odoric of Pordenone, or Forli Julii.[3] Then, for his account of his travels in the Middle East and the Orient, he follows, step by step, the genuine Itinerary of Odoric of Pordenone,[4] also published about 1330. He uses these reports as the canvas, upon which he embroiders, tapestry-wise, with the vari-colored threads of his armchair labors, revising these pedestrian journeys into a book of wonder and high romance.

First of all it must be recognized that in the years before 1356, while the *Travels* was being written, the beginning of the Hundred Years' War had destroyed the plans and hopes

---

[2] Originally a Dominican Friar of Minden, he became a Knight of the Holy Sepulchre. C. L. Grotefend, ed., "Itinerarius Guilielmi de Boldensele," in *Zeitschrift des Historischen Vereins für Niedersachsen* (1852, rptd. Hanover, 1855), pp. 236-286. The same work, ed. H. Canisius, "Hodoeporicon ad Terram Sanctam," in *Lectiones Antiquae*, ed. J. Basnage (Antwerp, 1725), IV, 331-357. A French translation was printed in *L'hystoire merveilleuse de Tartarie* (Paris, 1529), pp. lxvi-lxxvii. There is an English extract in C. D. Cobham, *Excerpta Cypria* (Cambridge, 1908), pp. 15-16. A. S. Atiya, *Crusade in the Later Middle Ages* (London, 1938), pp. 160-161 and notes, gives an account of Boldensele, alias Otto von Neuhaus.

[3] "Liber de Terra Sancta," in J. C. M. Laurent, *Peregrinatores Medii Aevi Quatuor* (Leipzig, 1864).

[4] Henri Cordier, "Les Voyages en Asie au xiv⁰ Siècle de Bienheureux Frère Odoric de Pordenone," in *Recueil de Voyages et de Documents pour servir à L'Histoire de la Géographie depuis le xiii⁰ jusqu'à la fin du xvi⁰ siècle*, x (Paris, 1891). An English version of a different text is in Sir Henry Yule, *Cathay and the Way Thither*, II (Hakluyt Soc., 2d Ser. No. 33 for 1913). A. W. Pollard reprints the English translation made by Hakluyt, in his ed. of Mandeville already cited.

for a new Crusade, and developments in the Near East had closed the trade routes to China and India. The first great era of European travel to the Orient was over. Mandeville was not an explorer, genuine or fictitious. He was a literary popularizer who used as his raw materials the reports of genuine travelers, embellishing them from his wide reading, transforming and vivifying them with literary skill and a genuine creative imagination.

Of the two parts of the *Travels* the second is probably more interesting today, as it must have been the more exciting part in the days when it was written. In the thirteenth century both a land and a sea route to China and India, the rich and fabulous Orient, were suddenly opened to European travelers and traders. In 1214 the Mongols, or Tartars, began their phenomenal conquest of Asia by taking Peiping. By 1259 "one empire stretched from the Yellow River to the banks of the Danube, and from the Persian Gulf to Siberia," comprehending all of southern and central Asia, from the frontiers of Europe to the China Sea.[5] In spite of the appalling violence of the Tartars' conquest, they proved excellent organizers who cultivated foreign trade, protected the trade routes, and were hospitable to all religions. The result was that, after the initial convulsion of fear that the Mongol hordes would engulf Europe, the Christians began to look upon the Tartars as possible allies against the Turks in Egypt and Asia Minor. Christian traders and missionaries began to travel freely in the vast reaches of the Mongol empire. In 1269 the elder Polos brought back from Kublai Khan a request for a hundred missionaries to work among his people. Some missionaries were sent—how

[5] Eileen Power, "The Opening of the Land Routes to Cathay," in *Travel and Travellers of the Middle Ages,* ed. A. P. Newton (London, 1930), p. 126. See also Yule's *Cathay,* I (Hakluyt Society, No. 38 for 1915), 146-173; M. D'Avezac, "Relation des Mongols ou Tartares par le Frère Jean du Plan de Carpin," in *Recueil des Voyages et de Mémoires,* pub. by the Société de Géographie, IV (Paris, 1839), 397-602; L. Olschki, *Marco Polo's Precursors* (Baltimore, 1943).

many we do not know. We do know that in the first third of the fourteenth century there was a Catholic Archbishop at Peiping, another at Sultânieh on the Caspian Sea, and several Franciscan churches in India and China, including three at "Zaiton," a Chinese seaport.[6]

In the days of Marco Polo, the last third of the thirteenth century, there was much intercourse between East and West. Even distant England was involved. In 1271, at Acre, Prince Edward of England and the Christian king of Armenia undertook to make an alliance with the Khan of Persia against the Turks. Embassies were exchanged in 1273-74, and again in 1277. In 1287 the Khan sent a Nestorian monk from Peiping to Europe to see Edward.[7] There were exchanges between these two monarchs in 1290, and again in 1291, on the eve of the fall of Acre. As late as 1307 a Persian embassy visited Edward II. But nothing was done, and after thirty years of disappointment, the Khan ruling in 1316 officially adopted Mohammedanism and thereby reestablished a hostile Islam across the overland trade routes to India and China. By 1340 the flow of traders and missionaries had shrunk to a thin trickle of hardy adventurers who managed to get around to the East by sea. In 1370 a revolution in China replaced the tolerant Mongols with a native Ming dynasty which was hostile to foreigners, and a glorious chapter of exploration was ended for centuries. Some of the information gathered by Marco Polo and Friar Odoric was not available again at first hand until after 1860.[8]

[6] Formerly identified as Canton, but Cordier argues, in his edition of Odoric (pp. 268-284), that it was Tsiouen-tcheou tou. Sir Henry Yule argues for Chwangchau-fu, modern Chinchew, in *The Book of Ser Marco Polo*, 3d ed. revised by H. Cordier (London, 1902), II, 219. For a description of the Oriental Sees of Rome, see Atiya, p. 24.

[7] René Grousset, *Histoire des Croisades: et du Royaume Franc de Jérusalem* (Paris, 1934-36), III, 658 ff., 692 ff., 710-719, 725-727; and see E. A. Wallis Budge, *The Monks of Kûblâi Khân* (London, 1928), pp. 63 ff.

[8] N. M. Penzer, *The Most Noble and Famous Travels of Marco Polo . . . edited from the Elizabethan Translation of John Frampton*, 2d ed.

The first two accounts of journeys into the Mongol empire were written by Jean du Plan de Carpin, an emissary of the Pope, who visited the Khan of central Asia in 1245-47, and Guillaume de Rubruquis, an emissary of St. Louis, who set out a decade later. Each wrote a priceless factual account of the Tartars of central Asia.[9] Marco Polo was the first European to write an account of China. His book began to circulate about 1290. The most popular of the later accounts was that of Friar Odoric, and the last was written by a contemporary of Sir John Mandeville's, John of Marignolli, papal legate to the Khan of Cathay, who set out in 1339 and returned in 1352, the last European to report about China for centuries.

Mandeville was not an explorer, but a popularizer; not the creator of a dishonest travel-book, but the author of a romance of travel which belongs, primarily, to the history of literature. In casting his materials in the mold of a first-person narrative he was doing no more than his predecessors in this genre had done before him and his successors were to continue to do. But his book was so successful that for centuries it deceived the historians of geographical discovery, and they have retaliated by placing the stigma of plagiarism upon it. In order to evaluate the *Travels* as literature, however, it is necessary to reexamine Mandeville's materials and his use of them.

By the time he was writing, travels to China were over and what accounts of the East had been written had achieved considerable circulation. The encyclopaedists, the translators, and the copyists had made reports of the Orient widely available. The earliest description of the Tartars was written by Matthew

---

(London, 1937), p. xxxi. The English part in the rediscovery of the Middle East is reviewed in S. C. Chew, *The Crescent and the Rose* (New York, 1937).

[9] See D'Avezac, op. cit.; and W. W. Rockhill, *The Journey of William of Rubruck to the Eastern Parts of the World, 1253-1255, . . . with Two Accounts of the Earlier Journey of John of Pian de Carpine*, Hakluyt Society, 2d Ser., IV (1900). Hakluyt's translations of Carpini, Rubruquis, and Odoric are reprinted in Pollard's ed. of *Mandeville*.

Paris, under the date 1240. The report of Jean du Plan de Carpin was largely incorporated in the encyclopaedic work of Vincent of Beauvais (ca. 1250-64). Roger Bacon met Rubruquis in Paris after his return from central Asia, and abstracted almost every detail of his geographical information in the *Opus Majus* (1264). Brunetto Latini, in his encyclopaedic *Trésor* (1268), made most of the information about the Saracens and the Tartars available in French.

By the time *Mandeville's Travels* was written, almost all of the accounts of Asia, including those of Marco Polo and Odoric, were available in both French and Latin. Accounts of the Near East, and especially of Palestine, were even more plentiful, and therefore Mandeville's sources for that part of the *Travels* are much more difficult to identify.

It is not necessary, however, to deal with them in any detail here, because two independent and exhaustive source-studies have been published, one by Albert Bovenschen,[10] and the other by Warner.[11] Hamelius incorporated much of this material, along with some additions of his own, in his edition; and other scholars have supplied further details.[12]

It is generally agreed that besides the Itineraries of William of Boldensele and Odoric of Pordenone, Mandeville made extensive use of Vincent of Beauvais' *Speculum Historiale* and *Speculum Naturale*.[13] The sketch of the history of the Saracens was drawn largely from William of Tripoli's *De Statu Sarace-*

[10] "Untersuchungen über Johann von Mandeville und die Quellen seiner Reisebeschreibung," *Zeitschrift der Gesellschaft für Erdkunde zu Berlin*, XXIII (1888), 177-306; also printed separately, without the biographical preliminary, as *Die Quellen für die Reisebeschreibung des Johann von Mandeville*, Dissertation (Berlin, 1888).

[11] In the notes to his edition.

[12] See the notes to the E.E.T.S. ed., and Victor Chauvin, "Le prétendu séjour de Mandeville en Égypte," *Wallonia*, x (1902), 237-242; Mary Lascelles, letter in *The [London] Times Literary Supplement* (April 6, 1933), p. 248; and her article, "Alexander and the Earthly Paradise in Mediaeval English Writings," *Medium Aevum*, v (1936), 173-175, 180-188.

[13] About 90 parallels are cited in Hamelius' notes. Letts (p. 29) says

THE MATERIALS 21

*norum* (1270),[14] and the account of the Tartars from Hayton of Armenia's *La Flor des Estoires de la Terre d'Orient* (1307), a work which circulated widely in the original French, in a Latin translation, and in a retranslation from Latin into French by Jean le Lonc of Ypres.[15] Mandeville used Carpini's account in the version given by Vincent of Beauvais, whose excerpts were so extensive that they were abstracted from the *Speculum* again and circulated as a separate work.[16] He may have also known Rubruquis' report and he had certainly read Marco Polo.[17] He knew well the famous *Letter of Prester John*, a fabrication of the latter half of the twelfth century. Mr. Letts reports that some twenty episodes in the *Travels* can be traced to this *Letter*.[18]

---

that he has traced 40 or 50 passages to Vincent, but these probably duplicate Hamelius.

[14] He was a Dominican friar of Acre. His "Tractatus de Statu Saracenorum et de Machomete pseudo-propheta et eorum lege et fide" was ed. by Hans Prutz, in *Kulturgeschichte der Kreuzzüge* (Berlin, 1883), pp. 575-598; and see Warner, xvii, n. 2.

[15] Both French and Latin texts are found in the *Recueil des Historiens des Croisades: Documents Latins et Français Relatifs à L'Arménie*, published by L'Académie des Inscriptions et Belles Lettres (Paris, 1906), II, 121-253, and 255-363. For other eds. of Hayton see A. S. Atiya, *The Crusade of Nicopolis* (London, 1934), p. 166, n. 3.

[16] Warner, p. 210, note to p. 123, l. 11, points out a borrowing from Carpini which must have come through Vincent, since it includes the episode of the pickled ears which is not in Carpini, but which Vincent interpolated from another source.

[17] See index, under "Marco Polo."

[18] Letts, pp. 31-32, 76-87, and see Index. His statement that Mandeville "first introduced the *Letter* to English readers" (p. 76) is puzzling. There are copies of the Latin *Letter* in England, as for example in a MS. from Bury St. Edmunds, now Corpus Christi College, Cambridge, 66, written in the first third of the 14th century. It contains several items used by Mandeville; besides the *Letter*, it has De Vitry, the *Journey of Macarius*, two books of the *Imago Mundi*, *Barlaam and Josaphat*, Pseudo-Methodius, some tracts on the Holy Land, the story of the Cross, and John Holywood, or Sacro Bosco's *De Sphera*; see M. R. James, *Descriptive Catalogue of the Manuscripts in the Library of Corpus Christi College, Cambridge* (Cambridge, 1911), I, 137-145. See also J. L. Lowes, "The Dry Sea and the Carrenare," *Modern Philology*, VII (1905-06), 1-46.

The *Travels* incorporates borrowings from many of the accounts of the Holy Land and the Near East. Some of the geographical confusions have been traced to the *History of the First Crusade* by Albert of Aix.[19] It makes extensive use of Jacques de Vitry's *Historia Orientalis, sive Hierosolymitanae*.[20] Traces of Burchard's *Descriptio Terrae Sanctae* have been detected, but Warner is of the opinion that Mandeville knew this work only through the extracts from it in Marino Sanudo's *Secreta Fidelium Crucis* (1321).[21] He used Peter Comestor's *Historia Scholastica Evangelica*, Josephus' *Bellum Judaicorum*, pseudo-Brocard's *Directorium*, Durand's *Rationale*, pseudo-Methodius, Eugesippus' *De distantiis locorum Terrae Sanctae*, and other itineraries of Palestine, including Ernoul's *Itineraries* and the *Pelerinaiges et Pardouns de Acre*.[22] He used Brunetto

---

Mandeville's debt to Prester John was studied by Friedrich Zarncke, "Der Priester Johannes," in *Abhandlungen der philologisch-historischen Classe der Königlich Sächsischen Gesellschaft der Wissenschaften*, Bd. VII, VIII (Leipzig, 1879, 1883), See VIII, 128 ff., and for copies of the *Letter* in England, VII, 907-908, 935-940. See also L. Olschki, "Der Brief des Presbyters Johannes," *Historische Zeitschrift*, CXLIV (Berlin, 1931), 1-14.

[19] In *Recueil des Historiens des Croisades. Historiens Occidentaux* (Paris, 1879), IV, pt. 3. See Warner's note to p. 4 and Hamelius' note to p. 4.

[20] The *Historia Hierosolymitana Abbreviata*, trans. by Aubrey Stewart, Palestine Pilgrims Text Society, XI (London, 1896). This and the "Historiae Orientalis," in Latin, ed. Jacques Bongars, *Gesta Dei per Francos* (Hanover, 1611), I, 1047-1145.

[21] Warner, p. xix. Burchard's work is edited by Jacob Basnage, *Thesaurus Monumentorum Ecclesiasticorum et Historicorum, sive Henrici Canisii Lectiones antiquae* (Amsterdam, 1725), IV, 9-26; trans. A. Stewart, P.P.T.S., XII (1896). This vol. contains also Marino Sanudo's "Secrets for True Crusaders to Help Them to Recover the Holy Land" (1321), III, xiv. For the full text, in Latin, see Bongars, II, 1-316. Sanudo, Burchard, and pseudo-Brocard or Burchard are summarized in Atiya, *Crusade of the Later Middle Ages*, pp. 95 ff.

[22] J. C. M. Laurent, *Peregrinatores Medii Aevi Quatuor* contains the "Liber de Terra Sancta" of pseudo-Odoric and the itineraries of Burchard, Ricold of Monte Croce, and Willibrand of Odenburg; fourteen itineraries appear in Henri Michelant and Gaston Raynaud, *Itinéraires à Jérusalem et Descriptions de la terre Sainte rédigés en français aux xi*, xii*, et xiii* siècles*, in Publications de la Société de L'Orient Latin, Série Géographique, III (Geneva, 1882).

Latini's *Trésor* and the *Imago Mundi* commonly attributed to Honorius of Autun.

Many of his literary embellishments have been traced to the romances. He evidently knew many of the Alexander romances, as well as those of Charlemagne and of Arthur. He seems to have known the *Chevalier du Cigne* and its sequel, *Godefroi de Bouillon*, as well as the *Chanson de Jérusalem*, the *Chanson d'Antioche*, and the *Legends of the Cross*.[23] He knew the *Legenda Aurea*, of course, and he used some linguistic work, such as Hrabanus Maurus' *De Inventione Linguarum*, for his account of the alphabets of the Greeks, Hebrews, Saracens, and the like.[24]

Among the ancients, he certainly knew Solinus, the contemporary and epitomizer of Pliny, though perhaps through the extensive abstracts in Vincent of Beauvais. Warner suggests that in making Andromeda a giant he was misunderstanding a reference in Solinus, but the mistake was apparently a current one and not original with Mandeville. A century later Bernard de Breydenbach, a genuine and intelligent traveler, reported seeing the bones of *the giant Andromeda* at Joppa, where Mandeville reported them.[25] Bernard suggests that what he was shown was really the rib of a whale. Solinus said that in his day the bones *of the monster* to whom Andromeda was to be sacrificed were taken to Rome and exhibited. The exhibition of a huge bone was evidently traditional at Joppa, and it is not surprising if, in the course of a thousand years and more, the Andromeda legend got a little confused. Mandeville says, "And yet there sheweth in the rock, there as the iron chains were fastened, that Andromeda, a great giant, was

---

[23] See Warner's useful summary of Mandeville's sources, in his Introduction, pp. xv-xxv, and his notes.

[24] Letts has a chapter on the alphabets, pp. 151-160, but bases his statements on an unreliable text; see below, Chapter 9 and see p. 146.

[25] *Le grand voyage de hierusalem diuerse en deux partes* (Paris, 1522), fol. xiii^v. Breydenbach was observant and apparently kept a diary, yet he imitates Mandeville by giving alphabets and including accounts of the religions of various peoples.

bounden with, and put in prison before Noah's flood, of the which giant, is a rib of his side that is forty foot long."[26]

In many cases we cannot be sure of the immediate source of Mandeville's information. Hamelius reduced the list as much as possible by attributing everything he could to Vincent of Beauvais, even when closer parallels had been noted elsewhere. Bovenschen cited parallels wherever he found them. Warner undertook the more exacting task of identifying the particular work used in each case, as far as that is possible with mediaeval texts which vary from manuscript to manuscript.

However, all attempts to identify Mandeville's sources have proceeded on the assumption that he neither traveled nor talked with anyone who had been in the East. No allowance has been made for the probability that some of the material especially about the Near East, was picked up orally—and that some may even have been gathered at first hand, if we allow the author such a minimum of travel as thousands of Englishmen achieved during his lifetime. Nevertheless, when such allowances have been made, a solid body of evidence remains to show that Mandeville was widely read in the literature of the East, in natural history, and in the romances. He had read as widely as was possible in his time about the Orient. That is not surprising, since the exploration of Asia in the fourteenth century created much the same kind of excitement as did the discovery of America in the sixteenth.

Unfortunately, some of what was written, and all of what was said, is lost to us, unless by some miracle of invention we learn to visit Chaucer's "House of Fame," for

>   this hous in alle tymes,
> Was ful of shipmen and pilgrimes,
> With scrippes bret-ful of lesinges [lies],
> Entermedled with tydynges,
> And eke allone be hemselve. (ll. 2121-25)[27]

[26] Pollard's text, p. 21. See Warner's note on p. 16, l. 1. Hamelius traces

We can be sure that the author of the *Travels,* whether he was a traveler or not, listened to many a pilgrim reporting of the wonders he had seen. And yet the evidence is overwhelming that Mandeville depended almost, or entirely, upon "the authorities" for his materials. But, like Chaucer or Shakespeare or any other writer, his quality depends, not on his borrowings, but on what he did with them.

---

this to Vincent in his note on p. 19, l. 3. The theory that men were much larger before the flood came down from antiquity through the Renaissance; see D. C. Allen, "Donne among the Giants," *Modern Language Notes,* LXI (1946), 257-260.

[27] *The Complete Works of Geoffrey Chaucer,* ed. F. N. Robinson (Boston, 1933).

# THE TRANSFORMATION OF THE MATERIALS

Mandeville has been called a forger, a "mere plagiarist," and even a "mere translator." His debt to William of Boldensele has been somewhat exaggerated, although it is real enough; but his borrowings from Odoric of Pordenone are not only extensive but continuous, and therefore they will serve best to illustrate how skillfully he transformed his materials to build up the illusion of reality which is the foundation of successful fiction. The comparison is easily made, because he follows Odoric's itinerary step by step. But he adds, deletes, revises, and changes the character of the whole, including the personality of the traveler, in a way which strikingly demonstrates his conscious artistry.

The two begin their journey together at Trebizond,[1] about which city Mandeville borrows some of Odoric's very words. He omits, however, Odoric's simple marvel of some partridges which followed a man like so many chickens. Instead he elaborates what Odoric has to say of St. Athanasius: that he "made the Creed," and is buried at Trebizond. Mandeville adds to this bare statement the story that the saint was put in prison for heresy and while there wrote a psalm which embodied his faith. He sent it to the Pope, who was thereby convinced that he was a true Christian and ordered his release.[2]

[1] For his account of the Holy Land, from Bethlehem on, Mandeville drew heavily on a *De Terra Sancta* which was attributed to Odoric; see Warner's notes to pp. 35 ff.

[2] The story seems to be a confused reflection of the troubles St. Athanasius had with various Roman emperors, and was probably not original with Mandeville. Warner, note to p. 73, 1. 4, comments on the confusion of two bishops named Athanasius. I quote the translation of Odoric in Sir Henry Yule's *Cathay and the Way Thither*, II, 97 ff.

Next Odoric says that he went to Armenia, to a city called Erzeroum (Erzrum). The mention of Armenia reminds Mandeville of a good story, and he proceeds to tell of the castle of the sparrowhawk—a story which accounts for the sorrows of that land. This is a beautifully proportioned little folktale, involving three men and three trials with different results. Whether Mandeville invented it, or not,[3] apparently he was responsible for the attachment of this story to the legend of the house of Lusignan. The king of Armenia, when the *Travels* was being written, was a member of the house of Lusignan (1342-75), as Mandeville undoubtedly knew.

Next Mandeville repeats, verbatim, what Odoric has to say of Erzrum, amplifying a little the account of the Euphrates.[4] Then Odoric mentions "Sarbisacalo," the "mountain whereon is Noah's Ark. And," he says boastfully, "I would fain have ascended it, if my companions would have waited for me," although the people of the country reported that no man could ever ascend it because it was not "the pleasure of the Most High."[5] Mandeville changes the whole spirit of the account and enriches it with graphic details. He says, first of all, that the mountain is also called "Ararat," and by the Jews "Taneez"; that it is seven miles high; and then, to Odoric's statement that Noah's Ark rests on its summit, he adds, "And men may see it afar in clear weather." In reporting the inaccessibility of the summit, he converts Odoric's futile boast into an impersonal but graphic explanation: "And that mountain

[3] See below, Chap. 15. Jean d'Arras added the story to the Melusine legend by making the heroine, Melior, a sister of Melusine. Leo Hoffrichter, "Die ältesten französischen Bearbeitungen der Melusinensage," *Romanistische Arbeiten*, XII (1928), 33-34, points out that the last king of Armenia of the Lusignan line died in Paris in 1393, *after* the romance of Melusine was completed, but the fairy curse falls on Armenia and the whole line of kings, not on any particular one. Hoffrichter says that the transfer of the castle from Arles to Armenia is probably due to the Lusignan connection, and R. S. Loomis agrees: *Arthurian Tradition and Crétien de Troyes* (New York, 1949), pp. 89-95.

[4] Pollard's ed., p. 100.
[5] *Cathay*, II, 102.

is well a seven mile high. And some men say that they have seen and touched the ship, and put their fingers in the parts where the fiend went out, when that Noah said, *Benedicite*. But they that say such words, say their will. For a man may not go up the mountain, for great plenty of snow that is always on that mountain, neither summer nor winter" (p. 100). So no man since Noah's time has been up, except one monk who brought away a plank from the ark which is preserved in the monastery at the foot of the mountain. Marco Polo, Hayton, and Friar Jordanus all mention the snow, and the inaccessibility, and Rubruquis tells the story of the plank, although not in quite the same form. Warner found no source for the height of the mountain, for the Jewish name for it, or for the hole in the ark where the fiend went out.[6] The last sounds like an episode in a Noah play.

Mandeville has not only changed the whole tone and spirit of Odoric's account, but he has created a visual image by adding details of sense impression—the ark can be seen afar in clear weather. He also injects a reassuring note of scepticism by his disbelief that anyone has been up to touch the ark, and he gives a characteristically reasonable explanation why it is impossible. Then he makes the difficulty of the ascent vivid by telling the story of the monk who got to the top only with the help of an angel. The economy of the whole episode, fifteen lines in Pollard's text, is perfect in its kind, and as far above Odoric as the work of a master artist is above that of an ordinary reporter.

Next, both Odoric and Mandeville speak of Tauris (Tabriz), where Odoric reports the famous "dry tree." Since Mandeville has other and more effective use for this marvel, he omits it here. He also omits Odoric's comment, "And there are many things else to be said of that city, but it would take too long to relate them."[7] The wandering friar often expresses his im-

---

[6] Notes to p. 74, ll. 17 and 23; and see Letts, p. 53 n.
[7] *Cathay*, II, 104.

## TRANSFORMATION OF THE MATERIALS

patience with his task and lets the reader down in this way, as Marco Polo does also. Mandeville seldom, or never, resorts to generalization, and one of his charms is that he has no set phrases.[8]

He follows Odoric past the summer palace of the Emperor of Persia, at Sultânieh, and on to Cassan (Kashan), which, Odoric remarks, is the city of the Magi. Mandeville drops out the "bread and wine, and many other good things," which interested Odoric, and concentrates his whole attention on the story of the three Magi. Neither does he stop here to describe the dry sea, to which Odoric devotes a sentence. Mandeville saves this marvel until near the end of his book, and then he draws upon the more imaginative *Letter of Prester John* for his materials.[9]

Odoric is fond of such flat and colorless generalizations as "And there are many other matters there" or "It aboundeth in many kinds of victual." Mandeville regularly omits such statements. For example, Odoric says, "At length I reached the land of Job called Hus which abounds in all kinds of victuals." Mandeville omits the victuals and concentrates on the story of Job.[10] Odoric next mentions some mountains good for pasturing cattle. Then he says, "There also is found manna of better quality and in greater abundance than in any part of the world. In that country also you can get four good partridges for less than a Venetian groat." Mandeville wastes no time on the cattle or the partridges, but he writes (out of Vincent of Beauvais) as if he had seen and tasted the manna: "In that land of Job there ne is no default of no thing that is

---

[8] Some of the later, but not the early MSS., begin almost every paragraph with the word "Item," and call every country an "isle," but it is not so in the original.

[9] Pollard, p. 180; and Zarncke, *Der Priester Johannes*, VII, 914.

[10] The story of Job, Warner's French text, p. 76, ll. 29-34, beginning "Iob fuist paen . . ." and ending "quant il Morust, CCXLVIII ans," is omitted in the 1371 MS., but appears on fol. 48 of the better text of this redaction, Bibl. Nat. MS. nouv. acq. fr. 10723. For discussion of these texts see below, Chap. 9.

needful to man's body. There be hills, where men get great plenty of manna in greater abundance than in any other country. This manna is clept bread of angels. And it is a white thing that is full sweet and right delicious, and more sweet than honey or sugar. And it cometh of the dew of heaven and falleth upon the herbs in that country. And it congealeth and becometh all white and sweet. And men put it in medicines for rich men to make the womb lax, and to purge evil blood. For it cleanseth the blood and putteth out melancholy" (p. 102).

Surely it is no wonder that there are four or five times as many manuscripts of Mandeville's *Travels* as there are of Odoric's. Mandeville knew how to select and develop his material. He takes the reader with him, giving a sense impression of what he describes, so that we can see and feel and taste it. As Lowes said of the later voyagers, he has a way "of clothing the very stuff and substance of romance in the homely, direct, and everyday terms of plain matter of fact."[11] He knows also the trick of comparing the strange with the familiar, cultivated to such good advantage by Hakluyt's worthies, two centuries later. Odoric says of the women of Chaldea that they wear short gowns with long sleeves that sweep the ground. Mandeville adds, "like a monk's frock."

Next Odoric describes inland India as a place where men live almost entirely on dates, "and you get forty-two pounds of dates for less than a groat; and so of many other things."[12] Here Mandeville, impatient at this dull commercial stuff, leaves him (pp. 102-108) to return to Ur of the Chaldees, and to remind us that here Abraham was born, and here Ninus, who founded Ninevah, was king, and Tobet lies buried. He speaks of Abraham's departure with Sarah to the land of Canaan, and of Lot and the destruction of Sodom and Gomorrah, and he says that beyond Chaldea is Scythia, the land of the Amazons,

[11] J. L. Lowes, *The Road to Xanadu* (Boston, 1927), p. 313.
[12] *Cathay*, II, 111-112.

TRANSFORMATION OF THE MATERIALS 31

to whose history he devotes a page, mentioning Tarmegyte (Merv?), where Alexander built cities, and Ethiopia and Mauritania, where live the men who have only one foot and use it for a sunshade.[13] Then he passes to India to tell, not of dates, but of diamonds. He gives us a wonderful story of how diamonds breed and grow like animals, and of how, in the far North, ice turns to crystal, and on the crystal grow the good diamonds. He goes on more soberly to the various uses and kinds of diamonds, ending with practical suggestions about how to tell a good diamond from an inferior one.[14]

Nor is he ready, even yet, to rejoin Odoric. First he must tell of the Indus with its great eels "thirty foot long and more" (according to Pliny and his successors), and of the vast population of India which travels but little because it is ruled by Saturn, whereas "in our country is all the contrary; for we be in the seventh climate, that is of the moon. And the moon is of lightly moving . . . , and for that skill it giveth us will of kind for to move lightly and for to go divers ways, and to seek strange things and other diversities of the world (p. 109).[15]

At last Mandeville is ready to rejoin Odoric at Ormes (Hormuz), where he repeats Odoric's surprising information that the great heat makes *ly perpendicles del homme, i.e. testiculi* hang down to their knees.[16] He adds, from Marco Polo or the *Letter of Prester John,* that "in that country and in Ethiopia, and in many other countries, the folk lie all naked in rivers and waters" to escape the heat.[17] Then, apparently of his

[13] They are described by Pliny, Solinus, Isidore, Vincent, Higden, and even St. Augustine; see Warner's note to p. 78, l. 22.

[14] See below, pp. 76-77.

[15] Warner, note to p. 81, l. 5, quotes a similar passage from Gower (ed. 1857, III, 109). Hamelius hastens to point out that both England and Liège are in the seventh climate; see his note to p. 108, l. 6.

[16] See Cordier's note 4, in Yule's *Cathay,* II, 112-113.

[17] This passage is cited by Warner, note to p. 81, l. 17, and Sir Henry Yule, "Mandeville" in the *Encyclopaedia Britannica,* as the only borrowing from Marco Polo in Mandeville, but there are others: the mark made by the crocodile's tail in the sand, details of the garden of the

own invention, comes the further detail that "men and women together . . . they lie all in the water, save the visage . . . and the women have no shame of the men, but lie all together, side by side, till the heat be past" (p. 109). Mandeville actually describes what he had not seen but only imagined, while Marco Polo, who had seen it perhaps, reports without attempting to describe.

Both Odoric and Mandeville speak of the ships built without nails (a procedure for which Mandeville supplies a reasonable explanation), and of the great rats at Thana. But next Odoric gives us a long, pious tale of four friars who got into trouble with the authorities and were slain. They were able to stand unharmed in fire, so their heads were cut off. Then their flesh refused to rot, and they were finally buried by the Christians. Odoric claimed that he gathered up their bones and carried them all the way to China (by sea), performing miracles with them along the way.[18] Mandeville shows no interest whatever in this typical medieval miracle. The only trace of the martyred friars in the *Travels* is the remark (borrowed from the midst of Odoric's recital) that at Thana the dead are not buried because the sun soon dries up dead bodies.[19] The comment is oblique but revealing, both of the personality of Mandeville and of his attitude toward Odoric. In place of the long account of the martyred friars, he devotes his attention to the strange religions of India. Odoric says, "The people thereof are

---

Assassins, etc.; see n. 31, below, and next chapter. The detail of the crocodile is not in Odoric, or in Vincent, as Warner notes on p. 98, l, 4. Marco Polo does not make the statement about the sexes; see A. C. Moule and Paul Pelliot, *Marco Polo: The Description of the World* (London, 1938), I, 124-125, and, on the mark of the Crocodile's tail, I, 279.

[18] Marco Polo also records miracles of this type, such as the moving of a mountain by prayer, and the existence of a church in which the roof is supported by pillars which do not touch the ground: Moule, I, 105-112, 144-146.

[19] *Cathay*, II, 137. Pollard, p. 112.

idolaters, for they worship fire, and serpents, and trees also."[20] He is not interested in the how or the why. Mandeville is interested in both, because he recognizes that these people of strange lands are human beings like himself. His attempts to understand them gives his narrative the human interest which vitalizes it and makes his imaginary travel more real than the actual peregrinations of Odoric, or even of Marco Polo.

He elaborates the account of the religion of these people, crediting them with natural religion, "for they know well that there is a God of kind [nature] that made all things, the which is in heaven" (p. 110). They worship the sun because it is so profitable that they know "God loveth it more than any other thing," and they worship the ox because it is the most patient and profitable of beasts. He is attempting to rationalize what Odoric and others have merely reported. He adds, moreover, an account of their superstitions, mentioning similar superstitions among Christians, and adding the charitable comment that, since Christians who are well instructed have such beliefs, it is no marvel that the pagans "that have no good doctrine but only of their nature, believe more largely for their simpleness." He has seen augurs foretell the future by the flight of birds, but nevertheless "therefore should not a man put his belief in such things, but always have full trust and belief in God our sovereign Lord" (p. 112).

Mandeville's tolerance and charity are in striking contrast to Odoric's rigid orthodoxy. To Odoric the heathen are simply "idolaters" and the Nestorian Christians, who befriended the Roman missionaries in all parts of Asia, are "schismatics and heretics," or "vile and pestilent heretics."[21] Mandeville, on the other hand, includes nine Nestorians among the fifteen men who went with him into the Valley of Devils, a feat which

[20] *Cathay*, II, 114.
[21] *Cathay*, II, 117, 142. On the importance of the Nestorians in China in the 13th and 14th centuries, see Budge, *The Monks of Kûblâi Khân*, pp. 36 ff.; and A. C. Moule, *Christians in China before the Year 1550* (London, 1930).

Odoric considered evidence of his own special holiness. Mandeville is sure that "all the divers folk, that I have spoken of . . . have certain articles of our faith and some good points of our belief . . . But yet they cannot speak perfectly (for there is no man to teach them), but only that they can devise by their natural wit" (p. 206). His tolerance and charity give an impression of urbanity which dignifies and enlarges the mind of the author. The field of his interests is much above Odoric's.

The divergence in the account of the pepper forests of Minibar (Malabar) shows another facet of the contrast. Odoric says that the pepper forests are full of snakes which must be burned out before men can gather the pepper.[22] Mandeville says that "some men say" fire is used to drive out the snakes, but it is not so, for fire would burn up the pepper. What they really do, he says, is to anoint themselves with the juice of lemons (the Cotton text mistranslates "snails"), and the snakes dislike the smell and do not trouble them (p. 113). Odoric's remedy for snakes in the pepper can be found in Isidore of Seville. Mandeville apparently invented his, taking a hint from another part of Odoric's Itinerary, where Odoric says that lemon juice is used in Ceylon to keep off leeches.[23] Neither man is reporting from first-hand observation. Both are dependent upon "the authorities," but Mandeville creates the impression of careful observation and good sense by saying, "For if they burnt about the trees that bear, the pepper should be burnt, and it would dry up all the virtue, *as of any other thing.*" Friar Jordanus denies the use of fire,[24] but it was not until John of Marignolli published his report, the same year the *Travels* was finished, that Europeans were told pepper did not grow in forests at all, but in gardens.[25] The passage

[22] *Cathay*, II, 136.
[23] *Cathay*, II, 171.
[24] *The Wonders of the East,* trans. and ed. Sir Henry Yule, Hakluyt Soc., No. 31 (1863), p. 27. Friar Jordanus was in India just before Odoric.
[25] Marignolli's Itinerary is translated in Yule's *Cathay,* III (Hakluyt Soc. 2d Ser. No. 37 for 1914), see p. 217; and see Warner's note to p. 83, ll. 17, 18.

illustrates Mandeville's tendency to disagree with his authorities and to look for a reasonable explanation which does not violate the laws of nature.

After the pepper forests, Odoric describes Polumbrum (Quilon, in Malabar) and reports the worship of the ox and the "abominable superstition" of anointing with its ordure. He also reports the sacrifice of children, the practise of suttee, and he says, "there be many other marvelous and beastly customs which 'tis just as well not to write."[26] Mandeville, in repeating all this, raises it from a depressing kind of anthropology to high romance. He begins by interpolating an account of the Fountain of Youth, which he borrows from the *Letter of Prester John* and locates at Polumbrum. He says, by way of authentication. "I have drunken there of three or four sithes, and yet me thinketh I fare the better" (p. 113)—surely a modest way of making a wild boast! Next he describes the worship of the ox, borrowing the name of the priest who officiates, the "archiprotopapaton," out of the *Letter of Prester John,* and making an elaborate religious ceremony out of Odoric's "abominable superstition."[27]

So this ill-sorted pair journey uneasily together, like the two horses of Plato's chariot of the soul, one all fire and spirit, the other pedestrian and earthy, interested chiefly in the quality of the victuals and the wickedness of the heathen. Both report the worship of the Juggernaut, but Mandeville alone is moved to say: "And them thinketh that the more pain, and the more tribulation that they suffer for love of their god, the more joy they shall have in another world. And, shortly to say you, they suffer so great pains, and so hard martyrdoms for love of their idol, that a Christian man, I trow, durst not take upon him the tenth part the pain for love of our Lord Jesu Christ" (p. 117). Odoric traveled in the flesh, but how much more truly Mandeville traveled in the spirit!

---

[26] *Cathay,* II, 140.
[27] See Warner's note to p. 84, l. 18. The Zoroastrians of India use the urine and ordure of the bull in their lustrations.

Odoric, following Marco Polo, remarks that at Lamary (Sumatra) "I began to lose sight of the north star, as the earth intercepted it."[28] Mandeville picks up this sentence and elaborates it into his famous account of the roundness of the earth and the practicability of circumnavigation.[29] Indeed, at every step of the way, Mandeville illuminates and vivifies and humanizes Odoric's account of his journey. He adds details which are picturesque, as in the case of the king of Campa (Cochin China), whose fourteen thousand elephants Odoric mentions.[30] Mandeville equips them with "castles of tree" which he says are put on their backs for fighting.[31] Both report the fish which come up onto the land every year, and Odoric says that the natives claim they come to pay homage to their emperor. Mandeville repeats this explanation, and then suggests that perhaps the real reason is that they come to feed the offspring of this king, who has a thousand wives (according to Odoric), and so obeys the commandment given to Adam and Eve: *Crescite et multiplicamini et replete terram.* Then he adds, more soberly: "I know not the reason why it is, but God knoweth; but this, meseemeth, is the most marvel that ever I saw. For this marvel is against kind [i.e., natural law] and not with kind . . . And therefore I am siker that this may not be, without a great token [i.e., miracle]" (pp. 128-129).[32] He never loses sight of the principle that God is also the creator and God of the heathen, though he has only revealed Himself to them through His works. Mandeville's assumption that the laws of nature operate even on the other side of the world is a fundamental part of his belief that it is possible to sail all the way around it. In fact, his conception of natural law as uni-

---

[28] Moule, I, 371, 373; *Cathay*, II, 146-147.
[29] See below, Chap. 15.
[30] *Cathay*, II, 164.
[31] Marco Polo mentions these "castles" on the elephants of Zanzibar; Moule, I, 433; and of Tibet and India, I, 287.
[32] Warner, in his note to p. 95, l. 24, cites records of the similar behavior of fish. Many fish, such as salmon and carp, spawn in shallow water, and one species actually buries its eggs in the sand at high tide.

versal makes it highly improbable that he believed at all in the unnatural marvels which he retold from Odoric and Solinus and the *Letter of Prester John*.

Twice, into Odoric's sufficiently fanciful account of the islands of the Indies, Mandeville inserts additional marvelous islands. After Odoric's account of the dog-headed men of Nacumera[33] he has some additions, and again after Odoric's Dondin, where men kill and eat the sick. After Dondin, Odoric goes directly to Manzi (Marco Polo's name for China), merely remarking that there are "a good twenty-four thousand islands" which he will omit. Mandeville says, at this point, that the king of Dondin has fifty-four (note the modest number) great isles in subjection, each with a king who paid him tribute. He populates these islands with a whole list of marvels collected out of Pliny by Solinus and incorporated in Isidore of Seville, Vincent of Beauvais, and others. Here are the islands of cyclops, men without heads, men with mouths in their backs, men without faces, men with upper lips so large they used them for sunshades, pigmies with mouths so small they had to eat through a pipe, men with ears that hang down to their knees, centaurs, men who go on all fours, hermaphrodites, men with eight toes, and "many other divers folk of divers natures" (pp. 133-135).

This perfect spate of absurdities, all crammed into a single page (fol. 191 of the MS. written in 1371), perhaps was brought on by Odoric's protest that "there be many other strange things in those parts which I write not, for unless a man should see them he never could believe them. For in the whole world there be no such marvels as in that realm. What things I have written are only such as I was certain of, and

---

[33] *Cathay*, II, 167. Odoric created them by combining what Marco Polo says about three different islands, "Necuveran," where the men behave like dogs (Moule, I, 377-378), and "Angerman," where the men have heads like mastiffs (Moule, I, 378), and "Maabar," where a miniature of the ox is worn on the forehead (Moule, I, 404); see Warner's note on p. 97, l. 13.

such as I cannot doubt but they are as I have related them."[34] Mandeville's outburst fills this omission in Odoric's text. Evidently he did not want to omit any marvels, but we might well ask ourselves whether he actually believed in them, or expected his readers to believe. John de Marignolli, in his account of his embassy to the Great Khan, explains that while freaks do occur in nature, such as six-legged calves and two-headed birds, whole races of them do not exist anywhere.[35] Marignolli was a learned man, but not an intellectual giant. He denied the possibility of circumnavigation, which Mandeville argued in favor of, and he confused the great rivers of Asia in an absurd way. But he was not simple and credulous, like Friar Odoric.

Odoric reported more marvels than Marco Polo, who reported enough to discredit him with such practical men as King John of Portugal in the days of Christopher Columbus. Mandeville certainly knew Marco Polo's book,[36] but he elected to follow Odoric, whose account of the East was much briefer and full of marvels. Odoric's contemporaries found his report hard to credit. Sir Henry Yule calls attention to the affidavit which Odoric was called upon to append to his narrative, and he mentions also the apologies made by Odoric's ecclesiastical biographers. Henry of Glatz, Odoric's contemporary, declares, "that if he had not heard such great things of Odoric's perfections and sanctity, he could scarcely have credited some of his stories."[37] Mandeville, in following and improving upon Odoric, was writing the first romance of travel in modern times.

[34] *Cathay*, II, 176.
[35] *Cathay*, III, 254-256.
[36] See index, under "Marco Polo."
[37] *Cathay*, II, 24.

# THE ROMANCE OF TRAVEL

THE STEP by step comparison of Mandeville's *Travels* with Odoric's Itinerary shows most clearly the differences between the two works. Odoric records, without selection, whatever came to his attention along the way; or rather, since he dictated his account after his return, whatever he happened to remember. Mandeville's is a literary undertaking, the product of much reading and of literary rather than purely geographical interests. He everywhere substitutes local history for Odoric's comments on the food supply. The two accounts differ in form, in substance, and in purpose.

Mandeville was writing in a literary genre which has a long history, from the *Odyssey* and the lost *Arimaspeia* of Aristeas, through Ctesias, Megasthenes, and parts of Herodotus, Strabo, Aelian, Photius, and the lost novel of Antonius Diogenes about the wonders beyond Thule. Pliny collected these travelers' tales indiscriminately, and Solinus, perhaps Mandeville's closest forerunner, made a selection from Pliny of choice geographical wonders. Lucian travestied the genre in his *True History*, but St. Augustine included a chapter on the fabulous races of men in his *City of God*. In his day, the romance of Alexander was beginning its long history with the *Pseudo-Callisthenes* and the Epistle of Alexander to Aristotle about the marvels of India. In the seventh century Isidore of Seville repeated much of this lore, and shortly afterwards the pseudo-Aethicus produced his *Cosmographia,* which shows the same disregard for the changes wrought by time, and the same appropriation of other people's experiences complained of in Mandeville. In the Renaissance the popularity of Solinus and Aethicus tended to eclipse Mandeville!

Sometime between the third and seventh centuries a letter was invented which purported to be from "Fermes" to the Emperor Hadrian, describing a journey to the East on which the writer saw all the traditional marvels of strange beasts and stranger men. A book of *Marvels of the East* was made, mostly out of "Fermes." It is preserved in both a Latin and an Anglo-Saxon text.[1] At the opening of the thirteenth century, Gervase of Tilbury included all of "Fermes" in his *Otia Imperialia*. Meanwhile, about 1165, the *Letter of Prester John* appeared and circulated widely. In the thirteenth century, when Europeans had an opportunity to visit China, they reported not only what they saw, but what they expected to see.

As a result, they merely added some fresh marvels to the old ones, and the better educated or more sceptical regarded all alike as "great liars." Marco Polo's difficulties with the incredulous are well-known, and even Friar Odoric's sanctity did not entirely protect him from the sceptics. Mandeville was free, therefore, to add and subtract, to polish, change, and interpret what he found in his sources. He does not omit the best of the traditional wonders of the earth, but he found, in the newer reports of the Orient, things more marvelous than in the old. For example, he took from Odoric the lake at Sylan (Ceylon) formed by the repentant tears of Adam and Eve. Marco Polo reported that the king of Nicoveran had a necklace of one hundred and four great pearls and rubies, which he used, like a rosary, to say his prayers.[2] Odoric raises the number to three hundred pearls,[3] and Mandeville follows Odoric.

---

[1] Edited by M. R. James for the Roxburghe Club (1929). In his Introduction (p. 25), James gives a brief summary of the genre. The letter to the Emperor Hadrian is discussed also by E. Farel, "Une Source Latine de L'Histoire D'Alexandre: La Lettre sur les Merveilles de L'Inde," *Romania*, XLIII (1914), 199-215, 353-370. On Solinus and Aethicus see C. R. Beazley, *The Dawn of Modern Geography* (London, 1897-1906), I, 250 ff., and 360 ff.

[2] Moule ed., I, 383-384.

[3] *Cathay*, II, 169. Mandeville and Marco Polo, but not Odoric, say that the king uses the jewels "as our ladies wear paternosters."

This same king had a famous ruby, which Marco Polo said was "a large palm long and quite as thick as the arm of a man."[4] Odoric makes it "a good span in length and breadth," and Mandeville reports it "a foot of length and five fingers large" (p. 131). Modern critics have called Marco Polo's statement "hearsay," Odoric's "gullibility," but Mandeville's "sheer mendacity." It was, rather, pure fiction.

In his account of Manzi, or China, Mandeville shows much less dependence on Odoric than in the earlier part of the journey. He omits the visit to Zaiton, where Odoric left the bones of the four friars; and he omits some of Odoric's cruder marvels, such as the mountain on one side of which everything is black, while on the other everything is white.[5] He uses other sources of information, as when he substitutes otters for the birds which, according to Odoric, are trained to catch fish for their masters.[6] Both otters and cormorants were actually used, but, perhaps because birds were used for hunting in Europe, the otter seemed the greater marvel. He does not approve of crude exaggeration, however. Where both Marco Polo and Odoric say that Cansay (Hang-chow) is a hundred miles in compass, Mandeville says it is fifty-one miles.

He is much interested in the monastery, reported by Odoric, where the monks feed animals which have human faces, and which they believe are the souls of men. Odoric claimed that he argued with the monks that they were only animals.[7] Mandeville substitutes a characteristic suggestion: "And I asked them if it had not been better to have given that relief to poor men, rather than to those beasts. And they answered me and said, that they had no poor men amongst them in that country; and though it had been so that poor men had been among them, yet were it greater alms to give it to those souls that do there their penance" (p. 137). The point of view which

[4] Moule ed., I, 380. Jordanus says much the same, op. cit., p. 30.
[5] *Cathay*, II, 187.
[6] Ibid., p. 190.
[7] Ibid., pp. 201-203.

he is attributing to the Chinese monks is the same as that taken by many Christian churchmen of his day about masses for the dead, but if his intention is ironic, it is gently and subtly so. Such implications as this constitute his commentary on mankind, and on the life of his time. He describes the strange customs of other lands and lets his reader draw what parallels he will. But we should observe that he has turned Odoric's reaction into something entirely different. He constantly assumes that human nature is the same everywhere, and he uses the familiar to explain the strange, and the strange to suggest comment on the familiar. Yet he is content to observe, clearly and simply, with the full, sympathetic, and imaginative understanding which is true charity.

The pigmies, whom Odoric reported,[8] interested Mandeville, and he adds to every statement that Odoric makes about them, adding also their war against the cranes, which had been traditional since Homer. His greatest contribution to the literature of the pigmies, however, is his account of their relationship to men of normal size. Here, it has been suggested, he set the model for Swift. He says that the pigmies do the finer work, such as weaving, while men of normal size do the farming, "And of those men of our stature have they as great scorn and wonder as we would have among us of giants, if they were amongst us" (p. 138). So Gulliver found it.

Mandeville's descriptive skill is beautifully illustrated by his account of the palace of the Great Khan. He turns Odoric's red leather walls[9] into panther skins which exude a sweet smell, are red as blood, and shine in the sun (p. 141). They are prized, he says, more than fine gold.[10] Odoric mentions next some mechanical peacocks, operated "by diabolic art, or by some engine underground."[11] He gives them about six lines.

[8] Ibid., p. 207.
[9] Ibid., p. 220.
[10] Warner suggests confusion with the stone *pantheros* which was described as red and shining; note to p. 106, l. 1. Letts (p. 66) cites Vincent of Beauvais, who mentions the sweet odor.
[11] *Cathay*, II, 222.

Mandeville, with a better sense for creating a word-picture, sets the stage first by describing the jeweled throne of the Khan with its three "seges" of graduated heights for his three wives. Next he explains how the Khan is served at table, and how his secretaries write down every word he utters. Then he is ready to tell how, at solemn feasts, mechanical peacocks are displayed in motion. The story is much more impressive at this point. He says that the peacocks "dance and sing, clapping their wings together . . . and whether it be by craft or by necromancy I wot never; but it is a good sight to behold, and a fair; and it is great marvel how it may be." Then he dramatizes his own curiosity and the cleverness of the Chinese by claiming, "I did great business for to have learned that craft, but the master told me that he had made a vow to his god to teach it to no creature, but only to his eldest son" (pp. 142-143).

Next he adds the famous vine, with leaves of gold and fruit of precious stones, out of the Epistle of Alexander, *De Situ Indiae,* and some cups of emerald, sapphire, and topaz, from which the Emperor is served, and then he mentions the practical detail of guards kept in the hall, and explains how he came to see it all: "And ye shall understand, that my fellows and I with our yeomen, we served this emperor, and were his soldiers fifteen months against the King of Mancy, that held war against him. And the cause was for we had great lust to see his noblesse and the estate of his court and all his governance, to wit if it were such as we heard say that it was" (pp. 143-144). Here he is adapting a story of Marco Polo's to his own use, but the suggestion of scepticism effectually reassures the reader and makes it possible for Mandeville to find everything more wonderful than he had heard that it was, "insomuch that we would never have lieved it had we not seen it. For I trow that no man would believe the noblesse, the riches ne the multitude of folk that be in his court, but he had seen it." Then he adds the comparison with things familiar which distinguishes his narrative from that of his sources. He says, "it is not there as it is here. For the lords here have folk of certain number as they may suffice; but the great Chan hath every day men at his costage and expense as without number. But the ordinance, ne the expenses in meat and drink, ne the honesty, ne the cleanness, is not so arrayed there as it is here; for all the commons there eat without cloth upon their knees, and they eat all manner of flesh and little of bread, and after meat they wipe their hands upon their skirts, and they eat not but once a day. But the estate of lords is full great, and rich and noble" (p. 144).[12] The comparison not only creates the air of simple candor which is Mandeville's specialty, but it also saves the pride of his readers and sets the seal of apparent authenticity on his work.

Having drawn the picture of the Great Khan, he turns next (Chapters XXIV-XXVII in the Cotton text) to a sketch of the origin and history of the Tartars, out of Hayton, Vincent, and others. Odoric has very little to say on these subjects, but he was apparently the first to bring to Europe the wonderful Chinese story of the vegetable lamb, which Mandeville could not possibly omit.[13] He has no use, however, for Odoric's unimaginative account of Tibet, the land of Prester John. Odoric says that not a hundredth part of the stories about it are true[14] (Carpini says not a tenth part). Here Mandeville turns to the *Letter of Prester John* and gives his readers what will delight them.

He makes use of both Odoric[15] and Marco Polo in his story

---

[12] Warner gives Carpini as the source; note to p. 108, l. 5. Jordanus gives a similar account of the eating habits of the Persians, op. cit., p. 10.

[13] See Warner's note on pp. 212-213, and *Cathay*, II, 240-241. Both Odoric and Mandeville compare this lamb which grows on a tree to the barnacle goose.

[14] *Cathay*, II, 244-245.

[15] Ibid., 257-260. Mandeville changes the name of the Old Man from Marco Polo's Alaodin (Ala-ed-din), the name of the last leader of the Assassins of Persia, destroyed in 1256, to Gatholonabes, and the name of the place from Marco Polo's Mulecte and Odoric's Millestorte to Mistorak. A recent account of the assassins is C. E. Nowell, "The Old Man of the Mountain," *Speculum*, XXII (1947), 497-519. The name of the place was Alamut in the Mulihet Mountains, according to Rubruquis.

of the Old Man of the Mountain, but as usual the interpretation is his own. Probably from Marco Polo, he got the "fair halls and fair chambers depainted all with gold and azure,"[16] but Marco Polo locates the garden in a valley between two mountains. Odoric puts the wall around two mountains. Mandeville is reminded of the Christian traditions of the Earthly Paradise, so he puts it on top of a mountain on an island (where Tasso put his garden of Armida).[17] Marco Polo says that it is in Saracen country, and that the Old Man represents it to his followers as the paradise promised by Mahomet. Odoric calls it simply "a paradise." Mandeville represents the Old Man as quoting the Bible on a land flowing with milk and honey—a concept which Coleridge caught up in the line, "For he on honey-dew hath fed, / And drunk the milk of Paradise." Mandeville even has the Old Man hint of the higher, heavenly paradise, which also belonged in the medieval Christian tradition (p. 184). Marco Polo mentions four conduits flowing with wine, milk, honey, and clear water.[18] Mandeville mentions these, but he adds three wells, "fair and noble, and all environed with stone of jasper, of crystal, diapered with gold, and set with precious stones and great orient pearls," which could, at will, be made to run with wine, milk, and honey. Like Marco Polo, he mentions the fruits and flowers, but he adds mechanical beasts and birds "that sung full delectably and moved by craft,

---

The story of the assassins was well-known in Europe by Mandeville's time, but the legend of the garden paradise does not go back of Marco Polo in Europe and seems to be of oriental origin: F. M. Chambers, "The Troubadours and the Assassins," *Modern Language Notes*, LXIV (1949), 245-251.

[16] Moule ed., I, 129. Lois Whitney, "The Literature of Travel in the 'Faerie Queene'," *Modern Philology*, XIX (1921-1922), 165, notes that the *Romans de Bauduin de Sebourc* has an account of the Old Man of the Mountain, out of Marco Polo, which includes the gold and azure palace and streams of claret, honey, and another wine.

[17] See below, Chap. 16. On traditions of the earthly and heavenly paradise see H. R. Patch, *The Other World* (Cambridge, Mass., 1950).

[18] Odoric mentions briefly a fountain of water, two conduits, girls, and horses.

that it seemed that they were quick." Perhaps he was remembering the mechanical peacocks, or similar mechanisms of the romances.[19] At any rate, he is probably responsible for the mechanical birds which appear in the artificial paradise described by Spenser.[20]

Mandeville owes to Odoric much of his account of the Valley of Devils, which follows next, but here Odoric is especially vainglorious, saying, "all the Saracens, when they heard of this [that he had traversed the valley], showed me great worship, saying that I was a baptized and holy man."[21] Mandeville, on the other hand, remarks whimsically of his courage at this point in the journey, "I was more devout then, than ever I was before or after" (p. 187). He says (in the French, but not in the English text) that his party consisted of fourteen: nine Nestorians, two Greeks, and three Spaniards. Only nine passed through, but some, he says, went around another way. He describes how the party debated whether they should go through, or not, and he says that they were "shriven and houseled" by two friars minor of Lombardy that were in their company. Odoric was a Franciscan friar of Lombardy, and he traveled with a single companion! It is characteristic of Mandeville's sly humor that he should imply that Odoric was his confessor in this tall tale he is borrowing from him.

His description is far better than Odoric's, however. Odoric says that the devils that infest the valley play "nakers" and make sweet harmonies to allure travelers.[22] Mandeville turns

---

[19] Earlier instances of singing metal birds are noted by Otto Söhring, "Werke bildender Kunst in altfranzösischen Epen," *Romanische Forschungen*, xii (1900), 582-586; and Frederic E. Sweet, in his edition of Johann von Konstanz, *Die Minnelehre* (Boston, n.d., ca. 1934), pp. lxxii-lxxiii.

[20] See below, Chap. 16.

[21] *Cathay*, ii, 266.

[22] Ibid., p. 264. J. L. Lowes suggests that Odoric's valley derives from Marco Polo's account of the desert of Lop, or Gobi, where also strange, alluring music is mentioned: *The Road to Xanadu*, pp. 489-490, n. 4, and "The Dry Sea and the Carrenare."

this into "great tempests and thunders, and ... great noise, as it were sound of tabors and of nakers and of trumps, as though it were a great feast" (p. 185). Odoric says the place was full of dead bodies. Mandeville marvels at the freshness of the bodies, and the great multitude of them, "as though there had been a battle between two kings, and the mightiest of the country, and that the greater part had been discomfited and slain." If he was not thinking of the fields of Crécy and Poitiers, his readers must have been reminded of them, and perhaps have drawn an inference from the fact that he makes the valley a test of covetousness. Here again, by comparing the strange with the familiar, a literary device which he did not find in his sources, he has enabled his readers to create a visual image.

After his account of the Valley of Devils, Odoric ends abruptly with profuse protestations of the truth of everything he has recounted.[23] How he got home he does not say. Obviously he had been in the land of hearsay and pure fantasy for some time. Mandeville ends in a more orderly way, bringing his reader home through India, past the land of the Bragmans which Alexander failed to conquer, and Taprobane with its hills of gold protected by ants (out of Herodotus via Vincent of Beauvais). He tells of the four rivers of Paradise, and of the land of darkness.[24] He makes skillful use of bits from Odoric, omitted earlier, such as the funeral service in Tibet where birds are fed the flesh of the dead, and a cup is made out of the skull.[25] From Odoric's account of China he is now ready to tell the story of the rich epicure who lives "in ease as a swine that is fed in a sty for to be made fat" (p. 205). Odoric follows this

[23] See above, p. 38.
[24] Marco Polo puts it in the far north: Moule ed., I, 472-473. He attributes the darkness to magic employed to rob the natives of their furs. He says the Tartars get in and out by using mares, since they will return to their colts without guidance.
[25] *Cathay*, II, 254. This Zoroastrian custom is still being reported: see Lt. Col. Ilia Tolstoy, "Across Tibet from India to China," *National Geographic Magazine*, XC (1946), 181. He does not mention the skulls.

by a mention of the Chinese fashion of wearing long fingernails. Mandeville puts the two together, using the nails as the reason that the man has to be fed by others, the inconvenience of long nails immediately occurring to him.

He ends with a defense of the beliefs of the heathen, and of his own. He says that they all have "some articles of our faith," but imperfectly, because they have only natural religion, and not the revelations of the Bible, to guide them. He defends the Christian use of "simulacres," which he distinguishes from idols, saying, "we worship not the images of tree or of stone, but the saints in whose name they be made after." Then, with characteristic humor (since what he is writing is fiction), he leaves the door of adventure open to his successor. He says that he has not told all of the marvels of the world, but only what he has seen (sic!); and he has not told all of those, so that other men who go thither may, as a reward for their labors, find enough that is new to tell of.

How much the travelers of the next two centuries found to tell can be read in the compilations of Hakluyt and Purchas, but in these later accounts we keep coming upon reminders that these men, in their youth, had read Mandeville as well as Pliny, Solinus, and Strabo and the more "authoritative" ancients. They could have learned some of their narrative art from Mandeville, for much that Lowes describes as the art of the voyagers—their simple, lucid style, their conveying of sense perceptions, their expression of the unknown by homely comparisons with the familiar—all these elements are characteristic of Mandeville.

There are other things which Mandeville did not borrow from Odoric or from Marco Polo. Odoric piles on his marvels indiscriminately, the bad with the good, without proportion or arrangement. Mandeville, like a careful gardener, weeds, prunes, transplants, and arranges his materials to insure variety, harmony, and continued interest. Obviously those who call Mandeville a "mere plagiarist" have not compared the two. Nor is he to be compared to Marco Polo, for Polo, as his most recent editors point out, was not writing a narrative of his travels, but a description of the world. He takes up China, province by province, and city by city, giving for each the location, size, government, religion, currency, taxes, measures, products, and the things which a merchant might want to know. His descriptions are informative catalogues, always expressed in general terms, never in pictorial detail. It has been said of him that he had "looked at everything and seen nothing."[26] His stories are artless and long-winded in a fashion which suggests that his amanuensis, the romance writer, Rusticiano de Pisan, was largely responsible for his literary form.[27] Mandeville, on the other hand, gains his effects by the proper selection and arrangement of details and the apt use of simile, in a way which could, and probably did, give lessons to such moderns as Defoe and Swift.

He writes like a man of reading and social experience, who brings to his travels more than he finds in books. He looks through the eyes of others and sees more than they have recorded. He was writing, at least in his account of Asia, entirely out of his reading; but he had read so widely that the source-hunters, intent on proving that he had not traveled at all, have succeeded in proving that he had read most geographical works from Pliny to Marco Polo. What is more important, he read with his imagination. In the school of Solinus and Aethicus he was writing an epitome of the new travel literature of his own time. He was writing literature, not a dishonest travel book.

He does not pretend to confine himself to the experience of

[26] Moule ed., I, 40.

[27] P. Paris suggested that Marco Polo's companion in prison, who wrote down his account of his travels, was Rusticiano, or Rustichello de Pisan, compiler of the *Table ronde*, and grandfather of Christine de Pisan: "Extrait d'une notice sur la relation originale de Marc-Pol, Vénitien," *Journal Asiatique*, 2d Ser., XII (Sept. 1833), 244-254, extracted from the *Bulletin de la Société de Géographie*, 1st Ser., XIX (1833), 23-31. L. F. Benedetto, *Marco Polo: Il Milione* (Florence, 1928), pp. xiii-xxxiii, has demonstrated the truth of this theory, and Moule and Pelliot, in their edition, accept the identification, I, 40-43.

an actual traveler. He enriches his narrative, wherever he can, by telling of the religious and literary associations of whatever place he is describing. In the first part of the book, he reports not only the religious associations of the Holy Land, but the classical and romance associations as well. He understands the use of literary allusion, and he combines the pleasures of novelty and of recognition.

He is artist enough to go a step further and create literary associations. He succeeded in attaching folk tales to new places. He has an unfailing instinct for what is appropriate. Warner remarks that his folklore is always right for the region to which it is assigned.[28] Perhaps he has had a larger share than has been recognized in forming our concepts of what is appropriate to various regions. At any rate he localized the castle of the watching of the sparrowhawk in Armenia, where it took its place quite naturally in the folklore of the East. He borrowed the story of the perilous kiss, perhaps from the romance of *Le Bel Inconnu* (the English version, *Libeaus Desconus*, by Thomas Chester, was written 1325-50), localizing it at Lango, or Cos, making the dragon-woman a daughter of Hippocrates. The association is plausible, because Hippocrates was born at Cos, was associated with the serpent cult of Aesculapius, and had a son or grandson named Draco. Whether Mandeville knew all this, or whether his invention was merely a fortunate one, its effectiveness is shown by the fact that it was adopted into both the romances and the local histories.[29] The dragon-woman of Cos is referred to in Bondelmonti's *Liber Insularum* (ca. 1420), in Porcacchi's *L'Isole più Famose* (Venice, 1576), and as late as Boschini's *L'Arcipelago* (Venice, 1658). Mortorelli incorporated it verbatim into his fifteenth century romance of *Tirante lo Blanch*.[30] Evidently Mandeville had the

[28] Note on p. 12, l. 16.
[29] Ibid. A discussion of Mandeville's source, with references to other discussions, is G. Huet's "La Légende de la Fille d'Hippocrate à Cos," *Bibliothèque de l'Ecole des Chartes*, LXXIX (1918), 45-59. Huet argues that it was a local legend at Cos.
[30] Warner, note on p. 12, l. 16.

same power to localize folklore which Washington Irving displayed so notably. It is a literary gift of great value.

Mandeville was not responsible for localizing the tale of the Gorgon's head at the Gulf of Adalia, or Satalia. It had been traditional there from the time of the early crusades,[31] but he modified the story in several ways. Where others say that the head was thrown into the gulf and made it dangerous, Mandeville says that because of it the city sank into the sea and the gulf was formed. He also suppressed the cruder elements of magic in the story, converting it into a romance of a lost city,[32] and created a more polished narrative without violating the nature of the folktale he was revising.

Perhaps the best example of his instinct for what is right in folklore appears in the case of the orb which he says has fallen from the hand of the statue of Justinian at Constantinople. He says that it will not stay when it is put back, because it "betokeneth the lordship that he had over all the world," much of which had been lost by the Eastern Empire. A careful checking of the reports of other travelers indicates that the orb was still in the statue's hand in Mandeville's day,[33] but

[31] It is reported in detail by Benedict of Peterborough, Roger of Hoveden, Gervase of Tilbury, Walter Map, and others. Warner's note on p. 14, l. 6, gives references and also notes that the story figures in the Vulgate version of the *Livre d'Artus*. See also Hamelius' note, II, 33-34.

[32] Several hundred local legends of engulfed cities, monasteries, etc., were recorded by René Basset, "Les Villes Englouties," *Revue des Traditions populaires*, v-xxxiv (1890-1919). The cities are usually under lakes, and were often engulfed because of sins or curses, but none of the stories resembles Mandeville's significantly. H. M. Smyser, "The Engulfed Lucerna of the *Pseudo-Turpin*," *Harvard Studies and Notes in Philology*, xv (1933), 49-73, summarizes Basset.

[33] Warner, note on p. 4, l. 16, says that the *cross* on the orb was blown down in 1317 and repaired in the same year. Boldensele does not mention the loss of the orb, nor does Bondelmonti in 1422. Stephen of Novgorod (1350), Zosimus (1420), and Clavijo (1403) describe it as still in place. Schiltberger (1427) repeats Mandeville's story, but he also tells Mandeville's story of the watching of the sparrowhawk, and several others of his fictions. His learned editor, evidently unaware of his debts to Mandeville, has some amusingly puzzled notes on these points: see *The Bondage and Travels of Johann Schiltberger*, trans. J. Buchan Telfer

symbolism required that it should have fallen out. A similar tale of a giant idol on the shore at Cadiz, said to have been erected by Mahomet, told of a key destined to fall out of the idol's hand when a king should be born in France who should restore Christianity to Spain.[34] Mandeville may have been imitating this story in his account of the statue of Justinian. At any rate he knew what was appropriate.

Warner comments on the aptness of his mention of St. Nicholas in juxtaposition with the Greek Sea, because the Greek islanders of the Middle Ages attributed to St. Nicholas what their forefathers had fabled of Poseidon.[35] On the other hand, sometimes Mandeville may make a bold transfer of a bit of folklore; for example, he attributes to a tribe in India a superstition about the breaking of maidenheads which Julius Caesar had attributed to the Britons. The historians of travel literature have been particularly outraged by this transposition, but Mandeville was certainly right in putting the belief in a far country. In fact, he may not have been following Caesar at all, but Solinus, who tells a slightly different version of the story about the Augyles, who live next to the Troglodites in Ethiopia (which in the Middle Ages was considered to be a part of

---

with notes by P. Bruun, Hakluyt Society, Vol. 58 (1879), Chaps. 30, 31, 38, and 57, with the note on pp. 228-229. *Clavijo: Embassy to Tamerlane, 1403-1406*, translated by Guy Le Strange, is in the Broadway Travelers Series (London, 1928), see p. 72. Robert Fazy, "Jehan de Mandeville: Ses Voyages et son séjour discuté en Egypte," *Asiatische Studien*, 1-4 (1950), 30-54, argues that this and other details of the account of the Near East are authentic and show that Mandeville had been there.

[34] C. Meredith-Jones, *Historia Karoli Magni et Rotholandi ou Chronique du Pseudo-Turpin* (Paris, 1936), Chap. IV, pp. 100-102; R. N. Walpole, *Philip Mouskés and the Pseudo-Turpin Chronicle* (Berkeley, 1947), pp. 327-433, provides a source study; and another text in "The Burgundian Translation of the Pseudo-Turpin Chronicle in Bibliothèque Nationale (French MS. 25438)," *Romance Philology*, II (1949), 177-215; also edited by H. M. Smyser, *The Pseudo-Turpin*, Mediaeval Academy of America Publications, 30 (1937), see p. 60 and p. 20 and note.

[35] Note on p. 11, l. 16.

India.)[36] He has been accused of transferring the castle of the sparrowhawk from Arles to Armenia, but there is no evidence that the watching test was a part of the *Mélusine* legend before Jean d'Arras borrowed it from Mandeville and added it to the end of his romance of *Mélusine* by calling the fairy mistress of the sparrowhawk Melior (Mandeville does not name her), and making her a sister of Mélusine.

Mandeville's dependence on his authorities, and especially on Odoric of Pordenone, is so great that it does not seem possible that he had traveled in the Far East. But if he did not travel with Odoric, neither did he merely plagiarize from him. He made of the bald and undiscriminating Itinerary of the Friar what is, indeed, another book, as different from Odoric's as the personality and education of Mandeville are different from Odoric's. The *Travels* is incomparably richer than the materials out of which it was made because the imagination of a writer of genius has shone upon those materials and brought them to life. Mandeville is neither a plagiarist nor a "forger," but the creator of a romance of travel, a field in which he holds his place with the best.

[36] See Chap. 31 of the *Polyhistor,* ed. Th. Mommsen (Berolini, 1864); or A. Golding's translation (London, 1587), Chap. 34.

## THE EXPERIENCE
## OF A TRAVELER

THE PROBLEM of whether or not Mandeville had traveled is partly biographical and will be discussed in Part II; but since it cannot be settled on a biographical basis, and since it is significant chiefly for our estimate of the author's literary genius, the evidence provided by the *Travels* must be discussed here. The discovery of sources for most of his facts has led critics to assert positively that he had never traveled at all, but that is not a necessary conclusion. His imaginative reporting of sense impressions makes it easy to believe that he had done some traveling. Moreover, there are some details in the first part of the *Travels* which show a familiarity with what the French called *outre-mer*, and which are entirely lacking in the second part, the account of the Far East, where he is much less likely to have been. This difference may be due to the greater wealth of information about the Near East available to him, or it may be the echo of a journey made in his youth and much overlaid by subsequent reading. As he says, "things passed out of long time from a man's mind or from his sight, turn soon into forgetting" (p. 6). Undoubtedly he had read widely in "the authorities," but there is a certain sureness in visualization, a certain aptness in supplying details for which no source has been found, which suggests that he had been as far as the Holy Land.

If, as he says, he set out in 1322 and did not finish the book until 1356, he could have had ten or fifteen years of travel, followed by fifteen or twenty years of reading, before he began to write. There were many interests, both religious and worldly, which drew men to the Near East in this century. There were

## THE EXPERIENCE OF A TRAVELER

pilgrimages and military expeditions against the "Saracens"; there were commercial interests and territorial struggles.

Of the great Crusading Orders, the Templars had been suppressed in 1311, but the Hospitalers, or Knights of St. John of Jerusalem, had set up their headquarters at Rhodes, where "representatives to every language and religion of the Levant jostled, haggled and quarrelled."[1] Of the two hundred Knights of this Order, the English contingent seems to have consisted of twenty-eight knights with their attendants plus a reserve in England of thirty-eight more.[2] In 1343 the Hospitalers, with the aid of the Venetians, the king of Cyprus, and the Papal forces, took Smyrna and aroused the enthusiasm of all Europe by that achievement. The English Crusading Order of St. Thomas of Acon was established at Nicosia, on Cyprus, and as late as 1357 it was receiving new members.[3] There was fighting in Spain and Greece and in the islands of the Mediterranean,[4] during the years in which the author of the *Travels* says that he was abroad and had been "in many a full good honourable company, and at many a fair deed of arms, albeit," he adds modestly, "that I did none myself, for mine unable insuffisance" (p. 208). The various efforts to identify Chaucer's knight furnish materials for illustration of the far travel of many Englishmen

---

[1] W. A. Phillips, "St. John of Jerusalem," *Encyclopaedia Britannica*, 11th ed.

[2] E. J. King, *The Knights of St. John in the British Empire* (London, 1934), pp. 52-55. See also *The Knights Hospitallers in England: being the report of Prior Philip de Thame to the Grand Master Elyan de Villanova for 1338*, ed. L. B. Larking with an Introduction by J. M. Kemble, Camden Society, No. 65 (1857), listing property in almost every county of England and naming 34 knights, 48 squires, and 34 chaplains.

[3] E. J. King, *The Knights Hospitallers in the Holy Land* (London, 1931), pp. 306-307. There is a tentative list of crusaders from England, 1150-1220, naming several Mandevilles, in Beatrice W. Siedschlag, *English Participation in the Crusades 1150-1220*, (Bryn Mawr Doctoral Diss., privately printed, 1939).

[4] See Atiya, *Crusade in the Later Middle Ages;* and J. Delaville Le Roulx, "La France en Orient au xive siècle," in *Bibliothèque des Écoles Françaises d'Athènes et de Rome*, No. 44 (Paris, 1886), I, 88-110.

in this period, and of the widespread interest in the Holy Land which supplied the audience for the *Travels*.[5]

Travel to the Holy Land was so common in Mandeville's day that it is hard to believe a man so interested in the East did not find some way to go there. In support of this hypothetical probability are the many specific and interesting details for which intensive source-hunting has found no authority earlier than the *Travels*. Some of these details concern Cyprus, an island which Mandeville mentions several times in different connections. If he had been to the wars in the East he would certainly have stopped there, for it was a common stopping place for pilgrims and a transfer point for merchandise, as well as an important kingdom in the politics of the Middle East. Its king was of the house of Lusignan and very active in trying to organize the Christian states against the Turks. Its chief port, Limasol, had been the headquarters of both the Templars and the Hospitalers until the former were suppressed and the latter moved to Rhodes.

Mandeville twice mentions a cross preserved at Cyprus, which he says was represented by its custodians as the True Cross, whereas it was only the cross of the good thief (pp. 8, 19-20). No one else mentions this fraud before 1727.[6] Mandeville was not hostile to relics, but interested in them and informed about them. It does not seem probable that he invented this story, but rather that, as he says, one half of the True Cross was at Constantinople and the other half at Paris. His intelligence might well be offended at being asked to venerate still another True Cross at Cyprus.

He mentions the good wines of Cyprus, especially the wine

[5] J. M. Manly, "A Knight ther Was," *Transactions and Proceedings of the American Philological Association*, XXXVIII (1907), 89-107; A. S. Cook, "The Historical Background of Chaucer's Knight," *Transactions of the Connecticut Academy of Arts and Sciences*, XX (1916), 161-240; and for a summary, Muriel Bowden, *A Commentary on the General Prologue to the Canterbury Tales* (New York, 1948), pp. 52 ff.

[6] Charles Rohault de Fleury, *Mémoire sur les Instruments de la Passion de N.-S. J.-C.* (Paris, 1870), pp. 324-325, reports the fraud.

## THE EXPERIENCE OF A TRAVELER

"de Marrea" which, he says, was much prized by the king there. Warner found no mention of this wine in any of the itineraries before 1395 when d'Anglure reported it.[7] However, an Augustinian monk of Verona who visited Cyprus in 1335 mentions a wine called "Marea."[8] Mandeville could hardly have seen the monk's report, but he was not inventing the name of the wine.

His most curious statement about the island is his assertion that the Cypriotes sit on the ground to eat and dangle their feet in pits dug for the purpose, "for greater coolness" (p. 20). It seems that the Cypriotes dug trenches for the storage of their wine, and it has been suggested that Mandeville mistook the purpose of these trenches.[9] But the mistake is the result of observation, not of reading. Mandeville could, of course, have got it at second hand from a returning traveler, but he could hardly have invented it.

Other details about Cyprus have been traced to Boldensele and Jacques de Vitry, including the story of the hunting leopards which he says are called "papiones" (i.e. baboons). Warner suggests that the name represents a misunderstanding of de Vitry.[10] D'Anglure describes the animals as *smaller than foxes* and names them "carables." Mandeville says they resemble leopards, and are somewhat *larger than lions* and more agile (p. 20). They were, undoubtedly, the hunting leopards, or cheetas, used immemorially in India and Persia, and known in Italy at least from the time of the Emperor Frederic II. Mandeville is right, therefore, about their appearance. If he makes them too large D'Anglure has them too small, although there is no question of the genuineness of D'Anglure's travels.

---

[7] Warner's note to p. 12, l. 11; and *Le Saint Voyage de Jherusalem du Seigneur d'Anglure*, ed. F. Bonnardot & A. Longuon, Société des Anciens Textes Français (Paris, 1878), p. 85, "vin de Marbao."

[8] C. D. Cobham, *Excerpta Cypria* (Cambridge, 1908), p. 18.

[9] Warner, note on p. 15, l. 2, and comment, p. xvii. And see Fazy, op. cit.

[10] Warner, pp. xvii and 165, col. 2; Hamelius, II, 35.

## 58   THE *TRAVELS* AS LITERATURE

If Mandeville had traveled in the East at all, he would have visited Jerusalem. He *says* that he has been there many times, but the evidence consists of small details and precise measurements for which no source is known. Again and again he differs from Boldensele and the others in the number of steps, the number of columns, and the number of paces from one place to another. In many cases his testimony is corroborated by later visitors.[11] Unfortunately, some of these visitors "borrowed" freely from Mandeville, and we cannot check the reports by modern surveys because many places have been much changed since Mandeville's day. He seems to have been the first to designate the chapel in which Indian priests sang their service. His statement is corroborated by D'Anglure and Poloner,[12] but from his own day down through the sixteenth century the *Travels* was used by travelers in the Holy Land, who borrowed from it in good faith.[13] Their corroboration is suspect.

Mandeville makes a good many mistakes, and these have been produced as evidence that he had not traveled at all; but all of the travelers made mistakes. Marignolli made one river out of four; Marco Polo put cities on the wrong side of rivers and doubled various distances. In describing the church on Mt. Sion, Mandeville follows pseudo-Odoric, who says that it was still in use (1330), but Symon Simeonis, who visited the Holy Land in 1323, says that it was in ruins.[14] We do not know which was right.

[11] See Warner's note on p. 46, l. 5. No one earlier had mentioned the "synagog" on the Hill of Evil Counsel, but D'Anglure and Poloner (1422) follow Mandeville. No earlier mention of the "Charnell of the hospitale of S. John" has been found. See also Warner's notes on p. 47, l. 7; p. 48, l. 1; p. 42, l. 4; etc. The dimensions of the temple, the height of the rock in its center, the fact that the well is dry, all are details not found earlier. See also Warner's notes on p. 45, l. 10; p. 39, l. 21; and p. 40, l. 27.

[12] Warner's note on p. 40, l. 17.

[13] See Schiltberger (Chap. 3, n. 33 above), especially chaps. 30-32, 38; 57, etc.; and *The Pilgrimage of Arnold von Harff, Knight*, trans. and ed. by Malcolm Letts, Hakluyt Society, 2d Ser., No. 94 (1946), cf. index.

[14] Warner's note to p. 45, l. 12.

Mandeville's account of the number of columns and of steps in the church at Bethlehem disagrees with the figures given by earlier writers examined by Warner, but he is followed by Poloner, and his figures can be reconciled with the findings of later surveys.[15] These seem like insignificant details, but Warner lists too many of them to be accounted for by any theory of lucky guesses. We can only suppose either that Mandeville observed for himself, or that he had access to a better itinerary than has been preserved.

He shows considerable independence of known sources in his account of the monastery near Mt. Sinai. His stories of the source of the oil supply and of the miraculous election of the abbots were copied by later travelers. To the relics of the place he adds, from some source unknown to Boldensele, a bloody cloth in which St. Katherine's head was wrapped. Symon Simeonis reported that *the head* of St. Katherine was preserved there.[16]

He reports that there was a field for jousting at Constantinople. Boldensele did not mention it, but it was observed and described afresh by Clavijo (1403-06).[17] His story about the statue of Justinian does not prove that he had never been at Constantinople. He certainly adapted to his own purposes what he took from others, and he surely would not have hesitated to do as much for what he had seen for himself. He borrows much of his account of the religion of the Greeks from De Vitry, but he does not echo De Vitry's hostility.[18] On

---

[15] Warner's note to p. 35, l. 17.

[16] Warner's notes to p. 36, ll. 10, 11, and p. 39, l. 21. See also *Itineraria Symonis Simeonis et Willelmi de Worcestre,* ed. James Nasmith (Cambridge, 1778), p. 54. There is a full summary of Symon's itinerary by Mario Esposito, "The Pilgrimage of Symon Semeonis: a Contribution to the History of Mediaeval Travel," *The Geographical Journal,* L (1917), 335-352, and LI (1918), 77-96.

[17] Ruy Gonzalez de Clavijo was sent by Henry III of Castile to the court of Timour Beg of Samarkand; *Clavijo: Embassy to Tamerlane,* pp. 69-71.

[18] Warner, note on p. 31, l. 17. De Vitry was a great crusading preacher

the contrary, he reports it with such independence and moderation as to give it a different tone entirely. He makes the mistake of saying that the Greeks, generally, could not marry a second time, whereas that rule applied only to the priests—but that kind of information is always a matter of books and hearsay. It cannot be observed.

His treatment of Boldensele is often that of a rival. For example, Boldensele says that he had a letter which enabled him to enter the Dome of the Rock at Jersusalem. Mandeville says that *he* had a letter *from the Sultan* of Egypt for that purpose.[19] He directly disputes Boldensele on several points. Where the latter claimed to have traveled between Babylon (Cairo) and Mt. Sinai in record time, Mandeville comments unfavorably on the great haste of some travelers. He also says that the desert cannot be crossed on horseback, in contradiction of Boldensele, who claims to have done so.[20] He contradicts Boldensele on the purpose of the pyramids, arguing that they are not tombs, but the granaries of Joseph (pp. 35-36). He supports his mistake with the plausible arguments of their great size, hollow interior (a mistake current at the time), gates, etc. If all this was mere pretense to cover his indebtedness to Boldensele, then he deserves more literary credit than a genuine rivalry would entitle him to. Cairo was visited by many pilgrims. Symon Simeonis, the Irish monk who crossed England on his way to the Holy Land in the same year that Mandeville says that he set out, spent some time in Cairo and has much to report about it.

---

and Bishop of Acre, born before 1180 and dead about 1240; T. F. Crane, *The Exempla . . . of Jacques de Vitry,* Publications of the Folk-Lore Society, No. 26 (London, 1890), pp. xxii-xxxiv, for an account of his life.

[19] Professor Chew says that this story of a letter of permission "may indubitably be numbered among his lies," but his witnesses are all from the 16th and 17th centuries; *The Crescent and the Rose,* p. 79. Ludolph von Suchen, writing about 1350, says that the Dome of the Rock had *recently* been forbidden to Christians because of some ill-mannered Greeks: *Description of the Holy Land,* trans. Aubrey Stewart, Palestine Pilgrim's Text Society, XII (1895), 98.

[20] Warner, p. xviii, and note on p. 29, l. 25.

## THE EXPERIENCE OF A TRAVELER

Mandeville's itinerary of the Near East is distinguished from its predecessors by an unusual number of native names for places and commodities. These strange words are effective as a literary device regardless of their value as evidence of travel. However, Mandeville frequently supplies place names that are reasonably correct for the language of the place. It would be unreasonable to expect complete accuracy, since there was no standard formula for transliteration, and since scribes in copying Mandeville's text were particularly inaccurate in the transcription of strange words. Yet, in spite of these handicaps, Mandeville frequently succeeds in suggesting the native name. He adds to Boldensele's account of the way to Egypt, the name of the wilderness of Et-Tîh, to which he adds the Turkish word ending of place names, -*lik*, calling it "Atthelek." He calls the citadel *El-Kalah*, "Calahelic."[21] For *Canopus* the best text reads "Canopac," and *Mersyn* and *Belboys*, or *Belbeis*, are recognizable. Warner reports that "Markaritot" is the native name for St. Karitot, and he could find no other western pilgrim who used the prefix.[22] Of the "Saracen" names that he gives for the three kinds of balm, "Enochbalse, Abebissam, Guybalse," Warner suggests that the second represents the Arabic word *anab-balsân*.[23] Sometimes, however, Warner did not look far enough in his search for Mandeville's nomenclature, for he gives no source for the Arabic word "Gibel," which Mandeville uses for Mt. Aetna, although *Mongibel* was the usual name for that mountain in the Arthurian romances of Italy.[24]

Warner says that Mandeville alone prefixed the article and gave the Arabic name for bitumen, "al katran."[25] His place name, "char dabago," appears to represent the Persian word,

---

[21] Ibid. p. xvii, and note on p. 17, l. 13.

[22] Ibid., p. xxi, and note to p. 38, l. 2.

[23] Note on p. 26, l. 4. Trevisa's translation of Bartholomaeus names them "orilobalsamum, carpobalsamum, and Opobalsamum," lib. 17, cap. 18; ed. 1535, fol. ccl.

[24] Warner's note to p. 29, l. 3; E. G. Gardner, *The Arthurian Legend in Italian Literature* (London, 1930), pp. 12-13.

[25] Warner, p. xxi, and note to p. 50, l. 4.

*Chār bāgh,* literally "four gardens," or a palace.[26] His name for the diamond, "hamese," is evidently the Arabic *almās*.[27] He says the red earth of Hebron is called "cambil." The Arabic is *canbîl*. One of his names for the three kinds of pepper is the Arabic *fulful*. Some of these words may, as Warner suggests, have come from some medical or scientific work.[28] The place names may have come to him from travelers. At any rate they add interest, and give the appearance of authenticity to his narrative.

His propensity for supplying native names, in his account of the Near East, is in sharp contrast to the lack of any trace of authenticity in such matters when he gets beyond Trebizond. The name of the Mongol Khan of central Asia he borrows from Carpini, whose information was a century out-of-date. His native Indian name for the parrot comes from Vincent of Beauvais. He took the name of the high priest of Polumbrum from the *Letter of Prester John.* Elsewhere he departs from Odoric's nomenclature, but not in the direction of authenticity.

In evaluating the significance of his Arabic and Persian and Turkish words, we must remember that in the fourteenth century there was a considerable missionary movement as well as many commercial and political contacts between Europe and the Near East. Rubruquis, in the mid-thirteenth century, seems to have known Arabic fairly well and even to have learned enough Mongol to control his interpreter.[29] Ramón Lull (1235?-1315) persuaded the Council of Vienna in 1311 to adopt his plan for teaching Hebrew, Arabic, and "Chaldee" at Rome and in the four leading universities of Europe in order to prepare missionaries.[30] Lull spoke and

[26] Ibid., p. xxiv, and note to p. 75, l. 10.
[27] Warner's note to p. 79, l. 5.
[28] Warner, p. xxiv.
[29] Rockhill, Introduction, p. xxxvii.
[30] Atiya, *Crusade,* pp. 78, 86, et passim. Pierre Dubois also urged the study of Greek and Arabic for missionary work, in his *De Recuperatione Terre Sancte,* Atiya, p. 52. Both Lull and Ricold de Monte Croce preached in Arabic, Atiya, p. 160.

taught Arabic, and lectured at the Universities of Paris and Lyons in 1287-89, 1298, and 1302-05. There is a little evidence that the teaching of Oriental languages was attempted at Oxford shortly after 1311.

In addition to the missionaries, the merchants provided a channel by which Arabic words, especially the names of items of commerce, might reach the West. Consuls and *funduqs,* or commercial centers, were maintained by several European governments at Alexandria, Cairo, Beyrouth, Damascus, Acre, and Aleppo.[31] Early in the century, in 1316-17, the Venetian galleys began to make "the Flanders voyage" and Gabriel Dandolo, Captain of the Fleet, was named agent in England. There were interruptions, but Edward III encouraged the trade with Venice, and the annual voyage linked England and Flanders directly with the center of European trade with the Orient. Spices and drugs from the East Indies were brought by the Arabs to Alexandria, Damascus, and the other commercial centers where there were European *funduqs,* and were there traded for European products, among other things English wool. So it was that the Venetian galleys carried to London such exotic spices as ginger from Malabar, cloves from Ternate, nutmegs from distant Malacca, wormwood from Persia, camphor from Borneo, belzoim from Siam and Sumatra, and pepper from India.[32] There grow all manner of spicery in Java, says Mandeville, "as of ginger, cloves-gilofre, canell, seedwall, nutmegs and maces" (p. 125), and Chaucer, in the *Romaunt of the Rose,* follows his French author over a very similar list.[33]

[31] Atiya, pp. 114-116, and notes on p. 115. See also W. Heyd, *Histoire du Commerce du Levant au Moyen-âge,* trans. F. Raynaud (reprinted Leipzig, 1923), II, 725 ff.

[32] *Calendar of State Papers . . . Venice,* ed. Rawdon Brown (Rolls Series, 1864), I, liii-liv, cxxii, lxviii-lxvix, cxxxv ff.; and see Francesco Balducci Pegolotti, *La Practica della Mercatura,* ed. Allan Evans (Cambridge, Mass., 1937), Glossary and Index of Commodities, pp. 411-435; and L. F. Salzman, *English Trade in the Middle Ages* (Oxford, 1931), pp. 420 ff. Not only spices, but marmosets, apes, and in 1305 a parrot, were imported.

[33] Ed. F. N. Robinson, p. 677, ll. 1367-70.

64                THE *TRAVELS* AS LITERATURE

Through this trade channel we would expect a good many Arabic words to reach the West along with the products. Both the Universities and the seaports, as well as the pilgrims and the military adventurers, provided means of intercourse between the Arab world and the West.

On the other side of the ledger, it has been noted that Mandeville reverses the order of the towns along the coast of Palestine from Gaza to Athlît.[34] He follows the order of Boldensele, who was traveling north, while he is traveling south. He is mistaken about the names of the sons of the Sultan of Egypt, but here he shows more knowledge than ignorance. He borrows from Hayton the names of the Sultans to Melik-en-Nasir, but Hayton ends in 1307, and Mandeville completes the account of this Sultan's reign to 1341 correctly. Melik was followed in very rapid succession by eight of his sons, four in a single year. Mandeville calls the first, Melik-al-Mansūr, "Melichmader," which is not far wrong, but the next name, "Melechmadabron," comes nearest to Melik-el-Mudhaffar, the sixth son (d. 1346).[35] However, the best informed Europeans must have found it difficult to keep up with the rapid changes. Mandeville has been accused of borrowing the statement that the Sultan had four wives, one of whom was a Christian, from William of Tyre, who reported that the much earlier Sultan Baîbars had a Christian wife.[36] But here again we must consider that even the most honest traveler cannot *observe* such facts as these. He must depend on rumor. The conversation which Mandeville says that he had with the Sultan about the state of Christendom is a literary device with many precedents. He may have been imitating Marco Polo's report of a conversation with Kublai Khan on the same subject.[37]

[34] Warner's note on p. 17, l. 9.
[35] Warner, p. xvii; but see Atiya, *Crusade*, p. 534, for the list of Sultans.
[36] Warner's note on p. 20, l. 13. Grousset, *Histoire des Croisades*, III, 645, says that Baîbars (mid-thirteenth century) married Marguerite, daughter of Philippe de Montfort.
[37] Moule ed., I, 201-202. V. Chauvin (Chap. 1, n. 12, above) cites parallels in earlier travelers, especially Cesaire de Heisterbach.

To Mandeville's interest in languages we must add the alphabets which form so unusual a feature of the *Travels*. In the best texts of the French original, the alphabets of six languages are given, with both the forms and the names of the letters represented. While the forms of the letters were sure to be distorted quickly, as the scribes tried to draw them, the names could be copied more easily and so are more likely to be as the author wrote them. The letters of the first, or Greek alphabet, are named correctly, and in the correct order. The "Egyptian," "Jewish," "Saracen," "Persian," and "Chaldean" range from unrecognizable to purely fanciful.[38] However, the invention of them was not Mandeville's. Warner points out that similar alphabets occur in Hrabanus Maurus, *De Inventione Linguarum*, and some are printed (in J. G. Eccard's *De Origine Germanorum*) which are said to derive from a Ratisbon manuscript of the eleventh century.[39] Mandeville's alphabets derive from his reading and not from travel, but no earlier traveler shows so much interest in languages. The alphabets were evidently an attractive feature of the *Travels*, for the second redactor[40] added alphabets for the Chinese and for the land of Prester John. One was invented for the Old Man of the Mountain. A Dutch version, copied in 1430, has no less than seventeen such alphabets.[41] Two subsequent visitors to the Holy Land, Breydenbach and Von Harff, in the sixteenth century, included alphabets in their itineraries and borrowed other

[38] Warner (p. xxi) says that the "Jewish" alphabet is tolerably correct in some early manuscripts. But he probably had in mind the alphabet in Bibl. Nat. MS. nouv. acq. fr. 4515, which was added at the end of the MS. by another hand. Mr. Letts, p. 156, mistakenly attributes it to the scribe of the manuscript, but see below, Chap. 9, note 8.

[39] Notes to pp. 71, l. 18, and 76, l. 1. Eccard, (ed. Göttingen, 1750), Pl. xiv, opposite p. 88; Maurus, ed. J. P. Migne, *Patrologiae cursus Completus . . . Latine*, cxii (1852), 1579-83; Hamelius, ii, 21.

[40] See below, Chap. 7.

[41] Arthur Schoerner, *Die Deutschen Mandeville-Versionen: Handschriftliche Untersuchungen* (Lund, 1927), describes two MS of this kind, see below, p. 325.

things from Mandeville.[42] Sir Thomas More provided an alphabet for his Utopians very much in the manner of Mandeville.

It is possible that Mandeville knew a little Greek. The letters in the extant manuscripts are, of course, badly drawn, but they are named correctly, and in the correct order. Moreover, in his account of Golgotha he quotes two Greek inscriptions (p. 51). They are sometimes garbled and sometimes transliterated by the copyists, but they are recognizable. One of them he could have got from Peter Comestor's *Historia Scholastica Evangelica*, but no source has been found for the second.[43]

In general, the oriental alphabets are not evidences of travel, but neither are they pure inventions, literary hoaxes, or secret ciphers, as has been suggested.[44] They reflect a genuine interest in languages. Sir Simon Burley, the friend and tutor of Richard II, owned a book "of divers words in divers languages,"[45] but such books were not common. At the end of his so-called Arabic alphabet, Mandeville comments on the unique characters which he calls "thorn" and "zogh," which "we in England have in our language" (p. 96), in a way which gives verisimilitude to an alphabet of strange characters, but it also attests a genuine interest. The use of native place-names, some details of fact, and especially his accuracy of association, his ability to catch (or recreate) the atmosphere of the places he describes, suggest, though they do not prove, that the author had been at least in the more common resorts of pilgrims and would-be crusaders in the Near East.

[42] See above, p. 23.

[43] The translator of the Egerton text recognized one of the inscriptions, and with a "sum bukez saise thus" he quotes Comestor: Warner's note to p. 39, l. 4. According to Warner, the other inscription was not recorded elsewhere until the 16th century.

[44] Hamelius (II, 22) argues that they were intended for use in secret correspondence by "sympathizers with Mandeville's heterodox views." There is not a scrap of evidence either for the heresy or for the secret cipher: see Letts, pp. 151-152.

[45] Laura A. Hibbard [Loomis], "The Books of Sir Simon Burley 1387," *Modern Language Notes*, xxx (1915), 169-171.

## THE EXPERIENCE OF A TRAVELER

Neither his borrowings nor his mistakes are substantial evidence that he had not traveled, but the evidence is fairly tenuous that he had. Travelers regularly made extravagant claims and geographical mistakes. Marignolli claimed that he had visited the Queen of Saba (i.e. Sheba), and that he was within forty miles of the Earthly Paradise, which, says he, reaches up to the sphere of the moon "as Johannes Scotus hath proven." He also claimed to have seen Adam's footprint at Ceylon.[46] He makes one river, the Phison, out of the Volga (or Oxus), the Ganges (or Indus), the Yang-tze-kiang, and the Hwang-ho.[47] Others, including Marco Polo and Odoric, reported marvels and made geographical mistakes. Others padded their narratives with what they had read. Odoric's editor points out that his account of Nicoveran is a composite of what Marco Polo reported of the dog-headed men of Andaman, the miniature ox-head worn on the foreheads of the people of "Maabar," and the great ruby of Ceylon.[48]

Mandeville's geography is, on the whole, as good as that of other travelers of his day.[49] It is remarkably learned for a literary man with what must, at best, have been a limited opportunity for firsthand observation. It is very nearly incredible as the work of a man who had never traveled at all. Warner remarks on Mandeville's reading that "we have to credit the author with the learning of a clerk and a range of reading more naturally associated with the studious seclusion of a monastic library."[50] On the contrary, in the seclusion of a monastic library it would have taken more genius than it seems reasonable to credit the author with, to have produced so *credible* a book as the *Travels*. It was not only much more popular than either Friar Odoric's or Marco Polo's, judging by the number of translations and of surviving manuscripts, but

[46] *Cathay*, III, 220 ff.
[47] Ibid., pp. 224-225, and note.
[48] Moule ed., I, pp. 378, 380, 404.
[49] For a discussion of his measures of distance, see below, pp. 178 ff.
[50] Warner, p. xxx.

it was also consulted and borrowed from by pilgrims to the Holy Land of both the fifteenth and sixteenth centuries. He had narrative and descriptive powers of the first order, but where did he learn, except by observation, of such optical illusions as that of the sea, which he describes as "so high that it seemeth as though it hung at the clouds" (p. 132)? He could have read that in western Libya the sea is higher than the land.[51] But he is describing the sea on the other side of the world from western Libya, and he is vivifying it by an optical illusion which anyone who has been to sea is likely to have had, but which seems incredible as an invention. He does not need to have been to the South Seas to have seen the sea so high that it seemed to hang from the clouds, but he does need to have been to sea. Otherwise, what we take from him in actual experience we must add to him again, with interest, as imaginative power and literary skill.

[51] As for example, in Brunetto Latini, *Li Livres dou Trésor*, ed. P. Chabaille (Paris, 1863), p. 169; or ed. F. J. Carmody (Univ. of California Press, Berkeley, 1948), p. 120.

## MOTIVES AND THE MAN

THE AUTHOR of the *Travels* has created a very attractive and convincing self-portrait. He has represented himself as a knight and a traveler, an Englishman to whom modesty and under-statement (as a method of boasting) come naturally. He sustains throughout the book the character of a modest and candid observer. Even when he is telling the tallest tales, he reassures the reader with the disarming observation that he would not have believed it if he had not seen it himself. Yet he is a first-rate story-teller with a rich and vivid recreative imagination which enabled him not only to see what others had recorded, but to touch and taste. And, though he loves to quote the Latin of the Bible, he represents himself as a layman with an open, inquiring, and intelligent mind and a quizzical sense of humor. So far as the book is concerned, that *is* the character of its author.

Something further can be learned about him, however, by a consideration of his purpose in writing. He was not one of the many men of his time who advocated a new crusade, although he opens the *Travels* on that note.[1] He begins by explaining that our Lord consecrated the Holy Land with his blood and left it to "us in heritage." Therefore, he says, "every good Christian man, that is of power, and hath whereof, should

[1] Atiya suggests that the purpose of the *Travels* was to promote a crusade: *The Crusade of Nicopolis,* p. 25; *The Crusade of the Later Middle Ages,* p. 163. Leonardo Olschki says that the purpose was entertainment: *Marco Polo's Precursors* (Baltimore, 1943), pp. 9-15. Letts says, "he was concerned only with the needs of pilgrims and the preservation of the Holy Places": *Sir John Mandeville,* pp. 41-42. A. C. Baugh says that he set out "to write a mere guidebook," but continued it with an account of his travels in Asia: *Literary History of England* (New York, 1948), p. 267.

pain him with all his strength for to conquer our right heritage, and chase out all the misbelieving men." Unfortunately, "now pride, covetise, and envy have so enflamed the hearts of lords of the world, that they are more busy for to dis-herit their neighbours, more than for to challenge or to conquer their right heritage before-said." If they would make peace, and with "the common people" take this holy voyage over the sea, then within a short time this heritage would be in "the hands of the right heirs of Jesu Christ" (pp. 4-5). At several points he returns to this theme. Edward III was fighting for his "heritage," the crown of France (1337-56), and the French were intent "to dis-herit their neighbours"—from an English point of view.

However, the *Travels* was written, as the author goes on to say, because for a long time there has been no "general passage ne voyage over the sea; and many men desire for to hear speak of the Holy Land, and have thereof great solace and comfort." He is writing for readers with crusading hopes, or dreams, but he is not writing a guidebook, as has been so often asserted, and he is not writing propaganda for a new crusade.

After the fall of Acre in 1291, the reconquest of the Holy Land remained a kind of ultimate objective of all good men for three centuries. Throughout the fourteenth century it was constantly being agitated for. Mandeville was born in the reign of Edward I, who fought at Acre in 1272, and who in his old age (1304) wished to lead another crusade. Peter Dubois dedicated to him the first draft of his *De Recuperatione terre Sancte*.[2] Ramón Lull (d. 1315) advocated both a missionary and a military effort against the Turks. Marino Sanudo wrote what he intended as a blueprint of a new crusade, in 1306-07, and revised it for Philip of Valois, the new king of France, in

[2] Atiya, *Crusade of the Later Middle Ages,* gives a full account of all the works mentioned here. See also J. Delaville Le Roulx, "La France en Orient au xiv⁰ siècle," I, 88-110. Dubois's tract was edited by Charles-Victor Langlois, in *Collection de Textes pour servir à l'étude et à l'enseignement de l'histoire,* IX (Paris, 1891).

1321. He called it the *Secreta fidelium crucis* and urged an alliance with the Tartars against the Turks. In 1332-33 Philip took the Cross, and the organization of a "last great crusade" seemed about to begin. Three hundred thousand of his subjects are said to have followed his example. In England, Friar Roger de Stavegni addressed a treatise, *Du conquest de la Terre Sainte*, to Edward III. Parliament was in favor of the crusade, and was assured that Edward wished to go.[3] In Scotland, Robert Bruce, dying without having realized his crusading hopes (1329), directed that his heart be carried to the Holy Land for burial. The *Directorium ad Philippum regem*, attributed to Burchard, or Brocard, of Mount Sion, was written about 1330, to promote a new crusade.

It is against this background of crusading agitation that the first part of the *Travels* must be viewed. There is a reminiscence of Sanudo in Mandeville's opening pages. Both compare the Holy Land to the "umbelico," or navel, of the world. Warner traces some of the materials in the Introduction to Sanudo.[4] The first route described by Mandeville is borrowed from Albert of Aix's itinerary of the first crusade. Even after the Hundred Years' War had begun, the Hospitalers and their allies took Smyrna (1343-47). In 1345 the Dauphin of Vienna undertook a crusade. And in 1362, as soon as the English and French had made peace, Pierre I de Lusignan, king of Cyprus, visited Europe to promote a new crusade. The kings of France, England, and Denmark supported his effort and some troops were raised. Chaucer's knight was "at Alisaundre . . . whan it

[3] *Oeuvres de Froissart*, ed. K. de Lettenhove (Brussels, 1867), II, 523-525, note to 320-328.

[4] On the navel of the world, see Ugo Monneret de Villard, *Liber Peregrinationis di Jacopo da Verona*, in *Il Nuovo Ramusio* I (Rome, 1950), p. 162 n. 56. Mandeville seems to follow Sanudo in locating the land of Prester John far beyond Cathay. Sanudo puts it in the extreme northeast of Asia. See Warner, notes p. 215. Sanudo's map is reproduced in J. Bongars, *Gesta Dei per Francos*, Pt. II. A bibliography of Sanudo's works is in G. Sarton, *Introduction to the History of Science*, III (Baltimore, 1947), Pt. I, p. 771.

was wonne" (1365), and "at Lyeys" (1367) "and at Satalye." This was just after the *Travels* was finished and probably stimulated the initial circulation of the book.

Mandeville was not writing to promote a crusade, but he was writing for the entertainment of would-be crusaders. He was writing "specially for them that will and are in purpose for to visit the Holy City of Jerusalem and the holy places that are thereabout," but he is writing for readers, not for the guidance of travelers. He neglects the practical information about money and supplies which interested Marco Polo and Odoric, and which marked the guidebooks to the Levant in his day. He is busy, instead, with the history and customs of the people. He is re-creating the countries he describes, for stay-at-homes, men whose desire to visit the Holy Land has been frustrated by the quarrels of their sovereigns.

He was interested in people and in their beliefs. Whether by accident or design, he begins with the Greeks and gives accounts of successively less orthodox religions, ending with the purely "natural" religion of the "Bragmans." After he has described the beliefs and practises of the Greeks, he comments: "And all be it that these things touch not to one way, nevertheless they touch to that, that I have hight you, to shew you a part of customs and manners, and diversities of countries . . . For many men have great liking, to hear speak of strange things of diverse countries" (p. 15).[5] It is his desire to show the customs and manners and diversities of countries which makes his work so much more than a guidebook.

Next he describes the religion of the Samaritans (pp. 72-73), the Jacobites, Syrians, and Georgians (pp. 79-81), and then he comes to the Saracens (pp. 88-96), whose beliefs are dealt with from the point of view of the things they already accept and believe about Christ. He assures his readers that "because that

[5] The Italian version of the *Travels*, printed at Venice from 1491 through the sixteenth century, mentions on its title page the accounts of "diuerse secte . . . christiani & infideli."

they go so nigh our faith, they be lightly converted to Christian law when men preach them and shew them distinctly the law of Jesu Christ" (p. 91). So Ramón Lull taught. It is noteworthy that he does not repeat the gross slanders about the Mohammedan religion which appeared in his sources of information, such as Vincent of Beauvais, Jacques de Vitry, and William of Tripoli.[6]

His report of the religion of the "Bragmans," or Brahmins, preserves a medieval tradition about a "natural religion" and probably gave More some ideas for the religion of his Utopians. Mandeville says, "And albeit that these folk have not the articles of our faith as we have, natheles, for their good faith natural, and for their good intent, I trow fully, that God loveth them, and that God take their service in gree, right as he did of Job, that was a paynim, and held him for his true servant. And therefore, albeit that there be many diverse laws in the world, yet I trow, that God loveth always them that love him, and serve him meekly in truth, and namely them that despise the vain glory of this world, as this folk do, and as Job did also" (p. 195). Here he quotes three texts from Scripture to show that God "had other servants than those that be under Christian law." Therefore, he argues that "no man should have in despite none earthly man for their diverse laws, for we know not whom God loveth, ne whom God hateth."

So wide a tolerance was not common in Christendom in the period between the Albigensian Crusade and the preaching of Wyclif. Hamelius charges that Mandeville was a heretic. The Church showed no concern about the *Travels*, however, unless the apocryphal claim in the English versions, that the author had been to Rome and secured the approval of the Pope, was invented to reassure English readers. It is not in the original, nor in any of the continental versions.

[6] See Hamelius' ed., II, 82, note to p. 85, l. 13. Gower, in *Confessio Amantis*, Langland, and Honoré Bonet, *Arbre des Batailles*, all protest the crusade as a method of conversion: see Atiya, *Crusade of the Later Middle Ages*, pp. 187-188.

Mandeville's tolerance is not simply indifference, as we can see when he comes to generalize at the end of the book: "And ye shall understand, that of all these countries, and of all these isles, and of all the diverse folk . . . and of diverse laws, and of diverse beliefs that they have, yet is there none of them all but that they have some reason within them and understanding, but if it be the fewer [perhaps here he bethought him of his monstrosities], and that have certain articles of our faith and some good points of our belief, and that they believe in God, that formed all things and made the world, and clepe him God of Nature . . . But yet they cannot speak perfectly (for there is no man to teach them), but only that they can devise by their natural wit" (p. 206).

The book is not a plea for missionaries, any more than it is a plea for a crusade. Mandeville did not have Lull's painful conviction that a vast army of souls was being lost every day for lack of Christian doctrine. His is a larger view of the infinite mercy and wisdom of God. He believed that there were other ways to be saved besides being an orthodox Christian, "we know not whom God loveth, ne whom he hateth" (p. 195).[7]

Mandeville never descends to the level of propaganda. He is writing for the entertainment of a cultured audience, not preaching or persuading. Yet, in its general purpose, the *Travels* is a serious, and for its day a very scholarly book, presenting in fresh and spirited form the best information obtainable (and the most entertaining from a literary point of view) about the legendary and mysterious East. It is, moreover, a very moral book, not because it preaches morality, but because it is the expression of a gentle and charitable mind—a mind free from prejudice and malice, and open with the natural gaiety of such freedom.

He seems to have been amused at Odoric's account of the

[7] E. Montégut writes a somewhat overdrawn and eulogistic account of the main current of Mandeville's thought; "Sir John Maundeville, L'homme et le Conteur, le philosophe," *Revue des Deux Mondes*, XCVI (1889), 277-312, 447-567, reprinted in *Heures de Lecture d'un Critique* (Paris, 1891), pp. 235-337.

naked men and women of Lamary who, seeing him clothed, scoffed at him, saying that God made Adam and Eve naked. Mandeville repeats this, turning Odoric's first-person narrative into an impersonal one, and making them say further, "no man should shame him to shew him such as God made him, for nothing is foul that is of kindly nature. And they say that they that be clothed be folk of another world, or they be folk that trow not in God" (p. 119).[8] These people practise community of wives, and of goods, and "all the land is common; for all that a man holdeth one year, another man hath it another year; and every man taketh what part that him liketh." At another point he mentions a people who practise the community of wives, apparently so that he can bring in the jest, "If any man say to them, that they nourish other men's children, they answer that so do other men theirs" (p. 190).

Neither nudism nor communism were new in the world,[9] and quite possibly it amused him to put in the mouths of the heathen, and of distant savages, arguments which he had heard advanced in all seriousness by the "free thinkers" around him. Or perhaps he was merely dealing with the other customs of the heathen in the same broadly humane spirit in which he deals with their religions.

He does not have the zest for crudities of the flesh, and especially for the scatological, which possessed Rabelais. He mentions the taboo of virginity, and the race of hermaphrodites, but he does not elaborate. He simply includes them among the wonders of the earth. His account of the worship of the ox in India is less gross than Friar Odoric's.[10] He shows no inclination to shock his readers. Hamelius goes so far as to call even Mandeville's mention of the plurality of wives in Oriental courts an exhibition of "lewd humor," but Mandeville is merely repeating facts as he found them in his sources.

---

[8] There is a very similar passage about the Tartars on p. 165.
[9] For Marco Polo's defense of nakedness, see Moule ed., I, 405.
[10] Marco Polo also reported that the "Braamins" anointed themselves with an ointment made of powdered ox-dung: Moule ed., I, 404-405.

He had a concept of nature as orderly; that is, of natural law as we understand it. A marvel is something "against kind," as he remarks of the Dead Sea where (according to tradition) iron floats and feathers sink. The fish that come up onto the land are acting "against kind," and so it must be a miracle. The theory that God is revealed in nature, and in the observation of natural law, was by no means unorthodox in the Middle Ages. The conflict between religion and natural science was as yet undreamed of.

We should, I believe, view his tall tales in the light of his conviction of the order of nature. It has been suggested that perhaps he was parodying the tales of credulous and lying travelers, since "surely some of his arguments are a little too preposterous for perfect simplicity."[11] Surely they are; but he was a master of the light touch and the swift retreat. We can see an educated contemporary's attitude about such things as whole races of monstrosities in Marignolli's denial,[12] and in Trevisa's remark, at the end of his translation of Bartholomaeus Anglicus' account of Ethiopia (lib. xv, cap. lii), including men with four eyes, "as it is said, not that it is so in kind [nature] but that it is feigned." Traditional good stories were not to be sacrificed in favor of a mere geographical vacuum.

Mandeville not only preserves these fictional and traditional decorations, but he arranges them in new and wonderful combinations. He takes the commonplace designation of two kinds of diamonds as male and female, and converts it into a sex relationship, saying that they engender and bring forth young, which grow when nourished by dew. Some lapidaries report that the onyx bears little onyxes within it,[13] and that pearls grow when fed by dew. Mandeville has combined similar absurdities,[14] to create a tall tale which outdoes the most absurd

[11] *Times Literary Supplement* (London, March 23, 1933), p. 197.
[12] See above p. 38.
[13] *Mirk's Festial*, Early English Text Society, Extra Series, xcvi (1905), 107.
[14] Pollard's text, pp. 105-108. Warner (p. 197a) points out that most

of the lapidaries. For he adds that in northern India (Siberia) it is so cold that for "pure cold and continual frost the water becometh crystal.[15] And upon these rocks of crystal grow the good diamonds" (p. 105). Shades of Paul Bunyan! Perhaps what inspired this fantastic collection of absurdities was Marco Polo's story of a valley full of diamonds which was guarded by venomous snakes. Men got the diamonds by throwing meat into the valley. The meat stuck to the diamonds and was picked up by eagles and storks. By this means the diamonds were carried out of the valley.[16] Sinbad the Sailor had visited this valley before Marco Polo. Mandeville has a more whimsical and fanciful touch. Moreover, he immediately follows with a sober explanation of the uses of diamonds, and the kinds, according to the science of his day.[17]

On the other hand, it seems very doubtful that he indulged in satire. It has been suggested, more than once, that he used the alleged customs of the heathen for that purpose, as in the case of the island called "Milke," which he adds to Odoric's account. He says of it, "there is a full cursed people. For they delight in nothing more than for to fight and to slay men. And they drink gladliest man's blood, the which they clepe Dieu. And the more men that a man may slay, the more worship he

---

of this account comes from Pliny, or from Solinus, Isidore, Marbode, Vincent, and similar works. Bartholomaeus reports that pearls are engendered and fed by dew, and that "Echite" consists of male and female stones, and some contain stones within, like a woman with child: lib. xv, cap. 39 (ed. of 1535, fol. ccxxx). F. de Mély, *Les Lapidaires de l'Antiquité et Moyen Age,* Histoire des Sciences (Paris, 1896-1902), III, xlv-xlvi, reports that Theophrastus describes a stone "de faire accoucher," which is another matter.

[15] Three centuries later Sir Thomas Browne devoted a long chapter to combating this error: "Vulgar Errors," II, i, in his *Works,* ed. G. Keynes (London, 1928), II, 87-99. Solinus also denied it, cf. Golding's trans., Chap. 24, sig. n$^{iii}$.

[16] Moule ed., I, 395-397. The same story forms the basis of the adventure of Sinbad on his second voyage: *The Arabian Nights' Entertainments,* trans. E. W. Lane (Philadelphia, 1879), pp. 485-486.

[17] The confusion of the diamond with adamant and the magnet was etymological at base and still current long after his time.

hath amongst them" (p. 129). This has been interpreted as a satire on war, but every detail, except the name given to human blood, appears in Solinus' account of the upland Tartars.[18] The name for blood is so appropriate, folklore-wise, that even that is probably not original.

Mandeville shows nothing of the intellectual and moral condescension of the satirist or the professional moralist. He is addressing his book to his peers, and that tells us much about his own station in life. He is free to mix truth with fantasy because he can trust his readers to distinguish between them. He is free to decorate the borders of his moral earnestness with delicate (and indelicate) grotesques without fear that those for whom he is writing will be unable to distinguish between the text and the decoration. The decoration is intended to amuse, just as the impish monsters and absurd postures in the borders of fourteenth century missals and psalters were intended to amuse, without detracting from the seriousness of the text they illuminated.

This mixture of the serious and the jocular is characteristic of the time. It was carried much further than would be considered good taste today, in the parody of religious services, the hymns turned into drinking songs, and the grotesque sculptures and indecent misericords used in the decoration of churches, as well as in the manuscript illuminations already mentioned. It gives a puckish quality to some of Chaucer's stories, and it underlies the poignant mixture of tragedy and farce in the knocking at the gate in *Macbeth* and the bawdy singing of the mad Ophelia. Great literary skill is required in this balancing of the emotions.

Mandeville had such skill. His story of Gog and Magog combines the romance of distant places with a gentle ribbing of his countrymen, and with the most terrifying of religious beliefs,

[18] Warner, note on p. 97, l. 6. See Solinus, *Polyhistor*, ed. cit., p. 95, or Golding's trans., Chap. 24. Hamelius, in his note to p. 129, l. 26, suggests that the name for blood is a sly glance at the doctrine of transubstantiation.

the belief in the end of the world. He identifies Gog and Magog with the mountains of Scythia where the ten lost tribes of Israel were fabled to have been enclosed. Apparently he invented (with ironic intent) the explanation that they could not escape across the Caspian Sea, because "they ne wist never where that they should arrive [if they set out]; and also they can no language but only their own, that no man knoweth but they; and therefore may they not go out" (p. 175). The very lameness of the excuse suggests a sly glance at the stay-at-homes around him. But if irony is intended, it is the touch of a foil, and not the thrust of a lance. He turns aside immediately to add that anyhow the Jews have no other country, and even here they pay tribute to the queen of the Amazons.[19] Some few have escaped over the mountains, but the climb is too hard for most. However, men say that "they shall go out in the time of anti-Christ, and that they shall make great slaughter of Christian men" (p. 176). Here the narrative rises into the realm of prophesy and fantasy. "And if that ye will wit how that they shall find their way, after that I have heard say I shall tell you." His story is that a fox shall burrow under the gates that Alexander set up to enclose them, and they will chase the fox until it returns to its burrow, and they shall dig after him till they find the gates and break them down, and so get out.

This is a variant of the story told by Friar Ricold of Monte Croce in his Itinerary of Palestine, where it is the "Mongoli," a contraction of Magogoli (i.e., the Tartars), who were enclosed by Alexander. He set up automata to make them believe that the gates were guarded on the outside, but one day some dogs followed a hare to the barrier and as a hunter approached, he saw an owl sitting on the gate. He said, "This is not the habitation of men, where a hare flees and an owl sings." So the Tartars broke through the gates and escaped.[20] Mandeville

[19] This tradition is mentioned in the *Pricke of Conscience:* Warner's note to p. 131, l. 5.
[20] Friar Ricold's Itinerary appears in J. C. M. Laurent, *Peregrinatores Medii Aevi Quatuor,* cited above, and see Ugo Manneret de Villard, *Il*

uses the story of the owl to explain how the Great Khan escaped from his enemies (p. 148). At Alexander's gate, instead of the automata and the hare, he uses a fox, apparently borrowed from the *Arabian Nights,* where Sinbad the Sailor escapes from a similar enclosure by following a fox to its burrow.[21] Mandeville's reason for the change is not apparent, but the resulting folktale has the ring of genuineness, and yet it is essentially fiction. We cannot believe that, after reading such sober accounts of Scythia as those of Carpini and Rubruquis, Mandeville believed the story of the enclosed tribes, or expected anyone else to believe it. It is good fiction, but it is fiction and must have been so recognized.

Mandeville's attitude toward religious relics is one of interest and respect, but not of gullibility. His protest about the Cross at Cyprus has already been mentioned. Much the same thing was true of the Crown of Thorns. Both Paris and Constantinople claimed to have the relic, so he says that it was divided into two parts. This crown was of "jonkes of the sea," as he says correctly.[22] But several other places, including Aix-la-Chapelle and Pisa, claimed to possess the Crown of Thorns, so he accounts for others with a story that Christ was first crowned with "albespine," or white thorn, and then with sweet thorn "that men call barbariens," then he was crowned with eglantine, and finally with the crown of "jonkes of the sea." Altogether five crowns are accounted for. The variety of crowns

---

*Libro della peregrinazione nelle parti d'Oriente di frate Ricoldo da Montecroce,* Institutum Historicum Ff. Praedicatorum Romae ad S. Sabinae. Diss. Hist., fasc. xiii, Rome, 1948. A modified version of the story is in Giovanni Villani, *Chroniche* (Trieste, 1857), I, 71, and in Giovanni Fiorentino, *Il Pecorone,* in *Racolta de Novellieri Italiani,* Vols. 16, 17 (Milan, 1815), II, 102-105.

[21] Lane ed., p. 501; and see Warner's note to p. 132, l. 8. Pausanias tells a similar story of an escape by holding onto a fox, IV, 18: Loeb Classics ed., II, 273. Hayton tells the story of the escape of Genghis Khan through the presence of "a bird": Backer, p. 166.

[22] Rohault de Fleury, *Mémoire sur les Instruments de la Passion,* pp. 199-202, 206-207. Cf. Pollard, p. 10.

## MOTIVES AND THE MAN 81

served also to explain a variety of thorns. A good many churches and private individuals claimed to possess thorns from the crown,[23] and undoubtedly these were of different kinds. Mandeville says, "I have one of these precious thorns, that seemeth like a white thorn; and that was given to me for a great specialty. For there are many of them broken and fallen into the vessel that the crown lieth in [in Paris]; for they break for dryness when men move them to show them to great lords that come thither" (p. 10).

There was a great flood of relics into Europe from the East, brought by pilgrims and crusaders, especially after the plunder of Constantinople in 1204. Wills of the later Middle Ages mention so many "crosses made from the true cross" and "thorns from the crown" that such things must have been as plentiful as blackberries. Chaucer's scornful reference to "pig's bones" probably gives us sufficient light to guide us in determining the degree of an educated man's gullibility in such matters. Mandeville knew his Bible well, and must have been thoroughly familiar with the story of the Crown of Thorns. But he is content to suggest the preposterous by a margin of excess—to those who can see it.

A similar case is his story of the supply of oil at the shrine of St. Katherine near Mount Sinai. He says that every year birds bring enough olive branches to the shrine to supply oil, not only for the lamps of the shrine, but for cooking for the monks. Now a miraculous oil supply was claimed for this place. Vincent of Beauvais says that the oil oozed from the tomb of St. Katherine. One of the itineraries says that the Virgin provided the monks with an inexhaustible oil jar. Mandeville's story

---

[23] De Fleury records the relics, including two crowns (p. 204), and lists 78 places which claimed to have thorns, pp. 204-224. Paul E. D. Riant, *Exuviae sacrae Constantinopolitanae*, 2 vols. (Geneva, 1877-78), gives a detailed account of the relics and has a good index. F. de Mély discusses "Les Reliques de la Sainte-Couronne d'épines d'Aix-la-Chapelle et de Saint-Denis," *Revue Archéologique*, 3d Ser., xxxv (Paris, 1899), 392-398.

seems to have been his own invention, at once more fanciful and more "natural" than the other two, which follow common medieval patterns.[24] Moreover, by making the supply adequate both for the lamps and for cooking, he has made his explanation "practical" to the point of being grotesque. He has invented a source reminiscent of the dove returning to the ark, wildly exaggerated, ludicrous with the artificial naiveté of the sophisticated. Elsewhere he says, "whoso that will may 'lieve me if he will, and whoso will not, may leave" (p. 144).

We can learn something about what his contemporaries saw in the *Travels* by observing into what company they put it. The great folios of the medieval library were often collections in some general field, like our anthologies. *Mandeville's Travels* is often included in collections of works about the East, as for example in the one formed by Jean Le Long, or Lelonc of Ypres, who has been called "in his way, the prototype of all the Ramusios and Hakluyts" of a later time.[25] In 1351 Le Long published a volume of translations into French which included the itineraries of both Odoric and William of Boldensele, as well as that of Friar Ricold of Monte Croce (ca. 1294), Hayton's history of the Tartars, an account of the Great Khan by the Archbishop of Sultânieh, who addressed it to Pope John XXII, and some letters from the Khan of Cathay to Pope Benedict XII (1338).[26] There is some evidence that Mandeville used this col-

---

[24] Warner's note to p. 31, l. 1; Hamelius' note to p. 39, l. 6. Symon Simeonis says that the oil distills from the head of St. Katherine "ut dicitur," op. cit., pp. 54-55. Breydenbach visited this monastery and reported the absence of insects and vipers (credited to a miracle of St. Katherine), but of the oil supply he reports simply, "There are olives and almonds, figs and vignes [sic]" in abundance: ed. cit., fol. lxxiij.

[25] Sir Henry Yule, in a review in *The Athenaeum*, 2598 (Aug 11, 1877), 174-175.

[26] Le Long's work is studied very inadequately in Louis de Backer's *L'extrême Orient au Moyen-Age*, pp. 7-9. See Yule's review, just cited, and Henri Cordier's review in *Revue Critique d'Histoire et de Littérature*, New Series, III (May 19, 1877), 313-317. On Le Long see Léon Van der Essen, "Jean d'Ypres ou de Saint-Bertin," *Revue Belge de Philologie et d'Histoire*, I, No. 3 (1922), 483-485.

lection.[27] At any rate, by the end of the fourteenth century Marco Polo and Mandeville had been added to Le Long's anthology of Eastern travel.[28]

Of course, travelers' tales enjoyed then the same reputation for exaggeration and even invention that they have today. Marco Polo was "Il Milione" (i.e., a great liar). Of one traveler it was said, "he says less than he saw, because of the tongues of detractors who easily impose lies on others, and rashly condemn as a lie whatever they cannot believe or will not understand."[29] One of Mandeville's English translators makes him say, "many men trow nought but that that they see with their eyes, or that they may conceive with their own kindly wits."[30] *Piers Plowman* speaks feelingly of the man who has been no further than Rome, and "had leave to lie all his life after." The works of Solinus and Odoric and Mandeville all go at times under the title *De Mirabilibus Mundi*. A manuscript of Mandeville in French is headed *Le Romant de Mandeville*.[31]

[27] According to Sir Henry Yule, Mandeville's *Pentoxoire*, the name for the land of Prester John, is a corruption of *Tendek-Shahr* which occurs also in Le Long's translation of Odoric: Warner's note to p. 133, and Yule's *Cathay*, II, 166n., and 244n. See also Warner on tortoises, n. to p. 96, l. 11. Both Le Long and Mandeville translate into snails (*limaces*) Odoric's huge tortoises. However, it is possible that, in the texts we have, Le Long's *Odoric* was "corrected" out of Mandeville. That seems to have happened in the case of Odoric's story of fishing with cormorants. Mandeville makes the animals otters, and in some manuscripts of Odoric they are called otters. Sarton, op. cit., pp. 778, 1603, says that both cormorants and otters were used by the Chinese from early times to catch fish. Jean de Vignay made an earlier translation of Odoric into French.

[28] For example, in Bibl. Nat. MS. fr. 2810, known as the *Livre des Merveilles*, and in MS. 125 in the public library of Berne, Switzerland, described by Benedetto, *Marco Polo*, p. xxxix.

[29] Moule ed., I, p. 32, quoting from Iacopo d'Acqui's *Imago Mundi*, on the subject of Marco Polo.

[30] Warner's text, p. 156.

[31] *Catalogue Générale*, Vol. 31 (1898), 10, in the Bibliothèque, Palais des Arts à Lyon, MS. 28 (Delandine, no. 683); also J. Camus, *Notices et Extraits des Manuscrits Français de Modène antérieurs au xvi<sup>e</sup> Siècle* (Modena, 1891), p. 41, extracted from the *Revue des langues romanes* (1891), pp. 212-216, for another *Mandeville* with this title.

84 THE *TRAVELS* AS LITERATURE

The word "Romant" refers to the language, but the implication of fiction was there also. This manuscript also contains the *Vision of Tundale*. Other manuscripts show the *Travels* in company with such romances as *Sir Gowther,* the romance of *Joseph of Arimathea,* the *Romance of Alexander,* and even the *Letter of Prester John.* It appears also in the company of the *Voyage of St. Brandan.*[32]

In English manuscripts it is included even more definitely with works of literature. It appears several times in company with *Piers Plowman;*[33] once (in a Huntington Library MS) with both *Piers Plowman* and Chaucer's *Troilus and Criseyde;* once with Richard d'Aungerville's *Philobiblon.* The Folger Shakespeare Library has a copy of Robert Mannyng of Brunne's *Handlyng Sinne,* written about 1400, which was formerly bound up with a copy of the *Travels* in the same hand.[34] In Arundel MS. 140 it is preceded by the religious legends of *Ypotys* and followed by *The Pricke of Conscience,* the moralizing *Gy Earl of Werwyke and Dekene Alquyne,* the *Seven Wise Masters,* and Chaucer's *Melibeus.* Obviously this is an anthology of moral literature.

On the other hand, in France the *Travels* appeared more than once in the company of the *Roman de Fauvel,* a violent satire on all classes of society. One manuscript adds also the *Testament* of Jean de Meun, another satirical work (Bibl. Nat. MS. fr. 24436). So far as this evidence of association goes, we may conclude that from the first the *Travels* was read not only for information but also for entertainment. It was put not only with books about the East but with works of the imagination, travel romances, and works of social criticism. In other words, it had a place, from the beginning, in the field of "belles lettres," where it still belongs.

[32] See the Checklist of MSS. in Appendix I.
[33] As in Harleian MS. 3954, and Cambridge Univ. MS. Dd. I. 17.
[34] This *Mandeville* is now in the possession of Mr. Boies Penrose, who very generously made it available to me and ascertained that it is a copy of the short version, or Pynson text.

Another kind of evidence about contemporary attitudes toward the book is the tampering with the text. It was, of course, not unusual for a medieval scribe to take liberties with the text he was copying; but various scribes seem to have undertaken to add to the *Travels* details intended to give it additional verisimilitude—a practice which indicates that they thought some of the stories might be doubted. Probably the additions indicate that at least some of the interpolators thought that they were dealing with fiction. For example, a Latin letter of dedication to Edward III appears in most of the French manuscripts preserved in England. The addition of alphabets to some manuscripts has been mentioned. Someone invented a Latin letter of defiance purporting to have been written by the eldest son of the Sultan of Egypt to the Pope. It appears in two Latin and two French manuscripts of the *Travels*, all written in England.[35] I have already mentioned the fictions, invented by the first English translator, that Mandeville wrote in three languages and that he took his book to Rome and got it approved by the Pope. The translator of the English version in the Egerton manuscript adds this story about the visit to Rome, interpolates a statement about the blackness of the Moors, and adds a story about a man from Thule who was the object of a miracle performed by St. Thomas of Canterbury. He also added to the story of the vegetable lamb the remark, "Of that frute I haue eten." This is in obvious imitation of Mandeville's statement that he had drunk of the Fountain of Youth. Again, in the account of the dry sea, he says of the fish in it, "I, John Maundeuill ete of tham, and tharfore trowez it, for sikerly it es soth."[36] This is not even in Mandeville's style, but it indicates that the writer was trying, somewhat clumsily, to bolster up, or improve on, what he considered a tall tale. Mandeville himself uses the much more effective method of apparent modesty and common sense. He says that

[35] See the Checklist, Appendix I.
[36] Warner, p. 134, ll. 23-24.

he would not have believed it if he had not seen it himself. This same (Egerton) translation shows a more serious type of interpolation, the insertion of references to corroborative material, to Comestor, Isidore, and Bàrtholomaeus.[37] Perhaps these were interpolated by some scribe who took the *Travels* seriously, and not by the same man who added the more fictional interpolations. Several manuscripts add references to Odoric at several points, and one or two even represent Odoric as the traveling companion of the more famous Sir John Mandeville!

Humor is so often a product of play with the beliefs and ideas current in a circumscribed time and place that it is easily lost sight of. But, judging by the available evidence of the book itself and of the additions made by others to it, and by the contents of the manuscripts in which it appears, it seems clear that the true nature of the *Travels* was reasonably well understood from the beginning and that it was enjoyed by its first patrons, noblemen and gentlemen interested in the East and fairly well-informed about it, as a new kind of literature based, not on fabulous history, like the current romances, but on geography. It combined information, the best available, with amusement, to provide that delightful teaching which was to become the Renaissance ideal of *belles lettres*. It is the work of a man not only of remarkable reading but of urbanity and culture as well—a man of reflective and independent mind with an imagination neither crude nor extravagant, but of the kind which begins in intelligence and ripens into wisdom.

---

[37] The Egerton text cites Isidore and Bartholomaeus in support of Mandeville's account of the diamond: Warner, p. 79, ll. 20, 21; and "the buke of the Miracles of oure Lady" on the delivery of Theophilus, Warner, p. 22, l. 12. Several of the Latin texts cite Odoric at various points. This "Odoric" version of the Latin Vulgate was printed by Gerard Leeu at Antwerp in 1484; and see Warner, p. vii and n. 3.

# PART II
# THE IDENTITY OF THE AUTHOR

THE LAKE ON THE ISLAND OF CEYLON FORMED BY
THE REPENTANT TEARS OF ADAM AND EVE

THE RACE OF MEN WITHOUT HEADS

# TWO LIÈGE TRADITIONS

WHAT the *Travels* reveals about the character and personality of its author provides us with valuable background for a fresh examination of the evidence of his identity. For five hundred years, and more, his biography has been written out of what the author says of himself in his book and an epitaph for him which was at Liège in Flanders by the end of the fourteenth century. The *Travels* furnishes a brief but precise account of his place of birth, travels, and the ailment which drove him home to write. He says in his Prologue:

> I, John Mandeville, Knight, albeit I be not worthy, that was born in England, in the town of St. Albans, and passed the sea in the year of our Lord Jesu Christ, 1322, in the day of St. Michael: and hitherto have been long time over the sea, and have seen and gone through many diverse lands . . . (p. 5).

Again, at the end of the book, he says:

> And I, John Mandeville, knight, abovesaid (although I be unworthy), that departed from our countries and passed the sea, the year of grace a thousand three hundred and twenty-two, that have passed many lands and many isles and countries, and searched many full strange places, and have been in many a full good honourable company, and at many a fair deed of arms (albeit that I did none myself, for mine unable insuffisance), now I am come home, maugre myself, to rest, for gouts artetykes that me distrain, that define the end of my labour; against my will (God knoweth).
>
> And thus, taking solace in my wretched rest, recording the time passed, I have fulfilled these things, and put them written in this book, as it would come into my mind, the year of grace a thousand three hundred and fifty-six, in the thirty-fourth year, that I departed from our countries (p. 208).[1]

[1] For discussion of the dates, see below, p. 149 ff. These two passages are in all versions of the French texts.

From this apparently simple, modest, and straightforward statement, it would seem that he was writing in England after his return, and that he would spend his last years there. However, a famous epitaph formerly at Liège, in the church of the Guillemins,[2] had this to say:

> Here lies Master John de Montevilla knight alias ad Barbam, Master of Compredi, born in England, professor of medicine and most devout in prayer, and most liberal giver of his goods to the poor, who traveled over the whole world. He ended the last day of his life in a house in Liège, in the year of our Lord 1372, the seventeenth day of the month of November.[3]

Mandeville's early biographers, confronted with these two documents, the *Travels* and the epitaph, put them together, giving the "Life" from the *Travels* and adding that he became a doctor and died at Liège in 1372.[4] This remained the standard

---

[2] This was a religious order of hermits of St. William, founded in 1152. The house of the order at Liège dated from 1287: Warner, p. xxxi. It was destroyed at the end of the 18th century.

[3] The earliest transcript, made in 1462 by a German traveler, Jacob Püterich von Reichertshausen, was printed by "Karajan" in the *Zeitschrift für Deutsches Alterthum*, vi (Leipzig, 1848), 56; and by Raymond Duell, *Excerptorum Genealogico-Historicorum libri duo* (Leipzig, 1725), pp. 281-282. He read: "Hic jacet Nobilis Dominus Joannes de Montevilla, Miles, alias dictus ad Barbam, Dominus de Compredi, natus de Anglia, Medicinae Professor, et devotissimus Orator, et bonorum suorum Largissimus pauperibus erogator, qui totum orbem peragrauit in stratu Leodij diem vitae suae clausit extremum, Anno Dom. MCCCLXXII mensis Februarij vii." Warner prints from Duell, pp. xxxiii-iv. "Karajan" read *Barbani* for *Barbam*, and *Compredri* for *Compredi*. A century later, Abraham Ortelius made a transcript which read *Mandeville* and *Campdi*, omitted *suorum*, inserted *vir* after *nobilis*, transferred *Miles* to follow *Barbam*, and instead of *totum orbem peragrauit in stratu* he read *toto qvasi orbe lustrato*. He read the date *1371 novembris die xvii*: G. Hagenitius, *Itinerarium Frisio-Hollandicum*, et Abr. Ortelius, *Itinerarium Gallo-Brabanticum* (Leyden, 1630), pp. 212-213. Later transcripts show that Ortelius misread the year but was correct about the month and day. However, either Püterich was very inaccurate, or the two were not reading the same inscription. Except for the date, the changes are all in the direction of greater elegance and a Latinity of a later date than 1400. Hamelius (II, 1-2) is neither clear nor accurate about the two versions.

[4] The earliest seems to have been John Bale's in *Illustrium Maioris*

biography down to the nineteenth century. A note of scepticism was sounded in 1839 by the first great modern historian of Eastern travel, D'Avezac, who remarked, "The profession of medicine and the surname A la Barbe, which have been attributed to Mandeville in a so-called epitaph, seem to be the result of some confusion which ought to be cleared up."[5] He did not give any reason, however, for his distrust of the epitaph. Further information about it came in 1866, with the publication of a passage from *Ly Myreur des Histors,* an enormous world-history compiled by the Liège romancer, Jean d'Outremeuse (1338-1400). He tells the following story:

> In 1372 died at Liége on the twelfth [sic] of November a man who was greatly distinguished for his birth. He was content to be known by the name of John of Burgundy [Jean de Bourgogne], called With the Beard [à la Barbe]. He, however, opened his heart on his death-bed to Jean d'Outremeuse, his gossip, whom he appointed his executor. In truth, he entitled

*Britanniae Scriptorum* (1548), fol. 149ᵛ, reprinted with an English translation in Richard Hakluyt's *Principall Navigations,* etc. (1589), pp. 23-24. J. Pits, *Relationum Historicarum de Rebus Anglicis* (Paris, 1619), pp. 511-512, quotes a fresh transcript of the epitaph made by Edmund Leukner, an English priest. John Weever, *Ancient Funerall Monuments* (London, 1631), pp. 567-568, follows Ortelius but adds that St. Albans "vaunts her selfe very much of the birth and buriall of Sir *Iohn Mandevill* Knight, the famous Trauailer, who writ in Latine, French, and in the English tongue, his Itinerary of three and thirty yeares. And that you may beleeve the report of the Inhabitants to bee true, they have lately pensild a rare piece of Poetry, or an Epitaph for him, vpon a piller: neere to which they suppose his body to have beene buried . . ." Mandeville is not mentioned in Konrad Gesner's *Bibliotheca Vniuersalis siue Catalogus omnium scriptorum* (Tiguri, 1545), but the *Epitome* edited by Conrad Lycosthenes (Basle, 1551), col. 585, reads: "Ioannes Mandeuyle, Anglus, armatae militiae eques auratus, scripsit Itinerarium suum xxxiii annorum de Mirabilibus mundi lib. 1, Obijt Leodij, an 1372." An edition of Lycosthenes' *Epitome,* published by Josiah Simler (Tiguri, 1555), fol. 104ᵛ reads: "Ioannis de Monteuilla, Angli, peregrinationum in terram sanctam & aliarum experientiarum lib. 5. in quibus multa uidentur inesse fabulosa." The 5-book version of the *Travels* contained the Ogier interpolations, as we shall see.

[5] *Relation,* p. 429, cited above, Chap. 1, n. 5. The translation is mine.

himself, in the deed of his last will, Sir John Mandeville, knight, Earl of Montfort in England and lord of the isle of Campdi and of the castle Pérouse. Having, however, had the misfortune of killing in his country an earl whom he does not name, he bound himself to travel through the three parts of the world. Came to Liége in 1343. Issued as he was from very high nobility, he loved to keep himself hidden. He was, moreover, a great naturalist, a profound philosopher and astrologer, especially adding a very singular knowledge of physics, rarely making mistakes when he told his opinion about a patient, whether he would recover or not. When dead at last, he was buried with the brethren Wilhelmites, in the suburb of Avroy, as you have been able to see more fully above.[6]

This passage throws an illuminating light on the origin of the epitaph. It reveals that Jean d'Outremeuse was, according to his own confession, the sole authority for the identification of this doctor with the famous traveler, and therefore ultimately for the epitaph.[7]

In the 1880's d'Outremeuse's story was adopted by two distinguished English scholars, E. B. Nicholson and G. F. Warner, and enshrined by them in the *Encyclopaedia Britannica* and the *Dictionary of National Biography,* as well as in Warner's edition of the *Travels* for the Roxburghe Club. It was not accepted

[6] Hamelius, II, 8. He is translating from S. Bormans' Introduction to *Ly Myreur des Histors, Chronique de Jean des Preis dit d'Outremeuse,* in Corps des Chroniques Liégeoises, 7 vols. (Brussels, 1864-87), vols. I-III, V, ed Ad. Borgnet, vols. IV, VI and VII, ed. S. Bormans; see VII, cxxxiii-iv. The passage occurred in Bk. IV of the *Myreur,* which is now lost. This passage was transcribed by a Liège herald, Louis Abry (1643-1720). His transcript was copied by a Liège historian, Le Fort, from whom it was first printed by Bormans in "La Librairie Collégiale Saint-Paul à Liége au xv⁰ siècle," *Le Bibliophile belge* [3 ser.], I (1866), 236. It was first discussed by E. B. Nicholson in 1884: *Encyclopaedia Britannica* article "Mandeville." The history of the text is also reviewed by Warner who suggests that the date, Nov. 12, is the result of the omission of a *v* by a copyist; see his edition, p. xxxvi, n. 3.

[7] Warner says that this passage "leaves little doubt indeed that, if his story be true, Jean d'Outremeuse himself was responsible for it [the epitaph]" p. xxvi. If the story was *not* true, it is even more probable that d'Outremeuse was responsible for the epitaph, as we shall see.

in full, however. The story in the *Myreur des Histors,* and on the epitaph, is that Jean à la Barbe, or de Bourgogne, a Liège doctor, was really Sir John Mandeville. But Nicholson and Warner decided that, while d'Outremeuse was probably telling the truth, the doctor must have been lying; that his real name was Jean de Bourgogne, and that, having written the book of *Travels* under an assumed name, he was trying to get credit for the book by claiming the assumed name as his own.[8]

At the time that Nicholson and Warner wrote, it was generally supposed that d'Outremeuse's *Myreur* was a genuine medieval attempt to write history. The early part was, of course, legendary, but it was assumed that the author was reporting faithfully the events of his own time. It has since been discovered, however, that d'Outremeuse's *Myreur* is fictionized throughout. Where he had reliable sources, such as Jean le Bel and Froissart, he revised to suit his own fancy, and elsewhere he wrote history out of imaginary sources and often invented documents to support his fictions. His editor, Stanislas Bormans, reports that he "outrageously altered" the text of his borrowings from the chronicle of Jean le Bel.[9] He did the same with Froissart, as we shall see in a moment.

In 1910 the great Belgian historian, Godefroid Kurth, published an *Étude Critique sur Jean d'Outremeuse,* in which he demonstrated the fictional character of the *Myreur* throughout. On the basis of his findings, he concluded that the deathbed confession of the Liège doctor was "purely and simply an invention."[10] Paul Hamelius, the latest editor of the *Travels,* accepted this judgment and went a step further; he argued that d'Outremeuse had invented both the story in the *Myreur* and the epitaph, and that d'Outremeuse himself was the true

---

[8] Their reasons for this conclusion will be discussed in Chapter 11.

[9] *Ly Myreur des Histors,* vi, 323, n. 5. See above n. 6. All references to the *Myreur* are to this edition.

[10] The *Étude* was published by the Académie Royale de Belgique. Classe des Lettres et des Sciences morales et politiques et Classe des Beaux-Arts. Mémoires. Collection in 8°. Second Series, Tome vii, fasc. 2 (Brussels, 1910). See p. 102.

author of the *Travels*. Hamelius' arguments are very flimsy, however, and have been accepted only by those who have not investigated the evidence, such as J. J. Jusserand,[11] and A. P. Newton, who, in his *Travel and Travellers of the Middle Ages*, says incautiously, "We now know that it [the *Travels*] was a spurious compilation of a citizen of Liége, one Jehan d'Outremuse" [sic].[12] J. E. Wells, in his *Manual of Writings in Middle English*, is more conservative, saying, "We probably do best to conclude that the Liège physician's true name was de Bourgogne, and that he wrote the *Travels* under the assumed name of de Mandeville. Possibly d'Outremeuse is responsible for the Latin *Travels*."[13] This is a return to the theory of Nicholson and Warner.

Meanwhile a whole galaxy of Belgian medievalists, Gobert, Bayot, Magnette, Michel, and Balau discussed and rejected Hamelius' conclusion, on several different grounds.[14] Their

---

[11] *English Wayfaring Life in the Middle Ages*, new ed., trans. Lucy Toulmin Smith (London, 1920), p. 407 n., "The identification of Mandeville with Jean de Bourgogne . . . seems certain," but in the *Literary History of the English People*, 3d ed. (London, 1925), I, 406-407, he decides that the author was "more probably . . . the contemporary mystificator and pretended chronicler."

[12] (London, 1930), p. 160.

[13] (New Haven, Conn., 1926), pp. 433-437. Wells's account is inaccurate at several points. He asserts positively that Jean de Bourgogne "fled from England" in 1322, a statement for which there is no evidence whatever; that d'Outremeuse wrote a work in much resembling the *Travels*, a statement which can only refer to the huge *Myreur* with its borrowings from the *Travels*; that the manuscript dated 1371 is "the best and oldest," whereas it is certainly not the best, and quite possibly not the oldest, merely the oldest *dated* manuscript; and finally, that "the versions manifest ignorance of English conditions, that (it is declared) no Englishman would show." Since the *Travels* is not about England and says nothing of "English conditions" this criticism is meaningless.

[14] Hamelius read a paper, setting forth his views, to the Bibliographical Society [London], reported in their *Transactions*, XIII (1916), 193-196. He published his argument in "The Travels of Sir John Mandeville," *Quarterly Review*, CCXXVII (April, 1917), 331-352. On July 25, 1919, he reported his arguments to the Institut Archéologique Liégeois; *Chronique Archéologique du pays de Liège*, 10 année, No. 5 (Oct., 1919), p. 54; and No. 6 (Nov.-Dec.), p. 54. Finally he incorporated his conclusions in

judgment seems to be reflected by two recent historians of English literature, A. C. Baugh in *A Literary History of England*,[15] and H. S. Bennett in *Chaucer and the Fifteenth Century*.[16] Both report that modern opinion inclines to Jean de Bourgogne. George Sarton, in his monumental *Introduction to the History of Science,* says, "It is more than probable that Mandeville and Jean à la Barbe are one and the same person."[17] He prefers, however, to call that person "Mandeville," thereby rejecting Warner's and Nicholson's conclusion. Most recently Mr. Malcolm Letts, while accepting the Liège evidence, expresses the conviction that the author of the *Travels* was an Englishman whose real name was Mandeville.[18] That position represents a return to the biography current from about 1400 until Warner and Nicholson published their conclusion.

---

his *Introduction à la Littérature française et flamande de Belgique* (Brussels, 1921), pp. 79-89. His Introduction to the E.E.T.S. ed. of *Mandeville's Travels* was published posthumously in 1923. In 1921 Théod. Gobert rejected the attribution of the *Travels* to d'Outremeuse and reported finding a record of the house of Jean à la Barbe: "Un célèbre voyageur: Mandeville," *Chronique Archéologique du pays de Liège*, 12ᵉ année (1921), 3-11; incorporated in his *Liège à travers les âges. Les rues de Liège* (Liège, 1924-29), III, 398-401, IV, 42-47, and V, 115. Alphonse Bayot rejected all of Hamelius' attributions to d'Outremeuse, in his review of the *Intro. à la Litt.: Revue Belge de Philologie et d'histoire*, I, No. 2 (1922), 355-356. This part of his review was reprinted by F. Magnette, "A propos de Jean d'Outremeuse et de Mandeville," *Chronique Archéologique du pays de Liège*, 13ᵉ année (1922), 46-48. Louis Michel, in his *Les Légendes Epiques Carolingiennes dans l'oeuvre de Jean d'Outremeuse*, Académie Royale de Langue et de Littérature françaises de Belgique. Mémoires, X (Brussels, 1935), 31-34, 116-119, rejects the attribution on the ground that d'Outremeuse cited Mandeville in his list of sources, and used the *Travels* to extend his account of the adventures of Ogier. He agrees with Gobert that Bourgogne wrote the *Travels*. Sylvan Balau also rejected the attribution of the *Travels* to d'Outremeuse, in his *Étude Critique des Sources de L'Histoire du Pays de Liége au Moyen Age*, Mémoires Couronnés et Mémoires des Savants Étrangers publiés par L'Académie Royale des Sciences, des Lettres et des Beaux-Arts de Belgique, Tome LXI (Brussels, 1902-04), 531, 613.

[15] (New York, 1948), pp. 267-268.
[16] (Oxford, 1947), p. 199.
[17] II (Baltimore, 1948), 1603.
[18] *Sir John Mandeville*, Chap. I.

## THE IDENTITY OF THE AUTHOR

No one has challenged the identification of the author of the *Travels* with the doctor of Liège. This doctor, Jean de Bourgogne, alias à la Barbe, was a widely known authority on the plague. A house in Liège was identified as that of "Mestre Johan ala Barbe" in a legal document of 1386, fourteen years after his death. When the same house is mentioned seventy years later, it is said to be that of "Mandavele ly chevalier d'Engleterre qui avoit esteit par universe monde solloit demoreir, qui gist a Willmins."[19] Obviously, the epitaph was well known. But the epitaph and the story in the fictionized chronicle which accounts for it are the only primary contemporary evidence that the Liège doctor was really Sir John Mandeville.

There is an account of Mandeville in the chronicle of Radulf de Rivo (d. 1403), a Liège ecclesiastic, under the year 1367 [sic]. He says, "In this year John Mandeville, an Englishman, noble and eminent in the art of medicine, who had traveled over the whole earth, having written of his journey most learnedly in three languages, went into the other world . . . 17 November. Buried in the church of the Wilhelmites not far from the walls of Liège."[20] De Rivo knew the place of burial, but not the year of death. Perhaps he misread the inscription, reading CCCLXVII for CCCLXXII. Balau, in his study of the sources of this chronicle, concludes that De Rivo was too frequently absent from Liège to keep in touch with local events.[21] The

---

[19] Gobert, See above; Hamelius, II, 2-3. For an account of the doctor, see below, Chap. 11.

[20] I translate from the Latin, which is quoted by Hamelius, II, 3.

[21] *Étude Critique,* pp. 527-531, for the life of De Rivo, and ff. for the sources of the *Chronique des évêques de Liége* (1347-86). Both Warner and Hamelius reject De Rivo's testimony as not independent. Henri Cordier was misled by a misprint in J. Chapeaville's *Qui Gesta Pontificum Leodiensium Scripserunt* (Liège, 1612-1616), III, 1, where the date of De Rivo's death is "1483." But the correct date appears on p. 3, and on p. 13 De Rivo says that he was in Italy when Innocent VI died and Urban V was elected (i.e., in 1362). Cordier's mistake appears in his edition of Sir Henry Yule's *The Book of Ser Marco Polo,* 3d ed. (London, 1903), II, 600; and "Jean de Mandeville," *T'oung pao,* II (Leyden, 1891),

statement that Mandeville wrote in three languages seems to be an echo of the fiction perpetrated by the first English translator, and it has been suggested that this notice of Mandeville was actually a later interpolation into De Rivo's chronicle.[22] At any rate it echoes the epitaph and cannot be accepted as independent evidence.

The fifteenth century *Chronicon* of Cornelius Menghers of Zantfliet does not follow De Rivo in the mistaken date, but Balau found that the *Chronicon* was compiled from those of De Rivo, d'Outremeuse, and d'Outremeuse's continuator, Jean de Stavelot.[23] Later chroniclers exhibit the well-known weakness of historians for repeating each other. Hartmann Schedel, in his *Nuremberg Chronicle* (1493) repeats the story and adds a "portrait" of Mandeville.[24] The *Chronica Summorum Pontificum Imperatorumque* of Riccobaldus Ferrariensis (Rome 1474, fol. 111$^v$) gives the same "facts" in the same order. But the chain of history is no stronger than its weakest link, and in this case that first link is the inscription on the gravestone.

D'Outremeuse makes an earlier reference to Mandeville in a huge lapidary which he compiled about 1390 and called *Ly Trésorier de philosophie naturelle des pierres précieuses*. At the end of an impressive list of authorities he adds, "and that also which bears the name of a noble man, Sir John Mandeville, knight, Lord of Monfort, of Castle Perouse and the isle of Camperdi, who was in the Orient and in parts thereabout

---

290. Warner dates De Rivo's visit to Italy in 1378 because in 1362 the Papal seat was Avignon. However, Urban V was in Italy, as De Rivo reports, at the time of his election. De Rivo's will, dated 1401, was printed by Camille de Borman, *Bulletin du Bibliophile Belge*, xviii (Brussels, 1862), 274-277.

[22] Balau, loc. cit.

[23] Ibid., pp. 606-615. Zantfliet's notice is reprinted in Edmund Martene and Ursin Durand, *Veterum Scriptorum et Monumentorum . . . Amplissima Collectio*, v (Paris, 1729), 299.

[24] Fol. ccxxvii. This is in a list of famous men of the 14th century. Petrarch is mentioned on the next page.

for a long time, so he made a lapidary according to the opinions of the Indians."[25] This is the earliest reference to a lapidary by the author of the *Travels*. It will be discussed in Chapter 8. At this point we should observe that, while the epitaph claims for Mandeville only the title *Dominus de Compredi*, the notice in the *Trésorier* makes him *seigneur de Monfort, de Castel Perouse et de l'isle de Camperdi*, while the deathbed confession, perhaps written last of all, says boldly that he was *comte de Montfort en Angleterre* and *seigneur de l'isle de Camperdi et du chateau Perouse*.[26]

We cannot be sure that the epitaph came first. It need not have been, and probably was not, set up immediately on the interment in 1372. But in any case its inscription would be limited by what d'Outremeuse could persuade the monks of St. William to believe about the doctor. In his books he was under no such restraint, and in making Mandeville a "Count of Montfort in England" he overreached everybody's credulity. No Mandeville ever bore that title, as Nicholson and Warner point out. Warner suggests that the title might have been the result of a misunderstanding,[27] but I believe the explanation lies elsewhere.

---

[25] Henri Michelant, "Notice sur un manuscrit de Jean d'Outremeuse," *Bulletin de l'Institut Archéologique Liégeois*, x (1870), 39-50. The passage was also transcribed for me by M. Marcel Thomas from Bibl. Nat. MS. fr. 12326, fol. 3. It reads, "et ce aussy que l'en dist ung noble homme, seigneur Jehan de Mandeville, chevalier, seigneur de Monfort, de Castel Perouse et de l'isle de Campdi, qui fu en Orient et es partes par della, par longtemps, si en fist ung lapidaire selon l'oppinion des Indois." Michelant reads *Castelpouse*.

[26] Hamelius suggests (p. 2) that *Camperdi* was *Champ perdu*, an old name for an island in the Meuse near Liège. He also reports (p. 8 n.) the suggestion that *château Pérouse* may have been suggested by *Pierreuse*, the name of an old street in Liège. Since it is on the tombstone, *Camperdi*, or *Compredi*, may actually have been an estate of the doctor's, though not necessarily an island in the modern sense.

[27] He suggests (p. xxxviii) that "Count of Montfort" might be a Frenchman's misunderstanding of "Country of Hertford" where St. Albans is situated.

D'Outremeuse wove into his *Myreur* an extensive romance about the Montforts, who were originally Counts of Flanders.[28] He devoted much of his literary effort to the celebration of Liège and of Flanders, but he was weak on genealogy and on English history generally. He mentions among the Montforts Simon de Montfort, Earl of Lancaster, who was a younger son of Simon IV, first Count of Montfort l'Amauri, and a descendant of the Counts of Flanders of that name; but he calls this English Earl, *Symon li conte de Monfort, qui estoit conte de Lancastre*.[29] Perhaps he did not know that the famous Earl was a younger son and not a Count of Montfort. He romances extravagantly about the Earl's sons, saying that among the canons of St. Lambert, the cathedral of Liège, were "John, Edward, Charles, and Ogier, children of the Duke of Lancaster; which Duke of Lancaster has indeed thirty sons, all of the same mother, of whom four were canons of Liège, and seven at Cologne, and the others were in England."[30] This reckless flight of the imagination is a fair sample of d'Outremeuse's inventive genius, and it illustrates also his trick of attaching famous figures to Liège.

The title of "Count of Montfort l'Amauri" was used, in d'Outremeuse's day, by the Dukes of Brittany, who were living mostly in England. Brittany had both a Montfort and a Château Pérouse[31] within a few miles of Rennes, its capital.

---

[28] He gives an account of Simon IV and the Albigensian crusade: *Myreur*, v, 6-15, 106-111, 157-175. He tells a long, imaginative tale of Henri de Montfort, son of the Count of Guilders and Prince-Bishop of Liège: *Myreur*, v, 276-442. See also Kurth, pp. 47-52. He tells of a Simon and Hughes de Montfort who fought with Louis IX: *Myreur*, v, 273-379.

[29] *Myreur*, v, 316, 368.

[30] *Myreur*, IV, 300. The translation is mine. See Kurth, pp. 82, and 80-84 where he lists the illustrious canons of St. Lambert's as they are named in the *Myreur*. A historical account of Simon's five sons is in Charles Bémont, *Simon de Montfort*, new ed., trans. E. F. Jacob (Oxford, 1930), pp. 258-273. They left no male heirs.

[31] Now Bazouges, or Bazouges-la-Pérouse, about 5 miles north of Rennes. Montfort is about the same distance west.

These are, in all probability, the castles which d'Outremeuse had in mind when he bestowed the title of Count of Montfort on Sir John Mandeville.[32]

As Kurth discovered, d'Outremeuse had no more idea of writing serious history when he dealt with contemporary events than when he wrote of the time of Charlemagne and Ogier le Danois.[33] If his borrowing from Jean le Bel is "outrageously altered," he is no more faithful to Froissart, from whom he took the story of the fall of Edward II. His handling of this story will serve to illustrate his methods and some of his obsessions. Where Froissart says that the King and Hugh le Despenser retreated to Bristol, d'Outremeuse says "to Montfort." He interpolates a circumstantial story of how a "castel de Montfort" in England was taken from "Jacque Laires" (a fictitious person), who was holding it for Queen Isabel. Where Froissart says that Hugh le Despenser was taken to Hereford and executed, he again substitutes "Montfort."[34]

This bit of reconstructed history sufficiently displays his preoccupation with Montfort. We can no longer be surprised that he should give Mandeville that title, in his *Myreur* and his *Trésorier*. It would seem that he managed to get at least an allusion to the Montfort claim on the tombstone also. For, besides the inscription which has already been quoted, Ortelius says that there was a representation of an armed knight with a forked beard, trampling on a lion. The knight bore a shield which was blank when Ortelius saw it (1575), but which he was told had formerly displayed a silver lion on an

[32] In 1294 Yolande (d. 1322), heiress of the Montforts of l'Amauri, married Arthur II, Duke of Brittany, who then added "Comte de Montfort" to his title. In 1345 Jean, Duke of Brittany and Count of Montfort, transferred his allegiance from the King of France to Edward III of England. His son, Jean V, called "le Vaillant," grew up under the guardianship of Edward and married first Edward's daughter Marie, and second Jeanne, daughter of Thomas Holland, Earl of Kent, half-brother of Richard II, and third Joan, princess of Navarre, who later became the Queen of Henry IV of England.
[33] *Étude*, pp. 565-568.
[34] *Myreur*, VI, 307-309.

*azure* field.[35] The lion had on its breast a crescent *gules*, and the field had a bordure engrailed or indented *or*. The Mandeville arms were very simple, "quarterly *or* and *gules*." No known branch of the family displayed a silver lion, but Simon de Montfort, and the Montforts of l'Amauri, bore "*gules*, a lion rampant tail fourchée *argent*."[36] Ortelius says that the field was described to him as *azure*, but colors were sometimes changed to difference a younger branch of a family.[37] The crescent was a common device of a younger son, and the bordure could also have that significance.[38]

Ortelius' report comes two full centuries after the death of the Liège doctor, and some discrepancies between his account and one written a century earlier (1462) by Jacob Püterich von Reichertshausen suggest that, as the show-piece in the church, the stone had been "done-over."[39] Püterich, however, mentions the *lion with a forked tail*, although he does not mention any colors.[40]

[35] See n. 3 above.

[36] Joseph Foster, *Some Feudal Coats of Arms and Others Illustrated* (Oxford, 1902), p. 141.

[37] J. H. Round places the origin of the Mandeville coat in the time of King Stephen: *Geoffrey de Mandeville* (London, 1892), pp. 393-396. Descendants of the younger branch of the family, seated at Highworth in Wiltshire, bore quarterly *vair* and *gules*: *Parliamentary Writs*, ed. Sir Francis Palgrave, I (London, 1827), 411b, from MS. Cotton Caligula A, XVIII. Another example of a change of colors is mentioned by G. Wrottesley, "The Giffards from the Conquest to the Present Time," *Collections for a History of Staffordshire*, The William Salt Archaeological Society, New Series, v (1902), 201, 202.

[38] John Fitz John, of a younger branch of the Mandevilles, bore quarterly *or* and *gules* within a bordure *vairé nebulée*: Wrottesley, 201-202 n.; *Parl. Writs*, I, 420a.

[39] Richard Garnett remarks of Ortelius' version of the inscription, "The Latinity seems to savour of a later time than Mandeville's," *English Literature* (New York, 1903), II, 196.

[40] Püterich's description of the stone, engraved with letters of brass, is contained in some crude and very difficult verses quoted by Warner, p. xxxiii, n. 6, and by Duell, see n. 3 above. He mentions a lion with a forked tail ("der Stern gezwifacht was"), and a "throat open with yawning." There is a monkey on the knight's helmet, apparently with a collar and chain ("knebl") arranged "the way the servants play the game so

## 102      THE IDENTITY OF THE AUTHOR

The connection between the shield and the Montfort claim has been overlooked because, in 1725, the editor of the first English translation of the *Travels* discovered a record of a similar shield, except for the crescent, which was borne by Sir Roger Tyrell of Hertfordshire in the time of Edward I.[41] But no link between the Tyrells and the Mandevilles has been discovered; none between the Tyrells and the Montforts has been looked for. Certainly if the arms on the tomb were suggested by Jean d'Outremeuse, the resemblance to the Tyrell coat is irrelevant.

The similarity has obscured the true significance of the arms, however. The whole purpose of the epitaph and the other decorations of the tomb was to identify the Liège doctor, who was no doubt buried there, with the author of the famous book of *Travels*. In addition, there was a further purpose to identify Sir John Mandeville with the Montforts through the much differenced arms. The silver lion, since it connects the Montfort claim put forward by d'Outremeuse with the epitaph, further links the Liège romancer with the designing of the tomb.[42]

Both Nicholson and Warner interpret the evidence of the coat of arms, which is not that of any known Mandeville

---

that one falls on his head." The medieval dialect is most difficult, and I am much indebted to my colleague, Professor Carl Selmer, for interpreting it for me. Ortelius says nothing of a monkey, but reports that there was a hand over the knight's head, blessing him. He also reports a line on the stone in the local dialect, "Vos ki paseis sor mi povr lamovr deix proies por mi," which indicates that the grave was in the floor, probably in an aisle, where it would be worn by passing feet. In the course of two centuries such a gravestone might well have to be recut, and the brass reset.

[41] See p. xii n., in either the 1725 or 1727 editions. The editor cites MS. Cotton Lib., Tiberius D.X, p. 155. Warner (p. xxxii) repeats the reference. Foster (p. 194) reports that Sir Roger Tyrrell, co. Hereford, bore at the tournament of Dunstable in 1308 "*azure* a lyon *argent*, a bordure indented *or* (engrailed *or:* Harl. MS. 6137, fol. 31b)." See also *Parl. Writs*, I, 419a.

[42] See above, n. 7.

family, to support their argument that the author of the *Travels* was really the doctor, Jean de Bourgogne. But we know nothing about the doctor's arms, and it is quite probable that he did not have any. If they were genuine Mandeville arms, they would lend weight to the story that the author of the *Travels* was buried at Liège, but since they are not, they have no value whatever as negative evidence, i.e., that the author of the *Travels* was not a Mandeville. The presence of the silver lion suggests instead that they were a part of d'Outremeuse's fiction that Mandeville was really Count of Montfort.

The process by which the Liège doctor becomes, first the author of the *Travels*, and then the Count of Montfort, is characteristic of the workings of d'Outremeuse's inventive genius. He spent his whole literary life in the glorification of Liège and its cathedral.[43] One of his favorite devices was to attach a fabulous previous history to a family of Liège of his own day. He created an extensive romance of the Du Pré family, and then had the impudence to connect himself with it by a false genealogy.[44] He created an extensive romance of the Montforts and their connections with Liège. It would be entirely in character for him to attempt to connect the author of the *Travels*, a work which he extravagantly admired, with Liège in some way. But before we can dismiss the whole story, now five hundred and fifty years old, we must deal with a rival story of equal antiquity, that Mandeville *knew* the Liège doctor.

* * *

All modern biographers of Mandeville, from Nicholson to Mr. Letts, accept as important evidence a passage at the end of the popular Latin abbreviation of the *Travels* commonly called the vulgate. This version was circulating in the last decade of the fourteenth century, and, like the first English

---
[43] Bormans, Introduction to the *Myreur*, vol. VII, xxx-xxxi.
[44] Kurth, pp. 86-96; Michel, pp. 17-21.

version, it claims, at least by implication, to be by Mandeville himself. The colophon reads:

> So ends the itinerary from the land of the English to the Holy Land, and to more distant lands beyond the sea, written first in the French language, by Sir John Mandeville, Knight, its author, in the year of our Lord 1355 in the city of Liège, and a little after, in the same city translated into this Latin form.[45]

This is the only Latin version to be printed (although at least four others were made), and it circulated widely and was selected by Hakluyt for the first edition of his *Principall Navigations*. It is, however, a faulty, as well as an abridged, translation. It could not have been made by the author of the original, as has been repeatedly demonstrated.[46]

In spite of its being an abridgement, it contains several interpolations, two of which tell a circumstantial story of two meetings between Sir John Mandeville and the doctor, Jean de Bourgogne, called à la Barbe. In Chapter VII of this version a paragraph has been inserted describing a meeting between the doctor and the traveler in Cairo. Hamelius translates it as follows:

> While I stayed at court I saw about the soudan a venerable and able physician hailing from our country. For he uses to keep about him physicians of various nationalities, whose reputation has reached his ears. We two had but few opportunities for con-

[45] The Latin reads, "Explicit itinerarium à terra Angliae, in partes Hierosolimitanas, et in vlteriores transmarinas, editum primò in lingua Gallicana, à Domino Ioanne Mandeuille milite, suo autore, Anno incarnationis Domini 1355. In Civitate Leodiensi; Et Paulò post in eadem ciuitate, translatum in dictam formam Latinam": Hakluyt's text, *Principall Navigations* (1589), p. 77. This is a version of the vulgate which interpolates several references to "Odoricus"; see Appendix II.

[46] In 1840 Carl Schönborn published *Bibliographische Untersuchungen über die Reise-Beschreibung der Sir John Maundevile* (Breslau), in which he argued that the Vulgate is an abridged and faulty translation which could not have been made by the original author. J. Vogels distinguished five Latin translations, four made in England, none of which can be credited to the author of the original: "Die ungedruckten lateinischen Versionen Mandeville's," in *Programm des Gymnasiums zu Crefeld* (Crefeld, 1886). Warner (p. viii) gives a good summary of the evidence.

versation, as my duties were widely different from his. A long time after, and a long distance away, viz. in the city of Liège, I by the advice and with the assistance of the same worshipful man composed the present treatise, as I shall more fully tell at the close of the whole book.[47]

In the last chapter this interpolator completes the story by describing the second meeting. He says:

In the year 1355 . . . while I was travelling home, I stayed near the noble city of Liége and was there laid up by disease and arthritic gout in the ward called Basse Sauvenière. For my recovery I consulted some doctors of the town, and by God's will it happened that one physician came in who was more venerable than the rest through his age and hoary hair and evidently expert in his art. He was there called Master John with the Beard. . . . [They recognize each other and renew acquaintance.] While displaying his knowledge of his art to my benefit he admonished and prayed me instantly that I should reduce to writing something of what I had seen while roaming through the world, that it might be read and heard for the use of posterity. So at last, through his advice and with his assistance, the present treatise was composed, of which I intended to write nothing until I finally reached my own country in England. . . . [He believes that his adventures have happened by divine providence, because while he was away France and England have been at war.] While now, thirty-three years after my departure, dwelling in the city of Liége, which lies only two days' journey from the English sea, I learn that through the grace of God the abovesaid enmity of these lords has been settled. Therefore I hope and intend, for the rest of my riper years to be able to attend to the rest of my body and to the salvation of my soul at home. Here then is the end of my writing. . . .[48]

We have to deal, it seems, not with one, but with two contradictory stories which connect Sir John Mandeville with Jean de Bourgogne and the composition of the *Travels* with the city of Liège. According to the one, told in d'Outremeuse's *Myreur*

---

[47] Hamelius, II, 5. He also quotes the Latin. And see Warner, pp. xxxvii-viii.

[48] Hamelius, II, 5-6. Hamelius argues that this date is a fiction. Note that the doctor is described as very old in 1355.

and on the tombstone, Jean de Bourgogne *was* Sir John Mandeville. According to the other, told in this Latin abridgement of the *Travels,* Jean de Bourgogne *was acquainted with* Mandeville and persuaded him to write the *Travels* while he was in Liège on his way home. The date is obviously false. The battle of Poitiers was not fought until 1356, and peace was not made until 1360. The earliest date, in any of the French texts, for the writing of the *Travels* is 1356, but since here the French and vulgate Latin versions are being represented as written at Liège on the way to England, the prior date of 1355 is given them.

However, what is important about this interpolation is that it represents a second (or first) attempt to connect Mandeville with de Bourgogne and with Liège. Not only Nicholson and Warner, but Hamelius, and more recently Mr. Letts, all admit this story as important evidence about the authorship of the *Travels.* All assume that the vulgate was either made by the author of the original, or by someone who knew him. Warner concluded that the vulgate must have been written by Jean d'Outremeuse, in spite of the fact that (1) all of his known works are in Liègeois French, and (2) he was not inclined toward brevity.[49] In most respects the vulgate resembles the work of a typical medieval abbreviator, since it omits many of the stories and most of the comments and reflections. It is entirely unlike the known works of d'Outremeuse, except that it contains, besides the two interpolations quoted above, more than a dozen references to Ogier le Danois.

Ogier was d'Outremeuse's chief hero. He says in his *Myreur* that he has written a new *Geste de Ogier le Danois,*[50] and Ogier figures extensively in his long *Geste de Liège,* and in his

[49] Warner, p. xl. And see Wells, quoted above, p. 94.

[50] *Myreur,* III, 111-112. Of the combat of Ogier with Agramont he says, "Toutes ses chouses sont declareis en la novelle gieste que nous meisme avons fait sour Ogier; partant me passoie briefment que je la mis là cleirement et planement." Other references to this work occur in III, 2, 134, 141, 203, 357, 371, 402, etc. and in the *Geste de Liège,* printed in the same vols., II, 661, ll. 12,810-15.

*Myreur.* In the *Myreur,* Ogier is the chief hero in the time of Charlemagne, and then he is said to have been held captive in fairyland by Morgan le Fay for 418 years, so that he can come back to earth for a second set of adventures in the early thirteenth century. During his first life on earth he is represented as making a journey to the Orient, where he conquers fifteen great kingdoms. For the geography of these adventures, d'Outremeuse borrows wholesale from *Mandeville's Travels.*[51]

The borrowing from the *Travels* in the *Myreur* is direct and obvious. D'Outremeuse lists Mandeville among his "authorities" in the *Myreur* and he does not list Odoric of Pordenone. The parallels between the *Travels* and the *Myreur* could not be the result of a mutual dependence on Odoric because, as Hamelius points out, d'Outremeuse makes use of Mandeville's additions to Odoric, and even of his mistakes.[52] For example, Mandeville adds the Fountain of Youth to Odoric's account of Polumbrum and says that he drank some of the water. D'Outremeuse, in turn, reports in his *Myreur* that Ogier and his men drank from that fountain when they visited Polumbrum.[53]

The adventures of Ogier which are interpolated into the Latin vulgate version of Mandeville's *Travels* represent brief restatements of the Eastern conquests of Ogier described in d'Outremeuse's *Myreur.* According to the *Myreur,* Ogier left Paris on the third of August, 819 (the exactness of the date is characteristic of d'Outremeuse's fictions) and, after a preliminary visit to Denmark and Rome, he arrived at Jaffa and proceeded to Jerusalem. Here the borrowing from the *Travels*

[51] Michel, pp. 81-105, gives a useful summary of the Ogier material in the *Myreur*. On p. 115 he mentions the borrowings from the *Travels* in the account of Ogier's voyage to the Orient.

[52] Hamelius used this similarity as an argument that d'Outremeuse wrote the original *Travels*. He says, "Minute coincidences have been pointed out in our notes. . . . It is hardly possible that such a mistake has been committed independently by two writers" (p. 9). There is no question of independent composition, however.

[53] *Myreur,* III, 58. A later Ogier romance takes him to the Fountain of Youth, under the influence either of the *Myreur* or of the vulgate *Travels.*

begins. Ogier conquers Palestine, Arabia, Samaria, and Nubia, baptizing as he goes. Then he proceeds to India and China, is crowned at Nyssa, and makes one of his followers, called Prester John, emperor of that country. He also visits the Earthly Paradise and the islands of the "Bragmans," conquering altogether fifteen great kingdoms.[54]

It is a curious fact that, while d'Outremeuse's debt to the *Travels* has been noted, no mention has been made of the borrowing from the *Myreur* for the Ogier interpolations in the vulgate *Travels*. Since the relationship makes it evident that either the same person wrote both *Myreur* and the vulgate *Travels*, or that whoever is responsible for the Ogier interpolations in the *Travels* had access to d'Outremeuse's *Myreur*, it seems necessary to summarize the parallels which show the extent of the relationship. The Ogier interpolations in the vulgate *Travels* begin in Chapter xix and are as follows:

*Myreur:* Ogier's conquest and baptism of the Samaritans (III, 55-56).
VULGATE: Mentioned in Chap. xix.
*Myreur:* Ogier fought and killed Brehier at Laudinum (Laon) (III, 283-300).
VULGATE: Mentioned Chap. xxii, which deals with Mohammedanism.
*Myreur:* Ogier conquers the land of Prester John and establishes there churches called Danois (III, 57).
VULGATE: Statement inserted that there were many abbots in this land because Ogier had formerly established churches there called "Dani" (Chap. xxi). "Dani" in Latin corresponds to the French "Danois."
*Myreur:* Ogier names two cities of India after his two grandmothers, Flandrine and Florentine (III, 57).
VULGATE: The original French text of the *Travels* mentions two cities of India, Flandrina and Singlant. The vulgate adds that Ogier founded them and named them for his grandmothers, but the name of the second was changed to Singlant (Chap. xxvii).
*Myreur:* Ogier conquers Calamye and builds there a church for

[54] *Myreur*, III, 51-68.

St. Thomas' bones, which had been in Mesopotamia for 63 years (III, 58-59).

VULGATE: The same story, even to the number of years (Chap. XXVIII).

*Myreur:* Ogier conquers Jona (III, 59-60). See the index for the whole list of his Eastern conquests.

VULGATE: The passage on the roundness of the earth is reduced to ten lines, and instead we have an account of the palace of the Emperor of Jona decorated with pictures of the whole history of Ogier, from his birth, through his exploits in France and his conquests in the East (Chap. XXIX). The best French texts read "Java," but the later redactions read "Jona" (see below).

*Myreur:* Ogier conquers Lancheri (III, 63).

VULGATE: In the region of Lachori are many churches and religious houses founded by Ogier when he conquered fifteen great kingdoms, "sic infra dicet" (Chap. XXXII).

*Myreur:* Ogier conquers Cathay (III, 62-63).

VULGATE: There are Christian abbots at the court of the Great Khan of Cathay because Ogier instituted them (Chap. XXXVI).

*Myreur:* Ogier conquered fifteen great kingdoms in the East and divided them among his followers, giving India to Prester John (III, 52 and 66, and *Geste de Liége,* II, 676, l. 13,924).

VULGATE: This information is interpolated briefly (Chap. XLI).

*Myreur:* Ogier is translated into St. Ogier after his visit to the Earthly Paradise (III, 66-68, 314).

VULGATE: Ogier visited the Earthly Paradise, and the writer affirms his belief that he reigns with Christ in heaven (Chap. XLVII).

*Myreur:* Ogier baptizes the heathen in the Ganges (III, 63).

VULGATE: Mention is made of this event (Chap. XLVIII).

The two accounts have so many details in common that the dependence of the vulgate on the *Myreur* seems clear. D'Outremeuse used the *Travels* for matter in his *Myreur,* as he acknowledges in his list of sources; and, in his turn, whoever made the "Ogier" version of Mandeville's *Travels* made use of d'Outremeuse's *Myreur.* However, the *Myreur* was far from completion when the vulgate *Travels* began to circulate. The Latin *Travels* was known in the last decade of the fourteenth century, whereas the *Myreur* was probably still incomplete when its author died in 1400. Book III was in progress in 1398.[55] It is an enormously long work, written in the last years of the author's life, and there is no reason to suppose that it existed in more than one copy before 1400.[56] There must, therefore, have been a very close relationship between the author of the *Myreur* and the interpolator of Ogier in the *Travels*, and therefore, presumably, between the author of the *Myreur* and the author of the story of Mandeville's two meetings with Jean de Bourgogne.

However, at this point a new fact must be taken into account, and that is that the vulgate is not an independent redaction, as all previous biographers have supposed, but a Latin abbreviation of a hitherto unrecognized French redaction of the *Travels* which will be described in the next chapter.

[55] Dormans discusses the date; Introduction, pp. xci-xciii.

[56] For a list of the extant MSS of the *Myreur* see J. van den Gheyn and E. Bacha, *Catalogue des Manuscrits de la Bibliothèque Royale de Belgique*, IX (Brussels, 1909), nos. 6515-6526. Sylvan Balau gives an account of the MSS in his *Étude*, pp. 563-564; and see Michel, *Légendes*, pp. 22-28, and index.

# THE CHANTILLY MANUSCRIPT

A VERY important source of evidence about the authorship of the *Travels* is the text. Yet it is one of the vagaries of scholarship that no study of the original text has ever been published. Studies have been made of every one of the translations, Latin, English, German, Dutch, Danish, Czech, Italian, Spanish, and Irish. In most of these languages texts have been edited. Yet the only French text to be published in recent times is the Norman-French text published by Warner in the Roxburghe Club edition of the English translation preserved in an Egerton manuscript. Mr. Malcolm Letts is just now publishing an edition of the earliest dated manuscript, but at this writing it has not appeared.

It has been assumed, and even asserted, that "unlike the Latin and English texts, the manuscripts [in French] are all substantially of a single type," and that the "oldest and best" manuscript is that copied in 1371 for Charles V and now in the Bibliothèque Nationale (fonds fr. nouv. ac. 4515).[1] This manuscript is in the dialect of Paris. In 1889 Ernest Langlois mentioned a "second redaction," but did not identify it clearly.[2] A decade later F.E. Sandbach clearly distinguished the Paris text of 1371 from an "Ogier version" which he found in a manuscript of a German translation.[3] Hamelius discovered a French

---

[1] Warner, p. ix. This MS. is described in Chapter 9, and see Chap. 11.

[2] "Notices des Manuscrits François et Provençaux de Rome antérieurs au xvi⁰ siècle," *Notices et Extraits des Manuscrits de la Bibliothèque Nationale et autres Bibliothèques,* pub. by L'Institut National de France, Tome 33, pt. 2 (Paris, 1889), p. 47. He says that it contains interesting details of the personality of the author, a remark which probably refers to the end of the Ogier version.

[3] "Otto von Diemeringen's German Translation of Mandeville's Travels," *Modern Quarterly of Language and Literature (Modern Language Quarterly),* II, No. 5 (1899), 29-35.

text with references to Ogier (Brussels 10,420-5) but did not distinguish it further than to cite Vogels to the effect that it was a "very good" text, and to remark that it was "corrupt in many places"! He printed several passages from it in his notes.[4]

This manuscript has several Ogier interpolations such as occur in the Latin vulgate. It also has, at the end, the story which also occurs at the end of the Latin vulgate of the meeting between Mandeville and de Bourgogne at Liège. Another exemplar of this version which, if not the oldest, is certainly the most complete, is now in the Musée Condé at Chantilly (no. 699, formerly 1414).[5] Examination of it throws a flood of new light on the Liège tradition of the origin of the *Travels*, as well as on the source of the Latin vulgate.

It can easily be shown that it originated at Liège, and that it is a redaction of the Paris text represented by the 1371 manuscript. But first, let us place it in relation to the other French texts. These have been preserved in about sixty manuscripts (see Appendix I), which fall into three main groups. One, in Norman French, is to be found chiefly in the English libraries, and this is the version printed by Warner. A second group of manuscripts is in the French of Paris and includes the text dated 1371. The third group consists of manuscripts of the Ogier redaction in a northern French dialect. The question of authorship has been discussed for more than sixty years in the vacuum created by the lack of any study of the relations of these three versions to one another, and indeed without its being discovered that there are three versions!

[4] See his edition of the *Travels*, II, 18, and his notes *passim*.
[5] The fullest description is in the three-volume catalogue: *Chantilly. Le Cabinet des Livres Manuscrits. Institut de France. Musée Condé* (Paris, 1911), III, 3-6. A summary appears in the *Catalogue Général des Manuscrits des Bibliothèques Publiques de France. Musée Condé à Chantilly* (Paris, 1928), p. 143. It has some marginal decoration, including borders for many pages, and ornamental initials throughout. A large initial on fol. 1 shows a knight, armed, wearing on his breast a chevron ermine. A small shield at the foot of the page has the same charge, which has been identified as the arms of the Ghistelles of Artois, for whom the copy was therefore probably made.

Since it is the missing key to our puzzle, let us begin with the Ogier version. Of the six copies which I have been able to identify, the Chantilly manuscript most fully preserves the work of the redactor. It contains not only the text of the *Travels* with the interpolations about Ogier and Jean de Bourgogne, but also four additional books, each described as by Sir John Mandeville. The *Travels* is called "Book I." "Book II" is an account of the shape of the earth, "III" describes the heavens, "IV" is a herbal, and "V" is a lapidary. No other copy of the *Travels* has these four additional books, but there is substantial evidence that they were an integral part of the Liège redaction. The redactor interpolated into the text of the *Travels* a reference to "my lapidary which is the last of the five books which I devised" (fol. 39). In another place there is a reference to a "second book." Moreover, the account of the diamond, usually found in the original *Travels*, is here transposed to the lapidary. Evidently, whoever made the Ogier version planned from the first to include four additional books.

Other copies of this version, while they lack the additional books, provide evidence that they descend from a five-book version. One of these, now in the Bibliothèque Nationale (fonds fr. 24,436), has an *Explicit* describing it as "the first book of the five books of Sir John Mandeville. . . . Written by me, Ogier de Caumont, in the city of Liège and finished the penultimate day of July, 1396."[6] This is the oldest *dated* manuscript of this redaction, but it shows that, although the Chantilly manuscript may not be older, it represents more fully the text of the Ogier version. Moreover, Ogier de Caumont's text shows that this five-book version was in existence, and known in Liège, at least four years before d'Outremeuse died.

Of the four remaining copies of this version, one reported at Liège in the nineteenth century is now lost. The pseudo-autobiographical passage at the end has been transcribed and

---

[6] Fol. 62 reads, "Explicit le premier liure des cinq liures messier Jehan de mandeuille. . . . Escript par moy Ogier de Caumont en la cite de liege & finy le penultiement Joyr de juillet lan mil ccciiij$^{xx}$ & xvi."

published, however.[7] It not only names the street where Mandeville stayed in Liège, but it even names the innkeeper, "Henkin Levo." The copy at Brussels (no. 10,420-5), examined and partly described by Hamelius, has been further described by Mr. Letts under the misapprehension that it is a good text.[8] Another copy of this version was written on the continent, although it is now in the Fitzwilliam Museum at Cambridge, England (MS. McClean 177).[9] The last of the six is a mid-fifteenth century manuscript preserved at Amiens. It contains a lapidary attributed to Jean à la Barbe and will be described in the next chapter.

It is quite evident that this Ogier version is not the original, but a redaction of the Paris-French text. It rephrases and even transposes many sentences. Some passages are condensed, others curtailed, and in many places the feats of Ogier le Danois have been interpolated. For example, the Paris version says of a church in Jerusalem: "En ce temple estoit charlemaine quant lange lui aporta le prepuse nostre siegneur [li jour] de la circumcision. et il le porta a ais ala capelle a .vij. lieues du liege. Et puis Charles le cauve le fist porter a poitiers. et puis fu il portes a chartres."[10] That is, "Charlemagne was in this church when the angel brought him the prepuce of our Lord on the day of the Circumcision. And he carried it to Aix la Chapelle seven leagues from Liège. And then Charles the

[7] Ferd. Hénaux, "Notice sur le Quartier de la Saunevière à Liège," *Bulletin de L'Institut archéologique Liégeois,* IV (1860), 171. Reprinted by Warner, p. xxxviii, n. 1. Hénaux reports it as in the Bibliothèque publique de Liège, à l'Université, no. 360, fol. 118. It dated the *Travels* in 1356, instead of 1357 as in the Chantilly and de Caumont texts. A copy of the *Travels,* on paper, which was at Liège in the 15th century, is also lost: S. Bormans, in *Le Bibliophile Belge,* [3 Ser.] I (1866), 236.

[8] See Letts, pp. 116-119, and elsewhere.

[9] M. R. James, *Descriptive Catalogue of the McClean Collection of Manuscripts in the Fitzwilliam Museum* (Cambridge, 1912). I am indebted to Mr. R. A. B. Mynors for the information that it was no. 9019, and no. 835 of the Phillipps sale of 1898, and for other information about it.

[10] I quote from Bibl. Nat. MS. nouv. acq. fr., 10,723, fol. 24$^v$.

Bald had it carried to Poitiers. And then it was carried to Chartres."

In the Chantilly manuscript this has been expanded to read: "Item en che temple dn̂i estoit li roys charles li ĝn̂s iadis de franche roys et de rome l'emp*er*eies un jour en ĝn̂t deuocion aveq*ues* lui na*m*le li ducs de bayuier Ogiers li danois rolans Oliuiers et m̂ît dautres de ses pers de franche qui la estoient ales en pelerinage. Et li angeles a porta al roy charle le prepucie n̂re sigñ ihû xprist de sa circu*m*cision lequelle charles emporta et le mist a ais la chapelle mais charles li chauls de quoy charles le grans fu taion assauoir peres al roy loeis pere a cheli charle li chauls le osta days si fist porter a poitiers et puis fu elle porte a chartres."[11] The redactor has added the titles of Charlemagne, and the names of four peers, and the genealogy of Charles the Bald, all matters utterly irrelevant to the event being recorded. This kind of padding occurs wherever Ogier has been interpolated, which is in at least twenty-three places in the text of the *Travels*. There is no mention of Ogier whatever in either the Paris or the Norman-French versions.

The Latin vulgate is, unquestionably, an abbreviation of this Ogier (or Liège) redaction. Where Ogier is mentioned in the Latin he is also mentioned in the French, which names him more often. Moreover, where the vulgate mentions Ogier, the French is more extensive and detailed in its account of him, and where the French mentions him, but the vulgate does not, the vulgate frequently omits other matter also at that point.

This Ogier redaction, like the vulgate, contains the story of Mandeville's visit to Liège, although in a somewhat less elaborate form. At the end of the paragraph, contained in all versions, in which the author says that he was forced by the

[11] MS. Chantilly, Musée Condé. No. 699, fol. 11. The Latin vulgate omits the whole story of the recovery of the prepuce, and so does not have this Ogier passage.

gout to return home and had solaced himself by writing the book,[12] the Chantilly manuscript adds to the last sentence, "dedens la noble cyte de lyege en la basse sabloniere en lostel hannechin dit le volt. A la requeste & proyere de honnorable & discreit maistre iehan de bourgoigne dis a le barbe phizitien qui en ma maladie moy vizitoit. Et en vizitant moy recognut & rauiza sy com chil qui mauoyt veu en la court le souldan de Egypte auoec le quel il demoroyt quant ie fuy la" (fols. 74ᵛ-75). Here are all of the elements in the story told more elaborately in the vulgate: the sickness at Liège, the meeting with the doctor whom he had known formerly in Egypt, and the statement that he wrote the *Travels* at the doctor's request. In addition, we have the name of the innkeeper.

There are other indications that the vulgate was made from the Ogier-Liège redaction. The account of diamonds occupies more than two pages in the Paris version of 1371, but in the Chantilly manuscript most of this matter is transposed to the lapidary in the "fifth book," and at the end of the curtailed fragment left in the text of the *Travels*, the redactor makes the author say, "whoever wants to know all its manners, natures, and virtues will find it in my lapidary which is the last of the five books which I devised and made and which follows, according to the true opinion of the Indians who in this are the most wise in the world and the most expert" (fols. 38ᵛ-39). The vulgate also abbreviates the account of the diamond, adding, "sicut plenius describitur in lapidariis" (Chap. xxvi). This remark is followed, however, by the remainder of the account of the diamond. Evidently the abbreviator worked from the five-book version of the Ogier-Liège redaction, and was able to turn back and supply the missing passage. At another point the redactor has interpolated a reference to Ogier ending, "Et aussy an treuue tout che en lor chroniquez et en celles de nostre pays mesmes de engleterre & dautre part" (fol. 46ᵛ). Here the vulgate reads, "per certas historias habetur Ducem Danorum

[12] Pollard ed., p. 208, quoted above, Chap. 6.

Ogerum conquisiuisse has terras" (Hakluyt ed. p. 49, Chap. 28). There is no such appeal to authority in either the Paris or the Norman-French versions. It is quite out of keeping with Mandeville's direct and simple style of narration.

It is perfectly clear that the vulgate is not, as has been assumed, an independent version made by someone close to the author. On the contrary, it was made from this hitherto unrecognized Ogier version of the French, perhaps by a professional redactor. There is no necessity, therefore, to attribute it to the pen of d'Outremeuse whose acknowledged works are all in Liègeois French——although it was certainly made in his lifetime and quite possibly by someone who knew him and was inspired, in the elaboration of the story of the influence of the doctor on Mandeville, by something d'Outremeuse had told him.[13]

The Ogier redaction of the French text is, on the other hand, fully in keeping with the known work of d'Outremeuse. It is in the language in which he wrote.[14] It celebrates his chief hero, Ogier le Danois. And it brings Mandeville and the writing of the *Travels* to Liége. In the *Geste de Liège* he regularly celebrates his native city by bringing everybody there, from Charlemagne to Ogier. The mention of the name of the street, and of the innkeeper, is almost a sign manual of Jean d'Outremeuse. Kurth says of him that he always names not only the principals in an action but also the servants and subordinates whom history so regularly forgets.[15] It is one of his devices for creating verisimilitude—but it was not Mandeville's way.

The Ogier redaction not only brings into the *Travels* many references to d'Outremeuse's chief hero, but in some places the text is curtailed as if to make room for Ogier, as in the case of

[13] Even this is not a necessary assumption. Other scribes, redactors, and translators tried their hands at interpolations of small, circumstantial details; see above, Chap. 5, and below, Chap. 9.

[14] Whether the original was in Liège patois we cannot now demonstrate. Ogier de Caumont's version is much nearer the French of Paris. The dialect of the Chantilly manuscript has been described as "Picard."

[15] *Étude*, pp. 31-36.

the trees whose sap can be made into flour. According to the Ogier version, the trees were made fruitful by a miracle of Ogier's when he conquered the island and found a famine there (fol. 46). On the next page we read of the island of Calonak, where the fish come up onto the land each year. In the other two versions of the *Travels*, the author speculates about whether the fish are sent by divine providence to feed the many children of the polygamous king. But in the Liège version all this is replaced by the statement that the fish are another miracle of Ogier's.

As I have shown in the last chapter, these stories in the vulgate Latin and in the Ogier redaction of the French agree in detail with the account of Ogier's eastern conquests in d'Outremeuse's *Myreur*. In the Chantilly manuscript we are told that "he conquered fifteen great kingdoms in one expedition and twelve in another" (fol. 23$^v$). In the *Myreur* Ogier is provided with eastern adventures in 819-821, 836, and 857, not counting several trips to the Holy Land. In 821 he conquered eight new realms, according to Michel's résumé of the best manuscript.[16]

The Liège redactor makes Mandeville claim that in India he found a chronicle in the church of Our Lady at Nyssa which said that in 816 Ogier conquered all of India and Cathay,[17] comprising fifteen great kingdoms, which he gave to his "cousins" who were with him, "And among the others he had a cousin, son of his uncle, King Gondebuef of Friesia, who was named John in baptism, who, in his youth, frequented the church and spent the whole day on his knees before the altars of the churches. And his father, King Gondebuef, said that it would make of him a priest. And it ended in his limiting his too eager frequenting of the churches to certain hours. And

[16] *Les Légendes*, p. 91.
[17] D'Outremeuse's *Myreur*, III, 51, reads 819 as the date of Ogier's setting out for the East, but the rest of the story is the same. The difference in date probably results from a copyist's error; see Michel, pp. 90-99.

because of the shame that was attached to anyone named Prester John, by the common people, he was not able to bear it all his life. He went overseas with Ogier. And Ogier gave him the kingdom of Pentexoire to have in India" (fol. 70ᵛ). This account of the identity of Prester John is characteristic of the inventions of d'Outremeuse, who says in his *Myreur*, "Et ly roy Gondebuef de Frieze luy livrat prebstre Johan son fil, et l'appellat ly roy son pere: prestre, portant que tous les jours alloit oreir al moustier, en genulhant devant chascon aulteir par devotion, se le nommat prebstre Johan por solas; chis fut roy d'Inde, car Ogier l'en coronat."[18] There is more than one mediaeval explanation of the name of Prester John and of his origin, but this one is peculiar to d'Outremeuse and it replaces a different explanation which occurs in the other two versions of the *Travels*. Finally, in addition to the interpolations already mentioned, the Ogier redaction is provided with two additional alphabets, one for the Chinese and the other for Pentexoire, the land of Prester John.[19]

It is too obvious to require extensive illustration that this Ogier version is a redaction, and not the original version of the *Travels*. These evidences of d'Outremeuse's responsibility for it are, therefore, evidence that he did not write the original *Travels*. Both in style and content the Ogier redaction is inferior to the Paris and Norman-French texts. The intrusion of Ogier destroys the great plausibility which is one of the most notable literary achievements of the original. There are also stylistic changes which are the work of a less skilful and effec-

---

[18] Letts translates this passage, p. 113, and another which he attributes to the vulgate text. He argues (see p. 111) that d'Outremeuse was responsible for the Ogier versions which he enumerates as "the version used by von Diemeringen for his German translation, the abridged Latin vulgate text of c. 1484, and a manuscript at Brussels (Bibl. Royale 10420)."

[19] The description of these alphabets is erroneous in M. J. Techener's *Description raisonnée d'une collection choisie d'anciens manuscrits . . . réunis par les soins de M. J. Techener* (Paris, 1862-64), I, 159-162. He is describing the Chantilly MS.

tive narrator. The Ogier redactor shows a preference for the nerveless and prolix sentence, as when he changes the effective word-order of "Et pres de Famagoche fut nez saint barnabe lapostle," to "Item saint barnabe lapostele fy nez de cypre de la cyte de famagoche." He has a taste for verbosity, as in the opening paragraph, where "the cruel Jews" becomes "felons and cruel Jews"; "perpetual death" becomes "terrible and perpetual death"; and the sentence "we were condemned for the sin of our father Adam, and for our own sins also [et pour noz pechiez meismes aussi]" is changed so as to end "for our sins also of which we become participants by the morsel of the apple [et por nos pechies aussi des quels nous estiens entechies par le morsel de la pomme]." The addition changes the meaning.

It appears that the Ogier version was made from a somewhat corrupt text of the Paris version of the *Travels*.[20] Many of the proper names are garbled, yet there seem to be few garbled sentences in the Chantilly manuscript. There are, however, misinterpretations which may be the result of garbles in the text from which the redactor was working. The situation suggests that the Chantilly manuscript is a good text of the redactor's version, although it is not the holograph of the redactor. For one thing, it is in a good text hand of a professional scribe. For another, it drops out words occasionally—words which occur in the text written by Ogier de Caumont at Liège in 1396. On page 143 the reader will find a table of proper names which are corrupt in the 1371 text of the *Travels*. About half of these names are even more corrupt in the Chantilly manuscript. For example, *Java*, which is spelled *Iaua* in the best Norman-French manuscripts, becomes *Iana* in 1371, and *Ionna* in the Chantilly manuscript. It is regularly spelled *Iona* in the Latin vulgate.

The discovery of this Ogier redaction accounts for the text of the vulgate, and it solves one further textual problem. There

---

[20] See below, Chap. 9.

is a translation of the *Travels* into German, made by Otto von Diemeringen some time between 1369 and 1398, when he died. He says in his preface, "I, Otto von Diemeringen, a 'Thumherre' of Metz in Lothringen, have translated this book from 'Welschs' and from Latin into German so that the German people may read it."[21] Since Otto has matter which is omitted or abbreviated in the Latin vulgate, but also has references to Ogier, it has been assumed that he translated from the Paris French text and added Ogier from the vulgate. But he also has the two additional alphabets which are characteristic of the Ogier redaction, and which are not in the vulgate (that version omits all alphabets). It is evident, therefore, that Otto's "Welsch" text was the Ogier redaction.[22] What use he made of the Latin is not apparent, but his statement shows that it existed before he made his translation.[23] He thought that there were five books of the *Travels*, however, for he divides his translation into five books. Probably he noticed the mention of five books in the Ogier redaction, and did not know that what he had before him was only the "first book" of that version. His translation is preserved in at least twenty-eight manuscripts and was the basis of the Czech and Danish versions of the *Travels*.

It is quite possible that further search will reveal other copies of the Ogier redaction, but the six manuscripts which I have identified provide all the evidence necessary to show that this version was known at Liège in d'Outremeuse's life-

[21] F. E. Sandbach gives an account of this translation, *Handschriftliche Untersuchungen über Otto von Diemeringens Deutsche Bearbeitung der Reisebeschreibung Mandevilles* (Strassburg, 1899). Otto's version was printed at Basel by Bernhart Richel in 1481 as *Reysen und wanderschafften durch das Gelobte Lande, Indien und Persien*. See also Arthur Schoerner, *Die Deutschen Mandeville-Versionen: Handschriftliche Untersuchungen* (Lund, 1927), pp. 11-30, and my appendices I and II.

[22] *Welsch* was a name applied to the Liège dialect by neighboring Germans.

[23] Three Middle Low German manuscripts of this text were edited by Sven Martinsson, *Itinerarium Orientale: Mandevilles Reisebeschreibung in Mittelniederdeutscher Übersetzung* (Lund, 1918).

time, and that it is a redaction, and not the original version. The interpolation of the pseudo-biographical story intended to make it appear that the work was written at Liège, and the many references to Ogier le Danois make it highly probable that Jean d'Outremeuse was the redactor. The four additional books to be found in the Chantilly manuscript contribute further evidence in the same direction.

# THE APOCRYPHAL WORKS

Each of the four additional books of the Chantilly manuscript is specifically represented as by Mandeville. "The second book of Sir John Mandeville, Knight, . . . makes mention of the form of the earth and explains in what manner it was made,"[1] according to the heading. Its author claims to derive his information from the mythical *Book of Seth* (which d'Outremeuse mentions in his *Myreur*).[2] The story is told (out of Josephus) of how the world was altered by the flood.[3] Then he wanders on to the state of man, his sins, confession, prayer, good works, et cetera, with quotations from the Scriptures and the Fathers in Latin (Mandeville quotes from the Latin Bible and the Fathers). After several pages of digression, the author wanders back to the roundness of the earth, borrowing a little from the *Travels* and adding some jejune statements about the stars and the relation of the earth to the constellations. Then comes a paragraph on the influence of the stars, the divisions of the day, the stability of the earth, its relation to the sea, et cetera. Then there is a series of recapitulations, an explanation of the seven "words" spoken from the cross, a page of reiterated assertion that all parts of the earth are inhabited, and a page explaining that the law of God extends to all people. We are told that the antipodes have mountains, plants,

---

[1] Che commenche li secons lyures mesire Jehan de mandeville chevalier qui fait mencion de la forme de la terre et comment et par quel maniere elle fu faite" (fol. 75).

[2] *Myreur*, I, 321. A summary of the traditions about Seth, with notes on sources, and quotations, occurs in J. A. Fabricius, *Codex Pseudepigraphus Veteris Testamenti* (Hamburg and Leipzig, 1713), I, 139-157. See also Lynn Thorndike, *A History of Magic and Experimental Science* (New York, 1923), I, 366; M. R. James, *The Lost Apocrypha of the Old Testament* (London, 1920), pp. 9-10.

[3] Josephus, *Antiquities of the Jews*, I, ii, 3.

and beasts, all created for man. Finally there is again more than a page of recapitulation. It is verbose and repetitious, as utterly unlike Mandeville's crisp and specific narrative as anything could well be.

The third book (ff. 88-96$^v$) is headed, "Here begins the third book of Sir John Mandeville which makes mention of the form of the heavens." It opens with the statement that this book is also "according to the book of Seth," but goes on to appeal to the experience of St. Paul when he was wrapt into the third heaven. Then it mentions the four elements, the seven spheres, the seven planets, the orders of the angels, the empyrean, the Trinity, the precious stones in the throne of God, the appearance of the Deity according to the Scriptures and the book of Seth, and the places of various people in heaven, such as St. John the Baptist, the Virgin Mary, the Apostles, Evangelists, Popes, Cardinals, and others. He also appeals to "the books of India." Then he discusses the pride of Lucifer, the fall of the angels, contemplation, the use of images, and the rewards of the saved. Here, as in Book II, there is a very different mind at work from the one which created Mandeville's *Travels*. It is a mind more pious and superstitious, but much less learned.

The fourth book is again described as by Sir John Mandeville. It "makes mention of herbs according to the Indians and the philosophers thereabouts." He is made to boast, "Je Jehans de mandeuille cheualiers" have visited the Indians, Chaldeans, Persians, Egyptians, and many other nations where there are philosophers and sages. Seth and Hermes are mentioned. The boastful, "I, John Mandeville," is not to be found anywhere in the *Travels*, where the author mentions his name only at the beginning and the end, and there with modesty. Jean d'Outremeuse, however, often names himself in his writings in this way.

Book IV goes on to say that there are many sciences, especially the calculations of Adam, "augurie, sytrille, pyromanchie, ydromanchie, geomanchie, phyzonomie, cyromanchy," and all the magic arts, but here the author will speak of herbs because that science is "the shortest." Then follows a paragraph of pseudo-autobiography, according to which "Meleth Naser," formerly Sultan of Egypt, showed "a valiant Christian knight" his precious stones and all his treasure. But he boasted of a still greater treasure which the knight did not appreciate and so lost the chance to learn about "this herb." "Nous en sauons pluzeurs selonc che que ly aucteur de phizique nous dient mais de celle scienche occulte il ne font nulle mention."[4] This is obviously a part of the fiction of the meeting of Mandeville and Jean à la Barbe in Egypt and later at Liège, which appears in the Ogier redaction and the Latin vulgate. The "author of physic" probably refers to the doctor.

The book goes on to say, "I wish to make my little treatise for the service of the very excellent, very powerful, and very noble lord, my very dear and very redoubtable natural lord, Edward by the grace of God king of England and Scotland, lord of Ireland, Duke of Guyenne, ruler of the western ocean

[4] The passage reads: "Et pour tant meleth naser iadis souldans degypte monstra a vn vaillant cheualier x̄pien ses pierres preciouzes & tout son trezor car il lauoit loyalment serui sy lamoit moult. La quelle trezorie ly cheualiers priza moult. Mais ly Roys ly dist ie uous monstray autre trezorie que ie plus ayme que tout che que vous vees puis mena le cheualier en son iardin en un prayel enmuret dont il mesmes portoit la clef sy ly monstra une genestre qui la estoit moult noblement cidissante & encore est car ie lay veue. Et ly dist voys chi le trezor que ie ayme tant. Et ly cheualiers le cōmencha a despiter & dist que che prizoit il moult pau. Car en son pays en auoit tant con en chaulfoit les fours. Et dist ly souldans puis que tant en aues & blamet laues jamais ne sares par moy sa virtu que ie vous eusse aprize. Ensi perdy ly cheualiers par son trop parler assauoyr les virtues de celle herbe qui sont moult bonnes." Here follows the sentence quoted in the text, and then the dedication: "Par quoy je uoeil fayre mon petit traytiet pour la Reuerenche de tresexellent trespoissant et tresnoble signeur mon treschier et tres redoubtet signeur naturel. Edwars par le diuine dispozition roys dengleterre et descoche signeur de yrlande dux de gyenne souverains de la mer de occident et de ses ysles. Et signeur redoubte et renomme par vniuerse monde regnant en ces partyes lan de grasce mil trois cens LVII" (fol. 97ᵛ).

and its isles. And lord redoubtable and renowned throughout the universal world ruling in these parts in the year of grace 1357."[5]

This dedication bears a curious resemblance to the dedication, in Latin, often found at the end of copies of the French texts preserved in England, which reads, "To the most excellent prince, to be chiefly reverenced above all mortals, to the Lord Edward, by Divine Providence most serene king of France and England, lord of Ireland, Duke of Aquitaine, ruler of the sea and of its Western Islands, credit and ornament of Christendom, patron of all men at arms and pattern of probity and strength, also to the unconquered prince, follower of the wonderful Alexander, to be feared by the universe, the contents of this book are offered. . . ."[6] However, since both follow the formal style for addressing a monarch, the differences are more significant than the similarities. The exchange of Scotland for France, and of Guyenne for Aquitaine, reflects a national difference in point of view. It shows too that the dedication in the Chantilly manuscript was written after 1360, when Guyenne was ceded to the English crown. The date given, 1357, is therefore fictitious. It reflects, however, the fact that the Ogier redaction was made from the Paris version of the *Travels,* which regularly gives the date of publication as 1357, where the Norman-French version usually reads 1356.

It is not probable that the creator of the version in the Chantilly manuscript was familiar with the Latin dedication, for he worked from the Paris redaction in which it never occurs. The idea that the *Travels* should be dedicated to the English king is obvious enough to have occurred to more than one person.

After the dedication, Book IV of the Chantilly manuscript mentions the magic properties of herbs as they were revealed to Adam by an angel and recorded by his son Seth. The science

---

[5] Concerning this date, see below.
[6] Hamelius gives both the Latin and the translation in his edition of the *Travels,* II, 14.

was handed down among pagan philosophers, "but a philosopher of Chaldea who was named Gathalabricā, for the great love that he had for me taught me the science and put himself and me in danger of death . . ."[7] When the writer finally gets down to business, all he has to tell is the science of selecting plants for medicinal purposes solely by the number of leaves they have, from two to thirty-four. Even for its day the herbal is singularly naïve. While it might possibly be described as a medical work, it can hardly be imagined that it was written by a physician, certainly not by Jean de Bourgogne, who was a learned man for his day, as we shall see. At one point (fol. 99$^v$) a reference to Ogier le Danois and his combat with Brehier points to a different authorship altogether.

Book v is the lapidary (fol. 102$^v$-108$^v$), compiled "according to the opinion of the Indians from whom all the sciences of stones comes." It begins, "according to reason and true philosophy and also the opinion of the Indians as it has been approved by confirmed faith, I, John Mandeville, Knight . . ." A series of stones is described, then there is a recapitulation of the "five books of Mandeville," and, finally, there follows a longer list of stones not described.

Jean d'Outremeuse attributed a Latin work on precious stones to Mandeville in his own lapidary, the *Trésorier de Philosophie Naturelle des pierres précieuses*, dated 1390 and probably completed in that year. It opens with an impressive list of sources, ending with Sir John Mandeville, who "made a lapidary according to the opinion of the Indians."[8] He quotes in Latin from this lapidary thirteen times in the course of his

---

[7] "Mais un philozophe de caldee qui ot nom Gathalabricā pour la grant amour quil auoyt a moy ensegna la scienche & mist en auenture de mort luy & moy" (fol. 98). The name suggests that of the Old Man of the Mountain which is usually given in the *Travels* as *Gathalonabes,* or *Gacholonabes,* but in MS 10723 it is *Gachalonabes,* and in the Chantilly text, *Satha la nobles* (fol. 64$^v$).

[8] The *Trésorier* is fully described, with the chapter headings, in Michelant's "Notice sur un Manuscrit de Jean d'Outremeuse." See above, Chap. 6, n. 25.

own (which is in Liègeois French). He also refers three times to the *Travels* and once he invents a reminiscence, saying that Mandeville was for seven years a resident of Alexandria, where a Saracen with whom he was intimate gave him some fine jewels, which d'Outremeuse claims to have purchased.[9] This story is very similar to the one in the herbal of the Chantilly manuscript, which I have just described, and to the one in the vulgate which tells of Mandeville's meeting with the Liège doctor in Cairo.

The Latin lapidary quoted as Mandeville's is not the same as this French lapidary, however. In only one instance does the description of a stone which d'Outremeuse credits to Mandeville's Latin lapidary correspond with the description of a stone in the Chantilly manuscript. The two lapidaries are distinct and independent works, although both are attributed to Mandeville. The Latin quotations agree, in several cases, with an alphabetical lapidary by Arnoldus Saxo, which derived in turn from one translated from Arabic and attributed in the Middle Ages to Aristotle.[10] D'Outremeuse was familiar

[9] Since this passage has figured in the discussions of the authorship of the *Travels*, but has never been printed, I quote from the transcript made for me by M. Marcel Thomas from Bibl. Nat. MS. fonds fr. 12326, a paper MS of the early 16th century containing 248 leaves: "item nous en avons achette de tres belles et telles que devise avons par dessus, qui nous vinzent de messir Jehan de Mandeville et les avoit apporteez d'Alexandrie ou ong Sarezin luy avoit donne per grant amour et pour noble joyel car ils avoient demeure leur tamps ensamble en Alexandrie, dont messire jehan estoit baillez adonc par le tamps, et la fut par l'espace de vii ans, si avoient esté compaignons en fais d'armes ensamble. Nous les gardons moult precieusement si come affiert, car il nous samble . . ." (fol. 79). Letts accepts this story as authentic: cf. p. 107.

[10] Valentin Rose, "Aristotele's de Lapidibus und Arnoldus Saxo," *Zeitschrift für deutsches Altertum*, N. S., vi (Berlin, 1875), 321-455. Rose says that the lapidary attributed to Aristotle by Albertus Magnus and Vincent of Beauvais is identical with *Le Livre de pierres d'Aristotle de Luca ben Serapion*. F. de Mély reports that this work is translated from Arabic; *Les Lapidaires de l'Antiquité et du Moyen Age*, in Histoire des Sciences, (Paris, 1896-1902), III, vi and xxxiv ff. He notices a copy of this work discovered at Liège! In the lapidary of Arnoldus preserved at Montpellier, Codex Montispessul 277, fol. 127, the accounts of

## THE APOCRYPHAL WORKS

with this work, which he cites in his list of authorities, and he apparently assigned some version of it to his hero and victim, Sir John Mandeville.

Did he also give him a French lapidary of entirely different antecedents? He must have had many such works in his possession. They were usually short, plain little manuscripts, and so not expensive to buy or copy. The *Trésorier* is a big work, describing over three hundred stones and adding three books of natural history, in much the same way that four books are added to Mandeville's *Travels* in the Chantilly manuscript.[11] D'Outremeuse says that he has been working on the *Trésorier* for thirty-two years, that is, from the time he was twenty. He must have seen and copied many anonymous lapidaries (many were anonymous). He may have been the dupe of some other forger. Once it became known that he had an enthusiasm for Mandeville's *Travels*, some unscrupulous bookseller may have made sure of a sale by pandering to two interests at once.

However, he was certainly romancing about Mandeville in his *Trésorier*, and in the course of several years he was quite capable of attributing two different lapidaries to the famous traveler. He not only put into the *Trésorier* the statement that Mandeville was Lord of Montfort and of Castle Pérouse, but he also told there the story of how he had acquired some of Mandeville's jewels. Again, as in the herbal and the Ogier version of the *Travels*, the story concerns a sojourn in Egypt. All three are so similar as to suggest that all are by the same inventor.

We are not through with the story of the lapidaries, however.

---

Melicites, Quandros, Medus, Ceremon, and Sapphire are wholly or partly similar to the accounts quoted as Mandeville's by d'Outremeuse. Rose prints the lapidary. Mély, III, vi, says that the Montpellier text is a translation from Hebrew which distorts the names fantastically.

[11] In the introduction to Book II, of the *Trésorier* (fol. 36ᵛ) Mandeville is cited in Latin on the creation of precious stones, but the passage he quotes does not correspond to anything in the Chantilly manuscript.

There is still a third, which follows the Ogier redaction of the *Travels* in the Amiens manuscript.[12] This lapidary is entirely different from either of the other two, and it is attributed in the heading, not to "Mandeville," but to "Maistre Johans a la Barbe," but at the end we read, "Chis libre est appelleis le liure Johans de mande ville cheualier." The manuscript was written in 1461 "en la ville de hotton, par le main lambert le clers, pour ... signeurs de Rochefort et dagymont."

This Amiens lapidary is a little work written in a rather large hand on five small pages. It describes only nine stones,[13] and it is of too late a date to have much importance for this discussion. It is chiefly interesting as a further indication that Liège was a fertile source of legends about Jean à la Barbe and Mandeville, once the stories got started. We are concerned only with who started them.

The lapidary in the Chantilly manuscript was probably copied from an older one and adapted to its place in the expanded *Travels* by interpolating into it the passage about the diamond deleted from the *Travels* proper by the Liège redactor. It was also abbreviated, since it describes twenty-eight stones, beginning with the three kinds of "escarboucle," or ruby (i.e., anthrax, epististes, and balays), the diamond,

---

[12] It is fonds L'Escalopier, no. 94. It was described by Dorothea Waley Singer in a note in the *Library*, 3d ser., ix (1919), 275-276; see also E. Coyecque, *Catalogue Général des Manuscrits des Bibliothèques Publiques de France. Départements.* Tome xix (Amiens, 1893), pp. 493-494. M. Thomas very kindly provided me with a photostat.

[13] The opening is a garbled version of the lapidary in *Sidrac*, a popular encyclopaedia of the 13th century, for an account of which see Ch.-V. Langlois, *La Vie en France au Moyen Age* (Paris, 1927), pp. 198-275. It describes the jargousce, toupas, esmeraude, rubis, garnit, termidor, reflambine, Otriche, and turcamans. The opening of *Sidrac* was also borrowed for *Le Lapidaire du Roi Philippe,* a popular 14th century lapidary made by combining excerpts, usually verbatim, from *Sidrac*, with material from a Latin verse lapidary called *Le Lapidaire Crétien*. Léon Baisier, in his dissertation, *The Lapidaire Crétien* (Catholic University of America, Washington, 1936) overlooked the debt to *Sidrac*, but he prints the text of the *Lapidaire du Roi Philippe* (from Bibl. Nat. MS. fr. 2008), in his Appendix.

agate, sapphire, emerald, topaz, amethyst, sardonix, garnet, "pierre de soleil, pierre de lune," jacinth, pearl, etc. Then it lists thirty-six more without describing them.

In the fifteenth century there was a lapidary in circulation which was attributed to Mandeville, and which described the same stones, in the same order, with very few exceptions, often in the same words. This lapidary continued the list, describing the stones which are named but not described in the Chantilly manuscript, and preserving the same order.[14] Either the Chantilly list was later expanded, or, more probably, the Chantilly lapidary was abbreviated from one already in existence and more fully preserved in the fifteenth-century pseudo-Mandeville. Pannier, in his extensive study of medieval French lapidaries, reports that he found no copy of the pseudo-Mandeville which was older than the fifteenth century (he did not examine the Chantilly manuscript), but he did find a seventeenth-century manuscript which he believed preserved the original of the pseudo-Mandevillean lapidary. It is called "Traité du lapidaire selon l'Opinion des Indois," but it does not mention Mandeville.[15]

The fifteenth-century pseudo-Mandeville was extensively revised in the early sixteenth century and printed several times. The printed version was fitted with an introduction which claims that it was translated *from the Latin* of Sir John Mandeville into French for King Réné of Anjou (1409-80).[16] It consists

[14] Two copies of this 15th-century pseudo-Mandeville are described by Léopold Pannier, *Les Lapidaires français du moyen âge des xii*e, xiii*e, et xiv*e siècles*, published by the Bibliothèque de l'École des Hautes Études, Sciences Philologiques et Historiques, fascicule 52 (Paris, 1882), pp. 189-196. These are Bibl. Nat. MS. fr. 9136, and Brussels MS. 11058.

[15] See end of n. 16 below.

[16] The text was reprinted by Js. del Sotto, *Le Lapidaire du Quatorzième Siècle . . . d'après Traité du Chevalier Jean de Mandeville* (Vienna, 1862). Five editions of this work are recorded by Pannier, pp. 201-202. It is a composite in five distinct parts, of which the first describes 30 stones and, for the most part, follows the order and descriptions of the Chantilly MS. lapidary. The second section describes 17 stones (del Sotto, pp. 73-93), many of them already described in the first list, but here

of five distinct parts, of which the first substantially reproduces the Chantilly manuscript lapidary for the first twenty-four stones and adds accounts of the first six stones of the undescribed list given there. But since it omits the distinctively Mandevillean portion of the account of the diamond (which was transferred from the text of the *Travels* to the Chantilly lapidary) it obviously descends, not from the Chantilly version, but from the common parent of that and the fifteenth-century pseudo-Mandeville. However, the fact that Mandeville's name is attached to both indicates that a tradition had been established by the creator of the five-book Mandeville and by d'Outremeuse's *Trésorier* with its quotations from a Latin lapidary attributed to Mandeville. The four additional parts of the printed pseudo-Mandeville have much in common with the *Trésorier,* including a book of engraved stones attributed to "Téchef."

It is possible that the Chantilly manuscript is a curtailed version of the original, five-book Ogier redaction of the *Travels,* and that in the original all of the stones which are named are also described. The fifteenth century manuscript lapidary could represent such a version. The absence of Mandeville's own account of the diamond from such a text is a little harder to account for—unless we postulate a prolific and

---

taken from a different source. The third section describes 20 stones taken from the bodies of various animals. The last two parts describe two series of engraved stones, one of 18, the other of 33 stones, the last attributed to "Téchef." Finally, there is a list of 12 stones of the high priest's breastplate, named only, and a formula for restoring the magic properties of stones which have lost their power through contact with sinful men. Jean d'Outremeuse includes "Du livre Thechel et des autres ymages" in his *Trésorier,* Bk. III. Several versions of the work are described by Joan Evans, *Magical Jewels of the Middle Ages and the Renaissance particularly in England* (Oxford, 1922), pp. 102-109. The 17th-century lapidary discovered by Pannier and believed by him to be the original of the pseudo-Mandeville (printed text) contains the first and third sections, but instead of the second section it has only "orindes" and the last 4 stones; see his account of Bibl. Nat. MS. fr. 4836 (Pannier, pp. 198-200).

irresponsible inventor (such as d'Outremeuse is known to have been), who put out a French lapidary, which he had copied or invented, as Mandeville's, and then later created the five-book version of the *Travels*, adding the lapidary and transferring Mandeville's account of the diamond to it.

Whatever the exact relationship between the various lapidaries attributed to Mandeville, it is obvious that all of them are spurious.[17] The discovery of the Chantilly manuscript is important, however, in connecting the pseudo-Mandevillean lapidaries with the fabricator of the Ogier redaction of the *Travels*. All signs point to Jean d'Outremeuse as the redactor. His attribution of a Latin lapidary to Mandeville in the *Trésorier* does not make it any the less probable that he attributed an entirely different French lapidary to him in the continuation of the *Travels*.[18] His powers of invention are well established, and he was not troubled by any narrow notion of consistency, or even, in the case of the sons of Simon de Montfort, for example, of verisimilitude.

The Chantilly manuscript is valuable not only in connecting the various lapidaries with the Ogier redactor, but also in

[17] That is the conclusion of Pannier and Joan Evans.

[18] Warner (p. xxxv, n. 5) says that the Latin quotations "agree closely" with the text of the printed lapidary. They agree in only 4 of the 10 (borax, ceremon, emanach, and quandros). There is no agreement on amarites, beril, criseletes, medus, melocites, and sapphire. The Chantilly text agrees with the Latin quoted by d'Outremeuse only in the case of beril, a stone omitted in the printed text, where onix occurs instead. In the four cases of agreement, borax is in the second part of the printed lapidary, not in the first part, which follows the Chantilly text. Quandros and emanach (as lapus demath) appear in the third part of the printed lapidary, and ceremon is only named in the Chantilly MS. but was described in the 15th century pseudo-Mandevillean lapidary. There are 4 Latin quotations about the sapphire attributed to Mandeville in the *Trésorier* and not one of them is like anything in either of the other two lapidaries attributed to Mandeville. They parallel the description of the sapphire in the pseudo-Aristotle. Since lapidaries were compiled, rather than composed, these four scattered parallels between the Latin quotations attributed to Mandeville and the printed French pseudo-Mandeville are probably purely accidental, even if we conclude that d'Outremeuse invented both. They come from different compilations.

showing us the extent and direction of that redactor's inventiveness. The parallelism between d'Outremeuse's acknowledged works and these additions to the *Travels* leaves little room for doubt that he was chiefly, if not solely, responsible for all of the Mandeville apocrypha discussed in this chapter. We have, on the one hand, the similarity of structure and content between the additions to the *Travels* in the Chantilly manuscript and the *Trésorier;* and on the other hand we have the intrusion of Ogier le Danois from the *Myreur* into the Ogier-Liège redaction of the *Travels*. And since this version could not possibly be the original one, all of this evidence militates against Hamelius' theory that d'Outremeuse wrote the original *Travels*.

# THREE FAMILIES OF FRENCH MANUSCRIPTS

THE TEXT copied at Paris in 1371 is the oldest *dated* manuscript of the *Travels*, and scholarly caution in describing the undated ones has made of it "the oldest surviving manuscript." Some have gone a step further and called it the "best and oldest,"[1] but the best it certainly is not. I have made use of it for purposes of comparison in my discussion of the Ogier redaction, but now it is time to consider more fully the character of the Paris version and to establish its relation to the Norman-French texts preserved mostly in England.

G. F. Warner, in the Roxburghe Club edition of the second English translation of Mandeville, printed along with his English text what he considered to be the best and oldest of ten French texts then in the British Museum. He selected Harley MS. 4383, but gave the chief variant readings which he found in Sloane MS. 1464 and Grenville MS. xxxix; and, since the Harley manuscript is defective at the end, he made use of Royal MS. 20 B.x to complete his text. A full collation of all copies of this version is highly desirable, but Mr. R. A. B. Mynors has most generously looked at all copies of Mandeville in French preserved in England for me and he reports that he could find none which was obviously better than the text printed by Warner. He collated the test passages which I shall discuss. The Norman-French version differs from the Paris version in many details, but the two forms of the text are most easily distinguishable by the presence, in all copies of the Paris (and Ogier) versions, of two passages which do not occur in any copy of the Norman-French text.

[1] Wells, *Manual*, p. 434.

One of these is a long passage, amounting to about three pages in the 1371 manuscript, inserted into the account of the Valley Perilous. At first glance it might seem that the absence of this passage from the Norman-French texts might be the result of a missing leaf from the archetype of this version (a manuscript enough larger than that of 1371 so that the whole passage could be written on two sides of one leaf), but such a theory does not fit the situation for two reasons. In the first place, the style and narrative method of this passage differs markedly from the text of the *Travels*. In the second place, the second passage which has been inserted into the *Travels* (and which agrees with the first in style) is not simply an insertion, but a substitution. Since this substitution is short, the simplest way to demonstrate the difference in style is to quote both passages. The Norman-French version reads:

> Et sachez qe solonc loppinioun anxiens sages philosophes et astronomiens nostre pais, ne Irland, ne Gales, ne Escoce, ne Norwaye, ne les autres isles cousteantz, ne sont mie en la superficie contez dessur terre, si come il appiert par totes les liueres dastronomie. Qar la superficie de la terre est departie en vii. parties pur les vii. planetes; et celles parties sont appellez climacz. Et noz parties ne sont mie de vii. climacz, qar ils sont descendantz vers occident en trehant vers la roundure de monde. Et la sont les isles de Ynde; et sont encontre nous, qi sont en la basse pais. Et les vii. climacz sentendent enuironant le monde (Warner, p. 93).

Here we have a specific statement that England is outside the seven climates into which the surface of the earth is divided, because "they be descending toward the west [drawing] towards the roundness of the world. And also these isles of Ind which be over against us be not reckoned in the climates. For they be against us that be in the low country" (Pollard, ed. p. 124). The conception of a round, stationary world, with Europe and the Near East on top, and England and India far on opposite downward slopes, is clear enough. Actually Jerusalem was supposed to be on the high point, or "top" of the sphere.

## THREE FAMILIES OF FRENCH MANUSCRIPTS 137

In place of this passage, the Paris and Ogier redactions substitute the following (I quote from the manuscript of 1371):

Et ne desplaise aus lisans ce q*u*e iay dit que une partie de Inde est dessouz n*os*tre pays. et que aussi n*os*tre pays est dessouz euls a lopposite ainsi que le droit orient est opposite au droit occident. Et ainsi q*u*e est la partie de bise a la partie de midy. des quelles parties ie v*o*us ay a deuant parle et verite est. car ie lay mesure a lastrolabe q*u*e ceuls qui demeurent en la partie de bise sont pie contre pie aus autres de lautre partie contre midy. Et aussi s*om*mes nous a une partie des ylles dynde. Et sil auoit signe ou estoilles estables vers orient et vers occident par les quelles on peust les p*a*rties mesurer si co*m*me on fait les parties de bise et de midy p*a*r les deux estoilles non mouuables ou trouueroit de certain les ylles et la terre prestre Jehan bien loing lors des climas. Et en auironnant la terre dessouz nous plus assez que lautre partie de bise et de midy ne soient dont iay fait mencion cy deuant. Et si scay bien que iay mise mainte iournee pour aler vers les parties de ynde. plus que ie ne feys a aler la droite voie de bise vers le droit mydi. Et puis que la terre est ronde autant y a de bise a midy co*m*me de droit orient au droit occident. Pour quoy ie dy que on passe celle mesure et dessouz n*ous* environnant la terre.[2]

This passage is not only repetitious within itself, but it repeats what had already been said more tersely earlier in the account of circumnavigation and the roundness of the earth, in a passage which is certainly by the author of the original, since it occurs in all three versions of the text. It will serve, therefore, as a sample of Mandeville's own style of writing. He says:

Quar iay este vers les parties de Braban et regarde al astrolabre

[2] The 1371 MS., Bibl. Nat. fonds fr. nouv. acq. 4515, fol. 57$^r$. I quote from a photostat provided for me through the generosity of the Widener Library at Harvard. It has been described several times by L. Delisle, *Les Manuscrits du Comte d'Ashburnham* (Paris, 1883), p. 100 f.; *Catalogue des Manuscrits des Fonds Libri et Barrois* (Paris, 1888), p. 252; *Fac-Simile de Livres Copiés et Enluminés pour le Roi Charles V* (Paris, 1903). Plate VI reproduces the first page with its 4 miniatures showing a reader in his chair, the writer presenting the book to a prince, and two scenes from the story of the dragon-woman. See also his *Recherches sur la Librairie de Charles V* (Paris, 1907), Pt. III, Atlas, Plates VI and VII.

> qe la transmontane est liii degrez de haut, et plus auaunt en Almaigne et Beome elle est a lviii degrez, et plus auant vers lez parties septemtrionels elle ad lxii degrez de haut et ascuns menues, qar ieo mesmes lay mesure al astrolabre. Ore deuez sauoir qe encountre celle transmontane est lautre esteille qi est appelle Antartike, si come iay deuaunt dit. Et celles deux esteilles sount noun [i.e., non] mouablez et par elles tourne tout le firmament, auxi come vn roe tourne par soun axis. . . . Qar vous sauez qe cils qi sont al endroit del antartik sont droitement pez contre piez de ceux qi demoerent dessouz la transmontane, auxi bien come nous et cils qi demoerent souz nous sumes pie contre pie; qar totes les parties de mer et de terre ont lour apposites habitables ou trespassables et isles de cea et de la. Et sachez qe, solonc ceo qe ieo puisse perceuoir et comprehendre, les terres Prestre Iohan, emperour de Ynde, sont dessouz nous. Qar, en alant Descoce ou Dengleterre vers Ierusalem, homme monte totdys. Qar nostre terre est en la basse partie de la terre vers occident, et la terre Prestre Iohan est la basse partie vers orient. Et ont la le iour, quant nous auons la nuyt . . . (Warner, pp. 90-91).

This is the vigorous and graphic prose of the *Travels* as a whole. The imaginative power to visualize what he is describing is illustrated by the simile "as a wheel turns on its axis," and the specific statement "and there they have day when we have night." He gives names and distances, and uses the astrolabe to measure the height of the stars, whereas in the substitute passage, it is vaguely appealed to as evidence that "the north is opposite to the south." The pole stars are used in describing the movement of the heavens, not to show that "the isles and the land of Prester John" are "bien loing lors des climas."

The longer passage intruded into the account of the Valley Perilous, or Valley of Devils, shows the same contrast in style to the rest of that account. Where the Norman-French version is clear, graphic, and terse, the additional passage is clumsy, wordy, and repetitious. Hamelius, although he was partial to the Ogier redaction (which also has these two additions) because it supported his theory of authorship, calls this addition "about three pages of redundant particulars."[3] Letts says of the

---

[3] Hamelius, II, n. on p. 189, l. 17.

vulgate that it "tells the story twice over" (p. 89). It attempts to intensify the terrors of the place by repetition and elaboration, devices very common among medieval story-tellers but not employed by the writer of the *Travels*. Like the passage already quoted, it embroiders upon the earlier part of the account, without adding anything new.

On the other hand, the passage on the seven climates, in the Norman-French text, is perfectly in keeping with the rest of the *Travels*. The reference to "our partes," meaning the British Isles, occurs several times and supports the reality, or pretense, that the writer was an Englishman. It is true that here he says that England is outside of the seven climates, and in another place he says that the Indians travel little because they are ruled by Saturn, while "we" are great travellers, "for we be in the seventh climate, that is of the moon. And the moon is of lightly moving . . ." (Pollard ed., p. 109). Both statements about England were current, however, and our author was merely echoing two different authorities. The notion that the British Isles were "beyond the earth" (i.e., the three continents of Asia, Africa, and Europe) in "another world" appears in such popular authorities as Solinus and Bartholomaeus Anglicus.[4]

Besides these two passages, there are many minor differences between the Norman-French and the Paris versions of the text. The author of the Norman-French text likes to put the most important word last, as in "en celle isle crest ly mastik." The Paris text prefers the Latin word-order, "en celle ylle le mastic croist."[5] The Paris version sometimes reads "isle" where the Norman-French text has "terre" or "pais"[6] and it tends to in-

[4] In Trevisa's translation of Bartholomaeus, England is described as "departyd fro the roundenesse of the worlde," lib. xv, cap. xiiii (ed. 1535, fol. cc). Here the roundness seems to be a two, not a three, dimensional concept.

[5] Warner, p. 11; Bibl. Nat. fr. 4515, fol. 7.

[6] For example, Warner, p. 14, l. 28, reads "Vne grande terre," Egerton MS. translates "a grete cuntree," while 4515 reads "Vne bonne ylle," fol. 8; again, Warner, p. 104, l. 30, reads "pais" where 10723 reads "ile."

trude the word "Item" at the beginnings of sentences. In a few places the Paris text adds an explanatory phrase or sentence,[7] and, somewhat rarely, words or even whole sentences are transposed.

The Paris, like the Norman-French version, presents the difficulty that the texts have not been collated. We can be sure, however, that the 1371 manuscript is a poor copy of this version. Raoulet d'Orléans, the scribe, did his work in a very mechanical and hasty fashion. He omitted the first two alphabets along with the sentences which introduce them. The next three occur in their proper places, but the sixth again is omitted. At the end of the text (fol. 96-96$^v$) he transcribed the three missing alphabets with an apology for his "oversight," and he added conspicuous marginal notes at two points (fol. 6$^v$ and 16) where alphabets should have occurred.[8]

[7] Warner's text, p. 30, ll. 37-38, "Et pur ceo passe homme par cest desert as camailles; qar ly camaille troeuent bien totdys a manger des arbres et des busshons qil broutent, et ieunent bien de boire ii. iours ou iii, et ceo ne pourroient les chiualx faire." MS. Bibl. Nat. fr. 4515, fol. 17$^v$-18 reads, "et pour ce passe on par les desers a chamos. car il treuient tousiours a mangier aus buissons. car il broustent. et jeunent bien de bour ij. iours ou iij. et *qũt il treuuent une foiz a boire il bouient pour iij. iours apres*. et ce ne pourroit le cheual faire." Another such expansion appears in the account of the fountain of youth. Warner, p. 84, ll. 43-44, reads: "Et dit homme qe celle fontaigne vient de Paradys et pur ceo est elle si vertuouse. Par tot ceo pais croist tres bon gerger. . . ." MS. 4515, fol. 52$^v$, ll. 8 ff. reads, "Et dist ou que celle fontaine vient de paradis et pour ce est elle si vertueuse. *et auec ce ceuls qui souuent en bouient semblent estre tousiours ieunes. dont les anciens lappellent et dient que cest la fontaine de iouuent pour ce que le fait ressembler a estre les gens Jovenes*. Par tout ce pays croist mlt bon gingembre . . ."

[8] Delisle's incomplete description of these alphabets has misled Warner. He mentions the four alphabets that occur at the end of the volume (*Cat. des MSS. des fonds Libri et Barrois*, p. 252), which led Warner to believe that there were only four in this MS. and to conjecture (p. xxi) that they were not a part of the original text. Besides the three omitted alphabets, there is, at the end of the volume (fol. 96$^v$) a Hebrew alphabet and a line of Hebrew, written by someone who knew that language, as a correction of the "Jewish" alphabet which occurs in its place in the text, but which is far from genuine. The three alphabets in the text occur on fols. 33, 43$^v$-44, and 46$^v$-47.

## THREE FAMILIES OF FRENCH MANUSCRIPTS 141

Throughout the text he omits words and phrases at the rate of two or three to a page, and sometimes he drops out whole lines and even sentences. Two or three missing words have been added in the margin, near the beginning, as if an overseer had glanced at a few pages.[9]

The whole text seems to have been hastily planned. There are four miniatures on folio 1, but only two others in the whole book.[10] These occur on folios 34 and 36 verso. Their proximity suggests that other illustrations were intended, but the scribe outran the illuminator and failed to leave space for them.[11]

A considerably better text of the Paris version is in the Bibliothèque Nationale, fonds françaises nouvelle acquisition 10723. It lacks the headings of chapters which were in Raoulet's archetype (and which he regularly ran into his text, at the ends of the first lines of the chapter, as if they had originally been in the margin). In fact, the text of 10723 is without punctuation or subdivision of any kind, with rare exceptions, and it is in an unsightly, cursive hand, but some pains have been taken with the many proper names, and M. Marcel Thomas, my correspondent at the Bibliothèque Nationale, is of the opinion that it is the best text of the *Travels* now in Paris. It seems to have been written in the last quarter of the fourteenth century.

A comparison of this text with that of Raoulet d'Orléans

---

[9] On fols. 9, 10ᵛ, 12, and 15.

[10] On fol. 34 the Transfiguration is represented, and on fol. 36ᵛ St. Paul is represented with a sword over his shoulder teaching St. Luke from an open book (Warner's text, Chap. xiv). This illuminator has also done two capitals, fols. 8 and 8ᵛ, in a style which differs markedly from that of other capitals which appear on almost every page of the MS.

[11] It would seem, from the first page, where 4 miniatures are arranged in the form of a square occupying about two thirds of the page, that the illuminator had planned and perhaps sketched pictures for a more profuse illumination. The first two, of the writer and his book, and of the presentation of the book to a king, are appropriate to the beginning of the MS., but the two illustrations of the story of the dragon-woman of Cos, or Lango, belong in what is Chap. iv of the Cotton text. The other two miniatures occur opposite the text they illustrate.

shows that in the first few lines Raoulet dropped out *terres,* omitted a line or more which included the end of one sentence and the beginning of the next, leaving an obvious garble, and changed *pies* to *ioies*. Many of the proper names are distorted, but probably some of these distortions began in the text from which he was copying. He makes *thiope* out of *Ethiope,* and *grans biens aus gregois* out of *Arabiens et Gregoys, les angels* out of *les Euangelies,* and *dauffrique* out of *dauffrate.* Where the Harley text reads (of the height of the north star), *en Almaigne et Beome* [i.e., Bohemia], MS. 10723 has *en alemaigne vers voesme,* which becomes in 1371 *en alemaigne vers rome*. In another place, where Harley says *portant un noun,* meaning "bearing a name" both 10723 and Raoulet's manuscript read *portant un mont*. Such mistakes may go back to the original of the Paris version.

The many and strange proper names in Mandeville's text presented a special difficulty to the scribes, and were most readily and therefore most rapidly corrupted. Following is a table of the readings of seventy-five names as they appear in two texts of the Norman-French group, two in the Paris-French redaction, and one text of the Ogier version. This list shows very graphically the degeneration of the text, and the superiority of the Harley manuscript (and of the French text from which the Cotton translation was made) over either the Paris or the Ogier versions. It can be seen also that Raoulet's is sometimes the worst garbled of the five texts.

We cannot know what mistakes the author himself may have made, but in every case where the word is known from other sources, the Norman-French reading is clearly the best, and the readings of 1371 are often the worst. Chantilly is usually nearer to 10723 than to Raoulet's text; occasionally it is better, but often it is worse corrupted, as in the case of "Ethiopie," or "Ararath," or "Besanzon," i.e., Byzantium. Some of these mistakes may be the work of the Paris redactor, although he seems to have been a scholarly and well-informed

# THREE FAMILIES OF FRENCH MANUSCRIPTS 143

| Norman French | | Paris Redaction | | Ogier Redaction |
|---|---|---|---|---|
| MS. Harley 4383 | MS. Cotton (Engl. tr.) | MS. Paris 10723 | MS. Paris 4515 | MS. Chantilly 699 |
| Any | Any | hany | lony | hanyo |
| Ararach | Ararath | arrarath | ararath | aralach |
| Argite | Argyte | argute | Agucte | argite |
| Atiron | artyroun | artiron | thiron | artyro |
| Ascopartz | Ascopardes | as cospas | ascopars | a chopars |
| auguries | augurynes | vrgvuien | om. | auguriens |
| Balean | Belyan | belian | bethleem | belyam |
| Bellynas | Belynas | Selmas | selynas | bellinas |
| Besanzon | Bezanzon | besanson | bizancium | vesaton |
| Betemga | Betegma | botaugo | bolengle | bothenygo |
| Bragmey | Bragman | brames | bragine | bragmem |
| Caffoles | Caffolos | cafo les gens | Boffo | Caffo |
| Camaalech | Camaalech | Comahaleth | Cambaleth | camaach |
| Canapos | Canopos | canopes | Campos | canapos |
| Celsite | Celsite | telsite | cohite | celsyte |
| Cesaire Philippoun | Cesaire Philippon | cesaires le phelipon | cesaures le fils oppon | cesar le phillippon |
| Changuys | Changuys | canguys | nom cuigis | can guys |
| Chieuetout | chieuetout | chiuetout | chievetot | chenetout |
| Cobooch | Caboogh | vboth | coloth | caboth |
| Cohos | Colcos | cohos | colus | cohos |
| Colbach | Golbach | cobach | Calac | gobach |
| Crynes (Hormuz) | Crues | ormes | ariguez | orines |
| Cusys | Cusis | cussie | caussie | Cusys |
| Dalay | Balay | dalay | dolay | dalach |
| Dayne | Dayne | laidenge | laidenghe | laudame |
| de ebreu | from Ebrew | de ebreu | de brief | de hebrieu |
| Elcana | Elchana | elcana | helena | elchana |
| Ethil (Volga) | Ethill | Tigre | tingre | ethil |
| Ethiopie | Ethiope | ethioppe | thiope | deropes |
| Eufrates | Eufrate | dauffrate | dauffrique | effrates |
| Euilac | Emlak | euilat | finblach | emlat |
| Eurach | Eurath | curach | Eurath | curach |
| Faxis | Faxis | faris | suza | faxis |
| Gachalonabes | Gatholonabes | gachalo nabes | galcat | Satha la nobles |
| Galilee | Galilee | galilee | gelboe | galilee |
| Geth | Geth | Teth | teth | geth |
| Gysonophe | Gynosophe | ginosophe | geuesophe | genozoph |
| Hur | Hur | hur | hur | vz |
| Iamchay | Ianichay | Ianchay | iocam | cuman |

|  | NORMAN FRENCH |  | PARIS REDACTION |  | OGIER REDACTION |
| --- | --- | --- | --- | --- | --- |
| MS. Harley 4383 | MS. Cotton (Engl. tr.) | MS. Paris 10723 | MS. Paris 4515 | MS. Chantilly 699 |

| Ianeweys | Janeways | ianoais | Janeuois | ronoyas |
| --- | --- | --- | --- | --- |
| Iaua | Iaua | Jana | Jana | ianna |
| Iol | Job | Iob | iob | Jacob |
| Lanteryn | Lanteryne | lauterm | lautenn | lancherin |
| Mancy | Mancy | {Manti / manci | {Marchi / Maach | Manchy |
| Marrea | Martha | {mairoa / maroa | {mairta / marta | {mayroa / mayro |
| Mengly | Mengly | mongli | entreghi | menghy |
| Merfyn | morsyn | melsin | aielfin | mersin |
| Milstorak | Milstorak | milstorach | millestorach | nilcora |
| Moritane | Moretane | mortaigne | morianne | moretaine |
| Nacumera | Nacumera | macumoram | Nacameran | Matumeron |
| Niniue | Nynyuee | niniue | nineue | nyayue |
| ninus | Nunus | minus | ninus | nymis |
| Ny | Nye | sternes | athenes | sterne |
| Orille | Orille | orielle | orrible | orille |
| Oxidrate | Oxidrate | oxidrate | Midrache | Oxidrate |
| Paten | Pathen | paten | panthy | pathen |
| Pateran | Paterane | patheram | pateran | pantheram |
| Pitan | Pytan | pitan | puchany | pytau |
| Psytakes | Psitakes | paisitast | priscat | phitaque |
| Saba | Saba | sabba | sabba | Gaba |
| Sabssacolle | Sabissocolle | sabissatolle | sabisatrolle | sabisacolle |
| Sarray | Sarra | Sarra | darrã | saray |
| Semoch | Semoch | semoth | semath | semoch |
| Sichie | Sichie | Sithie | sithie | Sychie |
| Suse | Suse | suse | busse | Suze |
| Sinnobor | Sumobor | simobar | Snnobas | simobor |
| Tanghot | Tanghot | tangoth | canghor | tangoch |
| Taprobane | Taprobane | taprobane | gaquebane | Taprobane |
| Tauriso | Taurizo | taurisse | tarsie | Tamize |
| Thamiso | Thauriso | Taurise | taurisse | tamyse |
| Thanez | Taneez | Thano | chnioielarche | chano |
| Thebe | Thebe | tebe | codre | Chene |
| Valeir | Valair | villon | vilanis | villan |
| Yndiens | yndyenes | Indron | Judyiens | yndois |
| Zarchee | Sarchee | *om.* | garbe | sarque |

## THREE FAMILIES OF FRENCH MANUSCRIPTS 145

man, able to make some corrections of his faulty archetype.

Among the many verbal changes, the Paris redactor adds a phrase to the description of the castle of the sparrowhawk in Armenia, the history of which has a bearing both on the history of the text and on the nationality of the author. The text of the Harley MS. reads, "vn chaustel anxien, qi siet sur vn roche" (p. 73, l. 41). Several pages later, in speaking of the cultivation of pepper, the same manuscript reads, "il est tot vert, auxi come les bayes de edre [Latin *hedera*] qe nous appellons yuy" (p. 83, ll. 42-43). This comparison to ivy has been transferred, in the Paris version, from the account of pepper to the story of the sparrowhawk castle. The redactor inserted after *ancien* the words "dont les murs sont angues tout couuert de eder que nous appellons yvi" (MS. 10723, fol. 46). This is corrupted in the 1371 MS. which reads, "couuers de i. yerre Eder" (fol. 45). The true reading of the Paris redactor is clear from the fact that the Brussels and Chantilly MSS. of the Ogier redaction follow MS. 10723, as do most other versions of the Paris text for which I have collations (see Appendix III), except that they vary in the spelling of "ivy." The garble in the 1371 text can be most simply accounted for if we suppose that a previous copyist had reduced the explanatory phrase, "que nous appellons yvi," to a marginal gloss, "i.e., yeue," which the next copyist then put back into the text, and "i. yerre Eder" was the result.

The little phrase illustrates the poor quality of Raoulet's original, as well as the tendency of the Paris redactor to tamper with his text. It also furnishes an example of the introduction of an English word into the original, to support the reality, or pretense, that the author was an Englishman.

Another passage which illustrates the history of the three versions is the one already quoted (p. 115) from the Chantilly manuscript, describing how Charlemagne was given the prepuce of Our Lord. The Harley MS. reads, "et il la porta a Ayes la Chapelle. Et puis Charles ly Chauues le fist porter a Poitiers, et puis a Chartres."[12] We know that the words *a Ays* were dropped out of an important early text, because the Sloan and Grenville MSS., collated by Warner, do not have them, and the Cotton translation reads, "to Parys into his Chapelle," which is an obvious attempt to rationalize *porta la chapelle*. The Egerton translation says "to Parysch." But the Paris redactor either had a good text of this passage, or he encountered the garble and corrected it out of his own knowledge, for he says (I quote the 1371 text), "il le porta a ays la chappelle a vij. lieues de liege." The explanation that Aix is seven leagues from Liège occurs in the Brussels MS. (of the Liège-Ogier version) examined by Hamelius, and he cited it as evidence that the author must have been a citizen of Liège. It is not in the original version, however. It was supplied by the Paris redactor and retained in the Liège-Ogier version.

From the examination of the three states of the text, it seems very clear that the manuscript written by Raoulet d'Orléans at Paris in 1371 is a poor copy of a redaction, and that the manuscripts written in England in Norman French represent most faithfully the work of the author. The Ogier version is a redaction of a redaction, the least authentic of the three versions. Yet this is the version selected by Vogels, Hamelius, and most recently by Mr. Letts, as it appears in Brussels manuscript no. 10420-5, as a very good text. When, however, the true nature of these three versions of the text has been recognized, we are in a position to deal finally with the whole problem of Mandeville's connection with Liège.

[12] Warner, p. 42, ll. 27-29; MS. 4515, fols. 24ᵛ-25. Warner, in his note on p. 42, l. 1, suggests that for Poitiers and Chartres we should read "Charroux in Poitou," to which Charles the Bald really did transfer the relics, but, as Warner says, Gaston Paris reports no fewer than six churches which claimed the prepuce: *Histoire Poétique de Charlemagne* (Paris, 1865), p. 57.

# ⟨10⟩

# THE CASE AGAINST JEAN D'OUTREMEUSE

THE DISCOVERY of the Ogier redaction of the French text clears up the problem of d'Outremeuse's relationship to the *Travels*. There is an embarrassing profusion of evidence that the Liège romancer made free with the *Travels* and with the name of the author. It seems a little excessive to charge that he produced two conflicting stories about Mandeville's identity and connection with Liège, a redaction of the *Travels* with large additions, and two or more lapidaries, one in Latin and the others in French, all attributed to Mandeville.

On the other hand, the Latin vulgate translation, usually assigned to d'Outremeuse by biographers of Mandeville, can now be removed from the catalogue of his works. It is possible that some of the other fabrications were the work of others; but the connection between his story of the death-bed confession and the epitaph created for Jean de Bourgogne is clear and immediate. The relation of the Ogier redaction of the *Travels* to the *Myreur* and *Trésorier* makes it certain that, if there were other fabricators, d'Outremeuse was the leading spirit among them. And there is no need to postulate other fabricators. Kurth, Michel, and Hamelius all observe that the Liège romancer frequently tells the same story twice, fitting it each time to different people and different sets of circumstances. He is not always consistent. Michel remarks on the fact that he makes Ogier both a saint in heaven and a captive of Morgane la Fay in an earthly paradise where he meets King Arthur.[1]

---

[1] *Les Légendes*, p. 105. See also p. 111 where he shows how two adventures are made out of one in connection with Ogier's visit to Morgane le Fay; and p. 374 on the trick of making two stories out of one.

Kurth has shown that he was not averse to forging documents to support his stories. We know that when he borrowed from the chronicles of Jean le Bel and Froissart he "outrageously altered" what he found. He took the same liberty with the *Travels*.

Michel has discovered a copy of the *Myreur* in which Mandeville is credited with *reigning* in India for a long time.[2] The passage (unknown to Hamelius) reads, "Cil pays d'Inde et de Ethioppie est ung divers lieu, selonc les croniques et selonc ce que mestre Jehan de Mandeville, chevalier, sire de Canpdi, de Monfort et del Case Perouse raconpte en ses escrips qu'il fist de ce pays d'Inde et des partiez où il fu regnant loing temps, plus de xxxiii ans et revint par dessa l'an de nativiteit nostre Seigneur Jhesu-Crist xiii$^c$ et xvi [sic!], ou il racompte toute ce que Ogier conquist et fist à son temps." Obviously, one of d'Outremeuse's ideas was to make the *Travels* "authority" for the conquests of Ogier in the East. Another was to have the *Travels* written in Liège. Another was to connect its author with the great Montfort family of English and Burgundian fame, just as he connected himself with the Du Pré family, by a false genealogy.

There is no reason to doubt that d'Outremeuse made the Ogier redaction, nor that it is a redaction and not the original version. The same author could not have made both versions; they differ not only in dialect but in literary quality, style, and method. The intrusion of Ogier le Danois destroys the candid and factual atmosphere which the author of the original so carefully and skillfully built up; and the evidence provided by the Chantilly manuscript that the redactor did not rest with perversion of the text of the *Travels,* but went on to add four books of apocryphal matter, puts the spurious nature of this text beyond question. Finally, since the vulgate Latin version

[2] Ibid., p. 91. This MS is an early and important text of part of the *Myreur*. It was acquired by the Bibliothèque Royale (MS. II, 3030) in 1903 and so was not available to the editors of the *Myreur*. The passage is quoted and translated by Letts, p. 109.

## THE CASE AGAINST JEAN D'OUTREMEUSE 149

was made from the Ogier redaction, we need not take more seriously its circumstantial story of the meeting between the doctor, Jean de Bourgogne, and Mandeville at Liège in 1355 than we take d'Outremeuse's story of Mandeville's "reign" in India—or the various anecdotes of his sojourn in Egypt, where, quite possibly, neither he nor Jean de Bourgogne had ever been at all.

However, in the process of arguing that d'Outremeuse wrote the *Travels,* Hamelius has raised a dust which has settled over several points and must now be cleared away. The most important of these is the question of when the *Travels* was written. The best Norman-French manuscripts read 1356, and the Paris version reads 1357, but some manuscripts and the printed text of the Pynson version read 1366; and since d'Outremeuse was only eighteen in 1356, Hamelius argued that 1366 was the true date of publication. He presented two arguments in support of this contention. He pointed to the statement in the text that it is "more than viij$^{xx}$ yeer" since the rise of the Tartars,[3] and Vincent of Beauvais dates that event in 1202. If Mandeville had this date in mind, his one hundred and sixty years would bring him to 1360 or later. However, the figure is a round number, and a Roman number in which the addition of a single "i" would make a difference of twenty years. There is a second reference to time in the text which produces a very different date. Mandeville says that Palestine has been in the hands of the heathen for "vii$^{xx}$ et xiiij ans,"[4] i.e., one hundred

---

[3] Hamelius' ed., p. 146, l. 26, and see Hamelius' note on this line. For Marco Polo's date, see Moule, I, 162.

[4] MS Harley 4383 (Warner, p. 38, l. 32) says Palestine has been in the hands of the heathen for "vii$^{xx}$ ans et pluis." The Cotton MS. says "forty year and more" (Pollard, p. 50). Hamelius' note on p. 49, l. 15, reports that both Brussels MSS which he consulted read "vij$^{xx}$ et xiiij ans." (MS. 4515 has "vii vins ans et xiiij" fol. 22$^v$). From the fall of Jerusalem in 1187, 140 years and 14 more would bring us to 1341, which is too early for the date of writing. The fall of Acre in 1291 is too late for the date meant, and no other date *post quem* has been suggested.

and fifty-four years. Jerusalem fell in 1187, which would give us a date of writing in 1341. These dates can be reconciled by adding an "i" to the latter, or subtracting one from the former —whichever one likes. They are round numbers, uncertain at best.

Hamelius' other argument rests on the genuineness of the Latin letter of dedication which occurs in most of the Norman-French manuscripts written in England[5]—and on a particular interpretation of a phrase in this letter. In it Edward III is addressed as "above all mortals," and Hamelius contends that this phrase puts him above the Pope and therefore that the letter was written in 1366 when Edward finally, and formally, denounced the papal claim to temporal supremacy over England.

Warner rejects the letter as spurious. Its extravagant language, and the fact that it is in Latin, certainly brings its authenticity in question, although the fact that it does not occur in any copy of the Paris redaction is understandable enough and does not militate against its authenticity. But whether it is authentic or not, the phrase "above all mortals" need have no reference to the Papal claim. This was the period of the "Babylonian captivity" and of the Avignon popes. The temporal power of the Pope had been denied philosophically by William of Occam and his associates, and practically by the German emperor. It is extremely doubtful whether anyone, thinking of the conquests of Edward III and comparing the Black Prince with Alexander the Great, would have in his mind this ineffectual Papal claim.[6] If he did, and if he was, or was pretending to be, English, he need not have waited until 1366 to deny that claim. The English generally, and the Barons particularly, had rejected the submission of King John and refused to pay the tribute. It had not been paid for many years before Edward III finally repudiated the debt.

[5] Hamelius, II, 13-15. In the list of MSS in the appendix I have indicated which have the letter.

[6] See above, Ch. 8, p. 126, for the text of the letter.

# THE CASE AGAINST JEAN D'OUTREMEUSE

The late Arpad Steiner attempted to date the *Travels* between 1365 and 1371 on the basis of its statement that Bulgaria was a part of the domain of the king of Hungary.[7] He pointed out that Louis the Great of Hungary conquered Bulgaria in 1365. But such an argument gives Mandeville too much credit for accurate and current information. It puts the *Travels* in the category of a "news letter." Moreover, the statement occurs near the beginning of the *Travels*, and so we would have to accept 1365 as the date of its beginning, rather than of its completion. But actually Louis the Great of Hungary included the title "Bulgariae Rex" in his official style from 1347 onward.[8] That official style, supported by vague rumors of his constant warfare and many conquests in the region of Bulgaria, was, in all probability, the basis of Mandeville's statement.

While the date 1356 is obviously the authentic date given in the best texts, it may, of course, be fictitious. However, with the discovery that the copy made in 1371 is not the "best and oldest," that it is not even a copy of the original but a poor copy of a redaction of the original text, it becomes more probable that 1356 is the genuine date of publication. It seems hardly possible that even so popular a book as the *Travels* could have been copied, in the five years between 1366 and 1371, as many times as the state of the 1371 text indicates.

D'Outremeuse was not only too young in 1356 to have written so mature and learned a work as the *Travels*, but, according to his own account of himself, he was writing verse

[7] "The Date of Composition of *Mandeville's Travels*," *Speculum*, IX (1934), 144-147.

[8] Georg. Féjér, *Codex Diplomaticus Hungariae*, Tome IX, Vol. I (Buda, 1833), pp. 460 ff. "Ludouicus, Dei gratia, Hungariae, Dalmatiae, Croatiae, Ramae, Seruiae, Galliciae, Lodomeriae, Cumaniae, Bulgariaeque Rex, Princips Salernitanus, et honoris montis Sancti Angeli Dominus." Mandeville says, "the King of Hungary . . . holdeth the kingdom of Hungary, Sclavonia, and of Comania a great part, and of Bulgaria that men call the land of Bougiers, and of the realm of Russia a great part, whereof he hath made a duchy, that lasteth unto the land of Nyfland, and marcheth to Prussia" (p. 7). And see Warner's note on p. 4, l. 2.

"giestes et histoires" for the first twenty years of his literary career,[9] i.e., until about 1380. Probably during the years when he was writing his huge *Geste de Liège* and other verse "histoires" (including, so he says, a *Geste d'Ogier* in three books, a *Geste de Jean de Launchon,* and a *Geste de Huon de Bourdeaux*),[10] he was merely collecting and copying lapidaries. The period of active composition of the *Trésorier* was the decade 1380-90, and the position of the reference to Mandeville, near the end of the list of authorities for that work, suggests that his acquaintance with that worthy, and with the *Travels,* came late in the period of writing of the *Trésorier.*

The compilation of the *Myreur* was later still. Bormans dates the redaction in the last five years of the author's life, 1395-1400,[11] although he had spent most of his adult life in the collection of materials for it. It was probably his interest in lapidaries rather than in geography which led him to the *Travels.* His *Geste de Liège,* the only one of his verse romances extant, shows a preoccupation with local history. Everything, including Ogier, is brought to Liège. Even in the *Myreur* he gives no evidence of being widely read in the travel literature known to Mandeville. He borrowed wholesale and verbatim from Brunetto Latini's *Trésor* for his account of India and the lands conquered by Alexander the Great.[12] And he borrows in the same way from the *Travels* for the adventures

---

[9] *Myreur,* III, 402. Hamelius gives the text and translation of this passage, II, 11.

[10] Bormans' Introduction, VII, xii-xx, xxxv, xci-xciii; Michel, op. cit.; and Sylvan Balau, *Comment Jean d'Outremeuse écrit l'histoire,* Académie royale de Belgique. Compte rendu de séances, Vol. 71 (Brussels, 1902), 227-259. Hamelius attributed to d'Outremeuse three very long verse romances written in Liège in his day, *Godfrey of Bouillon, Baldwin of Sebourc,* and the *Bastard of Bouillon,* but no reputable scholar has accepted his conclusions; see for example, A. Bayot's review of his *Intro. à la Litt.,* in *Revue Belge de Philologie et d'Histoire,* I, No. 2 (1922), 355-357.

[11] Bormans, Introduction, p. xciii.

[12] *Myreur,* I, 282-305, and the editor's note, p. 285.

## THE CASE AGAINST JEAN D'OUTREMEUSE

of Ogier in the same region. In Book I he has also borrowed Mandeville's story of the fox which led the ten lost tribes out of their prison. His editor comments on his ignorance of notables and place names and his lack of any notion of geography.[13]

Here we come to a second bit of debris which must be cleared away before the relation of d'Outremeuse to the *Travels* is perfectly clear. Warner remarks, very inaccurately, that the great bulk of sources of the *Travels*, except Boldensele and Odoric, occur in the list of authorities for d'Outremeuse's *Myreur*.[14] Hamelius regards this as important evidence that d'Outremeuse wrote both works. The absence of Boldensele and Odoric is enough to destroy any theory that d'Outremeuse wrote the *Travels*, but these are not the only notable omissions. In his list of seventy-five authorities, d'Outremeuse names many chronicles and encyclopaedias. He cites Carpini, Hayton, and Prester John, all of whom he could have found in Vincent of Beauvais. But we look in vain for Rubruquis, Marco Polo, Friar Jordanus, or any of the Palestine itineraries, or for such works as de Vitry, Burchard, or Marino Sanudo.

In fact, the two lists have little except the encyclopaedists in common. Mandeville was using the latest accounts of the near and far East which were available to him. There is no evidence, either in the list of authorities or in the text of the *Myreur*, that d'Outremeuse knew any more of these writers than he found in Vincent and Brunetto. Certainly he did not know the later ones, including not only Boldensele and Odoric but also Sanudo and Marco Polo.

The fallacy is sufficiently obvious in Hamelius' second argument, that d'Outremeuse must have written the *Travels* because in his borrowings from Odoric he made mistakes which coincide minutely with mistakes made in the *Travels*.[15] These

[13] Balau, *Étude*, pp. 566-567, quoting Bormans; and Kurth, p. 11.
[14] Warner, p. xl; Hamelius, II, 21; and for this list of authorities, A. Borgnet's edition of the *Myreur*, I, pp. 2-4; and Bormans' discussion, Vol. VII, pp. xcix-cxvi.
[15] Hamelius, II, 9.

## THE IDENTITY OF THE AUTHOR

"coincidences" are simply proof that d'Outremeuse knew Odoric only through Mandeville.

A progressive succession of misstatements seems to be responsible for a fourth mistake, the allegation that "Outremeuse declared he inherited Mandeville's library."[16] He made no such claim, but in the late seventeenth or early eighteenth century Louis Abry, the Liège herald (1643-1720), reported that Mandeville, i.e., Jean de Bourgogne, left his library to the Church of the Guillemins, whom he made his heirs. He says, "he left the said monastery many very fine manuscripts *of his works*, as well of his travels as of medicine, written in his own hand; there are still in the aforesaid house many belongings that he left there for remembrance." To this statement a nineteenth century editor, S. Bormans, has added: "He left some books of medicine which have never been printed: *Tabula astronomicas, De chorda recta et umbra*, and *De doctrina theologica*."[17] Books "written with his own hand," "manuscripts of his works," are not "his library" in the modern understanding of the words and cannot be used to support a statement that d'Outremeuse had access to Mandeville's library in any sense which would account for the similarity between Mandeville's sources and d'Outremeuse's list of authorities. But, as a matter of fact, the three titles mentioned by Bormans happen to be exactly the same three titles of works attributed by John Bale to "Ioannes Manduith," a fellow of Merton College, Oxford, who flourished about 1340.[18] Manduith was a doctor and

[16] Wells, *Manual*, p. 437; A. W. Pollard, in *The Academy*, 957 (Sept. 6, 1890), 190. Warner, p. xl, says d'Outremeuse's list of authorities "very possibly had been De Bourgogne's own library."

[17] " 'Il laisse audit monastère plusieurs MSS. de ses oeuvres fort vantés, tant de ses voyages que de la médecine, écrits de sa main; il y avait encore en ladite maison plusieurs meubles qu'il leur laissa pour mémoire.' Il a laissé quelques livres de médecine qui n'ont jamais été imprimes, des *tabulae astronomicae, de corda recta et umbra*, de *doctrina theologica*," S. Bormans, from Le Fort's transcript, in *Le Bibliophile Belge*. [3 Ser.] I (1866), 236.

[18] John Bale, *Illustrium maioris Brytanniae Scriptorum* (Basle, 1557, 1559), p. 426. Mandeville is noticed on p. 478.

astrologer. In the *Bibliotheca Universalis* of Konrad Gesner (1583), the entry for "Ioannes de Mandauyle" is immediately followed by that for "Ioannes Manduith," whose three works are listed.[19] In J. A. Fabricius' *Bibliotheca Latina Mediae et Infimae Aetatis* (Hamburg, 1736), the titles of Manduith's three works appear under the names of both Mandeville and Manduith.[20] What happened seems obvious enough. A confusion of similar names, or a mistake in transcription, led to the attribution of Manduith's works to Mandeville and to the identification of Manduith with Mandeville; then to the allegation that he (as Jean de Bourgogne) left a library *of his works* "written in his own hand"; then Warner suggests that d'Outremeuse had access to "de Bourgogne's own library"; and finally we read that "Outremeuse declared he inherited Mandeville's library." So history is sometimes made.

One other point has been made in the attempt to connect d'Outremeuse with the *Travels*. Bormans pointed out that in the *Myreur* (IV, 587) d'Outremeuse writes that he will not stop to describe Tartary because it has already been described elsewhere. Since such a description was not found in the earlier part of the *Myreur*, Hamelius seized upon this as an "admission" of the authorship of the *Travels*.[21] Such an "admission" by d'Outremeuse would hardly be proof of authorship; but what he actually says is not that *he* has written an account of Tartary, but that Hayton and John de Plano Carpini have described Tartary, and he does not need to repeat, for "it would take too long, and it has been well devised in another

---

[19] *Bibliotheca Instituta et Collecta primum a Conrado Gesner*, ed. I. Simler, and re-ed. Johann Jacob Fries (Tiguri, 1583), p. 470.

[20] Fabricius, Vol. IV, 289, 290. See Dorothea W. Singer and Reuben Levy, "Plague Tractates," *Annals of Medical History*, I, (New York, 1917), 394-411. No books are mentioned by either Püterich (1462) or Ortelius. Bormans, in *Biblio. Belge* I (1866, p. 236), says, "Jean Mandeville, ou Manduith, theologien, médecin, et mathematicien."

[21] Hamelius, Introduction, p. xc; Warner also makes this point in his Introduction, p. xl, n. 1.

place, of that same state."[22] He is introducing a passage (out of Mandeville) about the Tartars, to whom he devotes the next four pages. He deals with them again, at greater length, in Book III (Vol. v, 185, 192, 197-199, 269, 357-361, etc.). Perhaps some of this material had already been written, and he intends to refer to it, but the vague and impersonal reference could equally well refer to the work of someone else. When he speaks of himself, he usually says, "I, Jean d'Outremeuse."[23]

It is possible that d'Outremeuse "discovered" the *Travels* in the 1370's. We know that what he had was a copy of the Paris redaction, and that this redaction was made some time before the end of 1371. But it seems more probable that he came upon it in the 1380's, when he was compiling his

[22] *Myreur*, IV, 587: "Item, en cel commencharent à monteir en sengnorie li Tartariens, selonc les croniques mesire Ayto [Hayton] dont ilh fut onclez mesire Ayto, le roy d'Ermenie; et li unc et li altrez, furent avecque les Tartariens en mains beais fais d'armes, ensi qu'il fait mencion en leurs croniques; car, si que j'ay did desus [p. 564] ilh commencherent devant, ensi que j'ay dit deseur, à monteir en signorie, solonc les croniques frere Johain de Plain, de Campine [Carpin], de ordre des Freresmenours, de saint siege de Romme messages à Tartars, et son compangnon, frere Benoit, de cel ordre meisme, qui à leur temps furent envoieis en ches partiez de là; et racomptent le manere de paiis, et de tout, ensi que vous l'oïreis chi-apres recordeir; et plus avant asseis en dient mesire Ayto et ansi chis freres, que je n'en doie dire ne racompteir, car il fais est trop long, et si l'ay bien deviseit altre part, de chel paiis meisme; mains ilh dient tous en leurs traitieis, parlant devant de mult de royalmes, de paiis et de gens, que li Tartariens sont gens qui de lonc temps habitoient as champs, en tentes, . . ." Here follows an account of Genghis Khan, probably out of Mandeville.

[23] With Hamelius' further argument that the *Travels* was put out by d'Outremeuse under an assumed name because the book was heretical, it does not seem necessary to deal. The Church never discovered the heresy. Hamelius' attempt to show that d'Outremeuse was critical of the Church is extremely feeble. Actually, he was devoted to the hierarchy, to the Cathedral of St. Lambert, where he had a house in the Cathedral Close in his later years, and to the Prince Bishop of Liège in whose court he was a minor official. Probably the reason he represented Mandeville as staying in the suburb of Avroy was that the Abbot and Convent of St. Laurent owned the market toll in that suburb: Em. Fairon, *Régestes de la Cité de Liége* (Liège, 1933), I, 381.

## THE CASE AGAINST JEAN D'OUTREMEUSE 157

*Trésorier*. Perhaps he first attributed the Latin lapidary to Mandeville, and then created the Ogier redaction of the *Travels*, with its four books of additions, including a lapidary in French. All that we know for certain is that in the 1390's the Ogier redaction was circulating. Someone made a Latin abbreviation of it. Otto von Diemeringen translated it into German. And in 1396 Ogier de Caumont made a copy of it which we still have.

With this clarification of d'Outremeuse's connection with the *Travels*, we are ready to deal definitively with the epitaph and with the passage in d'Outremeuse's *Myreur* telling the story of the deathbed confession, which accounts for it by identifying Mandeville with Jean de Bourgogne and naming d'Outremeuse himself as de Bourgogne's executor and the author of his will.

## ꞌ 11 ꞌ

# DOCTOR JEAN DE BOURGOGNE

SCHOLARS who have rejected Hamelius' theory that d'Outremeuse wrote the *Travels* have all fallen back upon the older identification of the Liège doctor, Jean à la Barbe, or de Bourgogne, with Sir John Mandeville. The discovery of d'Outremeuse's unreliability has weakened confidence in Nicholson's and Warner's theory that the author's real name was de Bourgogne, but this has merely produced a return to the older belief that the man buried in the convent of the Guillemins was really Sir John Mandeville[1]—although that theory also rests solely on the reliability of d'Outremeuse. No one has so much as suggested that the author of the *Travels* was not buried at Liège at all.

The evidence of an epitaph is hard to refute, even though it rests on a "confession" reported by so unscrupulous a fabricator as Jean d'Outremeuse. Hamelius raised the question whether the Guillemite fathers would have allowed the erection of a false epitaph in their church,[2] but we have no reason to doubt that it marked the grave of Jean à la Barbe. It merely fails to mention that he called himself "de Bourgogne," naming him instead "Johannes de Monteuilla Miles, alias dictus ad Barbam," and neatly combining a reference to his travels with mention of the doctor's genuine reputation for piety and charity. We need not suppose that the monks were accomplices in a conspiracy. Why should they question the story which d'Outremeuse tells in his *Myreur*, and which he undoubtedly told them, of de Bourgogne's "confession" on his deathbed of

---

[1] So Mr. Letts asserts, p. 17. See also Chap. 6 above.
[2] See his article in the *Quarterly Review*, 227 (1917), 331-352.

## DOCTOR JEAN DE BOURGOGNE

his "true" identity? D'Outremeuse was a distinguished citizen of Liège, "clers ligois, ... notaire et audienchier," of the court of the Prince Bishop.[3] Since he claimed to be executor of the doctor's will, he undoubtedly paid for the monument. He had forged other documents to support his fictions,[4] and this was perhaps his most elaborate and grandiose, as well as his most successful, forgery.

That the epitaph was a forgery is made probable by what we can learn of the doctor, Jean de Bourgogne, as well as by what we can learn from the study of the manuscripts. De Bourgogne was an eminent man with an international reputation as an authority on the plague. In 1365 he published a *De Pestilentia*, which quickly became famous. In this work he mentions that he had also written a *De causa et natura corrupti aeris, sive iudicia Astrologie* and a *De distinctione moribus pestilentialium*.

His works had a considerable circulation, if we can judge from the number of manuscripts preserved.[5] The plague tract

---

[3] This was his title as legal officer in the household of the Prince-Bishop of Liège: Bormans, Introduction, xi; Hamelius ed. II, 9.

[4] S. Balau, *Étude Critique des Sources de L'Histoire du Pays de Liége au Moyen Age*, pp. 571 ff.; G. Kurth, *Étude Critique sur Jean d'Outremeuse*, pp. 20-24.

[5] Karl Sudhoff, "Pestschriften aus den ersten 150 Jahren nach der Epidemie des 'schwarzen Todes' 1348," *Archiv für Geschichte der Medizin*, v (1911), 58-80, argues that the shorter plague tract, which has also been attributed to de Bourgogne, was by a John of Bordeaux; but Herbert Schöffler suggests that the Latin "Burdeus" is not Bordeaux but simply a contraction of Bur[gun]deus," *Beiträge zur mittelenglischen Medizinliteratur* (Halle, 1911), in "Sächsche Forschungsinstitute," in *Leipzig, Forschungsinstitut für neuere Philologie III, Anglistische Abteilung*, I, 145 ff. Schöffler prints the shorter English version of the *De Pestilentia*. It is also in David Murray, *John de Burdeus, or John de Burgundia, otherwise Sir John Mandeville and the Pestilence*, privately printed (Paisley and London, 1891), with descriptions of 37 MSS.; reprinted, and Latin and English versions of the longer tract added, in his *Black Book of Paisley* (Paisley, 1885). The treatise of 1365 was turned into Hebrew by Benjamin, son of Isaac, of Carcassonne, and appears in Paris MS. 1124, dated 1399: E Renan, *Histoire Littéraire de la France*, Tome XXXI (Paris, 1893), 723-725. The shorter pest tract is in the MS.

was translated into English, and then retranslated from English back into Latin and exists in that form in several manuscripts. It was also translated into French and Hebrew.

There is no evidence, however, that he wrote anything in French, or that he traveled or was interested in travel books. The story of his sojourn in Cairo comes entirely from d'Outremeuse. The doctor says, in the pest tract of 1365, that he had been practising medicine for forty years (i.e., since 1325). He does not say where. D'Outremeuse claims, in his story of the deathbed confession, that the doctor came to Liège in 1343, but since he, himself, was only five at that time, he hardly remembered the event for himself. He had a motive for putting the date as late as possible, since he was telling the story of the deathbed confession and so had to make room in the doctor's life for the alleged travels. In 1399, when the story in the *Myreur* was written, there was little danger that anyone living could remember when Doctor Jean à la Barbe first practised medicine in Liège. He had been dead for almost thirty years.

We do not know when the grave, with its stone inscribed with letters of brass, was marked. We need not assume that this was done in 1372. The interpolation at the end of the Ogier redaction and of the Latin vulgate shows that d'Outremeuse at first told a story of how the doctor knew Mandeville and persuaded him to write the *Travels* in Liège. It was not until he wrote the last book of the *Myreur* that he

---

(Lincoln Cathedral, A i 17) of the Thornton Romances, ed. J. O. Halliwell for the Camden Society (London, 1844), see pp. xxv-xxxvi. Most recently these works have been edited by Dorothea Waley Singer, "Some Plague Tractates (Fourteenth and Fifteenth Centuries)," *History of Medicine*, in *Proc. of the Royal Society of Medicine*, ix, (1916), pp. 159-178; and with Reuben Levy, in *Annals of Medical History*, i (New York, 1917), 394-411. She suggests that the tract of John of Bordeaux in 1390 was made from the 1365 tract which she edits from MS. Bibl. Nat. fr., nouv. acq. 4516: *Proc. of the Royal Society of Medicine*, pp. 200-212. For a résumé see E. Wickersheimer, *Dictionnaire Biographique des Médecins en France au Moyen Age* (Paris, 1936), "Jean de Bourgogne."

## DOCTOR JEAN DE BOURGOGNE

made the claim that the doctor *was* Mandeville, who was the Count of Montfort. We can hardly assume that the epitaph was cut in 1372, and that afterwards the Ogier redaction was made with its claim that the doctor *was acquainted with* Mandeville. The more natural growth of the tale would be from acquaintance to identity.

It might be asked why, if there were no grounds whatever for connecting Jean de Bourgogne with Mandeville, d'Outremeuse should have thought of making a fictitious connection. It may have been that the doctor was English, or that d'Outremeuse thought that he looked English. The connection may have been one of first names, or of beards. The name "cum barbam," or "à la barbe," was commonly used for the doctor,[6] and a beard must have been unusual in Liège if it could be used as a distinguishing mark. Beards were common in England, as we know from Chaucer's account of his pilgrims and from his own and other portraits.[7] D'Outremeuse needed no excuse, however, for romancing about a citizen of Liège, and this one was sufficiently famous, safely dead, and probably without heirs to question any story the chronicler might invent about him.

In the light of what is now known about d'Outremeuse's historical irresponsibility it seems almost superfluous to examine the theory of Nicholson and Warner that the doctor wrote the *Travels*, but that his real name was Bourgogne and not Mandeville. Warner says, "Assuming the substantial correctness of the latter's [d'Outremeuse's!] report, it certainly seems most probable that, in spite of his own declaration, the bearded doctor's real name was, and always had been, Jean de Bourgogne, but that, having written his book of *Travels*

---

[6] See Murray, *John de Burdeus*, p. 1, n.; Warner, p. xxxvii, n. 1; British Museum MS. Royal 12 G. IV, written in the 14th century, describes him as *Johannes de Burgundia, aliter vocatus cum Barba civis Leodiensis ac artis mediciniae professor.*

[7] See also H. Bateson's ed. of *Patience*, English Series III, Publication LXX, 2d ed. (Manchester University Press, 1918), xxx.

under the assumed name of Mandeville, he was tempted by its success to secure to himself a posthumous fame by reversing the facts and claiming as his veritable name that which was fictitious."[8] We can no longer suppose that the irresponsible d'Outremeuse was telling the truth in this place, while the pious and learned mediaeval doctor was telling a lie on his deathbed "to secure posthumous fame" under an assumed name. What of his very considerable fame as a doctor, under his own name? As a matter of fact, it is an anachronism to attribute the Renaissance thirst for literary "immortality" to a man who died in 1372. Even Petrarch would hardly have jeopardized his soul for that end.[9]

The reason for arguing that the doctor wrote the *Travels* under the assumed name of "Mandeville" is that, in looking for a Sir John Mandeville who left England in 1322, Warner discovered a John de Burgoyne, chamberlain to Sir John Mowbray, who was pardoned for his part in an attack on the Despensers, 20 August 1321, and then the pardon was revoked in May 1322.[10] Nicholson imagines that this man fled overseas,[11] became a doctor, and eventually settled at Liège. But this is pure conjecture, based solely on the similarity of a name which was almost as common as "John Smith." "John of Burgundy" is not a sufficiently distinguishing mark to warrant the

[8] Warner, p. xxxix; and see his article in *D.N.B.* Hamelius rejects the deathbed confession as an invention of d'Outremeuse's, yet he calls the doctor "Sir John Mandeville"; see his notes, II, 67-68, and elsewhere.

[9] See H. Pirenne, "Mandeville, Jehan de," *Biographie Nationale . . . de Belgique*, Tome 13 (Brussels, 1894-95).

[10] *Encyc. Brit.*; see also Warner, p. xxxix; *Calendar of Patent Rolls, Edward II (1321-1324)*, p. 20; *Parliamentary Writs*, ed. Sir Francis Palgrave (London, 1834), II$^2$ Appendix, p. 167, and II$^3$, p. 619, where the pardon is described as "afterwards revoked." Warner cites II$^2$, 168, for the revocation. I do not find it there.

[11] He also suggests that the name "Mandeville" was suggested to de Bourgogne by the fact that a John Mangevilayn was named with him on the pardon. Apparently Nicholson and Warner between them concocted the theory that "Mandeville" was the pseudonym of de Bourgogne; see "Mandeville, Jean de" in *Encyc. Brit.*, 9th ed. ff.

identification of Sir John Mowbray's chamberlain of 1322 with the doctor who died at Liège in 1372. The commonness of the name is attested by the fact that another John of Burgundy was practising medicine at Pisa at this very time, and his writings are sometimes confused with those of the doctor of Liège. We know nothing of the age, education, or subsequent history of Mowbray's chamberlain. We do not even know that he ever left England.

We are dealing with a time when the practise of adopting fixed surnames was just being established.[12] Several different principles of identification were in use, of which "John with a Beard" represents one and "John of Burgundy" represents another. The Liège doctor's use of an alias should not suggest that he was a shady character. It merely indicates that he had no fixed surname but used two different names, as many men did as much as a century later.[13] What is important to recognize is that "John of Burgundy" was too common a name, especially in the Low Countries, to create the probability that the chamberlain of Sir John Mowbray was the same man as the Liège doctor.

Neither Nicholson nor Warner could find a record of a John Mandeville who left England in 1322, and their argument for Bourgogne's authorship of the *Travels* is partly based on this negative evidence. But we do not even have a list of all the noblemen and knights who fled from England after the defeat of the Barons at Boroughbridge early in that year, although we know that many fled. How could we expect, therefore, that the name of one young gentleman who set out on his travels in 1322 must have been recorded, and the record survive—if he really existed.

[12] See, for example, Gustav Fransson, *Middle English Surnames of Occupation, 1100-1350, with an Excursus on Toponymical Surnames*, Lund Studies in English, III (1935), 20-30.

[13] See, for example, the practise of the Russell family as described by Gladys Scott Thomson, *Two Centuries of Family History* (London, 1930), pp. 58 ff.

There was, however, another consideration which led Warner to prefer the doctor as author of the *Travels* to "a simple knight," and that was the nature of the *Travels*. He says, "We have to credit the author with the learning of a clerk and a range of reading more naturally associated with the studious seclusion of a monastic library. To have read and assimilated, however clumsily, Boldensele and Odoric, Carpini and Hayton, Vincent of Beauvais and Brunetto Latini, Albert of Aix and Jacques de Vitry, the *Historia Scholastica* and the *Legenda Aurea*, the Palestine Itineraries, Latin and French, and all the other works with which the writer shows himself more or less intimately acquainted, is an achievement not easily to be believed of a simple knight and soldier of fortune in the 14th century."[14] It does not follow that if the author was not "a simple knight and soldier of fortune" then he must have been a doctor of Liège. Boldensele, for example, was a monk before he became a traveler and a knight of the Holy Sepulchre. The Liège doctor was a learned man, but in a different field from that of the author of the *Travels*. His works were all in Latin. Almost certainly he could have written in French, but we do not know that he ever did. If, by chance, he was an Englishman, he might even have written in Norman French like that of the first version of the *Travels*, but it is highly improbable that, if he had written the *Travels* in Norman French at Liège, the version known to d'Outremeuse should be so far removed from the original. It would also be very strange that early copies in the original dialect should be so very rare on the continent—but I will deal with the distribution of manuscripts in the next chapter.

The author of the *Travels* was not merely a learned man. He was a literary genius. There is no evidence that the Liège doctor had any particular literary skill, though of course a Latin medical treatise is hardly a fair basis for judgment. But, to return to Warner's argument—the author of the *Travels*

[14] Warner, Introduction, p. xxx.

was well-educated, although not necessarily from the "studious seclusion of a monastic library." Laymen had considerable access to the monastic libraries in the fourteenth century, and it was a period in which wealthy laymen in France, and even in England, were interested in books and sometimes had magnificent libraries.[15]

There is one other fact which has been brought forward as evidence that Jean de Bourgogne and Sir John Mandeville were the same man. Both Warner and Hamelius make much of the fact that the earliest dated manuscript of the *Travels* (1371) contained also a copy of the *De pestilentia* of Jean de Bourgogne. The juxtaposition is curious and striking, but I believe it is not significant. Medieval manuscripts were often miscellaneous, and both these works, being relatively short, were frequently bound up with other pieces.[16] This manuscript (now identified as Bibliothèque Nationale, nouvelles acquisitions françaises, nos. 4515 and 4516) was stolen at one time and broken into two parts which were bound separately. Both parts were made by the same copyist, the famous scribe, Raoulet d'Orléans, who says in his colophon that he made the book for Master Gervaise Chrétien, Master in Medicine, and first physician to King Charles V: "Ce liure cy fist escrire honnora-

---

[15] The collections of Charles V, Jean Duc de Berry, Philippe Duc de Bourgogne, and the Duc d' Orléans are famous. Records of English collections are more scanty but enough evidence has been preserved to show that they were fairly common: see below, Chap. 14.

[16] In Charles V's library, no. 404 was *L'Ymage du monde, ryme, et de Cirurgie:* Gilles Mallet, *Inventaire ou Catalogue des Livres de l'Ancienne Bibliothèque du Louvre, fait en l'année 1373* (Paris, 1836), p. 79. The short version of the *De Pestilentia* occurs in the same manuscript with a chronicle of Scotland: cf. Murray, *The Black Book of Paisley.* M. R. James says, "We all know how little the medieval people cared about preserving uniformity of complexion in the contents of their books. Tracts of the most diverse kinds might be collected in one volume, consideration being only had to their bulk and not to their subject," *Lists of Manuscripts formerly in Peterborough Abbey Library* (Oxford, 1926, printed as a Supplement to the Bibliographical Society's Transactions, No. 5), p. 13.

bles homs sages & discirt [sic] maistre Geruaise crestien. Maistre en medicine. et premier phisicien de tres puissant noble et excellent prince. Charles par le grace de dieu. Roy de france. Escript par Raoulet dorliens. lan de grace mil. ccc.lxxi. le xviij[e]. Jour de Septembre." A note at the end of the manuscript records that Chrétien presented the book to his master, the French king. The *Travels* comes first in the manuscript and has the usual statement about the identity of the author at the beginning and end.[17] The treatise on the plague which formed the second part of the manuscript is described as by "Maistre Jehan de Bourgoigne, autrement dit à la Barbe, professeur en Medicine et cytoien de Liége." Again, at the end, we read: "Explicit le traictié maistre Jehan à la Barbe, docteur en medicine, compilé a Liége, en laquelle ville il fait moult d'autres nobles traictiez de la science, non oys autrefois, et le fist l'an mil ccc lxv."[18] Nothing in the manuscript suggests any connections between the two authors.

If we could assume that the manuscript from which Raoulet d'Orléans copied contained both works and came from Liège, i.e., that it was a manuscript which came from de Bourgogne, then the presence of the two works together in Raoulet's copy might provide grounds for belief that both works were by the same author. But actually we can be very sure that *neither* work came at all directly from its author. The text of the *Travels* which he was copying was neither in the original Nor-

---

[17] See above, Chap. 6.

[18] It was in the Louvre library of Charles V and was withdrawn by Charles VI in 1392. It was in the Royal library in the 17th century, but was abstracted by Barrois and sold to Lord Ashburnham, and so is described among his manuscripts. It was recovered by France through his generosity and the researches of L. Delisle; see his *Catalogue des manuscrits des fonds Libri et Barrois,* pp. 251-253. Warner gives a brief account, vi n. 1. See above, Chap. 9. Facsimiles of the first and last pages have been published in *Fac-Simile de Livres Copiés et Enluminés pour le Roi Charles V.* Souvenir de la Journée du 8 mars 1903 offert à ses amis par Léopold Delisle. Plates vi and vii. The Harvard College Library now has a photostatic copy of this text of the *Travels*.

man French nor a good copy of the first redaction. The plague tract was originally written in Latin, yet it appears here in French. Raoulet was a scribe and not a translator. We can therefore be sure that the archetype from which he worked was also in French,[19] and therefore not the original.

Since neither manuscript from which Raoulet copied could have come directly from its author, we must look upon the appearance of the two works together, in this one instance,[20] as of no significance whatever for the identification of the author. Chrétien wished to present a book to his monarch. He was a bookish man, the founder of a college which bore his name down to the Revolution.[21] He himself wrote a work on the pest,

---

[19] Delisle, *Le Cabinet des Manuscrits de la Bibliothèque Impériale* (Paris 1868), I, 36 ff., and *Recherches sur La Librairie de Charles V* (Paris, 1907), I, 70-79, 275-76, gives a list of the books Raoulet copied for Charles V between 1367 and 1396.

[20] Bibl. Nat. fr. 5634 is a 15th century MS on paper which seems to have been copied from Raoulet's text. It has a table of contents at the beginning, the first leaf of which is missing, and at the end of this table we read, "Et en la fin de cest livre est escripte le preservacion de epidimie . . . faicte de maistre Jehan de Bourgogne . . . et ce commence én feullet 93." But the manuscript is mutilated and stops at fol. 87. It has not been fully collated, but all I can learn about it points to its being a direct copy of MS. 4515. Among other things, it has what seems to be a copy of the genuine Hebrew alphabet which was added at the end of 4515. See also MS. Bibl. Nat. fr. 5637, 2129, and 6109, described in Appendix I.

[21] See Gilles Mallet, *Inventaire*, p. 99, note by the editor. Two works on ethics from the Louvre library (nos. 560 and 566) were given by the king to "the schools of master Gervaise." The foundation dated from 1370. There is a biography by S. Le Paulmier, "Notice sur Gervaise Chrétien Fondateur du Collège de Maître Gervaise, à Paris, et sur Guy Chrétien Trésorier du Roi." *Revue Catholique de Normandie*, VII (Evreux, 1897), 40-60, 97-129. He was physician to Jean le Bon both before and after he was king, but was probably not with him in England. He was a Norman. A summary biography of him is in E. Wickersheimer, *Dictionnaire Biographique des Médecins en France au Moyen Age*. As a bibliophile he is mentioned in Delisle, *Recherches*, I, 74, 343, II, 81, 131-2, 142. He published a work on the pest. See the Society des Antiquaires de la Morinie's *Bulletin historique trimestriel*, x (1897-1901), 617-622.

and the *De Pestilentia* was a new medical work which interested him. It had been in circulation for only six years. The king was a collector of books about the East, and the *Travels* was probably selected and put first in the volume on that account.[22] The two together made a sufficiently substantial volume for presentation to royalty.

Paris was a book-buyer's paradise in this century, and commercial scriptoria flourished. Richard of Bury described it as he found it in the first half of the century; and after the peace of 1360, the book collecting of Charles V and his two brothers, Jean Duc de Berry and Philippe Duc de Bourgogne, set a fashion and created a market which made the scriptoria flourish again in the last third of the century.[23] It is against this background of demand and supply that we must set the fact that one copy of the *Travels*, the earliest *dated* manuscript, but not a good copy, and not a copy of the original text, was put with a translation of Jean de Bourgogne's pest tract. Obviously, in this context, the juxtaposition has no significance for the problem of the identity of Sir John Mandeville.

In the end we have nothing but the story of a thoroughly discredited witness to connect the author of the *Travels* with the Liège doctor—or with Liège at all. On the contrary, a survey of the French texts shows that the oldest version is the one in Norman French which, so far as we can tell, was unknown

---

[22] Charles V took from his Louvre library on one occasion a *Traittie de l'Épidemie, en prose: Inventaire*, no. 482. For other medical books and accounts of the East see the *Inventaire, passim*.

[23] See the *Philobiblon;* and H. Fierens-Gevaert, *Les Très Belles Heures de Jean de France Duc de Berry* (Brussels, 1924), Introduction; Paul Delalain, *Étude sur le librarie parisien du xiii⁰ au xv⁰ siècle* (Paris, 1891), *passim*, especially his list of licences to stationers in the years 1316-1350, naming ten Englishmen. Jean de Jandun's *Tractatus de Laudibus Parisiis* (1323) praises French scribes, illuminators, and binders. See also Henry Martin, *La Miniature Française* (Paris, 1867), pp. 54 ff.; Laura Hibbard Loomis gives valuable references in her article, "The Auchinleck Manuscript and a Possible London Bookshop of 1330-1340," *PMLA*, LVII (1942), 595-627.

in Liège, where the Paris redaction was used to make the Ogier version. We have, therefore, good reason to believe that the work originated elsewhere, and that it had been circulating for some time, probably as much as fifteen or twenty years, before a copy came into the hands of Jean d'Outremeuse. In all probability the famous Liège doctor, Jean de Bourgogne, or à la Barbe, who died in 1372, had never even heard of it.

# 12
# THE PLACE OF WRITING OF THE *TRAVELS*

THE DISTRIBUTION of the three versions of the French text is what we would naturally expect if the Ogier redaction originated at Liège, the Paris-French at Paris, and the Norman-French in England. Copies of the Norman-French version are usually written in English hands and are still to be found, almost exclusively, in England.

The evidence of provenance and distribution goes far beyond this generalization. Of the seventeen French texts preserved in England, all but two are of the Norman-French version, and those two are modern importations.[1] On the other hand, of the fifteen texts in French preserved at Paris, only ten are of the Paris version, one is of the Ogier of Liège redaction, and four are copies of the Norman-French representing two different importations.[2] Three of these four belong to a sub-group characterized by the presence of a life of "St. Alban of Germany." This Life occurs also in two manuscripts preserved in England, one of which is probably earlier than any of the Paris exemplars. It is Sloan MS. 1464, in the British Museum, one of the four texts selected by Warner for colla-

---

[1] According to Mr. R. A. B. Mynors, Harley MS. 3940 was written in the early 15th century, and was owned in France in the 16th century. It is a copy of the Paris version, and so probably originated in France. MS. McClean 177, in the Fitzwilliam Museum in Cambridge, is a copy of the Ogier version, written in the 15th century in a hand which is not English.

[2] MS. Arsenal 3219 is described as in an Anglo-Norman hand of the 14th century, but it is a text of the Paris version, and the dialect is rather Picard than Norman French, according to my informant, M. Thomas; see Henry Martin, *Catalogue des MSS. de la Bibliothèque de l'Arsenal* (Paris, 1887), III, 294.

tion. The other is in the Bodleian, Additional MS. C. 280, written somewhat later. The three manuscripts of this group now in the Bibliothèque Nationale were written on the Continent, although they are copies of the Norman-French version of the text. One of them is dated 1402, one occurs in the beautiful *Livre des Merveilles*, written about 1403. The third is later.[3] A fourth is in the public library of Bern, Switzerland, No. 58. All but one of these manuscripts have the Life of St. Alban of Germany at the end of the *Travels*. The 1402 manuscript transposes it, along with the author's concluding statement about himself (to which it was originally attached), to the beginning of the text. As a result we have, in this manuscript, a prologue in which the author says that he went abroad in 1322 and that he put his *Travels* into writing in 1356, in the thirty-fourth year after he set out. These are the dates given in all early copies of the Norman-French version of the text. But one of the distinguishing marks of the Paris redaction is that it gives the date of writing as 1357 and corrects the number of years to read thirty-five,[4] and these are the figures given when this autobiographical passage occurs again, in its proper place, at the end of the 1402 manuscript. The situation suggests that the scribe made use of both the newly imported Norman-French version and the older Paris-French text.

Since the Paris redaction was circulating as early as 1371, it must have been made from a much earlier copy of the text than this "St. Alban of Germany" version. One manuscript in the Bibliothèque Nationale (fonds français 25,284) may descend from the earlier Norman-French importation. It is a fifteenth-century copy, on paper, but it lacks the two passages which characterize the Paris redaction, the addition to the account of the Valley Perilous, and the substitute passage on

[3] The MS written in 1403 is Bibl. Nat. fr. 2810. That of 1402, written and dated by G. Mayes, is now Bibl. Nat. fr. 5635. The third, Bibl. Nat. fr. 5633, is a 15th-century MS on paper. All three preserve the peculiarities of the English version.

[4] For a fuller description of all the manuscripts, see Appendix I.

circumnavigation. It is a poor copy, lacking three alphabets, and omitting the representations of the characters of the other three, but in the account of the castle of the sparrowhawk it has the words, "les murs sont couers de une yerre." This may represent a contamination with the Paris version, or it may indicate that this particular interpolation was made by some Norman-French scribe, and that it was in the archetype from which the Paris redaction was made.

If, as the best texts assert, the *Travels* was completed in 1356, or shortly thereafter, it is easy to see why it found its way so quickly to Paris. In that year the battle of Poitiers resulted in a mass importation of French noblemen into England to be held for ransom. Chief among them was King Jean le Bon, who lived in John of Gaunt's palace of the Savoy in London, and at Hertford and elsewhere, in suitable state for a king, for most of the remaining four years of his life. He occupied himself while there partly with books, buying and borrowing manuscripts.[5] His mother had been a patroness of French letters, and her son would have been noteworthy in

[5] On the king's books, see L. Delisle, *Recherches sur la Librairie de Charles V*, Pt. I, pp. 326-336; and *Le Cabinet des Manuscrits*, I, 15 ff. On his patronage of translators, see Petit de Julleville, *Histoire de la Langue et de la Littérature française des Origines à 1900* (Paris, 1896-99), II, 258-269. For a general account of the captivity of King Jean, see J. J. Britton, "The Captivity of King John of France," *The Antiquary*, XXXV (Nov., 1899), 331-334; G. F. Duckett, ed., *Original Documents relating to the Hostages of John, King of France, and the Treaty of Brétigny in 1360* (London, 1890); Herbert C. Andrews, "John, King of France: A Prisoner at Hertford Castle," *East Herts Archaeological Society Transactions*, VI, (1921-22), 160-179; Edward Trollope, "The Captivity of John, King of France, at Somerton Castle, Lincolnshire," *Reports of the Associated Architectural Societies*, IV (1857), pp. 49-68; S.A.R. le Duc d'Aumale, "Notes et documents relatifs à Jean, Roi de France, et à sa Captivité en Angleterre," *Miscellanies of the Philobiblon Society*, II, no. 6 (1855-6), p. 21; and "Nouveaux Documents . . . ," ibid., V, no. 1. Among the books in the Louvre library, listed in Gilles Mallet's *Inventaire ou Catalogue des Livres de l'Ancienne Bibliothèque du Louvre, fait en l'année 1373* (Paris, 1836), are some that had belonged to Jean and his mother. No. 37 is a copy of *Godefroi de Bouillon* "which was of the Countess of Pembroke." She was one of his chief

that respect if he, in his turn, had not been so far surpassed by his three sons. Of the three, Jean, Duc de Berry (1340-1416), and Philippe, later Duc de Bourgogne, were among the captives. Jean served as a hostage in 1356-57, and he was in London again, or still, in 1364 when he obtained a year's parole. He did not recover his liberty until 1367, but it is not clear just how many of these ten years he actually spent in England.[6] Many French noblemen were in England during this decade, waiting for their families, tenants, or friends to ransom them. Many were paroled and lived as guests of their captors, and there was much travel between England and France.

The *Travels*, as a new book about the Near and Far East, would naturally be of interest, something that an English host could offer for the entertainment of a French guest. The Paris redaction may have been made in England by a clerk of one of these men.[7] Whoever made it was an educated man who understood what he was transcribing, as some of his additions show. But he was not working from the author's holograph, but from a copy into which had crept errors he could not detect. Again, between his transcription and the copy made in 1371, several manuscripts intervene. Raoulet copied from a manuscript which had been supplied with frequent sectional headings, and several other manuscripts with these same headings can be identified. One of them reached Milan sometime before 1388, when a copy of it was made for Valentine

---

friends in England. See Louis C. Douët-d'Arcq, *Comptes de l'Argenterie des Rois de France au xiv$^e$ siècle,* published by the Société de l'Histoire de France (Paris, 1851), Vol. 64, pp. 15, 224, 227, 240, 251 (the last a record of 2 romances bought when the king was preparing to go home in 1360). See also L. C. Douët-d'Arcq, *Nouveau Recueil de Comptes de l'Argenterie des Rois de France,* published by the same (Paris, 1844), No. 170.

[6] Duckett, op. cit.

[7] King John had at least 70 attendants, according to Andrews, op. cit. Duckett mentions 40 hostages pledged to secure his return to England. His physician, Guillaume Racine, bought books for him.

Visconti, who had just been formally contracted to Louis, Count of Valois (Duc d'Orléans after 1391).[8] Valentine was the

[8] There is a copy now at Modena, Bibliothèque Est, fonds Francese, no. 33 (XI F. 17), with a colophon saying it was copied for her by "Perre le Sauvaige de Chaalons en Champaigne, maistre en ars," and completed December 10, 1388. Jules Camus argued that it came from the Visconti library at Pavia, where a copy is reported in the catalogues of 1426 and 1459: "Les 'Voyages' de Mandeville copiés pour Valentine de Milan," *Revue des Bibliothèques*, IV (1894), 12-19; see also his "Notices et Extraits des Manuscrits Français de Modène antérieurs au xvie Siècle," *Revue des langues romanes*, xxxv (1891), 212-215. There are two difficulties. First, Valentine took her copy to France with her; see J. Camus, "La Venue en France de Valentine Visconti, Duchesse d'Orléans et l'inventaire de ses joyaux apportés de Lombardie," *Miscellanea di Storia Italiana*, Ser. III, Tome v (Torino, 1900), p. 39, no. 101, where it is listed as "un Mandeville, couvers de cramoisy." Which brings us to the other difficulty, the copy listed in the catalogue of the Visconti library in 1426 is described as "in gallico et in litterina notarina, copertus corio albo vetere hirsuto." The catalogue is printed by A. Thomas, "Les Manuscrits Français et Provençaux des Ducs de Milan au Château de Pavie," *Romania*, XL (1911), 571-609, see no. 79. Thomas points out the further difficulty that while the Modena manuscript is on paper, this must have been on parchment because in this inventory the paper manuscripts were expressly so described. Giulio Bertoni, "Intorno al Codice dei 'Viaggi' di Jean de Mandeville posseduta da Valentina Visconti," *Giornalia storia della letteratura Italiana*, XLIX (Torino, 1907), 358-366, argues that the Modena manuscript, which is unornamented and a somewhat rough copy, was not Valentine's copy but one made from the MS. recorded at Pavia to serve as an intermediate from which her more elaborate copy was to be made. Just why such an intermediary copy was required is not altogether clear. More probably it is a copy of her copy, and the scribe copied also the colophon in her copy. Camus shows, however, that the paper on which it is written came from the Visconti chancelleries about 1388: See "La Venue. . . ." Valentine's mother was a sister of Charles V of France, who had a copy of the *Travels* in 1371. One of the traits to be observed about these French princes is the frequency with which they gave books as presents, to one another and to servants. It is not surprising that a copy of the book should have reached the Este library by 1388, or that Valentine should have one in her personal library. But the Modena copy, made by (or from the copy of) Perre le Sauvaige, who describes himself as in her service and who was in the service of her son, Charles d'Orléans, in 1412, and was secretary, treasurer, and counselor of the Duc in 1444, may have been made for his own use, or (the date, December 10 is suggestive) as a gift for someone

daughter of Jean Galeazzo Visconti, Duke of Milan, who in 1360 had married Jean le Bon's daughter Isabella. By 1395 there was a copy of this version of the *Travels* in the royal library of Spain, where the text was translated into both Catalan and Aragonese.[9] And, of course, by the 1380's, or earlier, a copy had reached Liège.

Manuscript reproduction was slow, at the beginning, but capable of multiplication at a constantly accelerating pace. The diffusion of copies of the Paris redaction suggests that a manuscript of this version was available in some large Paris scriptorium by 1371.

Occasionally the *Travels* was richly illuminated, as in the *Livre des Merveilles,* and in the manuscript from which only twenty-eight pictures survive and are reproduced by Warner.[10] But usually the manuscripts are unpretentious, often they are described as "on paper," and many of them must have perished in the Renaissance, when the compositions of the Middle Ages were so freely discarded as out-of-date, erroneous, superstitious, "Popish," and worthless. It is surprising that so many of them have survived, and that the history of the text can be traced so clearly, once the initial mistake of believing that it originated at Liège has been corrected. It is fortunate for this

---

who did not take it to France. It was probably not a part of the Pavia library, which was captured by Louis XII and taken to Blois. Part of it is now in the Bibliothèque Nationale. Another 14th century copy of the *Travels* is in the Vatican Library, MS. Reg. 750, from the collection of Queen Christina of Sweden (d. 1689). It was copied by Jean Hazart, who has been identified as a physician of the King of France and author of a medical work in the Louvre library: E. Langlois, "Notices des Manuscrits Français," see above Chap. 7, n. 2, and see E. Wickersheimer, *Dictionnaire Biographique des Médecins en France au Moyen Age.*

[9] A copy in the library of Don Juan, King of Aragon, recorded in that year, is apparently in Aragonese. A copy of this version still survives in one manuscript: W. J. Entwistle, "The Spanish Mandevilles," *Modern Language Review,* xvii (1922), 251-257.

[10] In his Roxburghe Club edition of the *Travels.* MS. B.M. Addit. 24, 189.

inquiry that enough manuscripts survive[11] to provide ample evidence that the original version was written in the French of Gower and the English court in the mid-fifteenth century, and that it was written, in all probability, in England, since the best texts are written in English hands and are still preserved in English libraries.

We must, therefore, give careful reconsideration to the author's claim that he was an Englishman. There are some indications in the text which have been minimized or overlooked by those who were convinced of the Liège origin of the work. Mandeville starts his itinerary from "England, Ireland, Scotland or Norway," and he says at other points, "in going from Scotland or from England toward Jerusalem," and again, "a man that comes from the lands of the West, he goes through France, Burgundy, and Lombardy and so to Venice." Now it would be easy enough for a Frenchman who was pretending to be an Englishman to start the journey each time from England; but here the English point of view is glossed over and presented with a modest show of generalization which is characteristic of the author as he represents himself, and which, if it is a pose, is a most successful one. There are several other and more subtle revelations of an English point of view. When he mentions the finding of the true cross by St. Helena, he adds "file choel roi Dengleterre." Anyone who had read the histories of England after Geoffrey of Monmouth wrote would know that Helena was the daughter of King Cole, but who but an English author writing for an English audience would mention it in this connection? Again, when he speaks of the time when Saladin was sultan, he adds, "en qui temps le roy Richart dangleterre y fut auec pluseurs autres qui garderent le passage de Roche." Further on he mentions the excursion to the Holy Land of "King Edward of England," i.e., Prince Edward, who became Edward I. In the account of

---

[11] See Appendix I. Very few of the paper manuscripts survive in England.

## THE PLACE OF WRITING OF THE *TRAVELS* 177

Beyrouth, where he is following Boldensele very closely, he adds "where St. George slew the dragon." These are artful notes of Englishry, if they were put in to sustain the pretense that the author was an Englishman, but they would be natural enough if he really was an Englishman.

Warner notes that the passage in which Mandeville represents the Sultan of Egypt as lecturing him on the follies of the Christians and especially the passage on extravagance of dress, is very like a passage in the *Brut Chronicle*[12] under the year 1345. Extravagance of dress was a characteristic of the English frequently assailed by the moralists, and it was particularly in evidence after the plunder of France by the armies of Edward III.[13] If the author was not English he knew a good deal about the English. He knew, for example, that they had two additional characters in their alphabet which they called "thorn" and "zogh."[14]

Some very careless statements have been made about his knowledge of England, in such standard reference works as the *Cambridge History of English Literature,* where we are told "that the writer was no Englishman may be deduced from the absence of any local colouring and from his ignorance of English distances, more surely than from the erroneous titles and coats of arms" (i.e., d'Outremeuse's fabrications). J. E. Wells is probably echoing this dictum when he says that the "versions manifest ignorance of English conditions, that (it is declared) no Englishman would show."[15] Since the author has no occasion to mention "English conditions" and had no opportunity, in writing about his travels in the Orient, to give his work "local [English] colouring," it is a little hard to see what the writers of these generalities had in mind.

[12] Warner, p. 69, n. 4.
[13] See, for example, Chaucer's "Parson's Tale" in the passage on pride, Robinson's ed., pp. 285-286. Warner quotes Egerton MS. 650, fol. 74; see his note on p. 69, l. 4.
[14] See above, pp. 65-66.
[15] Wells, *Manual,* p. 434. Warner, on the other hand, says (p. xxxix) that Mandeville "shows a certain knowledge of England."

By "ignorance of English distances" is probably meant ignorance of English measures of distance. Mandeville speaks several times of "miles of our country," and at one point he explains, "and that containeth a forty mile of Lombardy, or of our country, that be also little miles; these be not miles of Gascony ne of the province of Almayne, where be great miles." Warner explains that the French league equalled two English miles, and in checking Mandeville's reports of distance allowance must be made for the fact that two old English miles, or a French league, were equal to three modern miles.[16] In fact, so many different measures of distance were used in the Middle Ages that it is very difficult, in any given case, to determine what measure is being used *except* by assuming that the writer is correct and then finding the unit of measure which fits his description! Mandeville does not always specify what measure he is using, although he sometimes says "leagues of Lombardy," sometimes "leagues of France," and at one point "English miles." His redactors and translators seem to have regarded "miles" and "leagues" as interchangeable. Moreover, in

[16] Warner's note on p. 11, l. 13. According to the article on "Weights and Measures" in the *Encyclopaedia Britannica*, 11th ed., the league was 1.59 British miles, old measure, according to the Bordeaux pilgrim. The old British mile was about a third longer than the modern mile, so that by this computation the league would be almost exactly equal to two modern miles. Some of the difficulties are evident in the statement of Schiltberger, *The Bondage and Travel of Johann Schiltberger,* p. 47, "a league is three Lombard miles, and four stadia is one Italian mile. One Italian mile should have 1,000 full paces and one pace should have 5 feet of 9 inches." An inch "is the first member of the thumb." We can only ask helplessly, "Whose thumb?" Much later, Thomas Fuller, in his *Pisgah-sight of Palestine* (London, 1662), p. 45, describes the confusion: "An *Italian* mile containeth seven, an *English* eight furlongs. A *French* is equall to two, a *vulgar Dutch* to three *English* miles, the *large Dutch* to four, the miles in Switzerland to five, not to say six of our English computation. . . ." Even in England a Middlesex is the shortest and a Yorkshire mile the longest! John Norden, in his *Speculum Britanniae* (1593), p. 8, says that an Italian mile contains 1000 paces of 5 feet. An English mile contains 8 furloughs of 40 perches of 16½ feet, or 5280 feet, "but our ordinary mile exceedeth both the Italian, and true English mile."

most manuscripts measures are given in Roman numerals, which are notoriously easy to misread. It is absurd, therefore, to try to deduce anything about Mandeville's nationality from the mistakes in measures of distance which occur in various versions of the *Travels*. Certainly the statement that the Paris version of 1371 is the "best and oldest" text (made both by the *Cambridge History,* II, 94, and by Wells' *Manual,* p. 434), is sufficient evidence of ignorance of the text to invalidate any judgments of this kind.

Mandeville does not consistently obtrude his English measures, any more than he does English words, or English comparisons. Where Odoric says that a city of China is as big as two Venices, Mandeville says "bigger than Paris," not "bigger than London," although London was bigger than Paris in his day. He is modest about his nationality, as he is (in his manner of writing) about everything else that he tells us of himself; but, considering the remoteness of England from his subject matter, a good deal of evidence of an English point of view appears in the course of the book. Moreover, these touches of Englishry slip in unobtrusively, in a way which would be natural enough if the author was an Englishman, but which, if they are a part of the fiction, would require us to credit him with even greater literary skill than is involved in his imaginative re-creation of other people's travels.

The clearest evidence of the English origin of the *Travels* is the style of the Norman-French text. The French unanimously condemn it as barbarous, not simply because of the dialectical spelling, but rather because of the choice and arrangement of the words. The whole cadence and word-order is more English than French, so that the first Englisher had little to do beyond finding English equivalents for the French words. For examples the reader has only to turn to the passages already quoted for other purposes, such as those on pages 136 ff. I have already remarked upon his tendency to put the emphatic word last in a sentence in English fashion. The opening of Chapter II in Warner's text gives a fair sample of his narrative style:

> A Constantinople est la croiz nostre Siegnur Ihesu Crist, et vne sue cote sanz coustures, et lesponge et larundine a quoi homme luy donoit a boire fiel et aigre vin en la croiz. Et si ad vn des claus de quoi il fuit atachez a la crois. Ascuns gents quidont qe la moitee de la crois nostre Seigneur soit en Cypre a vne abbeye de moignes qe homme appelle la Montaigne de Seinte Croiz; mes y nest mie ensi. Qar celle croiz de Cypre est celle en quelle Dismas le bon laron fuist penduz. Mes chescun nel sciet mie; et ceo est mal fait. Qar pur auoir lemolument des offerendes ils la fount a honurer et donent entendant qe ceo soit de la croiz nostre Seignur.

The Paris redactor did a little to smooth his text into a more French idiom and cadence, as when in the very first sentence he changed "Come il ensi soit qe la terre doutre mer . . ." to "Comme il soit ainsi . . ." but he did not rewrite, and the Englishman's French comes through. It is not probable that the Paris version was written first, and that an English redactor changed the word-order for the worse. The very "barbarousness" of the French is, therefore, the best evidence that the author was an Englishman.

# THE ENGLISH MANDEVILLES

As I have already pointed out, the argument that Jean de Bourgogne was the author of the *Travels* rests partly on the assumption that there was no Jean de Mandeville of the right age and of sufficient education to have written the book. Nicholson asserts recklessly, "There was no contemporary English mention of any English knight named Jehan de Mandeville, nor are the arms said to have been on the Liége tomb like any known Mandeville arms."[1] Since the arms are fictitious, they prove nothing. As for an English knight named John Mandeville, the real trouble is that there were many men of that name in England in the fourteenth century who were either knights or of families capable of knighthood.

Before we consider any of these men, however, we must free our minds of the incubus of the Liège tradition and go back to the text of the *Travels* as the only possibly authentic clue to the identity of the author. Moreover, we must limit ourselves to what can be found in the oldest and best French texts, discarding the fictions added to the vulgate and to the Ogier redaction, and also those in the English translations, which so confused Warner, Hamelius, and more recently Mr. Letts.

According to the best text, which I believe is the French text published by Warner, the author asserts that his name is Sir John Mandeville, that he was born and bred at St. Albans, that he left England on St. Michael's eve in 1322, that he traveled in many lands, and, returning home because of arthritis, he wrote and compiled his *Travels*, finishing the work in 1356.[2] Since the *Travels* is the product of wide reading

---

[1] Nicholson, *Encyc. Brit.*, "Mandeville, Jehan de."
[2] See above, Chap. 6 for quotation.

rather than, or in addition to, actual travel, I believe there are three alternative possibilities: either (1) there really was a Sir John Mandeville, a student and something of a traveler, who *wrote* the book; or (2) there was a famous traveler of that name upon whom a student of travel literature *fathered* the book in question; or (3) the author was a student of travel literature who *invented* Sir John Mandeville. We cannot ignore the third possibility, but neither can we accept it until the first two have been thoroughly explored. Both of these involve a real traveler to whom (presumably) the biographical data would apply.

Warner, in his Introduction (pp. xxx-xxxi), notices several John Mandevilles in fourteenth-century England, but he concludes, "there is nothing in the circumstances of any of these bearers of the name . . . to make it at all likely that the author of the Travels was included among them; while, on the contrary, there is the strongest evidence that he must be sought on the other side of the channel." This conviction that the Liège records were authentic prevented a serious search being made in England by either Warner or Hamelius.

In 1928 Professor Isaac Jackson called attention to records of a Sir John Mandeville who, he thought, had reason to flee from Ireland in 1333 because he had murdered his overlord, the Earl of Ulster.[3] This man can be quickly dismissed for several reasons. First, 1322 and not 1333 is the authentic date given for the departure from England. Second, the story that Mandeville fled because he had killed an earl comes from the *Myreur* of Jean d'Outremeuse. The motive for the departure is not stated in the *Travels*. Third, it was not Sir John Mandeville, but Robert Mandeville, who killed the Earl of Ulster. Sir John was still in the king's service in 1335, and still a tenant in Ireland in 1338-42.[4]

---

[3] "Who was Sir John Mandeville? A Fresh Clue," *Modern Language Review*, XXIII (1928), 466-468.

[4] A statement that Sir Richard Mandeville struck the fatal blow may be found in R. F. D'Arcy, *The Life of John, First Baron Darcy of*

In 1936 K. W. Cameron published records of thirty-four John de Mandevilles in medieval England, with notes on twelve others described as "unidentified."[5] Most of these forty-six can be quickly eliminated. The first nine are clearly too early, and three others are too late. Of the twelve "unidentified," five are too early, three are too late, and the last is a notice of the inscription for our traveler, put up at St. Albans in the sixteenth century but never credited. Of the remaining twenty-two plus three "unidentified," some are duplications,[6] and some are clearly too humble men.[7] A further reason for eliminating most of these Jehan de Mandevilles is that they were in England while our Sir John was on his travels. None was from St. Albans.

In general, Cameron paid too little attention to the evidence of the descent of lands, which is the surest guide to the identi-

---

*Knayth* (London, 1933), pp. 62-63. But Robert, son of Martin Mandeville, is named the assassin in Edmund Curtis's more scholarly *History of Mediaeval Ireland from 1110 to 1513* (London, rev. ed., 1938), p. 210; see also pp. 167, 186, 238-239. These Mandevilles settled in Ulster before 1221. Other records of the family can be found in C. Moor, *The Knights of Edward I*, Publications of the Harleian Society, 80, (1929), and 82 (1930), 103-106; M. V. Clarke, *Fourteenth Century Studies* (Oxford, 1937), p. 32; *Chronicle of the Isle of Man*, in *Church Historians of England*, ed. Joseph Stevenson, v, Pt. I (1858), 405; *Historic and Municipal Documents of Ireland* (1172-1320), ed. J. T. Gilbert, Rolls Series (London, 1870), pp. 350, 378, 450. In 1335 John de Mandeville was among the Irish knights ordered to Scotland with horses and arms; *Rotuli Scotiae in Turri Londinensi*, I (1814), 344b.

[5] "A Discovery in John de Mandevilles," *Speculum*, XI (1936), 351-359.

[6] Nos. 17, 19, and 24 concern one or more Irish Sir Johns, and G (among the "unidentified") is also an Irishman, probably the same. Nos. 9 and 11 concern a man who had lands in Dorset and Wiltshire as well as at Buckhorn Weston. Nos. 6, 8, 27, D and K all concern members of this family, who also held land at Nettlebed in Oxfordshire and at Coker in Somerset. Nos. 15 and 16 are probably the same man. Desertion from the army was a felony. See also Warner, p. xxx.

[7] Such as the tinker of Oxford wanted for theft (no. 7), the girdler of London in 1336 (no. 20), and the foot-soldier of London sent to Scotland in 1334 (no. 18).

fication of men in this period. Moreover, he limited his search to men named John, rather than to families who might have had a John capable of knighthood and of the right age in the right neighborhood. Our search is for a young man "born and nurtured" at St. Albans, who was out of England for many years after 1322 but had returned before 1356.

There were a great many Mandeville families in England in the fourteenth century descended from Geoffrey de Mandeville, a companion of William the Conqueror. Geoffrey was granted an enormous estate chiefly in the Home Counties, amounting to 118 lordships, of which 19 were in Hertfordshire, where St. Albans is situated, 40 in adjoining Essex, 30 in Suffolk, and the other 29 scattered over England. The Essex estates were central, and the family seat was established very early at Pleshy, near the middle of that county.

The founder of the family had at least three sons who left heirs. His eldest was William, and according to the recent editors of the Falaise Roll[8] a second son was Stephen, father of Roger, castellan of Exeter and founder of the Devon branch of the Mandevilles. A third was Geoffrey, who was granted fifteen knight's fees and a seat at Marshwood in Dorset, which was still in the family in the fourteenth century. William, the heir of the first Geoffrey, had sons Geoffrey and Walter. Geoffrey was created Earl of Essex by King Stephen, but was outlawed, along with his eldest son, Ernulph, Arnulph, or Arnold. After his father's death in 1144, Ernulph was not restored to his heritage, but was granted other lands, amounting to ten knight's fees, and left several sons who founded families.[9] Walter, the

[8] *Falaise Roll, Recording Prominent Companions of William Duke of Normandy at the Conquest of England*, ed. M. J. Crispin & Leonce Macary (Frome & London, 1938).
[9] J. H. Round, *Geoffrey de Mandeville* (London, 1892), pp. 228 ff. His wife is said to be Alice, sister of Simon de Beauchamp, but this could not be the Simon de Beauchamp who was a son of Pain de Beauchamp and Rohaise de Vere, widow of the first Earl Geoffrey and mother of the second, since Ernulph had grown-up sons and daughters by 1157 or 1158, and Rohaise could not have remarried until after

younger brother of this first Earl Geoffrey, founded the branch of the family seated at Black Notley in Essex, to which we shall return.

Henry II bestowed the forfeited Earldom of Essex on Geoffrey, a younger son of the outlawed Earl, but he had no heirs and his younger brother, William, who inherited the Earldom next, also died without issue. The title and estates passed to Geoffrey Fitz Piers in the right of his wife, a granddaughter of the first William de Mandeville. Fitz Piers took the name of Mandeville, but this line lasted only two generations, and in 1227 the title and estates passed, through marriage with the heiress, to Humphrey de Bohun. The Bohuns held the Earldom for six generations, from 1227 to 1373.

After 1227, therefore, the descendants of this great house who still bore the name of Mandeville, and who were by that time scattered over most of the counties of England, looked to the Bohun Earls as holders of the Honour of Mandeville and representatives of the senior line. Moor, in his study of *The Knights of Edward I* (1239-1307), lists eleven knights named Mandeville, of whom two were named John. One of these is a

---

1144; see G. H. Fowler and M. W. Hughes, *A Calendar of the Pipe Rolls of the Reign of Richard I for Buckinghamshire and Bedfordshire, 1189-1199*, in *Publications of the Bedfordshire Historical Record Society*, VII (1923), 170; and W. Farrer, *Honors and Knights' Fees* (University of Manchester Press, 1925), III, 249. Rannulf, son of Ernulf, witnessed a charter for his uncle, the Earl Geoffrey, in 1157-58; G. F. Warner and H. J. Ellis, *Facsimiles of Royal and Other Charters in the British Museum*, I (London, 1903), No. 43, and note citing *Pipe Rolls, 2-4 Henry II*. For descendants taxed in the castle and hundred of Colchester, see the *Great Roll of the Pipe, Henry the Third*, ed. H. L. Cannon (Yale University Press, 1918), pp. 165, 170. There are records of this branch of the Mandevilles in Yorkshire: see *The Red Book of the Exchequer*, ed. H. Hall (London, Rolls Series, 1896), I, 424, 434. An Ernulph was with Richard II in Palestine in 1191; Lionel Landon, *The Itinerary of King Richard I*, Pipe Roll Society, LI, N.S. XIII (London, 1935), 50, 120, 136. See also *The Great Roll of the Pipe*, ed. D. M. Stenton (1933-40). And for this line at South Mimms in Middlesex, see below, n. 19.

combination of two Johns, so that there were really three.[10] But this is not the place for a catalogue of all the Mandeville families recorded in England in the fourteenth century. We must limit ourselves to Mandevilles in the St. Albans neighborhood, and to two whom I have not been able to connect certainly with that neighborhood, but who are too interesting to pass over in silence.

A record missed by Cameron has been called to my attention by Mrs. Laura Hibbard Loomis and Miss Bertha H. Putnam. It involves the Mandevilles of Marshwood in Dorset, who traced their line back to the companion of the Conqueror.[11] In 1275 the head of the house, a Sir John Mandeville, died, leaving a son and heir named John in the wardship of the king. This John came of age in 1281 and was knighted, and had sons, John and Robert. He died about 1317,[12] leaving his

[10] Moor (n. 4 above) confuses the Sir John Mandeville of Marshwood in Dorset, who died in 1275, with the man of the same name seated at Black Notley in Essex, who died in 1303: see III, 103-104.

[11] John Batten, *Historical and Topographical Collections relating to the Early History of Parts of South Somerset* (Yeovil and London, 1894), traces the pedigree from the first Geoffrey, but is clearly mistaken on several points. For an authoritative pedigree, see *Historical Manuscripts Commission Report. Dean and Chapter at Wells*, I (1907), 527-528; also John Hutchins, *History and Antiquities of the County of Dorset*, 3d ed. II (1863), 260-261. *The Calendar of Inquisitions Post Mortem*, II (1906), 97-100, shows that Sir John Mandeville, the head of this family in 1275, left to his heir East Coker, Hardinton, and Kington, in Somerset, Marshwood, Marteshorne, Weston, and Pyneforde in Dorset, Nettlebed in Oxfordshire, Sutton Mandeville in Wiltshire, and a long list of knight's fees in Devon. Robert, father of Geoffrey, father of this John, bore quarterly *argent* and *vair*, the Mandeville arms with the colors changed to represent a younger branch: see J. Bratten, "Arms of de Mandeville of Coker," *Notes and Queries of Somerset and Dorset*, IV (1894-95), 170-171.

[12] *Cal. of Inq. Post Mortem*, V (1908), 248; Sir Harris Nicolas, *Historic Peerage of England*, ed. W. Courthope (London, 1857), p. 309; *Inquisitions Miscellaneous*, II, 17; W. St. C. Baddeley, *A Cotteswold Manor: being the History of Painswick*, 2d ed. (London, 1929), p. 81 n.; John Collinson, *History and Antiquities of the County of Somerset* (London, 1791), II, 341. In 1316 John, the father of Robert, was certified as one of the lords of Buckhorn Weston, in Dorset; *Parliamentary Writs*,

second son, Robert (said to have been in orders), as his heir. Meanwhile, in 1305, he had alienated Marshwood to Robert Fitz Payn. It has been assumed that his heir, John, predeceased him, but the *Yearbooks of Edward II* for the years 1307-09[13] preserve an interesting record: "Robergia, wife that was of John de Maundeville, demands against Robert Fitzpayn a third part of the manor of Marshwood and of the hundred of Whitchurch as her dower. The tenant [i.e., Fitzpayn] pleads that John has taken the habit of religion in the order of the Hospital of St. John of Jerusalem in England and is still alive, and that Robergia likewise of Buckland Somerset, diocese of Bath and Wells, has taken the habit in the same manner and is professed therein. The Bishop of Bath and Wells is to inquire, and on July 1 he reports that Robergia is professed." Robergia denied that she was professed, and in her interest a certain Willoughby testified that John "died in the town of 'Ypota' in the Greek sea." The John who was the husband of Robergia can hardly be the Sir John who came of age and inherited the Marshwood estates in 1281. As a tenant-in-chief he was active in the king's service, and there are abundant records of him down to 1317, the year of his death (see Cameron's no. 8). More probably Robergia was the relict of his son and heir, named John, who predeceased him. If this John was dead, and she had not herself become "dead" legally by virtue of religious vows, she could apparently claim a dower right in the Marshwood entail.

This record of a Sir John Mandeville, Hospitaler, is sugges-

---

II, pt. iii, p. 1138. Robert's son John (1320-1360) left lands in Buckhorn Weston and Coker in Dorset, Cloverley manor in Devon, and Painswick and Egge in Gloucestershire; *Inq. Post Mortem*, II (1808), 142, 219. Baddeley gives the descent of Coker and Buckhorn Weston, and see John Hutchins, *History and Antiquities of the County of Dorset*, 3d ed. (1870), IV, 115; and *Inq. Post Mortem*, IX (1916), 84, and X, 247.

[13] Ed. for the Selden Society by F. W. Maitland, Vol. 17; Year Books Series, Vol. I (London, 1903), 21-23 and xxxii.

tive, although Marshwood is a long way from St. Albans, and this is a record of 1307-09, not of 1322 or later. It is very interesting as illustration of what might have happened, but this is not our traveler.[14] It calls attention, however, to the activity of the Hospitalers in England in this century. There were five English knights at Cyprus in 1303, each with two squires, and when the headquarters of the order was moved to Rhodes the number of knights was raised to twenty-eight. The order was divided into "Tongues" at Montpellier in 1331, and in 1338 the English "Tongue" had a Grand Priory at Clerkenwell and 137 bailiwicks, manors, or cells in England.[15]

Another John Mandeville of this period (Cameron's no. 25) is recorded as having distinguished himself at Crécy. He is named as "John Mandevill of Belisby" in a long list of men granted a general pardon as reward for their good services at Crécy in November 1346. He was recommended by Walter de Wetewang, keeper of the king's wardrobe.[16] The general pardon did not, of course, mean that these men were criminals. It was, like the general absolution or pardon of the Church, a form of special recognition and a safeguard in case of trouble. Belesby, or Beelsby, in Lincolnshire was held partly of the Bishop of Lincoln, and as early as 1148-68 a Walter de "Amundaville" (a variant of Mandeville) was dapifer, or steward, of the Bishop. He had five knight's fees in Kirkby, where his brother William also had lands.[17] In the fourteenth century the head

[14] See Maitland n. on p. 23, for a similar conclusion.
[15] E. J. King, *The Grand Priory of the Order of the Hospital of St. John of Jerusalem in England* (London, 1924); Charles Cotton, *A Kentish Cartulary of the Order of St. John of Jerusalem*, Kent Records, Kent Archaeological Society, Records Branch, Vol. XI (1930), x, and see above Chap. IV, n. 2 and 3.
[16] George Wrottesley, "Crécy and Calais. From the Public Records," *Collections . . . William Salt Archaeological Society*, XVIII (1897), pt. II, p. 238. Wetwang was Treasurer for the Wars at Calais (1345-48): Joseph Foster, *Some Feudal Coats of Arms* (Oxford, 1902), p. 205.
[17] For records of this family see *Registrum Antiquissimum of the Cathedral Church of Lincoln*, IV, ed. C. W. Foster and Kathleen Major, Lincoln Record Society, XXXII (1937), and V (1940), and see Vols. I-III.

of the Belesby branch of the Mandevilles seems to have been a Robert who held additional land of the manor of Waltham (near St. Albans) of John de Bohun of Midhurst, knight. The John Mandeville who fought at Crécy was probably a younger son, or brother,[18] of this house. He could, conceivably, be our traveler, since this family, although chiefly of Lincolnshire, had interests near St. Albans.

However, the original Mandeville grant lay partly around St. Albans, and there are records of several Mandeville families in this neighborhood. St. Albans is near the southern border of Hertfordshire, having Middlesex on the south and Essex on the East. There were Mandevilles at South Mimms on the border of Middlesex, surrounded on three sides by Hertfordshire parishes belonging to the Abbey of St. Albans. Ernulf, the disinherited son of the first Earl Geoffrey de Mandeville, held land here, for he granted the advowson of the church of

---

Bishop Hugh de Welles of Lincoln made a will in 1212 leaving money to the widow of a Geoffrey de Mandeville and to Thomas, William, Robert, and Robert's wife "Hill'"; see *H. M. C. Report. Wells*, I, 431. His last will, dated 1233, makes no mention of Mandevilles: see *Giraldi Cambrensii Opera*, ed. J. F. Dimock, Rolls Series (London, 1877), VII, Appendix G, pp. 223 ff. But see his register: *Rotuli Hugonis de Welles, Episcopi Lincolniensis 1209-1235*, Lincolnshire Record Society, Vols. 3, 6, 9 (Lincoln, 1912-14), I, ed. W. P. W. Phillimore, pp. v ff; II, 57; III, ed. F. N. Davis, pp. 42, 108, 153, 154, 177, 210 bis.

[18] See *Parl. Writs*, II, iii, 1138; *H.M.C. 14th Report. Appendix, Part VIII. The Manuscripts of Lincoln, Bury St. Edmund's and Great Grimsby* (London, 1895), p. 259; *Cal. of Inq. Post Mortem*, XII (1938), 104, 105. *Feudal Aids*, III, 230; C. W. Foster and T. Longley, *The Lincolnshire Domesday and the Lindsey Survey*, Publications of the Lincoln Record Society, XIX (1924), 64, 246; Rosamond Sillem, *Records of Some Sessions of the Peace in Lincolnshire, 1360-1375*, Lincoln Record Society, XXX (1936), 71; Doris M. Stenton, *The Earliest Lincolnshire Assize Roll (1202-1209)*, Publications of the Lincolnshire Record Society, XXII (1926), 24, 34, 37, 84, 129, 229, 231. Jolani de Mundevile held land of the Bp. of Lincoln at Ouresby in temp. Edw. I, and Robert de Brus had land there also: *Rotuli Hundredorum*, I, 360. See also *Lincolnshire Notes and Queries*, XII (1913), 180; *Cal. of Pat. Rolls, Edw. II*, III, 180. Cameron's no. 13 is a John Mandeville of Cheyle in 1318 who had Lincolnshire connections.

South Mimms to Walden Abbey in Essex, a Mandeville foundation.[19] In 1218-19 Ernulf, son of Ernulf, held the manor of South Mimms and gave lands in that parish to the Abbey of St. Albans.[20] In 1257-58 his son John granted seventy-six acres in Norton, in the liberty of St. Albans, to the Dean and Chapter of St. Paul's in London. In 1335 the charter was confirmed by John de Mandeville of Mimms.[21] A Richard de Mandeville was living at South Mimms in 1337.[22]

Several other John Mandevilles have been noticed in the neighborhood. One, who had a son, John Jr., witnessed a charter at Edmonton in 1313. One witnessed a deed at Little Stanmore in 1300. One was born about 1315 and was living at Enfield, in the same corner of Middlesex, in 1353, but he had apparently lived there all of his life, and so he is not our traveler.[23]

Both Edmonton and Enfield belonged to the estates of the Earls of Essex. They also held Mimms as one knight's fee.[24]

[19] F. C. Cass, *South Mimms* (Westminster, 1877), pp. 8, 14, 18.

[20] He was sued for 300 pounds which his father owed at his manor of Mimms. Crusading was very expensive: *Curia Regis Rolls, 3-4 Henry III* (London, 1938), VIII, 110-111. He also confirmed the gift of the advowson of the church of South Mimms to Walden Abbey (Saffron Walden); F. Brittain, *South Mimms* (Cambridge, 1931), pp. 8-9. And see Cass, pp. 14, 18. A record dated 1334 says these lands were given to the Abbey "in the time of Henry, late King of England, before the statute of Mortmain was enacted," T. Walsingham, *Gesta Abbatum*, ed. H. T. Riley, Rolls Ser. (London, 1867), II, 325. This Ernulph married Galyena de Daunmartin, and was living in 1250-51; *Feet of Fines for Essex*, ed. R. E. G. Kirk, Essex Archaeological Society Publications (Colchester, 1899-1910), I, 187. He was dead by 1253-54; ibid., p. 225; and *Hist. MSS. Comm. Report*, IX (1883), I, 38, nos. 1, 116 and 119. His heir was John, but he also left a son, Sir Hugh, who settled in Ireland.

[21] *Hist. MSS. Comm., Ninth Report*, I, 31, no. 266.

[22] Brittain, pp. 9, 10.

[23] The Edmonton record is noticed by Warner, in his article on Sir John Mandeville in the *D.N.B.* They are Cameron's nos. 33 and 34. The Little Stanmore record is Cameron's no. E, and the Enfield man is Cameron's no. 26.

[24] *Calendar of Inq. Post Mortem* I (1904), 212, Inquisition of 52 Henry III. *Liber Foedorum, The Book of Fees commonly called Testa de Nevill* (1920 ff.), p. 474.

As I have already explained, these Earls were Bohuns who held the Honour of Mandeville through marriage with the Mandeville heiress in 1227. Their lands were intermingled with those of the Abbey, and they numbered several Mandevilles among their tenants. North Mimms was a part of their estates, and they held the manor of Stapleford and had an interest in the next manor of Gobions, in Hertford hundred, and in East Barnet, in Cashio, a hundred which was practically all included in the liberty of St. Albans.[25] They also held the manor of Lockleys in Welwyn, just north of St. Albans. In 1214 Adam de Mandeville had a free tenement in Lockleys. His son and heir was Wilkin. Again in 1288 an Adam de Mandeville was connected with Welwyn, and from 1309 to 1325 a man of that name was sub-tenant of Lockleys, holding of Aymer de Valence, Earl of Pembroke, who went abroad in 1322 and died in France in 1324. This Adam de Mandeville's eldest son was William—but he might have had a younger son John in the service of the Earl.[26]

St. Albans was a substantial town belonging entirely to the Abbey, and since Abbey tenants had to attend the Abbot's court at frequent intervals, probably many found it convenient to keep a house in town. There is a record, for example, of Abbot John's leasing in 1255 the capital messuage of Cashio and a fulling mill to Petronilla de Ameneville (a possible variant of Mandeville) for as long as she should wear a religious habit. She was the widow of Hugh de Ameneville, and in 1271 she married again and released to the Abbot all claim to the manor, saving the right to hunt and fish in the demesne and *the use of a house in St. Albans*.[27] She was evidently a lady

[25] *Victoria History of the County of Hertford*, ed. W. Page (London, 1912 ff.), III, 507; II, 252-253, 331-333.
[26] *Curia Regis Rolls*, VII, 121, 177; *Victoria History*, III, 166. Lockleys was rated as a quarter fee in Welwyn; see *Inq. Post Mortem*, VI, 332; *Feudal Aids*, II, 429, 436; H. C. Andrews, "Lockleys and Some Perients," *East Herts Arch. Soc. Trans.*, VII, pt. 1 (1923) 56, records an Adam de Mandeville in 1282.
[27] *Victoria History*, II, 453. She was the daughter of Roger de Croxely,

of considerable wealth and may have had children by her first marriage. At any rate she was an Abbey tenant who kept a house in town.

The author of the *Travels* says that he was "neez et norriz Dengleterre de la ville Seint Alban." The St. Albans grammar school was famous throughout the Middle Ages. In the early fourteenth century it produced Richard Wallingford, "one of the greatest mathematicians of the middle ages."[28] He was Abbot, 1326-35, having been at Oxford, 1317-26. Born about 1292, he was close to the same age as the author of the *Travels*.

Warner (p. xxx) looked for Mandevilles in the neighborhood of St. Albans, and considered the family seated at Black Notley in central Essex; but he rejected them because in 1322 the head of the house was named Thomas, and his heir was named Walter, and the arms of this family do not correspond with those reported at Liège. He does not consider that there might have been a younger son named John. There are two reasons why our traveler was more likely to have been a younger son than an heir. An heir had inducements to stay at home, for one thing; and, for another, younger sons were usually given more bookish educations than heirs, since there was always the possibility that they might find a living in the church.

The Mandevilles seated at Black Notley were descended from Walter, younger brother of the first Earl Geoffrey. Walter was granted four knight's fees in Essex, at Black Notley, Bromfield, Great Lees, Redleigh, and Chatham.[29] This estate was

---

see H. M. Chew, *English Ecclesiastical Tenants-in-Chief and Knight's Service* (Oxford, 1932), pp. 125-126; Round, *Mandeville*, p. 232, n. 1, mentions the custom of having a house in the county town attached to a manor.

[28] Sarton, *Intro. to Hist. of Science*, III, 278.

[29] The eminent genealogist, J. H. Round, asserts that this family was wholly distinct from the noble line and that they were only feudal tenants of Mandevilles, because they held no lands in chief, and bore *argent*, on a chief indented *gules*, three martlets coupled at the legs *or*: "Architecture and Local History," *Transactions of the Essex Archaeological Society*, xv (1919), pt. 2, pp. 129 ff., and "Descent of Foulkbourne,"

held of the Earl of Essex and continued in the same family of Mandevilles until 1400. In 1261-62 the head of the house was a Sir John Mandeville who died in 1303,[30] leaving Thomas his son and heir. Sir Thomas Mandeville was seated at Bromfield as early as 1296, and had married Ismamian, or Ismena, daughter of Robert de Roos and sister of Sir John Roos, probably of the family of that name which held Great Samford and Radwinter in Essex, and Gildeston in Hertfordshire of the Earl of Essex.[31] Sir Thomas had land and feudal obligations in Hertfordshire in 1301, for in that year he was summoned for military service as of *Essex and Hertfordshire*.[32] He inherited Black Notley and Chatham in 1303, and in 1307-08 he settled the manor of Chatham on his son Walter and Agnes, his wife, probably at the time of their marriage.[33] If Walter was of age at that

---

ibid., xv, n.s. (1918), pt. 1, pp. 54-56. But his evidence is refuted by the clear record of descent of the estate from Walter, younger son of the first William, son of the first Geoffrey de Mandeville. Walter held his lands of his older brother, the first Earl Geoffrey, and so his descendants continued as feudal tenants of the Earls of Essex. P. Morant, *History and Antiquities of the County of Essex*, (London and Chelmesford, 1816), II, 123, citing the *liber ruber*, fol. 92. For other early records of this family, see Farrer, *Honors and Knight's Fees*, III, 252; and *Curia Regis Rolls*, IV, 107, 108; and *Feet of Fines for Essex*, I, 127, 188, 189, 245, also 96, 108, and 118.

[30] This is Cameron's no. 5, and also no. 4, since Borham and Little Waltham are in Essex and formed part of the estates of the Black Notley family, not in "Staffordshire or Warwickshire." This Sir John is confused by Moor with the Marshwood Sir John, and so missed.

[31] *Ancient Deeds*, I, 121, and II, 220. Sir Thomas had a command in the king's army in Scotland in 1298 and 1301: *Parl. Writs*, I, 723; and *Calendar of Documents relating to Scotland*, ed. Joseph Bain (Edinburgh, 1884), II, 317. On Robert de Roos and his son John, see Morant's *Essex*, II, 526, 536; T. Wright, *The History and Topography of the County of Essex* (n.d.), II, 73. Sir John Roos held 10 acres in Walden, a Bohun fief, in 1326.

[32] An Inquisition taken "after 1303," into the extent of the lands of Humphrey de Bohun, sometime Earl of Essex, lists Thomas de Maundevil second among his tenants, holding Bromfield, Notele, and Great Waltham in Essex; *Cal. of Inq. Misc. (Chancery)*, II (1916), 508-510. This was probably taken after the Earl's death in 1322.

[33] *Feet of Fines for Essex*, II, 117.

time, he must have been born by 1287 and could easily have had a younger brother John old enough to go abroad in 1322.

There are records which connect a John Mandeville with this family at this time. As one of his chief tenants, Sir Thomas Mandeville followed Humphrey de Bohun, Earl of Hereford and Essex, to Scotland in 1301. In 1312 he was involved when Earl Humphrey and Guy de Beauchamp, Earl of Warwick, seized Piers Gaveston and executed him. In 1313 when Edward II issued a pardon to all those involved, Sir Thomas Mandeville's name was on the list.[34] It is probable that most, or all, of the five hundred men pardoned were feudal tenants of the two Earls chiefly responsible for the execution. It is also probable that the names were arranged, roughly at least, in the order of precedence.[35] Thomas de Mandeville is seventy-sixth on this list, and numbers 322 and 323 are John and Jordan de Mandeville, numbers 325 and 326 are Simon and Walter de Mandeville. This Walter was, in all probability, Sir Thomas's son and heir.[36] A Simon de Mandeville of Essex appears in the service of one of the Bohuns in 1342.[37] Jordan de Mandeville was certainly of this family, since he acted with Sir Thomas as a witness of a deed for the rectory of Black Notley and also as a witness in a grant which concerned Bromfield. A Jordan de Mandeville, quite possibly this one, is named in a letter of protection for those going to France with the King and Queen later in 1313.[38]

[34] *Calendar of Patent Rolls, Edward II*, II, 21-25; T. Rymer, *Foedera*, ed. A. Clarke and F. Holbrooke (London, 1818), II, i, 230-231.

[35] For an account of the affair, see J. H. Ramsay, *Genesis of Lancaster* (Oxford, 1913), I, 44-51. Immediately after the two Earls, who head the list, the pardon names Henry de Percy, who allowed Gaveston to be taken from his custody, but who had no part in the execution, and Robert Clifford, son-in-law of Earl Humphrey.

[36] Walter died before his father, but he was still living in 1334: *Ancient Deeds*, I, 89, and V, 217.

[37] He was one of the mainpernors to whom the Priory of Priterwell was committed at the request of William de Bohun, younger brother of the Earl of Essex: *Fine Rolls*, V, 262.

[38] T. Rymer, *Foedera*, II, i, 212; Ramsay, pp. 50-51; for his witnessing

The John of this pardon has been identified by both Warner and Cameron as Sir John Mandeville of Marshwood in Dorset.[39] But there is no reason to believe that the Dorsetshire man was concerned in the execution of Gaveston. On the contrary, he was not a tenant of the rebellious earls but held his land partly "in chief," that is, directly from the king, and partly from Sir Hugh Courtenay, who was not involved in the Gaveston affair. Moreover, if he had appeared on the list his name would have been above that of Sir Thomas Mandeville, not far below it because he was a far greater land owner. The John who appears with Jordan was probably a son or brother of Jordan's, and therefore also of the Black Notley family.

There are other records of a John Mandeville in neighborhoods where the Black Notley family had lands, but before we discuss them it will be necessary to dispose of another objection. It has been said that the John of the 1313 pardon would have been too old to have written the *Travels* in 1356. But a boy began his service as a squire when he was fourteen; and even if he was twenty-one in 1313 he would be only sixty-four in 1356. A contemporary, John de Marignolli, went as papal legate to the Great Khan of Cathay in 1339, returned in 1353, and wrote his recollections in 1356 or after—and he is said to have been born before 1290.[40] The John Mandeville of the 1313 pardon could have been of age and still have written a book in 1356.

A John Mandeville (not on Cameron's list) disposed of property and feudal obligations at Borham in Essex in 1320-21. The Black Notley family had property at Borham, as well as at Little Waltham, three or four miles to the east, and at

---

of deeds in 14-15 Edward II, and 19-20 of the same: *Ancient Deeds*, I, 52, 89.

[39] See Warner, Introduction, p. xxx; Cameron's no. 8 citing *Parl. Writs*, II, iii, 1138.

[40] His account of his journey was included in his *Monumenta Historia Boemiae*, which he compiled after his return: see Sir Henry Yule, *Cathay and the Way Thither*, III, 209 ff.

Great Waltham, five or six miles from Borham. According to this record: "John atte Tye of Terlyng and Alice his wife had a settlement with John Mandeville of Borham and Agnes his wife by which the former secured for 20 marks of silver one messuage, sixteen acres of land and one and a half acres of wood in Borham, John atte Tye and his heirs to hold of the chief lords."[41] About the same time, Richard Fillol and Emma his wife had a very similar settlement by which they secured ten acres in Borham from "John de Maundevile and Agnes his wife."[42] Men disposed of land for many different reasons, but one of those reasons was to acquire money for a journey. If this is the John of the pardon, and of the Black Notley family, he had evidently married and had family lands at Borham settled on him.

A John Mandeville appears, or reappears, at Waltham in 1358 as a witness to a grant of property.[43] Again, in 1381, a "John Maundevile of Waltham" (a son or namesake of the former?) was pardoned for killing a man, on a plea of self-defense.[44] In 1386 and 1387 a John Mandeville, Junior, witnessed charters at Waltham.[45] In 1390 letters of attorney were issued to several men of Waltham Holy Cross authorizing them to deliver seisin of lands, etc., in Waltham aforesaid, and the hamlet of "Halyfield" which they had by feoffment of John Caiper, chaplain, John Maundevylle the younger, etc.[46] How

[41] *Feet of Fines for Essex*, II, 199. For a record that Sir John Mandeville, father of Sir Thomas, had lands at Borham, see Cameron's no. 4.
[42] Ibid., II, 203. The record is assigned to 1312-22.
[43] *Cal. of Close Rolls* (1354-60), v, 510.
[44] *Cal. of Pat. Rolls, 1381-85*, p. 51.
[45] Warner, p. xxxi; Cameron, nos. 28 and 29.
[46] *Ancient Deeds*, I, 92-93. A Thomas de Maundeville witnessed a deed of a tenement at West Haningfield, n.d., ibid., I, 91. Haningfield includes three parishes in Essex which lie three or four miles south of Little Waltham and Borham, and here also the Black Notley family had interests. In 1257-58 Sir John Mandeville was sued by Brother Amadaeus de Moriscallo, Master of the Knighthood of the Temple in England, of this "that John should acquit him from the service which William de Albo Monasterio exacts from him for the free tenement which he

many different John Mandevilles of Essex are involved in these records, it is impossible to say, or whether either the Borham or the Waltham man could have been our traveler. But they show at least that there was no lack of John Mandevilles in England and in the vicinity of St. Albans at this time.

But let us return to the problem of whether Simon, John, and Jordan, as well as Walter de Mandeville, were sons of Sir Thomas. Sir Thomas Mandeville lived until 1346. Walter died before him, without issue, and the estate passed to a nephew, who was also named Sir Thomas Mandeville.[47] It is evident, therefore, that the older Sir Thomas had one or more brothers; but if he had other sons, they all died before him without heirs, or they were in orders, or long abroad. Simon seems to have been a clerk, and so probably did not marry. John and Jordan may have been younger brothers of Sir Thomas rather than sons.[48] There is record of a John de Maundeville, clerk, described as "Magister," and therefore a tempting candidate for the authorship of the *Travels*. He served in 1312, and again in

---

holds of John in Haningfield": *Feet of Fines for Essex*, I, 223; see also *Ancient Deeds*, v, 193. In 1338 this tenement, valued at 6 marks, belonged to the Hospitalers: *The Knights Hospitallers in England*, ed. L. B. Larking, Camden Society 65 (1857), 95.

[47] *Feudal Aids*, II (1900), 159, "Dominus Thomas de Maundevill tenet un f. in Bromfield et Chatham, quod Thomas de Maundeville avunculus predicti Thome aliquando tenuit"; the same for Black Notley, ibid., p. 170. Morant is mistaken in making this Thomas the son of Walter, and husband of the de Dronkensford heiress: *Essex*, II, 123. The wife of this Thomas was Elizabeth, probably a Wanton, or Walton: see Morant, II, 411; *Cal. of Inq. Post Mortem*, II, (1808), 162; *Inq. Misc.*, III, 15, 48; *Ancient Deeds*, VI, 214. It was Thomas, the son and heir of this Thomas and Elizabeth, who married Anne de Dronkensford (b. ca. 1357): see Morant II, 75, and cf. I, 179, 444. The *Visitations of Essex*, Harleian Society, XIV (1879), II, 591, omits this generation. For Anne's age: *Cal. of Inq. Post Mortem*, III, 242; for this Sir Thomas: *Ancient Deeds*, III (1900), 311, and I, 390; Farrer, *Honors and Knight's Fees*, II, 25; *Cal. of Inq. Post Mortem*, III, 265; Clutterbuck, *Hertford*, III, 163-164; *Victoria History . . . of Hertford*, III, 317-319.

[48] That would account for their names' appearing above Walter's on the pardon, although the list is probably not rigidly in the order of precedence.

1320 on commissions sent to mediate between Edward II and Robert Bruce.[49]

A member of the Black Notley family would have made a very likely choice for such a mediator, for Robert Bruce was born and reared at Hatfield Broadoak in Essex, in the neighborhood of Black Notley, and Walter de Mandeville's wife was the daughter of Bruce's steward, Nicholas de Barington.[50] When Sir Thomas Mandeville was captured along with his overlord Humphrey de Bohun in the battle of Bannockburn in 1314, the Earl was exchanged for Bruce's wife, and Bruce contributed £94 towards the ransom of Sir Thomas Mandeville, as a way of repaying a debt he owed to Nicholas de Barington.[51] A son or a brother of Sir Thomas, who was also a clerk, would not be an unsuitable choice for a mediator. A man old enough to serve in that capacity in 1312 must have

---

[49] He was thanked by Edward II in 1312 along with two English knights, John de Vallibus and David de Graham: *Rotuli Scotiae in Turri Londinensi*, I (1814), 111b. In 1320 he is one of four clerks, five knights, and three yeomen granted a safe conduct as envoys to Robert Bruce: *Cal. of Patent Rolls, Edw. II*, III, 414. Cameron lists him as no. 10, but suggests that he was a Scot. I see no reason for thinking so.

[50] Morant, *Essex*, II, 502. The de Baringtons had intermarried with the Mandevilles before. According to Sir Philip Sidney's pedigree, Sir Nicholas Barington's mother was Eva, daughter and heiress of Sir William de Mandeville, son of Sir William, son of Sir Geoffrey, son of a Sir William who was a brother of Geoffrey, Earl of Essex: *Miscellanea Genealogica et Heraldica*, II, 161. We read also of a Dru de Barintyn whose daughter Agnes married the Sir John Mandeville, seated at Marshwood in Dorset, who died in 1275. After 1306, the Essex estates of Bruce were granted to the Earl of Essex.

[51] William of Malmesbury's *Chronicle* mentions the capture of Humphrey de Bohun: *Chronicles of the Reigns of Edward I and Edward II*, ed. W. Stubbs, II, (1883), 206. The story of Sir Thomas's ransom is told by G. Alan Lowndes, "History of the Barrington Family," *Trans. of the Essex Archaeol. Society*, N.S., I (1874-76), 262; but he is mistaken in dating the transaction 18 Edw. II. The *H.M.C. Appendix to the Seventh Report*, p. 537, records the license granted 8 Edw. II to Nicholas de Barington to release Robert de Brus from the debt of £94, which sum "Brus" wishes to contribute toward the ransom of Thomas de Mandeville.

THE ENGLISH MANDEVILLES 199

been born at least by 1290 but would not be too old to be our traveler—he need have been no older than John de Marignolli.

There are several records which connect this family with St. Albans. The founders of the line, Walter and Gunnilda de Mandeville, gave to the Abbey a third of the tithes of Notley, Brumfield, Chatham, and Redlegh, as the *Liber Benefactorum* of St. Albans compiled in 1380 records.[52] But a more immediate connection between Sir Thomas Mandeville and St. Albans may have resulted from his marriage with the daughter of Robert de Roos. A Robert de Roos (probably the same) held the manor of Sarratt, in Cashio hundred where the Abbey was situated.[53] Sir Thomas was probably married by 1286, but the family manor of Bromfield was not settled on him until ten years later. It would not have been at all unusual if the young couple had begun their married life in the bride's family home or on her dower lands. The record that in 1301 Sir Thomas had military obligations in Hertfordshire as well as in Essex seems to indicate something of the kind. If he had a younger son John, born before 1296, he might well have been born and sent to school at St. Albans.

One fact emerges from this mass of records. There were many John Mandevilles of families capable of knighthood in England in the fourteenth century. There were several who lived near St. Albans. With all of the records of descendants of

[52] W. Dugdale, *Monasticon Anglicanum*, new ed. by J. Caley, H. Ellis, and B. Bandinel (London, 1819), II, 220. The medieval tithe was commonly divided into three parts, one for the local church, one for the Bishop, and one for the poor, including monks and friars who claimed voluntary poverty: R. H. Snape, *English Monastic Finances in the Later Middle Ages* (London, 1926), pp. 75-76. St. Albans no longer held these tithes in 1290, and perhaps the gift was for one generation only: see *Taxatio Ecclesiastica Angliae et Walliae, ca. 1290*, ed. J. Caley (1802), pp. 26, 27.

[53] In 1336 the manor of Sarrett was settled in fee tail on Robert's son, Sir John Roos, and Alice, his wife: *Feudal Aids*, II, 426; *Feet of Fines, 10 Edward III*, no. 9; *Victoria History of Hertford*, II, 439; H. M. Chew, pp. 124-125. The next two Sir Thomas Mandevilles to hold the Black Notley estate also took brides from Hertfordshire: see above, n. 47.

Ernulph de Mandeville seated at Mimms, and of possible connections of the Black Notley Mandevilles with Abbey lands in Cashio hundred, and of Mandevilles at Edmonton, Enfield, Mimms, and Welwyn on lands held by the Bohun Earls, it is not improbable that there was a John Mandeville born at St. Albans before 1300. However, because the name is so common in this neighborhood it does not seem probable that we will be able to single out the author of the *Travels* for positive identification.

A good reason for going abroad in 1322 is not far to seek. In March of that year occurred the battle of Boroughbridge, in which the followers of Thomas of Lancaster were decisively defeated. Humphrey de Bohun, Earl of Essex, who was among the rebellious Earls, was killed. After his victory, Edward II took stern vengeance on the rebels and their followers. Many were executed, many more were fined and imprisoned, and many fled overseas.[54] Earl Humphrey's sons were disinherited and thrown into prison and his estates were taken into the custody of the crown. His heir, John de Bohun, remained in prison until Edward was deposed in 1326. Sir Thomas Mandeville did not follow his lord into this battle,[55] but all of the Earl's tenants would be required to contribute toward the fines and would share in the consequences, if not in the treason, of their overlord.

I have already mentioned the departure abroad of the Earl

---

[54] See D. H. Leadman, *Battles Fought in Yorkshire* (London, 1891), pp. 52-66; J. H. Ramsay, *The Genesis of Lancaster*, I, 120 ff.; and for the names of many killed in the battle, executed afterwards, fled overseas, or otherwise punished, see *Parl. Writs,* II, ii, Appendix, pp. 200-201, 261 ff., and G. L. Haskins, "A Chronicle of the Civil Wars of Edward II," *Speculum,* XIV (1939), 73-81.

[55] He was appointed by the king to be one of the special conservators of order in Essex, and in July, after the battle, he was summoned for duty against the Scots. In 1324 he was summoned to the Great Council: *Parl. Writs,* II, iii, 1138. He was not a Baron by writ, but in 1324 the Bohun estates were still in the king's hands, and he was therefore temporarily a tenant-in-chief.

of Pembroke after this battle. A band of exiles formed around Roger Mortimer and Queen Isabella at Paris in 1325 and 1326, but there seems to be no record even of the names of the principals, certainly not of their followers. There is a record, however, of a John de Mandeville in Paris in 1327.[56] There is also a record, on a fragment of a Computus Roll of the University of Paris, for 1329 to 1336,[57] of a "Johannes de Sancto Albano" among a large group of students living "in vico Sancti Victoris." There is also a "Johannes Mande vilani" on this roll, but he has been identified (not too convincingly, I think) as the man who became Dean of Nivers in 1332 and Bishop the next year. The Bishop had been a clerk of Charles IV (d. 1328) and seems a little old to have been a student of the University of Paris in 1329 and after.[58] Moreover, this "Johannes Mande vilani" is listed as living in a neighborhood frequented by foreign students. Among them were Oliver Salhadi and his brother, two sons of Douglas with a master, and the son of the Count of Hanover "cum familia."

Our traveler must have been a student at some time in his life, and there is a tradition that he studied at the University of Paris, but it rests on a misinterpretation of a seventeenth-century text.[59] It is a tempting theory, however, in view of the

[56] Noticed by Kervyn de Lettenhove, *Oeuvres de Froissart* (Brussels, 1870-77), I, pt. i, 85, n. 2, citing "Recueil de jugements de la cour de l'Echequier, Bibl. imp. de Paris, f. fr. 5577, fol. 12." The Thomas de Mandeville also mentioned by Lettenhove belongs to the year 1377: see G. Wrottesley, "History of the Bagot Family," *Collections . . . Salt Archaeol. Society*, XI, N.S. (1908), p. 46.

[57] *Chartularium Universitatis Parisiensis*, ed. H. Denifile and A. Chatelain (Paris, 1891), II, i, 668b.

[58] Ibid., 661b, 720. C. Eubel, *Hierarchia Catholica Medii Aevi*, Editio Altera (1913), I, 116, 175, 369; *Gallia Christiana* (Paris, 1771), XII, 647-649, 663. This man was of Clermont in Auvergne and was canon of St. Quentin before he became Dean of Nevers in 1332. In December of 1333 he preached before the King on the state of the soul after death. He died in 1339.

[59] The *Historia Vniversitatis Parisiensis*, by Caesare Egassio Bulaeo (Paris, 1668), has a "Catalogus illustrium Academicorum sexti Seculi," which reports, "Ioannes Mandevylle vir Equestris Ordinis Natione Anglus.

## 202  THE IDENTITY OF THE AUTHOR

fact that in 1322 William Ockham and Marsilius of Padua and John of Jandun were making all Europe ring with their attacks on the temporal authority of the Pope. In 1327 John Buridan was made rector of the University. His discussion of whether the earth rotated on its axis and whether the antipodes were inhabitable is discussed in Chapter 15, below. If our traveler was not in Paris in this decade, he must nevertheless have owed something of his free and inquiring spirit to the intellectual atmosphere created by these men.

Out of this maze of records it would be possible to construct a tentative biography of a Sir John Mandeville, born and educated at St. Albans, who went abroad in 1322. He

---

Studiosissimus si quis vnquam fuit; Theologicis disciplinis instructus, transtulit demum sua studia ad Medicinam, qua in facultate Doctor Parisiensis fuit, vt legitur in Chronico Belgico Magno, p. 293. peregre coepit proficisci an 1332. totumque fere Orientem lustrauit: qua in peregrinatione consumpsit annos 33. vt in Itinerario docet. Obijt an 1372. Leodij, vbi inter Guillelmitas sepultus est" (IV, 964). But if we look in John Pistorius, *Rerum Familiarumque Belgicarum Chronicon Magnum* (Frankfort on Main, 1654), where the *Chronicon Belgiae Magnum* is printed, we read on p. 293, under 1323, a paragraph which begins with the statement that at that time there were the greatest astronomers at Paris, namely, etc. (going on to list an astronomer) and then "Ioannes Mandevil Doctor in Medicina & miles in armis, natione Anglicus, qui mirabilem peregrinationem quasi totius mundi perfecit, et eam tribus linguis explicauit, Odoricus," etc. The account goes on to report the burning of heretics in Paris, but it is not clear that the author intends to associate any but the first name with the University. In any case, it is clear that he is following no better authorities than Radulphus de Rivo (see Chap. 6. n. 20, and Hamelius, Introduction, p. 3) and the *Nuremburg Chronicle* which reads, "Johannes Mandena [sic] qui a ceteris de monte villa appellatur nominatissimus doctor medicine fuit. *as* miles siue eques armatus natione anglic*us* hic magnas partem orbis terre peregrinando p*e*ragravit. & maximus orbis circulator mirabilia mundi p*e*rcipue asie & indie varijs linguis ad oblectationes p*e*rscripsit. & per hec tempora felici fine quievit" (Hartmann Schedellus, *Libri Cronicarum* [1493], fol. ccxxvii). It is possible that Bulæus had other evidence that Mandeville was a Doctor of Theology at Paris, but the authority he cites contains no such record. He may have confused the traveler with the Bishop of Nivers. Sir John was also confused with Henri de Mandeville, author of a work on surgery.

might have been a younger brother or son of Sir Thomas Mandeville, born about 1290 in a town house attached to a manor in the vicinity of St. Albans and left at school at St. Albans when the family took up residence at Bromfield in 1296. By 1312 he would be of age and might have been sent on the royal commission to Scotland to treat with Robert Bruce. The next year he could have been involved in the execution of Gaveston, and so named in the pardon of 1313. The man who went to Scotland in 1312 is probably the same man who went also in 1320. Sometime before 1322 he could have married and had the family lands at Borham settled on him and in 1321-22 disposed of them and gone abroad, perhaps to Paris to study at the University. Let us suppose that his interest in the East led to his wandering off in that direction, probably in the service of some English knight, as a squire who was eventually knighted, or as a member of one of the crusading orders. Let us say that he had taken religious vows, or that his family had lost track of him, and that when Sir Thomas died in 1346 John was presumed to be dead or *was* legally dead, and the estates passed to his cousin as the nearest kin. When he returned to England, perhaps about 1350, we might suppose that he found employment with the current Earl of Essex, Humphrey IX de Bohun; for, when this Earl died in 1361, he remembered among the members of his household a John Mandeville, to whom he left twenty marks.[60]

Such a weaving together of records would make a coherent and plausible story, but the truth is that we do not know, and probably never will know, whether these records concern one man or several men named John Mandeville—or whether any of them are actually records of the man who wrote the *Travels*. They are worth collecting, nevertheless, because they establish the probability that there was such a

[60] J. Nichols, *A Collection of all the Wills ... of the Kings and Queens of England*, etc. (London, 1780), pp. 52 ff. A mark was about two thirds of a pound, and a knight's fee was 20 pounds per annum at that time.

person as the author of the *Travels* represents himself to be. There is further evidence that his account of himself was accepted by those of his contemporaries who were in the best position to know the truth about him, but this matter will take another chapter to explore.

# ⟨14⟩

## SOME FURTHER CLUES

IF THERE was a real traveler named Sir John Mandeville, born and bred at St. Albans, the two places where knowledge of him can be most certainly presumed would be at the Abbey, and at Pleshy in Essex, the seat of the Earls of Essex, representatives of the Honour of Mandeville, whose manors lay around St. Albans in Essex, Hertfordshire and Middlesex. There are records of active interest in the *Travels* and in its author at both of these places before 1400.

Of all the John Mandevilles recorded in fourteenth-century England, perhaps the one most likely to be our traveler is the one who was in the service of the Earl of Essex in 1361. Humphrey IX de Bohun, Earl of Hereford and Essex, who died in that year aged about fifty-three, was a chronic invalid who never married. He was, however, a patron of arts and letters. He inherited the Earldom from his elder brother John in 1335, and in 1338, on the outbreak of war with France, he relinquished his hereditary office as Constable of England to his younger brother William, "because of the feebleness of his body, which, because of long weakness, had kept him from exercising his office of Constable. . . ."[1] Froissart says, however, that he was with his brother at Sluys in 1340, and he apparently took some part in military affairs. He was interested in building, and had the king's license to embattle his houses in Gloucestershire, Essex, Middlesex, and Wiltshire.[2]

---

[1] Rymer, *Foedera*, II, 1042. A document, dated June 12, 1338, describes him *qui tam ob corporis sui imbecillitatem, quam propter infirmitatem diuturnam, quâ detinetur, ad officium Constabulariae praedictae excercendum,* . . . But for his services in the war in '42 and '47 see Rymer, *Syllabus,* pp. 331, 355.

[2] There is an account of him in W. W. Skeat's ed. of *The Romance of William of Palerne,* E.E.T.S., Extra Series, I (1867). He did extensive

He acquired Cold Harbor in London, and he rebuilt the London church of the Austin Friars in 1349, giving it the "small, high, and straight" spire which Stow described as the finest in all London.[3] He was also a patron of letters and collector of beautiful books. There is a famous group of finely illuminated service books still in existence which was made for a Humphrey de Bohun, in all probability this one,[4] and it was for him that *William of Palerne* was written about 1350, very early in the alliterative revival.[5]

When this Earl Humphrey died at Pleshy in 1361 he remembered a John Mandeville among the members of his

---

building at Enfield, which he had the king's license to embattle in 1347: D. Lysons, *Environs of London*, II (1795), 282; R. Clutterbuck, *History and Antiquities of the County Hertford*, III (London, 1827), 370.

[3] *Transactions of the London and Middlesex Archaeological Society*, II (1862), 1-20.

[4] They are described by M. R. James, *The Bohun Manuscripts. A Group of Five Manuscripts Executed in England about 1370 for members of the Bohun Family*, with an Introduction by E. G. Millar, Roxburghe Club Publications, No. 200 (Oxford, 1936). The date in the title is conjectural. I believe that they were made for this Humphrey de Bohun, since they include a request to the reader to pray for the soul of "Humphrey." This could be either the Earl who died in 1361, or his nephew who died in 1373, but the illumination shows the arms of various members of the family, including those of the two sisters of the first Humphrey. It seems to me much more probable that this bachelor would celebrate the marriages of his two sisters than that the young Humphrey (who had married the Earl of Arundel's daughter) would remember the marriages of his aunts, but not record his own in these armorial coats. James's dating involves the arms of Castile which also appear. I think he had the wrong connection in mind. The mother of Humphrey IX (d. 1361) was a daughter of Edward I and Eleanor of Castile. James connects the arms of Castile in the Bohun MSS. with the fact that Mary, the younger of the two daughters of Humphrey X (d. 1373), married the heir of John of Gaunt, and in 1372 John had married Constance of Castile and laid claim to the throne of Castile. It seems more likely that the son would record his grandmother's arms than that the book was made for Humphrey's daughter and recorded the pretensions of her father-in-law and her husband's step-mother.

[5] See Skeat's ed., n. 2 above. The Bohuns were probably the patrons of at least one other poet of the alliterative revival; see below, p. 223.

household, leaving him the substantial sum of twenty marks.[6] The bequests ranged from £100 and a silver service left to his confessor to a mark apiece for the humbler servants. John Mandeville's name occurs well above these servants, along with the names of four knights who were left from 100 marks to £10 apiece. The bequests were probably graduated both by the beneficiary's rank and by length of service. If there was such a man as the author of the *Travels* represents himself to have been, there could hardly have been a more likely place for him to find refuge in his old age than in the service of this Earl of Essex.

The successive masters of Pleshy in Essex were bookish men whose literary patronage has curious connections with Mandeville's *Travels*. The invalid Earl Humphrey who died in 1361 left as his heir his nephew, Humphrey X, to whom John Erghom dedicated his satirical *Prophecies of John of Bridlington*. There is a good Norman-French text of the *Travels*, described as "written about 1400 (or a little earlier)," bound up with an early and important text of Erghom's *Prophecies*.[7] It is unique in that it describes Erghom as "Laici." He was an Austin Friar (an order which was under the special patronage of the Bohuns),[8] but the *Prophecies* may have been written before he joined the Order. There must have been a presentation copy of his work in the Bohun library, and it may have been in that library that the *Prophecies* and the *Travels* came together and were copied into the same manuscript. The *Prophecies* are usually dated 1362 or 1363, about five years after the *Travels*.

There was a copy of the *Travels* at Pleshy in 1397, but how

---

[6] See Chap. 13, n. 60.

[7] This is Ashmole 1804: see W. H. Black, *A Descriptive . . . Catalogue of Manuscripts bequeathed unto the University of Oxford by Elias Ashmole* (Oxford, 1845), cols. 1510-11. The *Prophecies* follow the *Travels*, beginning on the verso of the last leaf.

[8] A. Gwynn, *The English Austin Friars in the Time of Wyclif* (Oxford, 1940).

long it had been there we do not know. There is reason to believe, however, that Thomas, Duke of Gloucester, master of Pleshy, 1380-97, was especially interested in the book. Humphrey X de Bohun had died in 1373, leaving two small daughters as coheiresses. The elder was Eleanor, who married Edward III's youngest son, Thomas, Duke of Gloucester. Gloucester took up his residence at Pleshy about 1380, and it was from there that he was lured to his death by Richard II in 1397. The Inventory of the Duke's goods, made after the murder, enumerates eighty-four volumes of a very interesting library, including a *Mandeville*, bound in red.[9] The record of books at Pleshy goes back to the Earl Humphrey de Bohun killed at Boroughbridge in 1322, who mentions several books in his will.[10] The invalid Earl Humphrey (d. 1361) certainly added to the collection. But Thomas of Gloucester was also a bookish man and a patron of letters.

One of his scholarly protégés was Thomas de Burton, author of the *Chronica Monasterii de Melsa*[11] in which appears one of the first notices of Mandeville. Thomas de Burton wrote his chronicle between 1388 and 1396. In it he tells no more of Mandeville than he could learn from a copy of the Norman-

---

[9] Viscount Dillon and W. H. St. John Hope, "Inventory of the Goods and Chattels Belonging to Thomas, Duke of Gloucester, and seized in his castle at Pleshy, Co. Essex, 21 Richard II (1397); with their Values, as shown in the Escheator's Accounts," *Archaeological Journal*, LIV (1897), 300-303. The books are listed in *Johanne Gower, Poema Quod Dicitur Vox Clamantis*, ed. H. O. Coxe, for the Roxburghe Club (1850), pp. xlvi-lii, n. Gloucester bought B.M. MS. Royal 19 B XIII from Sir Richard Stury. MS. Harley 2942 belonged to him, and Bodley 316. For books he gave to the college he founded at Pleshy: see M. R. James, *Transactions of the Essex Archaeological Society*, N.S. 21 (1933), 34-46.

[10] T. H. Turner, "The Will of Humphrey de Bohun, Earl of Hereford and Essex, with Extracts from the Inventory of his Effects, A.D. 1319-1322," *The Archaeological Journal*, II (1846), 339-349.

[11] *Chronica Monasterii de Melsa*, ed. E. A. Bond, Rolls Ser. (London, 1866-68), Introduction, pp. lxii ff. For the notice of Mandeville, see Vol. III, 158. Thomas de Burton was forced upon his house, Meaux Abbey in Yorkshire, as Abbot (1396-99), by the Duke of Gloucester, who, as Lord of Holderness, stood in the relation of founder to the Abbey.

French text of the *Travels* which contained the dedication to Edward III. This may have been the copy in the Duke's own library, for the dedication must have been written either before Edward's death in 1377, or as a compliment to one of his sons.

There are records of two other copies of the *Travels* owned by men within the Duke of Gloucester's sphere of influence. In 1399 Thomas Roos, son of Sir Robert Roos of Ingmanthorp in Yorkshire, willed a "Maundevyl" to a friend,[12] The Rooses were an important northern family with estates chiefly in Holderness, where the Duke of Gloucester was overlord. The will of John of Scardeburgh, rector of Tichmarsh in York diocese, proved in 1395, mentions a copy of *Mandeville* in French, on paper, worth 2 shillings.[13] From the list of his benefices it appears that John enjoyed the patronage of the Duke of Gloucester.

Either the *Travels* was especially popular in Yorkshire or the connection of these three men with the Duke of Gloucester is significant. One surviving manuscript also comes from this district. Harleian MS. 212 is a fairly good Norman-French text probably written in the fourteenth century. In 1425 it was given to "the lady house of Bolton in Craven," an Augustinian Priory in the West Riding of Yorkshire.[14]

These bits of evidence that the masters of Pleshy took a special interest in the *Travels* do not help us to determine whether the interest issued from family pride, interest in the Holy Land, or literary taste. However, if the name "Sir John

---

[12] *Testamenta Eboraciensis*, Publications of the Surtees Society (1836), I, 251-253.

[13] *Test. Ebor.*, III, 6. He was a man of considerable wealth who left a remarkable library. In 1380, when Richard II was a minor and Gloucester was a leading member of the regency council, he was presented "by the king" to a stall in the chapel of St. Mary and the Angels at York. He made a handsome bequest to Thomas Arundel, Archbishop of Canterbury, formerly Archbishop of York, and uncle of Gloucester's mother-in-law.

[14] See Appendix I, p. 265.

Mandeville" was fictitious, or if the attribution of the *Travels* to a famous traveler of that name was spurious, the deception was not discovered by those best able to ascertain the truth. Thomas de Burton accepted the autobiographical matter in the *Travels* in good faith, and so did the famous St. Albans chronicler, Thomas Walsingham, who also enjoyed the favor of Thomas of Gloucester. Walsingham compiled a list of the distinguished people connected with St. Albans, including "Sir John de Mandeville, Knight, wanderer over almost the whole earth, and in many wars against the adversaries of our faith active, but not at all weary, he composed a book in French about what he had seen. This man was brought forth from his mother's womb in the town (*villa*) of St. Albans."[15] There is nothing in this notice which could not be inferred from the text of the *Travels*, but Walsingham evidently had no suspicion that what he found there was not true. Moreover, if he was writing after the first English translation began to circulate (ca. 1390), he was either unaware of it or aware that its claim that the author wrote in three languages was not true. Walsingham's notice may have been written as early as the 1370's or as late as 1396.[16]

There are two further early evidences of belief in a real Sir John Mandeville at St. Albans. The treasury had one or more rings which he was believed to have presented,[17] and before

---

[15] *Annales Monasterii S. Albani a Johannes Amundesham*, ed. H. T. Riley, Rolls Ser. (London, 1871), dates the list 1391-94. For the Notice, see II, 306, Appendix E, from British Museum MS. Cotton Claudius E. IV.

[16] V. A. Galbraith, *The St. Albans Chronicle, 1406-1420* (Clarendon Press, 1937), pp. lviii-lix dates the composition 1393-96, the actual date of writing of the extant manuscript. The list in which this notice occurs is bound up with the *Gesta Abbatum*, along with several other small tracts probably written earlier.

[17] *Annales*, II, 331. This manuscript is now bound up with MS. VII of Corpus Christi College, Cambridge. It is printed in *Johannis de Trokelowe et Henrici de Blaneforde Monachorum S. Albani, Chronica et Annales*, ed. H. T. Riley, Chronicles and Memorials Series (London, 1866), p. 454. Riley argues (p. xliii), that the version in Cotton Nero

## SOME FURTHER CLUES

the end of the fourteenth century the library had a Latin translation of the *Travels* made from the Norman French. This translation appears in a manuscript which was certainly written at St. Albans and at the direction of Thomas Walsingham, since it contains also his chronicle of England from 1272 to 1393.[18]

Walsingham's *Chronicle* was compiled before he left St. Albans in 1394 to become Prior of the cell at Wymundeham.[19] After his return, and probably after the accession of Henry IV, the *Chronicle* was revised and shifted from the beginning of the volume to the end, and the Latin *Travels*, originally contained in quires 21, 22 and 24 (quire 23 contained a complete short history of England) was brought together, although that involved the rewriting of the outside leaf of quire 22.

Whether this translation of the *Travels* was actually made at St. Albans, or merely copied there, we do not know, but we do know that Walsingham was aware that the original was in French, and not in three languages, as the English translation asserted. There are four other surviving copies of this Latin translation, all made in the fifteenth century, and this Latin version was turned into English.[20]

Walsingham's interest in Mandeville, which produced the

---

D. VII is the later one, but Galbraith (pp. xxvi-vii) points out that it is clearly dated 1380, while the Cambridge manuscript belongs to the later years of the Abbot Thomas (d. 1396). There are additions after 1413, and this item is among the additions. But the items are arranged in the order of importance of the donors, not in chronological order. Walsingham died in 1420.

[18] See Galbraith, op cit. The MS is B.M. Royal 13 E IX.

[19] Galbraith, p. li, n. 1, and pp. ix-x, xlvi-vii; Thomas Walsingham, *Historia Anglicana*, ed. H. T. Riley, Rolls Ser. (London, 1864), II, ix ff.

[20] These are B.M. Cotton Appendix IV, fols. 59-102; Harley 175; Hunterian Museum (Glasgow) T 4.1; and Durham University Library, Cosin v. iii. 7. For the identification of this last I am indebted to Mr. R. A. B. Mynors. This version of the *Travels* is described by Vogels, but he does not mention the fact that the earliest copy was written at St. Albans. For the English translation see Appendix I. The Egerton MS. version may also have come from St. Albans. See below, p. 237 ff.

notices in the appendix to the *Gesta Abbatum* and in the *Liber Benefactorum* and (whether he actually translated, or copied it, or not) the Latin version of the *Travels* in the manuscript of his *Chronicle*, evidently was inspired by Mandeville's statement that he was born and bred at St. Albans. It is possible that this recognition of the traveler was merely a manifestation of local pride which accepted an honor thrust upon the community, without knowing the identity of the man who, nevertheless, bore a name familiar in the neighborhood. Probably the attribution of the rings was a fraud, like that practised by the monks of St. William of Liège at a much later date. But if anyone in England knew the identity of the author of the *Travels*, the St. Albans chronicler is the most likely person to have known it, since he was a historian and antiquarian, and a contemporary. Next to him, the masters of Pleshy in Essex are most likely. The records of interest in the *Travels* and in Sir John Mandeville, preserved in both places, point to some knowledge, though they do not prove it. The man who completed his book in 1356 could easily have been in the service of the Earl of Essex who died in 1361; but he was almost certainly dead before the Duke of Gloucester became master of Pleshy, about 1380, and there is no certainty that Thomas Walsingham's notices were written earlier than 1380.

However, we must take into account the fact, overlooked in earlier discussions of Mandeville's identity, that two reputable English chroniclers before 1400 accepted as genuine Sir John Mandeville and the biographical data in his *Travels*, so that the English records are fully as early as the Liège fabrications of Jean d'Outremeuse. The fact that he is mentioned both by the St. Albans chronicler and by a historian in the service of the Duke of Gloucester makes it less probable that the name "Sir John Mandeville" was assumed, or that the work was written by a man who had not traveled at all, but who fathered it on a famous traveler of that name.

One other record of the *Travels* in England before 1400 is a second translation of the work into Latin. It is preserved in a manuscript written at Abingdon, near Oxford, by a monk named Richard Bledelewe, in 1390.[21] It is a different and fuller translation than that in the St. Albans manuscript. Abingdon was a Benedictine house, like St. Albans; the two had a close relationship in financial matters and a mutual interest in Oxford, and especially in the college of their order there.

Other records of Mandeville, in England, belong to the sixteenth century, and carry very little weight. We cannot put any confidence in the tradition, reported by Norden in 1599, that there was once a cross-legged effigy of Mandeville, in armor, in the Abbey of St. Albans. Weaver in his *Ancient Funerall Monuments* (1631) ridicules the tablet set up there in his day to commemorate the traveler. He was convinced by the Liège epitaph. But the Elizabethan tradition of Duke Humphrey's monument at St. Paul's in London shows how unreliable such traditions could be. Neither can we credit the note in Douce MS. 109 in the Bodleian (a fifteenth-century copy of the *Travels* in English), that "the original manuscript of his travels was late the property of George Scott, esq., and, before 1746, in the possession of Mr. William Thompson, fellow of Queen's College, Oxford," who noted in it, "N.B. I had this book from a descendant by the mother's side, from Sir John Mandeville, W. T."[22]

John Leland's remarks are of a different order, however. Unlike the reports of Burton and Walsingham, they are not based entirely on the text of the *Travels,* nor has he heard of the Liège tradition picked up soon afterwards by Bishop Bale. He says, "I remember having heard much of Mandeville when I was a little boy, from a certain Jordan, a very old man, not

---

[21] Leyden MS. Vulcaniani 96; see *Bibliotheca Universitatis Leidenensis. Codices Manuscripti,* I (1910), 39; and see Warner's Introduction, p. vii, and Vogels. Bledelewe is named in the refectorer's account in 1422-23: R. E. G. Kirk, ed., *Accounts of the Obedientiars of Abingdon Abbey,* Camden Society, 51 (1892), 19.

[22] R. Clutterbuck, *History . . . of Hertford,* I, 82, n. h.

only of the things that he had done, but also of the place of his burial, of which my memory now holds hardly a shadow."[23] Leland grew up in London and was educated at St. Paul's School. The name "Jordan" is tantalizing, therefore, because there is a connection between the Mandevilles of Black Notley in Essex and a Jordan, or Jurdan family of London. I have already discussed the Jordan Mandeville of the 1313 pardon, who was certainly a member of the Black Notley family. In 1317 Avice Jurdan *of London* complained that Sir Thomas Mandeville of Essex, with many others, had broken into "Great Leighe" and carried off charters and valuable papers.[24] The manor of Great Lees had formerly been a part of the estates of the Mandevilles seated at Black Notley, and Sir Thomas' raid was obviously a move in a quarrel over property, probably a family quarrel.[25] The Jordan to whom Leland talked in London may have been a descendant of the same family as this "Avice Jurdan of London" and Leland's lapse of memory may have cost us a positive identification of the author of the *Travels*.

Leland goes on to say, however, that Mandeville was of the family of noble Mandevilles and he adds, "Some think he was of Hainville, where Sir Thomas Lovell built a splendid house in our memory." According to Camden,[26] Sir Thomas Lovell built a house at Enfield. There were several manors at Enfield, of which Lovell inherited Worcesters, or Wroths Place, and built Elsynge Hall, on the manor of Elsynges, where he died.[27]

---

[23] J. Leland, *Commentarii de Scriptoribus Britannicis*, ed. A. Hall (Oxford, 1709), II, 366-68.

[24] *Cal. of Patent Rolls, Edward II*, III, 81.

[25] I did not find any trace of Sir Thomas Mandeville's mother's name. His father was Sir John Mandeville, son of Sir Thomas Mandeville, who in turn was grandson and heir of Ralph de Mandeville. In 1212 Milisent, widow of Ralph, sued for land in Brumfield which she claimed as her dowry. Ralph was the heir of his uncle, Walter de Mandeville. Mirabilis de Mandeville, wife of Walter, also had lands as her dowry (*Curia Regis Rolls*, VI, 396). Perhaps Great Lees had been alienated in this way.

[26] W. Robinson, *History and Antiquities of Enfield* (London, 1823), I, 103-132.

[27] J. S. Brewer, *Calendar . . . Domestic and Foreign, Henry VIII*, IV, Pt. I, 154, n. 366.

## SOME FURTHER CLUES

Enfield was one of the chief seats of the Earls of Essex, and the Earl Humphrey who died in 1361 did extensive building there. In the time of Edward III a "Jordan de Elsynge" had two-fifths of a knight's fee at Enfield which he held of the Earl of Essex and Hereford, and a man of the same name was there in 1417.[28]

"Hainville" seems a curious corruption of "Enfield" although it is an easy auditory mistake. I have found no "Hainville," although Morant says that Haningfield in Essex was vulgarly called "Hanville."[29] And there was a Haningfield in East Barnet, just west of Enfield, in the St. Albans neighborhood. East Barnet is in Cashio hundred, in Hertfordshire, which belonged to the Abbey lands.[30] Records of John Mandevilles in this neighborhood have already been noticed. Leland's story has coherence and plausibility, and it has the virtue of being independent, although he took his dates for the *Travels* from Pynson's text, which read 1332 and 1366 instead of 1322 and 1356. He also credits the story that the book was approved by the Pope, whom he names Urban V (1362-70), obviously inferring the Pope from the mistaken date of completion in the printed text. He compares Mandeville to Marco Polo and Ulysses, saying that on his return he was recognized by few, a remark which may have been prompted by the comparisons, but which Bale picked up and elaborated upon. Leland was also acquainted with the notice of Mandeville in the *Nuremberg Chronicle*,[31] but his most important fact he had forgotten.

Once the web of fiction which has for so long connected the author of the *Travels* with Liège is swept away, the superiority of the Norman-French texts and their English provenance make it probable that Sir John Mandeville was in fact an Englishman, writing in England. The evidence of Mandeville families capable of knighthood living near St. Albans in the early fourteenth century gives credibility to his statement

---
[28] Robinson, I, 158.
[29] *Essex*, II, 35.
[30] See above, chap. 13, n. 46.
[31] Hartmann Schedel, *Libri Cronicarum* (Nuremberg, 1493), fol. ccxxvii.

that he was born and nurtured there. The interest in the *Travels* shown by Thomas of Walsingham, the St. Albans chronicler, and by Thomas Duke of Gloucester, the head (in the right of his wife) of the family descending from the senior line of noble Mandevilles, while it does not prove that they knew any more than they read in the *Travels*, at least suggests that they had no reason to doubt the biographical information given there. If the name "Sir John Mandeville" was a hoax, it was a very clever and plausible one, not detected by those most likely to know the truth. With the records now available, we cannot hope to produce a positive identification, but there is plenty of circumstantial evidence to support the author's claim. There is no valid evidence to refute it. We must therefore accept it and look upon it not as a part of a fictitious narrative but as part of the documentation by which the author gave his fictions verisimilitude. It could not serve that purpose, however, unless Sir John Mandeville had indeed been abroad for many years.

In the end we know no more about him than he tells us in his book; the investigations reported in the last several chapters are, nevertheless, very much worth while if they clear away the debris of mistakes and misinformation under which the author of the *Travels* has been buried and which has prevented the enjoyment of a literary treasure of considerable importance. Because it is a finished work of art, the *Travels* would still tell us more that is pertinent to literature about the author than a whole volume of dates and circumstances could. But the incrustation of *false* biographical data and of mistaken criticism, which has been accumulating for over five centuries, has made it impossible to see the *Travels* at all as a sincere work of art. It is as a work of art—the expression of a personality and of a point of view giving form and color to interesting matter, shaping and arranging and proportioning it, and giving it permanence through appropriate utterance—that the *Travels* should be read.

# PART III
# THE REPUTATION AND INFLUENCE OF THE *TRAVELS*

PRESTER JOHN HONORS THE CROSS

THE VEGETABLE LAMB AND SOME BARNACLE GEESE

# THE FIRST TWO CENTURIES

THE IMMEDIATE popularity of the *Travels* is indicated both by the rapid multiplication of manuscripts and translations and by borrowings and allusions too numerous for more than an exploratory survey here. Of about 250 surviving manuscripts, 73 are in German and Dutch, 37 in French, about 50 in Latin, and about 40 in English. The rest are in Spanish, Italian, Danish, Czech, and Old Irish.[1] Over three times as many manuscripts of Mandeville's *Travels* survive as of either Odoric's or Marco Polo's. Before the Reformation the *Travels* was especially popular in England, where the forty manuscripts in English represent at least three different translations. The English also made four translations into Latin, and eighteen of the surviving French manuscripts are written in English hands.

Yet many more manuscripts must have perished than survive. Mandeville's mention of relics, saints' legends, and even of popes made the *Travels* suspect to the early Protestants. Some of the extant English manuscripts show mutilation where a pope is named. The destruction of the monastic libraries which Bishop Bale so eloquently described, when books were shipped abroad by the boatload, probably accounts for the fact that the Latin manuscript copied at Abingdon by Richard Bledelewe in 1390 has long been at Leyden.[2]

The popularity of the *Travels* in Germany and the Low Countries was hardly second to that in England. Most of the manuscripts of the Latin vulgate are preserved there. It was on the continent that Odoric's *Itinerary* was sometimes recom-

---
[1] See Appendix I.
[2] See p. 213, & n. 21. Pinelo's epitome of Barcia, I, 21, lists it in 1737.

mended to its readers as the work of a companion of the more famous Sir John Mandeville.[3]

Originating in England in the year of the great victory at Poitiers, the *Travels* was quickly carried to France, where we know that it was circulating in a revised version before 1371. This version was carried to Italy, Spain, and Germany, as well as to Liège in Flanders. Michel Velser, or Felser, made a translation of it into German which proved popular. It was translated into Italian and twice into Spanish. At Liège a second redaction was made, probably before 1390, and this Ogier version served as the basis both for the Latin vulgate and for Otto von Diemeringen's translation into German. Otto's version served, in turn, as the basis of the Danish and Czech translations, as well as for one Dutch version. By 1400 the *Travels* was available in all the major languages of Europe.

From the first, the *Travels* was a popular work. It was written in French because literate English laymen could more easily read French than Latin, and it was turned into the other languages of Europe for a similar reason. It was written for the entertainment of laymen, and was therefore "popular" in the sense of "non-learned." But it was popular in the other sense also. It appealed to the many. Most of the manuscripts are inexpensive ones,[4] often on paper, seldom illuminated—although a few were expensively made for noble and royal readers. Most of the manuscripts are in a cursive hand which, if it does not actually mark the amateur copyist, was certainly faster, and therefore cheaper, than the book hand.

The fabrications of Jean d'Outremeuse are testimony of the

---

[3] A manuscript in the Wolfenbüttel National Library, no. 40, and another in the Mayence Cathedral Library make this claim. The latter reads: "Oderici, socii militis Mandavil per Indiam"; see H. Cordier, *Mélanges*, I, 7, 52, and his edition of *Odoric*, pp. lxxii, lxxv. The statement occurs also in *De orbis situ ac descriptione . . . epistola* (Martin Caesar for Roland Bollaert, Antwerp, ca. 1524).

[4] John of Scardeburgh's copy was on paper and valued at 2 shillings: see Chap. 14, n. 13. The copy at Pleshy was valued at 5 shillings: Chap. 14, n. 9.

popularity of the *Travels*. His invention of lapidaries, and even of the tombstone, would not have been successful if others had not shared his enthusiasm for the English traveler. Other evidence of Mandeville's popularity is provided by the references to, and borrowing from, his book in the writings of his immediate successors in both England and France. His *Travels* seems to have been popular with the creators of the English alliterative revival, several of whom show indebtedness to it.

It has been recognized that the *Pearl* poet borrowed from the French text of the *Travels* for a passage in his early poem, *Purity*, or *Clannesse*.[5] In fact, misinformation about the *Travels* has affected the dating of this poem. Because of the belief that the *Travels* was not written before 1366, and that it began to circulate at Liège and was not known in England before 1370, the composition of *Clannesse* has been dated "1370 or after."[6] But, so far as the debt to the *Travels* is concerned, it could have been written over a decade earlier.

A second poet of the alliterative revival, the author of the *Morte Arthure*, shows an acquaintance with the *Travels*. Near the beginning of the poem a banquet is described which includes on the bill-of-fare "Pygges of porke despyne" (line 183). The *New English Dictionary* cites this as the first appearance of the word "porcupine" in English. However, Mandeville says

---

[5] Carleton Brown, "The Authorship of *The Pearl*, Considered in the Light of his Theological Opinions," *PMLA*, XIX (1904), 149-153; and W. H. Schofield, "The Nature and Fabric of the *Pearl*," ibid., 189-190.

[6] Brown argues that the poem, *Clannesse*, must have been written after 1370 because *Mandeville* was not known in England before that date. Sir Israel Gollancz points out a parallel passage in the *Book of the Knight of La Tour Landry* (1371-72 or '73), but it is by no means a certain borrowing: *Selected Early English Poems*, VII (London, 1921), xxiii-xxviii. Attempts to show that *Clannesse* borrowed from the B-text of *Piers Plowman* prove nothing, because the borrowing could have been the other way: R. J. Menner, ed., *Purity*, Yale Studies in English, LXI (1920), xxviii-xxx. See also the introductory essays of Mable Day and Mary S. Serjeantson to Sir I. Gollancz's ed. of *Sir Gawain and the Green Knight*, E.E.T.S., O.S., 210 (1940).

of India, "And there be also urchins (hericons, Fr. hérissons), as great as wild swine here; we clepe them Porcz de Spine" (Pollard, p. 191; Warner, p. 143, "Porcz Spinous"). There are other references in the poem which strongly suggest a reading of the *Travels*. Another item on the menu is "Barnakes" (line 189). "Bernakes" is the *Travels*' name for barnacle geese (Pollard, p. 174). The Norman-French text reads "oisealx" (Warner, p. 130), however, and the name supplied by the English translator must have been a current one which must have come from other sources. Near the middle of the poem, Lucius is represented as having sent for help to many lands, "To Inde and to Ermony, as Eufrates rynnes," summoning kings "of Crete and of Capados" and from "Tartary and Turkey" and "The flour of the faire folke, of Amazonnes landes" and of " Perce, and Pamphile, and Prester Iohne landes,' with the "Sowdane of Surrey and sextene kynges" (ll. 570-609). Evidently the author had been reading about the Orient; the reference to porcupines seems to indicate a particular work that he had been reading.

The poets of the alliterative revival borrowed so freely from one another that it is probable they comprised a "school" or group of poets who knew each other and took a special interest in each other's productions. A study of the dialects they used points to the West and Northwest Midlands as the place where they originated, and the very probable suggestion has been made that the revival was patronized by the nobility of the Welsh Marches.[7] The Bohuns were prominent among the Marcher Earls, with estates in Gloucestershire, Herefordshire, and farther west in Pembrokeshire. They also held the Honour of Brecknock in North Wales.

Their connection with the poets of the alliterative revival is established by the dedication of perhaps the earliest poem of

[7] J. R. Hulbert, "A Hypothesis Concerning the Alliterative Revival," *Modern Philology*, XXVIII (1930), 405-422. For discussion of the dialects of the poems, see J. P. Oakden, *Alliterative Poetry in Middle English* (Manchester University Press, 1930), Pub. of the Univ. of Manchester, No. 205, English Series, XIX.

THE FIRST TWO CENTURIES 223

the revival, *William of Palerne*, to the invalid Earl Humphrey de Bohun. The alliterative *Romance of the Chevelere Assigne* was almost certainly written for a member of the Bohun family. It is a version of the first part of the swan-knight story, omitting all of the genealogical matter which, in the French version, connects the swan-knight with Godfrey of Boulogne. The Bohuns used the swan as their badge and showed a special interest in the story, although I cannot find that they claimed descent from Godfrey. The Bohun Earl who died at Boroughbridge (1322) left a bed "powdered with swans," and one of his sons was named Enias, the name of the swan-knight.[8] His great-granddaughter Eleanor, wife of the unfortunate Duke of Gloucester, left to her son a copy of the *Historie de chevaler a cigne*. She also mentions in her will a bed embroidered with swans, and a Psalter decorated with swans.[9] It is a natural assumption that the author of the alliterative poem about the swan-knight wrote under Bohun patronage.

Because of these suggestive connections——that of the Bohuns with the alliterative revival, that of the *Pearl* poet with the *Travels*, and that of the Bohuns with at least the name "Mandeville"——one further document seems worth noticing. Macray suggested that Bodley MS. 264, one of the great treasures of the Bodleian Library, is to be identified with the book described in the inventory of the Duke of Gloucester's library at

[8] T. H. Turner, "The Will of Humphrey de Bohun, Earl of Hereford and Essex . . . 1319-1322," *The Archaeological Journal*, II (1846), 339-349. In 1301 the seal of this Bohun Earl showed a swan: Nicholas Harris Nicolas, "Remarks on the Seals affixed to two Documents . . . in the Year 1301. . . ." *Archaeologia*, XXI (1827), 196-198. The contemporary Earl of Warwick (d. 1315) was named Guy, and two of his grandsons were Guy and Reynburne.

[9] J. Nichols, *Collections of . . . Wills*, p. 181; or Sir Nicholas H. Nicolas, *Testamenta Vetusta* (London, 1826), I, 148. The families of Tony, Beauchamp, and Stafford also used the swan as a badge in the 14th and 15th centuries: Laura A. Hibbard, *Mediæval Romance in England* (New York, 1924), p. 250. The Beauchamps were intricately interrelated with the Bohuns, and the Tonys with both, while the Stafford claim clearly derived from the Bohuns.

Pleshy as "un large livre en ffraunceis tresbien esluminez de la Rymance de Alexandre et de les avowes al poun."[10] This manuscript was written in 1338 and illuminated by a Flemish artist in 1344. It seems to have originated on the continent but may have been commissioned by someone in the retinue of Edward III, who was in Flanders in 1338-39.[11] This manuscript is connected with the alliterative revival in a curious way. About 1400 the alliterative fragment known as *Alexander and Dindimus* was added to the French text, and a note was inserted into that text, indicating where this matter had been "omitted." If this manuscript is from the Bohun library at Pleshy, it is one more link between that family, the alliterative revival, and interest in the Orient.

Some effort has been made to find echoes of Mandeville in Chaucer's works, but without any unquestionable results.[12]

---

[10] W. D. Macray, *Annals of the Bodleian Library, Oxford*, 2d ed. (Oxford, 1890), p. 21, n. 2. And see M. R. James, *The Romance of Alexander: A Colotype Facsimile of MS. Bodley 264* (Oxford, 1933), which suggests that the book was made for the Scotch king because the shield given to Alexander the Great, "*or,* a lion rampant *gules*" lacks only the "double tressure" of the arms of Scotland. But the traditional arms of Alexander, as in the 14th century tapestry in The Cloisters (New York, Metropolitan Museum of Art), were "*Gules,* a lion rampant *or* in a chair." It seems about as likely that the arms were intended for Alexander as for Scotland.

[11] James notes (pp. 4-5) that Edward III was in Belgium in 1338-39. He arrived in July 1338 with the Queen and the Earls of Derby, Suffolk, Salisbury, and Northampton (William de Bohun, Duke Humphrey's brother), and the Bishops of Canterbury, Lincoln, and Durham (Richard of Bury). The party stayed chiefly at Antwerp, where Lionel, Duke of Clarence, was born. The king returned to England in September 1339, leaving the Queen at Ghent (Gaunt) where John was born. The King was in Flanders again from June to November 1340: Octave Delepierre, "Edouard III, roi d'Angleterre en Flandre," *Miscellanies of the Philobiblon Society*, x (1866-67), fasc. 5.

[12] Hugo Lange, "Chaucer und Mandeville's Travels," *Archiv für das Studium der neueren Sprachen*, 174 (1938), 79-80; "Die Paradies-Vorstellung in *Mandeville's Travels* im Lichte mittelalterlicher Dichtung," *Englische Studien*, LXXII (1928), 312-314; and see *Archiv*, etc., 175 (1939), 209.

Curiously enough, a clear allusion to Mandeville has been overlooked. It occurs just where we would expect it, in the *Squire's Tale*. In describing the feast of Cambyuskan, Chaucer says,

> Eek in that lond, as tellen knyghtes olde,
> Ther is som mete that is ful deynte holde,
> That in this lond men recche of it but smal;
> Ther nys no man that may reporten al. (ll. 69-72)[13]

J. L. Lowes, in his study of "The Squire's Tale and the Land of Prester John,"[14] suggests that the strange food referred to is that mentioned in an English version of the *Letter of Prester John* which occurs in a single manuscript that Chaucer might have seen. However, the much more accessible *Mandeville* says that the Tartar subjects of the Khan "eat hounds, lions, leopards, mares, foals, asses, rats and mice and all manner of beasts, great and small . . . and they eat all the beasts without and within." (p. 164). It is a striking passage. Chaucer could have found such a statement elsewhere, of course, but of what other source would he remark, "as tellen knyghtes olde"? Most of the accounts of Asia were written by friars. No other by a knight is known, so that if the reference is not to Mandeville, we must imagine an oral source. The Squire's father had been in the Near East but not in Tartary proper. And such an allusion would be rather far-fetched. Surely, when he said "as tellen knyghtes olde" Chaucer expected his audience to remember Mandeville's *Travels*. He makes the Squire add, "Ther nys no man that may reporten al," which seems to echo the close of the *Travels*, where Mandeville protests that there are many more wonders than he has reported, "for it were too long thing to devise you the manner [of them]." And if he told all, then another traveler would find nothing new to report,

---

[13] Robinson ed., p. 155.
[14] Washington University Studies, I, pt. ii (Oct. 1913), No. 1, pp. 3-18; and see W. F. Bryan and Germaine Dempster, *Sources and Analogues of Chaucer's Canterbury Tales* (University of Chicago Press, 1941), p. 359.

"wherefore I will hold me stil, . . . to that intent and end, that whoso will go into those countries, he shall find enough to speak of, that I have not touched of in no wise" (p. 207). This is the last paragraph before the autobiography with which he concludes. It is an example of the elfin humor which the two Englishmen have in common, and which Chaucer would therefore especially appreciate in the older writer. The "as tellen knyghtes olde" is accompanied therefore not by one, but by two, statements which Chaucer could expect his audience to recognize because they would be familiar with the most popular and available account of the strange world of the Orient.

The problem is not whether Chaucer had read Mandeville. There is no reason to question that he had. The problem is, rather, how many of Mandeville's sources had Chaucer also read?[15] For example, in his *Parliament of Fowls*, he describes the earthly paradise as "walled with grene ston" (l. 122). Both Mandeville and the *Iter Paradisi* of the Alexander cycle describe the wall as moss covered,[16] i.e., green with moss. Hugo Lange called attention to several details which both writers use, including mention of the river "gysen," the ruby that shines in the dark, travels *west* to Paradise, the magnet, etc.[17] Since all of these details occur in one or another of Mandeville's sources, the tendency has been to discount Chaucer's debt to Mandeville. However, when it is recognized that the *Travels* (in Norman French) was circulating in England in the 1360's (rather than in Latin and not before 1370, as has been generally supposed), then both the possible borrowings and the dates of

---

[15] Robinson in his headnote to the *Squire's Tale*, pp. 821-822, suggests as possible sources Marco Polo, Carpini, Simon de St. Quentin, Rubruquis, Ricold, Hayton, Odoric, and the *Letter of Prester John*, but not Mandeville!

[16] M. M. Lascelles, "Alexander and the Earthly Paradise in Mediaeval English Writings," *Medium Aevum*, v (1936), 98-100.

[17] See n. 12 above. The dry tree in the *Squire's Tale* is another such detail.

works which clearly borrow from Mandeville will have to be reconsidered.

Two of Chaucer's French contemporaries, Jean d'Arras and Christine de Pisan, borrowed openly from the *Travels*. In his famous romance of *Mélusine,* Jean d'Arras tells a story of Melior (whom he makes a sister of Mélusine), and her castle of the sparrowhawk, which is so close to Mandeville's story of the castle in Armenia that Mandeville has often been accused of borrowing from the romance of *Mélusine.*[18] But Jean d'Arras did not write his story until long after the *Travels* had reached Paris and found a place in the royal library of the Louvre. Jean says that he began it in 1387 and finished it in 1394. He was "libraire" to the Duc de Berry, brother of Charles V to whom the famous copy of the *Travels* written in 1371 was presented. In 1392 this manuscript was withdrawn from the Louvre library by Charles VI, quite possibly for the use of Jean d'Arras.[19] Jean says that he got his story of Mélusine out of some old chronicles of Lusignan which he found in the castle library, and part he got from the Earl of Salisbury, who was a commissioner treating with France in 1389 and 1392.[20] The Melior story is an addition to the story of Mélusine, not an integral part of it. Jean was probably led to borrow it from

[18] For an account of Jean d'Arras, see Jules Baudot, *Les Princesses Yolande et les Ducs de Bar de la Famille des Valois* (Paris, 1900), pp. 248 ff. Baudot suggests (p. 282) that Jean got the story from the Earl of Salisbury. The *Otia Imperialia* of Gervase of Tilbury is commonly mentioned as a possible source of the Melior story. There is a "Chateau de Esparvier" (III, lxvii) with a fairy mistress, and another fairy mistress story (III, xv). Both have points of similarity to *Mélusine,* but no trace of the watching test. The editor of the English *Travels* (ed. 1727, p. v) attributes Mandeville's Melior story to *Mélusine,* and others have repeated the mistake.

[19] Mallet, *Inventaire,* pp. xvi ff., where the editor, Boivin le Cadet, cites Christine's tribute to Mallet and remarks that the court seems to have used the library freely. Mallet recorded the withdrawal of the book, p. 33, no. 131.

[20] See the opening of *Mélusine.* The castle of Lusignan was in English hands for some years in the 14th century. The Earl of Salisbury was William de Montacute (1328-97).

Mandeville because, like the Mélusine story, it was attached to the house of Lusignan.

Christine de Pisan made extensive use of the *Travels* in her *Chemin de Long Estude* (ll. 1191-1568), which she presented to the Duc de Berry early in 1402. In this work she describes an imaginary trip with the Sibyl to see all that is worth seeing in this world before passing into the next. She makes a point of seeing everything that Mandeville reports as inaccessible, such as the Earthly Paradise and the head-waters of the Nile. Mandeville mentions several places which he says that he did not actually visit, and in each case Christine pretends to visit that place.[21]

The Duc de Berry and his brother Philippe, Duc de Bourgogne, both showed their admiration for the *Travels*. In January of 1403, the Duc de Berry bought a copy of *Mandeville* which he gave to his *valet de chambre*, Jean Barre.[22] In 1401 the Duc de Bourgogne bought three books called *La Fleur des Istories de la terre d'Orient* from Jacques Raponde, a Lombard merchant in Paris, for the huge sum of 300 livres d'or. He gave one book to the Duc de Berry, another to the Duc d'Orléans, and the third he put in his own library. From the title it has been assumed that all three were copies of Hayton's book,[23] but the price suggests a collection of such works, a book like the *Livre des Merveilles*, which was bought by the Duc de Bourgogne about this time and given by his son to the Duc de

---

[21] P. Toynbee, "Christine de Pisan and Sir John Mandeville," *Romania*, xxi (1892), 228-239. Marie-Josèphe Pinet, *Christine de Pisan* (Paris, 1927), pp. 290 ff.

[22] L. Delisle, *Recherches sur la Librairie de Charles V*, ii, 217 ff., no. 168.

[23] Gabriel Peignot, *Catalogue d'une partie des livres composant la Bibliothèque des ducs de Bourgogne en XV$^e$ Siècle* (Dijon, 1841), pp. 31-32. P. Paris identifies the Duc de Berry's copy as MS. Bibl. Nat. fr. 12201: *Histoire Littéraire de la France*, xxv (Paris, 1869), 503. Alfred Hiver de Beauvoir, *La Librairie de Jean duc de Berry, au Château de Mehun-sur-Yèvre, 1416* (Paris, 1860), p. 61, describes the Hayton in that library. Delisle, no. 256 dates the gift "22 May, 1403 n.s."

Berry in 1412, and which was valued a decade later at 125 livres.[24] The *Livre des Merveilles* is indeed the flower of the accounts of the Orient. It contains the works of Marco Polo, Odoric, Boldensele, two letters written by the Great Khan of Cathay in 1338 to Pope Benedict XII, the Pope's reply, an account of the estate and government of the Great Khan written by an Archbishop of Sultania to Pope John XXII, and the accounts of the Orient by Mandeville, Hayton, and Friar Ricolde of Monte Croce. It is illustrated with 265 large miniatures.[25] The compiler has added Marco Polo and Mandeville to the collection made by Jean Le Long of Ypres and translated by him from Latin into French. It is possible that his translations were used by Mandeville.[26] At any rate, by 1403 Mandeville's own work had been added to this collection.[27]

This Duc de Bourgogne's son, Jean sans Peur, who led the disastrous crusade defeated at Nicopolis in 1396, owned a copy of *Mandeville*.[28] Louis, Duc d'Orléans, had a copy for which he had not paid, and for which his poet son paid in

[24] Hiver de Beauvoir, pp. 59-60. The copy was bought by Philippe le Hardi, Duc de Bourgogne (d. 1404), and given by his son, Jean sans Peur, in 1413 to the Duc de Berry: see H. Omont, below, and above p. 82.

[25] The best account of this manuscript is by Henri Omont, in his edition of the *Livre des Merveilles. Reproduction des 265 Miniatures du Manuscrit Français 2810 de la Bibliothèque Nationale*. 2 vols. Pub. by the Bibl. Nat. Département des Manuscrits (Paris: Imprimerie Berthaud Frères, 31 Rue de Bellefond [1907]). The illustrations are said to be mostly by Jacques Coene of Bruges: *Les plus beaux Manuscrits français du VIII*ᵉ *au XVI*ᵉ *siècle,* published by the Bibl. Nat. (Paris, 1937, p. 52). The book has been described many times; see below p. 270. Jean Flamel, secretary of the Duc de Berry, wrote his name in the book, but was not the scribe: see Omont's Introduction.

[26] See above Chap. 5, n. 27.

[27] Two copies of Le Long's translations in Bibl. Nat. fr. 12202 and 1380 do not contain Mandeville and Marco Polo, nor does the B.M. Cotton Otho D. II (ruined by fire): see T. Smith, *Catalogues Librorum Manuscriptorum Bibliothecae Cottonianae* (Oxford, 1696), pp. 74-75. The copy in the Public Library of Bern, Switzerland, no. 125, has the additions, however: see Appendix I below, p. 277.

[28] Described as on paper: see Peignot, p. 68.

1411.[29] Still another copy of *Mandeville*, bound with other works, has been recorded from the Duc de Bourgogne's library.[30] And Charles V also had other copies besides the 1371 manuscript.[31] Evidently Paris, as well as Liège, had developed considerable enthusiasm for the *Travels* by 1400.

In another connection I have indicated that Thomas, Duke of Gloucester, and the Abbey of St. Albans in England appear to have been centers for the dissemination of the *Travels*. It had been translated into Latin at least twice before 1400, and while the Cotton Manuscript text of the first English translation has been conjecturally dated 1410-20,[32] the translation itself is certainly substantially earlier, because several manuscripts of the shorter version made from it were written at least as early as 1400.[33]

Most of the surviving manuscripts were, of course, copied in the fifteenth century. They show that the *Travels* continued to be in demand. When it was first printed we cannot be sure. Two copies of a primitive edition in Dutch have been dated about 1470.[34] Anton Sorg, probably in 1478, produced the first illustrated edition at Augsburg,[35] and in 1480 a stream of editions began to pour from the presses of France, Germany, Italy, and the Low Countries at the rate of almost two a year.

---

[29] L. Delisle, *Cabinet*, I, 105; Pierre Champion, *La Librairie de Charles d'Orléans* (Paris, 1910), pp. xxi, 71 (where the price is quoted as 40 écus). It was Charles, later Comte d'Angoulême, who acquired the 1371 *Mandeville*, and from him it was returned to the Royal Library of France: Champion, p. 119, and no. 115.

[30] J. B. J. Barrois, *Bibliothèque protypographique, ou Librairies des fils du Roi Jean* (Paris, 1830), no. 2251.

[31] L. Delisle, *Recherches sur la Librairie de Charles V*: no. 877 is identified as the copy presented by Gervaise Crétien; no. 878 is a *Mandeville* (defective), and no. 1106 is a *Mandeville* bound with a copy of *Florimant* (in verse).

[32] Hamelius, II, 19, quotes Warner as definitive.

[33] See Appendix I.

[34] See Appendix II.

[35] See Appendix II, and my note on the "First Edition of *Mandeville's Travels*," forthcoming.

THE FIRST TWO CENTURIES 231

Copies survive from at least thirty-five incunabula editions, and since seven of these copies are unique, it is most probable that whole editions have been lost.[36]

This record of enthusiasm for *Mandeville* in the early days of printing is significant because these were also the early days of exploration and discovery. Modern historians of travel books, having reduced Mandeville to a mere plagiarist (as they thought), have done their best to ignore the *Travels* and so banish it altogether from the history not only of exploration and discovery but also of ideas and of letters. In contexts where all of Mandeville's sources and rivals are named, he is left out. It is as if scholars were ashamed to admit that such great men as Christopher Columbus were "taken in" by Mandeville. It is refreshing to find such a scholar as E. G. R. Taylor, in his study of *Tudor Geography*, observing, "The value of this book has been obscured by the incredible tales which it contains, but it embodies also the real advances in geographical knowledge and geographical thought that were made in the thirteenth century, and great geographers like Mercator showed no lack of judgment when they gave it due consideration."[37] Abraham Ortelius also cited Mandeville and visited his grave.[38]

The more usual attitude is illustrated by G. F. Warner, who asserts that there is "nothing to show that he was in advance of his time in his knowledge of the roundness of the earth."[39] That is beside the point. The knowledge that the earth is round

[36] See Appendix II on the French, Dutch, English, and German editions.
[37] (London, 1930), p. 5. On Mercator's *Weltkarte* (Duisburg, 1569), in the lower right-hand corner, under the heading, "De meridianae continentis ad Iavam maiorem accessu," he says, "cui Io: Mandeuillanus, autor licet alioqui fabulosus, in situs tamen locorum non contemnendus consentit."
[38] In his *Theatrum Orbis Terrarum* (1572), he lists "Ioannes Mandevilius et eius comes" among his authorities; and he comments on the map of Asia, listing as authorities, "M. Paulus Venetus, Ludouicus Vartomannus, et Ioannes Mandeuilius (sed fabulis refertus hic)." His account of Mandeville's tomb [sic] is discussed in Chap. 6.
[39] Introduction, pp. xxiv-xxv.

has a long history, going back to the ancients. It could have reached Mandeville through such popular medieval works as those of Sacro Bosco, Bartholomaeus Anglicus, or Vincent of Beauvais. But the available evidence for the fact was not sufficient to overcome theological prejudice in favor of the Biblical account of the world. Vincent, for example, after citing several authorities who assert the roundness of the earth, ends with Augustine's vigorous argument against it.[40]

What Mandeville did in aid of geographical advancement was to assert confidently that a man could sail around the earth and return home safely. A century and a half before Columbus sailed, Mandeville claimed that he had been as far north as 62°, as far south as 33° and 46 minutes, and the same distance fom East to West, and he adds: "If I had had company and shipping for to go more beyond, I trow well, in certain, that we should have seen all the roundness of the firmament all about. . . . By the which I say you certainly that men may environ all the earth of all the world, as well under as above, and turn again to his country, that had company and shipping and conduct. And always he should find men, lands and isles, as well as in this country. . . . For all the parts of sea and of land have their opposites, habitable or trespassable . . ."[41] He "proves" his point with a story, which he says that he had heard in his youth, of a man who sailed to the East till he came to an island where he heard his own language spoken; then, not realizing where he was, he turned back westward and after a long journey reached his home again. Years later he happened to go into Norway and there he recognized the island which he had previously visited. In other words, the man had sailed entirely around the world in both directions.

When Columbus found "company and shipping" and courage to sail westward to find the Indies, the fears which beset his

---

[40] *De Civit. Dei, lib.* 16. See *Speculum Naturale*, vi, Chaps. viii-xii (ed. 1524), i, cols. 374-376; and Warner's note on p. 90, l. 1.

[41] Pollard ed., pp. 121-122. See also p. 202, the opening of Chap. 34.

way were not so much doubts that the earth was round as fear that if a ship ventured "down under" the earth it could never get back "up" again. Some thought that "men should fall toward the heaven from under," but Mandeville explains that "from what part of the earth that men dwell, either above or beneath, it seemeth always to them ... that they go more right [i.e., upright] than any other folk. And right as it seemeth to us that they be under us, right so it seemeth to them that we be under them" (p. 123).

John of Marignolli, Papal emissary to China and Mandeville's contemporary, denied very positively the possibility of circumnavigation and of men dwelling at the antipodes, quoting St. Augustine.[42] In fact, when Mandeville asserted that the earth was "habitable or trespassable" in all parts, he was directly contradicting a whole galaxy of the Church Fathers. As late as 1588, Father Joseph de Acosta, in his *Natural and Moral History of the Indies*[43] undertook the refutation of Chrysostom, Lactantius, Jerome, Procopius, Augustine, and others who argued that the heavens did not extend all around the earth, but were only above, so that the antipodes were not 'inhabitable or trespassable."

Columbus was most interested in this point. His copy of the *Imago Mundi* of Pierre d'Ailly shows underscoring and notes when it speaks of the inhabitability of the whole earth.[44] At one point in his journal of the first voyage, Columbus records his satisfaction at the mountainous seas, "because it encouraged the sailors," i.e., that they were not going "down under" the earth.

[42] "Recollections of Travel in the East" (1338-53), in Yule's *Cathay* III, 260-261. For other references to disbelief in the inhabitability of the antipodes and fear of going "down under," see Taylor's Introduction to Vol. II of Cecil Jane, *Selected Documents Illustrating the Four Voyages of Columbus,* Hakluyt Society, 2d Ser., 70 (1933 for 1932), lxxviii-lxxix.

[43] Ed. C. R. Markham, from the tr. of Edward Grimston (1604), Hakluyt Society, 1st Ser. 60, 61 (1880), I, 1 ff.

[44] Ed. with the annotations of Christopher Columbus (Boston, 1927), especially pp. 39-41$^v$.

When Mandeville was a young man, John Buridan lectured at the University of Paris on whether the earth rotated on its axis, and whether the torrid and south temperate zones were inhabitable.[45] His discussion is not only theoretical but it avoids any definite conclusion. The step from academic speculation to practical exploration is a long one and must first be taken by the imagination. It is for this imaginative preparation that Mandeville deserves considerable credit. A recent geographical historian, Leonardo Olschki, has pointed out the importance of ancient and medieval legends about the East in inspiring and directing the efforts of the early explorers of America.[46] Most of these legends are to be found in Mandeville; and for more than a century before America was discovered, they were most readily accessible in this popular book.

Columbus' copy of Marco Polo, with his annotations, has been preserved, but not his copy of Mandeville's *Travels*. Irving had no doubt, however, that Columbus studied Mandeville as well as Marco Polo.[47] Ferdinando Columbus cites the two together in his account of the reasons which led the Ad-

[45] E. A. Moody, "John Buridan on the Habitability of the Earth," *Speculum*, XVI (1941), 415-425.

[46] *Marco Polo's Precursors* (Baltimore, 1942), p. 16; "What Columbus Saw on Landing in the West Indies," *Proceedings of the American Philosophical Society*, LXXXIV (July, 1941), 633-659; and especially "Ponce de León's Fountain of Youth: History of a Geographic Myth," *Hispanic American Historical Review*, XXI (1941), 261-385. See also Luis Weckmann, "The Middle Ages in the Conquest of America," *Speculum*, XXVI (1951), 130 ff.

[47] Washington Irving, *The Life and Voyages of Christopher Columbus*, revised ed. (New York, 1873), III, 494. Irving asserts positively that Columbus read Mandeville, but his authority was probably the old version of the letters of Toscanelli, now discredited: see Clements R. Markham, *The Journal of Christopher Columbus*, Hakluyt Society, 1st Ser. 86 (1893), pp. 3-11. But Columbus' familiarity with the *Travels* is asserted also by Justin Windsor, *Christopher Columbus*, 5th ed. (Boston, 1892), pp. 112-117; and S. E. Morison, *Admiral of the Ocean Sea* (Boston, 1942), I, 320, 340, 359. II, 34, 128, 129, 133. He discusses the influence of Mandeville on men's minds. Morison is mistaken in crediting the search for men with tails entirely to Mandeville. Marco Polo also reported them: see Moule's ed., I, 376.

## THE FIRST TWO CENTURIES

miral to undertake his voyage.[48] Andrés Bernáldez, the historian of the second voyage, describes Columbus as very learned in cosmology, having, he says, studied "Ptolemy and other books and John Mandeville."[49] Bernáldez himself cites Mandeville several times, giving references to particular chapters of the *Travels*.[50] Columbus could have read the *Travels* before 1492 in any one of several Italian, French, or Latin editions, or in manuscript in Spanish.

Mandeville's story of the man who sailed around the world is not the first of its kind. Strabo and Cornelius Nepos tell similar yarns.[51] But Mandeville's version was fresher and more graphic and was appended to an argument for the practicability of circumnavigation, imbedded in an account of the wonders and vast wealth of the Orient—all of which gave it great persuasive power. The generation of Columbus was ripe for the attempt to sail westward to find Cathay. It was full of stories of the explorations of the Norwegians in the North Atlantic and of the Portuguese in the South.[52] Columbus investigated a tale of two Orientals cast up on the coast of Ireland.[53] Mandeville's

[48] "La Historie de D. Fernando Colon en la Quale se da Particular, y verdadera relacion de la vida, y hechos de el Almirante D. Christoval Colon, su padre" . . . trans. Alfonso de Ulloa, in D. Andres Gonzalez Barcia, *Historiadores Primitivos de las Indias Occidentales*, etc. (Madrid, 1749), I, fol. 5ᵛ. Chap. VII cites Marco Polo and Mandeville.

[49] *Historia de los Reyes Catolicos D. Fernando y Dona Isabel* (Seville, 1870), I, 357-358. The first edition was printed in 1513.

[50] Ibid., II, 43, 53, 58; or see Cecil Jane, *Selected Documents*, Hakluyt Society, 2d ser., 65 (1930), I, notes on pp. 116, 130, 138, 144. Bernáldez cites Mandeville on the cleverness of the Chinese, the 5000 islands of the Indies, the people who go naked, and on griffins (they thought they saw griffin tracks).

[51] Frederich J. Pohl, *Amerigo Vespucci* (New York, 1944), p. 213. Strabo said that India could be reached by sailing west. Seneca predicted discovery of a land beyond Thule. Cornelius Nepos told of Indians whom a storm had carried to the coast of Germany. See also C. R. Beazley, *The Dawn of Modern Geography* (London, 1897-1906), I, 364.

[52] A recent bibliography and anthology of pre-Columbian documents is R. Hennig, *Terrae Incognitae* (Leyden, 1936-39), esp. Vol. III.

[53] A note in Columbus's hand in a copy of the *Asiae Europaeque Elegantissima descriptio* of Pius II reads: "Men have come eastward from

great popularity in the two decades, 1480 to 1500, was certainly partly the result of this ferment; but it was also partly the cause.

From rational hypothesis to creative act there is a long step which must be taken by the imagination. It is in this area of imaginative preparation that Mandeville's *Travels* had an important place. It helped to fire the imagination not only of the leaders but of the all-important followers and supporters of the explorers. It helped the leaders to "find company and shipping for to go more beyond." It helped to create a demand for a route to China and the Indies, and so served as both imaginative preparation and motive force for the explorations and discoveries of the fifteenth and sixteenth centuries. Even after the discovery of America, it continued to play a part in quickening the imaginations both of those who risked their fortunes and of the more humble sailors who risked their lives in looking for the wealth and wonders of the East in the new world in the West.

The immediate effect of the new discoveries on the popularity of the *Travels* was not unfavorable. Lyons, which produced at least six editions in the decade between 1480 and 1490, produced no more until about 1508; but Italy, with six editions before Columbus' return, printed six or seven more before the end of the century. In Germany the inhibiting force seems to have been the Reformation and not the discovery of America. No edition is recorded between 1507 and 1580.

In England at least four editions of the short English version appeared between 1496 and about 1510. Sir Thomas More supplied his Utopians with an alphabet, in direct imitation of the alphabets in the *Travels*. The natural religion of his Utopians undoubtedly also owed something to the medieval tradi-

---

Cathay. We have seen many a remarkable thing, and particularly in Galway, in Ireland, two persons hanging on to two wreck planks, a man and a woman, a beautiful creature," trans. in Salvador de Madariaga, *Christopher Columbus* (New York, 1940), p. 81.

tion of a natural religion of the "Bragmans," an account of which he could have found in *Mandeville*.

Other members of More's immediate literary family show a familiarity with the *Travels*. John Heywood was evidently recalling it, perhaps even intentionally alluding to it, in his interlude of the *Four P's*, where the Palmer mentions visiting the Holy Places around Jerusalem and adds, "On the hylles of Armeny, where I saw Noe's arke." John Rastell, in his interlude, *The Nature of the Four Elements,* represents Experience explaining to the Student the geography of the earth. He mentions the discovery of the new lands in the West "within this xx yere," but he also speculates on the distance of this new world from the "Cane of Catous lande." He mentions India the Great as the land of Prester John, discusses whether the earth is round, and speaks of the height of the north star in different latitudes, in a way which suggests that he knew the *Travels* in some form which included the passage (omitted in the printed English text) on the circumnavigation of the earth.[54] The French texts printed at Lyons, with their German woodcuts from Anton Sorg's press, were copied by Wynkyn de Worde, and were therefore available in London.[55]

It is possible that More and his circle had access to the Eger-

---

[54] Chap. xx in the Cotton text, Chap. lv in the Pynson text, but with this passage omitted. Rastell's debt to Mandeville was argued by G. B. Parks, "The Geography of the *Interlude of the Four Elements*," *PQ*, xvii (1938), 251-262. M. E. Borish, "Source and Intention of *The Four Elements*," *SP*, xxxv (1938), 149-163, argues that Gregor Reisch's *Margarita Philosophica* (1503 ff.) was Rastell's source. Johnstone Parr, "More Sources of Rastell's *Interlude of the Four Elements*," *PMLA*, lx (1945), 48-58, points out contemporary parallels for everything that has been traced to Mandeville, but concedes that the information could have come from the *Travels* as well, and that Mandeville at least constitutes an analogue for the account of the inhabitants of the New World, the argument that the earth is round, and the description of a star below the horizon.

[55] See my article, "The Woodcut Illustrations in the English Editions of *Mandeville's Travels*," *Papers of the Bibliographical Society of America*, xlvii (March, 1953), 59-69.

ton Manuscript of the only complete English version of the *Travels*.[56] This manuscript has in it a note by a former owner, E. Hill, M.D., dated 22 March 1803, saying that on a slip of paper pasted inside the old cover (destroyed in the process of rebinding) was the inscription, "Thys fayre Boke I have fro the abbey at Saint Albons in thys yeare of Oure Lord MCCCCLXXXX the sixt daye of Apryll. Willyam Caxton." It also contained the name "Richard Tottyl, 1579." In his memorandum Hill further asserts that he got the book from the Reverend Hugh Tuthill, a descendant of the famous publisher. Warner does not credit this story,[57] in the absence of the slip of paper to prove it. But the story is not improbable. We have seen how the monks of St. Albans began to treasure the memory of Sir John Mandeville before the end of the fourteenth century. At that time they had a Latin translation of the *Travels*, and, in all probability, the French text from which the translation was made. In the course of the next century they could certainly have acquired, or even produced, an English version. It will be objected that the Egerton translation is in a somewhat northern dialect, while the premier abbey of all England was near London. But St. Albans had extensive and important connections with the North. It had a cell at Wymundeham in Yorkshire, and another at Tynmouth on the Scottish border. There was much visiting and exchange of personnel, and surely of books, between the mother house and the cells. For that matter, the translation could have been made at St. Albans. A dialect is a very portable piece of baggage, which a man acquires in his youth and usually carries with him wherever he may go thereafter.

According to Vogels,[58] this translator made use of a copy of

[56] Edited by Warner for the Roxburghe Club.
[57] Introduction, p. xii.
[58] J. Vogels, "Handschriftliche Untersuchungen über die englische Version Mandeville's," *Jahresbericht über das Realgymnasium zu Crefeld* (Crefeld, 1891), pp. 3-52.

the earlier translation preserved in the Cotton manuscript. But the text used by the translator had a large gap (corresponding to p. 22, l. 3, to p. 41, l. 21, in the Early English Text Society edition), which was filled from the short, unprinted translation of the Latin text preserved in MS. Royal 13 E. IX which, we know, was available at St. Albans. The author of the Egerton text must also have had a good French text available, for he corrects mistakes which occur in the Cotton text. He does not repeat the claim, made in both the Cotton and the so-called Pynson version, that the author wrote in three languages. He was not deceived by the first translator's claim to be the original author, or he would hardly have undertaken to make another and more correct translation from the French.

The author of the Egerton version was a scholar, whether of St. Albans or not. He shows considerable independence of the Cotton translation, and maturity of style (see Appendix IV). If he did not refer to a good Latin translation of the *Travels*, as well as to the French and two earlier English translations, he shows, at any rate, the influence of Latin on his sentence structure and vocabulary. Moreover, he was a man working in a library well supplied with texts of the *Travels*. The interest in Mandeville which we know existed at St. Albans makes that a likely place—but we do not know what other centers of enthusiasm may have developed, places like Abingdon where we know that there was a Latin translation (and presumably a French text from which it was translated) as early as 1390.

If William Caxton owned the Egerton manuscript it could have reached Richard Tottel through Wynkyn de Worde, Caxton's apprentice and successor, some of whose materials were used, in turn, by Tottel. Or the link may have been through More and the Rastells. William Rastell edited and Tottel printed More's *English Works*. The two men had in common not only interest in the law and legal publications but also interest in the memory of Thomas More and in the publication of literature in English.[59] It would not be at all surprising if, near the end of his active printing career, in 1579, Tottel acquired the only complete manuscript of Mandeville's *Travels* in English.

However, if Caxton acquired the Egerton manuscript in 1490, he did not print it. He died the next year, and Pynson and Wynkyn de Worde both printed the short version of the Cotton text, thereby increasing the English circulation at the expense of the literary value of the book.

As the sixteenth century wore on, the extent to which Mandeville suffered from competition with his classical predecessors increased. For example, John Boemus, in his *Omnium Gentium Mores*, written in the early sixteenth century, shows the same interest in strange customs and religions which Mandeville had, but Boemus cites Pliny, Solinus, Ptolemy, and even Herodotus, but not Mandeville. He mentions several of the strange races of men to be found in his classical sources, and in Mandeville, but he ends abruptly: "But in these and such like tales of the Indians, and their countrie: for that a manne had neede of a redie beliefe that should take them for truthes, one had not neede to bee to longe. . . ."[60] Trevisa had made a similar comment well over a century earlier.

The new school of geographers and cartographers which grew up in the sixteenth century did not believe Mandeville's stories, yet they could not do without him. Mercator thought that, while he was somewhat "fabulous," his geography ought not to be condemned.[61] Ortelius took much the same position.

---

[59] H. R. Plomer, "New Documents on English Printers and Booksellers of the Sixteenth Century," *Transactions of the Bibliographical Society*, IV (1898), 153 ff., discusses Tottel and the Rastells, and lists William Rastell's library at Sergeant's Inn in 1558. It did not include a Mandeville. See also H. R. Plomer, "Richard Tottel," *Bibliographica*, III (1897), 378-384.

[60] Tr. by William Watreman as *The Fardel of Facions* (1555), reprinted in 3 vols. (Edinburgh, 1888), II, 15.

[61] See below, p. 244.

THE FIRST TWO CENTURIES 241

Münster, whose *Cosmographie* (1544) largely replaced the *Travels* as popular information about the Orient, took over all of the marvels, man and beast, without once mentioning Mandeville. His publishers even took over the woodcut illustrations.

No edition of Mandeville's *Travels* printed in England between about 1510 and 1568 is known to have survived,[62] but the book was not forgotten. Its influence on More, Rastell, and Heywood is apparent. We know of John Leland's boyhood interest. Leland reported that Canterbury (apparently the shrine of St. Thomas) had a gift from Mandeville, a crystal globe enclosing an apple which showed no signs of decay. John Bale included Mandeville in his dictionary of English writers, and, about the same time (in mid-century) Richard Eden quoted from the printed text of the *Travels* the wonderful story of the vegetable lamb and the barnacle goose.[63] A ship setting out for Moscow in 1576 carried a copy of the *Travels* in its library.[64]

Spain produced at least five editions of the *Travels* between 1515 and 1547. Cervantes borrowed from it in his *Persiles y Segismunda*. Antonio de Torquemada used it in his *Jardín de Flores Curiosas* (Salamanca, 1570), a very popular work which was turned into English by Ferdinard Walker as *The Spanish Mandeville of Miracles* (London, 1600, 1613, 1618).[65] The *Travels* was also heavily plagiarized by "Gomes de Santo Estevão" of Leon, in his *Libro del Infante don Pedro de Portugal* (1544, 1547, etc.). Professor Entwistle noted nineteen

[62] Evidence of at least one lost edition is provided by the state of the pictures in the 1568 edition: see reference above, n. 55. The single leaf now in the Harleian collection may be from an otherwise unknown edition, see below, Appendix II.

[63] *Decades of the newe world or West India* (1555), reprinted by Edward Arber (Birmingham, 1885), p. 329.

[64] G. B. Parks, *Richard Hakluyt and the English Voyagers*, American Geographical Society, Special Publications, No. 10 (New York, 1928), p. 46.

[65] Entwistle, op. cit., and Letts, *Mandeville*, p. 36.

editions of this last work in Castilian between 1602 and the present, ten in Portuguese.

In Italy ten editions of the *Travels* appeared between 1504 and 1567. Most of them were printed in Venice,[66] partly, no doubt, because the Aldine Press made that the chief printing center of Italy, and partly because the *Travels* had a ready sale among pilgrims to the Holy Land, who most frequently went by way of Venice. Several of the later Itineraries of the Holy Land borrow from, and are modeled upon, Mandeville's *Travels*.

Even the French, who have shown the least interest in the *Travels*, produced at least six editions in the sixteenth century. Rabelais mentions "Monteville" along with "Orlando Furioso, Robert the Devil, Fierabras, William without Fear, Huon of Bordeaux, and Matabrune." These he calls "gallant stately books, worthy of high estimation" (Prologue to Book II). Montaigne, in his "Apology for Raimond de Sebonde,"[67] cites Pliny and Herodotus for a list of the races of strange men which is very similar to Mandeville's list. But even after the Paris redactor had done his work, Mandeville undoubtedly sounded crude and strange to a French ear. He is one of those few writers who gain by translation, as the record of his popularity testifies. Like the *Pearl* poet, he wrote in a dialect which did not become a literary language. But because of his immediate popularity and many translators, he escaped the obscurity which the *Pearl* poet, Gower in his Norman-French works, and others of his contemporaries suffered.

Indeed, his very English French clearly guided the hands of his English translators and entitles him to some of the credit for the translation. At this late date, with the record of his success so clearly written on the pages of literary history, it would be absurd to cavil at his "barbarous French" or to judge him by the literary standards of Paris. A comparison

---
[66] See Appendix II.
[67] Bohn ed. (1913), II, 223.

with the French of Gower would be more just. But it is only in French that he suffers from his dialectal handicap.

In England and Germany the Reformation seems to have brought the *Travels*, for a time, into disrepute. The scarcity of English editions between 1510 and 1568 is matched by a similar gap in the sequence of German editions between 1507 and 1580. Mandeville's accounts of saints and relics, his reminiscence of the Crusades, and concern with pilgrimages and miracles would naturally bring him into disfavor in the Protestant countries. The fiction, inserted into the Cotton and Pynson versions, that the *Travels* had been approved by the Pope would not recommend it to early Protestant readers. In the English manuscript which is now in the Henry E. Huntington Library in California, the word "Pope" has been erased from this passage. Probably in the general destruction of "superstitious" and "Popish" books, many copies of Mandeville were destroyed—including almost all of the manuscripts which contemporary records report as "on paper." Mostly the parchment manuscripts were saved, but not all of those.

In general, Mandeville's *Travels* can be said to have attained two peaks of popularity in the first two centuries of its history. The first, attested by the number of surviving copies, occurred in the last decade of the fourteenth, and first decade of the fifteenth, centuries. The second, evidenced by the multiplication of editions, in all major languages of Europe, dated from 1480 to about 1505, and ended rather abruptly in the North with the rise of religious controversy. Elsewhere the *Travels* suffered from competition with the discoveries of the New World and the revival of classical geography which created a prejudice in favor of Herodotus, Pliny, Strabo, Solinus, and even pseudo-Aethicus. However, as Mandeville's authority as a traveler waned, his reputation as a great and wonderful liar grew.

# ‹16›

# A BRIGHT IMAGINARY WORLD

BEFORE the end of the sixteenth century, the *Travels* had made the difficult portage from the realm of "redie beliefe" to the land of the imagination, with gain rather than loss, for it was assuming its natural and rightful place in literature by that change. In the long calm of the Elizabethan settlement, Thomas East reprinted the popular English version in 1568 and again about 1582. There is good reason to believe that one or more lost editions were printed between de Worde's last (of about 1510, only two leaves of which have survived), and the first East edition. De Worde had a set of seventy-five woodblocks (copied from a French edition of the *Travels*), which he used in 1499, again in 1503, and in the edition of about 1510. East's first known edition is illustrated with seventy-five woodcuts which were copied from de Worde's. They are not printed from de Worde's woodblocks, yet they have every indication of being from old blocks, not new ones cut for the 1568 edition. Many of them have broken borders and other evidences of previous use. Some even show wormholes. The total number of de Worde's pictures is eked out by printing eight pictures twice. Obviously these are old blocks, cut sometime after 1510, but used, probably more than once, before 1568.[1]

William Bullein provides us with evidence that the *Travels* was circulating in 1564, for in his *Dialogue against the Fever Pestilence*, which appeared in that year (and again in 1573 and 1578), he satirizes the *Travels* and travelers' tales, among other

---

[1] Edward Hodnett, *English Woodcuts, 1480-1535* (London, 1935), p. 35, so describes them; and see my article, "The Woodcut Illustrations in the English Editions of *Mandeville's Travels*," cited in Chap. 15, n. 55.

## A BRIGHT IMAGINARY WORLD

subjects, making use of several of Mandeville's stories.[2] Such a use of the book assumes familiarity with it on the part of readers, greater familiarity, it would seem, than could be assumed of a book which had not been republished since 1510.

Drake's voyage around the world, ending in 1580, did much to reawaken English interest in the Far East. Sir Walter Raleigh testifies that it brought new respect to Mandeville, "whose reports were holden for fables many yeeres, and yet since the East Indies were discovered, we find his relations true of such things as heretofore were held incredible."[3] This remark is part of his argument that the race of men without heads lived somewhere in his precious Guiana. Nevertheless, he was not forced to seek out Mandeville for a witness. They were described and pictured also in editions of such popular classics as Pliny's *Summarie of the Antiquities and Wonders of the World* (1566), Solinus' epitome of Pliny, translated by Arthur Golding in 1587, or Ptolemy's *Compost*, as it was Englished in the 1530's. There were at least thirty-five editions of Ptolemy before 1600, many in Latin. Münster's *Cosmographie* also appeared in many editions, and in a popular English abridgement of 1572, reprinted in 1574. Even earlier, his *Treatyse of the Newe India*, as Englished by Richard Eden, appeared in 1553.

Probably, in the end, Mandeville's agreement with these classical and popular geographers gained him some readers besides Raleigh among the Elizabethan sea-dogs. At any rate, Richard Hakluyt printed the Latin vulgate text of the *Travels* in the first edition of his *Principall Navigations, Voiages*, etc. (1589). He adds, however, an "Admonitio ad Lectorem" in which he defends Mandeville's learning and reputation, citing Bale, Mercator, Ortelius, "and others." He also defends Mandeville's monstrous races of men by pointing out that Pliny, whom

[2] Noticed by S. C. Chew, *The Crescent and the Rose* (New York, 1937), pp. 3 ff.; also by Letts, pp. 39-40.

[3] *Discoverie of Guiana* (1595), reprinted in Hakluyt's *Voyages*, Everyman edition, VII, 328-329.

he quotes (pp. 77 ff.) for two pages, also has them. But in the second edition, Hakluyt omitted Mandeville, substituting Odoric, Johannes de Plano Carpini, and William de Rubruquis. Perhaps the state of Mandeville's reputation in England about 1600 can be fairly represented by two examples. Samuel Rowland, in his *Letting of Humors Blood* (1600), says of the boastful traveler: "His wondrous travels challenge such renowne/ That Sir John Mandeville is quite put down."[4] But John Stow wrote in the margin of his copy of Norden's *Description of Hertfordshire* (1598), "Sir John Mandeville . . . whose travayles in forraine regions and rare reportes are at this time admired through the world."[5]

It was the account of the races of men without heads, men with the heads of dogs, men with tails, and so forth, which delighted the imagination of the Elizabethans while it offended their reason. These creatures appeared in a succession of plays and masques extending at least from *The History of the Cenocephali*, acted at court in 1577, to Milton's *Comus*. The lost play of *Tamar Cam* (acted in 1592, a second part in 1596) had outlandish *dramatis personae*.[6] Dekker, Shakespeare, and Ben Jonson, each made use of such creatures in their plays. Evidently Desdemona was displaying a popular weakness when she showed her delight to hear

> . . . of antres vast and deserts idle,
> And of the Cannibals that each other eat,
> The Anthropophagi, and men whose heads
> Do grow beneath their shoulders. . . .[7]

There are many references to these geographical marvels

[4] Chew, loc. cit.

[5] Letts, p. 13. Another antiquarian, Francis Thynne, in a collection of epitaphs made in 1589-1601, records the inscription at Liège: British Museum Sloan MS. 3836, fol. 6.

[6] Chew, loc. cit.

[7] *Othello*, I, iii, 140-145. J. M. French, "Othello among the Anthropophagi," *PMLA*, XLIX (1934), 807-809, calls attention to the pictures in various editions of Ptolemy's *Geography*. Similar pictures also illustrated Münster and Mandeville.

## A BRIGHT IMAGINARY WORLD 247

scattered through Shakespeare's plays. Lear, for example, mentions the Scythians who eat their parents (I, i, 119). Two plays in particular, *A Midsummer Night's Dream* and *The Tempest,* are full of the wonders of the Indies, East and West. Prospero says that Caliban is "not honour'd with a human shape" (I, ii, 283), and the drunken Trinculo thinks that he sees a man "of Inde" with four legs and two heads (II, ii, 60 ff.). The magic banquet is served by "strange shapes" which make Sebastian declare that he will now believe in the unicorn and the Arabian phoenix (III, iii, 21 ff.), and Gonzalo reminds them that:

> . . . When we were boys,
> Who would believe that there were mountaineers
> Dewlapp'd like bulls, whose throats had hanging at 'em
> Wallets of flesh? or that there were such men
> Whose heads stood in their breasts? which now we find
> Each putter-out of five for one will bring us
> Good warrant of. (III, iii, 43 ff.)

Here too are the "Sounds and sweet airs that give delight and hurt not" (III, ii, 145), which were traditional, after Marco Polo.[8] The storm and the darkness produced by magic are also in Marco Polo and in Mandeville. They are as old as the Odyssey, and as new as the New World. Travelers, their minds conditioned by what they had read, often found the traditional wonders which they expected to find, and the new travelers' tales, like the old, were full of mingled observation and imagination.

If *The Tempest* arrives at the Indies by a suggested westward journey, *A Midsummer Night's Dream* turns the imagination to the East. The occasion is the wedding of Hippolyta, the Amazon queen, and it is appropriate that Oberon should come from India and that Titania's love should be a little Indian boy. It is a world-ranging play on a toy globe that

---

[8] J. L. Lowes, *The Road to Xanadu* (Boston, 1927), pp. 489 ff., discusses the Desert of Lop in English literature. See also p. 10 for other parallels. Marco Polo mentioned the calling voices. Odoric and Mandeville have only the noises and the music.

Puck can fly around in forty minutes. He flies to the east and creates a new monster, the donkey-headed Bottom, reminiscent of the cynocephali, or dog-headed men of the Andaman Isles, who had already appeared on the Elizabethan stage. At the height of the quarrel (III, ii) Helena's hand is compared to "high Taurus' snow" (l. 141), while Hermia is called an "Ethiope" (l. 258), a "tawny Tartar" (l. 262). The scene is Athens, but it is Hippolyta that Oberon has come "from the farthest steep of India" to honor (II, i, 69).

It cannot, of course, be said that these details necessarily came from Mandeville. They were the common property of the classical and the medieval geographers. They must have been familiar to Shakespeare's audience from several sources, but Mandeville's *Travels* was one, and a very popular one, of those sources. In fact it was so popular that its influence sometimes appeared to be both direct and indirect, as in the case of Spenser's Garden of Acrasia. Spenser borrowed heavily and directly in this passage from Tasso's Garden of Armida, and Tasso's garden, in its turn, borrows from Ariosto's Garden of Alcina. Tasso and Spenser are indebted also to the Garden of the Assassins as it was described by Marco Polo and Friar Odoric and Mandeville. Ariosto's debt to Marco Polo has been studied,[9] and there is no reason to doubt that he had also read the more popular and readable *Travels* of Sir John Mandeville. He makes his great traveler Astolpho an Englishman, and the places he visits are suggestive of Mandeville. Canto XV of the *Orlando Furioso* reports how Astolpho was given a pre-view of the geographical discoveries of Ariosto's day, but then he goes to the Holy Land by way of Joppa, where the relics of Andromeda are mentioned (st. 98). Astolpho also visits the land of the Amazons (canto XIX), the realm of Prester John (canto XXXIII), and the Earthly Paradise (canto XXXIV). Ariosto was, of course, following Boiardo in making his romantic heathen, such as Ferragus, Mandricardo, and Argail, not Sara-

[9] Benedetto, I, ccxiv.

cens, but Tartars. Angelica is the daughter of the King of Cathay and she places her lover on that throne.

However, Ariosto's Island of Alcina borrows no distinctive details from the Garden of the Assassins, or the Old Man of the Mountain, as he was called. But Tasso, in creating a similar garden, adds several details which he could have found in Mandeville. He put his Garden of Armida on an island on a high mountain top, above the snow-line, and he says that it is among the "Happy Isles" (cantos xv-xvi). Mandeville was the first to associate the Garden of the Assassins with the Earthly Paradise, as I have already pointed out (p. 45). Spenser in turn adds elements to his borrowing from Tasso which are reminiscent of Mandeville. He emphasizes the artificial character of the place, making the vines, and even the birds, artificial as they are in Mandeville but not in Tasso. In other places Spenser shows his acquaintance with Mandeville. He combines features of several of the monstrous races of men in his description of the giant who seizes Amoret (IV, vii, 5, 6). He is covered with hair, has the long underlip "like a wide deep poke" and the "wide long ears" which hang down to the waist (see Pollard, pp. 134, 196). Other parallels have been noticed,[10] and there is no reason to question the usefulness of the *Travels* as a source of familiar allusions.

The extent of Mandeville's fascination for the young is curiously illustrated by the use of his name in William Warner's *Albion's England*. Warner begins with the remark: "Who reads Sir Iohn de Mandevil his Travels, and his Sights,/ That wonders not? and wonder may, if all be true he wrights."[11] But after this skeptical beginning he interlards a review of Hakluyt's *Voyages* with sections of a romance about Sir John Mandeville and his love for "Elinor," whom he describes as a

[10] Lois Whitney, "The Literature of Travel in the 'Faerie Queene'," *MP*, xix (1921-22), 143-162.

[11] (London, 1612), p. 267. The romance is contained in Books 11 and 12. I am indebted for this reference to Professor Franklin B. Williams of Georgetown University.

cousin of Edward III. Chapters of the romance are alternated with recapitulations from Hakluyt, obviously for the purpose of sugar-coating the instruction. We are told that he was of rich parentage, and his love affair is made the excuse for his travels which end happily at Rome where the lovers are reunited through the good offices of "Stafford" and his lady-love (pp. 276-313).

The *Travels* had passed into the safekeeping of those who dwell largely in the world of the imagination. Mandeville is mentioned in the popular ballad known as "Saint George's Commendation" (1612), along with other English knights who "Pagans did convert": "Sir Isonbras and Iglesmore, they were Knights bold./And good sir Iohn Mandeuile of travell much hath told . . ."[12] In the same year (1612) Thomas Snodham reprinted the *Travels*. His sales must have been satisfactory, for he reprinted the book in 1618 and again in 1625. These were cheap popular editions, using the same Black Letter type which East had used and the now worn and worm-eaten woodblocks for pictures which East had used in 1582.

As a serious report of travel, *Mandeville* was now beyond the pale. Purchas attempted an apology, calling him "the greatest Asian traveler that ever the world had," with the possible exception of Marco Polo; but adding that "some later Fabler out of the Tales of Ogerus the Dane hath stuffed this storie."[13] He is referring to the text of the Latin vulgate which Hakluyt had rejected from his second edition. In another place Purchas refers to "our Countrieman, that famous Traveller Sir John Mandeville, whose geographie Ortelius commendeth, howsoever he acknowledgeth his worke stuffed with fables." He thinks that the true text of Mandeville has been lost, and "cannot but deplore the losse of such a

---

[12] *The Pepys Ballads*, ed. H. E. Rollins, 8 vols. (Harvard Univ. Press, 1929), I, 39 ff.; cf. stanza 7.
[13] *Hakluytus Posthumus, or Purchas his Pilgrims*, 20 vols. (Glasgow, 1905), XI, 363, 364.

Treasure," which he would like to recover as Ramusio did the text of Marco Polo. However, he contents himself with referring the reader to Hakluyt's first edition, abbreviating the text to a few pages in his own edition of books of travel. He says that he has "been forced to deal with him as Historians doe with our famous Arthur, daring to say little, because others have dared so much and such incredibilities." Then he reprints Bale's *Life*, with its account of the Liège epitaph from Ortelius.[14] It is evident that both Hakluyt and Purchas had been misled by the fictions (in the Latin vulgate and in the English translation) that these versions as well as the French were by the hand of the original author.

However the lovers of English antiquities might defend him, by the opening of the seventeenth century Mandeville's name had become a byword for the lying traveler. Ben Jonson, in *The New Inne*, makes Lord Frampull confess that he has traveled over all England to see strange people: "And here my wife, like a she *Mandeville,/*Ventred in disquisition, after me" (V, v, 81 ff.). And Richard Brome, in his play of the *Antipodes* (1630), has an amusing passage which is predicated on his audience's familiarity with the *Travels:*

PEREGRENE: Drake was a Dy'dapper to Mandevile,
　　　　　　Candish, and Hawkins, Furbisher, all our voyagers
　　　　　　Went short of Mandevile. But had he reach'd
　　　　　　To this place here—yes here—this wildernesse,
　　　　　　And seen the trees of the Sunne and Moone, that spake,
　　　　　　And told King Alexander of his death, he then
　　　　　　Had left a passage ope for Travailers:
　　　　　　That now is kept and guarded by wild beasts,
　　　　　　Dragons, and Serpents, Elephants white and blue

---

[14] *Purchas his Pilgrimes* (London, 1625), III, "The Third Part in Five Books," I, 128-138. He follows Bale in giving the dates from the printed English edition, 1332 and 1366, says that he wrote in three languages, also from the English edition, and that "he dyed at *Leege,* in the yeere 1372. . . ." Then he prints the text of the vulgate, which gives the dates of the journey as 1322 and 1355!

|             | Unicornes and Lyons of many colours,           |
|-------------|------------------------------------------------|
|             | And monsters more, as numberlesse, as namelesse. |
| Doctor:     | Stay there,                                    |
| Peregrene:  | Read here else: can you read?                  |
| Doctor:     | No truer than I ha' seen't.                    |
| Diana:      | Ha' you bin there Sir, ha' you seen these trees? |
| Doctor:     | And talk'd with 'hem, and tasted of their fruit. |

The last remark would lose much of its point if the audience did not recognize it as an echo of Mandeville's boast (in the English, not in the French text) about the vegetable lamb, "I have eaten of that fruit."

Robert Burton, in his *Anatomy of Melancholy* (1621), announces "I would censure all Pliny's, Solinus', Strabo's, Sir John Mandeville's, Olaus Magnus', Marcus Polus' lies, correct those errors in navigation," etc.[15] Sir Thomas Browne, in his *Vulgar Errors* (1646), lists Mandeville among those who have most promoted such errors, but he offers an interesting excuse for still reading him:

> He left a book of his travels, which hath been honoured with translation of many languages, and now continued above three hundred years; herein he often attesteth the fabulous relations of Ctesias, and seems to confirm the refuted accounts of antiquity. All which may still be received in some acceptions of morality, and to a pregnant invention may afford commendible mythology; but in a natural and proper exposition, it containeth impossibilities. . . .[16]

The suggestion that Mandeville might be made to serve for "mythology" probably refers to the plays and masques which often employed grotesque figures, especially in the antimasque. Milton's *Comus* (1634), with its "rout of Monsters headed like sundry sorts of wilde Beasts, but otherwise like Men and Women," is of this type. It has been suggested that the magic banquet provided by the Devil in *Paradise Regained*

---

[15] Edition of London, 1923 (Bohn ed.), II, 46.
[16] *The Works of Sir Thomas Browne,* ed. Simon Wilkin (Bohn ed., 1852), I, 63-4.

# A BRIGHT IMAGINARY WORLD 253

(II, 340-365) was suggested by the *Gerusalemme Liberata* (x, 64) which, in turn, borrows from Mandeville's artificial paradise of Gathalonabes.[17] The story of the assassins was well-known from the time of the Crusades, but the legend of the garden-paradise has not been traced back of Marco Polo. Milton was familiar with the account of it in *Purchas his Pilgrimes*, but it is probable that in his boyhood he had also read *Mandeville*.

Five editions of the *Travels* appeared in English between 1600 and 1640. There is a gap of ten years in the Puritan period, but editions appeared again in 1650, 1657, 1670, 1677, 1684, and 1696. We catch the note of Puritan disapproval in William London's *Catalogue of the most Vendible Books in England* (1657). He remarks, "too many idly sit down in the Chaire of Ignorance, travelling by the fire side, with the *Wandering Knight Sir John Mandevil*, or it may be *Bevis of Southampton;* whilst the Laws of Nations, admirable foundations of Common-wealths, pass undiscovered or dived into" (p. 1). The tribute is a left-handed one, but a testimonial nevertheless to the popularity of the *Travels*. It was no longer regarded as serious reading. Long ago it had lost prestige to the classics, but by the time of the Restoration it had itself become a classic, a book of wonders for the education of the imagination. It had passed into that small class of timeless books beloved of the young, where it would later be joined by *Pilgrim's Progress* and *Gulliver's Travels*, and still later by *Alice in Wonderland* and *The Wizard of Oz*——all of them accounts of imaginary travels, which have found a permanent place in the very heart of our literary heritage.

Bunyan has repeatedly been credited with borrowing from Mandeville's Valley of Devils for his Valley of Despond,[18] but the two accounts have little in common except that both

---

[17] John Milton, *Paradise Regained*, etc., ed. M. Y. Hughes (New York, 1937), p. 482.
[18] Montégut, op. cit., pp. 294-295.

writers compare their valleys to battlefields. More probably Mandeville's Valley was in Spenser's mind when he created the Cave of Mamon, since Mandeville made it a test of covetousness. The existence of such parallels is significant not so much as evidence of borrowing as of the imaginative quality of the *Travels*.

"Isaac Bickerstaff" [Steele], in *The Tatler* for November 22, 1710 (No. 254) comments perceptively: "There are no Books which I more delight in than in Travels, especially those that describe remote Countries, and give the Writer an Opportunity of showing his Parts without incurring any Danger of being examined and contradicted. Among all the Authors of this kind, our renowned Countryman Sir *John Mandeville* has distinguished himself, by the Copiousness of his Invention, and Greatness of his Genius. . . . One reads the Voyages . . . with as much Astonishment as the Travels of *Ulysses* in *Homer*, or of the *Red-Cross* Knight in Spencer. All is enchanted ground, and fairy-land." With these words the Age of Reason acclaimed the *Travels*; for, while ten editions satisfied the seventeenth century, the eighteenth absorbed at least twice that number. There were printings in 1704, 1705, 1710, and 1722. In 1725 the full text of the first English translation was edited for the first time from the Cotton Manuscript (Titus C. xvi), and in 1727 a second edition was called for. Thereafter the *Travels* in English led a double life. The popular edition, with its traditional pictures, shrank to a chapbook of a few pages, while the unabridged edition gained a new fame for its author. The translation was admired for its literary quality. Dr. Johnson quoted two passages from it in his famous *Dictionary* (1755), and praised it "for the force of thought and beauty of expression." He placed the quotations from Mandeville before those from Gower, whom he called "the father of our poetry," thereby implying the same priority for Mandeville in prose. A later critic made the attribution specific.[19] Dr. Johnson's admiration for

---

[19] See above, p. 2 note 1.

## A BRIGHT IMAGINARY WORLD 255

the *Travels* was not limited to the translation falsely represented as Mandeville's. He also recommended the *Travels* to a friend for information about China.[20]

Indeed, the interest in the Orient which grew up with the eighteenth century may have restored a little of Mandeville's prestige. At any rate, Fabricius, in his *Salutaris Lux Evangelii Toti Orbi per Divinam Gratiam Exoriens* (Hamburg, 1731), quotes the vulgate *Travels* several times.[21] And the collection of voyages which goes under the name of Burgeron turned into French Purchas's excerpts from the vulgate.

Probably it is largely coincidental that *Gulliver's Travels* appeared the very next year after the full Cotton-manuscript text of Mandeville was published. Both works seem to have been evoked by the enthusiasm created by William Dampier's accounts of his voyages to the South Seas, which began to appear in 1697. Swift and Mandeville show considerable similarity in narrative technique, but in spirit they have little in common. They were at opposite poles in temperament and point of view. Swift's criticism of mankind was largely local and temporal. He lashed the follies of his contemporaries as only a supreme egotist can. The gentle and modest Mandeville looked through the other end of the telescope. He observed in strange lands the common humanity of all mankind, the common human weaknesses, and the similarities of reason and religious faith. One is a satirist, the other a philosopher.

There are some similarities of content between the two books of travel. Both emphasize the strange languages, and Swift provides an alphabet for Balnibarbi, a traditional decoration of such travels which goes back to Mandeville. Both compare huge rats to mastiffs, and sheep to beeves. Both make apologies for nakedness. Both describe a race of pigmies who keep men of normal size to work for them. Both visit an

---
[20] "Extracts from Windham's Diary," in *Johnsonian Miscellanies*, ed. G. B. Hill (Oxford, 1897), II, 387.

[21] On the Christians of St. Thomas, p. 626; on the Tartars, p. 688; and on Prester John, p. 692.

island inhabited by giants. But all of these might be accidental parallels. Swift had probably read Mandeville in his youth, in one of the editions of the popular English version, but he was hardly the man to appreciate the gentle humor and urbane tolerance and breadth of sympathy of the older writer. He was not concerned with the elements of feeling and behavior which bind all mankind into one great race.

Mandeville's new reputation as "the father of English prose" ran through the eighteenth and most of the nineteenth century side by side with his popularity in the "gilt-cover little books" and "uncovered tales of Tom Hickathrift, Jack the Giant-Killer, etc." works which delighted Lamb, Wordsworth, and Coleridge, and the boys of their generation.[22] Coleridge was especially fond of the old writer. In his notes on Sir Thomas Browne's *Vulgar Errors,* he comes to Mandeville's defense, albeit mistakenly, with the comment, "Many if not most, of these Ctesian fables in Sir John Mandevill were monkish interpolations."[23] The reminiscences of Marco Polo in *Kubla Khan* have been noticed.[24] Coleridge had fallen asleep over *Purchas His Pilgrimage,* but it was Mandeville who first combined Marco Polo's and Odoric's accounts of the Garden of the Assassins with Biblical descriptions of the Christian heaven. Therefore Coleridge's "honey dew" goes back ultimately to Mandeville's account of manna, and his "milk of paradise" flows from the well in Mandeville's *Travels.*[25]

There is another striking reminiscence of Mandeville in Coleridge which illustrates how this little book entered into the imagination of the poets and became part and parcel of the rich fabric of English literature. Coleridge, writing of a walking expedition, says in one of his letters, "I applied my mouth ever

[22] *Letters of Samuel Taylor Coleridge,* ed. E. H. Coleridge, (Boston, 1895), I, 11-12. Crabbe Robinson also mentions these chapbooks: see Lowes, *Xanadu,* pp. 16, 459, and 461, n. 60.

[23] Written in 1804: see T. M. Raysor, *Coleridge's Miscellaneous Criticism* (London, 1936), p. 265.

[24] Lowes, *Xanadu,* loc. cit.

[25] See above, pp. 44-46.

## A BRIGHT IMAGINARY WORLD

and anon to the side of the rocks and sucked in droughts of water cold as ice, and *clear as infant diamonds in their embryo dew.*"[26] Coleridge was recalling Mandeville's wonderful passage in which he describes how, in the far north, the ice turns to crystal, and on the crystal grow the good diamonds. He also says that diamonds grow when fed by dew.

The generation of Coleridge valued the *Travels*. In his *Library Companion* of 1825 (p. 416), Dibdin complained that the edition of 1725 "maintains a stiff price." He records a sale at which it brought three pounds and seven shillings. Even the poor edition of 1722, with "wretched woodcuts," brought a pound and nine shillings at the Towneley sale. Dibdin comments, "Whatever may be the estimation in which his work is held abroad, there are certainly good proofs of its having been long favorable received at home." The magnificent collections of Harley manuscripts and Grenville editions in the British Museum attest Mandeville's popularity among the great bibliophiles.

Mandeville's stories, having passed into folklore, returned again to literature. The dragon-woman of Cos,[27] the watching of the sparrowhawk,[28] and the earthly paradise of Gathalonobes have already been discussed. The story of the rich voluptuary of China, which Mandeville improved from Odoric, was adopted by La Fontaine in the seventeenth century,[29] and in the eighteenth, Defoe used it in the *Further Adventures of Robinson Crusoe*.[30] In the nineteenth century Peacock converted it into a story of the English countryside. Leigh Hunt

---

[26] *Letters*, I, 79. Browne cites the opinion, which Pliny affirms, but Solinus denies, that crystal is nothing else but ice strongly congealed: *Vulgar Errors*, II, Cat. 1.

[27] See above, p. 50.

[28] See p. 227.

[29] *Fables inédites des XII,ᵉ XIII,ᵉ et XIVᵉ Siècles, et Fables de La Fontaine*, 18th fable of the 4th book: Apollin Briquet, "Le Vieillard et ses enfants," in J. Techener's *Bulletin du Bibliophile* (Paris, 1849), pp. 107-109.

[30] Observed by Montégut, pp. 311-312; Cordier, *Odoric*, p. 468. See the edition of London, 1895, Part II, Chap. VI, p. 259.

borrowed the story of the dragon-woman in the *Indicator,* and William Morris retold it in *The Earthly Paradise.*[31] Kipling's description of the postal service in India, with its runners wearing bells to warn of their approach, is very similar to Mandeville's account of the messengers of the Great Khan of Cathay. It is possible that the system had survived through the intervening centuries. More probably it had been re-created, and perhaps here we have an instance of the influence of literature on history. In any case, Kipling was the poorer if he was not aware of the antiquity of the picturesque service he was describing.[32]

In the nineteenth century Mandeville continued to have admirers as well as detractors. He continued to be cherished as an old English worthy. Halliwell-Phillipps reedited the 1725 edition in 1839 (republished in 1866 and 1883). In 1820 Hugh Murray denounced the *Travels* as "a pure and entire fabrication" borrowed from Odoric, Carpini, Rubruquis, and others. "What he added of his own consists, quite exclusively, of monstrous lies."[33] Yet in 1841 Isaac D'Israeli, old and blind, came quixotically to his defense in the *Amenities of Literature* (I, 243), asserting stoutly, "Sir John Mandeville's probity remains unimpeached; for the accuracy of whatever he relates from his own personal observations has been confirmed by subsequent travellers." Evidently D'Israeli had forgotten the Fountain of Youth from which Mandeville said that he had drunk at Polumbrum. He goes on with more perspicacity, however, to say, "it is the spirit of these intrepid and credulous minds which has marched us through the universe. To these children of the imagination perhaps we owe the circumnaviga-

[31] (London, 1868-70), pp. 524-525, "The Lady of the Land."

[32] Marco Polo has a long account of the Chinese postal system, in which he mentions the bells of the runners as a minor detail: Moule's ed., I, pp. 243-247. Mandeville picks up this detail and makes it vivid and graphic as usual: Pollard's ed., pp. 159-160.

[33] *Historical Accounts of Discoveries and Travels in Asia* (Edinburgh, 1820), I, 192; and *Retrospective Review,* (1821), II, ii, 269.

tion of the globe and the universal intercourse of nations."

Certainly Mandeville belongs to the history of the exploration of the world. But he belongs also to literature; it is in the comparison of his book with the chief masterpieces of English literature that his quality and influence appear. In that company, the *Travels* reveals itself as a rich and varied piece of imaginative writing, containing elements which anticipate some of the greatest flights of the imagination in English, indeed in European, literature and anticipates them in no fumbling or unworthy fashion. More important than the demonstrable borrowings are the parallels which suggest that Mandeville left a recognizable footprint on the sandy shore of many a gifted child's imagination; or that the human imagination, like the human reason, has patterns of a universal kind —patterns which the changes of the last six centuries have not altered; for Alice's entrance into Wonderland bears a strong resemblance to the way the ten lost tribes are to escape from their prison behind Gog and Magog; and the pool of tears in which Alice almost drowns is a miniature replica of the lake made by the repentant tears of Adam and Eve. Perhaps the dwarfish little Alexander Pope's love of the smell of apples arose from a childhood self-identification with the race of pigmies which Mandeville says subsist solely on that smell.

The fourteenth century, the first great century of English literature, still has some unexplored fields. One of its finest poets, the creator of the *Pearl* and *Gawain and the Green Knight,* has only recently been given his rightful place in English letters, and *Piers Plowman* still awaits a complete edition. The eminence of Chaucer has tended to obscure his forerunners and contemporaries, and the literature created in England in French and Latin, in that trilingual century, has not received its rightful due. Indeed, the work of the Early English Text Society, which has produced a revival, almost a renaissance, of fourteenth-century English literature, has all but reduced Mandeville to nonentity.

It is to restore the *Travels* to its rightful place in English literature that this study has been dedicated. When it is recognized that its author was, after all, an Englishman, born and bred, so far as we know, at St. Albans, the *Travels* will surely find the editors it needs. It has had appreciative readers, from Chaucer's time to our own, but it has suffered much from the vagaries of printers and editors. The French text has not been edited at all, one English translation is just being printed for the first time, another has been printed only in one very limited edition and in so huge and unwieldy a volume as to repel all but the sturdiest scholars. The short popular edition is available, appropriately enough, in the Everyman's Library, but there it lacks the little pictures which have belonged with it since the time of Wynkyn de Worde. The best English text of all, the text of the Cotton manuscript, has not been reprinted since it appeared in the publications of the Early English Text Society—unless we count the very limited and expensive edition issued by the Grabhorn Press, which is more concerned with the art of printing than with the text.

Yet, in spite of these handicaps, and in spite of the abuses the book has suffered because of its popularity, wherever there are readers of English, there will always be readers of Mandeville. He is an ancient mariner we cannot choose but hear, for he knows how to tell a traveler's tale. His book has stimulated the imagination of many gifted children, from the sixteenth century through the nineteenth, and it should find a place again on the shelves of those who will create the literature of all English speaking people in the generations coming on.

# APPENDICES

# APPENDIX I
# THE MANUSCRIPTS

## TABLE OF MANUSCRIPTS

**FRENCH**

- A. Norman French .............................. 265
- B. Paris French, or the First Redaction ............ 271
- C. Ogier-Liège, or Second Redaction ............... 280
-     Unidentified ................................. 284

**ENGLISH**

- A. Cotton Translation ........................... 288
- B. Egerton Translation .......................... 288
- C. Short Translation from Latin .................. 288
- D. Common, or Pynson Version .................... 289
-     Unidentified ................................. 296

**LATIN**

- A. First Translation Made in England .............. 298
- B. Second Translation Made in England ............ 299
- C. Third Translation Made in England ............. 300
- D. Fourth Translation Made in England ............ 301
- E. Fifth, or Liège Translation ................... 301
- F. Latin and North German ....................... 310

**GERMAN**

- A. Otto von Diemeringen's Translation ............. 312
- B. Michel Velser's Translation ................... 316

**DUTCH** ............................................. 323
**DANISH** ............................................ 326
**CZECH** ............................................. 327
**ITALIAN** ........................................... 329
**SPANISH** ........................................... 332
**IRISH** ............................................. 333
**PICTORIAL** ......................................... 334

# NOTE

A survey of the manuscripts is a necessary basis for discussion of the authorship and influence of the *Travels;* but final classification must follow, not precede, the determination of the origin of the text. My interest has been primarily in the texts—that is, it has been literary rather than bibliographical. However, in the interest of those who may be able to carry the study further, I am appending a finding list with rough classification and arrangement by date, and for the manuscripts in French some indication of the most significant test passages on which the classification is based.

The last attempt at a complete list of manuscripts of the *Travels* is that in Reinhold Röhricht's *Bibliotheca Geographica Palaestinae* (Berlin, 1890), pp. 79-85, 223, 666. He gives no information except the location (now frequently out-of-date), language (mistaken in a few cases), and date of writing (usually given only in centuries and often inaccurate). The present list makes use of such partial studies as Schoerner's of the manuscripts in German, of library catalogues, and, for the manuscripts in French, of information supplied by correspondents, especially my husband in Vienna, M. Marcel Thomas in Paris, and Mr. R. A. B. Mynors, the distinguished English bibliographer, who has supplied me with invaluable information about every one of the French manuscripts in England and has also examined for me those at Brussels and Bern.

It is to be hoped that the following list, however imperfect, will be of assistance to those undertaking further study of the texts, and that it will bring out information about additional manuscripts—for although I have made substantial additions to Röhricht's list, I do not doubt that there are unrecorded copies in private collections, and even in public libraries.

I have prefaced the lists, in languages other than French, with a short explanation of the classifications. For the French manuscripts, the reader is referred to the text, especially Chapter 9.

I have undertaken to account for all manuscripts listed in Röhricht (R), but have not included him in the references for each manuscript, merely indicating where I am correcting or adding to his list, or where he notices manuscripts which do not contain Mandeville's *Travels.*

# IN FRENCH

## A

### Norman-French Version

1. **LONDON: BRITISH MUSEUM. HARLEY 4383.** 14 century. English hand. Vellum. 273 × 178 mm. (i$^{12}$ ii$^{10}$ iii$^{12}$ [lacks 7] iv$^{13}$ [foll. 39-40 are in a later hand, replacing one canceled leaf]). 38 long lines. *Mandeville*, incomplete, on foll. 1-46 [text ends in the middle of Chap. 22; 23-34 missing]. No letter of dedication. Bound with a contemporary but originally quite separate *Formulae Epistolarum Latinae*, and 1 leaf of *Rentale Manerii de Southtawton*, foll. 47-55. Begins: "Come il ensi soit qe la terre doutre mer . . ." Headings and plain caps. in red. No ornamentation, illustration, or marks of early ownership. 3 alphabets. Text printed by Warner.

    Ashton *Voiage*. Halliwell *Voiage*. *Harl. Cat.*, III, 139. Warner, *Buke*, p. ix ff. Letts, p. 173. Examined for me by R. A. B. Mynors.

2. **OXFORD: BODLEIAN. ASHMOLE 1804 (25174).** ca.1400 "or a little earlier." English hand. Vellum. tall 2° size. 2 cols. *Maundeville* on foll. 1-42, ends with letter of dedication, followed by the *Prophecies of John of Bridlington*, foll. 42$^v$-46$^v$. Foll. 47-48 blank. Foll. 49-104$^v$ *Le Chronique nommé Le Brut* continued to temp. Edw. III (text agreeing with Royal 20 A. III, and 19 C. IX). *Maundeville* has red headings, blue caps. flourished in red. Good texts of all 3 works. See above p. 207.

    *Ashmole*, pp. 1510-11. Mynors.

3. **LONDON: BRITISH MUSEUM. HARLEY 212.** Late 14 century. Current English hand. Vellum. 4° size (i-vii$^{12}$ [v and vi each lack 1 and 12] viii-ix$^{14}$). 28 lines. Original title on fol. 1, S$^r$ *John Maundeuille de meruailles de mounde*. Latin letter of dedication at the end, fol. 107. Begins: "Comme il ensi soit . . ." Red headings, blue paragraph marks, small blue caps. flourished in red. No illustrations, 4 alphabets. At the foot of fol. 107 is a contemporary inscription recording that the book was given in 1425 to "the lady house of Bolton in Craven," i.e., the Augustinian Priory of Bolton in the West Riding of Yorkshire. The date of setting out is given as 1332.

    Ashton. Halliwell. *Harl. Cat.*, I, 68. Letts, p. 173. Mynors.

4. ——— ROYAL 20 A. I. Late 14 or early 15 century. English hand. Vellum. 222 × 159 mm. 1 + 122 foll. (in 12s, except vi[11]). No catchwords. 31 lines in 2 cols. Text ends fol. 119: "Explicit le geste de sire John Maundevill Chevaler de Seint Albanz en Engletere," followed by a table of chapters, and the letter of dedication, in the same hand. Red and blue paragraph marks and caps. Some scribal blunders in the placing of rubrics.

   Halliwell. Warner and Gilson, II, 349. Letts (p. 174) says no alphabets. Mynors.

5. DURHAM: CATHEDRAL LIBRARY. B. III 3, PART II. Early 15 century. Neat current English hand. Vellum. 298 × 196 mm. (in 8s). 77 leaves. 35-40 long lines. Bound ca. 18 century with a 12 century MS. which precedes it. Text has a preface, 33 caps., letter of dedication on 134$^v$. Fol. 1 has initial and partial border of foliage in gold and color. Red headings, blue caps. flourished in red. No marks of ownership.

   Rud, p. 147. *Cat. Vet.* p. 140, no. 10. Mynors.

6. OXFORD: BODLEIAN. BODL. 841 (8714). ca 1430. Neat small English hand. Vellum. 246 × 160 mm. i + 89 foll. Lacks letter of dedication. Rubrics as far as Chap. 22 only (those for 23-34 om.). Fol. 1 has small initial and partial border, foliage and a little gold. Blue caps. flourished in red. Good contemporary stamped binding. "Christopher Wiswick" inside lower cover. Presented after 1632 to the Bodleian by Charles King, A.M. Christ's College.

   Vogels *LV*. Madan, II, ii, 1216. Mynors.

7. LONDON: BRITISH MUSEUM. HARLEY 204. 15 century. Poor current hand. Vellum. 4° size. 100 foll. (i-ii[8] iii[6] iv-xii[8] xiii[8] [lacks 8, blank]). 2 leaves numbered 35 and 2 numbered 69 by mistake. ca. 30 lines. Letter of dedication at the end. No ornamentation. Owner's name, 16 century, on fol. 1.

   Ashton. Halliwell. *Harl. Cat.*, I, 63. Letts (p. 174), says first 2 alphabets only. Mynors.

8. ——— HARLEY 1739 [bound with Harley 204]. 15 century. Small neat hand. Vellum and paper. Small 4° size (i-vii[10] viii[5]). 75 leaves. 30-35 lines. Good text. Letter of dedication at the end. Red headings and small plain caps. in red. Fol. 1, "Suthwell" in red, in late 15 century hand, replaces an earlier name.

On the flyleaves are many scribbles of accounts, etc., including names of Tudor owners.

Ashton. Halliwell. *Harl. Cat.*, II, 193. Letts (p. 174), reports the first 3 alphabets only. Mynors.

9. DURHAM: UNIVERSITY LIBRARY, COSIN V. i 10. Late 15 century. Several fairly good hands. Paper. 292 × 203 mm. (mostly in 12s). ca. 30 lines. Incomplete (ends in the midst of the account of the throne of Prester John, Hamelius, p. 183). Caps. and rubrics never filled in. Codex was George Davenport's.

Not in R. Described for me by Mynors. See also *The Durham Philobiblon*, I, pt. 2, p. 16. *Cat. Vet.*, p. 140.

*Three Manuscripts of this Version in French Hands*

10. LONDON: BRITISH MUSEUM. ADDIT. 33757 (formerly Grenville XXXIX). Late 14 century. Vellum. Small 2° size. 2 columns. 75 foll. No letter of dedication. Not divided into chaps. A good initial and partial border in red and blue penwork, with inner border fringed with fleurs-de-lis on fol. 2. Rubrics and caps. in red. Fair text of the Anglo-Norman version, but in the dialect of Paris, and with very corrupt proper names. Text nearest Sloane 1464, especially in its omissions. It has been inferred, from an L and crown with fleurs-de-lis stamped on the late 17 century binding, that it once belonged in the French royal library. This MS. has all 6 alphabets but lacks the Greek characters. All important variants are given by Warner in his notes.

*Bibl. Gren.* Ashton. Warner, *Buke*, p. ix. B. M. *Cat. of Addit. MSS, 1888-1893*, p. 103. Letts, p. 173. Mynors.

11. PARIS: BIBLIOTHÈQUE NATIONALE. FONDS FR. 25284. 14 century. Paper. 205 × 145 mm. 157 leaves. Follows the Norman-French text in the critical passages, but uses mostly Parisian spelling. Names of owners, "Philopot, oblat des celestins [de Paris]," on fol. 153$^v$, and "Louis Dotruy" on fol. 157. No alphabets. dates *cccxxii* and *mil lvi*. Fol. 51 has an addition on Nazareth; fol. 61 reads: "les murs sont couvers de une yerre" as in the Paris redaction. Begins: "Comme il soit ainsi que la terre d'Outremere . . ."

Omont, *Cat. Gen.* 8° Anc. Petits fonds fr., II (1902), 553-554. Thomas.

12. BERN: BÜRGERBIBLIOTHEK. NO. A. 280. 14 century. Vellum. 207 × 195 mm. 261 leaves. In a composite MS of which the first 5 items are on paper, and the last 4 are on parchment. Mandeville, the first item in the second part, is unrelated to either what precedes or what follows. The text occupies foll. 81-136$^v$, and lacks about 3 leaves at the beginning, perhaps 4 in the middle, and a leaf or two at the end. It is roughly written in 28-32 long lines to a page. The first extant leaf begins just before the chapter opening, "En Constantinople est la croix Nre Seigneur J.C." The text ends on 136$^v$ shortly after the account of the Valley Perilous (foll. 133-135), near the beginning of the chapter, "Par le pais dinde a grant foison de cocodrilles." Fol. 96 reads, "Et il la porta a une chappelle qui est a viii lieues du liege." On the "ivy" passage see Appendix III. But the passage on circumnavigation (fol. 130) follows the Norman-French text, and the addition to the Valley Perilous is not present. Belonged to Bongars.

Hagen, *Cat.*, pp. 305-307. Examined for me by Mr. Mynors.

## SUB-GROUP I

Two French and two Latin texts [Leyden: UB, Vulcan 96; and London: B.M. Egerton 672] contain an interpolated Latin letter purporting to be from "Balthazardy," son of Melik-en-Násir, Sultan of Egypt, to the Pope, reproaching him for the state of Christendom. The letter is printed by Vogels, *LV*, p. 15. Hamelius, II, 40-42, prints and translates it. The two French manuscripts are:

13. LONDON: BRITISH MUSEUM. ROYAL 20 B. X. Late 14 or early 15 century. Current English hand. Vellum. 267 × 178 mm. 83 foll. (in 8s, except the last in 4s), catchwords. Foll. 1-2 (before 1st gathering) have table of 34 chaps. in a later hand. Letter of dedication on fol. 83$^v$. Text nearest to Harley 4383. Warner suggests that it descends from the same archetype, because in 2 places both omit the same word. He used it to complete his text, printing foll. 48-83$^v$. This MS was at Richmond Palace in 1535. Only 3 alphabets, Greek, Hebrew, and Egyptian, and names of letters only, no forms. Letter to the Pope on f. 10$^v$. No illustrations.

Halliwell. Warner, *Buke*, pp. ix, xxix n. Warner and Gilson, II, 364. Letts, p. 173. Mynors.

## APPENDIX I

14. LONDON: BRITISH MUSEUM. SLOANE 560. 15 century. Neat English hand. Vellum. 229 × 152 mm. 55 leaves. (1 + i$^{12}$ ii$^{12}$ [whole sig. missing] iii$^{12}$ [lacks 6 and 7] iv-v$^{12}$ vi$^{12}$ [lacks 6 and 7] + 4). ca. 40 long lines. Has letter of "Balthazardy" but no letter of dedication. No ornamentation, not even rubrication. Chapter division missing in most of the book. "George Browne" and "Elizabeth Browne" among late 15 century scribbles on the guard leaves. Contemporary foliation shows 16 missing leaves.

    Ashton. Halliwell. Scott, *Index*, 335. Letts, p. 173. Mynors.

### SUB-GROUP II

Six MSS have a life of St. Alban of Germany added. These are:

15. LONDON: BRITISH MUSEUM. SLOANE 1464. Late 14 century. Vellum. Neat current English hand. 185 × 171 mm. (i-xx$^8$ xxi$^5$ [1 leaf lost after fol. 149]. ca. 24 lines. Lacks letter of dedication, but has, at end of text, in same hand as rest of MS, on foll. 161$^v$-164, a life of St. Albàn of Allemagne, beginning: "Pur ceo que ieo su de la ville de Seint Alban et meintes gents de nos pays guident qil nia autre seint Alban fors q*ue* cely de nos pays jeo voielle q*ue* vous sachetz q*ue* lia un autre Seint Alban en Almaigne . . ." and ending: "nous doyre bon fyn et saluacõn de corps et alme Amen." No illustration or ornamentation, but much rubrication. No marks of early ownership. Collated by Warner. Letts reports Egyptian and Hebrew alphabets, and Greek forms given for Saracen.

    Ashton. Halliwell. Scott, *Index*, 335. Warner, *Buke,* p. ix. Letts, p. 173. Mynors.

16. OXFORD: BODLEIAN. ADDIT. C 280 (29572). Late 14 or early 15 century. English hand. Vellum. 267 × 191 mm. 127 leaves. Table of chaps. unfinished. Lacks letter of dedication and has the Life of St. Alban at the end of the text, foll. 119$^v$-120$^r$. Foll. 124-127 contain 2 English poems added in mid-15 century. Inscribed: "Iste liber constat Johanni Heruy de Lyncolnes In." He was admitted to the Inn in 1509. Tends to agree, in omissions and mistakes, with Sloan 1464; as in the omission of "Aix la Chapelle," and the reading "Emperor" for "Espervier."

    Madan, v, 646. Mynors.

17. PARIS: BIBLIOTHÈQUE NATIONALE. FONDS FR. 5635 (anc. 10261.[3] Colbert 3112). 1402, written by G. Mayes. Vellum. 1 + 65 leaves. Foll. 1-2, table. 2$^v$, miniature, followed by the passage from the end of the text, beginning: "Je Jehan de Mandeville chevalier, passay la mer l'an de grace mil iii$^c$ xxii . . ." through the Life of St. Alban of Allemagne. This passage gives the date of return as 1356, but when the autobiographical passage is repeated, in its usual place at the end of the text, this date is 1357 as in the Paris redaction. The additions which distinguish the Paris redaction are not present, however. Beginning reads: "Comme qu'il soit que la terre d'O . . ."

*Bibl. Nat. Cat.*, Ancien fonds, 2° Sers., v, 48. Thomas.

18. ———— ANCIEN FONDS FR. 2810. ca. 1403. Vellum. 420 × 298 mm. 297 leaves. This is the famous *Livre des Merveilles*, described in Chap. 5, pp. 82-83; see also Chap. 15, n. 25. It contains Marco Polo, foll. 1-96, Mandeville, foll. 141-225$^v$, and Le Long's translations of 6 other works about the Orient. Fol. 141, miniature of the author taking leave of an English king, and six other pictures from this MS reproduced, see "Illustrations." The text is headed: "Cy commence le livre mesire Guillaume de Mandeville," but he is called "Jehan" in the text proper. Fol. 224$^v$ contains the Life of St. Alban of Germany. Letter of dedication is not present. The text lacks the additions which distinguish the Paris redaction, and gives the date of return as 1356. MS made for Philippe Duc de Bourgogne, and given in 1413 by his son Jean sans Peur to the Duc de Berry. It passed through the hands of the Duc de Nemours, at whose death it came into the hands of the house of Bourbon.

*Bibl. Nat. Cat.*, Ancien fonds, 2° Ser., I, 485-486. H. Omont, *Livre des Merveilles*. Introduction, for the best account of the MS. and bibliography of descriptions and reproductions of the pictures. Benedetto, p. xxxv-vi. Many of the pictures are represented in Cordier's *Odoric*, cviii-cxiii, 174, 202, 207, 267, 303, 358, 377, 427, 439, 490. L. Delisle, *Recherches sur la Librairie de Charles V*, II, 305, traces its history, but see Omont. Thomas.

19. ———— FONDS FR. 5633 (anc. 10261). 15 century. Paper. Table on foll. 1-4, followed by text. Life of St. Alban of Allemagne at the end, foll. 185$^v$-188. Text is similar to that of Bibl. Nat. fr. 5635, but more correct. The date of return is 1357, but the

additions of the Paris redaction are absent. 3 alphabets, Egyptian and Hebrew names only. The St. Alban addition begins: "Pour ce que je suis nés de Saint-Albain, et maintes gens de nostre païs cuide qu'il ne soit nul autre Sain Albain que celui de nostre païs, je vueil que vous sachies qu'il y a ung autre Saint Albain en Almagne. . . ." Incipit: "Comme il soit ainsy que la terre . . ." Fol. 188$^v$ ex libris of "Pierre Godet Barbier" and "Jehan Bouhard 1584." Also on fol. 1, "Tulloüe." Once used to press flowers, and foll. 47, 65, 80, 87, and 96 damaged.

*Bibl. Nat. Cat.*, Ancien fonds, 2° Ser, v, 47. Thomas.

20. BERN: BÜRGERBIBLIOTHEK. NO. 58. Written 1468. Paper. 290 × 205 mm. 100 leaves, unnumbered. 34 lines. Red and blue caps. Initial with the coat of arms of the original owner; *argent* a chevron *gules* between three bunches of grapes *azure*. A note in the MS. attributes them to J. Budè, and refers to the Gumuchian & Co. *Catalogue* (1941?) "Belles reliures." Contains the Mandeville only, with the short Life of St. Alban at the end. No title. This is the Norman-French version giving the date of writing as 1356. In 2 hands, the second beginning on f. 42. Begins, "Comme il soit ainsi que le terre . . ." and ends, "Car dieu prent toujours amer cy seulx qui meurent en bonne entencion et qui vraiement se repentent de bon cuer." It does not have the substitution in the passage on circumnavigation (fol. 57), nor the addition to the Valley Perilous. Fol. 23 on the prepuce reads, "et il la porta a poitiers et puis a chartres" (no mention of Aix), and see the reading on the sparrowhawk castle. At the end: "Explicit Mandeuille lequel fut assouuy le xvij$^{me}$ jour de mars lan mil iiij$^c$lxviij." Below the Explicit is an ownership mark, black with reagent. Inside the front cover is the ex-libris of Jean Garroy(?) in a 16 c. hand. Later it belonged to Bongars who transmitted it to Bern.

Hagen, Cat., I, 85. Sinner, *Cat.* II, 415-418. Mynors.

# B

## Paris French

Two early MSS define two families of MSS of this redaction, one divided into chapters, and the other not. I have designated them P and Q without intending to suggest which is the earlier.

*P TEXT*

21. PARIS: BIBLIOTHÈQUE NATIONALE. FONDS FR., NOUV. ACQ. 4515 (Formerly Bibl. Nat. 886 in 1645; 10262 after 1682; 185 in Barrois' library; Barrois 24 in Lord Ashburnham's library [not Libri xxiv, as listed by Vogels]; also once numbered 5636, and so listed by R.) Vellum. 230 × 155 mm. 96 leaves. Originally followed by the *De pestilentia* of Jean de Bourgogne, foll. 97-102$^v$, now nouv. acq. 4516 (formerly Barrois 282). Text begins: "Comme il soit ainsi que la terre . . ." *Mandeville* illustrated by 6 miniatures, 4 on the title page, the others on foll. 34 and 36$^v$. Other ornamentation, including the arms of the king, Charles V, and many fleurs-de-lis. The text is divided by ornamental caps. into 123 chapters. After the first 50, chapter headings are sometimes missing. A note (erased) on the last page of 4516: "Ce livre est à nous, Charles le V$^e$ de no/tre roy de France, et le nous donna metre Gervese Cretien, notre premier/fisicien, l'an M.CCC.LXXI./ Charles." A note in Mallet's *Catalogue* records that Charles VI took the volume out of the library 20 November 1392.

For its subsequent history, see Delisle, *Cat. Libri et Barrois*, pp. 251-253; *Recherches*, etc. Photostat in the Harvard College Library, xlli, 426. Photographic reproduction of the first and last leaves in Delisle's *Recherches*, album, pl. vi and vii. The text is being printed by Malcolm Letts for the Hakluyt Society (1953). For further description, see above, Chap. 9, pp. 135 ff., and 11, pp. 165 ff. R. lists twice, under both old and new numbers. Letts, pp. 172-173. Vogels, *LV*, pp. 10 ff. quotes from this MS.

22. —— FONDS FR. 5637 (anc. 10270[a.a.] Ant. Faure 111). 14 century. Vellum. 102 leaves, A-D, 1-98. B and D blank. Foll. 1-2, table of chaps. Fol. 3 miniature of presentation, followed by an ex libris entirely erased. Text on foll. 3-98. There are traces of Picard(?) dialect. All alphabets omitted. Probably copied directly from 4515. Begins: "Comme il soit ainsi . . ."

*Bibl. Nat. Cat.*, Ancien fonds, 2° Sers., v, 48. Thomas.

23. —— FONDS FR. 5634 (anc. 10261$^2$. Baluze 392). 15 century. Paper. Imperfect. Lacks leaves 1, one between the present 6 and 7, and 2 at the end. 87 leaves present, but 79-87 are mutilated. Foll. 1 [missing] and 2, table of chaps, same headings as in 4515. At end of table is the statement: "Et en la fin de cest livre est escripte le preservacion de epidemie . . . faicte

# APPENDIX I

de maistre Jehan de Bourgogne autrement dit A la barbe professeur en medecine et cytoyen de Liege, et ce commence on feullet 93." All leaves after 87 missing. Owned in 1633 by Brodeau. More carefully written than nouv. acq. 4515, it attempts to make sense of "de i. yerre Eder," reading "de une pierre (Vaire) Eder." As in 4515, the Hebrew alphabet occurs twice, once in its place in the text, fol. 28$^v$, where as in 4515 it is fancifully drawn and named, and again on fol. 73, where the correctly written Hebrew alphabet at the end of 4515 is clearly imitated. Begins: "Comme il fust ainssi . . ."

*Bibl. Nat. Cat.*, Ancien fonds, 2° Ser., v, 47. Thomas.

24. ——— FONDS FR. 6109 (anc. 10532). Early 15 century. Vellum. 136 leaves. Fol 1 has a miniature [in a bad state] of a knight, followed by text ending on fol. 136. Last leaf has some names of 15 century owners: "harlay——Marguery de Hudebert——Jehan Bonin, prisonier à la Consiergerie." The rubrics are analogous to those in 4515, and like that text the first paragraph has the reading *joies* for *piés*, i.e., feet. There are no alphabets. Fol. 63 reads: "les murs sont couers de un yerre." Begins like 4515.

D. Zarncke, *Der Priester Johannes* (1876), pp. 180-184. *Bibl. Nat. Cat.*, Ancien fonds, 2° Ser., v, 213. Thomas.

25. ——— FONDS FR. 2129 (anc. 7972²). 15 century. Vellum. 4° size. Incomplete at beginning and end, and lacks 6 other leaves. The reading "murs sont couvers de une yerre eder" indicates that this is a copy, direct or indirect, of 4515, but M. Thomas found it difficult to check fully because of the lacunae. It has the addition to the Valley Perilous. Egyptian alphabet only.

*Bibl. Nat. Cat.*, Ancien fonds, 2° Ser., I, 361. Thomas.

## Q TEXT

26. ——— NOUV. ACQ. 10723. 14 century. Vellum. Current hand. 250 × 170 mm. 100 leaves. 33 lines. Text foll. 1-100$^v$. No ornament except a small initial and a few leaves of vine on fol. 1. No chap. headings, rubrication, or punctuation. Begins: "Cõme il soit ainsi que la terre doultremer Cest assauoir la terre sainte de promission entre toutes autres terres soit la plus excellante et la plus digne . . ." Has all 6 alphabets, also the

addition and the substitute passages which distinguish the Paris redaction. Gives dates 1322, 1357, and 35th year. Probably the best text of this version: see further above, p. 141 ff.

Not in R. *Bibl. Nat. Cat.*, Nouv. acq. fr., IV (1918), 90. Acquired by Bibl. Nat. 1891-1910, probably from Quaritch, see *Cat. of Ancient, Illuminated, and Liturgical MSS.* (1902), p. 33, no. 76.

27. ——— ARSENAL 3219 (formerly 21 H. F.). 14 century. Vellum. Norman-French hand. 232 × 162 mm. 107 leaves. Single col. Foll. A and B preceding the text contain some fragments of Ovid's *Heroides* in an Italian hand of the 14 century. Large initial in gold and color on fol. 1. Almost as good a text as 10723, from which it perhaps descends. Until the 18 century it was no. 82 of an Italian library. It passed to the Arsenal from the library of M. de Paulmy, where it was "Histoire No. 8010 A." Haenel, p. 357, describes the dialect of this MS as "provenzale." M. Thomas suggested Walloon. Begins, "Com il soit ensi..."

Martin, *Cat.*, III, 294. See above, p. 170, n. 2.

## Other MSS probably of the P Text

28. TOURS: BIBLIOTHÈQUE DE. No. 947. 14 century. Vellum. 320 × 223 mm. 192 leaves. 2 cols. Contains, foll. 1-66, *L'Image du Monde*, with over 1500 verses of the voyage of St. Brandan; foll. 67-154, *Mandeville*, followed by the *Roman de Fauvel*, and the *Advocacie Notre-Dame*. First item only illuminated. Fol. 67 has the table of chaps. 68$^r$ begins: "Ci Commence... Comme il soit ainsi...," and opening and close suggest the P text. Lacks the usual colophon identifying the writer. Belonged, temp. Henri IV, to Père Matthieu Giron. Came to the Public Library of Tours from the Abbey of Marmoutier (no. 86).

Cordier, *Biblio. Sin.*, III, 2042-43. Dorange, *Cat.*, pp. 417-418. *Cat. Gen.*, Vol. 37$^2$, pp. 681-683.

29. MODENA: BIBLIOTECA ESTENSE. FRANCESE NO. 33 (formerly XI. F. 17). 1388. Paper. 275 × 210 mm. 92 leaves. 27-36 long lines. Three unnumbered leaves at the beginning were added later, and the title and table of chaps. written on them in a 15 century hand. Fol. 2 begins: "Comme il soit ainssy que la terre d'oultre mer..." Text ends on fol. 82 with the biographical passage giving the dates 1322, 1357, and 35 years.

# APPENDIX I 275

Text ends: "et par tous temps. Amen." Foll. 83 and 87 are blank. Foll. 85-89$^v$ contain a fragment of *L'évangile de l'enfance* written in mid-15 century. At end of *Mandeville* text, fol. 82, is the colophon: "Explicit le romant messire Jehan de Mandeville chevalier de la nacion d'Angleterre, escript et accomply l'an de grace Nostre Seigneur; Mil CCC LXXXVIIJ le x$^e$ jour de decembre par la main maistre Perre le Sauvaige de Chaalons en Champaigne maistre en ars; demour' adonc a excellent et puissant Princesse, la Duchesse de Tourainne, countesse de Valoiz et de Beaumont." For a discussion of this MS, see p. 174, n. 8. Camus, *La Venue*, shows that the paper came from the Visconti chancelleries about 1388. It was at Modena in 1757.

R. gives old number. Camus, *Notices et Extraits*, p. 212; and *Revue des Bibl.* IV, 12-19. And see Bertoni.

30. ROME: BIBLIOTHECA APOSTOLICA VATICANA. CODEX REG. LAT. 750 (formerly Regina Christina 542). 14 century. Vellum. 294 × 200 mm. 83 leaves. 2 cols. 37 lines. Some miniatures. The explicit is an acrostic in bad verse which gives the name of the scribe as Jean Hazart. A man of that name was mentioned as the physician of the King of France in MS. Reg. 1334. Langlois describes this as an early and good text, and quotes the beginning and end. He distinguishes it from what he calls a "second redaction," by which term he evidently means the Liège version. The 18 cent. binding is decorated with the arms of Pope Pius IX. The date of return is given as 1358.

R. gives the old number. E. Langlois, *Notices des Manuscrits*, Vol. XXXIII, Pt. II, 46-48. And see above, p. 174, n. 8.

31. MILAN: TRIVULZIANA. CODEX 816 (formerly Belgioioso, 166). written 1396. Vellum. 298 × 208 mm. 112 leaves numbered in a recent hand, the last 3 blank. 33 lines. Illuminated initials and borders throughout. In its original binding of red velvet. Colophon: "Explicit li romans de Messire Jehan de Mandeville chevalier de la nattion dangleterre escript et acompli l'an de grace M CCC LXXXXVI le mercredi XIII iour de Septempre par la main de Richart Hemon clerc." Followed by 2 cancelled lines, ending "Deo gratias." Gatherings of 4 leaves, with catchwords. Inside the back cover is the inscription, "Questo libro e Joh. Jacobo Vincemalo/ fiolo del magnifico sig.

re Redolfo Vincemala," in a hand of the 16th century. There is also the inscription in a 17th century hand, "Viaggi e navigatione e descrittione de paesi de Giovanni de Mandavilla Francese."

R. makes 2 of this ms. He lists Belgiojoso, no 166 as French, and Trivulziano no. 816 as Italian. Porro, *Cat.*, pp. 231-232. For additional details I am indebted to Prof. Caterina Santoro, the Director of the Biblioteca Trivulziana.

32. ROME: BIBLIOTHECA APOSTOLICA VATICANA. CODEX. REG. 837 (formerly Regina Christina 742). 2nd half 15 Century. Paper. 248 × 205 mm. 90 leaves. The beginning is lacking. Rubrics and table of chaps. in Latin. Same text as no. 30, but inferior to it. Gives the dates 1332 and 1347, for 1322 and 1357. Copied by Frater Johannes Descallis. Belonged to A. Petau in 1638.

R. gives the old number. Langlois, *Notices des Manuscrits*, xxxiii, Pt. II, 64-65.

## Other MSS of the Paris Redaction

33. MADRID: BIBLIOTECA NACIONAL. NO. 9602 (Ee 65). 14 century. Vellum. 52 leaves. 2 cols. 38 lines. Begins: "Come il soit ainsi que la terre doultremer . . ." and ends: "et Regne per touz temps et per touz siecles. Amen. Explicit le liure de mādeuille." It is more recent in Spain than the Spanish versions.

Not in R. Entwistle, p. 253 n.

34. BRUSSELS: BIBLIOTHÈQUE ROYALE. NO. 14787. 14 century. Vellum. 310 × 250 mm. 87 leaves plus 2 guard leaves at the beginning and one at the end. 34 long lines. Caps. in red and blue make 23 sections. Fol. 21, "et il la porta a Ays la chappelle a viii lieues du liege." F. 39$^v$ the "ivy" passage, see Appendix III. Fol. 51 has substitute passage on circumnavigation, and the date is 1357, but the addition to the Valley Perilous seems to be missing. Compare No. 39. 16 century binding. There are entries of ownership of members of the de Marisy family, seigneurs de Cernel, in the xv, xvi, and xvii centuries. In 1647 it belonged to Claude Desmares, whose mother had been Pauline de Marisy. Bought by Bassange in 1837 from Rosny.

*Cat. of B. R.*, ii, 79. Examined for me by Mr. Mynors.

## APPENDIX I

35. LONDON: BRITISH MUSEUM. HARLEY 3940. Early 15 century. Vellum. 4° size, much cut by the binder. 42 long lines. Neat, probably French hand. Text on foll. 1-49 (i-vi,[8] vii[3]), followed by an Old Testament history from the creation to Isaac. No ornamentation, no rubrics. 1 leaf lost after fol. 12, and 1 after fol. 22. Fol. 27[v] has the substitute passage on circumnavigation, and foll. 43-44 have the addition to the Valley Perilous, beginning, "Ceste uallee a asses belle entree et bel chemin au commencement . . ." and it includes a story of a black spot which Mandeville bore for over 18 years until it was removed by patience. Warner describes this MS. as "almost" in "a class by itself" with the names "more than ordinarily disfigured." It seems to have been the only copy known to him of the Paris redaction. Letts reports that it has only the first 2 alphabets, the Greek without forms. Begins: "Cy commenche le livre de Jeh. de Mandeville Chavalier." On the last leaf, in a 16 c hand, "Ce livre apartient a Jhan Vauguelin escuyer sieur des Quetcaulx'." It has the bookplate and binding stamp of Nicolas Joseph Foucault.

    Ashton. Halliwell. *Harl. Cat.*, III, 97. Warner, *Buke*, p. ix. Letts, p. 173. Mynors.

36. BERN: BÜRGERBIBLIOTHEK. NO. 125. Early 15 century. Vellum. 325 × 235 mm. 2 cols. of 34-35 lines, ruled in red. 287 leaves. Foll. 1-93, Marco Polo; foll. 95-180[v], *Mandeville*, followed by Le Long's 6 translations, as in B.N., f. f. 2810. Two (?) leaves of text are lost at the end of the *Mandeville*, which is headed: "Ci commence le liure Jehan de Mandeuille cheualier lequel parle de lestat de la terre Saincte et des merueilles que il ya veues." F. 116[v] reads: "Et il le porta a ays la chappelle a vii lieues de liège," and f. 135 reads "de l yerre Eder" as in the P text copied in 1371. F. 146 has the substitute passage on circumnavigation, and 170[v]-172[v] the account of the Valley Perilous. The text breaks off in the chapter headed: "Cy parle des ymaiges de pierre et de fust et des ydoles du pais." The text proper begins: "Comme il soit ainsy . . ." and ends: "Car ilz ne porroient riens dire de nouuel de quoy les oyans peussent prendre soulas."

    No pictures, but many illuminated margins of formal foliage of good French work, embellished with the arms of the person for whom the book was made: *argent*, a fess bendy of 6, *or* and *gules*. From the library of J. Bongars of Orléans. The first quire is in a different hand from the rest.

Sinner, *Cat.*, II, 419-502. Hagen, *Cat.*, pp. 178-180. Cordier, *Odoric*, pp. cxiv-v. Benedetto, *Marco Polo*, p. xxxix. Examined for me by Mr. Mynors.

37. AMIENS: BIBLIOTHÈQUE MUNICIPALE. FONDS L'ESCALOPIER 95 (5201). 15 century. Vellum. 340 × 250 mm. 154 leaves. Fol. 106 has the substitution on circumnavigation, and fol. 142 has the addition on the Valley Perilous. Reads *pieds* in the first paragraph, where the P text has *joies,* and omits *ivy* in the passage, fol. 74 reading, "murs sont couvers de edere que nous appelons et siet sur une roche." Begins, "Comme il soyt ainsy que la terre . . ."

Fol. 1 has a miniature showing someone presenting the book to a Duc de Bourgogne, whose arms appear at the foot of the page. Margins illuminated. The name "Philippe de Cleves" appears on the last leaf, at the end of the text, and the binding has his arms. Has 6 alphabets but lacks the names of the "Persian" letters.

Not in R. *Cat. Gen.*, XIX, 494-495. *L'Escolopier Cat.*, II, 381. Thomas.

38. BRUSSELS: BIBLIOTHÈQUE ROYALE. NO. 10439 (in a Vol. press-marked 10437-40). Mid 15 century. Paper. 290 × 220 mm. 200 folios. 33 long lines. The volume is made up of 4 separate works, in different hands, which have been bound together. Fol. 53 is a blank leaf, except for the title *Mandeuille*. Text begins on fol. 54 and ends of fol. 138 with the colophon, "Iehans Grouz escripsi cest liure." At the foot of the text, in another hand, "Ce liure est appelle le mandeuille traittant de touttes nacions, le quel est a monsieur Charles de Croy Comte de Chimay," whose collection passed into the Bibliothèque de Bourgogne, and so into the Bibliothèque Royale. The text begins, "Comme il soit ensi . . ." Fol. 75 reads, "et il le porta a ays le chappelle a viii liuwes de liege." It has the "ivy" passage on fol. 93, and the substitute passage on circumnavigation on fol. 104$^v$. The Valley Perilous on 128-129$^v$ seems to lack the addition. The date of writing is given as 1357. Compare No. 34. The text is divided into 18 sections by rough red caps. 6 alphabets.

*Cat. de B. R.*, II, 79. Mynors.

## APPENDIX I

39. —— NO. 11141. Written 1463. Paper. 282 × 205 mm. 85 leaves. 2 cols. 40-45 lines. Red caps. make 50 sections. Fol. 20$^v$ "et il le porta a ays en allemaigne a la chappelle a viii lieues de Liege." The "ivy" interpolation on fol. 38. The substitute passage on circumnavigation on fol. 49$^v$ but the Valley Perilous on fol. 74 without the addition. The date of completion is given as 1357. 6 alphabets. Colophon at the end: "Che liure chy fu escript de ma main G. Judocy en ce present papier ou chasteau de duersteden Emprez la ville de Wijck sur la riuiere du Rin lan mil cccc lxiij."

*Cat. de B. R.*, II, 79. Occasionally quoted by Hamelius, but not described. Mynors.

40. DIJON: BIBLIOTHÈQUE DE. ANCIEN FONDS 549 (313). 15 century. Paper. 275 × 205 mm. 68 leaves, the last 2 mutilated. Reads *piés*, has the "ivy" passage on fol. 37, and the addition to the Valley Perilous on fol. 64. It has the substitute passage on circumnavigation. 5 alphabets, the Hebrew very incomplete. An ex libris of the end of the 15 century: "Nycolas Flutelet vigneron demourant à la Bouquerie (?) dudit Dijon." In the 16 century it belonged to St. Benique de Dijon.

*Cat. Gen.*, V, pp. 135-136. Thomas.

41. PARIS: BIBLIOTHÈQUE NATIONALE. FONDS FR. 5586 (anc. 10024). Dated 1477. Paper. Fol. 1-88$^v$, followed by the Romance of the Seven Sages, incomplete. Has 6 alphabets, but lacks figures of all, and both names and figures of the last, which has an attempt (apparently) at transliteration instead. Colophon: "Escript l'an de grace mil IIII$^c$ LXXVII, de par ung très noble seigneur et escuier, sire Amy Robe, seigneur de la Mureicte a qui Dieu doient bonne vie et longue et a la fin de ces jours paradis. Amen.// Lequel livre a fait escripte à frère Johan Ragot, frère mineur du convent d'Angiers quant il demoroit au convent de Moyrenc[ourt], l'an mill cccc lxxvii et fini le xxii$^e$ jour de octobre./ Jo*h*a*n*nes Ragot."

*Bibl. Nat. Cat.*, 2° Ser., ancien fonds V (1902), 29-30. Thomas.

42. —— FONDS FR. 20145. 15 century. Paper. 380 × 250 mm. 91 leaves. Fragmentary. With a chronicle of the kings of France, 376-1461. The text of *Mandeville* is defective at beginning and end, extending from Warner's Chap. VI (fol. 14) to XXV (fol.

82). Fol. 52 reads: "les murs sont couvers de edron que nous appellons plomb." No alphabets. No rubrics. Chap. divisions very different from those of the P text.

*Bibl. Nat. Cat. Gén.* anc. petits fonds fr., I (1898), 20. Thomas.

43. ——— FONDS FR. 1403 (anc. 7511). 15 century. Paper. Defective at beginning and end, and other leaves lacking. Text begins on fol. vii of an old foliation, at a point corresponding to 4$^v$ in Bibl. Nat. fr. 4515 and ends on fol. cxi$^v$ at a point corresponding to fol. 74$^v$ of 4515. Foll. ix, xxi-xxiii, xxxiv, lix, etc. missing. Leaves containing all 6 alphabets are preserved. Some marginal rubrics in Latin. The "ivy" passage is missing, but the passage on circumnavigation is present. Owned at end of 15 century by Simon de Ribo. Some marginalia of 16-17 centuries.

*Bibl. Nat. Cat.*, 2° Ser., ancien fonds fr I (1868), 222. Thomas.

44. **CAMBRIDGE, U.S.A.: HARVARD UNIVERSITY LIBRARY.** RIANT 50. Late 15 century. Paper. 210 × 150 mm. 245 + 3 leaves. Cursive hand, Latin in large Gothic letters. 18 lines. A curiously jumbled text, such as would result if it had been copied from an unbound MS in which leaves, especially at the beginning, were misplaced. The mistake was not made in binding this MS, because here the confusions occur in the middle of the page. There are frequent omissions of words, but great care was taken in transcribing the alphabets. Little ornament, but a sketch of a dog at the foot of one page. Text in several hands, with notes in various later hands.

Not in R. De Ricci, *Census*, I, 1005, described as "unbound." Now in a modern binding.

45. **AIX: BIBLIOTHÈQUE DE.** NO. 437 (148-R. 339, 616, 659). 17 century. Paper. 430 × 282 mm. 571 leaves. *Mandeville* on pp. 255-571, following a "Chronique de Louis douze." Text follows that of the printed editions.

R. calls it "Aix 659." *Cat. Gen.*, xvi (1894), 224.

## C

### Ogier-Liège Version

46. **CHANTILLY: MUSÉE CONDÉ NO. 699 (1414).** 14 century. Vellum. 293 × 112 mm. 118 leaves. 34 lines. Foll. 1-75: text

of the *Travels*. Foll. 75-88: "Chi comenche li secons lyures mesire Jehan de mandeuille cheualier qui fait mencion de la forme de la terre & comment & par quel maniere elle fu faite." Foll. 88-96$^v$: "Chi commenche ly tiers liures mesire iehan de mandeuille qui fait mention de la forme del cyel." Foll. 96$^v$-102$^v$: "Chi commenche li luurs quars sire iehans de mandeuille chlr fait mention des herbes selonc les yndois & les philosophes par de la." Foll. 102$^v$-108$^v$: "Chi commenche ly lapydayres complis de par mesire iehan de mandeuille chlr selonc le oppinion des yndois de cui toutes les sciences des pierres vienent & est ly chiuncismes & ausy daerams des chiunc liures qui de par lui fuirent ordines sy com ly autres vous sont deuises par dessus." Foll. 108$^v$-118: "Chi endroit commenche la venianche de nostre signeur ihesu crist fayte par vaspasian fil del empereur de Romme & comment ioseph daramathye fu deliuers de la prison." Fol. 1 has full border and large initial showing a man in the arms of the Ghistelles of Artois, "de gueules au chevron d'herminis." Same on a shield at the foot of the page. Ornamental initials in gold and colors, with border extensions, throughout, dividing the text into 145 paragraphs. Borders on all title pages. Fol. 118, in a contemporary hand, "Dieu en ayde a Jacqueline." Fol. 88 has a marginal inscription, "Monasterii SS Trinitatis Vindocin" (18 century), and on fol. 1 is the press-mark "C 113" of the abbey of the Trinity of Vendôme (near Orléans). Foll. 17-24 are misplaced in binding. The Chantilly *Cat.* omits the opening of pt. 2, and the fol. no. of pt. 3, confusing the two parts. This is probably the copy described in the Heber sale *Cat.* Pt. XI (1836), p. 105, no. 1009, as "appears to be considerably more ample than in the printed copies." Other details agree, including the opening: "Cy commence le livre des parties doultre mer lequel fu fait et ordonne par messire Jhan de Mandeville Chevalier qui fu nes en Engleterre de la ville qui on dist sainct Albain . . ." According to the Newberry Library's annotated copy of this Heber catalogue, no. 1009 was bought by Techener for £ 32. 11 s. Techener owned the MS now in the Musée Condé. It is described in the *Description raisonnée d'une collection choisie d'anciens manuscrits . . . réunis par les soins de M. J. Techener*, I (Paris, 1862), 159-61, no. 104. Heber's MS is described as from the White Knights and Watson Taylor collections.

Halliwell (1839) called it a fine MS. Not in R. *Chantilly. Le Cabinet des Livres*, III, 3-6. *Cat. Gen. Chantilly* (1928), p. 143. See above, Chaps. 7 and 8.

47. PARIS: BIBLIOTHÈQUE NATIONALE. FONDS FR. 24436. Written in 1396. Paper and Vellum. 260 × 205 mm. 160 leaves. Foll. 2-62 contain the text of the *Travels*. Foll. 64-114 contain poems and prayers in many hands. Foll. 115-130$^v$, the *Testament* of Jehan de Meun. Foll. 130$^v$-154, *Roman de Fauvel* by Gervais Du Bus. The *Mandeville* was originally a separate MS. On fol. 62 is the note: "Hunc librum acquisivit monasterio Sancti Victoris prope Parisius frater Johannes Lamasse, dum esset prior ejusdem ecclesie. Scriptum anno Domine 1424." This is the MS copied by Ogier de Caumont at Liège, see p. 113 for the text of the colophon. This MS has the 8 alphabets and the pseudo-autobiographical interpolation at the end, naming the innkeeper *Hennequin dit le volt*. On fol. 13$^v$ some Latin verses on the pyramids are interpolated. In 1899 F. E. Sandbach compared this text with Bibl. Nat. fr. 4515, and with Otto von Diemeringen's German. He recognized that Bibl. Nat. fr. 24436 was related to Otto's version, but did not pursue the problem to a positive identification of the French Ogier version: *Mod. Quart. of Lang. and Lit.*, pp. 29-35.

Omont, *Cat. Gen.*, 8° Anc. Petit fonds fr., II (1902), 373-376. A. Långfors, in *Romania*, XLI (1912), 206-246. Thomas.

48. AMIENS: BIBLIOTHÈQUE MUNICIPALE. FONDS L'ESCALOPIER 94 (5200). Written in 1461. Vellum, 220 × 153 mm. 134 leaves. The last 3 leaves contain a short treatise "des pieres precieuze" described above p. 130, followed by the colophon: "Chis libre est appelleis le livre Iohans de mande ville chevalier qui fut fait, escrit, copileit et extrais hors d'une aultre en la ville de hotton par le main lambert le clers Pour et ou nom de mon tres vailhant et tres honoreis signõur Mon damoysiaux Lowy Signeurs de Rochefort et Dagymont et cet. Sur l'an de grasce de la sainte natiuiteit nostre signeur Ihsucriste Milhe quatre cens et sissante et unck. En moy de May. et cet." The pseudo-autobiographical passage was published by M. Coyéque in the *Cat. Gen.*, and by Dorothea Waley Singer in the *Library*, 3d Ser., IX, 275-276. It names the innkeeper "Henkin Levolt," or Levoit. It reads 1322, 1356 and xv$^e$ [sic] an. Begins: "Comme il soit ensi . . ."

*Cat. Gen.*, XIX (1893), 493-494. Thomas.

49. CAMBRIDGE: FITZWILLIAM MUSEUM. McCLEAN 177 (Formerly Phillipps 9019 [no. 835 in the sale of 1898]). 15 cen-

tury. Vellum. 83 leaves (i⁸ii[lacks 1,2,7,8] iii-xi⁸ [lacks last leaf]). 302 × 217 mm. 27 lines. Of continental origin. Handsome copy, well written. Divided into numerous paragraphs beginning with large script and decorative initial. Fol. 82ᵛ has the note, "Nobilis Vir Jacobus bodueler [or bourueler] pocessor est huius voluminis" in a 15-16 century hand. The end of the text, fol. 80ᵛ, lacks the autobiographical interpolation, but foll. 60ᵛ and 79 contain the passages characteristic of the Paris version, and fol. 24 has the Ogier version of the prepuce story. The text is divided into numbered paragraphs. See above, p. 114. At the foot of fol. 1, erased, "Ex libris Cl. F. Mar[ra?]cher." Phillipps bought this MS of Thorpe in 1836. According to the annotation in the Newberry Library copy of the Heber *Cat.*, Pt. XI (1836), p. 105, Thorpe bought Heber No. 1008 (for £3.11s). It seems probable, therefore, that this is Heber's no. 1008.

Not in R. James, *Cat.*, I, 335-336. Phillipps, *Catalogus* (1837), p. 142. Mynors.

50. BRUSSELS: BIBLIOTHÈQUE ROYALE. NO. 10420-25. (Bound in 1913 with other items). 15 century. Paper. 217 × 145 mm. 148 leaves. Ca. 20-35 lines. Roughly written, with rough red caps. Mr. Letts, pp. 115 ff., describes it as late 15 or early 16 century, untidy and often illegible. It has neither rubrics nor a table. Hamelius made use of it in his notes, but says it is full of crabbed abbreviations. He quotes p. 97, l. 7, n: "de eder que nous appelons ivy"; p. 124, l. 10, the substitute passage on the antipodes; pp. 168, l. 27, and 184, l. 32, the alphabets of the Tartars and of Pentoxoire; p. 189, l. 17, the interpolation in the account of the Valley Perilous; p. 181, ll. 1, 10, p. 198, l. 30, p. 199, l. 10, references to Ogier; and p. 210, l. 33, he quotes the pseudo-autobiographical interpolation which names the innkeeper "herbin levo." Letts, pp. 116-118, quotes the 4 Ogier passages and the interpolation, and reports 6 alphabets.

*Cat. B. R.*, II, 78, indicates it came from Stavelot. Letts, pp. 115-118. Mynors.

51. LIÈGE: BIBLIOTHÈQUE DE L'UNIVERSITÉ. NO. 360. 15 century. This copy has disappeared, but in 1860 Ferd. Henaux published the pseudo-autobiographical passage from fol. 118, as follows: "Si en ay compileit che petit livre et mis en escript ensy quilh me puet sovenir. La quele ouvres fut ordonné lan

de grasce milhe ccc et lvi, alle xxxiiii an que me parti de mon pais, dedens la noble ceteit de Liége, en unc hosteil en la basse Savenir que on dist al hosté Henkin Levo, ou je gisoy malade. Sy me visetoit uns venerable homme et discreit, maistre Johans de Bourgogne, dit ala barbe, phisechiens, liqueils . . . moi recognuit . . ."

See "Notice sur le Quartier de la Sauvenière à Liége," *Bulletin de L'Institut archéologique Liégeois,* IV (1860), 171. Warner, *Buke,* p. xxviii n. partly transcribes from Henaux and reports that he could not find the vol. in the Catalogue of 1875. The present librarian could find no trace of it between 1860 and 1875.

UNIDENTIFIED

52. CAMBRIDGE: FITZWILLIAM MUSEUM. CFM. 23. Late 15 century. Paper and vellum. 290 × 210 mm. 114 leaves. 35 long lines. Written in neat French bâtardes, and bound with a fragment of the *Communeloquium* of John le Walleys. Begins: "Je Jehan de mandeville chevalier passay la mer lan de grace mille ccc. xxij. & fu partout ou homme peut aler . . ." This copy was Barrois 380 in the Ashburnham library, sold at Sotheby's 12 June 1901, lot 375. It was bought by C. Fairfax Murray and given to the Fitzwilliam Museum in 1904.

*Ashburnham Library,* p. 136. Wormald and Giles, *Handlist,* p. 205, no. 50. J. & J. Leighton, *Catalogue* (1901-1905), no. 3284.

53. GRENOBLE: BIBLIOTHÈQUE PUBLIQUE. ANCIEN FONDS 962. 15 century. Paper 203 × 145 mm. 150 leaves. Incomplete. Begins: Comme il soit ainsi . . ." and ends with the land of Prester John: "à la region tenebreuse où l'on . . ."

R. gives the no. as 393A. *Cat Gen.,* VII, 290.

54. LYONS: PALAIS DES ARTS. NO. 28 (Delandine No. 683). 15 century. Paper, except 1 bis, 14, 156, vellum. 207 × 140 mm. 192 leaves. *Le Romant de Mandeville* on foll. 1-132, followed by the *Visio Tundal* and 6 other pieces. It has armorial decorations and the inscription: "Ce livre est à messire Charles de Dysimyeu, chevalier, S$^r$ de la Féole." It has been at Lyons at least since 1759. It has the unusual opening: "Comme il soit ainsi que en la louange du Pere, du Filz, et du Saint Esperit, ce livre est establiz par Mandeville, chevalier, qui parle des merveilleuses choses qu'il a veu . . ." Ends: "et regne par tous siecles."

*Cat. Gen.,* XXXI, 10-12. Cordier, *Bibl. Sin.,* III, 2043. Delandine *Cat.,* I, 444.

55. LILLE: BIBLIOTHÈQUE DE. FONDS GODEFROY 121. Written 1472. Paper. 280 × 197 mm. A-K +. 106 leaves. Begins: "Comment il soit ainsi que . . ." Fol. 100ᵛ has the inscription: "Hic liber est scriptus per me Anthonium Ravillionis et finitus die martis ultima marcii, anno Domini millesimo quatercentesimo septuagesimo secundo. Deo gratias."

Not in R. Brunet, III, col. 1356. *Cat. Gen.*, XXVI, 578.

*Present Whereabouts Unknown*

56. PARIS: BIBLIOTHÈQUE FIRMIN-DIDOT, NO. 59. Late 14 century. Vellum. 4° size. 90 leaves. Fol. 1 begins: "Cy apres cōmence le liure Iehan de Mandeuille/ chlr lequel est fait et compilé de plus's choses et meruueilles que le dit chlr a veues par les parties/ du monde ou il a esté . . ." Followed by a table of 100 chapters on foll. 1-3. Fol. 4 blank. Foll. 5-12 lost and replaced in a hand which is a good imitation of the original. Text begins on fol. 5 with the rubric: "Cy apres cōmence le liure Iehan de Mandeuille/ chlr lequel parle de la terre sainte et de merueille'/ que il y [a] veues." Chap. 99 ends on fol. 89ᵛ with the words: "Cy fine Mess. Iehan de Mandeuille." This is followed by the epilogue giving the date of departure as 1322 and of writing as 1356 "à l'âge de 68 ans" (a statement not found elsewhere, so far as I can learn). The MS ends on fol. 90 with the words: "Qui en Trinitè vit et regne par touz les siecles des siecles amen. Explicit Mandeuille." Fol. 1 has a miniature of presentation with fleur de lis and a shield of France at the top of the page, and a picture showing Mandeville as an old pilgrim on his knees offering his book to a man, standing, dressed as the Grand Master of the Hospitalers—a red cross on a white mantle over a scarlet tunic. This has been taken for a figure of Charles V, because of the shield and fleur de lis. Well written, and richly ornamented with initials. Bound in "velours cramoisi."

*Catalogue Illustré* (1881), pp. 82-84.

57. PHILLIPPS NO. 1930. Vellum. 4° size. At the foot of fol. 1, the arms of Louis of Bruges, seigneur de la Gruthuse (d. 1492). Formerly Meerman, no. 885. *Biblio. Meerman.*, IV, 152-153, describes it as "tel qu'il l'a descrit à Liége en langue Gauloise, l'an 1355." Sold by Meerman in 1824. Bought by Phillipps of Payne in 1834. Listed by Haenel, p. 869, as Middlehill 1930/885. Kervyn de Lettenhove calls it "un fort bel exem-

plaire"; *Oeuvres de Froissart* (Bruges, 1870), I*, p. 85 n. 2. Praet, *Recherches*, p. 261.

*Fragment*

PHILLIPPS NO. 4439. 2 leaves only. Bound at the end of a *Regula Monachorum* of the 14 century. *Phillipps Cat.*

*Extract*

LONDON: BRITISH MUSEUM. ADDIT. 34802. Copied from Bodley Addit. C 280, about 1884, by George Parker of the Bodleian Library. Small 4° size: "Vita Sancti Albani de Allemannia, secundum dominum Johannem Mandeuille militem gallice scripta." Begins: "Pur ce qu ioe Iohan Mandeuille fu de la ville Seinte Alban . . ." *Cat of Addit., 1894-1899.*

Röhricht also Lists

a. DOUAI NO. 313. The number is the same as his number for the Dijon Mandeville. There is no *Mandeville* recorded at Douai.

b. PARIS, BIBLIOTHÈQUE NATIONALE. FONDS FR. 13423. This is a 17 century MS on paper of "Chronologica, historica et geographica." M. Marcel Thomas has confirmed for me that this is a series of extracts of travels, but has no Mandeville. See *Cat. Gen.*, anc. Supp. fr., III, 55.

c. ———— FONDS FR. 25519. This is not Mandeville, but Jehan du Pin's *Livre d'Amendavie*. See. Omont, *Cat. Gen.*, Anc. petit fonds fr., II, 619.

d. MARSEILLES, A b, 14. No Mandeville is listed in the *Cat. Gen.*, xv, but no. 1141 (Ab 14-R 97) a 17 century MS on paper, has some itineraries, an "alphabet de toutes les langues," and extracts from lapidaries: see *Cat. Gen.*, xv, 320.

e. MIDDLEHILL (PHILLIPPS) 8252, listed by R. as French, is in English and is now Huntington Library, HM 114. No. 16 below.

f. BELGIOIOSO 166. See No. 31 above, Milan, Trivulziana 816.

## IN ENGLISH

Four translations into English were identified by J. Vogels, "Handschriftliche Untersuchungen über die englische Version Mandeville's," *Jahresbericht über das Realgymnasium zu Crefeld* (Crefeld, 1891), pp. 3-52. Two, existing in single copies, are named from the manuscripts which preserve them, the Cotton and the Egerton versions. The third is the common manuscript and printed version, called from its first printer "the Pynson" or common version. The fourth was translated from Latin and is being published for the first time, by Mr. Malcolm Letts, for the Hakluyt Society.

Nicholson and Warner argued that the "Pynson version" represents the earliest translation into English and that the Cotton version made use of it, filling in gaps with the aid of a French text. Vogels argues that the Cotton version is the older and that the differences, especially the small omissions, are the usual marks of a degenerating text. One gap (see Introduction n. 11 above) is clearly the result of blindly following a French manuscript which had leaves missing. The Pynson text is not, therefore, merely a degenerated form of the Cotton translation. It corrects the Cotton translator's obvious blunders. Hamelius agreed with Vogels that the creator of the Pynson version compared the Cotton with a French text and removed the worst errors, but introduced a new and serious one, the gap, sometimes called "the Egypt gap" which occurred in his French text but not in the Cotton and Egerton versions.

The relation of the other two translations to the Cotton and Pynson texts is even more puzzling. Vogels argued that the Egerton is a composite version, taking the main body of the text from the Cotton, and filling the gap where several leaves of the Cotton manuscript are missing from the fourth or Anglo-Latin version. He does not seem to consider that the Egerton translator might have had access to the Cotton manuscript before those leaves were lost from it——or may have used another copy of this translation, now lost. Appendix IV shows in parallel lines the beginning of the French text (from Harley 4383) and of the Cotton and Egerton translations. It seems to me to suggest that the two may be independent translations, resembling each other because both follow very closely the eminently translatable Norman French. The relations of the four English versions to each other need further study.

## A

### The Cotton Version

1. LONDON: BRITISH MUSEUM. COTTON TITUS C. XVI. Late 14 or early 15 century. Vellum. 216 × 152 mm. 132 leaves (after fol. 53, three leaves are missing). Title: *Maundeville*. First printed in 1725 with the gap supplied from Royal 17 B. XLIII. Reedited by J. O. Halliwell in 1839; described by Ashton, and edited in the original spelling for the Early English Text Society by Paul Hamelius. Simple ornamentation, the first initial in gold, red, and blue, the others and rubrics in red and blue. Belonged to Sir Edward Walker, who gave it, between 1645 and 1662, to Sir Thomas Cotton. Text divided by rubrics into 35 unnumbered chapters plus a prologue and epilogue. No illustrations. Alphabets, names and forms, Greek, Egyptian, Hebrew, and Saracen. The chap. divisions correspond with those in the French text in Harley 4383.

Halliwell. Warner, *Buke*, p. xii. Vogels, pp. 8-9. Letts, pp. 127, 168.

## B

### The Egerton Version

2. LONDON: BRITISH MUSEUM. EGERTON 1982. Late 14 or early 15 century. Now 216 × 152 mm. but more closely cropped than the Cotton MS. Vellum. 129 leaves. Title: *Here begynneth the buke of John Maundevill*. Large initial at the beginning lacks gold. Other initials plain red and blue. No chap. divisions, but place names noted in the margin. Of the same period as the Cotton MS and a very similar hand but a more Northern dialect. No illustrations. Has all six alphabets, but the forms are omitted for the Egyptian and Persian, and names for the Chaldean. There are two versions of the Saracen.

Edited for the Roxburghe Club by Sir George F. Warner: see p. xii. Described also by Ashton, Vogels, pp. 9-10, and Letts, pp. 133, 134, 168. An edition by Malcolm Letts is forthcoming in the Hakluyt Society Series.

## C

### The Short Translation From Latin

This version is a translation of the second Anglo-Latin version. See the list of Latin MSS. Nos. 4-9.

3. OXFORD: BODLEIAN. E. MUSEO 116 (3617). Written between 1420 and 1450. Vellum. 274 × 197 mm. iii + 153 leaves. fol. 6$^v$: "Hic incipit tractatus Maundevyle militis de mirabilibus mundi . . ." omits the usual prologue, and begins: "For thy that manye men desyryn to heryn of dyvers londis . . . I John Maundeville knyght . . ." Ends, fol. 49$^v$: "Explicit Johannes maundevyle, cuius anime propricietur deus." There are no illustrations; no alphabets. Foll. 1-5 latter part of Chaucer's treatise on the Astrolabe. Foll. 49$^v$-64 some works on fruit trees & wine making. Foll. 65-149 Liber Uricrisiarum. Names of some 15 and 16 cent. owners of Kent and Essex.

Vogels, pp. 15, 46, identified the version. Letts, says (p. 170) that some episodes are omitted and others are rearranged. Madan II, ii, 703-704.

4. ——— RAWLINSON D.99 (12917). 15 century. Paper. 2°. 31 leaves. Short prologue, and text like E. Museo 116. Where the Cotton translation has the statement that Mandeville wrote first in Latin, then in French, and then in English, this MS reads: "and thus in proce I shal bigynne this werke, because that oftene in Romaunce and Ryme is defawt and nouzt accordement founden to the natur, but be bestyghes sekande, as they wole come to mynde . . ." 69 chaps.

Macray *Cat.*, v, iii, 49. Vogels, p. 16. Edited for the Hakluyt Society by Malcolm Letts. Forthcoming.

## D

The Common, or Pynson Version

5. CAMBRIDGE: UNIVERSITY LIBRARY. Dd I 17. Late 14 or early 15 century. Vellum. 424 leaves. Large folio. 2 cols. ca. 60 lines. Miscellany of 23 items, of which the *Travels*, foll. 544-594, is item 20. Items 18-21 constitute a section in a more cursive hand than the rest. It includes *Piers Plowman*, 4 chaps. on visiting the sick, *Mandeville*, and, in another hand and in 3 cols., the *Romance of the Seven Sages*. The date of departure is given as 1332. No illustrations, 2 alphabets. Illuminated letters and marginal notes as in B.M., Royal 17 B. XLIII.

Camb. U. *Cat.*, I, 15-26. Vogels, p. 12. Letts, p. 171.

6. DEVON, PA.: BARBADOS HILL. MR. BOIES PENROSE. ca. 1400. Vellum. 360 × 250 mm. 42 leaves gathered in 8s plus

2 at the end. Catchwords. 2 cols. 37 lines. Fol. 1, illuminated initial and border. Red initials. Has the "Roys–Ils" gap, pp. 42-67, of the Everyman edition, and another corresponding to pp. 118 "Tortouse . . ." to 121, in Chap. 44. 2 alphabets. No illustrations. Bought from the Giffard family of Chillington Park, Staffordshire, before 1937, by William H. Robinson. It was formerly bound with the copy of Robert Manning of Brunne's *Handlyng Synne*, now in the Folger Shakespeare Library, advertised in Robinson's *Catalogue*, 65 (1938), no. 52. This part of the manuscript has a border around the first page, in bell-flower design, and at the foot of the page are three shields bearing arms: 2 parted per pale, first *sable* 2 bars *gules* fretty *argent;* second, *gules,* a bar *or* between 6 pears pendant of the same. On the left the shield is *gules,* a bend *sable* crossed by 2 bars *argent.* On the right the shield is *argent,* a white lion rampant, langed *gules.* These have been identified as the arms of Sir William Clopton (1350-1421), but they are no part of the original design of the page. They were added later, perhaps in 15 or even 16 century, by a much poorer artist. The Folger MS 420312 is one of 3 perfect copies of Robert Manning's poem, and was unknown to the Roxburghe and E.E.T.S. editors.

Penrose, *Travel,* p. 5. Examined in consultation with Mr. Penrose. Not in R. or Vogels.

7. OXFORD: BODLEIAN. RAWLINSON D 100 (12918). 14 or early 15 century. Paper and vellum. Small 4° size. 73 leaves. Beginning, end, and other leaves missing. Mr. Hunt, Keeper of Western Manuscripts at the Bodleian, described it to me as "a dirty manuscript in two hands, probably 14th century." Names of former owners, John Longby and Johannus Churchman.

Vogels, p. 16. Macray, *Cat.* v, iii, 49.

8. LONDON: BRITISH MUSEUM. ROYAL 17 C. XXXVIII. Early 15 century. Vellum. 247 × 171 mm. 3 + 61 leaves. 2 cols. The three preliminary leaves contain part of an itinerary from the north of Europe to Florence, a diagram of the points of the campass, and names of winds, in Italian. There are also scribbles: "Osborn" and "Knottesford." It has belonged to E. Bannyster and [John Lord] Lumley. 110 illustrations in the lower margins are listed by Warner and Gilson. Many are of the same subjects as later woodcuts. 22 chaps., a few words missing at the end.

## APPENDIX I

Dates given are, as usual in this version, 1332, 1366, and the 34th year. This text adds: "for xxxiiii yeer he was in travelyng."

Halliwell. Vogels, p. 10. Letts, p. 169. Warner and Gilson, II, 249-250.

9. ——— ROYAL 17 B. XLIII. Early 15 century. Vellum. 216 × 146 mm. 184 leaves (first 3 fly leaves). ca. 30 lines. 4 parts in 4 different hands, of which the *Mandeville* is the oldest and best, on foll. 4-115; *Sir Gowther*, foll. 116-133; William Staunton's *Vision in St. Patrick's Purgatory, A.D. 1409*, foll. 133-148$^v$; Tundale's *Vision*, foll. 150-184. Initials and borders flourished in colors or roughly illuminated. No illustrations. 2 alphabets. Marginal comments. The usual gaps. This MS was used by the editor of the 1725 edition to complete his text.

Warner and Gilson, II, 233-234. Halliwell. Vogels, p. 11. Letts, p. 169, and facsimile of a page, opposite p. 145.

10. ——— HARLEY 3954. Early 15 century. Vellum. 4° size. Foll. 1-69 *Johne Maundevyille*, followed by *Piers Plowman*, and 6 other pieces. Good text with many illustrations in ink, red, green, and blue. Many unfinished. 2 alphabets in red.

Halliwell. Douce, *Cat.*, III, 98. Vogels, p. 11. Letts, p. 169.

11. MANCHESTER: CHETHAM'S LIBRARY. NO. 6711,4. Early 15 century. Vellum. 4° size. 82 leaves. 2 cols. "Here begynneth the Book of John Mawndevyle, knyght." On 1$^r$: "translatus in Anglicum de lingua Gallicana" (Graesse, 4:360 says "Latina"). Much rubrication but no illustrations. Saracen alphabet only.

Röhricht describes it as "17391 Bibl. Clothawiens, IV, 440." Halliwell, *Account*, p. 10. Vogels, p. 17. Letts, p. 171.

12. OXFORD: BODLEIAN. BODLEY ADDIT. C 285. Written 1400-15. Parchment. 274 × 191 mm. iii + 91 leaves. Foll. 1-70 *Mandeville*, followed by a ghost story. See no. 14 below. Bought of C. J. Jefferies & Sons, Bristol, 25 June 1886.

Vogels, p. 14. Madan v, 662-663.

13. CAMBRIDGE: TRINITY COLLEGE. R 4.20. Early 15 century. Vellum. 257 × 191 mm. 172 leaves. 28 lines. Foll. 1-87, *Mandeville;* foll. 89-169$^v$ Lydgate's *Destruction of Thebes*. Fol. 1 has a good border. Shield at the foot of the page erased (party

per fess *arg.* and *sa.* a lion rampant countercharged, upper part *sa.* lower, *arg.*). Initial, man in plate armour and red cap (?), red mantle lined with ermine, stands holding a sword. 4 leaves missing.

Vogels, p. 12. James, *Cat.* II, 147-148. Bernard's *Cat.*, no. 579.

14. OXFORD: BALLIOL NO. 239. 15 century. Vellum. Folio. 141 leaves, 2 cols. Contains 5 religious and moral works in Latin, and foll. 112-141 *Mandeville,* in a neat, current hand, but defective at the beginning and end. Leaves much transposed. Gift of Wm. Dukins, M.A. 1656, and Fellow.

Coxe *Cat.*, I, 81. Vogels, p. 13. Mynors.

15. ———QUEEN'S NO. 383. 15 century. Vellum. Very small 4° size. 166 leaves. Fol. 1. Kalendarium. Foll. 15-135$^v$ the *Travels,* followed by a story of a ghost, of ca. 1330. This is the same story as in Bodley Addit. C 285. The *Mandeville* text is close to that of Balliol 239. Written by Edward Jenkyn. Formerly owned by Wm. Barnard, and after 1671 by Thomas Pargiter of Lincoln.

Coxe, *Cat.*, I, 88. Vogels, p. 13.

16. SAN MARINO, CALIF.: HENRY E. HUNTINGTON LIBRARY. HM 114 (formerly Phillipps MS from Middlehill and Cheltenham 8252/1088). Written 1430. Vellum and paper. 220 × 140 mm. 327 leaves. Fol. 16 lost; top half of fol. 146 missing. Foll. 1-130 *Piers Plowman,* foll. 131-184 *Mandeville.* Followed by the story of Susan, and Daniel, the Flight into Egypt, an account of the Garden of Bawme, Chaucer's *Troilus,* etc. Owned ca. 1550 by Thomas Browne, ca. 1580 by Henry Spelman (named on the top of fol. 131). Also belonged to Askew, R. Gough, Richard Heber (Sale cat. of 1836, XI, No. 1088).

Phillipps *Cat.*, p. 125. De Ricci, I, 51. R. and Vogels give old location. Vogels (p. 17) classified it as the C version, but he had not seen it.

17. OXFORD: BODLEIAN. RAWLINSON B 216 (11568). Before 1450. Vellum. Large 4° size. 171 leaves. 2 cols. 1. Chronicle from Brute to the siege of Rouen. 2. *Mandeville,* foll. 131-160. 3. *Proverbs of Solomon.* 4. Lydgate's Life of St. Edmund. Con-

tents agree with the description given by Bernard, *Cat.*, B no. 613, of the MS. at Naworth Castle, Yorkshire before 1674.

Vogels, p. 14. Macray, *Cat.*, v, i, 545-546.

18. ——— DOUCE 109 (21683). Mid 15 century. Paper 225 × 152 mm. v + 76 leaves. 2 leaves, about half of the prologue, lost. Wm. Thomson of Queen's College, Oxford, wrote in this MS in 1746: "I had this Book from a Descendant by the Mother's Side from S$^r$ John Mandeville. W.T." See below, No. 33. The text is a sister to that in Rawlinson B 216.

Vogels, pp. 14-15. Madan IV, 524.

19. LONDON: BRITISH MUSEUM. ARUNDEL 140. Written 1450-60. Paper. 276 × 209 mm. 181 leaves. Fol. 1 *Ypotys.* 5$^v$ *Mandeville.* 41$^v$ *Prick of Conscience.* 147 *Gy Earl of Werwyke and Dekene Alquyne.* 152 *Seven Wise Masters.* 166 Chaucer's *Melibeus.* Finely written; no illustrations. Letts, p. 169, suggests it is a copy of Harley 3954 (no. 10 above).

*Cat. of Arundel Mss.*, I, 38. Ward's *Cat. of Romances*, II, 224-226. Manley and Rickert, *Text of the Canterbury Tales*, I, 52. Ashton. Halliwell. Vogels, p. 11.

20. CAMBRIDGE: UNIVERSITY LIBRARY. Ff V. 35. mid-15 century. Vellum. 4° size. 128 leaves. 37 lines. Foll. 1-49 *The Book of Ion Maundeuyle Knyght of Seyne Albones;* followed by *Piers Plowman* in the same hand. Incomplete. Reads *1302* for 1322. Former owner Thomas Jakeson.

*Cat.*, II, 495. Letts, p. 171. R. lists twice, once as "535 Ff." Vogels, p. 13, lists as "Ff. 5.35."

21. ——— MAGDALEN COLLEGE. PEPYSIAN LIBRARY 1955. 15 century. Vellum and paper. 254 × 200 mm. 76 leaves. 30 lines. Foll. 16-76 *Mandeville.* Ugly current hand. A late 16th century inscription on fol. 76 notes the Liège tomb.

Vogels, p. 13. James, *Bibl. Pepys.*, Pt. III, 56-57.

22. OXFORD: BODLEIAN. LAUD 619 (formerly 1428). Mid-15 century. Vellum. Small 4° size. 92 leaves. Foll. 1-78 *Mandeville.* Followed by the ten commandments with an exposition, *de mirabilibus mundi* in Latin, *Oratio ad Christum ante Com-*

*munionem, Chronicon* from the Creation to the Coronation of Richard II, and *Sententiae* from the Fathers.

Coxe, *Laud*, p. 501. Vogels, p. 14, says it is very like no. 17 of this list.

23. ———E MUSEO 124 (3562). Mid-15 century. Vellum. 248 × 172 mm. i + 44 leaves. First half missing. Some notes of early owners.

Vogels, p. 16. Madan II, ii, 682.

24. EDINBURGH: NATIONAL LIBRARY (formerly Advocates Library, 19. i. ii). Mid-15 century. Paper. Folio. Defective at the end.

Vogels, p. 17.

25. DUBLIN: TRINITY COLLEGE, E 5. 6. 15 century. Paper. 4° size. 54 leaves. End missing. Bound with *Gospel of Nicodemus, Pseudo-Matthew,* an epistle of St. Bernard, and other works.

Vogels, p. 17. Abbot's *Cat.*, no. 604.

26. LONDON: BRITISH MUSEUM. HARLEY 2386. 15 century. Paper. 4° size. 139 leaves. MS contains 42 items, of which *Mandeville* is no. 41, on foll. 74-130. Foll. 1-70 contain many short historical pieces in Latin. Nos. 37 following are in English, in other hands. Beginning and end of the MS have notes of household accounts by Wyllyam Cresset, a butler or servant. *Mandeville* has Hebrew alphabet only.

Douce, *Cat.*, II, 678. Vogels, p. 11. Letts, p. 170.

27. LONDON: W. H. ROBINSON, 16&17 PALL MALL SW 1. 2nd half 15 century. 4° size. Contents: foll. 1-99 *Mandeville*. Foll. 100-118, an account in English of the Translation of St. Anthony, Abbot of Constantinople. Foll. 119-120, English poem on Count Ugolino of Pisa, adapted from Chaucer and 5 times as long. Foll. 123-130, the Long Charter of Christ. Foll. 131-132, John Skelton's Elegy on the death of King Edward IV. The last is a very early transcript of Skelton's poem, containing a suppressed stanza. MS lacks leaves of Mandeville's prologue. No illustrations. 2 alphabets.

Not in R. or Vogels. Robinson, *Cat. no.* 77 (1948), no. 144, and pp. 148-149 print a photograph of fol. 131. Letts identifies, p. 171,

# APPENDIX I

with the Naworth MS, but the contents of that MS are quite different; see Bernard, *Cat.*, B, no. 613 and above, no. 17. Robinson reports that this MS belonged in the early 18 century to John, Lord Somers, and in the early 19 century to Miss Frances Currer. It *then* passed to the library of Castle Howard in Yorkshire, and is not the MS seen by Bernard in the 17 century.

28. LONDON: BRITISH MUSEUM. SLOAN 2319. 2nd half 15 century. Small 4° size. Paper. 42 leaves. Imperfect at beginning and end (leaves missing between 3 and 4, 8 and 9, and 2 leaves between 9 and 10). 4, 5, 6 mutilated. No illustrations. Saracen alphabet only.

Vogels, p. 12. Letts (p. 169) dates it "early 15."

29. CAMBRIDGE: UNIVERSITY LIBRARY. Gg I.34³. 2nd half 15 century. Parchment. Small 4° size. 385 leaves in various hands. Contents: 1. Four humanistic letters. 2. Moral sayings of the Philosophers Englished. 3. *Liber de Mawdeville* (88 leaves). 4. Alexander and Nectanabus. Poorly written. Saracen alphabet only. "Ex dono William Thornton."

*Univ. Cat.*, III, 46-47. Vogels, pp. 12-13. Letts, p. 171.

30. OXFORD: BODLEIAN. RAWLINSON D 101 (12919). 15 century. Parchment. Small 4° size. 115 leaves. Add to the usual text: "And oure holy fader hath graunted to al tho that redith or wrytith or heryth this boke with good devocion, an C dayes to pardon and goddis blessynge on hye. Explicit Maundevyle." See the end of Bodleian, E Museo 116 (No. 3 above). *Ex libris* Caroli Ashburnham, & Ed Tayler 1703/4.

Vogels, p. 15. Macray, *Cat.*, v, iii, 49.

31. ——— DOUCE 33 (21607). Mid-15 century. Parchment. 137 × 96 mm. iv + 157 leaves. First leaf and a gathering in the middle missing after fol. 47.

Vogels, p. 15-16. Madan, IV, 499.

32. ——— TANNER 405 (10232). 2nd half 15 century. Parchment and paper. 8° size. 42 leaves. Poor condition. Leaves missing.

Vogels, p. 16. Hackman *Cat.*, p. 763.

33. LONDON: BRITISH MUSEUM. ADDIT. 33758 (formerly Grenville XL). End of 15 century. Paper. Small folio. 50 leaves.

A good hand but a poor text. No illustrations, no alphabets. Reads *1300, 1336* for 1322 and 1366. "Here begynneth the boke of Maundeuyle knyght . . ." Has a note in Douce's hand: "Mr. Rodd, I return your MS Mandeville, because it agrees word for word with one I have, and as that came from the author's family, this agreement may add to the value of yours." Douce's copy is now Bodley. Douce 109 (No. 18 above). The Old B.M. *Cat.* and Ashton call this MS. "Grenv. xii."

*Cat. of Addit. 1888-1893*, pp. 103-104. Vogels, pp. 11-12. Letts, p. 169.

### Unidentified

34. RUGBY SCHOOL, ARNOLD LIBRARY, BLOXHAM COLLECTION. Has a MS of Mandeville in English, according to R. W. Hunt, Keeper of Western Manuscripts of the Bodleian Library. Not in Vogels.

35. OWNER UNKNOWN. From Keele Hall, Co. Stafford. Property of the late Rev. Walter Sneyd. Sold by Sotheby, Wilkinson & Hodge, Dec. 1903, and described by them as 14 century. Vellum. 222 × 140 mm. 64 leaves, neatly written in long lines 31 to a page. Begins: "For as moche as ye lond on ye see yat ys to say ye holy lond . . ." 2$^a$ "I jon de mandevyle Knight yawh yt y be noht wordi . . ." Ends: "God without end. Amen—quoth Berstede."

*Hist. MMS Commission. Report,* iii Appendix, p. 290. Vogels, p. 17. Sotheby, Wilkinson, & Hodge, *Cat.* for Dec. 1903, 3d day, p. 70, no. 495.

36. JAMES P. R. LYELL OF ABINGDON, BERKSHIRE, had a MS of Mandeville in English some years ago. "Not very distinguished to look at, but having the arms of the first owners on fol. 1," according to Mr. Mynors. Possibly the same as the next.

UNKNOWN. MAGGS BROS. *Catalogue* no. 572 (1932), item 910. Early 15 century. Vellum. Small 4° size. 118 leaves. 23 lines. On 6 preliminary pages, medical advice for every month of the year, and a list of the Archbishops of York. Fol. 1 of the *Travels* has an F in gold with a scroll in the margin.

The lower margin has the arms, in red, blue, and silver, of a (Norton?) Yorkshire family. Other initials in red and blue. At the end, the life of St. Wilfred, Archbishop of York, analysed. Last 2 leaves blank. Described as "the shorter version." *The* [London] *Times Literary Supplement,* for July 16, 1931, p. 568, reported the sale of this copy (to Maggs?). The arms of the Norton family on the binding.

LOST? COVENTRY SCHOOL, NO. 12. "Sir John Maundeville's Travels, much different from the printed Books." Vogels, p. 18, did not find this copy. Bernard's *Cat.,* B 1457, describes it as "written painted, and gilded very well," containing Lydgate's *De Regimine Principum, De Incendio Amoris, Dialogus, Fabula,* and other of his works, followed by the *Travels,* and then by the *Siege of Jerusalem,* and the *Siege of Thebes.*

NAWORTH CASTLE, YORKSHIRE. The Earl of Carlisle had a MS which he showed to Vogels (see *EV,* pp. 17-18), but see above, no. 17. Possibly Vogels saw no. 27.

*Abridgment*

LONDON: BRITISH MUSEUM ADDIT. 37,049. First half of 15 century. Part misplaced. An abridgement of the Pynson version, foll. 3-9. A map showing 3 continents, a T-shaped ocean, and a picture of Jerusalem with some 20 buildings within a wall. No alphabets. Letts, p. 169. *Cat. of Addit. MSS. 1900-1905,* p. 324.

*Extracts*

OXFORD: BODLEIAN. ASHMOLE 751. Late 14 or early 15 century. Paper. 4° size. 155 leaves. Foll. 48, 49, 50$^v$ contain legendary extracts "Secundum Johannem Maunduyle." Fol. 142$^v$-143 "Nota secundum Johannem Maunduyle."

Black's *Cat.,* pp. 362-366, describes this collection of 45 excerpts from various sources. Listed by Vogels, p. 17.

────── DOUCE 45. (21619). 15 century. 143 × 105 mm. vi + 123 leaves. Chiefly medical and astronomical notes. Fol. 118, no. 20: "Responcio cujusdam imperatoris constantinopolitani D. Papae, ut patet in libro Johannis Maundeville." *Cat.* p. 5. Madan iv, 502-503 does not mention Mandeville.

## IN LATIN

J. Vogels, "Die Ungedruckten Lateinischen Versionen Mandeville's" in *Programm des Gymnasiums zu Crefeld* (Crefeld, 1886), distinguishes four Latin versions produced in England and never printed. A fifth version, made from the Liège redaction of the French text, has been discussed above, pp. 103 ff. and 115 ff. Since the first of the Latin versions produced in England is probably earlier than the Liège, or vulgate, Latin version, I have put the whole group of unpublished translations together and ahead of the manuscripts of the vulgate, although at least the third and fourth are later than the earliest vulgate text.

### A

#### First Translation Made in England

1. LEIDEN: RIJKSUNIVERSITEIT BIBLIOTHEEK. VULCAN 96. Written 1390. Vellum. 125 × 80 mm. 25 lines. 147 leaves. Fol. 1 illuminated border. No alphabets or illustrations, except on fol. 91 the circle of signs of the zodiac. Rubricated. At the end: "Finito libro sit laus et gloria Xpo. Explicit itin*er*arium Ioh*ann*is Maundevyle militis script*um* in anno iubileo p*er* manus Ricardi Bledelewe monachi Abendon*ensis* Anno d*o*mini M.CCC. nonagesimo. Et anno regni Regis Ricardi S*ec*u*n*di post conquest*um* quartodecimo." It has the letter from the son of the Sultan of Egypt to the Pope (printed by Vogels, p. 15) which is also (in Latin) in French MSS. Sub-Group I (cf. Vogels, pp. 5, 15, and Letts, p. 166). Vogels, p. 10, prints the opening in parallel cols. with "Libri XXIV" (i.e., Barrois xxiv), now Bibl. Nat. fr. 4515. This MS was at Leyden before 1737-38; Pinelo's epitome of Barcia, i, 21.

Described in *Bibliothecae Universitatis Leidenensis. Codices Manuscripti. I. Codices Vulcaniani*, p. 39. Tobler, p. 37. Vogels, p. 5.

2. LONDON: BRITISH MUSEUM. EGERTON 672. Early 15 century. Vellum. 118 leaves. Foll. 1-62 a history of England to the end of Edward III's reign, in a contemporary hand. Foll. 63 ff. *Itinerarius* in an early 15 century hand. No illustrations; no alphabets. Text close to Vulcan 96. Contains the interpolated letter. Last third of the text missing (after the middle of Chap. xx of Pollard's text).

Ashton. Vogels, p. 5. Letts, pp. 166-167. See below, Clarke MS 218. On p. 309.

3. CAMBRIDGE: CORPUS CHRISTI COLLEGE, NO. 275. 15 century. Vellum. 275 × 183 mm. 3-255 leaves. 2 cols. 42 lines.

The MS contains 21 items, including Odoric, St. Brandon, and Prester John. No. 11 on foll. 69-145 is the *Itinerarius*. Written in England. Left to his college in 1439 by Thomas Markaunt. It was not noticed by Vogels, or Letts, but Mr. Mynors has identified it as of this translation.

James, *Cat.*, II, 35-38. Cordier, *Odoric*, pp. lxv-vi.

### B
#### Second Translation Made in England

This is a somewhat abbreviated version from which the short English version contained in Bodleian E. Museo 116, etc., was made.

4. LONDON: BRITISH MUSEUM. ROYAL 13 E IX. Ca. 1400 (after 1394). Vellum. 450 × 328 mm. 326 leaves. 2 cols. 58-61 lines. Usually in 12s with catchwords. Item 12 (of 25 articles), Foll. 40-71$^v$ *Itinerarium Iohannis Maundevile de mirabilibus mundi*. No illustrations; no alphabets. Written at Albans. Item 20, foll. 116-137$^v$, is a fragmentary inventory of relics at St. Albans. Item 25 is Walsingham's *Chronicle* 1373-93. Vogels reports the interpolation, also in the English translations, telling of the visit to Rome and the Pope's approval.

Halliwell. Warner and Gilson, II, 113-116. Vogels calls this MS "Harl. 13 E IX," pp. 5, 20-23. See above, pp. 211 ff. He argues (*LV*, p. 22) that the Latin was translated from the English, but later (*EV*, p. 46) decided that the many French forms of Latin names showed that the Latin was translated from French, and the English version was from Latin.

5. LONDON: BRITISH MUSEUM. COTTON APPENDIX IV. 15 century. Vellum. 124 leaves. Foll. 2-58 Guido on letter-writing; foll. 59-102 *Itinerarius;* fol. 102$^v$ Prophecies of Merlin; fol. 103 *Philobiblon;* fol. 120 a *Provinciale* of 1343. Text very similar to no. 4. Name of an owner, R. Ascouh, in a contemporary hand.

Ashton and Halliwell date in late 15 century. Vogels, p. 6, says first half. *Cat. of Mss. . . . Cottonian Lib.*, p. 614. Letts (p. 167), designates this "Cotton App. 59."

6. ——— HARLEY 175. 15 century. Vellum. Small 4° or 12° size. 106 leaves. *Itinerarium . . . de mirabilibus mundi*.

Ashton. Halliwell. Vogels, p. 6. *Harley Cat.*, I, 61. Letts, p. 167.

7. GLASGOW: HUNTERIAN MUSEUM. T.4.I. (84). 15 century. Vellum. 273 × 183 mm. 340 (originally 352) leaves. 36 lines. Illuminated initials in gold and colors. MS contains Guido de Colonna, *Destruction of Troy;* Julius Valerius, *History of Alexander the Great;* Archbishop Turpin, *Itinerary;* Marco Polo; Odoric; and foll. 269-340 Mandeville's *Itinerarium, De mirabilibus mundi.* Written by "Ricardus plenus amoris fframpton." Belonged to Thomas Martin of Palgrave (1697-1771). The first part has the colophon of another scribe which was probably copied, along with the text, by Richard plenus amoris of Frampton.

R. lists this as in French. Haenel, 795. Vogels, p. 6. Young and Aitkin, pp. 89-91, no. 84. Letts, p. 167. Benedetto, p. cxxxvi describes it as "84 (ant. S 5 7)."

8. DURHAM: UNIVERSITY LIBRARY. COSIN V. iii 7. 15 century. 4° size. *Liber Peregrinationis Domini Johannis Maundevyle Militis.* Prologue begins: "Quia plures audire desiderant de Terrâ Sanctâ . . ." Cap. 1: "Nunc ergo in nomine Domini qui voluerit mare transire . . ." Ends: "qui in trinitate perfecta vives et regnas per cuncta secula Deus. Amen. Explicit Itinerarium domini Johannis Maundeville Militis de Mirabilibus Mundi." Followed by several short pieces. Secretary hand of a little after 1460. Codex was George Davenport's.

Not in R. or Vogels. Described in *Catalogi Veteres,* pp. 162-163. Classified for me by Mynors.

9. CAMBRIDGE: JESUS COLLEGE. NO. 35. 15 century. Paper. 225 × 156 mm. 160 leaves. 35 and 27 lines. Foll. 1-64, *Itinerarium Domini Joh. de Maundevill Militis de Mirabilibus Mundi.* In 88 sections. Fol. 65$^v$ blank, followed by *Gesta Romanorum.* The last quire contains 2 cancel-leaves of Mandeville, corresponding to foll. 24a and 56a. On the last leaf: "Sumr. tome rysyng du . . . a Orforthe." Probably from Durham. Gift of Mr. Man, a fellow (B.A. 1674).

Not in R. or Vogels. James, *Cat.,* pp. 56-57. Classified by Mynors.

C

THIRD TRANSLATION MADE IN ENGLAND

Distinguished by Vogels, pp. 5, 16-20, who prints a passage from Harley 82 in parallel with Vulcan 96 to demonstrate that they are different translations. This is a full-length translation, but "quite distinctive" and of a somewhat more classical Latinity.

10. LONDON: BRITISH MUSEUM. HARLEY 82. 15 century. Vellum. 4° size. 104 leaves in 2 hands. Fol. 1 is a fragment of a register of an Abbot of Reading, temp. Edw. II. Foll. 4-34 contain a martyrology, readings for certain days, legends, and similar matter. Foll. 35-104, the *Itnerarium*, lacks the first leaf and is defective at the end. The forms of the Greek letters are noteworthy.

> Ashton. Halliwell. *Harley Cat.*, i, 21. Vogels, p. 5. Letts, p. 167. Mynors.

### D

#### Fourth Translation Made in England

Distinguished by Vogels, p. 23 as another, and rather poor, translation from the French.

11. OXFORD: BODLEIAN. ASHMOLE 769 (8080). Ca. 1450. Vellum and paper. 4° size. 108 leaves, of which the last 9 are described as blank, but only 2½ are present. Neat small hand. Foll. 1-89ᵛ *Itinerarium domini Johannis Maundevile militis, de territorio sancti Albani prothomartiris Anglorum*.

> *Ashmole Cat.*, p. 388. Vogels (p. 6) calls it no. 679. Letts, p. 167. Madan ii, ii, 1151 (not described).

### E

#### Fifth (Liège) Translation

This is an abbreviated translation of the third, or Ogier, redaction of the French text, described on pp. 103 ff. It has been printed several times (see Appendix ii). A few manuscripts are described as "fourteenth century" but none is certainly earlier than 1390.

12. VIENNA: NATIONALBIBLIOTHEK. COD. 5363 [Rec. 3046]. 14 century [?]. Paper Foll. 1-60, *Libri duo de Amore, et Cortesia* of Andreas Capellanus, and *De Reprobatione Amoris*. Foll. 61-115ᵛ *Itinerarium à terra Angliae in partes Hierosolimitanes et ulteriores transmarinas*.

> Not in Röhricht or Vogels. Described by H. Cordier, *Revue de l'Extrême-Orient*, i, 314. *Tabulae* iv, 109. Classified for me by Roger E. Bennett.

13. CHARLEVILLE: LA BIBLIOTHÈQUE DE. NO. 62. 14 and 15 century. Paper. 4°. *Itinerarium* has no title; begins: "Cum terra Iherosolimitana terra promissionis filiorum Dei . . ." Followed by Sacro Bosco and *Mappi Mundi*.

   Not in R. or Vogels. *Cat. Gen.* Old Series, v (1879), 575-576.

14. ERFURT: STADTBÜCHEREI. (BIBLIOTHEK BOINEBURGICA), QUART. 3(2). *Io de Mandeeveld itinerarius*. The same (?) as no. 21, "Item itinerarium . . . Mandeville/ de regno Francorum Gregorius Turonensis/ de partibus iterum transmarinis Ludolphi/ Marchipolo de Sarracenia et Tartaria," in the catalogue of the Collegium Amplonianum, made in 1410-12; in Lehmann, *Mittelalterliche Biblio.*, II, 46.

   Listed in Pertz, *Archiv*, XI (1858), 725. Not in Vogels. R. calls it "Amplon. no. 6." But Pertz does not list it in the Amplonian collection. Not in Schum, except in his ed. of the 1412 *Cat.*, p. 821.

15. TURIN: BIBLIOTECA NAZIONALE. H-III-1 (formerly L-III-33). Early 15 century. Paper. 269 leaves. *Itinerarium* on foll. 137-212, in 50 chapters, preceded by Geraldus Clericus, *Historiae Trojanae* (written 1373); Bernardus, *Epistola;* Julianus, *Vita Alexandri Magni;* and followed by Jacobus de Cessolis, *Liber de ludo Scacchorum*. Mazzatinti describes it as "xiv cent. (Pasini Lat. 580)" but Vogels (p. 7), reports it is more probably dated first quarter 15 century. Has the usual explicit of the vulgate version.

   *Codices . . . Taurinensis Athenaei*, II, 133-134. Mazzatinti, *Inventari*, XXVIII, 125, No. 1221. Vogels. p. 7.

16. BELLUNO: BIBLIOTECA LOLLINIANA. NO. 39. Dated 1415. 44 leaves, with *Lectura Iohannis Andreae*, 16 ff.

   Not in R. or Vogels. Mazzatinti, *Inventari*, II, p. 124.

17. NEW YORK, OWNED APRIL, 1953 by H. P. KRAUS, DEALER. (Formerly Cheltenham/Middlehill 6650). Vol. II of a pair bound uniformly by Phillipps, but originally unrelated. Dated 1424. Vellum and paper. 8° size. 217 leaves. Contains foll. 1-85, *Mandeville;* 87-173, Jacobus de Verona *Peregrinationes* (dated by the scribe, August 12, 1424); 177-187, Johannes de Witte de Hese *Itinerarium;* 188-204, Jordanus Osnabrugensis [or Cardinal Jacobus Colonna] *de Prerogativa Romani Imperii;* 204$^v$-210 Henricus de Hyspania *Itin. de locis*

*Terrae Sanctae;* 211-217, Alexander of Tralles, *De Quatuor Complexionibus. De Mensibus.* Written in a round German hand by Johannes de Purmereynde of Witten on the Ruhr. In mid-15 century was in the library of St. Heribert's in Deutz opposite Cologne. End of volume has some notes of events in the archdiocese of Cologne, 1350-1414. Purmereynde dated the completion of his work 21 Nov. 1424.

> Not in R. or Vogels. Phillipps, *Catalogus,* p. 99, under the heading, "Payne 1834." Bought in London in February, 1947, by H. P. Kraus, New York dealer, and described in his *Catalogue,* no. 49, item 14. Also described in Ugo Monneret de Villard, p. xi.

18. —— Vol. I (bound by Phillipps uniformly with the preceding). Written after 1427, in a sharp, small 15 century hand. Foll. 2-63, Hayton; 64-88, Guilelmi de Belopen (i.e. Boldensele); 89-119, Theodericus *Libellus de locis sanctis;* 120-121, *Prodigia in Cathalonia Anno 1427;* 124$^{r,v}$ Latin satiric poem; 125-171, *Gesta Godefridi Ducis de Boulyon,* etc.; 173-223, *Itinerarius terre sancte et ulteriorum partium orientalium* (i.e., Mandeville). In the subscription it is stated that the work was originally written in French and "eventually translated into Latin by another man." At the end of the text of Mandeville is a note about Odoric's travels, running over onto the next folio. Designated Vol. I when these two MSS came together in the Phillipps collection.

> See above (no. 17) for references. Not in R. or Vogels.

19. BRUSSELS: BIBLIOTHÈQUE ROYALE. NO. 1160-1163. 1st third of 15 century. Vellum and paper. 290 × 210 mm. 3 + 145 + 1 leaves. Fol. 1$^v$, index; 2-29, *Navigatio sancti Brindani;* 30-54$^v$, *Visio Tungdoli;* 55-62, *Epistola presbiteri Iohannis;* 63-65 blank; 66-145$^v$, *Itin.* (Mandeville). Begins: "Qui de Angliâ, Hiberniâque . . ." From Bethleem, Lovanii.

> Vogels, p. 7. Cordier, *Melanges,* I, 33, and *Bibl. Sin.,* III, 2032, records a note on fol. 34 in a different hand from the scribe's, but an ancient one, which relates the text to Odoric. Van den Gheyn, *Cat.,* v, 101 (No. 3142).

20. BERLIN: STAATSBIBLIOTHEK. CODEX ELECTORALIS. 868 (LAT. FOL. 179). Early 15 century. Paper. 232 × 141 mm. 194 leaves. *Mandeville* on foll. 73-136$^v$ in 50 chaps. On fol. 96, opposite Chap. 23, is: "Nota. Hic incipit secunda pars."

Foll. 1-72 contain Jordanus of Osnabrug's *De Translatione Imperii,* and 2 other tracts. The *Mandeville* is followed by a chronicle and other works. The vol. is inscribed: "Honorabilis dn̄s Conradus Richardi psbr myndensis hunc dedit librum Monasterio. sc̄orum Mauricii & Symeonis Myndensi M CCCC LXXXIX ipso die lucie virginis.

Vogels, p. 6. Rose, *Verzeichnis,* II, pt. 3, 1021-23.

21. COPENHAGEN: DET KONGELIGE BIBLIOTEK. GL. KGL. S 445. Written 1434. Vellum. 296 × 212 mm. 41 leaves. Begins: "Itinerarius a terra Angliae in partes Jerosolimitanas et in ulteriores transmarinas, editus primo in lingua Gallicana ab auctore suo milite anno Domini 1355 in civitate Leodiensi et paulo post translatus in eadem civitate in hanc forman Latinam." At the end: "Finito 1434 in bona sexta feria."

Not in R. Vogel lists but does not describe (p. 7). Jørgensen, *Catalogus,* p. 372.

22. OXFORD: BODLEIAN. BODLEY ADD. A. 187 (29156). Written 1445. Vellum and paper. 242 × 162 mm. ii + 70 leaves. Written in northern Italy by Antonio. Parts badly damaged. Usual ending of the vulgate.

Was no. 37 of a 19 century French auction sale cat. Bought of T. Boone of London, Oct. 29, 1879. Madan v, 572.

23. LONDON: BRITISH MUSEUM. HARLEY 3589. 1st half 15 century. Paper. 74 leaves. Preceded by Ludolph de Suchen, *Liber de Terrâ Sanctâ* (1336). Table of 50 chaps. on foll. 74-74$^v$. Begins: "Itinerarius magistri Johannis de Mandevelt, ad partes Hierosolymitanas, et ulteriores partes transmarinas; qui obiit Leodii, A.D. 1382."

Ashton. Halliwell. *Cat. Harl.,* III, 45. Vogels, p. 6. Warner, p. vii, no. 2, says it was written on the Continent. See below, no. 40.

24. LEIDEN: RIJKSUNIVERSITEIT BIBLIOTHEEK. VOSSIANUS LATINUS. FOL. 75. 1st half 15 century. Vellum. 51 leaves. Preceded by Marco Polo: see Benedetto, p. cxxxvi.

R. lists as French. Not in Vogels. *Cat. Univ. Leid.,* p. 373.

25. GIESSEN: UNIVERSITÄTSBIBLIOTHEK. NO. 160 (B. S. MS 37 FOL.) 15 century. Vellum. 147 leaves. Folio in several

hands. Foll. 1-21, *Ioh de Mandevilla itinerarius;* 23ᵛ, in another hand, in a blank space, a poem concerning the Marienkirche in Utrecht; 24, in another hand, a poem on Daventer; 25, Compendium Cronicarium; 91, Martinus Polonus. Written in Utrecht before 1451. Belonged to Baron de Crassier.

Pertz, *Archiv*, IX (1847), 575. Not in Vogels. Adrian, p. 55.

26. KLOSTERNEUBURG: STIFTSBIBLIOTHEK. CANONICORUM REGULARIUM S. AUGUSTINI. NO. 132. Written 1452. Vellum and paper. 404 ×282 mm. 2 cols. 42 leaves. Foll. 1-37, *Itinerarium;* 38, table of chapters; 38ᵛ-42ᵛ blank. Fol. 1 is inscribed: "Can. reg. Claustroneoburgensi bibliothecae iure sum inscriptus 12. May, 1656." At the end of the text: "Finitum a.d. 1452 currente 16. die iunii."

Not in Vogels. Pfeiffer & Cernik, *Catalogus*, p. 87.

27. OXFORD: BODLEIAN. LAUD MISC. 721 (formerly 1296). Written 1454. Vellum. 393 leaves. Fol. 1 *Godefridi Viterbiensis Pantheon;* fol. 340 ff. *Mandeville,* with a table of 50 chapters. The date of writing (usually 1355) is here given as m ccc lviii. Written and dated by John von Oistrich of Eberbach in Bavaria.

Vogels, p. 6. Warner, *Buke.* Coxe, *Catalogus*, II, pt. 1, 512-513.

28. BERLIN: STAATSBIBLIOTHEK. DIEZ C FOL. 2 vols. Dated 1455, 1456. Paper. 290 leaves. 2 cols. Contains Guido de Colonna, *De bello Troyano,* lib. 35, *Historia de praelis, Vita S. Brandan, Mandeville,* Hayton, *Historia de anima,* Gui de Tour, *Historia Tundali.*

Described in *Recueil des Historiens des Croisades. Historiens Occidentaux*, IV, ci. (Same as 'Diez 75. 4° 15 c.' listed by R.?) Not in Vogels.

29. NEW YORK: COLUMBIA UNIVERSITY LIBRARY. PLIMPTON 264. Written 1456. Paper. 139 × 98 mm. 121 leaves. 22-24 lines. Foll. 1-2ᵛ, table of 50 chaps. At the end of the table and on fol. 119: "Ista pertinet monisterio bonorum puerorum in Leodio. Scriptus per me fraterum Sibertum Herkenbosch de sittart natum." After the *Explicit* is the date, 31 March 1456. Foll. 120-121 blank.

Not in R. or Vogels. Maggs, *Cat.* no. 536 (1930), item 1305 and plate LVII. De Ricci, *Census*, II, 1801. Plimpton, *Education of Chaucer*, pp. 10-12, Pl. VII, facs.

30. LONDON: BRITISH MUSEUM. ADDIT. 37,512. Written 1457. Vellum and paper. 4° size. Fol. 1, *De Itineracione terre promissionis et aliis mirandis insulis liber iohis demandeuille militis.* 52 chaps. including the pseudo-autobiographical passage at the end. Followed by Georgii de Hungaria *Visiones in Purgatorio* S. *Patricii, Vita* Malchi Monachi Captivi, *Vita* Pafnucii Monachi, *Opus* S. Basilii; fol. 146: "Explicit libellus ... scriptus per me fratrem iohannem Swanfelder ordis fratrum ... de monte carmeli ... Anno dni C cccc lvij." Foll. 147-148, table of chaps. Belonged to the Duke of Sussex, then to Phillipps (no. 13660).

Described in *Bibliotheca Phillippica* Catalogue of Sotheby, Wilkinson, & Hodge (May, 1897), p. 64, no. 498. Then in B. Quaritch, *Cat. of Ancient . . . Mss.* (London, 1902), p. 56, no. 122. *Book-Prices Current*, 1907, no. 6766 (Quaritch). Not in R. or Vogels. Letts, p. 166. Mynors.

31. MAIHINGEN: FÜRSTL. ÖTTINGEN WALLERSTEIN' SCHE BIBLIOTHEK. HS. 1, 2, FOL. 31. Latin MS written in 1457.
No mention of other contents.

*Cat.* Grupp (1897), p. 20, no. 578. Not in Vogels.

32. LIÈGE: BIBLIOTHÈQUE DE L'UNIVERSITÉ. NO. 354. Written 1458. Half parchment and half paper. 2 cols. *Mandeville* on ff. 13-55, followed by the *Itinerarius* of Ludolph. Scriptus per manus goeswin de susteren novicii conventus fratrum sancte crucis huyeñ." Dated 12 July 1458. Blue initials. Bound in 19 century.

Not in R. Vogels, p. 7. *Catalogue* (1875), p. 353, no. 723.

33. OXFORD: BODLEIAN. FAIRFAX 23 (3909a). Mid-15 century. Paper. Foll. 7-8 missing. Vogels (p. 6), says it is like Harley 3589 and Laud Misc. 721. Warner, *Buke,* p. vii, n. 2, says it is in an English hand, but Mynors reports that the hand is poor and a little strange, perhaps Scotch. Bound with 9 miscellaneous tracts: 1. Edw. I's claim to Scotland. 2. Descent of the Kings of Scotland, to the Stuarts, et cetera.

Barnard, Cat., II, 181. Madan II, ii, 783. Mynors.

34. WOLFENBÜTTEL: BRAUNSCHWEIGISCHE LANDESBIBLIOTHEK. 23.2 AUG. Written 1461. Paper. 210 ×150

mm. 168 leaves. Foll. 1-75, Johannis Hildishemensis . . . Fol. 75ᵛ-168, *Mandeville*. Thiodericus Roleues, vicar of the chapel of the Blessed Virgin, gave it to the church of Mt. Saint Mauritii extra Muros, Hildesheim.

Heinemann, *Cat.* No. 3266(2). Not in R. or Vogels.

35. —— 18.6 AUG. Written 1471, 1472. Paper. 210 × 155 mm. 379 leaves. Foll. 320-379ᵛ: *Johannis de Mondevilla itinerarium in terram Promissionis*, with a register of chaps. at the end. Preceded by 17 miscellaneous tracts, mostly devotional.

Heinemann, *Cat.* No. 3137(18). Not in R. or Vogels.

36. BRUSSELS: BIBLIOTHÈQUE ROYALE. NO. 21520. 15 century. Vellum. 209 × 145 mm. 93 leaves. Paper guard leaves at beginning and end. Foll. 1-2, table, 2-93ᵛ, text. Note on fol. 1: "en février 1877, un ms de Mandeville de la fin du xivᵉ S. a été présenté à la Biblioth. royale, par M. Eckstein, libraire, 105, rue de la Province à Anvers. On y trouve à la suite des mots: 'in eadem civitate translatus' de l'incipit, les mots suivants: 'per eumdem una cum adjutorio cujusdam Mgri Johannis ad barbam qui etiam multas partes transmarinas perambulavit'," and on fol. 93, "Godin 1652, martii die 9a."

*Catalogue* (1927), xi, 304. No. 7437. Not in R., Tobler, or Vogels.

37. BERLIN: STAATSBIBLIOTHEK. GÖRRES 153—LAT. QU. 711 (before 1911 at Coblenz, Gymnas. 1844 Sectio Görres). 15 century. Paper. 195 × 132 mm. 307 leaves. Foll. 1-236, originally a separate MS, contains several works of Aeneas Silvius. *Mandeville*, on foll. 237-307 in a different hand, begins with a table of chaps. divided into 3 books.

Pertz, *Archiv*, xi (1858), 741. R. lists under old location. *Verzeichnis der Lat. HSS zu Berlin*, iii, 220-222. Not in Vogels.

38. BONN: UNIVERSITÄTSBIBLIOTHEK. n.d. Listed Pertz, *Archiv*, xi (1858), 739, as with a copy of *Imago Mundi*.

R. Not in Vogels.

39. DRESDEN: ÖFFENTLICHE BIBLIOTHEK. F. 69 a. 15 century. Paper Folio. 41 leaves. Title lacking. Fol. 1, table of chaps.

Vogels, p. 7. *Katalog* (1882), i, 377.

40. DÜSSELDORF: LANDES- UND STADTBIBLIOTHEK. G 12. 15 century. Vellum. Folio. *Itinerarius magistri Ioh. de Mandevelt . . . qui obiit Leodii A.D. 1832.* (See no. 23 [B. M. Harley 3589]).

Pertz, *Archiv*, xi, 752. Not in Vogels.

41. STRASBOURG: BIBLIOTHÈQUE UNIVERSITAIRE ET RÉGIONALE. NO. 30 (Lat. 28). 15 century. Paper. 312 × 205 mm. 2 cols. 326 leaves. *Mandeville* on foll. 286-326. Contains also chronicles, the Wars of Charlemagne, Martinus Poloner, and Guido de Colonna, *Historia Troiana*. Defective at the end.

Not in R. or Vogels. *Cat. Gen.*, 47 (1923), 21.

42. TRIER: STADTBIBLIOTHEK. NO. 334. 15 century. Paper. 2 cols. Fol. 1, table of 50 chaps.; 2, *Incipit Itinerarius a terra anglie*. Mandeville is followed by Ludolph.

Vogels, p. 7.

43. VIENNA: NATIONALBIBLIOTHEK. COD. 4459 (Theol. 286). 15 century. Folio. 200 leaves. Foll. 112-131 *Itinerarium* with table of chaps. at the end. Very difficult hand. Begins like Vienna Cod. 5363 (see above, no. 12), but ends differently.

Noticed in Cordier, *Revue*, i, 314, where it is described as item 13. Not in R. or Vogels. Roger E. Bennett has identified it for me as the Ogier version, and reports that it is item 15. The items include Odoric.

44. KÖNIGSBERG: UNIVERSITÄTSBIBLIOTHEK. NO. 334. 15 century. Paper. Folio. 228 leaves. Miscellaneous. Foll. 57-115$^v$, *Historia Alexandri Magni;* 116-120$^v$, 122-126, *Prester Johannis;* 126-133, 121, 134, *De Translatione Imperii;* 134$^v$, medical notes in verse; 135-143, *Mandeville,* mutilated at beginning and end. Ends with the Valley Perilous. Followed by several pieces, mostly religious.

*Catalogus*, Fasc. ii, "Codices Historici," pp. 64-66. Not in Vogels.

45. GOTHA: HERZOGLICHE BIBLIOTHEK. NO. 192. 15 century. Paper. 4°. 111 leaves. Foll. 1-54, *Itinerarium,* divided into 50 chaps.

Vogels, p. 6. All MSS from this library have been carried into Russia.

46. MIKULOV (NIKOLSBURG): FÜRSTLICH DIETRICH-STEIN'SCHE BIBLIOTHEK. SIG. II. 162. 15 century. Paper. Folio. 276 leaves. 20 items. Foll. 1-27, Marco Polo; 28-82, *Mandeville* ("a good text, with an index"); 83-113, *Solacii ludus Scacchorum*. The next 3 leaves are blank, followed by 17 items, mostly humanistic. The Mandeville in 50 chaps. From Hoffmann'sche Bibliothek, and later Biblio. Dietrichsteinianae.

*Archiv für österr. Gesch.*, xxxix, 492-493 (no. 51). R. lists this as German. Not in Vogels. Professor P. O. Kristeller tells me that this library was sold at auction in 1930. The whereabouts of this MS at present is unknown to me.

47. LIÈGE: BIBLIOTHÈQUE DE L'UNIVERSITÉ. WITTERT COLLECTION, NO. 99. 15 century. Paper. 216 × 14 [sic] mm. 77 leaves. Foll. 1-75$^v$, *Mandeville*, foll. 76-77 table of chaps. 77$^v$ blank.

Not in R. or Vogels. *Catalogue . . . Wittert*, p. 153.

48. LIBRI MS. 645 in Sotheby's *Catalogue* (March, 1859), p. 141. Latin *Itin.* 15 century. 4°. Paper, bound in calf. Sold to Quaritch for 3/5/0/. Perhaps the same as the following.

LORD AMHURST of Hackney's Library sold Dec. and March, 1908-09. Described in Sotheby, Wilkinson, & Hodge's Sale Catalogue, no. 581, p. 121, as early 15 century. Paper. 222 × 140 mm. 104 leaves. Neat English Gothic hand. 31 lines. Several original blanks. Rubricated. The end is quoted and shows it to be the vulgate text. Bound in old calf. Listed in *Book-Prices Current*, 1909, no. 4785, as for sale by Tregaskis.

CLARKE MS. 218. 4°. 234 pp. [117 leaves]. History of England to 1377 and Travels of Sir John Mandeville to Jerusalem, in Latin; see J. B. B. Clarke, *Manuscripts of . . . Dr. Adam Clarke* (1835), p. 96. This is probably now Egerton 672, no. 2 of this list.

49. LIÈGE: BIBLIOTHÈQUE DE LA EX-ABBAYE DE ST. JACQUES. NO. 490. 4° Paper. Fol. 1 Liber Internae Consolationis, seu Allocutionis Christi ad Animam fidelem; qui videtur esse Jacobi Grytrode, Catrusiensis juxta Leodium. Fol. 71 Itinerarius a Terra Angliae in partes Iherosolimitanas & in

Ulteriores transmarinas editus 1° in Lingua Gwallicana ab Autore suo Dompno Johanne de Mandeville Milite, anno Incarnationis Dni M.CCC. quinquagesimo quinto. in Civitate Leodiensi, & paulo post translatus in eadem Civitate in hanc formam Latinam. *Sale Cat.*, p. 485. Present location unknown.

HAMBURG: (?) HIST. GERM. FOL. 31[b]. Fol. 1, *De expeditione terre sancte facte per dominum Gotfridum Bollonenem;* fol. 37, *Incipit itinerarius Iohannes de Mandeville,* which ends on fol. 56. The next 4 leaves are missing; then, in another and older hand, Jordanus of Osnabrug's *De translacione imperii Romani* and several chronicles, the last beginning on fol. 236.

Pertz, *Archiv,* xi, 386-387. Vogels (p. 7) reports he could not locate it and cites J. C. M. Laurent's note of it in *Peregrinatores Medii Aevi Quatuor,* p. 154, n. 102. Prof. Kristeller tells me the shelf mark is that of the Stadtbibliothek now Bibliothek der Freien und Hansestadt.

## F

### Latin and North German

GÖTTINGEN: UNIVERSITÄTSBIBLIOTHEK. HIST. 61. 15 century. Paper. 315 × 210 mm. 489 leaves. Fols. 1 and 80 decorated, 1-79 in Latin, almost entirely from *Mandeville,* much of it given in both Latin and North German; 80-129, Alexander the Great; 129, the "Bragmans"; 132-196, Ludolph; 196-254, Chronicle of John of Hildesheim; 255-263, Epistle of Prester John; 276-301, Carpini; 367-486, Marco Polo in Pipini's translation into Latin.

Not in R. or Vogels. Schoerner, D. Benedetto, p. cxxxvi. Meyer, *Verzeichnis,* i, 2, pp. 19 ff.

### Uncertain

ROME: BIBLIOTHECA APOSTOLICA VATICANA. FONDO CHIGI F VII, 171. 14 century. Paper. MS contains a *Chronicon Compendium* to 1386; Martinus Polonus; *Istud est extractum ex libro gestorum pontif. Leodiensum; Hist. regum Franc. et comitum Flandriae; Geneal. ducum Lotharingie; Itin. ab Anglia in partes Hieros.* ca. 1300. Translated from French into Latin, detailed, very long description of lands. Noticed in Pertz *Archiv,* xii (1874), 391-392. The last item begins like a copy of the vulgate *Mandeville.*

PARIS: BIBLIOTHÈQUE NATIONALE. NO. 6447 (formerly 4847).
Listed by R. Not in Vogels.

AUGSBURG: KREIS- UND STADT-BIBLIOTHEK. NO. CXXIX. 15 century. Paper. 160 leaves. 2 cols. Red and blue initials. Marginalia. Foll. 1-103, Comedies of Terence; 104 ff. *St. Cyrilli epistola;* 121 ff. *Modus procandi Mulieres, et dicitur amatorium parvum;* 125 ff. *Commendatio brevis terrae Hierosolemytanae.*
R. lists as Mandeville. Not in Vogels. Metzger, *Geschichte,* p. 86, describes as above.

HOHENFURT. (?) 12 xvi fol. 133 N. Probably a fragment of Mandeville. Not in R.

### Excerpts—Version Unidentified

CAMBRIDGE: CORPUS CHRISTI COLLEGE. NO. 426. 15 century. Paper. Foll. 55-71, *Mandeville* followed by other data on the Holy Land on 3 leaves of vellum. Small, neat hand, 30-31 lines to a page.
Listed by R. James, *Cat.,* II, 332-334.

COPENHAGEN: DET KONGELIGE BIBLIOTEK. Ny kgl. S. 172. 8° size. 15 century. Vellum. 145 × 104 mm. Fol. 125 has the date 1455. Foll. 1-64, *Chronicon Angliae to 1437;* 65-83, *Memorabilia;* 95 ff., *Mirabilia mundi, Angliae, Hiberniae;* 137-138, "ex libro Johannis de Mandevilla," in a second hand. MS partly written and owned by William Horton, Monk of Lewes, ca. 1475.
Not in R. Vogels (p. 7) had not seen it. Lorenzen, p. xxxiv, n. *Hist. MSS. Commission,* 46th Report, App. II, 64. Jørgensen, *Catalogus,* pp. 391-394.

LONDON: BRITISH MUSEUM. COTTON OTHO D I. No. 8 "Extractus Itinerarii Johannis Mandeville." No. 9 is from Odoric. The vol. includes a description of England written in 1444. Damaged by fire.
Not in R. Smith, *Catalogue,* p. 74.

VIENNA: NATIONALBIBLIOTHEK, NO. 3529 (Hist. prof. 720). 15 century. Paper. 4° size. 331 leaves. Item 5, the *Itinerarium,* on fol. 156: "Quedam excerpta de itineraria . . ." corresponds to fol. 62ʳ of Vienna Cod. 5363. The account of

Mahometanism is much shortened. Fol. 190 corresponds to fol. 113 of Cod. 5363. The extract ends on fol. 191 and the end differs somewhat from that of 5363. There are extracts also from Boldensele, Hayton, and Brunellus. The volume has the inscription: "Liber presbyterorum et clerisorum in Wydenbach Coloniae."

R. lists *both* as Latin and as German. Vogels, p. 7. Cordier, *Revue* I, 314. Examined and identified as the Ogier version by Roger E. Bennett.

## IN GERMAN

There have been several studies of the manuscripts written in German. Carl Schönborn published *Bibliographische Untersuchungen über die Reise-Beschreibung des Sir John Maundevile* (Breslau, 1840), which distinguished two German translations and argued that the Latin vulgate was not written by the author of the original French version. A study of some value was made by Karl Simrock in the introduction to his edition of *Die deutschen Volksbücher* (Frankfort an Main, 1867) XIII, XIV-XVI, although he chiefly describes early editions. Francis E. Sandbach published *Handschriftliche Untersuchungen über Otto von Diemeringen deutsche Bearbeitung der Reisesbechreibung Mandeville's* (Strasbourg, 1899), and "Otto von Diemeringen's German Translation of Mandeville's Travels," *Modern Quarterly of Language and Literature*, II, 5 (1899), 29-35. He noticed 18 passages in B.N. fr. 4515 which are missing in Otto, and 35 in Otto but not in 4515.

The most recent and comprehensive study is Arthur Schoerner's *Die deutschen Mandeville-Versionen: Handschriftliche Untersuchungen* (Lund, 1927), which classifies and describes 27 MSS of Otto von Diemeringen's version, 33 of Michel Velser's, 7 of the Dutch MSS, and 1 of a translation into a mixture of German and Latin (See Latin F above). He gives the beginning and end of the text in each.

### A

#### Otto von Diemeringen's Version

1. BERLIN: STAATSBIBLIOTHEK. COD. GERM. FOL. 205. 14 century. Paper. v + 69 leaves (foll. 15 and 41 missing). 2 cols. Initials and flourishes in red. Once belonged to Jac. Twingei of Königshofen; later to Dan. Sudermann of Cologne.

Schoerner no. 1. *Kurzes Verzeichnis*, I, 31.

## APPENDIX I

2. KARLSRUHE: BADISCHE LANDESBIBLIOTHEK. NO. 167 (formerly St. Märgen 2). Written 1416. Paper. 96 leaves. 2 cols. R. gives old number. Schoerner no. 2.

3. PARIS: BIBLIOTHÈQUE NATIONALE. MS. ALLEMAND 150. 15 century. Paper. 210 × 140 mm. 356 leaves. Foll. 1-191$^v$, *Mandeville* (foll. 1-10, table, 11-191, text); foll. 192-200, Letter of Prester John, dated at the end 1418, St. Luke's day; foll. 201-245, *Aperçu de l'histoire universelle jusqu'à Alexandre;* foll. 246-261, Purgatory of St. Patrick; foll. 262-344 on St. Nicholas, with a colophon (fol. 344) dated 1419 St. Stephen's day. An *Explicit* on fol. 263: "Corin (?) Schriber. Ein gut geselle."

Schoerner no. 3. Huet, *Catalogue*, pp. 66-67. Sandbach, p. 12.

4. SÉLESTAT: BIBLIOTHÈQUE MUNICIPALE. NO. 25 (1101). Begun 1419 and finished 1421. Paper. 4° size. 2 cols. *Mandeville* has Otto's introduction and table of 45 chaps. Text, followed by *Gesta Romanorum*. Colophon names the scribe: Velmar Luczelstein, rector of the Church in Owenheim.

Schoerner no. 4. *Cat. Gen.* III (1861), 554-555. Cordier, *Bibl. Sin.*, 3:2043.

5. MUNICH: BAYERISCHE STAATSBIBLIOTHEK. CGM. 329. Written ca. 1430-1435. Paper. 90 leaves. 2 cols. 2° size. Leaves 1 and 90 lacking. Fol. 2, Otto's preface. Red initials.

Schoerner no. 19. Schmeller's *Catalogus*, I, 47.

6. ERLANGEN: UNIVERSITÄTSBIBLIOTHEK. SAMMELMAPPE 2112 NO. 35. 1st half 15 century. Vellum. 4° size. 2 cols. 1 leaf missing at end of Chap. 7 and beginning of 8 in Book II.

Not in R. Schoerner no. 13.

7. MUNICH: BAYERISCHE STAATSBIBLIOTHEK. CGM. 693. Written 1459. Paper. 4° size. 214 leaves (lacks foll. 11, 12, 23).

Schoerner no. 6 Sandbach, pp. 12 ff. Schmeller's *Cat.*, I, 113.

8. WÜRZBURG: UNIVERSITÄTSBIBLIOTHEK. MS. FOL. 38. Written before 1464 for the Dominicans of Würzburg. Paper. 303 leaves. Initials, alphabets, and flourishes in red. Foll. 2-5 blank; 6, register of chaps. and Otto's preface; 6-125, text.

Schoerner no. 7.

## GERMAN MANUSCRIPTS

9. GOTHA: HERZOGLICHE BIBLIOTHEK. NO. A 26. Written 1472 by Martin Scherffenberger. Paper. Mandeville on pp. 127-248. Begins: "Hie her nach hebt sich an das puch Johann von Montevilla . . ."

   Sandbach, p. 15. Tobler. Schoerner no. 8, reports it "misplaced." All MSS from this library have been removed to Russia.

10. WOLFENBÜTTEL: BRAUNSCHWEIGISCHE LANDESBIBLIOTHEK. COD. 14. 10 Aug. Written 1473. Paper. 210 × 155 mm. 210 leaves. Begins with Otto's preface. Places left for initials. Belonged to a Nürnberg family named Thill.

    Schoerner no. 9. Heinemann no. 3048.

11. VIENNA: NATIONALBIBLIOTHEK. COD. 2838. Written 1476. Paper 3 + 179 leaves (1-3 and 179 blank). 2 cols. 2° size. *Mandeville*, foll. 1-163, followed by a German tract on Antichrist. Red initials and flourishes and profuse illustrations. Fol. 178$^v$, colophon: "Don mit harr Hannsen Minner geschreiben von Costeniz aleman zalt tusent vier hundert und alzo sechz und siebenzigisten Iar off Sant Thomas abent." From the Imperial Library.

    Schoerner's no. 10. *Tabulae*, II, 141. Cordier, *Revue*, I, 314. Examined for me by R. E. Bennett.

12. BAMBERG: STAATLICHE BIBLIOTHEK. J. H. MISC. HIST. 112 (I, 17). 15 century. 320 × 220 mm. Paper. 164 leaves. Initials. Foll. 1-4 in another hand, dated 1477; 5-162$^v$, *Mandeville*, begins with Otto's preface; 163-164, other matter dated 1469 (3 leaves of a Würzburg Chronicle of the 15 century).

    Schoerner no. 11. Not in R. Leitschuh, *Cat.*, no. 145.

13. BERLIN: STAATSBIBLIOTHEK. GERM. FOL. 1268. (formerly Coblenz: Gymnasiumbibliothek Sectio Görres 33) 15 century. Paper. 91 leaves. 2 cols. Intro. and table lacking. From St. Maximin in Trier.

    R. lists as Coblenz. Schoerner no. 12. *Kurzes Verzeichnis*, I, 170.

14. GOTHA: HERZOGLICHE BIBLIOTHEK. NO. 584. 15 century. Vellum. 108 leaves. 2 cols. 36 lines. Otto's preface and (foll. 1-5) table.

Tobler. Schoerner no. 14. Jacobs, I, 423. All MSS from this library have been removed to Russia.

15. HEIDELBERG: UNIVERSITÄTSBIBLIOTHEK: PAL. GERM. 65. 15 century. Paper. 139 leaves. 2 cols. Fol. 35$^v$ arms of Erpachs and Hirshorns.

Schoerner no. 15. Sandbach, p. 12.

16. ——— PAL. GERM. 138. FOL. 15 century. Paper. 116 leaves.

Schoerner no. 16. Sandbach, p. 12.

17. LONDON: BRITISH MUSEUM. ADDIT. 17335. 15 century. Paper. 61 leaves. 2° 2 cols. Illustrations. Some leaves missing.

Ashton. Schoerner no. 17. Letts, p. 175. *Cat. of Addit. MSS* (1868), p. 6.

18. MUNICH: BAYERISCHE STAATSBIBLIOTHEK. CGM. 593. 15 century. Paper. 117 leaves. 2°. 2 cols. Lacks foll. ix, x, cix of old foliation; fol. 99 is in another hand. The last chap., 117$^v$, has been supplied from Velser's translation. Otto's preface lacking. The Table (which omits the heading for Book IV), begins on 2; Text, fol. 6 ff. "Ulmer Bürgern" on foll. 1, 5.

Schoerner no. 20. Schmellers *Cat*, I, 96.

19. PRAHA: FÜRSTLICH LOBKOWITZSCHE BIBLIOTHEK. NO. 421. 15 century. Paper. 154 leaves. 282 × 200 mm. Red initials, flourishes, and alphabets. Has Otto's preface.

Schoerner no. 21. Pertz *Archiv*, IX, 479. *Serapeum*, XXVIII (1867), 321-322. Lehmann, *Mitteilungen* III, p. 48.

20. ST. GALLEN: STIFTSBIBLIOTHEK. NO. 628. 15 century. Paper. 940 leaves. 2°. 2 cols. All in one hand, well written. Contains a world history to 1348, the letters of Alexander and Dindimus, the legend of the Three Kings, *Mandeville* on foll. 854-917, followed by Schiltburger. *Mandeville* lacks Otto's preface and is incomplete at the end.

Haenel 702 reports that it was formerly the property of "nobilibus Rink de Baldenstein." Schoerner no. 22. *Verzeichniss*, pp. 204-205.

21. STRASBOURG: BIBLIOTHÈQUE UNIVERSITAIRE ET RÉGIONALE. NO. 2119 (All. 195). 15 century. Paper. 2°. 2 cols. *Mandeville* on foll. 236-276, lacks Otto's preface and the

table and is defective at the end. It is preceded by chronicles and voyages, and followed by Schiltburger.

Haenel 469. Schoerner no. 23. *Cat. Gen.*, 47, p. 444.

22. TRIER: STADTBIBLIOTHEK. NO. 1935,13. 15 century. Paper. 229 leaves. 2°. 2 cols. *Mandeville* on foll. 122-199. Colophon: "Dit boich hort zo broder Johanne dem snyder yn Euerhartzclusen und hat es selber geschryben myt groisser arbeit."

Schoerner no. 24. Borchling, IV, 172. *Besch. Ver.*, VII, 107.

23. WIESBADEN: STAATSARCHIV. NO. B 25 (formerly Idstein). 15 century. Paper. 2 cols. *Mandeville*, foll. 1-73 (leaves 5 and 41 lacking; Otto's preface and the heading of the table missing).

R. lists twice (under both old and new locations). Schoerner no. 25. Friedemann, *Zeitschrift*, I, 1, p. 73 (see Gotha).

24. VIENNA: NATIONALBIBLIOTHEK. NO. 12449. 16 century. Paper. 234 leaves. 2°. 2 cols. *Mandeville* on foll. 150-233$^v$. Places left for initials Foll. 1-149 originally a separate MS in Latin in a very different hand. Mandeville has illustrations. Alphabets.

Reported by R. E. Bennett. Schoerner no. 26. Cordier, *Revue*, I, 315.

25. WOLFENBÜTTEL: BRAUNSCHWEIGISCHE LANDESBIBLIOTHEK. COD. 32. 8 Aug. 16 century. Paper. 205 × 200 mm. 2°. Foll. 1-77, Chronicle of Alexander the Great; 79-190$^v$, *Mandeville*.

Schoerner no. 27. Heinemann no. 2328.
(Schorner nos. 5 and 18 are listed with the Dutch MSS.)

# B

## Michel Velser's Version

26. HALLE: UNIVERSITÄTSBIBLIOTHEK. YD. QUART. 8. 14 century. Vellum and paper. 4° size. Foll. 1-10, on paper of the early 15 century, replace missing leaves; 48-69 also missing. Caps. with red flourishes. Rubrics in Latin. Dialect "oberdeutschefränkische." Title "Job. von Mandeville Reisen."

Schoerner no. 1. Pertz, *Archiv*, XI, 727.

## APPENDIX I

27. GIESSEN: UNIVERSITÄTSBIBLIOTHEK. NO. 992. (B.S. MS. 132. fol. min.) Written 1390-1400. Paper. 166 leaves. 2 cols. Red initials and flourishes. *Reise* on foll. 54-104. Begins: "Do ich da haim usz für in dem mût das ich wolt varen uber mer . . ." At the end: "Iste liber est Marquardi Waltheri Custodis ecclesie Sti Mauricii Aug." (Belonged in 1400 to Ulrich Walther, the elder of Augsburg.)

    Schoerner no. 2. Adrian, p. 300.

28. MUNICH: BAYERISCHE STAATSBIBLIOTHEK. CGM. 332. Written 1409. Paper. 109 leaves (last 2 blank). 2°. Fol. 83 damaged. Table in red on foll. 1-3; text, 4 ff.: "Do ich . . ." Foll. 15, 22, 74 and 96 all contain interpolations in which Michel Velser names himself. At the end in red: "Das püch ist volbracht wörden jnder iar Zahl nach Christi gepürde tawsent vierhundert iar dar nach jn dem newnten iar."

    Schoerner no. 3. Schmellers, I, 48.

29. WARSAW: BIBLIOTEKA UNIWERSYTECKA. NIEM. Q.4.1 (formerly at St. Petersburg, Q IV, 1). Written 1412. Paper. 120 leaves. 4° size. Last leaf mutilated. Cursive hand with illuminated initials and rubrics in red. Given to Poland in 1924. Probably lost.

    Minzloff, pp. 122-126. Schoerner no. 4. R. gives old location.

30. BRESLAU: STADTBIBLIOTHEK. M. 1073 (formerly in the Church of St. Mary Magdalen, no. 78). Written 1414. Paper. 2°. 195 leaves. Table in a 16 century hand on last 3 leaves, previously blank. Colophon on fol. 192 gives the date of writing. Many places in the MS. illegible from dampness.

    Schoerner no. 5. Pertz *Archiv*, XI, 711. Schönborn, pp. 10-11.

31. BAMBERG: STAATLICHE BIBLIOTHEK. MISC. HIST. 182 (formerly Nürnberg. Stadtbibliothek Ebneriana 60). Written 1415. Paper. 91 leaves. 2°. Fol. 1 damaged. Text ends on 90$^v$. Written by "Nicolaus Hohenstat de Winnpia, Presbyterus Bambergensis."

    R. gives old location. Schoerner no. 6. Murr, *Memorabilia*, II, 68 (see Nürnberg).

32. KLOSTERNEUBURG: STIFTSBIBLIOTHEK. NO. 1083. Written 1425. Paper. 2°. 228 leaves. Foll. 1-173, *Mandeville*, 174-219, Odoric. Initials in gold and colors. Colophon of the scribe, Johannes Levoch and date on fol. 219.

Schoerner no. 7.

33. LONDON: OWNED BY HEINRICH EISEMANN of 102 Clive Court, Maida Vale, dealer, who bought it at the Rauch sale in Geneva, March 2, 1953. Formerly belonged to Albert F. Zimmerman, dealer, who sold it at the Swenn Auction Gallery, 146 East 56 Street, New York, on April 10, 1952. Formerly Dresden: Sächsische Landesbibliothek. F. 184b. Written 1433. Paper. Small 4°. 23 lines. 3 + 184 leaves. First of 3 leaves of table missing. Painted caps. and scrolls. In original red sheepskin binding. Colophon with the scribe's name at the end of the table, and again at the end of the text: "Schriptum [sic] et Finitum Anno dni. m cccc.xxxiij. in die Corpus xpi. Melius scripsissem. Sy [sic] manum meum Usitassem. Man*us* mea non Consueuit. Ergo male scripsit. Fratr Ulricus Gampler Conuentual in Etal. Orate deum p*er* me."

R. lists at Dresden, as does Schoerner no. 8, and see Carolsfeld, *Katalog*, I, 421. Described in Zimmerman's *Catalogue*, no. 114.

34. MAIHINGEN: FÜRSTL. ÖTTINGEN WALLERSTEIN' SCHE BIBLIOTHEK. HS. I, 3. 4°. 8. Written 1434. Paper. *Mandeville* on foll. 2-171$^v$.

R. (no. 21), Schoerner no. 9. *Neues Archiv*, VII (1882), 175 (see Pertz). *Handsch.-Ver.*, p. 20. Grupp, no. 579.

35. MUNICH: UNIVERSITÄTSBIBLIOTHEK. COD. OCTAVO 179. Written 1434. Paper. Text on foll. 3-103. "Explicit phemanum Mendel de Valli Angeli anno M. CCCC. XXXiiij jn vigilia asumpcionis beate Marye Virginis . . . Et hoc jussit Conradus Haÿden dum tempus Ambergk . . ."

Schoerner no. 10.

36. DONAUESCHINGEN: FÜRSTLICH-FÜRSTENBERGISCHE HOFBIBLIOTHEK. No. 483. Written 1435. Paper. 107 leaves. 2 cols. Foll. 1-2, register; 3-106$^v$, text, 107$^r$, colophon. Written by Nicholaus Burger von Weilheim.

Schoerner no. 11. Barack, p. 328.

37. WOLFENBÜTTEL: BRAUNSCHWEIGISCHE LANDESBI-
BLIOTHEK. COD. 23.10 AUG. Written 1436. Paper. 210 ×
145 mm. 218 leaves. Flourished in red. Said to be translated
from Latin into "Deutsch" and calls him "Hans von Mon-
dauilde."

Schoerner no. 12. Heinemann 3274.

38. TAMBACH: GRÄFL. ORTENBERG'SCHE BIBLIOTHEK.
NO. 7. Written 1444. Paper. 63 leaves. 2°. 2 cols. 2 leaves
missing at the beginning. End: "Ich Hans von Montevilla fur
aus meyne land . . ." Scribe was Johen Klen in Vilshouen.

Schoerner no. 13. *Serapeum* III (1842), 345-46.

39. LONDON: BRITISH MUSEUM. ADDIT. 18026. Written
1449. Paper. 4° size. 2 cols. Foll. 1-65$^v$, *Mandeville*. No illustrations; no alphabets. At the end: "explicit per me Johanes
Segnitz de Castel M cccc xlviiij jn die palmarum."

Ashton. Letts, p. 174. Schoerner no. 14. *Cat. of Addit. Mss.* (1868),
p. 72.

40. MUNICH: BAYERISCHE STAATSBIBLIOTHEK. CGM.
594. Written ca. 1449. Paper. 2°. 107 leaves. Foll. 1-72,
*Mandeville;* 73-83, *Visio Tungdale* in German; 84-107,
Thomaus Prisschuch von Augsburg *Reimspruch* of the Council of Constance. Last item written 1449. Red initials and
flourishes.

Schoerner no. 15. Schmellers, *Cat.*, I, 96.

41. ———— CGM. 4872. Written 1456. Paper. 197 leaves. 4° size.
Foll. 1-68, George of Hungary's visit to St. Patrick's Purgatory;
69-197, *Hansen Monteville's Reise*. Red initials and flourishes.
"Explicit liber per me Johannem Fritzen per manus et non
per pedes." Schoerner says defective at the end, but quotes
the usual conclusion.

Schoerner no. 16. Schmeller's *Cat.*, I, 493.

42. NEW YORK: PULIC LIBRARY. SPENCER COLLECTION
(formerly Wernigerode, Fürstl. Stalberg'sche Bibliothek, Zb
25). Bought for the Spencer Collection from H. P. Kraus,
dealer, in 1941. Described in A. Rosenthal's *Cat.* I, "Secular

Thought," no. 25 (London, 1939). Completed 7 Sept. 1459. Paper. 168 leaves, last 12 blank. 214 × 150 mm. in 8s. Foll. 1ᵛ, a colored picture of "Johannes de Montefilla"; Text 2-156ᵛ. Colophon: "Et sit est finis huius opusculi D anno lix. In vigilia natiuitatis ble Marie vij"; 157-168 blank except for some notes on 166ᵛ and 167ʳ Text begins, 2: "Ich Johannis von monte silla . . . ," and 3 "von Englland von Nŭremburg oder von der nijder londen . . ." Michael Felser (Velser) names himself in an interpolation on fol. 31ᵛ. There are 81 pictures (3 reproduced by Rosenthal), some like Sorg's, such as the concept of Samson, men without heads, etc. Pictures and text were done together, after the pages had been ruled for text only. Apparently colored inks, mostly red and brown, a little yellow and purple, were used for the pictures.

R. gives old location. Schoerner no. 17. Letts, p. 175.

43. BASEL: UNIVERSITÄTSBIBLIOTHEK. E II 8 FOL. (formerly E IV 1). Written 1460. Paper. 142 leaves. 2 cols. 2°. Foll, 1-54ᵛ, *Mandeville;* 54ᵛ and 56ʳ contain other matter, interpolated.

R. gives the old number. Schoerner no. 18. Haenel 469.

44. BERLIN: STAATSBIBLIOTHEK. GERM. FOL. 1066 (formerly described as Sectio v. Stahremberg 55. Also formerly at Efferding, Signatur 55, no. 2). Written 1462. Paper. 393 leaves. Contains the History of Alexander the Great and *Mandeville,* foll. 231-393, with some short interpolations, in 98 chaps. Register on foll. 390-393. Defective at the end. The scribe was Petrus Seltzem von Sautterför. In 1652 it belonged to Heinrich Wilhelm Graf von Staarhemberg of Riedegg.

R. lists this MS 3 times: under Berlin, old number; under Coblenz; and under Effering. Schoerner no. 19. Lohmeyer in *Germania* 31 (1886), p. 227. *Kurzes Verzeichnis,* I, 149.

45. VIENNA: NATIONALBIBLIOTHEK. COD. 12475 fol. Written 1465. Paper. 139 + 1 leaves. 2 cols. Red initials. Begins: "Do ich dohayme ausfur in dem mut das ich wolt faren . . ." Ends 139ᵛ: "Johannes de Montevilla seu Mandevilla, Iter in terram sanctam in linguam versum germanicam a Michaële Velser." No illustrations.

Schoerner no. 20. R. E. Bennett.

46. GÖTTINGEN: UNIVERSITÄTSBIBLIOTHEK. HIST. 823.
Written 1470. Paper. 280 × 205 mm. 1 + 132 leaves. 2 cols.
Red initials and flourishes. First leaf damaged. Fol. 49$^v$ names
the translator. *Mandeville* ends on 72. Followed, 72-98, by John
of Hildesheim's legend of the three Kings. 132 has the colophon:
"Finitus ist liber iste per me Conradum Blannckhen de Kyemsee . . ." A.D. 1470.

Schoerner no. 21. Meyer, *Verzeichniss*, I, 2, pp. 274-275.

47. MUNICH: BAYERISCHE STAATSBIBLIOTHEK. CGM 695.
Written 1473. Paper. 141 leaves. 4° size. Foll. 1-128, *Johann's
von Mandevilla Reise;* 128-140, three religious tracts. Red initials and flourishes. At the end of the *Reise* (fol. 128$^v$): "1473
jar an Symon vnd Judas aubent."

Schoerner no. 22. Schmellers, I, 113.

48. ——— CGM. 252. Written 1477-80. Paper. 213 leaves. 2°.
Decorative initials. Miscellany containing a fragment of Marco
Polo; foll. 79-87, a fragment of *Mandeville;* 158-163, Petrarch's
*Griselda;* 177-191, *Melusine;* 194-201, *Godfrey of Bologne;*
202-213, Boccaccio's *De claris mulieribus,* etc., all in German.

Schoerner no. 23. Schmellers, I, 27-28.

49. HEIDELBERG: UNIVERSITÄTSBIBLIOTHEK. Pal. Germ.
806. Written 1478. Paper. 2°. 2 cols. Foll. 2-47, *Mandeville,*
defective. Bound with another, but quite distinct MS, 48-131.

Schoerner no. 24. Bartsch, *Katalog,* I, 179.

50. LONDON: BRITISH MUSEUM. ADDIT. 10129. 15 century.
Paper. 120 leaves. 2°. Foll. 3-120, *Mandeville.*

Not in R. Schoerner no. 26. Ashton. Letts, p. 175. Heber, *Sale
Cat.* No. 11, p. 105, no. 1010?

51. BERLIN: STAATSBIBLIOTHEK. GERM. FOL. 912. 15 century. Paper. 203 leaves (bound with Konrad v. Megenberg, *Das
Buch der Natur.*) *Mandeville* in 2 cols., foll. 145-201$^v$. Old
foliation, lvij leaves + 3 of register. Formerly belonged to
Freiherr v. Richthofen.

Not in R. Schoerner no. 25. *Kurzes Verzeichnis,* I, 125.

52. MAIHINGEN: FÜRSTL. ÖTTINGEN WALLERSTEIN'
SCHE BIBLIOTHEK. HS. I. 3, FOL. 11. 15 century. Paper.

*Mandeville,* foll. 2-138. Colophon: Scriptus est liber iste per me Fridricum de Swobach."

Not in R. Schoerner no. 27. *Handsch.-Ver.,* p. 20. Grupp, No. 580.

53. MUNICH: BAYERISCHE STAATSBIBLIOTHEK. CGM. 299. 15 century. Paper. 156 leaves. 2°. 2 cols. Red initials and flourishes. Fol. 1 lacking. *Mandeville,* 2-120$^v$, followed by 3 other works.

Schoerner no. 28. Schmellers, I, 41.

54. ——— CGM. 694. 15 century. Paper. 88 leaves. 4° size. *Mandeville,* foll. 1-88$^v$, very incomplete; 22-23 exchanged with 34-35.

Schoerner no. 29. Schmellers, I, 113.

55. SALZBURG: STIFTSBIBLIOTHEK ST. PETER. B. IV 37. 2nd half 15 century. Paper. 4° size. 122 leaves. Red initials and flourishes.

Schoerner no. 30.

56. ST. PAUL IN KÄRNTEN: STIFTSBIBLIOTHEK. COD. HOSP. 210. (or St. Paul im Lavantthal). Early 15 century. Paper. 190 leaves. 4° size. *Mandeville* on foll. 107-190, incomplete at the end. 2 stubs show between 106 and 107.

Schoerner no. 31.

57. VIENNA: NATIONALBIBLIOTHEK. COD. 2850. 15 century. Paper. 2°. 128 leaves. Red initials and flourishes. *Mandeville* on foll. 2-128$^v$. Last leaf damaged.

Schoerner no. 32. *Tabulae,* II, 144, describes it as Otto's version. Cordier, *Revue,* I, 315, says 129 leaves, Otto's version. Roger E. Bennett has examined the MS for me and reports that it is like 12475, and not at all like 2838, Otto's version. No alphabets.

58. NÜRNBERG: STADTBIBLIOTHEK. SOLGERIANA 34. 15 century. 2°. Paper. Item (1) Edition of Marco Polo, Augsburg, 1481 (Sorg ed.). (2) St. Brandan, written 1488. (3) "Ioh de Mandeville Itinerarium, MS German," ca. 15 century. (4) Odoric, written 1488. (5) Schiltberger. This is evidently the same as no. 66, listed separately by R. as lost and described by Murr, I, 391-392 under the heading: "tam membranacii,

# APPENDIX I

quam characei." The 2 descriptions mention the same items, in the same order, including the edition of Marco Polo.

Schoerner no. 33. Murr, I, 383-384. (In *Odoric*, lxxxii, Cordier claimed to have seen no. 66 in 1886 and that it was in *Latin*.) R lists twice.

### Röhricht Lists Also:

LÜBECK 63b.
NÜRNBERG: Stadtbibliothek. Solgeriana 27 (lost).
STUTTGART (cf. Graf. *Diutiska,* II, 77). Schoerner does not list these three and I have not been able to find any further description of them.
NIKOLSBURG. Sig. II, 162, R. lists as German. See Latin no. 46.
VIENNA No. 3529. R. lists both as Latin and as German see above p. 311.

## IN DUTCH AND LOW GERMAN

Schoerner (p. 54) reports that there are two Dutch translations from the French, one (or both?) from the Ogier version, and at least two from the German, one from Otto von Diemeringen's translation. Two groups of manuscripts have been edited. N. A. Cramer, in *De Reis van Jan van Mandeville* (Leiden, 1908) edited a text from the Leiden, Göttingen, Brussels, and The Hague MSS and the earliest incunabulum (see pp. xxxviii-xli). Sven Martinsson edited a text from the Hamburg and Magdeburg MSS and collated Lüneburg, but did not print his collations: *Itinerarium Orientale: Mandeville's Reisebeschreibung in Mittelniederdeutscher Übersetzung* (Lund, 1918). Schoerner described and classified the 4 Berlin MSS and those at Soest and Düsseldorf, and made an extended refutation of Cramer's stemma: see pp. 48-71.

### A

#### From Otto's German

1. MAGDEBURG: STADTBIBLIOTHEK. NO. XII, 15 (III, 209 4° 75d). Paper. 75 leaves. 2°. 2 cols. Translated into Low German in 1420 by Otto vom dem Ringe.

    Not in R. Collated by Martinsson. Schoerner no. 18 (Otto). Borchling, III, 250.

2. HAMBURG: STAATS- UND UNIVERSITÄTSBIBLIOTHEK. COD. GEOG. 58. Written 1447. Paper. 290 × 210 mm. 88

leaves. 2 cols. Begins: "Ek Otto van Dimeringen eyn domhere to Mertze in Lotringhen hebbe ik dut buek ghewandelt . . ."

Martinsson's text. Schoerner no. 5 (Otto). Borchling, I, 139. From Uffenbach's library. In Middle Low German.

3. BERLIN: STAATSBIBLIOTHEK. GERM. QUART. 322 (formerly Bibliothek Paulina at Münster). 14 century. Paper. 215 leaves, last 2 blank, last damaged. Foll. 2, 9, 97, 105 misbound. Space left for initials. Text breaks off on 213$^v$ at the end of the 4th book (in Otto's version). Dialect, Niederdeutsch.

Cramer's Bl. Schoerner Niederländisch no. 3, or Bl. R. lists twice, in both old and new locations. *Kurzes Verzeichnis*, II, 55. Borchling, I, 139-140.

B

From French

4. LEIDEN: RIJKSUNIVERSITEITS BIBLIOTHEEK. HS. BPL. 14 F (formerly Univ. Biblio. Geel 661). Early 15 century. Vellum. 200 × 145 mm. 74 leaves in 6s. 2 cols. 40 lines.

Not in R. Cramer's L. Schoerner's A. Lelong, *Cat.*, p. 8, no. 55.

5. GÖTTINGEN: UNIVERSITÄTSBIBLIOTHEK. HISTOR. 823 b. 15 century. Vellum. 185 × 125 mm. 60 leaves. Red initials and flourishes. Text mixed up as in Riant MS. (Fr. 44) through being copied from a MS which had leaves out of order. Imperfect. Bought at auction in Leyden.

Not in R. Cramer's G. Schoerner's B. Meyer, *Verzeichniss*, I, 2, p. 275.

6. BRUSSELS: BIBLIOTHÈQUE ROYALE. NO. 720. Mid-15 century. Paper. 260 × 175 mm. 50 lines. 2 cols. Register at the beginning. Text begins: "Want dat alsoe . . ." From the French Ogier version. MS from Vallis S$^{ti}$ Martini, Louvain.

Cramer's B. Schoerner's C. *Cat. B.R.*, II, 79, dates in the late 14 century.

7. THE HAGUE: KONINKLIJKE BIBLIOTHEEK. Y 302 (1191). Written 1462. Paper. 280 × 200 mm. 161 leaves. 2 cols. 26-30 lines. From the French Ogier version.

Not in R. Schoerner says that it agrees with Brussels (Fr.) 10420 and 11141(!). Cramer's H. Schoerner's D. *Cat.* of H. van der Hoop (La Haye, 23 March, 1801), p. 102, no. 505.

## C

### The 17-alphabet Version (from French)

8. BERLIN: STAATSBIBLIOTHEK. GERM. FOL. 204. Written 1430. Paper. 151 leaves in 4 hands. Many pictures. Alphabets for Hebrew, Jewish, Greek, Greek caps., one unspecified, Saracen, Jew (bis), Russian, Slav, Saracen (bis), Persian, Chaldean, Indian, Tartar, Georgean, Turk. Formerly bound with *Summa Johannis Thodude,* printed at Magdeburg in 1498. The MS belonged, 15 and 16 centuries, to "Frid. Jac. Roloff." Marginal references to Sebastian Münster's *Cosmography,* and to travels of Jerome Scheidt of Erfurt (1616). On fol. 7: "In anno 1430 was dit bok geschreuen." Begins: "Wante also ist dat land van over see dat men heet dat hilge land . . ."

Cramer's Bi. Schoerner's N. no. 5, or Bi. *Kurzes Verzeichnis,* I, 31.

9. LÜNEBURG: RATSBÜCHEREI. MS C 8 FOL. 15 century. Paper. 168 leaves (plus 10 blank). In 2 or 3 hands. Has the same pictures, alphabets, and table of contents as the preceding. Martinsson, p. iii, reports 4 miniatures. He says that it has the same opening as "der englische Text," and is not Otto's translation. Begins: "Want dat also in dat dat landt van ouersee dat men hetet dat hilghe landt . . ." Red initials and flourishes.

Cramer's Lu. Schoerner's N. no. 6, or Lu. Borchling, I, 170, quoting its claim to be translated from Latin.

### Unclassified

10. BERLIN: STAATSBIBLIOTHEK. GERM. FOL. 550. 14 century. Vellum. 83 leaves. Fol. 1 half missing; 7-44 damaged; defective at the end. Dialect, Ripuarisch. Ends: "Bi deisem konineriche sint zwey andere eylande de eine heyst Orille und dat ander Argite. Vnd al dat lant van deisen eylande . . ."

Cramer's Be. Schoerner's N. no. 1, or Be. *Kurzes Verzeichnis,* I, 61.

11. ———— GERM. QUART. 271. 14 century. Vellum. 131 leaves. Table on foll. 1-2. 2$^v$ blank. Text on foll. 3-131. Several leaves missing after fol. 7. At the end in another hand: "Jn jaeren vns herrn M cccc ix." 64 chaps. Dialect, Ripuarisch. Red decorations. Formerly belonged to "Danyel Schillynck van Lausney [sic]," and "Biblio. Blanckenheim" [?].

Cramer's Br. Schoerner's N. no. 2, or Br. *Kurzes Verzeichnis,* II, 48.

12. SOEST: STADTBIBLIOTHEK. NO. 28. Written 1490. Paper. 92 leaves. 2°. 2 cols. Table on foll. 90-92. No alphabets. Fol. 1 defective, 12 missing. Written by Johannes Köp in the Soest Order of Preaching Friars in 1490.

Cramer's S. Schoerner's N. no. 7, or S. Pertz, *Archiv*, xi, 738. Schoerner classes it with Br.

13. CAPE TOWN, SOUTH AFRICA: PUBLIC LIBRARY. 15 century. Fine Gothic book-hand. Illuminated. Picture of the round world on fol. 2 shows Mandeville sailing across a blue sea with a book open before him. 6 alphabets, but the names of the Egyptian letters omitted. Formerly belonged to Sir George Carey, Governor of Cape Colony.

Described by A. Lodewyckx, "Een Nieuw Mandeville Handschrift," *Tijdschrift voor nederlandsche taal—en Letterkunde*, Pt. 30 (1910), 1-53. Letts, in *Quarterly Bulletin of the S. A. Library* (Cape Town), June, 1949; and *Mandeville*, pp. 175-176. Not in Schoerner.

### FRAGMENTS

14. DÜSSELDORF: STAATSARCHIV. 14 century. Vellum. 4°. 1 leaf. 2 cols. Dialect, Niederdeutsch.

Text printed in Crecelius, *Altdeutsche Neujahrsblätter für 1874* (Wiesbaden, 1874), p. 88. Not in R. Schoerner's N. no. 4. Borchling, iv, 76.

15. LÜNEBURG: RATSBÜCHEREI. MS. D. 25. In 2 parts. 15 century. Pt. 1, a life of St. Peter. Pt. 2, a fragmentary *Mandeville*. 175 × 115 mm. 2 cols. Fol. 1 begins: "ander riuiere heet nil och te gvon Dats te segghene in egypscher spraken tourble dat es donker. . . ." Otto's translation. Fol. 2 contains the conclusion of the 4th book.

Not in R. Borchling, i, 174.

### IN DANISH

The Danish version of the *Travels* was studied by J. C. J. Brandt, *Gammeldansk Laesebog* (Copenhagen, 1857), i, 115-123. More recently the text was edited from four manuscripts by Marcus Lorenzen, *Mandevilles Rejse i gammeldansk oversaettelse tillage med en Vejleder for pilgrimme, after håndskrifter udgiven*, 3 pts. (Copenhagen, 1881-82), in Samfund til udgivelse af gammel nordisk litteratur, vols. a, b, c. Text of the *Travels* in 50 chaps. from the Latin vulgate, with a table at the end, pp. 205-206. He lists 4 MSS (p. xlii):

1. STOCKHOLM: KUNGL. BIBLIOTEKET. K 31, in 2 pts. 1459 and 1534. This is Lorenzen's A and B, from a translation made about 1444. The first part has the colophon: "Explicit libellus, scriptus per fratrem Olauum Iacobi ordinis sancti Francisci, quem fecit scribi ffrater Johannes Michaelis, gardianus Nestuedensis. Anno domini MCDLnono in profesto assūpcionis Virginis gloriose."

    Listed by Molbech, in *Historisk Tidskrift*, IV (Copenhagen, 1843), 149-152.

2. —— NO. 55. 1601. *Mandeville* on the first 151 leaves, followed by a register of chaps., and another work on 27 leaves. Inscribed: "Thenne Boug Hør Müg Palle Friis Thüll Met Rete och Er Müg Forerret off mien guode Venn Her Peder skytt Gudtz Ordt Thiienner vdj Leiderdalls Prestegirell Thüll En Vennlliig Forerenng Anno 1601. Palle Friis. Egenn Hanndt."

    Not in R. Molbech, IV, 15. Brandt, V. See also Lorenzen, pp. lvi-lxiii. Lorenzen's C text.

3. ODENSE: KAREN BRAHES BIBLIOTEK. 4° size. "Joh. Mandivels Rejse-Bog of Latin fordansket 1544," in Linds *Cat.* (1725), p. 159.

    Vogelsangs, p. 87. "Rejsebeskrivelser." Lorenzen's E text.

4. COPENHAGEN: DET KONGELIGE BIBLIOTEK. NO. 3559. 16 century. 8°.

    Not in R. Lorenzen's D text.

## IN CZECH

Otto von Diemeringen's German version was translated into Czech about 1400 by the Hussite historian, Vivřincem Vavřinec of Březov (1370-1436). Ten manuscripts, three of them modern, are listed in Frantisek Simek's edition of the printed text, *Cestopis t. zv. Mandevilla*, in *Sbirka pramenův ku poznání literáního života v Čechách*, &., Skulpina I, Rada I, Cis. 9. (Praha, 1911), reprinted in a popular edition in 1912. I have not had access to this work. The encyclopaedia, *Ottův Slovnik Naučný* (Prague, 1900), art. "Mandevilla," lists eight manuscripts.

1. PRAHA: NÁRODNÍ MUSEUM. CODEX III E 42 (formerly III F 26. Formerly owned by the historian i Balbin, at Ossek; later in the library of Venceslas Hanka at Prague). Mid-15 century. This is the oldest MS.

    R. lists twice, at Ossek and at Prague, bibl. Hanka. It contains also a copy of Marco Polo and is described by Benedetto, i, cxlvi.

2. MIKULOV, i.e. NIKOLSBURG: FÜRSTLICH. DIETRICHSTEIN'SCHE SCHLOSSBIBLIOTHEK. Dated 1445. Paper. 4°.

    Dobrowsky, p. 166.

3. PRAHA: KNIHOVNA ŘÁDU PREMONSTRÁTU NA STRAIIOVE (formerly belonged to the Minorites). Dated 1449. Paper. Folio.

    Listed R. *Bohemia docta*, III, 803, and Dobrowsky, pp. 165-166.

4. MIKULOV, i.e. NIKOLSBURG: FÜRSTLICH. DIETRICHSTEIN'SCHE SCHLOSSBIBLIOTHEK. SIG. I 33. 16 century. 4° size. Paper. Begins, "Já Otta z Dymerinku kanovnik w Meci v Luturingii . . ." 119 chaps. Inscribed: Generosus Dominus Ferdinandus Hoffmann, Liber Baro in Grunbuchel et Strechaw. dominus in Grewenstein, &c.

    Listed by R. Dobrowsky, pp. 165-166. Dudík, pp. 466-467, no. 19. This library was sold at auction in 1930.

5. PRAHA: NÁRODNÍ MUSEUM. V E 11 (formerly owned by a nobleman, z Ričan). Dated 1484.

    Not in R. *Ottův Slovnik Naučný*.

6. KRIZOVNIKU MONASTERY. Dated 1576.

    Not in R. *Ottův Slovnik Naučný*.

7. MS in the hands of Kremerius, who published the first edited edition from it in 1687.

    *Ottův Slovnik Naučný*.

8. PRAHA: NÁRODNÍ MUSEUM. V E 12. Copied by Václav Nemasta, teacher at Provodov, in 1783.

    *Ottův Slovnik Naučný*.

## APPENDIX I

### Fragment

PRAHA: UNIVERSITY. XVII J. 12. 17 century. Paper. 160 × 95 mm. 137 leaves. Foll. 33-36ᵛ: Též vybrané některé věci z knihy Jana Mandyvilly rytíre pamĕti hodné (Výpisky z vydání Mandevilly r. 1600. Srovn. Hanuš Dod. I, 13). Jungmann, v, 505. Inscribed: "Ego Casper Antonius Norbertus Klimess Moravus Lascoviensis A.D. 1643."

Truhlář, *Katalog*, no. 377.

## IN ITALIAN

The translation from French into Italian was edited by Francesco Zambrini, "I Viaggi di Gio. da Mandavilla," in *Scelta di Curiosità Letterarie inedite o rare*, Vols. 113, 114 (Bologna, 1870). A partial list of the MSS was published by Enrici Narducci, "Opere Geografiche esistenti nelle Principali Biblioteche Governative dell' Italia," part III of *Studj Bibliografici e Biografici sulla Storia della Geografia in Italia*, by Pietro Amat di San Filippo (Rome, 1875). An attempt to study the translation was made by J. Vogels, "Das Verhältnis der italienischen Version der Reisebeschreibung Mandeville's zur französischen," in *Festschrift dem Gymnasium Adolfinum zu Moers ... vom Lehrercollegium des Gymnasiums zu Crefeld* (Bonn, 1882), pp. 37-45. In his first study of Mandeville, Vogels argues that the French, and not the Italian, was the original language. He attempts to construct a *stemma* from entirely inadequate materials, but provides no list of Italian manuscripts.

1. FLORENCE: BIBLIOTECA NAZIONALE CENTRALE. COD. MAGL. XXXV, 221. Mid 15 century. Paper.

    This is the text printed by Zambrini, see CXIII, xxii ff.

2. MILAN: AMBROSIANA. H 188. 15 century. Paper. 2°. With 6 other pieces, including Odoric.

    Described in Cordier's *Odoric*, p. lxxxvii.

3. MANTOVA: BIBLIOTECA COMUNALE. Written 1432. Vellum. 70 leaves. 2 cols. Historiated initials. Colophon: "Compilatione fornita questo di XI dicembre 1432 en Venezia per me Antonio de Mathe de Corado da Cardino da Firenze per lo Referir da fier Christofallo fioravente et per Michelo de Michielle Veneciani, trovatosi a li presenti periculi come prolixamente si

dichiara." Foll. 71-80: "Avegna ch'infiniti exempli et degni miraculien." Foll. 81-85, "Tractatus de vita et morti religiosi viri Galeoti Roberti Malatestis tercii ordinis sci Francisci principis Armin."

Narducci, no. 82.

4. OXFORD: BODLEIAN LIBRARY. ADDIT. C 252 (29437). Written 1442. Paper. 309 × 220 mm. i + 87 leaves. 1 illum. cap. Fol. 83, "Antonio delgayo do la cuntra de Sam quilicho Scripsi de lano de 1442. del messe de zenaro e finito a vltimo de febraro del ano[?] suprascritto."

Bought at Costa sale at Sotheby's (lot 376), Aug. 11, 1884. Madan v, 622-623. Vogels *LV,* p. 3 n.

5. PARMA: BIBLIOTECA PALATINA. NO. 1070. Written 1465. Paper. 2°. 40 leaves. Begins. "Qui incomenza el libro del Famosissimo cavalieri Miser Iohani de Mandavila de Ingletera del suo peregrinazo ultra mare. . . ." Colophon: "Scripto per me Bernardo del pra da Parma Canzellero del Magnifico di. Gandolfo di Rossi da Bologna Castelano del Castello de Parma de l'ano MCCCCLXV del messe di marzo."

Narducci, no. 157.

6. NEW YORK: PIERPONT MORGAN LIBRARY. NO. 746 (V 5 D). Written 1465. Vellum, 270 × 190 mm. 138 leaves. 31-33 lines. Gathered in quires of 10, except the 6th, which has 8. Illuminated. Arms on fol. 1 erased (see De Ricci, II, 1495, for a description). Colophon on fol. 138$^v$: "Questo libro he stato scrito per mane de Nicholo Mascharino del lano 1465 in ferrara." A handsome, large manuscript in an excellent large humanistic hand. Initial "D" in blue, framed in gold, with a band of illumination in red, blue, green, and gold on 3 sides of fol. 1. Other initials (43) in blue with red penwork, or in red with purple. Frequent marginal headings. This is a translation of the Paris redaction, giving the dates 1322 and 1357, but "xxv" years between. It has 6 alphabets, foll. 8$^v$, 21, 45$^v$, 48$^v$-49, 63, 64$^v$ (lacks names of the letters). Foll. 126 ff. have the addition to the Valley Perilous, and 78$^v$-79 have the substitute account of the roundness of the earth. On 109 "Nicolaus Companz" and "loningo" (?) in the margin, erased. Bought in 1928 from W. Toscanini.

Not in R. De Ricci, *Census,* II, 1495. Letts, p. 174. See also Bradley, *Dictionary of Miniaturists,* II (1888), 269.

7. NAPOLI: BIBLIOTECA NAZIONALE. XII D 57. Written 1467. Paper. 2°. 79 numbered leaves. Title: "Johannes de Mandevilla de mirabilibus in orbe. . . ." Date of completion given as 1357. Colophon: "Ego Notarius stephanus johannis delecto ad instantiam Mag. Leonardi de legistis de Aquila locumtenentis Ill. et ex. domini Mathei de capua ducis Aarie comitisque palen propria manu scripsi Die penultimo Junii xv Ind. Anno domini MCCCCLXVII."

Narducci, no. 128. R. lists as Latin. Title and Colophon are in Latin, but the text is in Italian.

8. LONDON: BRITISH MUSEUM. ADDIT. 41329. Completed March 10, 1469. Paper. 285 × 204 mm. 91 leaves. First 2 blank. Acquired in 1926. Bookplate (a shield and motto) erased, and no indication of previous ownership. Text begins: "Tractato delle piu meravigliose cose e piu notabili che si trovino in le parte del mondo." Fol. 3$^r$ "Questo libero fu composto per ulo nobilissimo cavaler dingeltera chimato per nome miser Zucani de Mediavila et questo lo principiato chapiar adi 10 Marzo 1469." The text differs considerably from the printed version of 1480, and from Zambrini's edition. There is an interpolation on fol. 17 which is pseudo-autobiographical.

I am indebted entirely to Mr. Malcolm Letts for calling my attention to this MS and providing me with this description of it.

9. FIRÉNZE: BIBLIOTECA RICCARDIANA. CODEX 1917. Written 1492. Paper. 2°. 87 leaves. 2 cols. Lacks rubrication. Colophon: "Io Bartolomeo di Benci da dicamano al presente provigionato nella Rocca vecchia del borgo San Sipolchro ho scripto questo libro, coe finito di scrivere questo di xx di giugno 1492. A stanza di Raffaelo di Michele di chorso ciptadino fiorentino."

Narducci, no. 59. Described by Zambrini, CXIII, xxii f.

10. ———— CODEX 1910. 16 century. Paper. 2°. The second of 10 items, beginning with Marco Polo. Contains also Piero Voglienti on the discoveries of the Portuguese, Amerigo Vespucci, Vasco di Gama, etc. Lacks rubrics.

Collated by Zambrini and the chief variants printed. Narducci, no. 55.

11. MUNICH: BAYERISCHE STAATSBIBLIOTHEK CODEX ITAL. 1009 (245). 15 century. 4° size.

Listed by R.

12. LUCCA: BIBLIOTECA GOVERNATIVA. NO. 304. 16 century. Paper. 2°.

Narducci, no. 81. Described by Zambrini.

13. FIRÉNZE: BIBLIOTECA NAZIONALE CENTRALE(?): (formerly Ashburnham, Libri 1699). 14 or early 15 century. Paper. It translates the statement about language: "Jo l'o totalmente in vulgare componuto," which makes of the sentence a claim that Italian is the original language. Vogels, p. 39, argued that it was early 15 century. In *LV*, p. 3, n. 2, he says it is essentially parallel to Zambrini's text. He lists it as in the British Museum, but Letts (p. 174), reports that he did not find it either in England or in the Bibliothèque Nationale.

### Extract

VENEZIA: BIBLIOTECA MARCIANA. IT. VI 208 (5881). Written 1518-20. 4° size. 270 leaves. Foll. 160-177 contain extracts, some from Mandeville. Compiled from MSS and printed texts by a Franciscan. Excerpts also from Odoric, Marco Polo, Don Manuel of Portugal, Columbus, Vespucci, etc.

Not in R. Described by Benedetto, p. cxxvi, and Mazzatinti, lxxvii (1950), 74-76.

## IN SPANISH

Two translations into Spanish survive, one made in the fourteenth century and the other apparently late in the fifteenth. No MS of the second is known, but it is preserved in the editions printed at Valencia in the sixteenth century. These are in the Castilian dialect and present a much shorter version than appears in the earlier manuscript. For a description of the two translations see W. J. Entwistle, "The Spanish Mandevilles," *Modern Language Review*, XVII (1922), 251-257.

1. ESCORIAL, EL. MS M iii 7—115 iii 7—Est. 15.4 15 century. Vellum. 258 × 192 mm. 91 leaves. 33 lines. Foll. 1-4 missing. Illuminated initials. The ending gives the dates 1322, 1357, but 55 years. Dialect and scribe Aragonese. Begins in the

account of "Famatroste." Entwistle identifies this translation with no. 22 of the inventory of King Don John of Aragon made in 1395. No. 22 contained an account of St. Patrick's Purgatory, as well as the *Mandeville*. The Escorial MS. bears the library mark of Conde-Duque de Olivares, from whom it passed to the royal library in the 18 century.

Cuevas, II, 288. *Miguelez*, II, i. Dr. John O. Marsh, Jr., has prepared *The Spanish Version of Sir John Mandeville's "Travels"; a Critical Edition*, as a doctoral dissertation (unpublished) at the University of Illinois. He has completed his text, and collated for sense and proper names, from the printed editions of 1521 and 1540.

## IN IRISH

The translation into Irish was made by Finghin Ó Mathghamhna, or Mahony, in 1475. It is a very free and abbreviated translation from a manuscript in English of the class of the Cotton text, but not from the common short version of that text, since it has the passage on circumnavigation which is missing from the "Pynson" version. The translator claims to have consulted English, Latin, Greek, and Hebrew. The Translation ends with Chapter 33, "Of Taprobane." The text has been edited, from the Rennes MS., by Whitley Stokes, "The Gaelic Maundeville," *Zeitschrift für celtische Philologie*, II (1898), 1-62, 226-312. Stokes prints the Irish and a literal English translation on facing pages, and adds, pp. 301-312, a vocabulary of Irish words and a table of corrigenda. The texts of the Rennes and Egerton manuscripts were compared by John Abercromby, "Two Irish 15th Century Versions of Sir John Mandeville's Travels," *Revue Celtique*, VII (1886), 66-79, 210-224, 358-368. Both are copies, not the original translation. Rennes is earlier and southern; Egerton is northern.

1. RENNES: BIBLIOTHÈQUE MUNICIPALE. NO. 598 (138). no. 18, foll. 52$^v$-69$^v$. 15 century. Vellum. Incomplete at the end. A leaf has been lost between 69 and 70. This is a collection of translations from Latin and French.

    *Catalogue General*, xxvi (Rennes), pp. 255-260. It was first noticed by J. H. Todd, "Some Account of the Irish Manuscripts," *Proceedings of the Royal Irish Academy*, MSS Series (1870), pp. 66 ff., and see above.

2. LONDON: BRITISH MUSEUM. EGERTON 1781, no. 23, foll. 129-146$^v$. In 2 hands, 1484 and 1487. Mandeville is in the sec-

ond. Vellum. 254 × 160 mm. 32 pieces in the collection, which consists of translations of romances, saints' lives, etc., chiefly from Latin. No. 3 is the Pseudo-Turpin.

Robin Flower, *Catalogue of Irish Manuscripts*, II, 526, 540-541. Stokes used the Egerton MS to supply the last leaf, missing in the Rennes MS. Letts (p. 175), says no illustrations, no alphabets.

### FRAGMENT

3. LONDON: BRITISH MUSEUM. ADDIT. 33,993, no. 6, foll. 6-7. Fragment. 16 century. Vellum. 184 × 130 mm. The text has been modernized from the older version. It was written in Co. Tipperary, and in 1648 belonged to Sir James Ware. The B. M. acquired it from the Crawford sale, Sotheby's, 18 March 1891, lot 1690.

Flower, *Catalogue*, II, 1-3.

## PICTORIAL

LONDON: BRITISH MUSEUM. ADDIT. 24189. Early 15 century. Vellum. 254 × 184 mm. 14 leaves. No text whatever. 28 full-page illustrations of the first 5 chapters only. This manuscript came from Samuel Maskell, who bought it from the dealer, Samuel Woodburn, who had it from M. Pesch, who said he got it from a monk in Rome. Warner, *Buke*, identifies the art as from "somewhere near the Meuse." It had been described by Woodburn as "old Spanish or *Moorisco* school," and Mr. Mynors tells me that the illustrations are now believed to be of Bohemian origin.

Since the pictures fill both sides of each leaf, and since they illustrate such a small segment of the text, it seems probable that the artist's intention was to create a pictorial Mandeville, or Mandeville in the universal language of pictures, without a text of any kind.

Described by E. G. Millar, *English Illuminated Manuscripts of the XIVth and XVth Centuries* (Paris and Brussels, 1928), and by Warner, who reproduces the pictures in full color, in the Roxburghe Club ed. of the *Travels*.

# APPENDIX II

# THE EDITIONS

### Table of Editions

| | |
|---|---|
| French | 337 |
| English | 346 |
| Latin | 359 |
| German | 364 |
| Dutch | 371 |
| Czech | 375 |
| Italian | 376 |
| Spanish | 383 |
| References cited in Appendices | 387 |

### NOTE

The listing of early editions of the *Travels* is very difficult, both because of the number of these editions in every major language of Europe, and because the surviving copies of this very popular little book are so very rare and widely scattered. I have attempted to list all the incunabula of which there is record, even where no copy is now known; and I have added all I could find of the equally rare sixteenth-century editions, and all of the English editions down to 1953. For other languages I have not made a systematic search for later editions, but have indicated briefly the continued popularity of the *Travels*, as far as my information goes.

For the convenience of students, I have given the location of all early copies known to me. There are others, I am sure, in private hands and in the smaller libraries. A renewal of interest in Mandeville may bring out of obscurity some further editions, and it is my hope that this list will aid in the identification of unrecorded copies and even in the discovery of new editions. I have seen all copies listed as HCL, PML, LC, Folger, Yale UL, NewbL, Rosenwald, NYPL, and Hisp. Soc. of Amer. In the list of references, I have put the BMC first, then Hain-Copinger-Richling, Klebs, Proctor, Cordier, Brunet, and the rest in alphabetical order. In the location of copies, I have put the American libraries first, then the British, then French, and after that the other countries in alphabetical order.

For languages such as Portuguese I found no record of manuscripts, or 15th- and 16th-century editions, and so I have not included modern editions. The Danish and Irish manuscripts, for which there were no corresponding early editions, have been studied in recent times, and editions have been noticed in the introductions to the manuscript lists.

## KEY TO LIBRARIES REFERRED TO IN BRIEF

| | |
|---|---|
| Berlin SB | Staatsbibliothek, Berlin |
| BM | British Museum, London |
| BN | Bibliothèque Nationale, Paris |
| BPL | Boston Public Library |
| BR Heredia | Bibliotheca Ricardo Heredia |
| CambUL | Cambridge University Library |
| Columbia UL | Columbia University Library, New York |
| Danzig SB | Danzig Stadtbibliothek |
| Folger | Folger Shakespeare Library, Washington, D.C. |
| Hanover KB | Hannover Königl. öffentlichen Bibliothek |
| HCL | Harvard College Library |
| HEHL | Henry E. Huntington Library, San Marino, Calif. |
| JRL, Manchester | John Rylands Library, Manchester |
| LC | Library of Congress, Washington, D.C. |
| L'Es. | Amiens, L'Escalopier |
| Magd. Col., Camb. | Magdalen College Library, Cambridge |
| Milan A. | Ambrosiana, Milan |
| Munich BSB | Bayerische Staatsbibliothek, Munich |
| NewbL | Newberry Library, Chicago, Ill. |
| NYPL | New York Public Library |
| PML | J. Pierpont Morgan Library, New York, N.Y. |
| U of Mich. | University of Michigan Library, Ann Arbor, Mich. |
| UB | Universitatsbibliothek |
| Yale UL | Yale University Library |

## FRENCH EDITIONS

1. 1480 APRIL 4 [LYONS: GUILLAUME LE ROY FOR BARTHELEMY BUYER]

BMC 8:235. C 3825 and 3830. Klebs 649.1. Pr 8504. Cordier 3:2027. Brunet 3:1357. Claudin 3:48. Picot 3:441. Thomas Fr. Copy: BM G 6775 (IB 41516).

2° 90 leaves a-k$^8$l$^{10}$ 30 lines 2 cols. 174 × 122-4 mm.

Fol. 1 blank (missing); fol. 2 (title): Ce liure est eppelle mā/ . . . (11 lines), followed immediately by text. l$^9$ (colophon): Cy finist ce tres plaisant/ liure nōme Mande ville par/lanc moult autentiquement/du pays et terre doultre mer/ Et fut fait Lā MilCCCC/lxxx le iiii iour dauril./ l$^9$ verso blank. l$^{10}$ blank (missing). Capital spaces. No illustrations.

BMC reports that several pages show miscalculation of copy at the foot of the page. Colophon reproduced in Claudin. Thomas misprints the Grenville number as 6755.

It has been argued that the next ed. is the earlier. Lyons dated the New Year from Easter, or Easter Eve, in this century, and Easter fell on April 2 in 1479/80 and April 22 in 1480/81; therefore, April 4 fell twice in "1480." J. Techener, quoted by Cordier, argues that this is the first French ed. Brunet describes this as the first ed. Picot argues that the Feb. 8 ed. is the earlier. However, it seems improbable that a second ed. would be called for in 2 months. Moreover, we know that in the spring of 1480/81 Le Roy was busy securing a new font of type in Venice, and apparently doing some retraining, in preparation for a very ambitious undertaking, a legal work in 8 large vols., of which the first was finished July 30, 1481. This 8 vol. work was Buyer's last undertaking, and Le Roy was probably helped by John Siber. But since the next 4 parts took almost a year to complete, the first could hardly have been done in less than 3 months, and the preparation must have been a time-consuming process, so that it is very improbable that the *Mandeville* was completed as late as April 1480/81. Concerning Le Roy's activities, see BMC 8:xlv.

BM copy lacks first and last blanks and a$^8$. The ed. is sometimes described as 88 leaves.

## 2. 1480 [1481] FEB. 8 LYONS [MARTIN HUSS] A LA REQUESTE DE BARTHOLOMEW BUYER.

> HC 10641. Klebs 649.2. Cordier 3:2027. Brunet 3:1357 and *Suppl.* 2:1056. Atkinson 495, 417. Claudin 3:20. Picot 3:441.
> Copies: Rothschild III, 2633 (in BN). Orléans. E 319 bis.

2° 106 leaves A⁷B-N⁸O⁶P⁴ KL is a single signature. The 4th leaf of K is signed KLiiij. 30 lines 2 cols. 164 × 50 mm. each column. No illustrations.

Fol. 1 blank (?) (missing). fol. 2 [ai] (title): Ce liure est appelle/ ... (12 lines) followed immediately by text. fol. Piiij verso (colophon): Cy finist ... Imprime a/ lyō sur le rosne Lan Mil/ CCCC lxxx le viii iour de/ freuier [sic] a la requeste de/ Maistre Bartholomieu/ Buyer. ...

Type similar to, but not identical with, that of the April 4 ed. There are 2 mistakes in the title and 2 in the colophon (cf. Brunet Suppl. and Picot), and very many in the text, a condition which suggests either very great haste, or that it was set up by another printer, on Buyer's press, during Le Roy's absence in Venice (see under April 4 ed.). BMC, VIII, xlviii suggests attribution to Huss. Pellechet N. attributes to Huss, and notes a second copy: Orléans E 319 bis. (Cat. Cuissard, FF.) 108 ff. 106ᵛ and last 2 foll. blank. Van Praet computed 113 leaves and described sig. L (8 leaves) as missing. Brunet followed him, but corrected himself in the Suppl. Van Praet was describing the La Vallière-Bright-La-Roche-Lascarelle-Rothschild copy.

## 2b. VARIANT: Same colophon, including date.

> Brunet (III, 1357). Picot, Cordier, Klebs, as above.
> Copy: BN Rés. 0² f. 3.

Title, with 4 corrections, reset in 13 lines, of which the last has only the word "isles." Brunet describes both titles. Picot says of the text, "L'exemplaire [in the BN] présente avec celui-ci de nombreuses différences, qui donnent lieu de penser que le volume a été, sinon réimprimé, du moins profondément remanié." Atkinson describes and (p. 417, fig. i a) reproduces the title page. Sigg. same as in Rothschild copy. Claudin reproduces first and last pages and traces the history of the type (pp. 22 ff.); see p. 173 for further connection of Huss with this type; and see BMC 8:xlvii ff. on Huss.

Unique copy lacks first and last blanks, 5 leaves of sig. B, and 5 leaves of sig. C. Picot, p. 442, gives a sample of the variants.

## 3. [BEFORE 1483. LYONS: NICOLAUS PHILIPPI AND MARCUS REINHART]

C 3828. Klebs 649.3. Cordier *Mél.* 1:21. Brunet, *Suppl.* 2:1056. Polain 2583. Quaritch *GC*, pp. 4038-39..
Copy: Univ. of Liège, xv$^e$s. C 66.

2° 90 leaves a-k$^8$l$^{10}$ 32-33 long lines. Woodcuts. Borders.

Fol. 1 blank (?) (missing). fol. 2 (title): Ce liure est appelle mandeuille & fut fait/ . . . title in 8 lines, followed by the text. Spaces left for caps. Col. on fol. 89, 89$^v$ blank. 90 blank (missing).

Polain describes the Liège copy as lacking a$^1$a$^4$b$^2$b$^7$h$^4$k$^1$k$^6$l$^1$l$^2$l$^{10}$. It lacks also h$^5$ and h$^8$. He reproduces the t.p. (Pl. cxi) showing the type and the woodcut border on the top and left margins, and woodcut initial. The reproduction, probably full size but atypical, measures with border 218 × 160 mm., without border 192 × 130 mm.

Several short pages, and several which have partial lines of text (not catchwords) added, at the foot of the page, attest the printer's difficulty in fitting text and pictures together.

The missing leaves identify this as the copy described by Crawford (June, 1887) and Quaritch, *Cat.* no. 375 and *GC* item 38418, pp. 4038-39. Both Crawford and Quaritch report a first leaf having on the recto a woodcut of a youth with a lance and streamer lettered "Iohannes de Montevilla." This was, undoubtedly, the Sorg frontispiece, used for the German ed. printed at Augsburg in 1481 and next used at Lyons by Nicolaus Philippi and Jean du Pré, ca. 1487. Copinger follows Quaritch in mentioning this leaf, but Polain describes fol. 1 as missing. When and why it was removed is a mystery.

There are 86 of the Sorg cuts present in this very defective copy. They are not copies of Sorg's cuts, but are actually printed from the same woodblocks as the Sorg cuts. Between July 18, 1481 and the end of 1482, the woodblocks must have been purchased and transported from Augsburg to Lyons; see below, "German Editions," 1 and 2.

Brunet described the Quaritch copy as 88 leaves, first and last blank (missing). 33-34 lines to a page. He read "appelle" in the title, where Quaritch read "apelle," and gave the number of missing leaves as 10, as in Polain. He also identified the press and dates the ed. 1477-82. BMC 8:241 dates the last book certainly from this press in Dec. 1482. The partners printed for Buyer in 1478 or 1478/9. The woodcut border was used next by Matthieu Huss in January 1482/3; and again April 9, 1486; cf. Polain.

## 4. [1487? LYONS: NICHOLAS PHILIPPI WITH JEAN DU PRÉ]

C 3826. Klebs 649.5. Cordier 3:2029, and *Mél.* 1:27. Brunet 3:1358 and *La Fr. Litt.*, p. 122. Atkinson, p. 497. Claudin 3:149.
Copy: Amiens, L.'Escalopier 5202. (?) Mazarine Library 18077B.

2° 76 leaves a-b⁸c-m⁶ 35 long lines. Woodcuts. Fol. 1 blank. 1ᵛ the Sorg frontispiece. a² (title): Ce liure est appelle Mandeuille et fut fait et compose par messire/ . . . (5 lines), followed immediately by text. Text ends on m³ 31 lines, followed by "Cy finist . . ." as in Brunet.

Claudin reproduces both the t.p. and the frontispiece, and (pp. 143 ff.) identifies the type as first employed by Philippi and Du Pré in 1486/7. It is a bâtarde type but not at all like that used in the Philippi-Reinhart ed. The capitals are distinctive, especially C and E. BMC 8: Pl. xlv, calls this type "Du Pré 121 B." Claudin 3:lvi calls it "Philippi-Du Pré bâtarde." Philippi was dead by 1489, and the capitals in the font were soon replaced by those of Gaspard Ortuin; Claudin 4:434-435. Du Pré had an active press by the end of 1487, important for woodcuts by 1491, employing 17 men in 1493, and ceasing in 1495: BMC 8:lvi, 280. Klebs assigns the ed. to 1488, but the only book signed by these partners is dated 15 Jan. 1486/7.

The Amiens copy lacks the first 3 leaves of sig. b, and the last 3 of sig. m. Brunet describes a variant, identical with this, except that it had "Mancduille" for "Mandeuille" in the title. It also lacked the first 3 leaves of sig. b, and had sigg. a-m₁₁₁, i.e., it lacked also the last 3 leaves of sig. m. It was sold by Hanrott in 1834 and by St. Maurys in 1841, and is probably the copy sold by H. Bohn, *Cat.* of 1830, no. 610. The whereabouts of this copy is unknown; the coincidence of the missing leaves suggests that Brunet was mistaken about the spelling "Mancduille" and that what he saw was actually the Amiens copy. If so he was mistaken in describing the ed. as a 4°. Claudin calls it a "small 2°."

ANOTHER COPY? Atkinson describes a *Mandeville* in the Mazarine library which he dates "[1505?]." It lacks the first and last leaves, and has been in bad condition since the 18 century. He quotes 2 lines from the title on a² and these agree exactly with the first lines of the title of the Amiens copy, including the awkward line division "saint a/lain" (i.e., St. Albans). The sigg. run a²-m⁵ and the page measures 209 × 128 mm. Claudin does not give the measures for the Amiens copy, but his reproduction of the t.p. measures 212 × 130 mm. The title page, with title above the first page of text, might well be a little larger than the average page, or the reproduction may be slightly oversize.

## 5. 1487 LYONS: PIERRE BOUTTELLIER.

> Du Verdier, p. 729. Le Croix du Maine et Du Verdier 4:476.
> No copy known.

4° Listed by H 10642; Claudin 3:425; Brunet 3:1358, and *La Fr. Litt.*, p. 122. BMC mentions 8:286, and lvii.

Pierre Boutellier, or Bouttellier, is identified as a German named Peter Schenck who printed in Vienne in 1484 and then migrated to Lyons where he was briefly in partnership with Ortuin in 1485. He married a French woman and translated his name. His French name appears in the tax lists of Lyons 1485-94. Only 2 books are "known to bear the signature of Bouttellier at Lyons, namely a French Mandeville dated 1487, of which no copy can now be produced, and an undated *Demandes d'Amours*": BMC 8:lvi. He printed mostly short, popular French books in a type described as "somewhat irregular bâtarde," following a fashion set by Le Roy (sample 108B and 112B): BMC 8:Pl. xxxv.

## 6. 1487 [1488] MARCH 26 [LANTENAC]: JEAN CRÈS.

> Klebs 649.4. Cordier 3:2027. Atkinson, p. 417, fig. 1 b. Claudin in *Bibliographica* III, 359. Thierry-Poux, p. 138, Pl. 34, nos. 10, 11 and p. 16. Berger p. 386.
> Copy: BN Res. 0² f. 4.

4° 123 leaves a-p⁸q³ 25-27 long lines. 140 × 90 mm. Fol. 1 has only the word "Mandeuille" on recto. fol. 1ᵛ blank. fol. 2 (title): Ce liure est appelle Mandeuille et fut faict/ . . . (7 lines), followed immediately by text. Spaces left for caps. No illustrations. Sig. a² (title and beginning of text) reproduced by Atkinson. Title and colophon reproduced by Thierry-Poux.

Earliest work known from this press: see BMC 8:lxxxiv, 404 and Claudin, op. cit. R. citing Hain 10642, makes a ghost by combining this with the Lyons ed. of 1487 as "Lyon, Jean Cres and Pierre Bouteillier 1487 4°." Cres was at Lantanec in Brittany. Vogels refers to an edition "Lyons 1487 Bartholomew Buyer." Buyer died in 1483.

## 7. [ca. 1490 LYONS: PIERRE BOUTTELLIER]

> C 3827. Klebs 649.6. Cordier 3:2028. Morgan *Cat.* no. 610. Quaritch

(see below). St M 141. Assign to Bouttellier in BMC 8: lvii.
Copy: PML 610.

2° 72 leaves a-b⁸c-k⁶l⁸ 29-37 long lines. 131-133 × 210-212 mm. to a full page of type. Woodcuts.
Fol. 1 [ai] blank. fol. 1ᵛ the Sorg "portrait" of Mandeville. fol. 2 (title): [C]e liure est appelle mandeuille et fust fait & compose/ ... (6 lines), followed by text ending on sig. 1ʳ. Verso blank. Last leaf blank. Spaces left for large caps.

103 of the Sorg woodcuts are reproduced. In fitting the text to the pictures, many pages are short of the full measure of type, as also in Sorg's edition.

The Sorg woodcuts, used in the German ed. July 1481, belonged to Philippi and Reinhart before 1483 (see notes on their ed.), and to Philippi and Du Pré about 1487 and passed (by the way of Du Pré and Ortuin?) to Bouttellier (after Philippi's death in 1489?). They were still in fair condition when the Morgan copy was printed, although the tails of the man and woman so equipped are broken off, and the hair (including the top of the head) of the woman catching fish (5th from the end in Sorg, 4th in Bouttellier) is gone.

The PML exemplar has the woodcuts beautifully colored and the caps. hand-lettered in red and blue. It lacks the final blank leaf, has the bookplate of the Hamilton Palace Library, Beckford Collection, bought at Sotheby's Dec., 1882, by B. Quaritch. Richard Bennett's bookplate is inside the back cover.

Quaritch first described this copy (Rough List, No. 82; dated Jan. 15, 1883, no. 62) as "Jehan de Mandevile. Tres plaisant livre nomme Mandeville ... small folio, n.p., n.d., not in Brunet, unique copy from the Beckford library with 103 colored woodcuts." Cordier was misled into making 2 editions out of 2 descriptions of this copy. The colophon reads: "Cy finist ce tresplaisant liure nomme Mandeuille parlant moult au/tentiquem ēt du pays & terre doultre mer & du sainct voiage de iherusalē ..." In *Cat.* no. 389, item 2558, Quaritch attributed this ed. to Philippi and Reinhart ca. 1485; see Copinger 3827. In his *GC*, pp. 1365, 2516, and 2852 (where it is given 130 woodcuts) the same attribution is made, but on p. 3811 it is described as "type larger but very like Topie & Hereberk 1488." The type is the somewhat irregular bâtarde used by Bouttellier: BMC 8: Pl. xlv, no. 110B, and see p. lvii, n. 2, where this ed. is assigned to Bouttellier.

R. gives this copy 76 pp. Cordier, *Mél.* 1:25, reports a few letters in a³ missing. The ancient tear at the top of the page has been mended, but some letters are missing in each of the first three lines.

## 8. [ca. 1508 LYONS: CLAUDE NOURRY DIT LE PRINCE]

Baudrier 12:93. FairMur (F) 350. Kraus 60, pp. 38-40.
Copy: NYPL Spencer collection (FairMur).

4°   64 leaves a-q⁴ 41 long lines. Woodcuts.

Fol. 1 (title) [M]onteuille cōpose par mes/ . . . (7 lines in red). Woodcut of a knight on horseback. fol. 1ᵛ the Sorg portrait. foll. 2-4ᵛ, the table. Half-title on the foot of 4ᵛ, Cy cōmence le liure . . . Chapter heading and beginning of text on fol. 5. Text ends on Q⁴. Verso blank. Last leaf mounted in the unique copy. Bâtarde type.

Listed in the *Bulletin Lib. Morgand* (1908), no. 422, with reproduction of 1 vignette. FairMur Cat. describes fully and reproduces the t.p., the Sorg portrait, and 3 other cuts, with a sample of the type. Exemplar from the library of the Comte d'Harcourt.

114 woodcuts (from Sorg's blocks), plus the picture on the t.p. (repeated at the end of the text), and one illustration on M$_{iii}$ which are not Sorg's. The full-page picture of the Great Caan on n$_i$ verso. Ornamental initials. Sorg's cuts frequently not in the original order. Baudrier reprints 8 lines of verse added to the end of the text, and records other descriptions of this ed.

This copy is bound with *Le liure des trois fils de Roys c'est/ assauoir de Frāce dangleterre et de scosse/,* which has the same type and the same small woodcut initials as the Mandeville. It has the colophon: Cy finissent les troys fils des roys imprimez a Lyon par Claude Nourry Lan mil. cccc & viii. le xvi iour de Mars.

## 9. [AFTER 1516] LYONS: BARNABE CHAUSSARD.

C 3829. Klebs 649.7. Cordier 3:2029 and *Mél.* 1:27. Brunet 3:1358, and Suppl. 1:932. Atkinson p. 498. Baudrier, Ser. II, pp. 35 and 529. Claudin 4:193.

Copies: Cambridge UL. Ste. Geneviève, OE$^{xv}$ 848 bis (Cat. no. 1200. Formerly coll. Yéméniz cat. 1867, no. 2688).

4°   64 leaves a-q⁴ 44 long lines. 200 × 134 mm. Woodcuts.

Fol 1 (title): [M]onteuille copose par/ . . . (6 lines, in red), followed by a picture of an armed knight, repeated at the end of text, as in Nourry's ed. Woodcut on 1ᵛ of the author presenting his book to the king of France. foll. 2-4ᵛ table. Text begins at the foot of 4ᵛ as in Nourry. Woodcut illustrations.

Listed in Cat. Coste, Cat. Yéméniz, no. 2688, Cat. Potier (1870), no. 1774. Reported as 66 leaves by Brunet, Copinger, Cordier, Daunou, Claudin, Baudrier 11:529 corrects to 64. He reproduces the t.p. on p. 350; as also Claudin.

Variously dated. Klebs says 1505. BMC 8:316 says that Chaussard was in partnership with Pierre Mareschal from 1492 until after the end of the century, Baudrier says until 1516. Atkinson dates the ed. after 1516. Baudrier suggests 1523 and contradicts Brunet's suggestion of the end of the 15 century. The woodcut on the t.p. (reproduced by Claudin) had been used by Martin Havard in 1505, was next used by Nourry in his ed. of *Mandeville* and, in 1525, in an ed. of *Ogier le Dannoys*. Chaussard died in 1525 and Cantarel married his widow: Baudrier, pp. 24-27.

The Ste. G. copy lacks sigg. i 1 and 4, and q 1 and 4.

### 10. [1521?] PARIS: LE VEUFUE FEU JEHAN TREPPEREL ET JEHAN IEHANNOT.

>Brunet 3:1358. Cordier 3:2030. Atkinson, pp. 497-498.
>Copy: BN Rés O² f. 5.

4°   100 leaves a-v⁴ except bdkmt in 8s. 33 long lines. 160 × 99 mm.

(Title) SEnsuit le Liure/ . . . (9 lines), followed by a vignette of an armed knight before a castle. Col. on fol. 99ᵛ. fol. 100, picture of a tower. Woodcut illustrations.

Cordier reports that sig. e lacks the last 2 leaves. Atkinson describes the BN copy as 88 leaves.

### 11. [ca. 1525] PARIS: PHILIPPE LE NOIR.

>Cordier 3:2030. Brunet 3:1359.
>Copy: whereabouts unknown.
>Reported by Brunet from the White Knights' sale and dated "after 1521."

### 12. 1542 LYONS: JEHAN CANTEREL, DIT MOTIN.

>Du Verdier, p. 729. La Croix du Maine et Du Verdier 4:476. Baudrier 11:51, and 63.
>Copy: Baudrier (fragment).

4°   56 leaves? A-O⁴ 56 long lines.

Woodcuts, numerous and curious, evidently following Nourry's. Baudrier's copy lacked sigg. A-H; see I:76, and XI:63.

Baudrier also spells the name "Cantarel." Canterel married Chaussard's widow.

13. [ca. 1550-1560] PARIS: IEHAN BONFONS.
>Cordier 3:2030. Brunet 3:1359. Atkinson, pp. 498-499. Thomas. Renouard, IP, p. 60, and *Les Marques,* pp. 20-24.
>Copy: BM 1074.K.4(1).

4°  68 leaves A-R⁴ 38 lines. 2 cols. 152 × 98 mm.

Title: Maistre Iehan Man/ . . . in black and red with a vignette of Bonfons.

Brunet, followed by Cordier, dates ca. 1550. Thomas and OBMC date "1560?" Ternaux-Compans, no. 34, dates the ed. 1487, and R. follows him but also lists an ed. by the same printer in 1550 citing Graesse, 4:361. Atkinson suggests 1515-25 because of the impression and [gothic] type. Renouard dates Bonfons' activities 1543-66. He was dead before May, 1568, and eds. assigned to him in 1533 and 1534 are "probably inaccurate." The colophon of the *Mandeville* describes Bonfons as living in "la rue neufue Notre Dame a lenseigne sainct Nicolas." See *Les Marques* for his printer's devices.

14. 1729 LEIDEN. "RECUEIL OU ABRIGÉ DES VOIAGES et Observations, de Sʳ Jean de Mandeville, Chevalier & Professeur en Médicine . . . Commencées en l'An MCCCXXXII, . . . Dans lequelles sont compris grand nombre des choses inconnues. Par Monsieur Bale," in *Recueil de divers Voyages Curieux, faits en Tartarie* . . . ed. Pieter Vander Aa. 4° 2 vols. in 1. Also attributed to Pierre Bergeron. II, 1-25.

This is simply a translation of Purchas' abridgement of the *Travels*. The editor has been misled by Purchas' title into attributing it to Bale: see under "Latin editions." He translates all that is in Purchas, the dedication, Bale's life of Mandeville and the epitaph (from Ortelius), and the abridged and truncated version of the *Travels* given by Purchas.

15. 1735 LA HAYE. Reprint of the preceding, in *Voyages faits principalement en Asie dans les* XII, XIII, XIV, *et* XV *siècles*, with an Introduction by Pierre Bergeron. 4° 2 vols. Vol. I, 4-25. Also attributed to Vander Aa.

. . . . . . . . . . . . . . . . . . . .

See also "English Edition," nos. 40, 59.

## ENGLISH EDITIONS

1. [1496 LONDON] RICHARD PYNSON.

STC 17246. C 3842. Duff 285. Klebs 648.3. Cordier 3:2022; *Mél.* 1:43. Esdaile 98. Dibdin 2:85. Herbert's Ames 2:568. Brunet 3:1356.
Copies: BM G 6713 (Ford-Freeling-Grenville). Bodley fragm. Microfilm in LC, NYPL, HCL.

4° 72 leaves a-g⁸h⁶i⁶k⁴ 30 long lines.

Fol. 1 missing. fol. 2 (text): For as moche as the Land ouer the see, that is/ to say . . . fol. 72 (colophon): Here endeth the boke . . . Emprented by Richard Pynson. fol. 72ᵛ printer's device 3.

No woodcuts, no chapter headings, no table of chapters.

BM copy lacks foll. 1, 8, 17, 24. C dated 1500. Freeling's note says that he purchased the copy of Dyer of Exeter, not of Ford of Manchester, as Dibdin (2:586) asserts.

2. 1499 [BEFORE DEC.] WESTMINSTER: WYNKYN DE WORDE.

STC 17247. C 3841. Duff 286. Klebs 648.4. Brunet 3:1356. Esdaile 98. Herbert 1775. Dibdin's H-A 2:85. Hodnett, pp. 14-15, nos. 1019-87. Lowndes-Bohn. Sayle 55.
Copies: Cambridge UL (imp.). Stonyhurst College (imp.).

4° 112 leaves A⁴A-S⁶ 29 long lines.

Fol. 1 missing. First quire contained t.p. and table of 109 chaps. fol. 5 (A¹ text): Here begynneth a lytell treatyse or booke na-/med Iohan Mandeuyll . . . fol. 112 (Colophon), 112ᵛ De Worde's device no. 1.

68 woodcuts (some supplied from the 1503 ed. where pages are missing) listed in Hodnett, who says: "There can be no doubt that the designs were copied," but does not suggest their source. The pictures are copies of woodcuts made by Anton Sorg of Augsburg who published two editions of the *Travels* in German. His wood blocks were carried to Lyons and used for the illustration of at least four editions in French, and it was probably from a Lyons ed. that De Worde copied Sorg's illustrations for his English Mandeville: see my article in the *Papers of the Bibliographical Society of America*, LVII (1953), 59-69.

The Cambridge copy lacks foll. 1-4, 18, 41, 46-47, 52, 77, 101-106. Vogels, *EV* p. 4n., says it was bought of Bennett, bookseller of Birmingham, in May 1881. And see *Camb. Univ. Reporter*, 1881-82. The Stonyhurst copy lacks foll. 1, 4, 77-112. Herbert described a copy lent him by John Chadwick of Healey-Hall in 1785. Dibdin quotes Herbert's memorandum in full. He gives only 108 leaves and mentions "several ordinary woodcuts." Four cuts are reproduced in Hodnett, figs. 36, 112, 114, 144.

The text is a modernization of Pynson's, as for example, in Chap. XIV: "hatte" has been replaced by "calle," and "trouthe" by "byleue," twice the phrasing has been expanded; and Pynson's "law of Greeks" becomes "Grekes lawe." Otherwise the text is the same.

## 3. 1503 LONDON: WYNKYN DE WORDE.

STC 17249. Brunet 3:1356. H-A 1:139. Dibdin's H-A 2:83. Hazlitt H., p. 368. Hodnett, pp. 14-15. Esdaile, p. 98. Nichols, *Illustrations*, 5:362, 359. Ames, p. 87.

Copies: Bodleian, Douce frag. e. 8 (sigg. $N^1$-$R^6$). Microfilm in LC, HCL, NYPL. Sotheby Sale Cat., 25 Nov. 1952, no. 362, lacks sigg. B, I, and $N^{3-4}$.

4° 108 leaves A-S⁶.

Herbert saw a copy belonging to W. Bayntun. Nichols saw Rev. Francis Peck's copy in 1740 and mentions "75 woodcuts." Ames reports 75 woodcuts. The copy recently at Sotheby's is described as 94 leaves, 66 woodcuts, and printer's device. Missing text supplied with leaves from a 17 century ed. Colophon (reproduced in facsimile): Here endeth the boke of Johan Maũdeuyil/ knyght of the wayes towarde Jerusalem// & of meruayles of Ynde & of other coũtrees/ Emprynted inthe Cyte of London in the fle-/testrete in the sygne of the sonne by Wynken/ de worde. Anno dñi M. CCCCC. iij.

The Cambridge fragment contains 9 cuts, 3 of which (Hodnett's nos. 1079, 80, 87) were not in the 1499 ed. The statement that the 1503 ed. also had a woodcut map derives from R. Gough, *British Topography* (London, 1780) I, 76, who says, "Sir John Mandeville, who lived in the middle of the 14th century, refers his readers, c 108, 109 to his *Mappa Mundi*." The reference is evidently to chap. 109 (on p. 108?), where the text mentions a *"Mappi Mundi."* Dibdin cites Gough as the basis for Herbert's statement that this ed. contained a map of the world. Brunet and Hazlett report "75 woodcuts and a map."

## 4. [1510? LONDON: WYNKYN DE WORDE]

STC 17248. Hodnett, p. 15.

Copy: (fragment of 2 leaves only) Bodleian Arch. G d 31(2). Microfilm in LC, NYPL, HCL.

4° The leaves are [g⁶?] and h₁ and have 2 pictures, Hodnett, nos. 1049, 50.

STC dates this fragment "1501?" Hodnett says "about 1510" and Mr. W. A. Jackson of the Houghton Library at HCL confirms this opinion. Hearne is said to have broken up a copy and distributed the leaves.

. . . . .

Probably a lost ed. ca. 1555-60. Possibly B. M. Harley 5919 (1 leaf), from the Bagford collection, according to Mr. W. A. Jackson, is from a lost ed.

5. 1568 OCT. 6 LONDON: THOMAS EAST IN BREADSTREAT AT THE NETHER END.

STC 17250. Brunet 3:1356. Esdaile 98. Cordier 3:2022; *Mél.* 1:43. *BMC to 1640.* (1884).

Copy: BM 1045 h. 2.

4° 94 leaves A⁴ B-M⁸N².

Fol. 1 (title): The Voiage and Travayle of Syr John Maundeuile Knight. Colophon at end of text.

75 woodcuts copied from those in De Worde's ed. (*not* from Pynson, as is commonly stated). Pynson printed no pictures. Brunet began the error by attributing the 1499 ed. to Pynson. The pictures are not printed from De Worde's woodblocks, but are copied from his pictures, and mostly reversed. Of the 75 cuts, 8 are repeats. Most of the cuts show that the blocks had broken borders, damaged corners, worm holes and other indications of age and previous use. The situation suggests that East was making use of an incomplete set (lacking 8 pictures) of old woodblocks made for some ed. intermediate between this and the last De Worde ed. If that is true it indicates an ed. no copy of which is known.

The t.p. of the BM copy is mutilated, also ll. 2, 3 and several at the end. This ed. has been reprinted with facsimile illustrations by John Ashton (London, 1887); and by the Oxford University Press (Oxford, 1932). Letts (p. 178), says reprinted from De Worde, but "one chapter seems to have dropped out."

6. [1582?] LONDON: THOMAS ESTE.

STC 17251. Cordier 3:2022; *Mél.* 1:43. Esdaile pp. 98, 99. Hazlitt H., p. 368. Ashton ed., p. 285. Herbert's Ames 2:1022.

Copies: Folger. BM G 6714 (imp.). Bodleian, Douce MM 489. HCL Microfilm of Bodley.

4° A-U⁴ 80 leaves.

2 preliminary blank leaves. All leaves faintly ruled in red in Folger copy. [A$_1$] (title): The/ Voyages and Trauailes of/ Sir John Maundeuile/ Knight./ Wherein is treated of the way towards Hierusalem,/ and of the meruailes of Inde, with other/ Lands and Countries./ (woodcut: 2 ships leaving port). London:/ Printed by Thomas Este/. Verso blank. A$^2$-A$^{3v}$ "The Preface" in BL., followed by Vignette. A$^4$ half-title and text begins. U$^{2v}$-U$^{3v}$ table of 109 chaps. U$^4$ blank. Large woodcut initials.

72 woodcuts + cut on t. p. and vignette. Nos. 19 and 55 omitted.

Entered in the SR (2:408) March 12, 1582. Esdaile dates "1581?" and p. 99 lists again under [1660?]. BM copy lacks t.p. and last leaf, which led Ashton to doubt that East was the printer. He says that the type and pictures are "totally different" from the ed. of 1568. Actually the pictures are a mixture of 50 old and 22 recut woodblocks, all copied from de Worde's. 2 are omitted, 2 repeated. The new cuts sometimes reverse the picture. Hazlitt H reports that the Bodleian copy lacks V$^4$ (blank).

The will of Robert Gourlaw, Bookbinder of Edinburgh, mentions in his stock, "Schir Johne Mandwell, ane, price iiij s." Probably a copy of this ed. This will was made in August, 1585 and proved April 22, 1586: in *The Bannatyne Miscellany*, II (Edinburgh, 1836), pp. 209, 211.

## 7. 1612 LONDON: THOMAS SNODHAM.

Not in STC. Hazlitt H. Cordier 3:2022; *Mél.* 1:43. Huth 3:896; Huth (SC) no. 4652. Esdaile, p. 98.
Copy: LC. G 370 M 2 Office (Huth).

4° A-U$^4$ 80 leaves. Woodcuts.

Fol. 1 (title): The/ Voyages and/ Trauailes of Sir Iohn Mandeuile/ Knight/ (woodcut of 2 ships). fol. 1$^v$ blank. A$^2$-A$^3$ preface, not in Black Letter. A$^{3v}$ blank. Text as in 1582 ed. same type, same caps. with a few exceptions, different catchwords. Page-for-page reprint largely. Same woodcuts, except in 4 cases where woodblocks from the 1568 ed. are substituted. One block reverses the picture, but shows wormholes, and so apparently was not cut for this ed. Last blank missing in LC copy.

SR 3:413 records that East's widow assigned her copyrights to Snodham 17 June, 1609. Hazlitt assigned this ed. to "Thomas Stansby." The Huth copy is from the libraries of Sir Harmon Le Strange and Lord Selsey. "Harmon le strange. 18 d" on the t.p.

## 8. 1618 LONDON: T. S[NODHAM].

STC 17252. Brunet 3:1356. Cordier 3:2022; *Mél.* 1:43. Esdaile, p. 98. Ashton ed., p. 285. Warner, p. xi, n. 3. *BMC to 1640* (1884). Copy: BM G 6715.

4° A-U⁴ First and last leaves blank. Woodcuts.

Imprint cut away and all authorities before STC follow Brunet in assigning to "T. Stansley" or "Stansby."

## 9. 1625 LONDON: THOMAS SNODHAM.

STC 17253. Cordier 3:2022; *Mél.* 1:44. Britwell *Handlist.* Esdaile, p. 98. Grenville (SC). 2:82, no. 2466. Hazlitt H., p. 368. Hoe 3:108; *Hoe (SC).* 1:350, no. 2112 (uncut).

Copies: Folger (Britwell). HEHL. Chatsworth 3:17.

4° A-U⁴.

Fol. 1 large picture of Fortune and her wheel. 1ᵛ blank. fol. 2, title and woodcut of 2 ships as in 1612. 2ᵛ blank. fol. 3-3ᵛ, preface in modern type. A⁴-U², text. U²ᵛ-U³, table of chaps. U⁴ blank (present in Folger copy).

Text set page-for-page from the ed. of 1612, but not always the same catchwords.

74 woodcuts, mostly the same as in the ed. of 1582, but 12 recut. T.p. reproduced in Hoe SC 3:107.

*Britwell Handlist* dates 1627, without brackets or question, but that copy is badly cropped at the bottom and no date appears. Hazlett reports the Freeling copy uncut.

## 10. 1632 LONDON: WILLIAM STANSBY.

Not in STC.

Copy: Yale UL, Ecd 322 gk (from the library of the Marquis of Lothian. Sold at the Anderson Galleries, Jan. 16, 1932. Cat. no. 135).

4° A-V⁴.

A¹ woodcut map of Venice. A² (title): The Voyages and Trauailes of Sir John Mandeuile Knight. (Followed by a woodcut of a ship.) 2ᵛ blank. A³ recto and verso, Mandeville's preface in modern type. A⁴, half-title followed by text in B.L.; text ends on V². V²ᵛ-V⁴, table of 109 chaps. V⁴ᵛ blank.

72 woodcut illustrations of the traditional subjects, but the cuts are new to sig. L, and in a different style. Beginning in sig. L new and old cuts are mixed.

This copy is in the original binding and has the preliminary blank

leaf, but no end paper. T.p. reproduced in sale cat., pp. 135-136.
Snodham's widow transferred all her copyrights to William Stansby, Feb. 23, 1625/6: see SR 4:152, 114.

11. [1640] LONDON: RICHARD BISHOP.

> STC 17254. Plomer's *Dict.* (1641-67).
> Copies: Folger (Harmsworth). HEHL.

4° A-V$^4$.

This is a reprint of 1632, including the map on fol. 1 and ship on the t.p., except that the table at the end is in different type from the text. It covers V$^{2v}$ to V$^4$. Last verso blank.

Stansby's new cuts (often reversing the picture) are used as far as sig. L. Thereafter the new cuts are interspersed with old as in 1632. All are of the traditional subjects.

The Folger copy has "Mary Cromwel" in a childish hand at the top of the map of Venice. It is in the original limp vellum binding.

SR 4:432, 458, records that on March 4, 1639, Stansby's widow assigned her copyrights to "Master Bishop." Plomer, II, p. 25, says that R. Bishop bought out Wm. Stansby in 1634, when he took up his freedom. He printed until 1653, although the last entry in the SR is for 1640.

12. 1650 [LONDON] R.B[ISHOP] FOR E. DOD & N. EKINS.

> Wing M 412. Grenville (SC) 2:82, no. 2467. JRL *Cat.* (1899).
> Copy: JRL, Manchester.

4° A-V$^4$. Title on A$^2$. Woodcuts.

13. 1657 LONDON: BY R.B.[ISHOP] AND ARE TO SOLD [sic] BY A. CROOKE.

> Wing M 413. Cordier 3:2022; *Mél.* 1:44. Ashton ed., p. 285. Esdaile, p. 99. Brunet 3:1356.
> Copy: BM G 6716.

4° Woodcuts. Black Letter.

Bishop's last book, according to Plomer, appeared in 1653.

14. 1670 LONDON: FOR A. CROOKE.

> Wing M 414. Cordier 3:2022; *Mél.* 1:44. Ashton ed., p. 285. Esdaile, p. 99. Brunet 3:1356.
> Copy: BM 10055 a. 6. 4° Woodcuts.

A. Crooke was at the Green Dragon in St. Paul's Churchyard,

1630-74. He was the brother of John Crooke, the Dublin printer; see Plomer II and III.

15. 1677 [LONDON] FOR R. SCOTT, T. BASSET, J. WRIGHT, AND R. CHISWELL.

> Wing M 415. Esdaile, p. 99.
> Copies: NewbL. HEHL. Magd. Col., Cambridge. Bodleian, Pepys 1244.

4° The traditional woodcuts.

15b. VARIANT: FOR B. TOOKE AT THE SHIP IN ST. PAUL'S CHURCHYARD.

> Arber (TC), 1:284.

B. Tooke set up at the Ship in St. Paul's Churchyard in 1670, having been apprentice to J. Crooke, whom he succeeded as King's printer in Dublin. He was Swift's bookseller. Plomer III.

16. 1684 [LONDON] FOR R. SCOT, T. BASSET, J. WRIGHT, & R. CRISWEL.

> Wing M 416. Cordier 3:2023; *Mél.* 1:44. Ashton ed., p. 286. Brunet 3:1356. Esdaile, p. 99. Huth 3:896; *Huth (SC)* no. 4653. Quaritch, *G.C.* (1887), 2852. Maggs Bros. *Cat.* 590, I (1933), 1130.
> Copies: BM G 6717, and 1045 h. 30.

4° 1 + 139 + 2 leaves A-S⁴ Woodcuts of poor quality.
Brunet calls it a reprint of 1568.

17. 1696 LONDON: PRINTED FOR RICH. CHISWELL, B. WALFORD, MAT. WOTTON AND GEO. CONYERS.

> Wing M 417. Cordier 3:2023; *Mél.* 1:44. Arber (TC) 2:593. Esdaile, p. 99. Quaritch, *G.C.*, 640. Brunet 3:1356.
> Copies: Folger (R. Farmer, from Dr. Dwight). BM G 6718.

4° A-S⁴. Text still in B.L. A ship on t.p. and 70 woodcuts, recut, but closely imitated from Bishop's miscellaneous set. Ashton says the woodcuts are "the same" as in the 1684 ed. So says Lowndes. Advertisement, at the end of the table, of "Lithgow's Nineteen years Travels."

18. 1704 [LONDON] R. CHISWELL.

> Hazlitt 2:380. Auction Book Prices. Livingston cites Currie's *Cat.* June, 1887, no. 173. W. H. Robinson, *Cat.* 69, no. 94 lists a copy for sale, with original wrapper bound in.

4° A-S² in 4s.

# APPENDIX II

19. 1705 [LONDON] R. CHISWELL, ... [as in 1696].

    Cordier 3:2023; *Mél.* 1:44. Esdaile, p. 99. Ashton, p. 286. Copy: BM 1077 g 35(2).

4° 135 + 2 pp. Woodcuts.

20. [1710] LONDON.

    Cordier 3:2023; *Mél.* 1:45. Ashton, p. 286. Copy: BM 10056 c.

4°

21. 1722 LONDON: PRINTED BY A. WILDE, FOR G. CONYERS, IN LITTLE-BRITAIN, T. NORRIS, AT LONDON-BRIDGE, AND A. BETTESWORTH IN PATER NOSTER-ROW.

    Brunet 3:1357. Cordier 3:2023; *Mél.*, 1:45. Huth 3:897; Huth (SC) no. 4654.

    Copies: Columbia UL. Plimpton 915/1722/M32, and Phoenix Po17 1 En/1722/M31 (Townley, Hy John Todd). NYPL, *KC. U of Mich., Hubbard Collection. HCL, Typ. 705.22.554. BM 10056 c 22. Bodleian, 206.e.3.

4° A-R⁴ 132 numbered pp., plus 4 unnumbered for table. T.p. has 2 woodcuts of ships, side by side.

69 woodcut illustrations from old blocks, some showing extensive damage. All are still in the Sorg-De Worde-East tradition. Besides the 5 East pictures omitted, 10 others are repeats, substituted for the pictures East put at corresponding points.

The BM copy has the date cropped. The HCL copy lacks pp. 15-30, 115 ff.

22. 1725 LONDON: FOR J. WOODMAN AND D. LYON ... AND C. DAVIS.

    First edited edition. Copies in many libraries. Brunet 3:1356.

8°. Pp. iii-xvi, 1-384 + 6 unnumbered pp. containing an index of obsolete words.

Title: "The voiage and Travaile of Sir John Maundevile, Kt., ... now publish'd entire from an Original ms. in the Cotton Library."

Edited by "Mr. Le Neve," according to Kerr, I, 432-4 [ed. dated 1727]; by David Caskey, according to Wellek, p. 220, n. 53. The editor claims to have collated 7 MSS, Eng., Fr., and Lat., and 4 eds., Lat., Eng., and Ital., but there are few notes. The preliminary leaves contain a preface by the editor and 4 leaves of alphabetical index. T.p. in two states, usually in black only, but some copies in black and red.

Huth reports 8 leaves of table, and 8 of glossary (2d ed. ?). HCL copies of 1725 and 1727 both have 4 unnumbered leaves of index in 2 cols. between xvi & p. 1. Ed. 1725 has Latin letter of ded. after p. 384. Index on V°.

23. 1727 REPRINT OF 1725, IN 2 STATES.

Esdaile describes BM 683 f. 18 as a reissue with a new t.p. The copies in HCL and NYPL have a t.p. in black and red (the 1725 ed. is usually in black), but everything else seems to be the same as in the 1725 ed. Ashton, p. 286, reports that the copy in BM Royal Library 149 b. 8, is another ed., with the old 1725 t.p. The situation suggests a second printing in 1725, for which a new t.p. was printed in 1727.

24. [ca. 1730-35] FOR J. OSBORNE NEAR DOCK-HEAD, SOUTHWARK AND J. HODGES AT THE LOOKING GLASS ON LONDON BRIDGE.

Cordier 3:2024; *Mél.* 1:47. Ashton, p. 286. Esdaile, p. 99.
Copies: BM G 2247, and 10055 a. 33. (Ashton makes 2 eds. here).

12° 138 + 3 pp. (title): "The Travels and Voyages of Sir John Mandevile, Knt. Containing . . . Faithfully Collected from the Original Manuscript, and Illustrated with Variety of Pictures."

This ed. is reduced to 77 chaps., of which the last is Chap. 103, "A Description of the Paradise Terrestre." Esdaile calls it "a different version" from the usual one.

Usually dated "1720?" or "1720-30" but the claim of a MS collation is an obvious attempt to capitalize on the ed. of 1725. In 1725 Osborne was in partnership with his son-in-law, T. Longman. In 1735 he was publishing alone: see Plomer III and IV. Sir James Hodges began to publish ca. 1730 or after. This is evidently the ed. Listed by Quaritch *GC* (1887), pp. 784, 2852, as "Southwark and London Bridge, 12°," rude woodcuts, "ca. 1700?" Cf. Letts, p. 179.

25. [ca. 1745-50] LONDON: PRINTED FOR J. HODGES, AT THE LOOKING-GLASS OPPOSITE TO ST. MAGNUT'S CHURCH, LONDON BRIDGE, AND J. HARRIS, THE LOOKING-CLASS AND BIBLE, ON LONDON BRIDGE.

Cordier 3:2024; *Mél.* 1:46. Ashton, p. 287. Esdaile, p. 99.
Copies: Columbia UL, O 17.1 En/1720/M 31. BM, 435 a. 1.

# APPENDIX II

12° 138 + 3 pp. Fol. 1ᵛ picture of a ship departing. Fol. 2 (title, same as the preceding). 2ᵛ blank. 3-3ᵛ, preface. A⁴, half title and chap. I. Text ends on F⁹ᵛ, followed by a table.

The preface is not Mandeville's preface, as in 1722 and earlier, but is by the publisher. Text omits chaps. 8, 10, 14, 15, etc. 10 pictures, besides the frontispiece, all set the wrong way of the page. The text, except for omissions, is the same as that of 1722. The pictures are closely imitated from those of 1722, but somewhat smaller (ca. 80 × 58 mm.), but since the type-page is only 70 mm. wide, the pictures, designed to run crosswise of the page, must all be set on end. Perhaps they were made for a larger edition, now lost.

J. Hodges remained at this address until 1758. J. Harris is supposed to have been an apprentice of J. Newbery of Reading, who went to London after 1744; see Plomer IV. On the fly-leaf of the Columbia Univ. copy, in a boyish hand, is written, "Robert Markes His Book 1756." The "56" has been inked over a "49." Ashton suggests as the date of printing "1730?"

## Chapbook Editions

According to Ashton, *Chapbooks*, p. ix, the principal factory was No. 4 Aldermary Churchyard, later moved to Bow Churchyard, and run by William and Cluer Dicey, afterwards C. Dicey, described in 1720 as of Northampton. Usually the texts were pirated at Newcastle-on-Tyne, but 22 other places are recorded where chapbooks were published in the 19th century.

26. [ca. 1750?] LONDON: PRINTED AND SOLD IN ALDERMARY CHURCH YARD.

> Cordier 3:2025; *Mél.* 1:47. Harvard *Chap-Books*, no. 312.
> Copies: NYPL. BM 1079 i. 14(23).

12° 24 pp. (title) "The Foreign Travels of Sir John Mandeville." Picture on t.p. of 3 men rowing out to a ship. Travels in the Holy Land reduced to half a chap. and the whole to 8 chaps.

6 other pictures, none of them in the Sorg tradition, in the copy in the NYPL. This ed. is reprinted in Ashton, *Chap Books*, pp. 405-416, with reproduction of the t.p. but no other pictures. Probably more than one ed. issued from this press. Ashton, p. 287, lists this ed., by mistake, as BM 1077 i. 14 (23).

27. [ca. 1780?] London 12° 24 pp.

> Cordier 3:2025; *Mél.* 1:47. Ashton, p. 287.
> Copy: BM 12315 aaa. 6(3).

28. [ca. 1785?] LONDON: BOW CHURCH YARD.

>Cordier 3:2025; *Mél.* 1:48. Ashton, p. 287. Halliwell, *Chap-Books*, no. 85.
>Copy: BM 1076 1. 3(12).

12°. Abridged "in 24 chapters," according to Halliwell. Letts (p. 179) says it is "less abbreviated than the others," but identifies it with the ed. reprinted by Ashton.

29. n.d. NEWCASTLE UPON TYNE.

>Herbert's Ames 2:86. Abridged.

30. n.d. LONDON: BOW CHURCH YARD.

>Harvard *Chap-Books*, no. 311 (58 [iv], 22).
>Copy: HCL.

16° 24 pp. Title: "The foreign travels and dangerous voyages of that renowned English knight, Sir John Mandeville . . ." Woodcut on t.p.

31. 1839 LONDON: EDWARD LUMLEY.

>Ed. J. O. Halliwell. Reprinted from the ed. of 1725, with an introduction, additional notes, and glossary. Cf. Brunet 3:1357.

8° i-xiv, v-xvii, 326 pp. OBMC says pp. xvii, 326.
69 illustrations from woodcuts in a 17 century ed., facsimile copies made by F. W. Fairholt. Halliwell reprints the editor's preface from the 1727 ed., which defends the author and gives the usual biographical misinformation. The pictures are crude but in the Sorg tradition. The frontispiece is reproduced from a MS (unidentified).

32. 1848 BOHN'S ANTIQUARIAN LIBRARY, IN *Early Travels in Palestine*, ed. Thomas Wright. 8°. pp. 127-282.

>Text from the 1725 ed. with spelling modernized.

33. 1866 LONDON: F. S. ELLIS. 8° xxxi, 326 pp. Reprint of Halliwell's ed. (1839). A page for page reprint on cheaper paper, and omitting the picture on p. 274. 12 large paper copies have further illustrations from an early German ed., according to Huth 3:897.

34. 1869 IN EDUARD MÄTZNER, ED., *Altenglische Sprachproben* I, pt 2, pp. 152-221. A reprint of Halliwell's ed. with notes. Some omissions.

35. 1875 LONDON: NIMMO'S NATIONAL LIBRARY, *English Explorers.* 8° A modernized abridgement.

36. 1883 LONDON: REEVES & TURNER. 8° xxxi, 326 pp. 1 plate. 3d ed. of Halliwell's ed., but disclaimed by him.

37. 1886 LONDON AND NEW YORK: CASSELL'S NATIONAL LIBRARY, no. 10. Ed. H. Morley. 24°. 192 pp. Abridged. Modern spelling. Copies: NYPL. HCL.

38. 1886 NEW YORK: SEASIDE LIBRARY. Pocket ed., no. 777. Ed. G. Munro. Copy LC, G370 M 25.

39. 1887 LONDON: PICKERING & CHATTO. Ed. John Ashton. Annotated and illustrated in facsimile [sic].

8° xxiv, 289 pp. Reproduces East's first ed., which Ashton mistakenly describes as a reprint of Pynson's (actually of de Worde's), with 74 woodcuts. In an appendix he reproduces 18 pictures from other eds., including Richel's 2 men without heads and other pictures in his style; p. 275 shows some in much later styles. Bibliographical appendix. 100 large paper copies.

40. 1889 WESTMINSTER: FOR THE ROXBURGHE CLUB.

2° xlvi, 232 pp. + 28 plates of BM MS. Add. 24, 189 (illustrations).
(Title) "The Buke of John Maundeuill. being the Travels of Sir John Mandeville, Knight 1322-1356. A Hitherto Unpublished English Version from the Unique Copy (Egerton Ms. 1982) in the British Museum, edited together with the French Text, Notes, and an Introduction, by Sir George F. Warner."

41. 1892 NEW YORK: E. MAYNARD & CO. ENGLISH CLASSICS SERIES, NO. 107. *Travels.* Selections (60 pp.). Ed. Eduard Mätzner with Introduction, notes, and etymological glossary. Copy: LC Pr 1120/ M 25.

42. 1894 CASSELL & CO. 2nd ed.

## ENGLISH EDITIONS

43. 1895 WESTMINSTER: CONSTABLE. 8°, xxx, 414 pp. Illustrated by Arthur Lanyard, with preface by J. C. Grant. Text modernized from the Cotton MS. version.

44. 1898 NEW YORK: D. APPLETON & CO. THE WORLD'S GREAT BOOKS. Ed. A. Lanyard & Jacques W. Redway. Copy: LC G370 M 28.

45. 1899 CASSELL & CO. 3 ed.

46. 1900 MACMILLAN CO. LIBRARY OF ENGLISH CLASSICS.

    8°. pp. 3-209 (with Hakluyt's trans. of Carpini, Rubruquis, and Odoric, pp. 213-262). Ed. A. W. Pollard. "The version of the Cotton Manuscript in modern spelling," with a bibliographical note.

47. 1901 COPY IN UNIV. OF MICHIGAN.

48. 1905 ELLIS.

49. 1905 CASSELL & CO. 4th ed.

50. 1905 Macmillan Co., 2 ed.

51. 1909 CASSELL & CO. CASSELL'S LITTLE CLASSICS. 12° 192 pp. Text from Bohn ed., 1848. Copy: HCL.

52. 1909 MACMILLAN CO. 3 ed.

53. 1915 MACMILLAN CO. 4 ed.

54. 1919 (for 1916) EARLY ENGLISH TEXT SOCIETY. Original Series, no. 153 (Vol. I, text). Vol. II (O.S. no. 154. 1923 for 1916). Introduction and Notes.
    *Mandeville's Travels* edited from Ms. Cotton Titus C. XVI, in the British Museum.

55. 1923 MACMILLAN CO. 5 ed.

56. 1928 SAN FRANCISCO (FOR RANDOM HOUSE, NEW YORK) GRABHORN PRESS. 2° 157 pp.

    Half-title: "The Voiage and Travaile of Sir John Maundevile Kt . . . table of chapters." Title repeated on p. 1. Text, 2-157. 31

woodcuts imitated from the English eds., but redesigned by Valenti Angelo. Decorative initials in color. Text from ed. of 1725. 150 copies only.

57. 1928 EVERYMAN'S LIBRARY No. 812. J. M. Dent & Sons, and E. P. Dutton. Ed. with an Intro. by Jules Bramont. Text of East's ed. "with certain passages restored, which the Elizabethan printers omitted in error." No illustrations.

58. 1932 LONDON: HUMPHREY MILFORD FOR THE OXFORD UNIVERSITY PRESS. 254 pp. 74 woodcuts. Reprinted from the edition of 1568 "with the addition" (Chap. xii, pp. 48-72). Full page picture of the devil omitted. Limited ed. 350 copies.

59. 1953 LONDON: HAKLUYT SOCIETY 2d Ser. No. 101 (for 1950), ed. Malcolm Letts. Editions of the Egerton Ms. Version, the hitherto unpublished English translation of one of the Latin versions made in England (see Appendix I, MS. in Eng. no. 4), and the French of BN 4515. 2 vols.

## Note

I have not included the numerous works on the history of the English language which have printed excerpts from Mandeville, beginning with a long quotation in the Preface to Johnson's *Dictionary* 1755. Some of these are: Morris and Skeat, *Specimens,* 164-172 cf. 320-22. Wülker, *Altenglisches Lesebuch,* II, 200 ff. A. S. Cook, *A Literary Middle English Reader* (Boston, 1915), pp. 248-261, 8 selections from the *Travels.* Kenneth Sisam, *Fourteenth Century Verse and Prose* (Oxford, 1921, and 8 times reprinted), pp. 96-106.

Also omitted are such compendiums, or retellings as J. Smith, *A Compendium of the Most approved Modern Travels,* ed. Hanway. Dublin, 1757. III, 202-245; and Merriam Sherwood and Elmer Mantz, *The Road to Cathay,* New York, 1928.

## LATIN EDITIONS

1. 1483 SEPT. 7 ZWOLLE: PIETER VAN OS.

   HC 10645. Klebs 652.1. Cordier 3:2031. Brunet Suppl. 1:932. Camp. 1197, and Suppl. 4:3. St. M137.
   Copy: PML 32727 (Wernigerode Fürstl. B. 61).

4°. 100 leaves? a⁷b-k⁸l⁶m⁸n⁶ 27 lines. 143 × 82 mm. 98 leaves, numbered at top center of recto.

First blank missing. String visible between leaves 3 and 4.

F. 2 (signed aJ) (title): [I] Ncipit itinerarius a terra anglie ī/ . . . (13 lines), followed immediately by the text, headed: Cōmēdatio breuis terre iherosolimitane./ Capittulū p̄mū./ fol. 97 [sig. n⁴]: Explicit ytinerarius domi iohannis de/ mandeuilla zwollis impressus per me petrū/ de os Anno dnī M.CCCC.LXXXJJJ in/ festo natiuitatis beate marie verginis Men/ sis septembris. [printer's device] foll. 97ᵛ-98ᵛ, table of chaps. (see below). n₆ blank.

The text is divided into 3 parts, and the chaps. are numbered for each part: Part I, chaps. 1-23 [with some mistakes, such as 28 for 18]. Part II has chaps. 1-17, beginning on fol. 38. Part III has chaps. 1-11, beginning on fol. 75 with the account of Prester John. In the table at the end, the chaps. are listed with fol. nos. for the leaves, instead of with chap. numbers. Sig. e⁷ is signed "CJ" and fol. 63 (h⁸) has one word added below the bottom line, not a catchword, but a miscalculation.

Hain said of this ed.: "Forte Belgice. Édition douteuse," and Brunet thought it: "fort douteuse, pour ne pas dire apocryphe." I have compared it with Van Os' ed. of Bonaventura's *Sermones* (1479), which lacks the printer's name and device in the colophon but shows signs of an attempt at page numbering, having consecutive letters of the alphabet on the top verso of many leaves. It is on paper watermarked with a b or p with a forked tail. One sig. of the *Mandeville* has this same, not uncommon, watermark. Other sigg. show: a shield, a monk seated teaching, a dog. A Pseudo-Jerome *Vitas Patrum* printed by Van Os in 1490, with his name and device, is in the same type as the *Mandeville*.

Probably the earliest printing of the Latin text, certainly the most primitive. It contains 5 citations of Odoric, pp. 76, 80ᵛ bis, 83, and 93. At the end of the preface (aJᵛ), before the author's introduction beginning: "Go iohannes de mandevilla—" is interpolated a moral tirade: "Verum quia iam temporibus nostris verius ös olim dici potest. Vertus ecclesie Clerus. Cessat. Calcatur. Errat. Et Demon Simonia. Regnat et duātur. Ecce iusto dei iudicio tradita est terra tam inclita et sacrosancta in impiorum manibus sarracenorum. quod nō absqz dolore piis metibus est audiendum et recolendum." These lines were reproduced in Hakluyt's ed., and translated in Fuller's Life of Mandeville.

Variant? Pinelo's *Epitome* of Barcia's *Cat.*, I, 21, says (fol. 373) there was an ed. in Lat. 4° n.p., n.d. for "Roberto Guormono" in Zuvvollis 1483.

2. [1483-6 STRASBOURG: PRINTER OF THE 1483 *Vitas Patrum*]

BMC 1:100. HC 10643*. Klebs 652.2. Pr 433. Cordier 3:2030. Brunet 3:1359, & Suppl. 1:932. FairMur (G), no. 282. Maggs *Cat.* 656 (1938), no. 305. Letts. Mazarine. Coll(S) 685. St M139.

Copies: PML 20615 (Ashburnham and FairMur copy). BM, G 6700 (IA1337). Maggs. Letts, p. 177 (Castle Howard). BN, Rés. 0²f.6. Paris; Mazarine 1300 (1138). Madrid. Stockholm.

4° 72 leaves a-i⁸ 30 lines 2 cols. 135 × 93 mm.

Fol. 1 (unsigned. title): Itinerarius domi/ . . . (3 lines). The rest of the page and the verso blank. a²-a³ table of 50 chaps. In 2 pts. a³ second column blank, verso blank. a⁴ text begins. The addition to the preface as in Van Os's ed., except that the order is slightly changed to: "Virtus, ecclesia. clerus. demō symonia. Cessat, calcatur. errat. regnat. domitiatur. Ecce . . ." Spaces left for caps. i⁸ blank.

FairMur (G) dates c.1486? Brunet, ca. 1485. St. ca. 1484.

Maggs' copy has last blank missing, initials in red and blue, and initial strokes in red. Same as Lett's copy? Brunet describes as 71 leaves a-I$_{iii}$. Cordier 3:2032, makes another ed. of this entry.

Part I has the same Chapter headings (with minor variants) as Van Os'. Part II agrees with Van Os' II + III, except that the heading of the 3d chap. from the end has been dropped, leaving just 50 chaps. The citations of Odoric do not occur in this ed.

3. [1484-85? ANTWERP: GÉRARD LEEU]

OBMC M:268. HC 10644*, 10309*. Klebs 652.3. Pr 8937, 8938. Cordier 3:2031, *BJ.*, p. 14. Ashburnham 2:81, no. 2461. Brunet 3:1359, Suppl. 1:931. Camp. 1198 and 1622. Hazlitt 4:242. Maggs 656 (1938), no. 368. Panzer 9:200. Polain (B) 2584. Quaritch GC 2606. Sinker, p. 49. St. M138. BPC 1900 (Ellis).

Copies: LC Incun. 1485 M 3. NYPL. BM 566 f 6 (IA 47355), and G 6728. 2 and 3. James F. Bell (Tho. Grenville copy). Bodleian. W. G. Kelso, Jr. Trinity Col., Cambridge. W. F. Robinson, dealer, *Cat.* 83 (1953), p. 107. BN Rés. 0²f.8 (3 copies). Belgian Royal Lib. A 1794. Univ. of Leyden. L'Es. 5203, 5204. Copenhagen. Letts. (p. 177) reports a copy sold by Sotheby's from the Sir J. A. Brooks sale, with Inglis bookplate. Bought by W. H. Robinson, 15 March, 1948, lot 4074, bound with Marco Polo, de Suchen, Johannes de Hese, and one other.

4° 62 leaves A-F⁸G⁶H⁸ 33-34 long lines. ca. 134 × 83 mm.

Fol. 1 usually blank; 2-4 table of 50 chaps.; 4ᵛ (at the bottom of an otherwise blank page, title): Liber pñs cui*us* auctor fert*ur* iohānes de mādeuille militari/ . . . (6 lines); 5-62ᵛ text. Spaces left for caps.

Leeu adds to his explicit: Quod opus vbi inceptū simul et cōpletū sit īpa elementa seu singularū seorsū characteres lrāmum quibus impressū vides venetica monstrant manifeste . . . which led Brunet at first to assign to "Venice?"——a mistake corrected in the Suppl. T. Tobler suggested Turin. Iseghem attributed to Théodoric Martin at Aloste, but Holtrop, *T. Martens,* pp. 48-57, shows that it was by Leeu. Panzer 9:200 assigns to Martens. Grenville assigned to Leeu at Antwerp. Proctor and Polain assign to Leeu's second press at Gouda. Camp. dates from the first year in Antwerp. Leeu left Gouda between 19 June and 18 Sept., 1484. Letts (p. 177), assigns to Gouda but dates "c. 1485."

This ed. is often bound up with other travel books from the same press. It is followed in BM 566 f. 6 and Amiens by the travels of Ludolph de Suchen (54 leaves, aa-hh6 in 8s). The Sunderland Library copy 7924 (sold by Quaritch), the Ashburnham (Libri 1527), and Maggs all have both de Suchen and Marco Polo (50? leaves). Maggs says 74 leaves a-k⁶ in 8 except i⁴ (Sunderland). BM G 6728. 2 & 3 has first de Suchen and then Mandeville. Ellis (*B. P. Current,* 1900) describes a copy in which fol. 1. has a large device of Gerard de Leeu s.a. and l., followed by Marco Polo, de Suchen, *Itinerarius Joannis de Hese Presbiteri a Jherusalem* (22 leaves), *Rabi Samuelis Redargutio contra Judeorum errores Messye adventum expectantes* (22 leaves), and another theological tract. The *Rabi Samuelis* has a colophon: "Impressum Antwerpie per me Gerardum leeu anno domini m cccc lxxxv., xv Kl. Novemb." All 6 of these pieces are described as printed with the same type. The first leaf of the *Mandeville* is A₁ of the first sig. and contains Leeu's device. The verso is blank.

The first leaf, missing in BM 566 f. 6, LC, NYP, and Bell L., is elsewhere described as blank, except by Hazlitt who reports a woodcut on fol. 1. Polain says fol. 1 is blank in the Belgian Royal Lib. copy.

The Bell library copy belonged ca. 1716 to Thomas Baker (*Cat.* p. 204). The LC copy has "Francis Egerton" stamped on the binding. The Amiens copy has the autograph of R. P. Vanhecke on fol. 1. Quaritch reported an unbound copy which had belonged ca. 1490 to Thomas Aleyne, ca. 1520 to John Barrett, and ca. 1570 to John Skelhorne. The Sunderland Library copy had, on the last leaf, a contemporary note of ownership dated 12 Aug. 1486.

The text of this ed. contains citations of Odoric in chaps. 33 (2),

## APPENDIX II

34 (4), 36 (3), as well as those to be found also in Van Os' ed., chaps. 43, 44, and 49.

4. [ca. 1495-1500. COLOGNE: CORNELIS DE ZIERIKZEE]

BMC 1:309. H 10643-44. C 3832-3831? Klebs 652.4. Pr 1498. Cordier 3:2032. Brunet Suppl. 1:932. L'Escalopier 5205. Huth no. 4648. Polain 2585. Voull(K) 682. St. M140.

Copies: HCL. 12436.28*. HEHL 925. LC Incun. 1485 M. NewbL Inc. 1498. NYPL. PML 1675. Boies Penrose (Harper). BM G 6699 (IA5205) and IA5204 (2 copies). Edinburgh, National Lib. Quaritch Cat. no. 713 (1953) item 301. BN Rés. O²f.7. Belgian Royal Lib. A 208. U. of Leyden. L'Escalopier 5205. Liège Univ. Lib., xv°s. C 66.

4° 48 leaves a-c⁶d-i⁴ ˣ ⁶ 37 long lines. 151 × 93 mm.

Fol. 1 (title): JOhannis de monte vil/la Itinerari[us] in partes/ ... (4 lines). fol. 1ᵛ-2 tables of 50 chaps. in 2 pts. 2ᵛ blank. fol. 3: "Incipit Itinerarius ..." (5 lines, followed by text. Text ends on i⁶ recto. Verso blank. Spaces left for caps.

VARIANTS: NewbL copy has "Mandeville" printed above the title. A copy with "Itinerarius" printed above the title is described in Brunet Suppl., citing the cat. of M. Asher (1865). It is listed also by Copinger 3831, but the whereabouts of the copy is unknown.

This ed. was assigned to J. Koelhoff, Cologne ca. 1490, by C3832 and BN Cat. OBMC M268 attributes to 1494, Mainz: P. Friedberg. Escalopier *Cat.* describes it as 1488: "Colonae apud Praedicatores." Both Koelhoff and Zierikzee used Venetian type, and Zierikzee described himself in the colophon of another of his books as "apud conuentum predicatorum"; Voull(K), p. lxxvi, and D.D., p. 45.

This text does not contain the interpolated references to "Ode" or "Odoricus" found in the Van Os and Leeu eds.

The NewbL copy is dated 1495 in a contemporary (?) hand. The HEHL suggests 1498. Polain collates a⁸c⁶, no b, but says fol. 7 is signed b₁, b₂ not signed. b₃ is signed! HCL (Sotheby, lot 5259) in old vellum binding, with notes of former owners. Letts (p. 178) notices the Leicester Harmsworth copy, formerly Sir Thomas Brook's, sold by Sothebys 15 March 1948 (3d section, lot 4073) to Quaritch.

. . . . . . . . . . . . . . . . . . . . . . . . . . . .

R. p. 83, lists an ed. "1564 Antwerp: Wouwer." He was misled by seeing the title in Latin. The ed. is in Dutch.

5. 1589 LONDON. IN *Principall Navigations, Voiages, and Discoveries of the English Nation* ... ed. Richard Hakluyt.

Pp. 24-77. Table of 50 chaps. in 2 pts. Latin ded. to Edward III on

p. 25, Bale's Life of Mandeville in both Latin and English, and a transcript of the epitaph. The text printed by Hakluyt has all the references to Odoricus found in Leeu's ed., but it has also the heading "Tertia pars" above chap. 41, as in Van Os's ed. but not in Leeu. The situation suggests a MS source or lost ed. which retained Van Os's division of the text into 3 pts., but had already suppressed his 51st chap. and added the further references to Odoricus. Leeu frequently calls him "Ode." Hakluyt never does.

Hakluyt omitted Mandeville from his second ed., 1598-1600, printing instead Carpini, Rubruquis, and Odoric, both in Latin and in his own English translation. His English translations were reprinted in the Macmillan ed. of the English *Mandeville*, 1900 ff.

**6. 1625 LONDON. IN *Purchas his Pilgrimes* by Samuel Purchas.**

Vol. III, "The Third Part in five Bookes," Chap. I, VI, 128-138 (misnumbered 158). This is a very much truncated Latin text. It is headed: "Briefe Collections of the Trauels and Obseruations of Sir Iohn Mandeville, written by Master Bale, Cent. 6." This is followed by Bale's Life, the epitaph (from Ortelius), the dedication to Edward III, and a brief résumé of the *Travels* in Latin. Purchas' title misled Vander Aa-Bergeron into attributing the epitome to Bale.

**7. 1809 LONDON: IN THE ROLLS SERIES.**

Hakluyt's Latin text reprinted in *Hakluyt's Collection of the early Voyages*, &c. Vol. II, 79-138.

## GERMAN EDITIONS

**1. [1478? AUGSBURG: ANTON SORG]**

Schramm 4:11.

Copy: Munich Bayerische Staatsbibliothek (formerly in Franziskaner-Kloster), Fragment.

Schramm says, "In der ersten undarierten Ausgabe steht der dritte Holzschnitt (das Kreuz Christi) richtig, während in der datierten Ausgabe der Holzschnitt falsch eingeszt ist: Abb. 583. Zwei Holzschnitte weichen in der ersten Ausgabe von der zweiten ab; siehe Abb. 699 und Abb. 700." He does not explain why he believes that the undated copy is earlier, but it is a different ed. from the next. The third woodcut could not have been turned while the book was in proof because the cut is oblong, 76 × 80 mm. and the type set beside it is too close to allow room. The two extra cuts which occur in this fragment, but not in the ed. of 1481, insure that this was indeed a different ed., and it is much more probable that the 2 cuts near the end would have been omitted in a second ed. than added. Sorg published another ed. July 18, 1481. October 18, 1482, another Augsburg printer, J. Schönsperger, published an ed. which borrows Sorg's text and copies Sorg's pictures. Schreiber 4800 says that the many damaged blocks used in Schönsperger's 1482 ed. suggest an earlier ed., now lost. Two Schönsperger eds. between mid-July 1481 and mid-October 1482 seem excessive. If, however, Sorg published an earlier ed. which Schönsperger copied, then his ed. of 1482 could easily have been his second. The condition of Schönsperger's woodcuts, as reported by Schreiber, lends weight to Schramm's assertion that Sorg printed his undated ed. about 1478.

Sorg was a very prolific printer who began to issue Almanacs and illustrated eds. of popular books about 1476, including such travels as Saint Brandan's and Schiltberger's, and such big books as a German Bible (1477), a Jacobus de Voragine, and *Historia Troiana* (1478). There is nothing in the history of his press which conflicts with Schramm's theory that he first published his Mandeville in 1478. That hypothesis is harmonious also with the evidence provided by the Richel ed.; see below. Richel shows some acquaintance with Sorg's cuts. Richel's last dated book was 20 Feb. 1482, and he was dead by August 1482. His Mandeville is dated ca. 1481-82, which puts it between Sorg's ed. of 18 July 1481 and Richel's death a year later. But those dates allow very little time for a copy of Sorg's book to reach Basel and for Richel to select his text (Otto von Diemeringen's tr.: Sorg printed Michael Velser's), and to design and cut over 150 woodblock illustrations. More probably he was inspired by an earlier ed. of the Sorg cuts. Sorg's source of inspiration seems to have been manuscript illustrations. H. Lehmann-Haupt, "Book Illustration at Augsburg in the Fifteenth Century," *Metropolitan Museum Studies,* IV, Pt. 1 (Feb., 1932), 3-17, presents evidence that in other works Sorg copied his pictures from manuscript illustrations of the Augsburg school of ca. 1350, and similarities have been noticed between such German MS illustrations of Mandeville as those in German no. 42 above and Sorg's pictures.

2. 1481 JULY 18 AUGSBURG: ANTON SORG.

H 10647*. Klebs 651.1. Cordier 3:2039. Brunet 3:1360. Castan 677. Hind p. 297. Muther 166. Schramm 4:11, 50, and nos. 579-698. Schr 4798. Simrock xiv-vi. Voull (B) KB 123* and Voull. (B Suppl.). St. M142.

Copies: BPL. LC (Rosenwald). PML 23215. Besançon 677. Berlin

SB 123 (formerly in Kupferstichkabinett frag.). Copies formerly at Wernigerode and Maihingen have been sold.

2° 92 leaves [a-h¹⁰i-k⁶] 34-35 long lines. 205-122 mm.

Fol. 1 blank. 1ᵛ full page woodcut of a youth standing, holding a pennant and sword. Over his head a streamer reads: "Iohannes de Montevilla." fol. 2 (title): Hie hebt sich an das bůch des ritters/ herr hannsen von monte villa./ (followed immediately by text.) Large woodcut letter I. No table of chaps. but chap. headings, unnumbered, in the text. fol. 67 blank, 67ᵛ has a full-page picture of the Great Khan of Cathay seated at table. A large woodcut initial on fol. 68 opens the section on China. fol. 91ᵛ (Colophon): "Das bůch hat gedruckt vnd vol enndet Anthoni/ Sorg zů Augspurg an der mitwochen vor sant/ marie Magdalene tag M.cccc.lxxxj. jahr./" Michael Velser's translation, mistakenly described as Otto's by Voull.

119 woodcuts (121 illustrations, 2 repeats) all reproduced by Schramm. Initials mostly in outline. Schramm, no. 580, reproduces the last page with colophon. Woodcuts next used at Lyons in a French ed. of ca. 1482.

Besançon 677 (described by Castan) belonged in 1609 to Sebastian Beyer of Stuttgart. BPL *Quarterly*, II (1950), 309, has a reproduction of fol. 65ʳ showing 2 pictures. PML and LC have last blank missing. BPL has first leaf supplied in facsimile.

In 1483 Sorg published a list of 35 books which he had for sale. No. 20 is "Item den grossen berůmpten land farer genamit jo/ hannes de monteuilla mit seinen figuren." See K. Burger[B], no. 26.

3. [ca. 1481-82 BASEL: BERNHARD RICHEL]

HC 10646. C 3833. Klebs 651.2. Cordier 3:2037. Brunet Suppl. 1:931. FairMur (G) 283. Kraus 56, no. 42. Schramm 21: nos. 398-552. Schr 4700. Weisbach, no. 8:11-14, 37. St. M143.

Copies: LC. X.M 29 (FairMur). PML (Melk). Cambridge, Fitzwilliam Museum, McClean 321 (Ashburnham lat. 2465). Basel. Danzig St. Wolfenbüttel.

2° 103 leaves [A-B¹⁰C⁸D⁹ (D⁵ disjunct) E-G⁸H-I⁶K-M¹⁰] 38-42 long lines. 195 × 114 mm. No catchwords.

Fol. 1 blank (present in LC copy). fol. 2: [I]Ch Otto von diemeringen ein/ Thümherre zü Metz in Lothoringen. han dises bůch verwandelt vsz welschs vnd vsz latin zü tütsch . . . 29 lines of Otto's preface, followed by the table, foll. 2-6. fol. 6ᵛ has the remaining 16 lines of the preface. Fol. 7, full-page picture 202 × 130 mm. of a knight with retinue taking leave of 2 ladies. fol. 7ᵛ-103ᵛ, text. Woodcut at the end. Otto von Diemeringen's tr.

148 woodcuts plus 8 woodcut alphabets, all reproduced by Schramm. FairMur (G) reproduces the first cut; and see Weisbach, pl. 3,4. Richel's cuts are more elaborate and sophisticated than Sorg's and often of different subjects. However, there are so many similarities between the two series that they can hardly have been independently produced. Sorg draws his figures naked when clothes are not mentioned in the text. His first picture, of the Emperor at Constantinople, shows him naked except for his crown. Richel's first illustration is also of a naked Emperor, although later Richel clothes all of his figures, even Adam and Eve, and the men without heads. The second Richel cut combines the objects (relics of the crucifixion) in Sorg's 2nd and 3rd. Richel's 3rd could be an enrichment of Sorg's 4th, but the next 5 Sorg subjects are omitted entirely. However, the first few pictures establish clearly that Sorg's and not Richel's were first. Apparently, Richel started to copy the Sorg cuts, but after the first began to "improve" on them, and very soon to design his own with occasional reference to Sorg. The picture of Jerusalem (fol. 45) shows the arms of Basel over the gate.

Brunet dates "vers 1475." Cordier (*Mél.*, 1:2, 14-17) owned and described the copy discovered by Tross and dated "Basle? 1475" and sold by M. Grant of Nancy in April, 1833. It is the FairMur copy, now LC Incun. X. M. 29. He discovered that it lacked fol. 89-90, old foliation. Stubs are present. But it also lacks fol. 60 (G⁷). In the new foliation foll. 89-90 become foll. 91-92. Cf. also Cordier's ed. of Odoric, which reproduces some cuts, pp. 212, 213, 326, 443, 466-67. This copy has a pencilled note, "Basle cir. 1472." The relation of the cuts to Sorg's suggest a date after July, 1481, unless there was an earlier Sorg ed. Richel's last dated book was 20 Feb. 1482, and he was dead by 8 Aug. 1482; cf. BMC I-III, 734.

Woodcuts are colored in the LC copy. FairMur (G) describes the part of Otto's preface at the end of the table as "misplaced by the printer from another part of the book," but see the Prüss eds. LC Cat. cards note slight variants from Cordier's description. PML has first blank missing. McClean, also colored, lacks A¹I¹M¹⁰. G⁵ and H⁵ are mutilated. Richel's cuts were used only once, but were copied by Prüss, Kistler, and Hüpfuff.

### 4. 1482 OCT. 18 AUGSBURG: J. SCHÖNSPERGER.

BMC 2:364. H 10648*. Klebs 651.3. Cordier, *Mél.* 1:17. Panzer, I, 130 ff. Pr. 1759. Schr 4800. Gemeiner S 107 no. 72. Brunet 3:1361. Copies: BM G 6774 (IB 6269). Munich BSB. Regensburg.

2° 88 leaves [a-h¹⁰i⁸]. 34 long lines. 204 × 132 mm.

Fol. 1 blank(?) fol. 2 (title): Hie Hebt sich an das pûch des Ritters/ herr Hannsen von Monte Villa./Fol. 88 Colophon. Michael Velser's tr.

120 woodcuts copied from Sorg's and mostly reversed. Many damaged blocks suggest an earlier ed. now lost, according to Schreiber. Most of the pictures are 82 × 60 mm.

BM copy lacks fol. 1, 20-22, 75, 76. BMC describes missing first leaf as blank. Burger [B], pp. 263-264), lists the known ed. of this prolific press (1481-1500).

## 5. 1483 STRASBOURG: JOHANNES PRÜSS.

Klebs 651.4. Cordier 3:2039; *Mél.* 1:18. Hind II, 337-8. Schr 4801. Schramm 20:1030-1184. Huth (SC) no. 4650. St M144. Letts, p. 180-181.

Copies: HEHL 306 (Robinson). NYPL (Spencer, from Maggs, 1948, via. Laudau-Finlay sale at Sotheby's 13/7/48, lot 79.) Karlsruhe, Grand Ducal Library (imp.).

2° 88 leaves a-m⁸ except c,d,f,h, in 6s. 41 long lines. 204 × 137 mm.

Fol. 1 (title): Johannes von Mon-/teuilla. Ritter/ (2 lines only). 1ᵛ blank. fol. 2 Das erste bûch. [Woodcut of knight taking leave of ladies before a castle.] Text begins below the picture. b⁴ signed b_{ii} and c² signed c_{iii}. m³-m⁷ Otto's preface, followed by a complete register of chaps. m⁷ᵛ has 18 lines of Otto's preface, as in Richel's ed., followed after a space by the col. in 3 lines. m⁸ blank. Xylographic title, initials, and headlines.

149 woodcuts (2 repeated, 8 alphabets in 11 parts, and 6 woodcut initials, 2 pictorial and 4 not, 1 a repeat). Woodcuts of various sizes. Pictures imitated from Richel, except 3 which had appeared earlier in an ed. of the antiChrist legend. The arms of Basel are replaced by those of Strasbourg in the picture of "Jerusalem" on fol. 25ᵛ. Muther 1:72 says the pictures are "Strassburger Originalarbeiten." He does not mention Richel's ed.

VARIANT: Huth 3:896 reports a copy which has on the verso of "the last leaf" the text and woodcut of i₆ "instead of the last 22 lines of the register." The NYPL copy has 23 lines of the register on m₇. The rest of the page is blank. The verso has 18 lines of Otto's preface, followed by 3 lines of colophon. m⁸ is missing.

The text, as well as the pictures, follow Richel's ed., except that Otto's preface and the table have been transposed from the beginning to the end of the text.

## APPENDIX II

### 6. 1484 STRASBOURG: JOHANNES PRÜSS.

BMC 1:119. HC 10649 + Add. Klebs 651.5. Brunet 3:1361. Cordier 3:2039; *Mél.* 1:18. Pr. 512. Schmidt 3. Schramm 20:9,15. Schr. 4802. St M145.
Copies: LC (Rosenwald). Cornell. Williams (Chapin L). BM G 6773 (IB 1563). BN Rés. 0² f. 13(2) and 0² f. 11 (incomplete). St. Florian. Augsburg. Hanover KB 45. Stuttgart BR. Wolfenbüttel.

2° 88 leaves a-m⁸ except cdfh in 6s. 41 long lines 206 × 138 mm. fol. 1 (title): Johannes von Mon/tuilla Ritter/(2 lines). Xylographic. $a_{ii}$: Do ich Johan von Monteuilla Ritter Geborn vsz En/geland, etc. m³-m⁷ᵛ same as in 1483. M⁸ blank. Otto's tr. same pictures as in 1483, with 1 exception. All pictures in Schramm. Letts says the type is from a different font from 1483.

LC copy has fols. 83-86 supplied in facsimile. In contemporary binding repaired.

This ed. was reprinted by Simrock.

### 7. 1488 STRASBOURG: J. PRÜSS.

H 10650. Klebs 651.6. Brunet 3:1361. Panzer 264. Pr 512. Schmidt 3. Schramm 20:9, 15. Schr 4803.
Copies: Strasbourg Univ. Darmstadt (incomplete). Stuttgart (incomplete). Budapest, Mus. Nat. Hungary, 314.

4° 88 leaves a-p (sic!) Fol. 1 title as in 1484. Text and pictures the same, but some initials are different.

### 8. 1499 SEPT.2. STRASBOURG: BARTHOLOMAEUS KISTLER.

H 10651. Klebs 651.7. Brunet 3:1361. Col(S) 686. Schmidt 4. Schramm 20:1887-2045. Schr 4804.
Copies: BN (cf. Lonchamp). Dresden. Göttingen. Munich BSB (Inc.). Stockholm.

2° 77 leaves a-l 2 cols.
Fol. 1 (xylographic title): Von. der. erfarüng./ des. strengen. Ritters./ iohannes. von. mon/tauille./ fol. 1ᵛ woodcut of a knight taking leave of ladies (after Richel's). Otto's preface and a register of chaps. at the end. Otto's tr. 157 woodcuts, mostly copied from Prüss, but with more shading and detail. Some from other sources. Pictures of various sizes, with full blackline borders. Drawing and perspective better than in Prüss.

Coll(S) reproduces the type and 2 pictures, pl. 95.
This ed. was reprinted by Matt. Hüffus, Strasbourg, 1856.

## 9. 1501 AUG. 16 STRASBOURG: MATTHIAS HÜPFUFF.

Copies: PML (Richard Bennett). Munich BSB. Basel. Danzig SB. Melk 553 (formerly?). Wolfenbüttel. Göttingen.

2° 70 leaves A⁴B-M⁶ 44 long lines.

Fol. 1 (title): Johannes Monteuilla/ der wytfarende Ritter./ (2 lines above the picture of departure, 167 × 125 mm. reduced from Richel's). fol. 1ᵛ Otto's preface and a list of the 5 books into which Otto's text is divided. A²-4ᵛ table of chaps. B₁ another picture of the departure, followed by the text. M⁶ᵛ blank. Otto's version.

137 woodcut pictures, 8 alphabets on 10 blocks, 4 large initials. Pictures copied closely from Richel's, except 2 in Hüpfuff's style (on B₁ and G₁). "Jerusalem" on F²ᵛ has the arms of Basel, as in Richel. Schr. 4799, says that 139 pictures are Richel's.

## 10. 1507 OCT. 31 STRASBOURG: IOH KNOBLOUCH.

Cordier 3:2040; *Mél.* 1:19. Pr 10055. Schmidt 7, no. 32.
Copies: NYPL, °KB. BM 148 C 3. Zurich, Bibl. Cantonale.

2° 70 leaves A-M.

Fol. 1 (title): Von. der. erfarüng./ des. strengen. Ritters/ iohannes von Mon/ tauille./ (woodcut: 2 compartments. a house. a knight with retinue.) Otto's tr. 141 woodcuts copied from Hüpfuff, except 12 in a better style.

## 11. 1580 FRANKFURT AM MAIN: [JOH. SPIESS.]

Cordier 3:2040; *Mél.* 1:19.
Copy: BM 10,076 a.

8° 6 + a-d⁵ + 1. Woodcuts. Otto's tr. Letts (p. 181) says "new and rather indifferent woodcuts."

## 12. 1584 FRANKFURT A. M. (*in Reyssbuch dess heyligen Lands*, fol. 405-432).

OBMC. Cordier 3:2040; *Mél.* 1:20. Ashton, p. 285.
Copy: BM 790 M. 16.

2° Letts (p. 188) says no woodcuts. Text modernized.

## 13. 1600 COLOGNE: WILH. LÜTZENKIRCHEN.

Cordier 3:2040; *Mél.* 1:19-20. Panzer 160.
Copy: Berlin, SB.

8° 266 + 3 pp. Otto's tr.

. . . . . . . . .

Eds. continued to appear through the 17, 18, and 19 centuries. R. reports eds. Frankfurt 1608 and n.p. 1608. The *Reyssbuch* was reprinted in 1609 (copy: BM 791 l. 12), and 1619 (pp. 759-812). Frankfurt a. M. 1630 (reprint of 1580). 1659 2° Nürnberg (in *Bewehrtes Reissbuch*..., I, 759-812), copy: BM 791 l. 25. Cologne 1690. Nürnberg 1690. Cologne 1692. n.p. 1692 (228 pp). n.p. 1696. Cologne 1696. A new tr. n.p., n.d., ca. 1700, in 16°. Copies: BM 12315 c 5(4), and NYP *C p.v. 1343, no. 1. A copy 1704 Cologne, in the NewbL. has 228 pp + 9 pp. of register.

1828 Nürnberg (Jäck, *Teschenbibl.*, II, I, 163-194). [1852] Reutlingen bei Fleischauer, von Ottomar F. H. Schönhuth, copy: Strasbourg D 164431 Cf. R.). 1856 Strasbourg, ed. Matt. Huffus; reprint of 1499 ed. [1865?] Reutlingen: O. F. H. Schönhuth copy: BM 1007 6. aa. [1866] Frankfurt a. M.: C Winter; copy: HCL 12436. 34.5: in *Deutsche Volksbücher* series of Karl Simrock, no. 51.

## DUTCH EDITIONS

1. [ca. 1470 PLACE AND PRINTER UNKNOWN]

OBMC M 40. Klebs 648.1. Pr 9181. Cordier 3:2032; *Mél.* 1.33. Brunet Suppl. 1:932. Camp. 1199. Cramer p. xli. Holtrop (H) 256. Holtrop (M), pl. 121 [4]. Lorenzen, p. xxxiii. Mus. M-W Cat. 2:244. Schoerner p. 54. Simrock. Techener, p. 444.

Copies: BM C2 m 5. Museum Meerman-Westr., The Hague KB 651.

2° 108 leaves without sigg. pag. or catchwords. 29-30 lines. 2 cols.

Fol. 1 blank (?) (missing). fol. 2: Dit is die tafel van/ desen boecke/ initials rubricated. Text ends fol. 107$^v$, l. 26 ff.: regneert in allen tiden/ Amen/ ¶Laus deo in Altissimo/ fol. 108 blank (?) missing.

Translator unknown. Not the Ogier version. No other work of this printer has been identified. That he was a beginner or amateur is clear from his failure to justify his lines or to keep them straight. He used no punctuation. Facsimile of the last page in The Hague copy in Holtrop (M), who observes that G. Leeu in 1477 used the "Laus deo ..." conclusion, but Leeu was a better printer. Van der Bergh calls it a 4° and assigns to Deventer. Techener described it as "in the genre of ... Laur. Coster, but not certainly from his press," and assigned it to 1465-8(?). H. Bradshaw: *Collected Papers* (Cambridge, 1889), p. 278, suggests G. Leeu, Gouda, before 1477.

Cramer reports "137 bladen" and fol. 1 (title): Jan van Madaville. The Hague copy has 107 leaves. Campbell reports 110 leaves; Fol. 1 blank and 110 blank. Brunet says 110 leaves.

Probably the same as 1483 "En flamand" reported by *Niceron*, T. 25, p. 254. Ashton (p. 283), gives the BM copy a Latin title and dates it "1500?" Letts (p. 181), reports 4 alphabets, the last imperfect.

2. 1494 JUNE 19 ANTWERP: GOVAERDT BACK.

> C 3839. Klebs 648.2. Brunet 3:161. Pr 9433. Cordier 3:2033; *Mél.* 133. Camp. 1200. Cramer, p. xli. *B. M. Grenv. Cat.*, p. 433. Heber 8: no. 1501.
> Copy: BM G 6707.

4° 139 leaves a-x⁴ 28 lines 2 cols.

Fol. 1 (title): Mandevil[l]e (a colored plate). fol. 2 (title): Hier beghint een genoechlijc boec gemaect/ . . . (5 lines). fol. 2ᵛ blank. fol. 139 blank. fol. 139ᵛ (printer's device).

3. [ca. 1530] ANTWERP: WILLEM VORSTERMAN.

> Cramer, p. xlii. Nijhoff and Kronenberg, pt. II, no. 3493.
> Copy: Ghent UB (Defective) lacks foll. 1 and 4.

4° 84 leaves A-X⁴ 33 lines 2 cols.

4. 1550 OCT. 31 "BIJ CONSENT VAN DEN HOVE GHEGEVEN TOT BRUSSEL . . ."

> Cramer, p. xlii. R suggests "Amsterdam" citing Le Long, no. 1208.
> No copy known.

Reproduced in 16–, 1734.

5. 1564 ANTWERP: CLAES VAN DER WOUWERE.

> Cramer (R, p. 83, lists as Latin, citing Adrichom 287 a.).
> Copy: Freiburg in Breisgau, UB.

4° 84 leaves 34 lines.

Fol. 1 (title): Jan Mandeuijl (in large red letters). fol. 1ᵛ (prologue). (Colophon) By consente van den houe ghegheuen tot Bruessel den/ lesten Octobris. Anno. M. CCCCC ende.1. (followed by) Gheprent Thantwerpen . . .

Christian Adrichom, *Urbis Hierosolymae,* Colonniae Agrippinae 1597, cites this ed. in his *Catalogus,* p. 131, giving the title in Latin.

## APPENDIX II

**6. 1578 ANTWERP: JAN VAN GHELEN.**

Cramer, citing *Cat.* of P. Kockx, 1887. No copy known.

**7. 1586 ANTWERP: JAN VAN GHELEN.**

Cramer. Copy: Göttingen UB.

4° 60 leaves A-P⁴ 43 lines 2 cols.
(Title): Die wonderlijcke Reyse van/ Jan Mandeuijl (large red letters, followed by a longer title).
Text follows Wouwer's.

**8. 1592 ANTWERP: BY DE WEDUWE VAN GIULLIAEM VAN PARIJS.**

Cramer. Copy: The Hague, Royal Library.

4° 46 leaves 47 lines 2 cols.

**9. 16– AMSTERDAM: B. JANSS.**

Not listed by Cramer. Copies: LC. NYPL, *KB 16—.

4° 48 leaves a-m⁴ 2 cols.
Fol. 1 (title): De Wonderlijcke Reyse/ van Jan Mandevijl . . . (8 lines), followed by a picture of a bishop blessing a man who carries baskets of grain. Gedruckt t'Amsterdam by Broer Jansz. Text begins on fol. 1ᵛ: De Prologie . . . catchwords and sigg., running title, no pagination. Table of 114 caps. on last leaf, r and v. Col.: "By consent van den Hove ghegheven/ tot Brussel den lasten October M.D. ende L." Not an Ogier version. No pictures after t.p.

**10. [ca. 1630] AMSTERDAM: CARNELIS DIRCKSS COOL.**

Cramer. Copy: Zürich Staatsbibliothek.

4° 48 leaves 48 lines 2 cols.
Cool printed 1614-48, according to Cramer.

**11. 1650? AMSTERDAM: IAN BOUMAN.**

OBMC M 270. Cordier 3:2033; *Mél.* 1:34. Ashton, p. 285. Cramer. Copy: BM 10,056 bbb/2. 4° no pagination. Slight cropping of t.p. makes date uncertain. Probably same as R. 1659 (?), 4°. 96 pp. Same place and printer. Title same as in Janss ed.

12. 1656 AMSTERDAM: JAN JACOBSS BOUMAN.
    Cramer. Copy: Jena UB.
    4° 48 leaves 48 lines 2 cols.
    Imitated from Cool's ed.

13. 1677 ANTWERP: JACOB DE BODT.
    Cramer. Cordier 3:2033; *Mél.* 1:34.
    Copy: BM 12410 f. 10.
    4° 79 leaves 2 cols.
    Vignette on t.p.

14. 1697 AMSTERDAM. 4°. Cited by Cramer, p. xlvi. Exemplar seen by Martin Nijhoff.

15. 1705 AMSTERDAM: WEDUWE VAN GYSBERT DE GROOT. Cramer citing J. G. Boekenoogen.

16. 1707 UTRECHT: J. VAN POOLSUM.
    4° Cordier 3:2033; *Mél.*, 1:34. Cramer.

17. 1734 AMSTERDAM: ERVE WED. GYSBERT DE GROOT. 4° 94 + 1 foll. A$^2$-M$^3$ "By consent," etc. Cramer cites *Cat. de la Collection Royaards van den Ham*, 1st part, p. 108, no. 1195. Cordier *Mél.*, 1:34. Waller No. 1147.

18. 1742 AMSTERDAM: GYSBERT DE GROOT KEUER. 4° 94 + 1 foll. 2 cols. Vignette on t.p. Table. R. Cordier 3:2033. Cramer. Copy: BM 10056 cc.

19. [ca. 1750] AMSTERDAM: ABRAHAM CORNELIS. 4° Ashton, p. 287. Cordier 3:2033. Cramer.
    Copies: BM 790 b 34. Utrecht UB. Leyden, Biblio. van de Maatsch. der Ned. Letterk (see Cramer).

20. [ca. 1750] ANTWERP: MARTINUS VERDUSSEN. Cramer. Copy: Ghent UB.

21. [ca. 1770] AMSTERDAM: ERVEN DE WEDUWE JACOBUS VAN EGMONT 4° 94 + 1 pp. A$^2$-M$^3$ 2 cols. Vignette on t.p. Table. Cramer dates 1730, but Waller dates this press 1761-

1804: see his no. 1148. R. lists an ed. "Jac. van Egmont," 4°. n.d. Cordier *Mél.*, 1:35. Copy: BM 10056 aa. Cramer cites *Cat. van Populaire Prozaschrijvers des 17<sup>e</sup> en 18<sup>e</sup> eeuw*, Fred. Muller & Co., No. 876.

22. 1779 AMSTERDAM: ERVE VAN DER PUTTE, EN BASTIAN BOEKHEUT. 4° 78 + 1 pp. 2 cols. Vignette. Cordier 3:2033; *Mél.*, 1:35. Cramer. Copy: BM 10055 b.

23. [ca. 1785] GENT: JAN GIMBLET. 4° 79 pp. 2 cols. Vignette on t.p. Cordier 3:2033; *Mél.*, 1:34. Cramer. Heurch, pp. 168-171. Copies: BM 1295.C.31. Ghent UB. Brussels, Bibliothèque Royale.

This is a revised ed. for use in the schools, as also the Amsterdam eds., according to Cramer, p. xlvii n. It gives the date as 1622 instead of 1322. See "La Bibliothèque Bleue en Belgique," *Le Bibliophile Belge*, vii (Brussels, 1872), 59.

24. [n.d.] AMSTERDAM: KOENE.
Cramer.

25. 1908 LEIDEN: CRAMER edited the chapbook.

## CZECH EDITIONS

1. 1510 PLZEN: MIKULÁS BAKALÁŘZE. 8°.

    R. Tobolka 5167. Graesse 4:361. Jungmann ii, 79.

    (Title): Knižka o Putowáni geho po Swietie, po Zemi, y po Morži. . . . No copy known.

2. 1513 PLZEN: MIKULÁS BAKALÁŘE. 8°.

    R. Tobolka 5168. Graesse 4:361. Jungmann ii, 79.
    No copy known

3. [1576] PRAHA: BUR. WALDA. 8°.

    R. Tobolka 5169. Graesse 4:361. B$^8$-R$^8$.
    Copy: Praha: Strahov. K. (FK I 143); (MK 29 G 6); and (29 G 7).

4. 1596 PRAHA: BURIANA WALDA. 4°.

    Tobolka 5170. Jungmann iv, 839.
    Copy: Roudnice. Lobkov. K. (III IB 12/47).

## ITALIAN EDITIONS

5. 1600 PRAHA: WOLDŘICH WALDA. 8°. A-R.

Tobolka 5171.
Copies: Praha, Museum, Král. čes. 29 g 3. Univ. Library 54 F 320.

(R. lists an ed. Prague 1610, also listed by Graesse 4:361 and Dobrowsky, 165 ff., described as a mistake of Jungmann. Not in Tobolka. The Czech encyclopaedia, *Ottův Slovník Naučný* (1900) also lists an ed. 1687, not in Tobolka.)

6. 1796 PRAHA: KRAMERIUS.

Tobolka 5172 (R. lists 1797). Grasse 4:361. 8° Edited from a MS. now lost.

7. 181– PRAHA: Revised ed. (of 1796).

R. *Naučný*. Graesse 4:361 says "Folkbook." Tobolka 5172 lists several copies.


## ITALIAN EDITIONS

1. 1480 JULY 31 MILAN: PETRI DE CORNENO.

BMC 6:758. HCR 10652. Klebs 650.1. Cordier 3:2033, 2036? and *Mél.* 1:35. Pr. 5972. Brunet 3: 1360. Huth 4649. St. M146.
Copies: LC (Thacher) 1488. HEHL 3501. Princeton (Grenville Kane). BM G 6702 (IA 26583). BN O²f. 10. Modena a C. 2. 10. Parma Inc. 142. Letts, p. 179.

4° 114 leaves $a^{10}b$-$o^8$ 31-32 long lines. 142 × 84 mm.
Fol. 1 blank. fol. 1$^v$ (title): Tractato de le piu marauegliose cosse e piu notabile che/ . . . (21 lines). fol. 2 (text): CONCIO Sia . . . fol. 114$^v$ (colophon): Explicit Iohannes d'Mādeuilla impressus Medio/lani ductu & auspicijs Magistri Petri de corneno pri/die Callendas augusti. M.CCCCLXXX Joha/ne Galeazio Maria Sfortia Vicecomite Duce no/stro inuictissimo ac principe Iucondissimo/.
Hazlitt II: 274 notices an ed. in Tite (May 1874), no. 1941, described as n.d., n.p., n.pr. ca. 1480. 4° a-b⁹c-o⁸ (title): Trattato de le piu marvegliose cose e piu notabile che se trouano, etc. Last fol. blank. On p. 491 he notices Corneno's ed. This may be another ed., imitated from Corneno's (?) or a faulty description of a copy lacking the first and last leaves (?).
Cordier 3:2036; but *Mél.* 1:40 describes the BN copy as 1530. He had previously described it correctly. He also says 1 fol. is intercalated between sigg a and b. BM copy has first leaf supplied

in pen and ink facsimile. Huth copy has last leaf in facsimile. Modena copy imperfect, from the library of Francesco III (1765). Huth reports that the long title usual in Ital. eds. is on a t.p. preceding $a_1$. Letts says no pictures, chapter heads, or alphabets.

## 2. 1488 BOLOGNA: UGO RUGERIUS.

BMC 6:808. CR 3835. Klebs 650.2. Cordier 3:2034; Mél. 1:36. Pr. 6569. Brunet 3:1360.
Copies: BM IA28809. BN Rés. O²f.818. Naples BN VI. B. 64. Parma Inc. 143.

4° 82 leaves a-i⁸k¹⁰ ca. 39 lines 2 cols. 152 × 98 mm.
Fol. 1 blank. fol. 1ᵛ (title): Tractato de le piu mauaue/gliose . . . (23 lines). fol. 2, text. fol. 82ᵛ, colophon and device.

BMC notes that the number of lines to a page is often short of 39, and the last sentences are sometimes shortened to keep from running over the page; therefore, this is probably earlier than the more regular ed. dated July 4. Reichling 3:100 reports 82 leaves but colophon on fol. 92b [sic].

## 3. 1488 JULY 4 BOLOGNA: UGO RUGERIUS.

BMC 6:808. H 10653. Klebs 650.3. Pr 6568. Panzer 4:247 (no. 116). St M147.
Copies: LC.X.M27 '88 (ex Bibliotheca Sobolewskiana). BM G 6703 (IA28807). BN Res. O²f. 818.

4° 80 leaves a-k⁸ 39 lines 2 cols. 152 × 100 mm.
Fol. 1 blank. fol. 1ᵛ (title): Tractato de la piu marauegliose cose e piu/ . . . Title in 23 lines. Spaces left for caps. fol. 80ᵛ colophon and printer's device in col. 2.

LC copy has first leaf mounted, a⁸, b¹, missing; several leaves damaged and repaired.

Chaps. not numbered and there is no table.

## 4. 1491 NOV. 17 VENICE :NICOLAUS DE FERRARIIS.

BMC 5:507. HC 10654. C 3834. Klebs 650.4. Brunet 3:1360. Cordier 3:2034; Mél. 1:36. Pr 5372. Panzer 1433. Rosenthal (IT) 1:939. St M148.
Copies: HCL, Inc. 5372*. HEHL 3151 (FairMur). NYPL. BM G 6704 (IA 23865). Rosenthal.

4° 70 leaves a-d⁸e¹⁰f-h⁸i⁴ 39-42 lines 2 cols. 165 × 104 mm.
Fol. 1 (title): Ioanne de mandauilla./ fol. 1ᵛ (long title): Tractato

de le piu marue/gliose cose . . . (ends) in diuerse secte de Latini Greci Iudei e Barbari Christiani & infideli & in molte altre prouincie como appare nel tractato de sotto. Text begins on a² and ends on i¹ᵛ col. 1, followed by the printer's device in col. 2, table of 182 chaps., colophon on i⁴ᵛ. sig. e¹ verso has the digression on Job. d⁸ verso lacks the phrase "coperti de edera." e¹⁰ has the substitute passage on climates. h²⁻³ has the addition to the Valley Perilous. The biographical passage at the end is omitted. Spaces left for caps. Guide letters.

Rosenthal describes a copy lacking sig. e (10 leaves) and i¹ and i⁴ (i.e., lacking the colophon), as "Venice 1491" no month date. 67 leaves. See also his *Cat.*, cv, no. 932 a. No. 2704, p. 435, reprints the description. MS notes on 2 first foll.

Hain quotes the title as "Zovanne de Mandevilla Angelico . . ." The spelling "Zouãe de Mãdauilla" occurs at the end of the text, above the printer's device.

BMC describes Nicolaus de Ferrariis as printing 22 Oct. 1491 to 8 June 1492. Only 4 books with his colophon known. BM copy lacks t.p.

HCL copy in very old vellum binding——a leaf of 11 century MS. Bought in 1918 from W. M. Voynich, 68 Shaftsbury Ave., Piccadilly Circus, *Cat.* No. 32.

5. 1492 JUNE 7 FLORENCE: LORENZO MORGIANI & JOHANNES PETRI DA MAGANZA.

BMC 6:681. HCR 10655. Klebs 650.5. Cordier 3:2034. Pr 6353. Brunet 3:1360. Sander 4169. St M149.
Copies: LC (Rosenthal) M 27 1492. BM G 6705 (IA 27785). Vatican, Inc. IV, 263. JRL, Manchester.

4° 80 leaves a-iK⁸ 39 lines 2 cols. 156-160 × 97 mm.

Fol. 1 (title): Tractato bellissimo delle piu marauigliose cose & piu/ . . . (5 lines). Woodcut. fol. 1ᵛ the long title usual in Ital. eds. Spaces left for caps. K⁸ᵛ colophon.

BMC reports that the woodcut on the t.p. represents an emperor mounted, attended by 4 men, confronted by a sage with a book at the edge of a wood, from an ed. of the *Fiore di Vertù* (1491) recently recovered: see *LC, Quarterly Journal of Current Acquisitions*, IX (1952), no. 3, pp. 156-157. Same text as Bologna 1488. Ends with a protest against sceptics.

## APPENDIX II

6. 1492 JULY 18 BOLOGNA: J. J. & J. A. DE BENEDICTIS.

BMC 6:835. C 3836. Klebs 650.6. Cordier 3:2035. Pr 6613. Brunet 3:1360. Caronti 515. St M151.
Copies: BM G 6706 (IA28974). Univ. of Bologna.

4° 56 leaves a-g⁸ 36 lines 2 cols. 165 × 111 mm.
Fol. 1 (title): IOHANNE DE Mandauilla. fol. 1ᵛ (usual long title): TRACTATO d'le piu marauegliose co/se &c. fol. 2, text begins. fol. 56ᵛ, colophon in col. 2, lines 23 ff.

7. 1496 AUG. 27 MILAN: U SCINZENZELER.

BMC 6:770. C. 3837. Klebs 650.7. Cordier 3:2035. Brunet, Suppl. 1:933.
Copies: BM IA26761. L. Rosenthal (*Cat.* cv, no. 1032).

4° 66 leaves a-p⁴q⁶ 40 lines 2 cols. 165 × 111 mm.
Fol. 1 (title): Iohane Mandauilla. fol. 1ᵛ, usual long title. fol. 2, text. 66ᵛ, colophon.

8. 1496 DEC. 2 VENICE: MANFREDUS DE BONELLIS DE MONTEFERRATO.

BMC 5:504. HCR 10656. Klebs 650.8. Cordier 3:2035. Brunet 3:1360. Pr 5366. Ess 907. Sander 4170. St. M150. Maggs Cat. 656 (1938).
Copies: Univ. of N. Carolina Library 5366. BM G 6708 and IA23823. Maggs 210 (*Cat.* 656). Rome, Corsini Lib. Venice, Marciana Misc. 2521(1).

4° 62 leaves A-N⁴O⁶P¹ 42 lines 2 cols. 170 × 116 mm.
Fol. 1 (title): Iohanne de mandauilla/ Tractato . . . (7 lines). Woodcut border. fol. 2, woodcut cap. at beginning of text. fol. 62. colophon. Verso blank.
VARIANT Colophon: BM G 6708 (IA23824) reads: "Qui finisse el libro de zouane de/ Mandauilla: elquale trata de le cose/ marauegliose del mondo. Stampado/ in Venexia per maestro Māfredo da/ Mōferato da Streuo da Bonello .M./ CCCC.LXXXXVI. Adi .ii. del me/se de Decembrio/ AMEN./" Copy IA23823 is probably earlier since it spells *fenisse* and omits the place. T.p. woodcut border had previously been used for Lucan's *Pharsalia*.

9. 1497 BOLOGNA: PIERO & GIACOPO DA CAMPII.

BMC 6:835. HCR 10657. Klebs 650.9. Brunet 3:1360. Cordier, 3:2035; *Mél.* 1:38. Pr 6612. St M151.

Copies: NYPL (Harper). BM 6710 (IA 28953). Amiens, L'Es. 5206 Venice, Musei Civ. A.99.

4° 72 leaves a-e F-I⁸ ca. 38 long lines. 143 × 96 mm.

Fol. 1 (title): Iohanne de Mandauilla che tracta de le piu/ ... (3 lines). fol. 1ᵛ, usual long descriptive title in 18 lines. fol. 2, text begins with large woodcut cap. fol. 72ᵛ, colophon.

### 10. 1497 OCT. 21 MILAN: U SCINZENZELER.

BM 6:772. HCR 10658. Klebs 650.10. Brunet 3:1360. Cordier 3:2035; *Mél.* 1:38. Pr 6035. Sander 4172. St. M152. Leighton (1905), 3285.

Copies: HEHL 3534. BM G 6709 (IA26771). Milan Ambrosiana.

4° 50 leaves a-l⁴m⁶ 45 lines 2 cols. 169 × 122 mm.

Fol. 1 (title): Iohanne de mandauilla/ TRactato ... (21 lines). T.p. imitates that of Bonellis (Milan 1496), including the decorations. Layout also follows Bonellis. Fol. 50, colophon. No woodcuts. Reprinted from Bonellis ed.

### 11. 149[7] DEC. 6 MILAN: U. SCINZENZELER.

BMC 6:772. H 10658? Klebs 650.11. Cordier 3:2035; *Mél.* 1:39. Pr 6043. Sander 4172.

Copy: BM IA26788.

4° 50 leaves acbed-l⁴m⁶ 45 lines 2 cols. 168 × 119 mm.

Title, etc. same as Oct. 21 ed. BM copy has title and last leaf mounted. Col. has last figure of the year date torn away, but a "vij" fits the space. On fol. 1 is written "Ad vsū Fratris Deodato De Brixia." Bought July, 1862. This is evidently the copy advertised by Sotheby & Wilkinson July 18 ff., 1861, *Catalogue of the Mathematical . . . & Miscellaneous Portion of the celebrated Library of M. Guglielmo Libri*, Pt. II, no. 4444, described as "1490 Milan: U. Scinzēzeler" perfect copy except title and last leaf mended. The *Cat.* does not mention the inscription. Proctor reports the ed. as not in Hain.

### 12. 1500 DEC. 23 VENICE: MANFREDUS DE BONELLIS & GEORGIUS RUSCONIBUS.

R. 1802. Klebs 650.12. Cordier 3:2036. Pr 5370.4. Ess. 908. Sander 4175.

Copies HEHL 3150 (FairMur). Milan, Ambrosiana, S.Q.P. IV. 19.

4° 59 [60] leaves A-P⁴ 43 lines 2 cols.

Fol. 1 (title): Iohanne De Mandavilla./[T]Ractato . . . fol. 60 blank.
Woodcut border on t.p. No other woodcuts.
Cordier describes Milan copy as 56 leaves, lacking A-A² and P⁴. Col. on P³.

13. [ca. 1500?] FLORENCE: [ANTONIUS TURBINI SOCIIQUE, A PETIZIONE] DI SER PIERO PACINI DA PESCIA.

> OBMC. R. 1260. Klebs 650.13. Cordier 3:2034. Pr 13486. Grenville (SC). Sander 4174.
> Copies: BM G 6701. Florence, Bibl. Riccard. E III 271 (3). Perugia, B. Civ.

4° 80 leaves a-k⁸ 39-40 lines 2 cols.
Fol. 1 (title): Tractato bellissimo delle piu Marauigliose cose . . . (woodcut from the ed. Florence, 1492).
Florence copy lacks f¹. Grenville dates "ca. 1512." Cordier dates ca. 1492. OBMC dates 1505? R. and Klebs suggest 1500? Excluded from BMC as not an incunabulum.

14. 1502 JUNE 26 MILAN: PIETRO MARTIRE DE MANTEGANTII.

> Sander 4176. Hazlitt 4:243, from Sotheby, Dec. 5, 1895, no. 830. Leighton's (1905), no. 3288.

4° 58 leaves a-h² in 8s 45 lines. 2 cols.
1 woodcut (on t.p.) reproduced by Leighton.

15. 1504 JULY 29 VENICE: I BAPT. SESSA.

> Pr 12553. Sander 4177. Ess. 909. Brunet 3:1360.
> Copy: BM G 6711.

4° 52 leaves A-N⁴ 47 lines 2 cols. Unusual woodcut on t.p. reproduced Ess. 2:301.

16. 1505 JAN. 26 VENICE: MANFREDUS DE BONELLIS.

> Cordier 3:2036. Pr 12614. Brunet 3:1360.
> Copy: BM 280 f. 32.

8° 111 leaves A-EE⁴. Last leaf missing.

17. 1515 VENICE: I. BAPT. SESSA. 4°.

> Panzer 8:424, no. 718. Brunet 3:1360.

## ITALIAN EDITIONS

18. 1517. JUNE 30 MILAN: ROCHO & FRATELLI DA VALLA.
    OBMC. Cordier 3:2036. Pr 13643. Huth 4651. Sander 4178 and 4171. Brunet 3:1360.
    Copies: NYPL, Spencer Coll. (FairMuir). BM G 6712. Milan, Ambrosiana.

    4° 58 leaves a-f⁸g¹⁰ 44 lines 2 cols. Large woodcut on t.p.

19. 1521 VENICE: I BAPT. SESSA.
    Grenville (SC) 2:80, no. 2464. Quaritch no. 9045 calls it 12°. Brunet 3:1360.

    8° A-P⁸. No woodcuts.

20. 1521 AUG. 26 VENICE: MARCHIO SESSA & PIERO DE RAUANA COMPAGNI.
    Cordier 3:2036. Ess 2:299n. Leighton (1905), 3286.
    Copies: HCL 12436.28.25* (FairMur). BM G 6656.

    4° 119 leaves, numbered, plus 8 for t.p. and table, plus final leaf with colophon and device. HCL lacks fol. 6, as did Leighton's copy. Leighton calls it small 8°.

21. 1534 AUG. VENICE: ALUISE DE TORTI.
    Cordier 3:2036. FairMur Cat. (1899), 1215. Hazlitt 4:243. Panzer 10:53, no. 1769b. Sander 4179.
    Copies: Yale UL. Ecd 322i. BM 10027. aa.6. BN Rés. O²f. 863. Amiens, L'Es. 5207.

    8° 8 + 119 numbered leaves A-P. 8 leaves in preliminary sig. l. Colophon at the end, and year date MDXXXIIII on t.p.
    Hazlitt notes 2 eds., one dated 1533.

22. 1537 OCT. VENICE: ALUISE TORTI.
    Cordier 3:2036. Quaritch Cat. 707 (1952), no. 207.
    Copies: NYPL *KB (Quaritch). U. of Mich. BM 1051.c.1(1). Milan, A.

    8° 8 + 120 leaves, last blank. Border on t.p. No pictures. 8 preliminary leaves have t.p. with long title on verso, 13 pp. of table of 184 chaps.

23. 1553 OCT. VENICE: NICOLO DE BASCHARINI.
    Cordier 3:2037. Quaritch (GC), no. 9046.
    Copies: HCL 12436.20*. LC. BM 1051.c.29. BN. Venice, Marciana.

    8° 119 leaves plus 8 leaves of t.p. and table of 184 caps.
    The t.p. reads 1553, but the colophon 1554. No woodcuts.

## 24. 1567 VENICE.

Cordier 3:2037. Hazlitt 1:274.
Copies: LC G 370 M 39. BM G 6657, and 1046. a.2614. Edinburgh, Nat.L.

8° 106 leaves single col. Picture (head of Caesar) on t.p. No other pictures. Printed on coarse paper like a chapbook.

(Title): Ioanne de/ Mandavilla,/ nel quale si contengono/ di molte cose marauigliose./ Con la Tauola di tutti i Capitoli, che nella/ presente opera si contengono/ Nouamente stampato, & ricorretto.

## 25. 1870 BOLOGNA.

8° 2 vols. pp. xxviii, 184, 217. "I viaggi di Gio. da Mandavilla, Volgarizzamento antico toscano . . ." ed. Francesco Zambrini in *Scelta di Curiosità letterarie inedite o rare dal secolo XIII al XVII, dispensa CXIII-IV*.

## SPANISH EDITIONS

Editions have been claimed for 1483, [1500], and [1513?] but the claims cannot be substantiated. All are attributed to Valencia. The first is cited in *Nicéron* xxv, p. 251, and Graesse, *Trésor* 4:361, who says "n'est pas constaté." Pinelo, 1.21, lists 4° 1496, 1507, 1512. An edition of ca. 1500 is described as used by Andrés Bernáldez before 1513, Castilian dialect, the "garrulity of the author strictly curbed." The edition is apparently inferred from Bernáldez' citation of chaps. 74, 85, 87, and 88. He could, however, have been referring to a manuscript, or even translating from a Latin, French, or Italian edition. Nothing but the suggested date appears for the third; and that is, perhaps, a confusion with the date of Bernáldez publication. All but the first are credited by Entwistle. No 15 century ed. cited in Vindel, *El arte tipográfico*.

## 1. 1515 VALENCIA.

Cordier, *Mél.* 1:50. R. Barcia notices, Pinelo, 1:21. Salvà-Palau doubts. Entwistle cites Burger, Gayangos. Cordier 3:2041 reports 2 eds. for this year.
No copy known.

4° Castilian dialect.

Vindel dates Jorge Costilla's press 1510-29. He does not notice the ed. of 1531. See his nos. 78-80.

## 2. 1521 JULY 15 VALENCIA: JORGE COSTILLA.

Cordier 3:2041; *Mél.* 1:50. Burnet Suppl. 1:932. Hazlitt 4:243. Heredia 2865. Palau. Thomas. Sp. Salvà 2:741 (no. 3782). Entwistle.
Copies: BM (Palau) C 20 e 32 (imp). Bibl. R. Heredia 2865.

2° 64 leaves a-h$^8$ 2 cols.
(Title): Libro d'las maraui-/llas del mūdo ... (6 lines). Last leaf blank. Collation as given by Brunet. *Heredia* describes the ed. as 62 leaves, a-k$^6$l$^2$, 4 figures, 8 vignettes, 120 woodcuts. 8 pictures reproduced by Salvà, pp. 742-743.

## 3. 1524 VALENCIA: [JORGE COSTILLA].

Entwistle p. 254 and n. Pinelo 1:21 reports the edition. 8°.
Copies: B.N. Madrid R 13149 (Gayangos' copy).

Collation same as 1521 ed. A table has been added at the end. 133 woodcuts. Title partly restored.

2° 2 cols. 64 leaves. Part of 63 and leaf 64 occupied by the table.

## 4. 1531 JUNE 30 VALENCIA: JORGE COSTILLA.

Hazlitt 4:243. Christie's, May 22, 1901, no. 456. Penny.
Copies: Hispanic Society of America, New York. 107 M31. Bedford Murray (Palau).

2° 62 leaves a$^6$b-h$^8$ 2 cols. 231-232 × 151-152 mm.
Fol. 1 (title): Juan d'mādauila (in red. top center). 8 pictures in 3 vertical rows of 3,2,3 of the monstrous men, below (on the last third of the page, in red and black): Libro d' las maraui-/ llas del mūdo y d' lvi/age dela tierra sancta de Jerusalen. V d'/ todas las prouincias y ciudades de las/ Indias ... (6 lines). Several borders on the t.p. a$_1$ verso and a$_2$ table of 66 chaps. with fol. nos. a$_{11}$ verso has full border and ornamental cap. Half-title: Comiēca el libro que compuso el/ noble cauallero ... followed by Prohemio, and then by Chap. 1. Text ends on fol. LXI$^v$. LXII has Mandeville's account of himself (giving dates: 1322, 1356, and xxiiii [sic] years), followed by col.: "Imprimio/ de el presente libro enla muyinsigne ciudad de Valencia/ por Jorge Costilla. Alcabose el postrero dia del mes de Ju/nio ... Año del nascimiento de nuestro señor Jesuchri-/sto de M D. XXXI./" (printer's device). Borders.

The text is divided into 2 books. *Libro Segundo* begins on fol. 37, which has an ornamental border and an introduction of half a page.

Last verso blank. Last leaf mounted in Hisp. Soc. copy.

123 illustrations (including several repetitions), plus the 8 on the title page (which are repeated in the proper place in the text), plus ornamental borders and woodcut initials. The illus., mostly 72 × 75 mm., some smaller—seem to show the influence of both Richel and Sorg, as well as other sources. Richel's influence is evident in the choice of subjects, and in some pictures which show his characteristic strong black areas. Many are free interpretations of his subjects. But the picture of the woman with no top to her head, fol. LIX, col. 2, seems to have been copied from Sorg after that cut was damaged; see the ed. of Lyons, ca. 1490. A few, like the virgin and child on fol. XXVII verso and the annunciation on fol. XXXV, are in a very different style.

5. 1540 VALENCIA: JUAN NAVARRO.

>Cordier 3:2041; *Mél.* 1:50. Pinelo 1:21 says 4°. Palau. Thomas Sp. Ashton, p. 283-284.
>Copy: BM 567.i.5 (Thomas says "C 55 g. 4").

2° 59 leaves 2 cols.
Title: Juan de Mandauila ... Colophon at the foot of 59ᵛ. Woodcuts. Salvà had not seen this ed. and questioned its existence. Letts (p. 180), says it is the same as 1521 except for slight variations in woodcuts.

6. 1547 MARCH 8 ALCALÁ DE HENARES.

>Cordier 3:2042; *Mél.* 1:50. Palau.
>Copy: BM 149.e.6.

2° 57 + 1 leaves 2 cols. Woodcuts.
Fol. 1 "preliminary" leaf for table. Title (in red and black): Selua deleytosa. Libro de las Maravillas del Mŭdo ... (vignette). Last leaf blank. Letts (p. 180), says "same as preceding."

7. 1564. PINELO 1:21 "segun Alricomio," citing D. Nicolás Antonio, fol. 559, among Spanish authors.

## REFERENCES CITED IN THE APPENDICES

The manuscript catalogues of public libraries and collections are arranged according to place; otherwise the arrangement is by authors, editors, owners, or sale catalogues.

*American Book Prices Current, 1895——.*

Ames, Joseph. *Typographical Antiquities: or an Historical Account of . . . Printing.* London, 1749. Ed. W. Herbert. London, 1785-90. 3 vols. Re-edited T. F. Dibdin 1810-19. 4 vols. Index, 1899.

Anderson Galleries. American Art Association. *Illuminated Manuscripts, Incunabula and Americana from the Famous Libraries of the Most Hon. the Marquess of Lothian.* [by Seymour de Ricci] Sat., Jan. 16, 1932. Sale No. 3945.

Arber, Edward, ed. [SR] *A Transcript of the Registers of the Company of Stationers of London, 1554-1640.* London, 1875-77. Birmingham, 1894. 5 vols.

—— *The Term Catalogues, 1668-1790.* London, 1903. 3 vols.

*Archiv,* see Pertz.

Ashburnham, Bertram. *The Ashburnham Library. Catalogue . . .* Sold by auction by Messrs. Sotheby, Wilkinson & Hodge. London, 1897-98.

Ashton, John. *Chapbooks of the Eighteenth Century.* London, 1882.

—— ed. *The voiage and travayle of Sir John Maundeville knight, which treateth of the way toward Hierusalem . . .* annotated and illustrated in facsimile . . . London, 1887. "Lists of Editions [including MSS] now in the British Museum."

Atkinson, Geoffroy. *La Littérature Géographique Française de la Renaissance: Répertoire Bibliographique.* Paris, 1927.

*Auction Prices of Books, 1850-1905.* ed. L. S. Livingston. New York, 1905. 4 vols.

Augsburg, G. C. Mezger, *Geschichte der vereinigten Königlichen Kreis- und Stadt-Bibliothek in Augsburg.* Augsburg, 1842.

Barcia, see Pinelo.

Bamberg. *Katalog der Handschriften der Königlichen Bibliothek zu Bamberg,* F. Leitschuh. Vol. II, Heller MSS. Leipzig, 1887.

Baudrier, J. *Bibliographie Lyonnaise. Recherches sur les imprimeurs,* *libraires, relieurs et fondeurs de Lettres de Lyon au XVI*ᵉ *Siècle.* Lyons & Paris, 1895-1921 (12 vols. published. No index.)

Beazley, C. R. *The Dawn of Modern Geography.* London, 1897-1906. 3 vols. III, 549, lists 19 MSS he has seen.

Bell, James F., *Jesuit Relations and Other Americana in the Library of* . . . ed. F. K. Walter and Virginia Doneghy. U. of Minn. Press, 1950.

Benedetto, Luigi Fascolo. *Marco Polo: Il Milione.* Comitato Geografico Nazionale Italiano. Pub. no. 3. Florence, 1928.

Bennett, J. W., "The Woodcut Illustrations in the English Editions of Mandeville's Travels," *Papers of the Bibliographical Society of America,* XLVII (1953), 59-69.

Berlin. *Die Handschriften-Verzeichnisse der Königlichen Bibliothek zu Berlin,* Valentin Rose. Vols. I-II, Berlin, 1893-1903.

—— *Verzeichnis der Lateinischen Handschriften von Valentin Rose.* [subtitle] Zweiter Band. Dritte Abteilung. Berlin, 1905.

—— *Verzeichnis der Lateinischen Handschriften der Preussischen Staats-Bibliothek zu Berlin.* Dritter Band. Die Görreshandschriften, Fritz Schillmann. Berlin, 1919.

—— *Kurzes Verzeichnis der Germanischen Handschriften der Preussischen Staatsbibliothek,* Hermann Degering. 3 vols. VII-IX of *Mitteilungen aus der Preussischen Staatsbibliothek.* Leipzig, 1925-32.

Bern. *Catalogus codicum. MSS. Bibliothecae Bernensis,* J. R. Sinner. Bern, 1760-72. 3 vols.

—— *Catalogus Codicum Bernensium* (Bibliotheca Bongarsiana), Hermann Hagen. Bern, 1874.

Bernard, E. *Catalogi librorum manuscriptorum Angliae et Hiberniae in unum collecti.* Oxford, 1697. 2 vols. in 1, indexed by Humphrey Wanley.

Bertoni, Giulio, "Intorno al codice dei 'Viaggi' di Jean de Mandeville posseduta da Valentina Visconti," *Giornale storico della letteratura italiana.* XLIX (Torino, 1907), 358-366.

Besançon, see Castan.

Bibliothèque Nationale [BN], see Paris.

Borchling, C., "Mittelniederdeutsche Handschriften in Norddeutschland und den Niederlanden," *Nachrichten von der Königl. Gesellschaft der Wissenschaften zu Göttingen.* Göttingen, 1895-1902. 3 vols.

*Book-Prices Current* [BPC] 1901, 1909.

Brandt, J. C. J. *Gammeldansk Laesebog.* Copenhagen, 1881-82.

British Museum. [BMC] *Catalogue of Books Printed in the XV*ᵗʰ *Century now in the British Museum.* London, 1908-49. 8 vols.

—— [OBMC] *The British Museum Catalogue of Printed Books* (1881-1900). Reprinted, Ann Arbor, 1946.

*Britwell Handlist*, S. R. Christie-Miller. London, 1933. 4 vols.

Brunet, Gustave. *La France Littéraire au XV$^e$ Siècle. Catalogue Raisonné.* Paris, 1865.

Brunet, J. C. *Manuel du Libraire de l'amateur de livres*, 6 vols. Paris, 1860-65. Supplément by P. Deschamps & G. Brunet, 1878-80.

Brussels. *Catalogue des Manuscrits de la Bibliothèque Royale des Ducs de Bourgogne.* [J. Marchal]. Brussels & Leipzig, 1839-42. 3 vols.

—— *Catalogue des Manuscrits de la Bibliothèque Royale de Belgique,* J. van den Gheyn & E. Bacha. Brussels, 1909-49. 13 vols. published. Incomplete.

Burger, K. *The Printers and Publishers of the 15th Century.* London, Supplement to Hain, by W. A. Copinger, indexed by Burger.

—— [Burger Dr. Sp.] *Die Drucker und Verleger in Spanien und Portugal von 1501-1586* . . . Leipzig, 1913.

—— [Burger MG&IT] *Monumenta Germaniae et Italiae typographica. Deutsche und italienische Inkunabeln in getreuen Nachbildungen.* Continued by Ernst Voulliéme. Berlin, 1892-1916.

—— [B] *Buchhändleranzeigen des 15. jahrhunderts.* Leipzig, 1907.

Cambridge. *Catalogue of the Manuscripts preserved in the Library of the University of Cambridge.* Cambridge, 1856-67. 6 vols.

—— M. R. James, *A Descriptive Catalogue of the Manuscripts in the Library of Corpus Christi College, Cambridge.* Cambridge, 1911-12. 2 vols.

—— M. R. James, *A Descriptive Catalogue of the Manuscripts in the Library of Jesus College, Cambridge.* London, 1895.

—— M. R. James, *Descriptive Catalogue of the McClean Collection of Manuscripts in the Fitzwilliam Museum.* Cambridge, 1912.

—— M. R. James, *The Western Manuscripts in the Library of Trinity College, Cambridge.* Cambridge, 1901. 4 vols.

—— M. R. James, *Bibliotheca Pepysiana: A Descriptive Catalogue of the Library of Samuel Pepys.* Part III—Mediaeval Manuscripts. London, 1923.

—— C. E. Sayle, *Early English Printed Books in the University Library, Cambridge.* Cambridge, 1900. 4 vols.

—— C. E. Sayle, *Fitzwilliam Museum. McClean Bequest. Catalogue of the Early Printed Books.* Cambridge, 1916.

—— Wormald, Francis & Phyllis M. Giles, "Handlist of Additional

MSS. in the Fitzwilliam Museum," Pt. I, in the *Transactions of the Cambridge Bibliographical Society*, I, pt. 3 (1951).

Campbell, M.-G.A.G. *Annales de la Typographie Néerlandaise au XV$^e$ siècle.* La Haye, 1874-90. 1 vol. and 4 supplements.

Camus, Jules. "Notices et Extraits des Manuscrits Français de Modène antérieurs au XVI$^e$ Siècle," *Revue des langues romanes*, 4th series, Vol. 35 (Modena, 1891), 212-15.

—— "Les 'Voyages' de Mandeville copiés pour Valentine de Milan," *Revue des Bibliothèques*, IV (1894), 12-19.

—— "La Venue en France de Valentine Visconti, Duchesse d'Orléans et l'inventaire de ses joyaux apportés de Lombardie," *Miscellanea di Storia Italiana*, 3d series, Vol. V (Torino, 1900), 39.

Caronti, Andrea. *Gli Incunaboli della R. Biblioteca Universitaria di Bologna.* Catalogo. Bologna, 1889.

Castan, A. *Catalogue des Incunables de la Bibliothèque Publique de Besançon.* Besançon, 1893.

*Catalogue Général des Manuscrits des Bibliothèques Publiques des Départements.* Old Series, III (1861), Sélestat; V (1879). Charleville.

*Catalogue Générale des Manuscrits des Bibliothèques Publiques de France.* Départements. New Series, V (1889) Dijon; VII (1889) Grenoble; XV (1892) Marseilles; XVI (1894) Aix; XIX (1893) Amiens; XXIV (1894) Rennes; XXVI (1897) Lille; XXXI (1898) Lyons; XXXVII (1905) Tours; XLVII (1923) Strasbourg; (1928) Chantilly.

Champion, Pierre. *La Librairie de Charles d'Orléans.* Tome XI, of the *Bibliothéque du XV siècle.* Paris, 1910.

Chantilly. *Le Cabinet des Livres Manuscrits. Institut de France. Musée Condé.* Paris, 1911. 3 vols.

Chapin Library. Williams College. *A Short-Title List*, Lucy E. Osborne. Portland, Me. and London, 1939.

Chicago, see Newberry.

Christie's *Catalogue*, May 22, 1901. No. 456.

Clarke, J. B. B. *Historical and Descriptive Catalogue of the . . . Manuscripts in the Library of the late Dr. Adam Clarke.* London, 1835.

Claudin, A. *Histoire de l'Imprimérie en France au XV$^e$ et au XVI$^e$ Siècle.* III, Paris, 1904. IV, Paris, 1914. 4 vols.

—— [Cl Paris] *The First Paris Press.* Illustrated Monographs issued by the Bibliographical Society, No. 6. London, 1898.

—— "Private Printing in France during the Fifteenth Century," *Bibliographica*, III (1897), 344-370.

Clausterneuburg. *Catalogus Codicum Manuscriptum, qui in Bibliotheca Canonicorum Regularium S. Augustini Claustroneopurgi asservatur*, H. Pfeiffer & B. Černík. Vienna, 1922.

Collijn, I. *Katalog der Inkunabeln der Kgl. Bibliothek in Stockholm.* Stockholm, 1914.

Copenhagen. *Catalogue Codicum Latinorum Medii Aevi Bibliothecae Regiae Hafniensis,* Ellen Jørgensen. Copenhagen, 1926.

Copinger, W. A. [C] *Supplement to Hain's Repertorium Bibliographicum.* London, 1897-1902. 2 parts in 3 vols.

Cordier, Henri. *Bibliotheca Sinica.* 2d ed. rev. Paris, 1906-07.

—— [Cordier, *Mél.*] *Mélanges d'Historie et de Géographie Orientales.* Paris, 1914-23. Vol. I reprints the Mandeville bibliography with few additions.

—— "Jean de Mandeville," *T'oung pao. Archives pour servir à l'Etude . . . de l'Asie Orientale,* II (1891), 288-323.

—— [Revue] *Revue de l'Extrême-Orient.* Paris, 1883. 3 vols.

—— [Odoric] *Les voyages en Asie au XIV$^e$ Siècle du Bienheureux Frère Odoric de Pordenone.* Vol. x, Recueil de Voyages et de Documents pour servir à l'histoire de la Géographie depuis le XIII$^e$ à la fin du XVI$^e$ siècle. Paris, 1891.

—— [BJ] *Bibliotheca Japonica: Dictionnaire Bibliographique des Oeuvres Relatifs à l'Empire Japonais.* Paris, 1912.

Cramer, Nicolaas A. *De Reis van Jan van Mandeville, naar de middelnederlandsche handschriften en incunablen.* Leiden, 1908.

Daunou, see Paris.

Davies, see Fairfax Murray.

Delisle, Léopold Victor. *Le Cabinet des Manuscrits de la Bibliothèque Impériale.* Paris, 1868. 3 vols.

—— *Mélanges de Paléographie et de Bibliographie.* Paris, 1880.

—— *Les Manuscrits du Comte d'Ashburnham.* Paris, 1883.

—— *Catalogue des Manuscrits des Fonds Libri et Barrois.* Paris, 1888.

—— *Fac-Simile de Livres Copiés et Enluminés pour le Roi Charles V.* Souvenir de la Journée du 8 Mars, 1903.

—— *Recherches sur la Librairie de Charles V.* Paris, 1907. 2 vols. and an Atlas.

De Ricci, Seymour, and W. S. Wilson. *Census of Medieval and Renaissance Manuscripts in the United States and Canada.* New York, 1935-40. 3 vols.

Dibdin, T. F., ed. Herbert's Ames, London, 1812. See Ames.

Didot, Ambroise Firmin- *Catalogue Illustré des Livres Précieux Manuscrits et Imprimés . . . de la Bibliothèque de M. Ambroise Firmin-Didot.* Paris, 1881. Sale 9-15 June.

Donaueschingen. *Die Handschriften der Fürstlich-Fürstenbergischen Hofbibliothek zu Donaueschingen,* K. A. Barack. Tübingen, 1865.

Dobrowsky, J. *Geschichte der Böhmischen Sprache und ältern Literatur.* Prague, 1818.

Dresden. *Katalog der Handschriften der Königl. öffentlichen Bibliothek zu Dresden,* Franz Schnorr von Carolsfeld. Leipzig, 1882.

Dublin. *Catalogue of the Manuscripts in the Library of Trinity College, Dublin,* T. K. Abbott. London, 1900.

Duff, E. Gordon. *Fifteenth Century English Books.* Illustrated monographs issued by the Bibliographical Society, No. 18. Oxford, 1917.

Durham. *Codicum Manuscriptorum Ecclesiae Cathedralis Dunelmensis Catalogus Classicus descriptus,* Thomas Rud. Durham, 1825.

—— *Catalogi Veteres Librorum Ecclesiae Cathedralis Dunelm . . . Mss. Preserved in the Library of Bishop Cosin, at Durham.* Publications of the Surtees Society, No. 7, 1838.

—— *The Durham Philobiblon,* I, pt. 2 (1949).

Du Verdier, Antoine. *La Bibliothèque d'Antoine Du Verdier . . . Contenant le catalogue de tous ceus qui ont escrit, ou traduict en françois . . .* Lyons, 1585.

See also La Croix du Main et Du Verdier.

Efferding. Eduard Lohmeyer, "Aus der Fürstliche Starhembergischen Schlossbibliothek zu Efferding," *Germania,* XXXI (1886), 215-232.

Entwistle, W. J., "The Spanish Mandevilles," *Modern Language Review,* XVII (1922), 251-257.

Erfurt. *Beschreibendes Verzeichniss der Amplonianischen Handschriften-Sammlung zu Erfurt,* Wilhelm Schum. Berlin, 1887.

Escalopier. *Catalogue de la Bibliothèque de M. Le Cte. Charles de L'Escalopier.* Paris, 1866-67. 3 vols. Collection presented to Amiens in 1870.

Esdaile, A. *List of English Tales and Prose Romances Printed Before 1740.* For the Bibliographical Society. London, 1912.

Essling, Victor Massena Prince d', [ESS] *Les Livres à Figures Vénitiens de la fin du XV$^e$ Siècle et du Commencement du XVI$^e$.* Florence & Paris, 1907-14. 6 vols.

Fairfax Murray, C. [FairMur (F)]. *Catalogue of a Collection of Early French Books in the Library of . . .* by Hugh W. Davies. London, 1910. 2 vols.

—— [FairMur (G)]. *Catalogue of a collection of Early German Books in the Library of* . . . by Hugh W. Davies. London, 1913.
Fava, D. [Fav (M)]. *Catalogo degli Incunaboli della R. Biblioteca Estense di Modena*. La Bibliofilia. Biblioteca de bibliografia italiana. Suppl. 7. Florence, 1928.
Gemeiner, see Regensburg.
*Gesamtkatalog der Wiegendrucke*. Leipzig, 1925-38. 7 vols. to "Eig" so far published.
Giessen. *Catalogus Codicum Manuscriptorum Bibliothecae Academicae Gissensis*, J. Valentino Adrian, Frankfurt a. M., 1840.
Glasgow. *Catalogue of the Manuscripts in the Library of the Hunterian Museum in the University of Glasgow*, John Young & P. H. Aitken. Glasgow, 1908.
Gotha. *Beiträge zur ältern Litteratur* . . . *der Herzogl. öffentlichen Bibliothek zu Gotha*, Fr. Jacobs & F. A. Ukert I, Leipzig, 1835.
—— F. T. Friedemann in *Zeitschrift für die Archive Deutschlands*, I, i (1846, 1847), "Gotha."
Göttingen. *Verzeichniss der Handschriften im Preussischen Staate*, W. Meyer. Berlin, 1893. II "Die Handschriften in Göttingen."
Gough, Richard. *British Topography*. London, 1780. 2 vols.
Graesse, J. G. T. *Trésor de Livres Rares et Précieux*. Revised and reprinted. Milan, 1950. Ed. London, Paris, Geneva, 1861. 7 vols. and suppl.
Grenville. *Bibliotheca Grenvilliana; or Bibliographical Notices of Rare and Curious Books forming Part of the Library of* . . . *Thomas Grenville*, J. T. Payne & Henry Foss. London, 1842—72. 4 vols.
Haebler, K. *The Early Printers of Spain and Portugal*. Bibliographical Society. Illustrated Monographs, No. 22. London, 1897.
—— *The Study of Incunabula*. With a foreword by A. W. Pollard. New York, 1933.
Haenel, G. *Catalogi Librorum Manuscriptorum, qui in Bibliothecis Galliae, Helvetiae, Belgii, Britanniae, Hispaniae, Lusitaniae, asservantur*. Leipzig, 1830.
Hain, L. [H] *Reportorium Bibliographicum*. Stuttgart & Paris, 1928-38. Reprinted Milan, 1948. 2 vols. in 4.
Halliwell, J. O. *Catalogue of Chap Books, Garlands, and Popular Histories in the possession of* . . . London, 1849.
—— *The Voiage and Traile of Sir John Maundevile, Kt.*, ed. by J. O. Halliwell. London, 1839.
Hamelius, P. *Mandeville's Travels, Translated from the French of*

*Jean d'Outremeuse*. Edited for the Early English Text Society, Original Series, 153 (1919), Vol. I, text. 154 (1923), Vol. II, introduction and notes.

Harvard. *Catalogue of English and American Chap Books and Broadside Ballads in Harvard College Library*. Bibliographical Contributions No. 56, W. Coolidge Lane. Cambridge, Mass., 1905.

Hazlitt, W. C. [Hazlitt H] *Hand-Book to the Popular, Poetical, and Dramatic Literature of Great Britain*. London, 1867.

—— [Hazlitt I] *Collections and Notes 1867-1876*. [First Series.] London, 1876.

—— [Hazlitt II] *Second Series of Bibliographical Collections and Notes on Early English Literature*. London, 1882.

—— [Hazlitt III] *Third and Final Series of Bibliographical Collections and Notes on Early English Literature*. London, 1887.

—— [Hazlitt IV] *Bibliographical Collections and Notes on Early English Literature. IVth Series (1893-1903)*. London, 1903.

Heber. *Bibliotheca Heberiana. Catalogue of the Library of the late Richard Heber*. Part XI, Manuscripts. Sold by Mr. Evans, 1836. And VIII, sold by Sotheby, 1834-37.

Heidelberg, *Katalog der Handschriften der Universitätsbibliothek in Heidelberg*, I, *Die Altdeutschen Handschriften*, K. Bartsch. Heidelberg, 1887.

Heitz, Paul & Fr. Ritter. *Versuch einer Zusammenstellung der Deutschen Volksbücher der 15. und 16. Jahrhunderts nebst deren späteren Ausgaben und Literatur*. Strasbourg, 1924.

Herbert's Ames, see Ames.

Heredia, Ricardo. *Catalogue de la Bibliothèque de M. Ricardo Heredia Comte de Benahavis*. Paris, 1893-94. 4 vols. in 2.

Heurck, E. H. van. *De Vlaamsche Volksboeken*. trans. Drs. J. Truyts. Antwerp, 1943.

Hind, A. M. *Introduction to the History of the Woodcut*. London, 1935. 2 vols.

*Historical Manuscripts Commission. Third Report of the Royal Commission on Historical Manuscripts*. Sneyd MSS. London, 1872. Also 46th Report, App. II.

Hodnett, Edward. *English Woodcuts. 1480-1535*. For the Bibliographical Society. Illustrated Monographs, No. 22. London, 1935 (for 1934).

Hoe, Robert. *Catalogue of Early English Books forming a portion of the Library of Robert Hoe*. New York, 1903.

—— [SC]. *Catalogue of the Library of Robert Hoe of New York*

... *to be sold by Auction by the Anderson Auction Co., New York, 1911-12.* 5 vols. in 4.

Holtrop, J. G. [Holtrop (H)] *Catalogus Librorum Saeculo XV$^e$ Impressorum. Quotquot in Biblotheca Regina Hagana asservantur.* The Hague, 1856.

Holtrop, J.-W. [Holtrop (M)] *Monuments Typographiques des Pays-Bas au Quinzième Siècle.* La Haye, 1867.

—— *Thierry Martens d'Alost.* La Haye, 1867.

Huntington [HEHL], see San Marino, Calif.

Huth, Henry. *Catalogue of the Printed Books, Manuscripts, Autograph Letters, and Engravings, collected by* . . . London, 1880. 5 vols.

——[Huth SC] *Catalogue of the Famous Library.* . . . *Collected by Henry Huth.* By Sotheby, Wilkinson & Hodge. London, 1913-20.

Iseghem, M. van. *Bibliographie de Th. Martens.* Malines et Alost, 1852.

Kerr, Robert. *General History and Collection of Voyages and Travels* . . . Edinburgh, 1811. 5 vols. Most of Vol. I from Hakluyt.

Klebs, Arnold C. *Incunabula Scientifica et Medica. Short Title List.* Bruges, 1938. Reprinted from *Osiris*, IV.

Koenigsberg. *Catalogus Codicum Manuscriptorum Bibliothecae Regiae et Universitatis Regimontanae,* A. J. H. Steffenhagen. Koenigsberg, 1867-72. Fasc. II, "Codices Historica."

Kraus, H. P. *Choice Manuscripts, Books, Maps and Globes. Important for the History of European Civilization and the Discovery of America, Catalogue 56.* New York, 1951.

—— *Fifty Select Books, Manuscripts, and Autographs, Catalogue 60.* New York, n.d.

—— *New Acquisitions. Fifty Outstanding Books and Manuscripts. Catalogue 49,* n.d.

La Croix du Maine, François Grudé, sieur de, et Antoine Du Verdier. *Les Bibliothèques Francaises.* Ed. A. Rigoley de Juvigny. Paris, 1772-73. 6 vols.

Långfors, A. "Notice du manuscrit Français 24436 de la Bibliothèque Nationale," *Romania*, XLI (1912), 206-246.

Langlois, E. "Notices des Manuscrits Français et Provençaux de Rome Antérieurs au XVI$^e$ Siècle," *Notices et Extraits des Manuscrits de la Bibliothèque Nationale et autres Bibliothèques,* XXXIII (1889), pt. II.

Laurent, J. C. M. *Peregrinatores Medii Aevi Quatuor.* Leipzig, 1864.

Lehmann, Paul (ed.). *Mittelalterliche Bibliothekskataloge Deutschlands und der Schweiz.* Munich, 1918, 1928. 2 vols.

Leiden. *Bibliotheca Universitatis Leidensis. Codices Manuscripti. I. Codices Vulcaniani.* Leyden, 1910.

Leighton, J. & J. *Catalogue of Early-Printed, and other Interesting Books and Manuscripts and Fine Bindings.* Pt. v. London, November 1905.

L'Escalopier, see Escalopier, Amiens.

Letts, Malcolm. *Sir John Mandeville: The Man and His Book.* London, 1949.

Library of Congress [LC]. *Exhibit of Books printed during the XVth Century and known as Incunabula.* Washington, 1930.

Libri. *Catalogue of the Choicer Portion of the Magnificent Library formed by M. Guglielmo Libri,* Sotheby & Wilkinson sale catalogue, Aug., 1859.

—— *Catalogue of the Extraordinary Collection* [MSS] ... *formed by M. Guglielmo Libri,* Sotheby & Wilkinson sale catalogue, March, 1859.

—— *Catalogue ... Miscellaneous ... Libri,* II (sale of 1861).

Liège. *Bibliothèque de L'Université. Catalogue des Manuscrits.* 1875.

—— *Catalogue des Manuscrits légués à la Bibliothèque de l'Université de Liège par le Baron Adrien Wittert,* Joseph Brassinne. Liège, 1910.

—— *Catalogue des Livres de la Bibliothèque de la célèbre Ex-Abbaye de St. Jacques à Liège.* Sale began 3 March, 1788.

—— S. Bormans, "La Librairie Collègiale Saint-Paul a Liège au xv$^e$ siècle," *Le Bibliophile Belge,* I (1867), 159-179, 223-237.

Lonchamp, F.-C. *Manuel du Bibliophile Français (1470-1920),* Paris and Lausanne, 1927.

London, see also British Museum.

—— *Catalogue of Additions to the MSS. in the British Museum,* 1848-1853 (1868).

—— *Ibid., 1888-1893* (1894).

—— *Ibid., for 1900-1905* (1907).

—— *Catalogue of* [Arundel and Burney] *Manuscripts in the British Museum.* New Series. London, 1840.

—— Thomas Smith, *Catalogus librorum MSS. Bibliothecae Cottonianae.* Oxford, 1696.

—— *A Catalogue of Manuscripts in the Cottonian Library ...* British Museum. London, 1802.

—— J. T. Payne & H. Foss, *Bibliotheca Grenvilliana; or Biblio-*

graphical Notices of Rare and Curious Books forming Part of the Library of . . . Thomas Grenville. London, 1842. 4 vols.
—— Francis Douce, Catalogue of the Harleian Manuscripts in the British Museum. London, 1808-12. 4 vols.
—— Robin Flower, Catalogue of Irish Manuscripts in the British Museum. London, 1926. 2 vols.
—— Sir George F. Warner & Julius P. Gilson, British Museum. Catalogue of Western Manuscripts in the Old Royal and King's Collections. London, 1921. 4 vols.
—— E. J. L. Scott, Index to the Sloane Manuscripts in the British Museum. London, 1904.
—— H. L. D. Ward, Catalogue of Romances in the Department of Manuscripts in the British Museum. London, 1883. 3 vols.
Lorenzen, Marcus, ed. Mandevilles Rejse, på dansk fra 15$^{de}$ Århundrede efter Handskrifter udgiven af M. Lorenzen. Skrifter No. 5 (3 parts), Samfund til Udgivelse af gammel nordisk litteratur. Copenhagen, 1881-82.
Lowndes, W. T. The Bibliographer's Manual of English Literature, ed. H. G. Bohn. London, 1883-85. 6 vols.
Lyons. Ant.-Fr. Delandine, Manuscripts de la Bibliothèque de Lyon. Paris, 1812. 3 vols.
Madrid. J. Z. Cuevas, Catálogo de los manuscritos castellanos de la Real Biblioteca de el Escorial. Madrid, 1926.
—— P. Miguélez, Católogo de los Códices Espãnoles de la Biblioteca del Escorial, II "Relaciones Históricas." Madrid, 1925.
—— García Rojo, D. and G. Ortiz de Montalván, Catálogo de Incunables de la Biblioteca Nacional. Madrid, 1945.
Maggs Brothers. Catalogue 536 (1930). 590 (1933). 656 (1938).
Maihingen. Handschriften-Verzeichnis. Öttingen Wallerstein'sche Sammlungen in Maihingen, G. Grupp. 1897.
Manchester. J. O. Halliwell, Account of the European Manuscripts in the Chetham Library, Manchester. Manchester, 1842.
—— [JRL] Catalogue of the printed books and manuscripts in the John Rylands Library, Manchester, England. Manchester, 1899. 3 vols.
Manley, J. M. & Edith Rickert, The Text of the Canterbury Tales. Chicago, 1940. 8 vols.
Martinsson, Sven. Itinerarium Orientale: Mandeville's Reisebeschreibung in Mittelniederdeutscher Übersetzung. Lund, 1918.
Mazzatinti, G. Inventari dei Manoscritti delle bibliotheche d'Italia. Forli, 1890—.
McKerrow, R. B. A Dictionary of Printers and Booksellers in England, etc. London, 1910.

Meerman, Jean. *Bibliotheca Meermanniana; sive Catalogus Librorum Impressorum et Codicum Manuscriptorum.* The Hague. Sale of 8 June, ff. 1824.

Mikulov, see Nikolsburg.

Milan. Lambertenghi Porro, *Catalogo dei Codici Manoscritti della Trivulziana.* ed. Giulio Porro. Biblioteca storica italiana, pub. per cura della R. Deputazione di Storia Patria, II. Torino, 1884.

Monneret de Villard, Ugo. *Il Nuovo Ramusio: I Liber Peregrinationis di Jacopo da Verona.* Rome, 1950.

Morgan, see New York.

Moule, A. C. and Paul Pelliot, *Marco Polo: The Description of the World.* London, 1938.

Munich. *Die Deutschen Handschriften der K. Hof- und Staatsbibliothek zu Muenchen.* Nach J. A. Schmellers *Kürzerem Verzeichniss.* . . . In Catalogus Codicum Manuscriptorum Bibliothecae Regiae monacensis. Tome v-vi ed. K. F. Halm. Munich, 1866.

Murr, see Nürnberg.

Muther, Richard. *Die Deutsche Bücherillustration der Gothik und Frührenaissance 1460-1530.* Munich & Leipzig, 1884.

Narducci, Enrico. "Opere geografiche esistenti nelle principali bibliotheche governative dell' Italia," in P. Amat di S. Filippo, *Studj Bibliografici e Biografici sulla Storia della Geografiche in Italia,* III, 391-470. Rome, 1875.

Newberry [NewbL]. Pierce Butler, *A Checklist of Fifteenth Century Books in the Newberry Library and in Other Libraries of Chicago.* Chicago, 1933.

New York. Pierpont Morgan Library [PML] A. W. Pollard, *Catalogue of the Manuscripts and Early Printed Books from the Libraries of William Morris, Richard Bennett, Bertram, Fourth Earl of Ashburnham, and other Sources, now forming a portion of the Library of J. Pierpont Morgan: Early Printed Books.* London, 1907. 3 vols.

—— Ada Thurston and Curt F. Bühler, *Checklist of Fifteenth Century Printing in the Pierpont Morgan Library.* New York, 1939.

Nicéron, J. P. *Mémoires pour servir à l'histoire des hommes illustres.* Tome xxv (1734), 250-255.

Nichols, John. *Illustrations of the Literary History of the Eighteenth Century.* Vol. v. London, 1828. 8 vols.

Nijhoff, W., & M. E. Kronenberg, *Nederlandsche Bibliographie van 1500 tot 1540.* 1938—.

Nikolsburg in Mähren. B. Dudík, "Handschriften der Fürstlich

## APPENDIX II

Dietrichstein'schen Bibliothek," *Archiv für osterreichische Geschichte,* xxxix (1868), 492-493.

North Carolina, University of. Olan V. Cook, *Incunabula in the Hanes Collection of the Library of the University of North Carolina.* Chapel Hill, 1940.

Nürnberg. Christopher Theophilus de Murr, *Memorabilia Bibliothecarum publicarum Norimbergensium et Universitatis Altdorfiae.* Pt. 1 Norimberga. Nürnberg, 1786.

Omont, Henri, ed. *Livre des Merveilles.* Réproduction des 265 miniatures Français 2810 de la Bibliothèque Nationale. 2 tomes. Pub. by the Bibliothèque Nationale Département des Manuscrits. Réproductions de manuscrits et miniatures de la Bibl. nat., xii, Paris [1907].

—— Omont. See also Paris. Bibliothèque Nationale.

Oxford. Bodleian Library. H. O. Coxe, *Catalogi Codicum Manuscriptorum Biblothecae Bodleianae,* Pt. ii, fasc. 1, Laud. Oxford, 1858.

—— W. D. Macray, *Catalogi Codicum Manuscriptorum Bibliothecae Bodleianae.* Pt. v Rawlinson. Oxford, 1862. Pt. ix Kenelm Digby. Oxford, 1883.

—— F. Madan, H. H. E. Craster, & N. Denholm-Young, *Summary Catalogue of Western Manuscripts in the Bodleian Library at Oxford.* Oxford, 1922-37. 6 vols.

—— W. H. Black, *A Descriptive, Analytical, and Critical Catalogue of Manuscripts bequeathed unto the University of Oxford by Elias Ashmole.* Oxford, 1845.

—— *Catalogue of the Printed Books and Manuscripts bequeathed by Francis Douce, esq. to the Bodleian Library.* Oxford, 1840.

—— H. O. Coxe, *Catalogus Codicum MSS. qui in Collegii Aulisque Oxoniensibus Hodie Adservantur.* Oxford, 1852-58. 2 vols.

—— A. Hackman, *Catalogi Codicum Manuscriptorum Bibliothecae Bodleianae, Pars Quarta. Codices . . . Thomae Tanneri.* Oxford, 1860.

Palau y Dulcet, Antonio. *Manual del Librero Hispano-Americano.* Vol. v. Barcelona & London, 1926.

Panzer, G. W. *Annalen der ältern deutschen Literatur.* Nürnberg, 1788-1805. 11 vols.

Paris. Bibliothèque Nationale. *Catalogue Général des livres imprimés de la Bibliothèque Nationale.* Reproduced 1924. 100 vols.

—— C. F. Daunou. *Catalogue des Incunables de la Bibliothèque Sainte-Geneviève,* ed. M. Pellechet. Paris, 1892.

—— *Catalogue des Manuscrits Français. Ancien Fonds.* Folio series, nos. 1-6170. Paris, 1868-1902.

## APPENDICES

—— H. Omont, *Ancien Supplément Français du Fonds Français, nos. 6171-15369 du Fonds Français*. Paris, 1895-96, 3 parts.

—— H. Omont & C. Couderc, *Ancien Saint-Germain Français, nos. 15370-17058 du Fonds Français*. Paris, 1898.

—— H. Omont, 8° Séries. *Anciens petits Fonds Français, nos. 20065-33264 du Fonds Français*. Paris, 1897-1902.

—— H. Omont, *Nouvelles Acquisitions Français*. 8° Séries, IV. Paris, 1918.

—— Gédéon Huet, *Catalogue des Manuscrits Allemands de la Bibliothèque Nationale*. Paris, 1895.

—— A. Vidier et P. Perrier, *Table Générale Alphabétique des ancien et nouveaux fonds 1-33264, nouv. acq. 1-10,000*. A. Vidier & P. Perrier. Paris, 1931-48.

—— Henry Martin, *Catalogue des MSS. de la Bibliothèque de l'Arsenal*. Paris, 1885-99.

—— P. Marais & A. Dufresne de Saint-León, *Catalogue des Incunables de la Bibliothèque Mazarine*. Paris, 1893-98 (with supplement).

—— H. Omont, ed. *Anciens Inventaires et Catalogues de la Bibliothèque Nationale*. Paris, 1908-21. 5 vols.

Paris, Paulin. *Les Manuscrits Français de la Bibliothèque du Roi*. Paris, 1836-48. 7 vols.

Pellechet, Marie. [Pell] *Catalogue Générale des Incunables des Bibliothèques Publiques de France*. Posthumous section, ed. Louis Polain. Paris, 1897-1901. 3 vols.

—— [Pell n.] Microfilm of unpublished notes in the Morgan Library.

Penny, C. L. *List of Books Printed before 1601 in the Library of the Hispanic Society of America*. New York, 1929.

Penrose, Boies. *Travel in the Old World from 1250 to 1650*. Philadelphia, 1945.

Pepysiana, see Cambridge.

Pertz, G. H. *Archiv der Gesellschaft für ältere deutsche Geschichtskunde* 1820-1874.

—— *Neues Archiv* ... Hanover, 1876-1935.

Phillipps. *Catalogus Librorum Manuscriptorum in Bibliotheca D. Thomae Phillipps, Bart*. Middlehill, 1837.

—— *Verzeichnis der von der Königlichen Bibliothek zu Berlin erworbenen Meerman-Handschriften des Sir Thomas Phillipps*. Berlin, 1892.

—— see also Sotheby.

Pierpont Morgan Library [PML], see New York.

Picot, E. *Catalogue des Livres composant la Bibliothèque de feu M. le Baron James de Rothschild.* Paris, 1884-1920. 5 vols.

Pinelo, Antonio Rodríguez de León. *Epitome de la Bibliotheca Oriental, y Occidental, Nautica, y Geografica de Don Antonio de Leon Pinelo.* [Pinelo's epitome of Barcia]. 3 vols. Madrid, 1937-38.

Plimpton, G. R. *The Education of Chaucer.* London, 1935.

Plomer, H. R. [Plomer I] *A Dictionary of the Booksellers and Printers who were at work in England, Scotland, and Ireland before 1640.* London, 1905.

—— [Plomer II] *A Dictionary of the Booksellers and Printers who were at work in England, Scotland, and Ireland from 1641-1667.* London, 1907.

—— [Plomer III] *A Dictionary of the Printers and Booksellers . . . 1668-1725.* London, 1922.

—— [Plomer IV], G. H. Bushnell & E. R. McC. Dix, *A Dictionary of the Printers and Booksellers . . . 1726 to 1775.* Oxford, 1932.

Polain, Louis. *Catalogue des Livres Imprimés au Quinzième Siècle des Bibliothèques de Belgique.* Brussels, 1932. 4 vols.

Pollard, A. W. & G. R. Redgrave [STC], *A Short-Title Catalogue of Books Printed in England, Scotland, & Ireland and of English Books Printed Abroad, 1475-1640.* London, 1926.

Proctor, Robert [Pr]. *An Index to the Early Printed Books in the British Museum . . . with notes of those in the Bodleian Library.* London, 1898-1903. 2 vols. with supplements.

[Praet, Joseph van]. *Recherches sur Louis de Bruges, Seigneur de la Gruthuyse.* Paris, 1831.

Quaritch, B. [Quaritch GC]. *A General Catalogue of Books Offered to the Public.* London, 1887-92. 7 vols. Supplements. Reprinted 1889-97. 10 vols.

—— *Catalogue no. 375* (Aug. 25, 1887). no. 389.

—— *Catalogue of Ancient Illuminated and Liturgical Manuscripts.* London, 1902.

—— *Rough List no. 82.* January 15, 1883.

—— *Catalogue no. 707* (1952).

*Recueil des Historiens des Croisades. Historiens Occidentaux.* Vol. IV. Paris, 1879.

Regensburg. Carl T. Gemeiner, *Nachrichten von den in der Regensburger Stadtbibliothek befindlichen merkwürdigen und seltenen Büchern aus der 15 Jahrhundert.* Regensburg, 1785.

Reichling, D. [R] *Appendices ad Hainii-Copingeri Reportorium Bibliographicum.* Munich & Münster, 1905-14. 8 parts.

Renouard, Ph. [Renouard IP] "Imprimeurs Parisiens," *Revue des Bibliothèques*, XXXII (Paris, 1922).

—— [Renouard *Les Marques*] *Les Marques Typographiques Parisiennes des xv et xvi Siècles*. Paris, 1926.

Riant. *Catalogue de la bibliothèque de feu M. le Comte Riant*, L. De German & L. Polain. Pt. 2, Vol. I. Paris, 1899.

Robinson, W. H. *Catalogue 77. A Selection of Extremely Rare and Important Printed Books and Manuscripts*. London, 1948.

Röhricht, Reinhold [R], *Bibliotheca Geographica Palaestinae*. Berlin, 1890.

Rosenthal, A., *Catalogue I, Secular Thought*, 1938.

Rosenthal, Jacques [Rosenthal IT], *Incunabula Typographica . . . à l'occasion du Cinquième Centenaire de Gutenberg*. Munich, n.d.

—— *Catalogue* CV.

Rothschild, see Picot.

St. Gallen. *Verzeichniss der Handschriften der Stiftsbibliothek von St. Gallen*. [Gustav Scherrer]. Halle, 1875.

Salvá y Mallen, Pedro. *Catálogo de la Biblioteca de Salvá*. Valencia, 1872.

Sandbach, Francis E. *Handschriftliche Untersuchungen über Otto von Diemeringen's Deutsche Bearbeitung der Reisebeschreibung Mandeville's*. Strassburg, 1899.

—— "Otto van Diemeringen's German Translation of Mandeville's Travels," *Modern Quarterly of Language and Literature*, II (1899), no. 5, pp. 29-35.

Sander, Max. *Le Livre à Figures Italiens (1467-1530)*. New York, 1941.

San Marino, California. H. R. Mead, *Incunabula in the Huntington Library*. San Marino, 1937.

Sayle, C. E. *Early English Printed Books in the University Library, Cambridge*. Cambridge, 1900. 4 vols.

—— *Fitzwilliam Museum. McClean Bequest. Catalogue of Early Printed Books*. Cambridge, 1916.

Schmidt, Charles. *Répertoire Bibliographique Strasbourgeois jusque vers 1530*. No. 3, "Jean Prüss père." Nos. 4, 7, "Hüpfuff," "Knoblouch," "Kistler." Strasbourg, 1893-96.

Schoerner, Arthur. *Die Deutschen Mandeville-Versionen: Handschriftliche Untersuchungen*. Lund, 1927.

Schönborn, Carl. *Bibliographische Untersuchungen über die Reisebeschreibung des Sir John Maundevile*. Breslau [1840].

Schramm, Albert. *Der Bilderschmuck der Frühdrucke*. Vol. IV

## APPENDIX II

(Sorg), Leipzig, 1921. Vol. xix (Richel), 1932. Vol. xx (Prüss, Kistler, etc), 1937.

Schreiber, W. L. [Schr.] *Manuel de l'Amateur de la Gravure sur bois et sur métal au XV$^e$ Siècle.* Vol. v. "Un Catalogue des incunables à figures imprimés en Allemagne, en Suisse, en Autriche-Hongre, et Scandinavie." Leipzig, 1910-11. 5 vols.

*Serapeum* xxviii (1867), III (1482).

STC, see Pollard and Redgrave.

Simek, Fr. *Cestopis t. zv. Mandevilla.* Prague, 1911 (not seen).

—— *Přehled dějin České Literatury od Počátku Literárního Tvoreni až po naše časy.* Prague, 1922.

Simrock, K. J. *Die Deutschen Volksbücher.* Frankfurt-am-Main [1850?]-1867. 13 vols. Reprinted Basle [1892].

Singer, Dorothy Waley. *The Library,* 3d ser. ix (1918), 275-276.

Sinker, Robert. *The Library of Trinity College, Cambridge. A Catalogue of the Fifteenth Century Printed Books in the Library of Trinity College, Cambridge.* Cambridge, 1891.

Sotheby, Wilkinson & Hodge. *Bibliotheca Phillippica.* Sale Cat., May, 1897. See also Phillipps.

—— *Catalogue . . . of a Selected Portion of . . . Manuscripts and . . . Books. The Property of the late Rev. Walter Sneyd.* Dec., 1903.

—— *Catalogue,* March, 1859, and Dec. 5, 1895 (no. 830).

—— *No. 581. Catalogue of the Magnificent Library . . . of the Rt. Hon. Lord Amhurst of Hackney* (by S. De Ricci), sold Dec., 1908, and March, 1909.

—— *Catalogue* of 25 Nov., 1952.

SR, see Arber.

Stillwell, M. B. [St] *Incunabula in American Libraries. A Second Census of 15th Century Books owned in the United States, Mexico and Canada.* New York, 1940.

Stockholm. C. Molbech, "Meddelser of Danske Handskrifter . . . Bibliothek i Stockholm," *Historisk Tidskrift,* iv (Copenhagen, 1843), 149-152.

Sunderland. *Bibliotheca Sunderlandiana. Sale Catalogue of . . . the Sunderland or Blenheim Library.* Puttick & Simpson. London, 1881.

Techener. *Description raisonnée d'une collection choisie d'anciens manuscrits . . . réunis par les soins de M. J. Techener.* Paris, i 1862. 2 vols. No more published.

Ternaux-Compans, Henri. *Bibliothèque Asiatique et Africaine; ou Catalogue des ouvrages relatifs à l'Asie et à l'Afrique qui ont*

*paru depuis la découverte de l'imprimerie jusqu'en 1700*. Paris, 1841 [42]. 2 parts. (Remarkably inaccurate.)
Thierry-Poux, O. *Premiers Monuments de L'Imprimerie en France au xv$^e$ Siècle*. Paris, 1890.
Thomas, Antoine. "Les Manuscrits Français et Provençaux des Ducs de Milan au Château de Pavie," *Romania*, XL (1911), 571-609.
Thomas, Henry [Thomas Fr] *Short-title Catalogue of Books Printed in France and of French Books Printed in Other Countries from 1470 to 1600 now in the British Museum*. London, 1924.
—— [Thomas Sp]. *Short-title Catalogue of Books Printed in Spain and Spanish Books Printed Elsewhere in Europe before 1600, now in the British Museum*. London, 1921.
Tobler, Titus. *Bibliographia Geographica Palaestinae*. Leipzig, 1867.
Tobolka, Z. *Knihopis Českých a Slovenských Tisků od doby nejstarší az do konce XVIII*. Století. Díl II. 1501-1800. Parts I-IV (A-O) so far issued. Prague, 1936-50. (A bibliography of books printed in Czechoslovakia, 1501-1800.)
Tours. A. Dorange, *Catalogue . . . Des MSS. de la Bibliothèque de Tours*. Tours, 1875.
Trier. *Beschreibendes Verzeichnis der Handschriften der Stadtbibliothek zu Trier*, Max Keuffer. Trier, 1894–. Pt. VII (1911).
Turin. *Codices Manuscripti Bibliothecae Regii Taurinensis Athenaei*, Joseph Pasin. Turin, 1749. 2 vols.
Truhlář, Josef. *Katalog Českých Rukopisů C.K. Veřejné a Universitní knihovny Pražské*. Prague, 1906.
Van Praet, Joseph B. B. *Catalogue des Livres de la Bibliothèque de feu le Duc de la Vallière*. Paris, 1788. See also Praet.
Vienna. *Tabulae Codicum Manuscriptorum Praeter Graecos et Orientales in Bibliotheca Palatina Vindobonensi Asservatorum*, P. Nelle. Vienna, 1864-99. 10 vols.
Vindel, Francisco. *Escudos y Marcas de Impresores y Libreros en España. . . . (1485-1850)*. Barcelona, 1942.
—— *El Arte Tipográfico en España durante el Siglo XV*. Madrid, 1945-51. 9 vols.
Vogels, J. "Das Vorhältnis der Italienischen Version der Reisebeschreibung Mandeville's zur Französischen," in *Festschrift dem Gymnasium Adolfinum zu Moers . . . vom Lehrercollegium des Gymnasiums zu Crefeld*. Bonn, 1882.
—— [LV] "Die Ungedruckten Lateinischen Versionen Mandeville's," *Programm des Gymnasiums zu Crefeld*. Crefeld, 1886.
—— [EV] "Handschriftliche Untersuchungen über die englische

Version Mandeville's" in *Jahresbericht über das Realgymnasium zu Crefeld.* Crefeld, 1891.

Voullième, Ernst [Voull (K)], *Der Buchdruck Kölns bis zum Ende des Fünfzehnten Jahrhunderts.* Bonn, 1903. Publikationen der Gesellschaft für Rheinische Geschichtskunde, XXIV.

—— [Voull (B)] *Die Inkunabeln der Königlichen Bibliothek und der anderen Berliner Sammlungen.* Leipzig, 1906.

—— [Voull (B Supp.)] *Die Inkunabeln der Preussischen Staatsbibliothek.* Neuerwerbungen der Jahre 1915-1922. Leipzig, 1922. XLIX Beiheft zum Zentralblatt für Bibliothekswesen.

—— [Voull (DD)] *Die Deutschen Drucker des XV. Jahrhunderts.* 2d ed. Berlin, 1922. 2 vols.

Waller, F. G. *Catalogus van Nederlandsche en Vlaamsche Populaire Boeken.* The Hague, 1936.

Warner, G. F., ed. *The Buke of Sir John Maundeuill: A Hitherto unpublished English version from the unique copy (Egerton MS. 1982) in the British Museum.* Edited together with the French text, notes, and an introduction. London, 1889. Roxburghe Club.

Weisbach, W. *Die Baseler Buchillustration des XV. Jahrhunderts.* Strasbourg, 1896. Studien zur Deutschen Kunstgeschichte, No. 8.

Weiss, Harry B. *A Book about Chapbooks.* Trenton, N.J., 1942. Biblio.

—— *Catalogue of the Chapbooks in the New York Public Library.* New York, 1945.

Wellek, René. *The Rise of English Literary History.* Chapel Hill, N.C., 1941.

Wing, Donald G. *Short-title Catalogue of Books Printed in England, Scotland, Ireland, Wales, and British America and of English Books Printed in other Countries, 1641-1700.* New York, 1945-51. 3 vols.

Wolfenbüttel. Otto von Heinemann, *Die Handschriften der Herzoglichen Bibliothek zu Wolfenbüttel.* Wolfenbüttel, 1897 ff.

Yéméniz, M. N. *Catalogue de la Bibliothèque de . . .* Paris, 1867.

Yule, Sir Henry, ed. and tr. *The Book of Sero Marco Polo.* 3d ed., revised by Henri Cordier. London, 1903. 2 vols.

Zambrini, Francesco. "I Viaggi di Gio. da Mandavilla," in *Scelta di Curiosita Letterarie inedite o rare,* Vols. 113, 114 Bologna, 1870.

Zarncke, Friedrich. *Der Priester Johannes.* Abhandlungen der Philologisch-historischen Classe der Königlich Sächsischen Gesellschaft der Wissenschaften, No. 7, 8. Leipzig, 1879-83.

# APPENDIX III: CASTLE OF THE SPARROWHAWK

Warner, *Buke*, p. 73 (Chap. 16).

*Norman French*

1. B. M. Harley 4383. fol. 31$^v$. Et en ceo pais il y ad un chaustel anxien qi siet sur un roche qils appellent le Chaustel del Esperuier . . .
2. Bod. Ashmole 1804. fol. 19$^v$. Et en ceo pays ya une chastell ancien qi seit sur un roche qils appellent le chastel de lesperuer
3. B. M. Harley 212. fol. 50. En ceo pais yad un chastel auncien qi siet sur une roche
4. B. M. Royal 20. A. I fol. 58. En ceo pais est une chastel anccien qi siet sur un roche
5. Durham C. L. B. III. 3 fol. 92$^v$. et en ceo pais yad un Chastel auncien q*ue* siet sur une Roche qills appallent la Chastel del Esperuier
6. Bod. Bodley 841. fol. 42. En ce pais ya un Chastell auncien q*ue* siet sur un roche qils appellent le chastell de Esperuier
7. B. M. Harley 204. fol. 49. Et en ce pais y ad un chastell auxien q*ue* siet sur un roche
8. B. M. Harley 1739. fol. 35$^v$. En ce pais yad un chastel auncien qi siet sur un roche
9. Durham, Cosin v.i.10. fol. 54. En ce pays ya ung chastel cest oultre la cite de Hayas et est ancien et siet sur ugne roche quilz appellent ainsy chastel de lempereur
10. B. M. Addit. 33757. fol. 37. En ce pais ya un chastel et est oultre la cite de layays et est auntien et siet sur une roche quil appellent ainsi chastel de lempereour
11. B. N. f.f. 25284. fol. 61$^v$. . . . a ung chastel ancien dont les murs sont couvers de une Yerre et sciet sur une roche
12. Bern No. 280. fol. 116. dont les murs sont touz couuers de edron q nous appellons rebun (?) et sciet sur une roche et est appelle le chastel de lessuier
13. B. M. Royal 20. B.X fol. 39$^v$. Et en ceo pais il yad un chastell auncien q sciet sõ un roch'
14. B. M. Sloane 560. fol. 21. en ceo pays Il yad une chastrel auncyen q*ue* siet sur une roche qils appellent le chastrel del Empero$^r$

15. B. M. Sloane 1464. fol. 81. en sa pais il ia un chastel ceo est outre la citee de Larais et est auncien et set sur un Roche qil appellent Ensuit [?] Chastel del Emp*ero*<sup>r</sup>
16. Bod. Addit. C 280. fol. 64<sup>v</sup>. En ce pahis il ya un chastel ce est outre la cite de Layais et est auncien et seet sur un roche qil appellent ensuit Chastel del Emperour
17. B.N. f.f. 5635. fol. 31. a un chastel et est toute la cité de laiais [Larais?] et est auncien et siet sur une roche
18. B.N. f.f. 2810. fol. 178. En ce pays y a un chastel ce est oultre la cité de Layais et est ancien et siet sur une roche qu'il appellent ainsis chastel de l'empereur .
19. B.N. f.f. 5633. fol. 85<sup>v</sup>. . . . . a ung chastel et est oultre la cité de layais et est auncien et siet sus une roche
20. Bern No. 58. fol. 44<sup>v</sup>. en ce pais ya ung chastel cest oult' la cite de laiz et sciet sur une roche quil appellent ainsi chastel de lay

### Paris French

21. B.N. f.f. 4515, fol. 45. En ce pays a vn chastel ancien, dont les murs sont couuers de i. yerre Eder et siet sur une roche et lappelle on le Chastel de Lespreuier, et siet oultre la cite de Layans.
22. B.N. f.f. 5637. fol. 46. i. castel ancien dont les murs sont couvers de eder c'est a dire yerre
23. B.N. f.f. 5634. fol. 39<sup>v</sup>. a un chastel ancien dont les murs sont couvers de une pierre [?] Eder et fut sur une roche
24. B.N. f.f. 6109. fol. 63. a un chastel ancien dont les murs sont couvers de un yerre et siet sur une roche
25. B.N. f.f. 2129. fol. 54<sup>v</sup>. un chastel ancien dont les murs sont couvers de une yerre eder, siet sur une roche
26. B.N. f.f. 10723. fol. 46. a un chastel ancien dont les murs sont augues tout couvert de eder que nous appellons yvi et siet sur une roche
27. Arsenal 3219. fol. 49<sup>v</sup>. En che pais a ii. chastiaus anchiens dont li mur sont augues tout couviert de eder que nous apellons yvi*m* et siet sur une roche et l'appiell'on le cashel del esprevier
34. Brussels 14787. fol. 39<sup>v</sup>. dont li mur sont augues tout couuert de eder que nous appellons ydm et siet sur une roche et lappellon le chastel de lespriuier . . .
35. B.M. Harl. 3940. fol. 22. En ce pais a un chastel ancien dont li mur sont couuers de Eder et sciet sur une Roche
36. Bern 125. fol. 135. dont les murs sont couuerts de l yerre Eder et siet sur une roche et lapelle on le chastel de lespreuier

37. Amiens, f. L'Esc. 95. fol. 74. ung chastel anchien dont le plus grant partie des murs sont couvers de edere que nous appelons et siet sur une roche et l'appellon le chastel de l'esprivier et siet entre la citè de Layas
38. Brussels 10439. fol. 93. dont le mur sont aucques couuierts de edron que nous appellons yviuy
39. Brussels 11141. fol. 38. dont les murs sont couuers de Eder que nous appellons yuy et siet sur une roche haulte et lappellon le chastre despreuier
40. Dijon 549. fol. 37. En ce pays a ung chastel dont les murs sont ausques tous couvers de cedre que nous apellons yvi et siet sur une roche et l'apellon le chastel d'esprevier
41. B.N. f.f. 5586. fol. 46. ung ancien chastel qui est sus une roche
42. B.N. f.f. 20145. fol. 52. a ung chastel ancien dont les murs sont couvers de edron que nous appellons plomb, et si siet sur une roche
43. B.N. f.f. 1403. lacuna of 2 leaves containing this passage.

*Ogier-Liège*

46. Chantilly 699. fol. 35ᵛ. vn chastrel viel & ancien dont ly murs sont couvert de Edere que nous appiellons lyre qui est vne herbe verde. Et siet sur vne Roche sy appiellon le chastiel de lespernier
47. B.N. f.f. 24436. fol. 31. a un chastel vielz et ancien dont les murs sont de edere [erased and *Lierre* written above] que nous appelons lyre [erased and *edera en latin* written above] qui est une herbe verde et siet sur une roche
48. Amiens, f. L'Esc. 94. fol. 63. Item en che paiis cit i. chastial anchiien dont ly murs sont alqueil tos covers de edere que nos apelons y. my [sic] et siet une rouche et l'apele on le chastial delle Espreuier et est oultre le citiet Layais
49. McClean 177. fol. 48. en laquelle a un chastel uiel et ancien dont les murs sont couvers de Cedre que nous appelons lire qui est un bois uert et siet sur une roche
50. Brussels 10420. j chastel anchien dont les muers sont pres tous couers de eder que nousappelons ivy et siet sur vne roche [quoted from Hamelius, II, 89].

# APPENDIX IV: THE FRENCH OF HARLEY 4383 COMPARED WITH COTTON AND EGERTON MSS. TRANSLATIONS

H. Comme il ensi soit qe la terre doutre mer, cest assauoir la Terre
C. For als moche as the lond beyonde the see that is to seye the holy
E. Sen yt es so that the land beyond the see, that es to say the

H. Seinte,      qe homme dit la terre de promission,
C. lond     that men callen the lond of promyssioun or of beheste
E. land of repromission,    that men calles the Haly Land,

H. vltre totes altres terres    soit la pluis excellente et la pluis dgne
C. passynge all othere londes    it is the most worthi lond most excellent
E. amanges all other landes    es the maste worthy land

H. et dame et soueraigne de touz altres terres,    et soit benoite
C. and lady and souereyn of all othere londes    and is blessed
E. and souerayne of all other,    and is blissed

H. et seintefie et consacree dul precious corps et du sang nostre
C. and halewed of the precyous body and blood of oure
E. and sacred and halowed of the preciouse blude of oure

H. seignur Ihesu Crist:    el la quelle terre il ly plesoit soy enombrer
C. lord jhesu crist;    jn the whiche land it lykede him to take flesch
E. Lorde Ihesu Criste;    in the whilke land it lykede him to take lief

H. et la virgine Marie et char humaigne prendre et noricion,
C. and blood of the virgyne Marie
E. and blude of oure Lady Saint Marie

H. et la dite terre marcher et enuironer de ses benureez piez.
C. to envyrone that holy lond with his blessede feet;
E. and to enuirun that land with his blissed fete.


H. . . . . . . .
C. And there he wolde of his blessedness enoumbre him in the seyd blessed and gloriouse virgine Marie and become man
E. . . . . . . .


H. Et ou il voleit meint miracle     faire et precher et enseigner la foy
C. and worche many myracles     and preche and teche the feyth
E. And there he didd many miracles     and preched and teched the faithe


H. et la ley de nous Cristiens,     come a ses enfantz;     et ou il veolt
C. and the lawe of crystene men     vnto his children.     And there it lykede
E. and the lawe of us Cristen men,     as vnto his childer;     and thare he


H. meint reproeche et meinte mokerie porter et soeffrer pur nous.
C. him to suffre many repreuynges and scornes for us
E. sufferd many reprufes and scornes by us.


H. Et de celle terre singulerement veolt estre appellez Roi
C. . . . . . . .
E. . . . . . . .


H. cil qi Roiz estoit de ciel,     de terre, de ayr, de meer, et de touz
C. And he that was kyng of heuene     of eyr of erthe of see and of all
E. And he that was King of heuen     and of erthe, of the air and of the see, and of all


H. choses contenues en y ceaux,     et il mesmes sappella Roi par
C. thinges that ben contayned in hem     wolde all only be cleped kyng
E. thingz that er contened in tham,     wald be called all anely king

## APPENDIX IV

H. especialtee de celle terre, en disant *Rex sum Iudeorum*
C. of that lond whan he seyde: *Rex sum Iudeorum:*
E. of that land,

H. . . . . . . .
C. that is to seyne: I am kyng of Jewes.
E. . . . . . . .

E. *interpolates:* as the prophete saise, *Noli timere, filia Syon: ecce, rex tuus venit tibi mansuetus,* that es to say, 'thou doghter of Syon, dred thou noght; for lo, thi kyng commes to the, dulye mylde and meke'

H. quar luy lors estoit celle terre proprement des Iuys;
C. . . . . . . .
E. . . . . . . .

H. et celle terre il auoit eslite pur luy entre totes altres terres
C. And that lond he chees before all other londes
E. and that land he chose before all other landes

H. come la meilleure et la pluis vertuouse et la pluis digne
C. as the best and most worthi lond and the most vertuouse lond
E. as the best and the maste worthy

H. de monde; qar ceo est luy corps et ly my lieux de totes la terre
C. of all the world. For it is the herte and the myddes of all the world,
E. of the werld; . . . . . . .

H. de monde, et auxi, come dit le philosophe, *Virtus rerum in medio*
C. Wytnessynge the philosophere that seythe thus *Virtus rerum in medio*
E. for as the philosophere saise, *Virtus rerum in medio*

H. *consistit.*
C. *consistit* that is to seye: the vertue of thinges is in the myddes.
E. *consistit,* that is to say, 'the vertu of thingez es in the myddes'

# INDEX OF MANUSCRIPTS

Aix 437 (F45),280
Amiens, fonds L'Escalopier 95 (F37),278
    fonds L'Escalopier 94(F48),282
Augsburg, CXXIX* (L?),311
Bamberg, J. M. Misc. Hist. 112 (G12),314
    Misc. Hist. 182 (G31),317
Basel, E II 8 Fol. (G43),320
Belgioioso, see Milan, 275
Belluno, Bibl. Lolliniana 39 (L16), 302
Berlin, Cod. Electoralis 868 (L20), 303
    Diez C Fol. (L28),305
    Görres 153-Lat. Qu. 711 (L37),307
    Germ. Fol. 205 (G1),312
    Germ. Fol. 1268 (G13),314
    Germ. Fol. 1066 (G44),320
    Germ. Fol. 912 (G51),321
    Germ. Quart. 322 (Du3),324
    Germ. Fol. 204 (Du8),325
    Germ. Fol. 550 (Du10),325
    Germ. Quart. 271 (Du11),325
Bern, A 280 (F12),268
    58 (F20),271
    125 (F36),277
Bonn (L38),307
Breslau, M 1073 (G30),317
Brussels, 14787 (F34),276
    10439 (F38),278
    11141 (F39),279
    10420-25 (F50),283
    1160-63 (L19),303
    21520 (L36),307
    720 (Du6),324
Cambridge, Fitzwilliam, M<sup>c</sup>Clean 177 (F49),114,282

Fitzwilliam, CFM 23 (F52), 284
UL, Dd I 17 (E5),289
Trinity, R 4.20 (E13),291
UL, Ff V 35 (E20),293
Magdalen, Pepysian 1955 (E21),293
UL, Gg I 34³ (E29),295
Corpus C., 275 (L3),298
Jesus 35 (L9),300
Corpus C., 426 (frag.) (L),311
Cambridge, Harvard U., Riant 50 (F44),280
Cape Town, S.A. (Du13),326
Chantilly, Musée Condé 699 (F46), 280
Charleville, 62 (L13),302
Copenhagen, Gl. Kgl. S 445 (L21), 304
    Ny Kgl. S 172 8° (L),311
    3559 (Da4),327
Coventry, 12* (E),297
Devon, Pa. (B. Penrose) (E6),289
Dijon, anc. fonds 549 (F40),279
Douai 313* (F a),286
Donaueschingen, 483 (G36),318
Dresden, F 69 a (L39),307
Dublin, Trinity, E 5.6 (E25),294
Durham, Cathedral, B III 3, Pt. II (F5),266
    Univ., Cosin V. i 10 (F9),267
    Univ., Cosin V. iii 7 (L8),300
Düsseldorf, G 12 (L40),308
    Frag. (Du14),326
Edinburgh, formerly Advocates 19. i.ii (E24),294
Erfurt, Bibl. Boin., Quart. 3 (2) (L14),302
Erlangen, Univ., Sammelmappe 2112, no. 35 (G6),313

* The asterisk indicates a ghost, or a lost manuscript. (F45) means French manuscript number 45, etc.

# INDEX OF MANUSCRIPTS

El Escorial, M iii 7-115 iii 7- Est 15.4 (S1),332
Florence, B. N. Cent., Cod. Magl. XXXV, 221 (It1),329
    Bibl. Ric., Cod. 1917 (It9),331
    Bibl. Ric., Cod. 1910 (It10), 331
    B.N. Cent., (It13),332
Giessen 160 (L25),304
    992 (G27),317
Glasgow, Hunterian, T.4.1 (84) (L7),300
Gotha, 192 (L45),308
    A 26 (G9),314
    584 (G14),314
Göttingen, Hist. 61 (L&G),310
    Hist. 823 (G46),321
    Hist. 823b (Du5),324
Grenoble, anc. fonds 962 (F53),284
The Hague, Y 302 (1191) (Du7), 324
Halle, YD, Quart. 8.14 (G26),316
Hamburg, Hist. Germ. Fol. 31b° (L),310
    Cod. Geog. 58 (Du2),323
Heidelberg, Pal. Germ. 65 (G15), 315
    Pal. Germ. 138 (G16),315
    Pal. Germ. 806 (G49),321
Hohenfurt, 12 XVI Fol. 133 N (L frag.),311
Karlsruhe, 167 (G2),313
Klosterneuburg, Canon Reg. S. Aug. 132 (L26),305
    1083 (G32),318
Königsberg, 334 (L44),308
Krisovniku Monastery (Cz6),328
Leiden, Vulcan 96 (L1),298
    Vossianus Lat. Fol. 75 (L24), 304
    BPL 14 F (Du4),324
Liège, Biblio. de l'Univ., 360° (F51),283
    Biblio de l'Univ., 354 (L32), 306
    Biblio. de l'Univ., Wittert 99 (L47),309
Biblio. de St. Jacques 490 (L49), 309
Lille, Fonds Godefroy 121 (F55), 285
London, B.M. Harl. 4383 (F1),265
    Harl. 212 (F3),265
    Royal 20 A. I (F4),266
    Harl. 204 (F7),266
    Harl. 1739 (F8),266
    Addit. 33757 (F10),267
    Royal 20 B. X (F13),268
    Sloane 560 (F14),269
    Sloan 1464 (F15),269
    Harl. 3940 (F35),277
    Addit. 34802 (F extract), 286
    Cotton Titus C. XVI (E1),288
    Egerton 1982 (E2),288
    Royal 17 C. XXXVIII (E8),290
    Royal 17 B. XLIII (E9), 291
    Harl. 3954 (E10),291
    Arundel 140 (E19),293
    Harl. 2386 (E26),294
London, Robinson, *Cat.* 77, no. 144 (E27),294
    B.M. Sloan 2319 (E28),295
    Addit. 33758 (E33),295
    Addit. 37049 (E abridgment),297
    Egerton 672 (L2),298
    Royal 13 E. IX (L4),299
    Cotton App. IV (L5),299
    Harley 175 (L6),299
    Harley 82 (L10),301
    Harley 3589 (L23),304
    Addit. 37512 (L30),306
    Cotton Otho D I (L extracts),311
    Addit. 17335 (G17),315
    H. Eisemann, dealer (G33),318
    B. M., Addit. 18026 (G39),319
    Addit. 10129 (G50),321

## INDEX OF MANUSCRIPTS

Addit. 41329 (It8),331
Egerton 1781 (Ir2),333
Addit. 33993 (Ir3 frag.), 334
Addit. 24189 (Pict.),334
Lübeck, 63b* (G),323
Lucca, 304 (It12),332
Lüneburg, C 8 Fol. (Du9),325
    D 25 (Du15),326
Lyons, Palais des Arts, 28 (F54),284
Madrid, 9602 (Ee 65) (F33),276
Magdeburg, XII, 15 (III, 209 4° 75d) (Du1),323
Maihingen, MS 1,2 Fol. 31 (L31), 306
    HS I,3. 4° 8 (G34),318
    HS I,3 Fol. 11 (G52),321
Manchester, Chetham's Library, 6711,4 (E11),291
Mantova (It3),329
Marseilles, A b 14 *(Fd),286
Middlehill, see Phillipps MSS.
Mikulov (Nikolsburg), Sig. II. 162 (L46),309
    Sig. I. 33 (Cz4),328
Milan, Trivulziana, Cod. 816 (F31),275
    Ambrosiana, H 188 (It2), 329
Modena, Bibl. Est., fonds franc. 33 (F29),274
Munich, CGM 329 (G5),313
    CGM 693 (G7),313
    CGM 593 (G18),315
    CGM 332 (G28),317
    Univ., Cod. Octavo 179 (G35), 318
    CGM 594 (G40),319
    CGM 4872 (G41),319
    CGM 695 (G47),321
    CGM 252 (G48),321
    CGM 299 (G53),322
    CGM 694 (G54),322
    Cod. Ital. 1009 (It11),332
Nápoli, XII D 57 (It7),331
Naworth Castle, Yorkshire* (E),297
Neuberg (Cz2),328
New York, H. P. Kraus (L17),302
    H. P. Kraus (L18),303
    Columbia Univ., Plimpton 264 (L29),305
    Public Library, Spencer Coll. (G42),319
    Pierpont Morgan Library, 746 (It6),330
Nikolsburg, see Mikulov.
Nürnberg, Solgeriana 34.15 (G58), 322
Odense, Karen Brahes Bibl. (Da3), 327
Oxford, Bodl., Ashmole 1804 (F2), 265
    Bodl. 841 (F6),266
    Addit. C 280 (F16),269
    E Museo 116 (E3),289
    Rawlinson D 99 (E4),289
    Rawlinson D 100 (E7), 290
    Bodley Addit. C 285 (E12),291
    Balliol 239 (E14),292
    Queen's 383 (E15),292
    Rawlinson B 216 (E17), 292
    Douce 109 (E18),293
    Laud 619 (E22),293
    E Museo 124 (E23),294
    Rawlinson D 101 (E30), 295
    Douce 33 (E31),295
    Tanner 405 (E32),295
    Ashmole 751 (E extracts), 297
    Douce 45 (E extracts),297
    Ashmole 769 (L11), 301
    Bodley Addit. A 187 (L22),304
    Laud Misc. 721 (L27),305
    Fairfax 23 (L33),306
    Addit. C 252 (It4),330
Paris, B. N., fonds fr. 25284 (F11), 267

f.f. 5635 (F17),270
anc. f.f. 2810 (F18),270
f.f. 5633 (F19),270
f.f. nouv. acq., 4515 (F21),272
f.f. 5637 (F22),272
f.f. 5634 (F23),272
f.f. 6109 (F24),273
f.f. 2129 (F25),273
f.f. nouv. acq. 10723 (F26),273
Arsenal 3219 (F27),274
B.N., f.f. 5586 (F41),279
f.f. 20145 (F42),279
f.f. 1403 (F43),280
f.f. 24436 (F47),282
Biblio. Firmin-Didot 59* (F56),285
B.N., f.f. 13423* (Fb),286
f.f. 25519* (Fc),286
6447 (?) (L),311
Allemand 150 (G3),313
Parma, 1070 (It5),330
Praha, 421 (G19),315
Museum, Codex III E 42 (Cz1),328
from Strahove (Cz3),328
Museum, Codex V E 11 (Cz5),328
Codex V E 12 (Cz8),328
Univ., XVII J 12 (frag.) (Cz9),329
Rennes, 598 (Ir1),333
Rome, Vatican, Lat. Reg. 750 (F30),275
Reg. 837 (F32),276
Fondo Chigi F VII, 171 (?) (L),310

Rugby, Arnold Lib., Bloxham Collection (E34),296
St. Gallen, 628 (G20),315
St. Paul in Kärnten, Cod. Hosp. 210 (G56),322
Salzburg, St. Peter, B IV 37 (G55), 322
San Marino, Calif., HM 114 (E16), 292
Sélestat, 25 (G4),313
Soest, 28 (Du12),326
Stockholm, K 31 (Da1),327
55 (Da2),327
Strasbourg, 30 (L41),308
2119 (G21),315
Stuttgart* (G),323
Tambach, 7 (G38),319
Tours, 947 (F28),274
Trier, 334 (L42),308
1935, 13 (G22),316
Turin, H-III-1 (L15),302
Venêzia, Marciana, It. VI 208 (extract) (It),332
Vienna, Cod. 5363 (L12),301
Cod. 4459 (L43),308
3529 (excerpt) (L),311
2838 (G11),314
12449 (G24),316
12475 (G45),320
2850 (G57),322
Warsaw, Niem, Q 4.1 (G29),317
Wiesbaden, B 25 (G23),316
Wolfenbüttel, 23.2 Aug. (L34),306
18.6 Aug. (L35),307
14.10 Aug. (G10),314
32.8 Aug. (G25),316
23.10 Aug. (G37),319
Würzburg, MS. Fol. 38 (G8),313

# MANUSCRIPTS FROM FAMOUS COLLECTIONS NOW DISPERSED

Ashburnham, Barrois 380 (F52),284
    Barrois XXIV (F21),272
    Libri 1699 (It13),332
Barrois 185 (F21),272
Belgioioso 166 (F31),275
Bernard's *Cat.*, B 613 (E17),292
    B 1457 (Coventry*),297
Bibliothèque Nat., f.f. 5636 (F21), 272
British Museum, Grenville XXXIX (F10),267
    Grenville XL (E33),295 [see also (E18),293]
Clarke 218 (L2),298 (see also p. 309)
Coblenz, Gym., Sectio Görres 1844 (L37),307
    Sectio Görres 33 (G13),314
Berlin, Diez 75 (L28),305
    Sectio v. Stahremberg 55 (G44),320
Dresden, F 184b (G33),318
Efferding, Signatur 55, no. 2 (G44),320
Heber 1008 (F49),283
    1009 (F46),281
    1010 (G50),321
    1088 (E16),292
Idstein (G23),316
Leighton, *Cat.*, 3284 (F52),284
"Libri XXIV," see (F21),272
Libri 645 (L48),309
    1699 (It13),332
Lord Amhurst of Hackney (L),309
Lyell, James P. R., of Abingdon,

Berks. (E36),296
Maggs *Cat.*, 572, no. 910 (E),296
Markaunt, Tho. (L3),299
Meerman 885 (F57),285
Münster, Biblio. Paulina (Du3),324
Naworth Castle (Bernard's *Cat.*) (E17),292
    (W. H. Robinson, *Cat.*, 77) (E27),294
    (Earl of Carlisle's),297
Nikolsburg (Cz4),328
Norton MS. (E),296
Nürnberg, Ebneriana 60 (G31),317
Ossek (Balbin MS.) (Cz1),328
Phillipps 1930/885 (F57),285
    4439 (F),286
    6650 (L17),302
    8252* (Fe),286
    8252/1088 (E16),292
    9019 (835 in sale, 1898) (F49),282
    13660 (L30),306
Quaritch (1902, p. 33, no. 76) (F26),274
    (1902, p. 56, no. 122) (L30),-306
Rosenthal *Cat.*, I (1939), no. 25 (G42),319
St. Märgen 2 (G2),313
St. Paul im Laventthal (G56),322
St. Petersburg, Q IV, 1 (G29),317
Sneyd MS., Keele Hall, co. Stafford. (E35),296
Techener, 104 (F46),281
Thornton, William (E29),295
Weringerode, Zb 25 (G42),319

## ADDENDA

Two more manuscripts, one in German and one in Italian, were brought to my attention after page proof was complete. Both are advertised for sale by Bernard M. Rosenthal, Inc., 19 East 71st St., New York (Catalogue I, issued in May, 1954, Nos. 65 and 66), with facsimile samples of text for each.

No. 65 is an excerpt of Otto von Diemeringen's German version. Paper. 15th century. 18 leaves. In one gathering. 305 × 197 mm. 2 cols. Cursive hand. Caps. and rubrication in red. Text begins on fol. 2 recto: Lamori dasz lant ist von Calamai do sant thomas list bij lij dagereisen vnd zehet man von sant thomas . . . Ends on fol. 18 recto: Die lercer spucchent daz alle waszer komment bz dean paradise . . .

From the shop of Jacques Rosenthal in München about 1932. This seems to be a sample, or trial piece. Fol. 1 is conjunct with fol. 18 which contains only 2 lines at the top of the recto. Fol. 1 is blank, but of the same paper as the rest of the MS. At 2 points corrections have been pasted over the text (3 lines on f. 12, and a few letters on f. 14). These slips are in the hand, and on the paper of the rest of the text, and suggest that the scribe had no way of erasing, since he was writing on paper and not on parchment. Some catalogue and library marks on the covers.

No. 66 Italian. Fragment. Paper. 15th century. 20 leaves in 1 gathering. 217 × 153 mm. 34 long lines. Small cursive hand. Rubrics faded, and pointing hands sketched in, in black ink. First 33 chaps. of text, covering the travels in Palestine.

Bookplate of Conte Paolo Vimercati-Sozzi, Cavaliere dell' Ordine de SS. Maurizio e Lazzario. Other catalogue numbers inside the covers of modern paperboard.

The outside of the first and last leaf of the MS are very brown, and the outer margins are badly damp-stained, affecting about an inch at the edge of the text throughout.

# INDEX

Abingdon, 213, 219
Abraham, 30
Abry, Louis, 92, 154
Acosta, Joseph de, 233
Acre, 15, 18, 60, 63, 70, 149
Adam and Eve, 36, 40, 67, 75, 120, 124, 126, 259
Aelian, 39
Aesculapius, 50
Aix-la-Chapelle, 80, 114, 115, 145
Albert of Aix, 22, 71, 164
Albertus Magnus, 128
Alexander, 31, 126, 150, 152; romances of, 23, 39, 43, 46, 84, 224, 226
Alexander's gate, 79, 80
Alexandria, 63, 128
alliterative revival, 206, 221, 222, 223, 224
alphabets, 23, 65-66, 85, 119, 121, 140, 172, 236, 255
Amazons, 30, 79, 248
Ameneville, Petronilla de, 191, Hugh de, 191
America, 1, 2, 12, 24, 231, 234, 236, 237
Amiens MS., 114, 130
Amundaville, 188
*Ancient Deeds in the Public Record Office, A Descriptive Catalogue of* (1890 ff.), 193, 194, 195, 196, 197
Andaman, 37, 67, 248
Andromeda, 23, 248
Anglure, Ogier VIII de, 57, 58
anthropophagi, 246
Anti-Christ, 79
antipodes, 123, 233, 251
Antonio de Torquemada, 241
Antonius Diogenes, 39
Arabia, 108
*Arabian Nights*, 77, 80
Arabic, 61, 62, 63-64, 66, 128

Ararat, 27
Ariosto, 1, 242, 248, 249
Aristeas, 39
Aristotle, 128
Arles, 27, 50
Armenia, 18, 27, 50, 145, 227, 237
Arnoldus Saxo, 128
Arsenal MS. *3219*, 170
Arthur, 23, 147, 251; romances of, 61
Arundel, Earl of, 206, 209; MSS., see British Museum
Asia, 24, 49, 225
Assassins, garden of, 31-32, 44-46, 248, 249, 253, 256, 257
astrolabe, 138
Athlît, 64
Atiya, A. S., *Crusade in the Later Middle Ages*, 16, 18, 55, 62, 63, 64, 69, 70, 73, *Nicopolis*, 21, 69
Athanasius, 26
Augustinian priory, 209
Augyles, 52
Austin Friars, 206, 207
automata, 79; see peacocks
Avignon, 97, 150
Avezac, 17, 19, 91
*Avowes al poun*, 224
Avroy, 92, 156
Aymer de Valence, 191

Babylon, 60
Babylonian Captivity, 150
Backer, L., 80, 82
Bacon, Roger, 20
Baîbars, 64
Balau, Sylvan, *Étude*, 94-95, 96, 97, 110, 153, 159, *Comment*, 152
Bale, J., 213, 215, 219, 241, 245, 251, *Illustrium*, 90, 154
Barbe, see Jean de Bourgogne

## INDEX

Barington, Nicholas de, 198; Dru de, 198
*Barlaam and Josophat,* 21
barnacle goose, 44, 222, 241
Barnet, East, 191, 215
Barre, Jean, 229
Bartholomaeus Anglicus, 61, 76, 77, 86, 139, 232
Basse Sauvenière, 105, 114, 116, 117
Bayot, A., 94-95, 152
Beauchamp, Guy de, 194, 223; Pain de, 184; Simon de, 184
*Bel Inconnu, Le,* 50
Belisby, 188, 189
Benedetto, L. F., 49, 83, 248
Bennett, H. S., 95
Bernard de Breydenbach, 23, 65, 82
Bern MS., no. *58,* 171; no. *125,* 83, 229
Bernáldez, Andrés, v, 235
Berry, see Jean Duc de
Bethlehem, 26, 59
Bevis of Southampton, 253
Beyrouth, 63, 177
Bible, 5, 45, 48, 69, 73, 81, 123, 256
Bibliothèque Nationale, MS. *2129,* 167; MS. *2810,* 83, 171; MS. *4515,* 37, 65, 111, 112, 116, 127, 135-146, 149, 151, 165-167, 173, 227, 230; MS. *4516,* 160; MS. *5633,* 171; MS. *5634,* 167; MS. *5635,* 171; MS. *5637,* 167; MS. *6109,* 167; MS. *10723,* 114, 139, 141, 142-143, 144, 145; MS. *12326,* 128; MS. *24436,* 84, 113; MS. *25284,* 171
Bickerstaff, Isaac, 254
Black Notley, 185, 186, 192ff., 214
Black Prince, 150
Bledelewe, Richard, 213, 219
blood, 77, 78
Bodley MS. *264,* 223; Addit. MS. *280,* 171

Boemus, John, 240
Bohemia, 9
Bohuns, 185, 191, 193, 200, 207, 222; estates, 190, 200, 215; library, 207, 208, 223-224; illuminated service books, 206; Eleanor, 208, 223; Humphrey VIII, 194, 198, 200, 208, 223; Humphrey IX, 203, 205, 206, 215, 223; Humphrey X, 207, 208; John, 189, 200; William, 194, 224
Boiardo, 248
Boldensele, 16, 26, 51, 57, 58, 59, 60, 61, 64, 82, 153, 164, 177, 229
Bondelmonti, 50, 51
Bongars, Jacques, 22, 71
*Book of Seth,* 123, 124, 126
books, see library
Borgnet, A., 92, 153
Borham, 193, 195, 196, 197, 203
Bormans, S., 92, 103, 110, 114, 152, 153, 154, 155, 159
Borneo, 63
Boroughbridge, 15, 163, 200, 208, 223
Boschini, 50
Bourgogne, see Jean de
Bourgogne, Ducs de, Philippe, 165, 168, 173, 228, 229, 230; Jean sans Peur, 229
Bovenschen, 20, 24
Bragmans, 46, 72, 73, 108, 237
Brahmins, 73, 75
Brehier, 108, 127
British Museum, 257; Addit. MS. *24189,* 175; Arundel MS. *140,* 84; Ashmole *1804,* 207; Cotton Appendix IV, 211; Cotton Otho D II, 229; Cotton Titus C XVI, 6-7, 8, 34, 44, 46, 141, 142, 143, 144, 149, 230, 237, 239, 240, 243, 254, 255, 260; Egerton MS. *1982,* 7-8, 66, 85, 86, 111, 135, 139, 146, 211, 237-240; Grenville XXXIX,

## INDEX

135, 146; Harley MSS 257; no. *175*, 211; no. *212*, 209; no. *3940*, 170; no. *3954*, 84; no. *4383*, 135, 140, 142-143, 144, 145, 149; Royal 20 B X, 135; Royal 13 E IX, 239; Sloan MS. *1464*, 135, 170; Sloan MSS., 146
Bristol, 100
Britain another world, 139
Brittany, Duke of, 99, 100
Brocard of Mt. Sion, 22, 71, 153; and see pseudo-Brocard
Brome, Richard, 251
Bromfield, 192 ff., 199, 203, 214
Browne, Sir Thomas, 77, 252, 256, 257
Bruce, Robert, 71, 189, 198, 203
Brunetto Latini, 20, 22-23, 68, 152, 164
Brussels MS. *10420*, 112, 114, 119, 145, 146, 149
*Brut Chronicle*, 177
Buckhorn Weston, 183, 186, 187
Budge, E. A. W., 18, 33
Bullein, W., 244
Bunyan, Paul, 77
Bunyan, John, 253
Burchard, see Brocard
Buridan, John, 202, 234
Burgeron, 255
Burgundy, see Bourgogne
Burley, Sir Simon, 66
Burton, Robert, 252
Burton, Thomas de, 208, 210, 213
Bury, see Richard d'Aungerville

Cadiz, 52
Cairo, 60, 63, 104, 128, 160
Calamye, 108
Calonak, 118
Cambridge Univ. MS. Dd I *17*, 84
Cambyuskan, 225
Cameron, K. W., 183, 186 ff., 190, 193, 195, 196, 198
Camden, 214
Campa, 36

Campdi, or Camperdi, 92, 97, 98, 148
Cansay, 41
Canterbury, 241; Archbishop of, 209, 224
Canton, 18
Carpini, Jean du Plan de, 17, 19, 20, 44, 62, 80, 153, 155, 164, 226, 246, 258
Carroll, Lewis, 1, 253, 259
Cashio, 191, 199, 200, 215
Caspian Sea, 79
Cassan, 29
Castile, Eleanor of, 206; arms of, 206
Catalan, 175
Cathay, 15-17, 71, 82, 109, 118, 235, 236, 249, 258; see China
*Cathay*, see Yule; Odoric; Jordanus
Caxton, W., 238, 239, 240
*Cenocephali*, 246
Cervantes, 1, 241
Ceylon, 34, 40, 67
Chaldea, 30, 62, 124, 127
*Chanson de Antioche*, 23
*Chanson de Jerusalem*, 23
Chantilly MS., 111-134, 142-143, 145, 148
Charlemagne, 23, 100, 107, 114, 115, 117
Charles the Bald, 114-115, 146
Charles IV, 201
Charles V, 165-168, 174, 227, 230
Charles VI, 166, 227
Chartres, 114, 115, 146
Chatham, 192, 193, 199
Chaucer, 5, 9, 24, 25, 63, 71, 78, 81, 84, 161, 177, 226, 227, 259, 260; Chaucer's knight, 55; "Knyghtes olde," 224-226
Chester, T., 50
*Chevalier du Cigne*, 25
Chew, S. C., 19, 60, 192, 195, 245, 246
China, 17, 18, 19, 32, 37, 40, 41, 47, 49, 108, 179, 233, 235, 236, 255, 257; and see Cathay

## INDEX

Chinese, 43, 65, 83, 119
Christian abbots, 109
Christine de Pisan, 1, 49, 227, 228
circumnavigation, 36, 38, 114, 115, 137, 172, 231, 233, 237, 258
*Cleannesse*, 221
Clavijo, 51, 59
climates, seven, 31, 136, 139
Clutterbuck, 197, 206, 213
Cochin China, 36
Coene, Jacques, 229
Coker, 183, 186, 187
Colchester, 185
Cold Harbor, 206
Coleridge, S. T., 12, 45, 256, 257
Columbus, C., 38, 231-236; Ferdinando, 234
Comestor, Peter, 22, 66, 86, 164
commercial interests, 13, 55, 56, 62-64
communism, 75
confession, deathbed, 93, 147, 157, 158, 160, 162
Constance of Castile, 206
Constantinople, 51, 56, 59, 80, 81, 180
Cordier, H., 16, 18, 31, 82, 96, 220, 257
cormorants, 41, 83
Cornelius Nepos, 235
Cos, 50, 141
Cotton translator, 6-7, 142, 179, 230, 257
Courtenay, Sir Hugh, 195
Crécy, 47, 188, 189
Crétien, Gervaise, 165-167, 230; schools of, 167
crocodile, 31, 32
Cross, 56, 80, 81, 176, 180
Crown of Thorns, 80-81
crusade, 15, 17, 51, 69, 71, 74, 253; Albigensian, 73, 99
crystal globe, Mandeville's 241
Ctesias, 39, 252, 256
customs, strange, 75, 240
Cyprus, 55, 56, 57, 71, 80, 180, 188
Czech, 111, 121, 219, 220

Dampier, W., 255
Danish, 111, 121, 219, 220
Danois, 108, and see Ogier
Dead Sea, 76
Dedication, letter of, 85, 125, 126, 150
Delisle, L., 137, 140, 166, 167, 172, 228, 230
Defoe, 4, 12, 49, 257
Dekker, 246
Delaville Le Roulx, J., 55, 70
*De Mirabilibus Mundi*, 83
Denmark, 9, 71, 107
Derby, Earl of, 224
Desert of Lop, 247
Despensers, 162; Hugh le, 100
Devon, 184, 186, 187
diamonds, 31, 62, 76, 77, 113, 116, 130, 132, 133, 257
Dibdin, T. F., 257
*Dictionary of National Biography*, 92, 190
*Directorium ad Philippum regem*, 22, 71
D'Israeli, Isaac, 258
doctor, 90, 101, 102, 154.
Dome of the Rock, 60
Dondin, 37
Don Juan, King of Aragon, 175
Donne, J., 25
Dorset, 183, 184, 186, 187, 195, 198
Douglas, 201
dove, 82
Draco, 50
dragon-woman, 50, 137, 141, 257, 258
Drake's voyage, 245
dry sea, 29, 85
dry tree, 28, 226
Dubois, Pierre, 62, 70
Duell, R., 90, 101
Dunstable, Tournament of, 102
Durand, 22
Durham, Bp. of, see Richard d'Aungerville
Durham MS, Cosin V. iii. 7, 211

## INDEX

Dutch version, 65, 111, 219, 220, 230

Early English Text Society, 259, 260; and see Hamelius
Earthly Paradise, 45, 47, 67, 108, 109, 226, 248, 249, 254, 257, 258
eating habits, 44
East, 74, 168, 203, 236; see Cathay, China, Far East
Eastern Empire, 51
East, Thomas, 244, 250
Eccard, J. G., 65
Eden, Richard, 241, 245
editions, 1, 5, 231, 236, 237, 250, 253, 256, 260; lost ed. 241; ed. of 1725, 102
Edmonton, 190, 200
Edward I, 70, 120, 176, 189, 206
Edward II, 15, 18, 100, 194, 198, 200
Edward III, 15, 18, 63, 70, 71, 85, 100, 125, 126, 150, 177, 208, 215, 224, 250
Egypt, 60, 61, 116, 125, 129, 149
Egyptians, 124
Elizabethan stage, 246-248
*Encyclopaedia Britannica*, 92
end of the world, 79
Enfield, 190, 200, 206, 214, 215
England, 63, 105, 139, 165, 167, 170, 176, 179, 183, 184, 203, 211, 243
English, 6, 111, 150, 161
English miles, 178-179
English version, 103, 210, 211, 238, 251, 252, 254, 260; shorter version, 230
engulfed city, 51
Enias, 223
Entwistle, W. J., 175, 241
epicure, rich, 47, 48, 257
epitaph, 89-92, 93, 96, 97, 98, 100, 102, 147, 157, 158, 159, 160
Erghom, John, 207

Ernoul, 22
errors in translation, 6, 7
Erzrum, 27
Essex, 184-186, 189, 190, 192, 193, 195, 197-200, 205, 207, 212, 214, 215; Earldom of, 184 ff.
Este library, 174
Ethiopia, 31, 52, 76
Eugesippus, 22
Euphrates, 27
Everyman's library, 260

Fabricius, J. A., 123, 155, 255
fairy mistress, see sparrowhawk
Far East, 15, 54, 173, 245; see China, Cathay, East
Farrer, W., 185, 193, 197
father of English prose, 2-3, 254, 256
Fazy, Robert, 52, 57
*Feet of Fines for Essex*, 190, 193, 196, 197, 199
"Fermes," 40
*Fierabras*, 242
fingernails, see epicure
fish, 36, 76, 85, 118
Flamel, Jean, 229
Flanders, 63, 99, 220, 224; Counts of, 99
*Fleur des Istories de la terre d'Orient*, 228; see also Hayton
*Florimant*, 230
Folger Shakespeare Library, 84
folklore, 50-53, 80, 257
Foster, J., 101, 102, 188
Fountain of Youth, 35, 85, 107, 140, 258
*Four P's*, 237
free thinkers, 75
French, 6, 8, 9, 71, 84, 109, 111, 126, 165, 176, 177, 194, 205, 230, 242
French editions, 235
Friars, martyred, 32, 41
Froissart, 71, 93, 100, 148, 201, 205
funduqs, 63

426                              INDEX

Ganges, 67, 109
gap, Egypt, see Pynson
garden, see Earthly Paradise, Assassins
Garnett, R., 10, 101
Gathalabrica, 127
Gatholonabes, see Assassins
Gaunt, John of, 206, 224
Gaveston, Piers, 194, 195, 203
*Gawain and the Green Knight*, 221, 259
Gaza, 64
Genghis Kahn, 80, 156
Geoffrey of Monmouth, 176
geographers, Renaissance, 231, 240
Georgians, 72
German MSS., 219
Germany, 9, 111, 121, 157, 178, 220, 230, 235, 236, 243
*Gerusalemme Liberata*, 253
Gervaise, see Crétien
Gervase of Tilbury, 40, 51, 227
*Geste de Houn de Bourdeaux*, 152
*Geste de Jean de Launchon*, 152
*Geste de Liége*, 106, 117, 152
*Geste de Ogier le Danois*, 106, 152
Ghistelles of Artois, 112
giant, 24, 25
Gildeston, 193
Gloucester, Thomas Duke of, 208, 209, 210, 212, 216, 223, 230
Gobert, T., 94-95, 96
Gobions, 191
*Godefroi de Bouillon*, 23, 172
Godfrey of Boulogne, 223
Gog and Magog, 78, 79, 259
Golding, A., 53, 77, 78, 245
Golgotha, 66
Gomes de Santo Estevão, 241
Gomorrah, 30
Gondebuef of Friesia, 118-119
Gorgon's head, 51
gout, 105, 116, 181
Gower, 3, 9, 31, 73, 176, 208, 242, 243, 254
Grabhorn Press, 260
Great Khan, see Khan

Great Lees, 192, 214
Great Samford, 193
Greece, 55
Greeks, 5, 46, 60, 66, 72
Greek Sea, 52, 187
Grenville editions, 257
griffins, 235
Grousset, René, 18, 64
guidebook, 70, 72
Guillemins, 90, 92, 96, 154, 158
Gulliver, 42, 253, 255
Guy, Earl of Warwick, 223
Guiana, 126, 245
*Gy Earl of Werwyke*, 84

Hadrian, Emperor, 40
Hainville, 214, 215
Hakluyt, 16, 19, 30, 48, 82, 91, 104, 117, 245, 246, 249, 250, 251
Halliwell-Phillipps, 258
Halyfield, 196, 215
Hamelius, 3, 6, 20, 21, 22, 24, 31, 51, 66, 73, 75, 78, 82, 93-94, 96, 98, 104, 105, 106, 107, 111, 134, 138, 146, 147, 148, 149, 150, 152, 153, 155, 156, 158, 162, 165, 181, 182, 202; opposition to, 94-95
Hang-chow, 41
Haningfield, 196, 197, 215
Happy Isles, 249
Hardinton, 186
Harvard College Library, 137, 166
Hatfield Broadoak, 198
Hayton, 21, 28, 44, 64, 80, 82, 153, 155, 164, 226, 228, 229
Hazart, Jean, 175
headless men, see monstrous races
heat, 31
Hebrew, 62, 79, 120, 129, 159, 160; alphabet, 65, 140, 167
Henkin Levo, 114, 116, 117
Henry of Glatz, 38
Henry II, 185
Henry III of Castile, 59
Henry IV, 100, 211
herbal, 113, 124-127

# INDEX

hermaphrodites, 37, 75
Hermes, 124
Herodotus, 39, 47, 240, 242, 243
Hertford, 98, 100, 172; hundred, 191
*Hertford,* see *Victoria History of*
Hertfordshire, 102, 184, 189, 193, 199, 205, 215, 222, 246
Heyward, John, 237, 241
Higden, 9, 31.
Hill of Evil Council, 58
Hill, E., 238
Hippocrates, 50
Historical MSS. Commission, 186, 189, 190, 198
*Historie de chevaler a cigne,* 223
Holderness, 208, 209
Holy Land, 15, 22, 26, 50, 54, 56, 58, 60, 65, 68, 69, 70, 71, 72, 118, 176, 209, 242, 248
Holy Places, 237
Holy Sepulchre, 164
Holywood, see Sacro Bosco
Homer, 42, 254
Honorius of Autun, 23
Hormuz, 31
Hospitalers, 55, 56, 71, 187, 188, 197
Hrabanus Maurus, 23, 65
Hundred Years' War, 16, 71, 105
Hungary, 151
Hunt, Leigh, 257
Hunterian Museum MS., 211
Huntington Library MS., 84, 243
*Huon of Bordeaux,* 242
Hwang-ho, 67

idol, giant, 52
illumination, 141, 175
images, worship of, 48
imaginary travels, 8, 253
*Imago Mundi,* 21, 23, 233
incunabula editions, 231
India, 17, 30, 31, 35, 36, 39, 46, 52, 53, 57, 63, 75, 77, 108, 118, 119, 148, 152, 222, 237, 258; books of, 124

Indian, 62, 116, 124, 127, 139, 235, 240
Indian priests, 58
Indies, 232, 235, 236, 247; East Indies, 63
*Indicator,* 258
Indus, 31, 67
Ingmanthorp, 209
inhabitability of earth, 234
interpolations, 6, 83, 85-86, 93, 97, 104-106, 108, 112, 113-134, 136-139, 145 ff.
interpolator, 105, 110
Ireland, 176, 182, 235, 236
Irish, 111, 183
Irish MSS., 219
Irving, Washington, 51, 234
Isabel, Queen, 100, 175, 201
Isidore, 31, 34, 37, 39, 77, 86
Ismena, 193
isle, 29, 139
Italy, 9, 57, 61, 97, 220, 230, 236, 242
Italian, 111, 220; editions, 235; MSS., 219, version, 72
itineraries of Palestine, 22
ivy, 145, 407-409

Jackson, Isaac, 182
Jack the Giant-Killer, 256
Jacobite, 72
Jacques de Vitry, 21, 22, 57, 59, 73, 153, 164
Jacques Laires, 100
Jane, Cecil, v, 233, 235
Java, 63, 109, 120
Jean le Bon, King of France, 15, 167, 172, 173, 175
Jean d'Arras, 27, 227
Jean le Bel, 93, 100, 148
Jean Duc de Berry, 168, 173, 227, 228, 229
Jean de Bourgogne, 3, 4, 11, 91-97, 101-106, 110, 112, 113-114, 125, 127, 128, 130, 147, 149, 154-155, 157, 158-162, 164-169, 181; works, 159, 165-168

## INDEX

Jean le Long of Ypres, 21, 82-83, 229
Jean d'Outremeuse, 3, 11, 91-94, 97-110, 113, 117-122, 123-134, 147-160, 164, 169, 177, 182, 212
Jean de Stavelot, 97
Jean de Vignay, 83
Jean le Vaillant, 100
Jerusalem, 58, 60, 71, 107, 114, 136, 149, 150, 176, 237
jewels, 128, 129, 210-211
Job, 29, 73
Johannes Scotus, 67
John, King, 150
John Fitz John, 101
John of Gaunt, 172
John of Jandun, 168, 202
John of Portugal, King, 38
Johnson, Samuel, 2, 9, 254
Jonson, Ben, 246, 251
Joppa, 23, 107, 248
Jordan, 214; and see Mandeville.
Jordan of Elsynge, 215
Jordanus, 28, 34, 41, 44, 153
*Joseph of Arimathea*, 84
Josephus, 22, 123
Juggernaut, 35
Julius Caesar, 52
Justinian, 51, 52, 59

Kashan, 29
Khan, Great, 38, 42, 43, 44, 62, 80, 82, 109, 195, 225, 229, 237, 258
Khan of Persia 18
Kipling, 258
Knights of St. John, see Hospitalers
Kublai Khan, 17, 64, 256; and see Khan
Kurth, G., 93, 99, 100, 103, 117, 147, 148, 153, 159

Lactantius, 233
La Fontaine, 257
Lamary, 36, 75

Lamb, Charles, 256
Lancaster, Thomas Duke of, 200
Lancheri, 109
land of darkness, 47
Lane, E. W., 77, 80
Lange, H., 224, 226
Langland, 73
Langlois, C. V., 70, 111, 130, 175
Lango, 50, 141
language, Mandeville's, 1, 2, 4, 6, 8, 61, 85, 97, 239
lapidaries, 76, 77, 97, 98, 113, 114, 116, 127-134, 147, 152, 157, 221
Lascelles, Mary, 20, 226
Latin, 6, 8, 86, 94, 103, 104, 106-110, 111, 112, 115, 118-119, 121, 125, 147, 211, 212, 220, 238, 239, 245, 250, 251; second trans., 213; MSS., 219; editions, 235
Laurent, J. C. M., 16, 22, 79
Lear, 247
leeches, 34
Leeu, Gerard, 86
Le Fort, 92, 154
*Legenda Aurea*, 23, 164
*Legends of the Cross*, 23
Leighe, Great, see Great Lees
Leland, John, 213, 214, 215, 241
Leon, 241
leopards, 57
Lettenhove, 71, 201
letter of defiance, 85
*Letter of Prester John*, 21, 29, 31, 35, 37, 40, 44, 62, 84, 225, 226
Letts, Malcolm, 4, 8, 20, 21, 23, 28, 42, 58, 65, 66, 69, 95, 103, 106, 111, 114, 119, 128, 138, 146, 158, 181, 241
Levant, 55, 72
Leyden, Vulcan MS. 96, 213, 219
*Libeaus Desconus*, 50
library, monastic, 164, 165, 219; medieval, 82

Libya, 68
Liège, 3, 4, 11, 31, 89-130, 146-169, 170, 175-176, 181-182, 212, 213, 215, 220-221, 230, 251; accent on, 3; dialect, 117, 121, 128; inscription, 246; Prince Bishop, 156, 159
Lincoln, Bishop of, 224
Lincolnshire, 188, 189
lion, silver, 100, 102, 103
Little Stanmore, 190
*Livre d'Artus*, 51
*Livre des Merveilles*, 171, 175, 228, 229; and see B. N., *2810*
Lockleys, 191
Lombardy, 46, 176, 178
London, 172, 179, 183, 206, 213, 214, 237
London, William, 253
Loomis, Laura H., 66, 168, 186, 223
lost city, 51
Lot, 30
Louis the Great, 151
Louis, Duc de Orléans, 229
Lovell, Sir Thomas, 214
Louvre Library, 166, 167, 227
Low Countries, 9, 163, 230
Lowes, J. L., 21, 30, 46, 48, 225, 247, 256
Lucian, 39
Lusignan, 27, 56, 71, 227, 228
Ludolph von Suchen, 60
Lull, Ramón, 62, 70, 73, 74
Lyon MS., 83; editions, 236-237; University of, 63

McClean MS. *177*, 114, 170
*Macbeth*, 78
Macray, W. D., 223, 224
Magi, 29
Mahomet, 45, 52; see Mohammedanism
maidenheads, 52
Malacca, 63
Malabar, 34, 35, 37, 63, 67

Mallet, Giles, 165, 167, 172, 227
Mande villani, Johannes, 201
Mandeville, Arms of, 101-102, 181, 186
Mandeville, Honour of, 185, 191, 205
Mandeville, Adam de, 191; Ernulf, 184, 189, 190, 200; Earl Geoffrey, 184, 186, 189, 192; Geoffrey Fitz Piers, 185; Gunnilda, 199; Henri, 202; JOHN, of Belisby, 188-189; of Black Notley, 193-197; of Borham, 195-196, 197; clerk, 197-199; of Edmonton, 190; of Enfield, 190, 215; of Little Stanmore, 190; of Marshwood, 186-188; of Paris, 201-202; of Pleshy, 205-207; Jolani, 189; Jordan, 194, 195, 197; Martin, 183; Sir Richard, 182; Robergia, 187; Robert, 182; Simon, 194, 197; Sir Thomas, 193-195, 197-200, 203, 214; Walter, 184, 192, 193, 194, 197, 198, 199; Wilkin, 191.
Mandeville, Sir John, autobiography, 89-90, 181, 212, 226; BIOGRAPHY, 3-4, 11, 90-106, 116, 147 ff., 163-164, 192-204, 208-216; dates, 15, 54, 89, 106, 135, 149, 151, 226-227; age of, 195, 202-203; Doctor of Medicine, 91, 154, 164; Doctor of Theology, 202; Englishman, 69, 139, 145, 176-180, 215-216, 260; a layman, 69, 220
  CHARACTER, 2, 5, 11, 49, 53, 69-86, 89, 111; charity, 5, 33, 34, 42, 74; faith, 5, 34, 66, 73-74, 156; modesty, 5, 35, 46, 124; tolerance, 73-74
  LEARNING, 15-25, 67, 164; geography, 38, 58, 67, 231-235; knowledge of England, 176-

179; mentality, 56, 76, 124; library, 154-155, 232-236; travel, 24, 54-68.
  LITERARY QUALITIES: use of allusion, 50; narrative art, 4, 42, 48, 80, 124; folklore, 50-53, 80, 257-258; genre of, 19, 38, 39-40, 53, 83-84; creation of illusion, 26; economy, 28; human interest, 33; on human nature, 42; humor, 5, 9, 36, 46, 48, 74-75, 76 ff., 86, 226; imagination, 69, 138, 236, 244, 250, 256-257, 260; interpretation, 45; literary devices, 61, 64, 65-66, 139; literary skill, 4-5, 9, 10-11, 17, 25, 26-39, 42-44, 48, 53, 68, 69 ff., 78, 216, 259-260; methods, 11, 26 ff., 40, 60, 68, 76-82, 136, 255; on miracles, 32; mistakes, 58, 60, 64, 67; purpose, 69-86; satire, 5, 42, 77-78; sources, 15-16, 19-24, 26-53, 54, 59, 67, see plagiarism; source-hunters, 3, 8, 49, 56; strange words, 61-63; item, 29, 140, zogh and thorn, 66, 177; style, 119-120, 136-138, 139-140, 148; Norman French, 1, 6, 10, 179-180, 242; symbolism, 51-52; verisimilitude, 29-30, 44, 66, 85 ff., 117, 216
  REPUTATION, 1-4, 8-11, 208-215, 219 ff.; borrowings from, 107-109, 219 ff., borrowing of style, 48; allusion to, 219 ff., 249; Father of English prose, 2-3, 254, 256
  TRANSLATIONS, English, 6-10, 85, 97, 236, 238-240, 243, 254; Latin, 103-110, 117, 147, 219, 238, 239, 245; many languages, 111, 219-220, 241-242
  APOCRYPHA, 123-134, 148, 157
  AUDIENCE, 1, 56, 74
Manduith, John, 154, 155
Mangevilayn, John, 162
manna, 29, 30, 256
manuscripts, 1, 29, 30, 84, 165; best MSS., 135; dated, 168; distribution, 170; number of, 219; reproduction of, 175, price, 220
Manzi, 37, 41, 43
Marco Polo, 8, 15, 18, 19, 20, 21, 28, 29, 31, 32, 33, 36, 37, 38, 40, 41, 43, 44, 45, 47, 48, 49, 58, 64, 67, 72, 75, 77, 83, 149, 153, 215, 219, 226, 229, 234, 235, 247, 248, 250, 251, 252, 253, 256, 258
Marignolli, 19, 34, 38, 58, 67, 76, 195, 199, 233
Marino Sanudo, 22, 70, 71, 154
Markaritot, 61
Marshwood, 184, 186, 187, 188, 193, 195, 198
Marsilius of Padua, 202
marvels, 24, 38, 40-41, 48, 67, 76, 246 ff.; and see monstrous races
*Marvels of the East,* 40
masques, 246
masses for the dead, 42
Matabrune, 242
Mauritania, 31
Meaux Abbey, 208
mechanical birds, 46
Megasthenes, 39
Melior, 27, 227
Mélusine, 27, 227, 228
Menghers, C., 97
Mercator, 231, 240, 245
merchants, 55, 56, 63
Merton College, 154
Michel, Louis, 94-95, 103, 107, 110, 118, 147, 148, 152
Michelant, Henri, 22, 98, 127
Middlesex, 185, 189, 190, 205
*Midsummer Night's Dream,* 247
Milan, 173; Duke of, 175
miles, 178
Milke, 77

## INDEX

Milton, 2, 11, 12, 246, 252, 253
Mimms, 190, 200; North Mimms, 191; South Mimms, 185, 189, 190
Ming dynasty, 18
miniatures, 141
*Miracles of Our Lady, Book of,* 86
missionaries, 17, 33, 62, 63, 74
Mohammedanism, 18, 73, 108
Mongol empire, 17
Mongoli, 79
Monks, Chinese, 41, 42
monstrous races, 31, 37, 39, 74, 76, 240, 242, 245, 246, 247
Montaigne, 1, 242
Montégut, E., 74, 253, 257
Monfort, 97, 98, 99, 100, 102, 129, 148
Montfort, Earl of, 92; Count of, 99-103, 161; Henri de, 99; Simon de, 99, 101, 133
Montpellier, 128, 188
Moor, C., 183, 185, 193
Moors, 85
Morant, P., 193, 197, 198, 215
More, Sir Thomas, 12, 66, 73, 236, 237, 239, 240, 241
Morgan le Fay, 107, 147
Morley, H., 3, 10
Morris, William, 1, 258
*Morte Arthure,* 221
Mortimer, Roger, 201
Mortorelli, 50
Moule, A. C. and Paul Pelliot, 32, 49, 64, 149, 234, 258
Moscovy, 241
Mt. Aetna, 61
Mt. Sinai, 59, 60, 81
Mt. Sion, 58
Mowbray, Sir John, 162, 163
Münster, 241, 245, 246
Murray, David, 159, 161, 165
Murray, Hugh, 258
Mynors, R. A. B., 114, 135, 170, 211
*Myreur des Histors,* 91, 92, 93, 99, 100, 105, 106, 107, 108, 109, 118, 123, 134, 147, 148, 152, 153, 155, 156, 158, 160, 182; date of, 110

Nacumera, 37
naked men, 75
natural history, 24, 129
natural law, 34, 35, 36, 76
natural religion, 33, 48, 72, 73, 74, 237
navel of the world, 71
Near East, 15, 22, 24, 54, 61, 62, 66, 136, 173, 225
Nestorians, 5, 18, 33, 46
Nettlebed, 183, 186
Neuhaus, Otto von, 16; and see Boldensele
Nevers, Bishop of, 202; Dean of, 201
Newton, A. P., 17, 94
New World, 12, 236, 237, 243, 247
Nichols, J., 203, 223
Nicholson, E. B., 3, 7, 92, 93, 94, 95, 98, 102, 103, 106, 158, 161, 162, 163, 181
Nicopolis, 229
Nicosia, 55
Nicoveran, 40, 67
Ninevah, 30
Ninus, 30
Noah, 28; the ark, 27, 237; the flood, 24
Norden, John, 178, 213, 246
Norman French, 10, 111, 112, 115, 117, 119, 126, 135, 136, 138, 139, 144, 149, 150, 164, 167, 168, 170, 171, 179, 211, 215, 222, 226
North star, 36, 138, 144
North Wales, 222
Norton, 190
Norway, 176, 232
Norwegians, 235
Nubia, 108
nudism, 75
*Nürnberg Chronicle,* 97, 202, 215

# INDEX

Nyssa, 108; Our Lady of, 118

Occam, William of, 150, 202
Odoric of Pordenone, 16, 18, 19, 20, 26-48, 62, 67, 72, 74, 75, 77, 83, 86, 104, 107, 153, 154, 164, 179, 202, 226, 229, 246, 247, 248, 256, 257, 258; companion of Mandeville, 219-220; and see pseudo-Odoric
Odyssey, 39, 247
Ogier de Caumont, 113, 114, 117, 120, 157
Ogier le Danois, 100, 106, 107, 108, 114, 115, 117, 118, 119, 121, 125, 127, 134, 147, 148, 152, 250
Ogier version, 65, 91, 111-118, 120-122, 126, 129, 130, 133-135, 137-138, 144-147, 149, 157, 160, 161, 169, 170, 220
oil supply, 59, 81
Olaus Magnus, 252
Old Man of the Mountain, see Assassins
Olschki, L., 17, 22, 69, 234
optical illusions, 68
orb, 51
Orient, 15, 17, 19, 24, 63, 177, 222, 224, 226, 229, 235, 241; see Far East
Oriental languages, 63
Orleans, Charles Duc d', 165, 174, 230; Louis Duc d', 229
Ormes, 31
Ortelius, A., 90, 100, 101, 102, 155, 231, 240, 245, 250, 251
otters, 41, 83
Otto van Diemeringen, 111, 119, 121, 157, 220
outre-mer, 54
owl, 79, 80
ox, worship of, 33, 35, 37, 75; ox-head, 67
Oxford, 63, 154, 183, 186, 192; Douce MS. *109*, 213
Oxfordshire, 183, 186
Oxus, 67

Painswick, 186, 187
Palestine, 16, 20, 64, 79, 108, 149; see Holy Land
Palestine itineraries, 153, 164
panther skins, 42
Paris, Matthew, 19-20
Paris, 56, 80, 107, 141, 168, 170, 172, 179, 201, 202, 203, 227, 230, 242; University of, 63, 201, 234
Paris redactor, 139 ff., 145, 167, 173, 180
Paris text, 112, 114, 115, 117, 119, 120, 121, 126, 135-146, 149, 150, 156, 169, 170-172
*Parliamentary Writs*, 101, 162, 186-187, 189, 193, 195, 200
Peacock, T. L., 257
peacocks, 42, 43, 46
*Pearl* poet, 1, 221, 223, 242, 259
Peiping, 17, 18
*Pelerinages et Pardouns de Acre*, 22
Pembroke, Earl of, 191, 201; Countess of, 173
pepper, 34, 35, 62, 63, 145
perilous kiss, 50
Pérouse, 92, 97, 98, 99, 129, 148
Perre le Sauvaige, 174
Persia, 29, 57, 63
Persians, 44, 61, 62, 124
Petrarch, 97, 162
Philip of Valois, 70, 71
Philippe le Hardi, 229
*Philobiblon*, 84
Phison, 67
phoenix, 247
Photius, 39
Picard, 117, 170
Pierre d'Ailly, 233
Pierre I de Lusignan, 71
*Piers Plowman*, 73, 83, 84, 221
pigmies, 37, 42
pilgrim, 25, 56, 66, 68, 242
Pisa, 80, 163
place names, 61-62, 66
plagiarist, 26, 48
plagiarism, 4, 8, 11, 26, 53

# INDEX

Pleshy, 184, 205, 206, 207, 208, 209, 212, 220, 223
Pliny, 23, 31, 37, 39, 48, 49, 77, 240, 242, 243, 245, 252, 257
plurality of wives, 75
Poitiers, 15, 46, 106, 114, 115, 145, 146, 172, 220
Pollard, A. W., 6, 7, 16, 19, 24, 27, 28, and edition quoted passim
Poloner, 58, 59
Polos, 17
Polumbrum, 35, 62, 107, 258
Pope, A., 259
Pope, 85, 150, 202, 243; Benedict XII, 82, 229; John XXII, 82, 229; Urban V, 97, 215
Porcacchi, 50
porcupine, 221, 222
Portugal, 9
Portuguese, 235, 242, 335
Poseidon, 52
postal service, 258
prepuce, 114, 115, 145, 146
Prester John, 22, 44, 65, 71, 83, 108, 119, 137, 138, 153, 237, 255
*Pricke of Conscience*, 79, 84
Procopius, 233
proper names, 7, 141, 144
pseudo-Aethicus, 39, 49, 243
pseudo-Aristotle, 133
pseudo-Brocard, 22
pseudo-Callisthenes, 39
pseudo-Mandeville, 113, 122, 131, 132, 133
pseudo-Methodius, 21, 22
pseudo-Odoric, 22, 58
pseudo-Turpin, 52
Ptolemy, 235, 240, 245, 246
Purchas, 48, 250, 251, 255; *Pilgrimes*, 253, 256
Püterich, J., 90, 101, 155
Putnam, Miss Bertha H., 186
Pyneforde, 186
Pynson, 7, 8, 84, 149, 215, 236, 239, 240, 243
pyramids, 60

Queen of Saba, 67
Quilon, 35


Rabelais, 1, 75, 242
races, see monstrous races
Radulph de Rivo, 96, 97, 202
Radwinter, 193
Raleigh, Sir Walter, 245
Ramsay, J. H., 194, 200
Ramusio, 82, 251
Raoulet d'Orleans, 140, 141, 144, 146, 165, 166, 167, 173
Raponde, Jacques, 228
Rastell, John, 237, 240, 241
rats, 32
Redleigh, 192, 199
Reformation, 219, 236, 243
relics, 80, 81; and see Cross, Crown
religions, 23, 48, 72; of the Greeks, 59; of India, 32
Renaissance, 39, 86, 162, 175
Réné, King, 131
Restoration, 253
Reynburne, 223
Rhodes, 55, 56, 188
Riccobaldus Ferrariensis, 97
Richard I, 176
Richard II, 66, 100, 185, 208, 209
Richard d'Aungerville, 84, 168, 224
Richel, B., 121
Ricold of Monte Croce, 22, 62, 79, 82, 226, 229
Robert fitz Payn, 187
Robert Mannyng, 84
Robert the Devil, 242
Rockhill, W. W., 19, 62
Roger de Stavegni, 71
Rohault de Fleury, C., 56, 80, 81
*Romance of the Chevelere Assigne*, 223
*Romance of William of Palerne*, 205
romances, 3, 23, 24, 84
romance of travel, 19, 38, 39-40, 53
*Roman de Fauvel*, 84
*Romant de Mandeville*, 83
Rome, 23, 73, 83, 85, 107, 250

## INDEX

Roos, Sir John, 193, 199; Robert, 193, 199; Sir Robert, 209; Thomas, 209
rosary, 40
rotation of earth, 234
Round, J. H., 101, 184, 192
roundness of earth, 109, 123, 136, 137, 231, 232, 233, 237
Rowland, S., 246
Rubruquis, 19, 20, 21, 28, 41, 44, 62, 80, 153, 163, 226, 258
Rusticiano de Pisan, 49
Rymer, *Foedera,* 194, 205

Sacro Bosco, 21, 232
St. Augustine, 31, 39, 232, 233
St. Albans, 8, 91, 98, 181, 183, 184, 186, 188, 189, 190, 191, 197, 199, 200, 202, 203, 205, 210, 211, 212, 213, 215, 216, 230, 238, 239, 260; Abbot John, 191; the school, 192
St. Alban of Germany, 170, 171
St. Chrysostom, 233
St. George, 177
St. Helena, 176
St. Jerome, 233
St. Karitot, 61
St. Katherine, 59, 81, 82
St. Lambert, 99; Cathedral of, 156
St. Laurent, 156
St. Louis, 19
St. Nicholas, 52
St. Ogier, 109
St. Paul, 124, 190, 213; St. Paul's school, 214
St. Thomas of Acon, 55
St. Thomas of Canterbury, 85, 109, 241, 255
St. William, 90, 98, 212
Saintsbury, G., 9, 10
Saladin, 176
Salhadi, Oliver, 201
Salisbury, Earl of, 224, 227
Samaria, 108
Samaritans, 72, 108
Samarkand, 59

Sandbach, F. E., 111, 121
Saracens, 46, 55, 61, 72, 128, 248
Sarah, 30
Sarratt, 199
Sarton, G., 71, 83, 95, 192
Satalia, Gulf of, 51
Scardeburgh, John of, 209, 220
sceptics, 40
Schedel, H., 97, 202, 215
Schiltberger, 51, 58, 178
Scotland, 126, 176, 183, 193, 203; arms of, 224
Scots, 200
Scott, G., 213
scribes, 61, 117, 120
scriptoria, 168, 175
Scythia, 30, 79, 80
Scythians, 247
sea, height of, 68
Selmer, Carl, 102
Seth, 123, 124, 126
*Seven Wise Masters,* 84
Shakespeare, 12, 25, 246, 247, 248
Siam, 63
Siberia, 77
Sidney, Sir Philip, 198
*Sidrac,* 130
Simon de St. Quentin, 226
Sinbad the Sailor, 77, 80
Singer, D. W., 130, 155, 160
Singlant, 108
*Sir Gowther,* 84
Smyrna, 55, 71
snails, 83
snakes, 34, 77
Snodham, T., 240
Sodom, 30
Solinus, 23, 31, 37, 39, 48, 49, 52, 77, 78, 83, 139, 240, 243, 245, 252, 257
Somerset, 183, 186, 187
Sorg, A., 230, 237
Spain, 9, 55, 220, 241
Spaniards, 46
Spanish, 111, 220, 242
Spanish, MSS., 175, 219, 235
sparrowhawk, 27, 50, 51, 53, 145, 172, 227, 257

## INDEX

Spenser, 12, 46, 175, 248, 254
spices, 63
Stapleford, 191
Steele, R., 254
Steiner, A., 151
Stephen, King, 101, 184
Stephen of Novgorod, 51
Stow, J., 206, 246
Strabo, 39, 48, 235, 243, 252
Suffolk, 184; Earl of, 224
Sultan, 60, 177; of Egypt, 64, 85, 125, 177
Sultânieh, 18, 29, 82; Archbishop of, 229
Sumatra, 36, 63
superstitions, 33
surnames, 163
suttee, 35
Sutton Mandeville, 186
swan, 223
Swift, 4, 12, 42, 49, 255, 256
Symon Simeonis, 58, 59, 60, 82
Syrians, 72

Tabriz, 28
*Tamar Cam*, 246
Taprobane, 46
Tarmegyte, 31
Tartars, 17, 19, 21, 44, 47, 71, 75, 78, 79, 82, 149, 155, 156, 225, 249, 255
Tasso, 1, 45, 248, 249
*Tatler*, 254
Tauris, 28
Taylor, E. G. R., 231, 233
Téchef, 132
Templars, 55, 196
ten lost tribes, 79
Ternate, 63
*Testament of Jean de Meun*, 84
test passages, 135 ff.
text, 4, 5, 11, 111 ff., 135 ff., 179, 250, 251
Thana, 32
Theophilus, 86
Theophrastus, 77
Thomas, Marcel, 98, 128, 130, 141, 170

Thompson, W., 213
thorn, 66, 177; see Crown of Thorns
Thule, 39, 85, 235
Thynne, Francis, 246
Tibet, 36, 44, 47
Tichmarsh, 209
Timour Beg, 59
Tobet, 30
*Tom Hickathrift*, 256
tortoises, 83
Tottel, Richard, 238, 239, 240
*Tour Landry, Book of the Knight of*, 221
*Traité du lapidaire*, 131
Trebizond, 26, 62
*Trésorier*, 97, 98, 100, 127, 129, 132, 134, 147, 152, 157
Trevisa, 61, 76, 139, 240
Troglodites, 52
Turkish, 61, 62
Turks, 17, 18, 56, 71
Tuthill, Rev. Hugh, 238
Tyrell, Roger, 102

Ulysses, 215, 254
Ulster, Earl of, 182
unicorn, 247
Ur, 30
Utopians, 66, 73, 236

Valley of Devils, or Valley Perilous, 33, 46, 136, 138, 171, 253
Vatican MSS., 175
Velser, Michael, 220
Venetians, 55
Venice, 63, 176, 179, 242
vegetable lamb, 44, 85, 241, 252
versions, English, 6-10, 236, 237, 240, 242, 244, 254
*Victoria History of Hertford*, 191, 197, 199
Vienna, Council of, 62; Dauphin of, 71
Vincent of Beauvais, 20, 21, 23, 24, 25, 29, 31, 32, 37, 42, 44, 47, 62, 73, 77, 81, 128, 149, 153, 164, 232

# INDEX

vine, 43
virginity, 52, 75
Visconti, Jean Galeazzo, 175; Valentine, 173-174; library, 174
*Vision of Tundale,* 84
Vogels, 8, 104, 112, 146, 211, 213, 238
Volga, 67
Von Harff, 58, 65
*Voyage of St. Brandan,* 84
vulgate, 116, 117, 120, 128, 139, 148, 157, 160

Walden, 193; Abbey, 190
Walker, Ferdinand, 241
Wallingford, Richard, 192
Walsingham, T., 212, 213, 216; *Annales,* 210; *Liber Benefactorum,* 199, 212; *Chronicle,* 211, 212; *Gesta Abbatum,* 190, 210, 212; *Hist. Angl.,* 211
Walter de Wetewang, 188
Waltham, 189, 196, 197; Great Waltham, 193, 196; Little Waltham, 193, 195, 196; Waltham Holy Cross, 196
Wanton, 197
Warner, G. F., 3, 6, 7, 8, 20, 21, 22, 23, 24, 26, 28, 31, 36, 44, 50-51, 57, 59, 61-62, 65, 67, 71, 76, 78, 80, 82, 92, 93, 94, 95, 98, 101, 102, 104, 106, 111, 112, 133, 135, 140, 146, 150, 151, 153, 154, 155, 158, 161, 162, 163, 164, 165, 166, 170, 175, 177, 178, 181, 182, 190, 192, 195, 196, 213, 231, 238; text, 180
Warner, W., 249
Warwick, Earl of, 223
Waterman, W., 240
Weever, J., 91, 213
Wells, J. E., 94, 106, 135, 154, 177, 179
Wells, Bishop of, 187

Welsh Marches, 222
Welsch, 121
Welwyn, 191, 200
Weston, 186
Whitney, Lois, 45, 249
Wickersheimer, E., 160, 167, 175
Wilhelmites, see Guillemins
William de Albo Monasterio, 196
William the Conqueror, 184, 186
*William of Palerne,* 206, 223
William of Tripoli, 20, 73
William of Tyre, 64
*William without Fear,* 242
Willmins, see Guillemins
Wiltshire, 183, 186
wines, 56, 57
*Wizard of Oz,* 253
wonders, 9, 75, 247; and see monstrous races
woodcuts, 237, 241, 244, 250
wool, 63
Wordsworth, W., 256
Worde, Wynkyn de, 237, 239, 244, 260
Wyclif, 9, 73
Wymundeham, 211, 238

Yang-tze-kiang, 67
*Yearbooks of Edward II,* 187
York, Archbishop of, 209
Yorkshire, 208, 209, 238; West Riding of, 209
Ypota, 187
*Ypotys,* 84
Yule, Sir Henry, *Cathay,* 16, 17, 26, 34, 38, 83, 195, 233; *Marco Polo,* 18, 96; *Mandeville,* 31; review, 82

Zaiton, 18, 41
Zantfliet, 97
Zanzibar, 36
Zoroastrians, 35, 47
Zogh, 66, 177
Zosimus, 51